DATE DUE

Business Plans Handbook

Highlights

Business Plans Handbook (BPH) is a collection of actual business plans compiled by entrepreneurs seeking funding for small businesses throughout North America. For those looking for real examples of how to approach, structure, and compose their own business plans, *BPH* presents 33 sample plans, including those for the following businesses:

- ❑Bed and Breakfast
- ❑Car Wash
- ❑Restaurant
- ❑Equipment Rental
- ❑Aerospace Supplier
- ❑Import Boutique
- ❑Inn/Resort
- ❑Magazine Publisher
- ❑Online Consultant
- ❑Florist
- ❑Toy Company
- ❑Virtual Reality Game Company
- ❑Software Developer
- ❑Business Consultant

OTHER FEATURES

BPH also provides additional resources for the small business owner preparing to research and compose their business plan, including:

- An **Instructional Foreword** providing advice on structuring your business, researching your plan, and other tips.

- A **Small Business Development Center (SBDCs) Directory** listing all 750 of these contact points for advice in the United States. These valuable resources can provide you with informative materials, offer business counseling and support, and provide you a place to begin networking with other business owners and contacts.

- A **Glossary of Small Business Terms** providing insight into the often confusing lingo of entrepreneurship.

- A **Bibliography** of materials for further study offering additional sources for research and advice.

Business Plans Handbook

A COMPILATION OF ACTUAL BUSINESS PLANS DEVELOPED BY SMALL BUSINESSES THROUGHOUT NORTH AMERICA

1st Edition

Kristin Kahrs,
Editor
Karin E. Koek,
Contributing Editor

An International Thomson Publishing Company

I(T)P

NEW YORK • LONDON • BONN • BOSTON • DETROIT • MADRID
MELBOURNE • MEXICO CITY • PARIS • SINGAPORE • TOKYO
TORONTO • WASHINGTON • ALBANY NY • BELMONT CA • CINCINNATI OH

Editor: Kristin Kahrs
Contributing Editor: Karin E. Koek

...rs: Gary A. Braun, Amy Lynn Emrich, Elaine Jirkans,
...y Lehman, Susan B. Martin, Bradley J. Morgan,
Holly M. Selden, AnnaMarie L. Sheldon

Production Director: Mary Beth Trimper
Assistant Production Manager: Evi Seoud
Production Associate: Mary Kelley

Art Director: Cynthia Baldwin
Page Design: Mark Howell

Data Entry Manager: Benita L. Spight
Data Entry Supervisor: Gwendolyn Tucker
Data Entry Associates: Merrie Ann Carpenter, Frances Monroe, Nancy Sheridan

ISBN 0-8103-9222-4
CIP 94-36046

Printed in the United States of America

Published simultaneously in the United Kingdom
by Gale Research International Limited
(An affiliated company of Gale Research Inc.)

Gale Research, Inc.,
an International Thomson Publishing Company.

10 9 8 7 6 5 4

Contents

Introduction

When Gale Research asked small business owners and business librarians what business resources they would like, the clear message was that current business planning aids were not quite what they were after. What they really wanted, they said, was examples of real business plans, not just mock-ups or artificial, untested samples. Librarians wanted to be able to point to "live" business plans that someone had actually used, to give their patrons a clear picture of what the finished product should look like. Entrepreneurs said that they wanted an idea of how to put together all the research, re-formulating, analysis, and revision. More importantly, they wanted a successful plan that would get them some money; and an example of a real plan that had been successfully used by a live business owner to get a loan was what they had in mind.

This clear vision of what people in the small business community were looking for led to the compilation *Business Plans Handbook (BPH).* It is designed to be used by those looking for direction...an example of where they should end up when the grueling business planning process is finally completed. After all, if you don't know where you're going, how can you get there?

COMPILATION AND ORGANIZATION

BPH provides a variety of plans presented on alphabetical order by their subject (Aerospace, Biscotti Bakery, Car Wash). Some are examples of home businesses, like consulting; others will help people flesh-out that dream of owning a bed and breakfast (p. 31) or restaurant (p. 315 and 325). Also included are plans in areas that entrepreneurs are just beginning to explore, such as virtual reality applications (p. 507 and 527). Others seem a product of people's everyday experiences, such as the toy company whose business plan arose out of two parents' desire to provide educational entertainment their children (p. 485) or the elder care facility that hopes to provide a comfortable and dignified alternative to sometimes inhospitable traditional nursing home care (p. 167). One of the most notable plans is for a restaurant that doubles as a training ground for mentally ill homeless people in the hope that new job skills will help get them off the street (p. 339).

The plans contained in *BPH* also reflect the differences in approachto planning with their varying levels of development, detail, and length; treatment of financial data; approach to competition and marketing; and evicence of research and rigorous examination that the planning process requires. As these plans show, there is no one way to write a business plan, it is an evolutionary process that takes time and patience.

While the plans contained in *BPH* are real plans, the majority have been fictionalized to protect confidentiality. Personal and company names, addresses, and sometimes product names were changed to protect the contributors. Additonally, in many cases financial data or charts were removed to protect the owners' privacy. The words "available upon request" usually appear in these cases to indicate that the charts would normally appear in the plan.

FEATURES AND BENEFITS

BPH offers many features not provided by other business planning references including:

❑ An instructional Foreword, written by an expert in business planning, offering advice on the most effective way to approach your business plan, providing sources that business owners need to consult in order to be well-informed, and explaining the process in easy-to-understand steps.

❑ Thirty-three real business plans, providing examples of what entrepreneurs in your situation have done. Each represents an owner's successful attempt at clarifying (for themselves and others) the reasons that the business should exist or expand and convincing a lender to fund the enterprise.

❑ A directory of all 750 Small Business Development Centers in the United States with full contact information, including phone and fax. It is strongly recommended that you contact these invaluable centers for support and advice for your plan and your business.

❑ A Glossary of Small Business Terms to help you decipher the sometimes confusing terminology used by lenders and others in the financial and small business communities.

❑ A Bibliography, citing sources mentioned in the Foreword for easy follow-up and further reading.

SOFTWARE ISSUES

While there are many software packages available to assist you with compiling your business plan, none provides a single example of a real, successful business plan in the same way *Business Plans Handbook* does. Furthermore, lenders may find that using business planning software circumvents any valuable lessons that may be learned by researching and preparing the document relying solely on your own resourcefulness. Consequently, banks and other lenders may refuse loans to those who take this apparent short cut.

However, if you are looking for a template with which to structure your research and coordinate the approach you will take with your own plan, *BPH* provides 33. Each plan can be viewed as a working outline that helps to identify the crucial elements needed for a successful business plan with examples of the level of detail your competitors have used.

ACKNOWLEDGEMENTS

The *BPH* staff would like to express our grateful appreciation to the entrepreneurs who allowed us to use their business plans. We would like to additionally extend our sincere thanks to the *Business Plans Handbook* Advisory Board, which is composed of Patricia A. Peacock, Director, Regional Small Business Development Center; Dr. Raymond M. Genick, Assistant Dean, Professional Development of the School of Business Administration at Wayne State University;

Frances V. LeDuke, Director of the Office of Regulatory Reform, Department of Regulatory Agencies of the State of Colorado; and Tim Dixon, Small Business Development Center, The University of Georgia; and the many people that offered their encouragement and suggestions to the project.

The editor would also like to sincerely thank Karin Koek, whose help was available whenever it was needed, and without whose contributions this project would not have been possible.

COMMENTS WELCOME

Your comments on *BPH* are welcome. Please direct all correspondence, suggestions for future volumes of *BPH*, and other recommendations to the following:

Business Plans Handbook
Gale Research Inc.
835 Penobscot Bldg.
Detroit MI 48226-4094
Phone: (313)961-2242
Fax: (313)961-6815
Toll-Free: 800-347-GALE
Telex: 810 221 7087
Email: gale@msen.com (Internet)

Kristin Kahrs

Foreword

By Patricia A. Peacock, Ed.D, of Rutgers University

"He who fails to plan, plans to fail."

An Ancient Proverb

Part I: An Introduction to Business Planning

Starting a small business appears deceivingly attractive because of the apparent lack of governmental interference. This hands-off approach is perceived as the exception, rather than the rule. Initially, few enterprises require much more than a local registration of a tradename, and the filing with the state and federal taxing authorities before opening their doors. Little or no evidence is required to verify that a venture is viable, let alone developed by someone knowledgeable and capable of delivering the agreed upon product or service.

Driven by demands of the lending community, often coupled with the need to compile accurate and timely information, individuals are now engaged in the pursuit of any knowledgethat will support their venture from concept to completion.

The business plan has evolved as a simple, albeit standard, well defined document. Its structure not only allows for the immediate evaluation of a business design against the backdrop of its industry, but also defines the manner in which the enterprise will measure success. This has become critical in an economy which still records a significant number of failures. Assurances are, therefore, defined by the data, and the procedures set in place to track and provide feedback on the implied and stated goals.

Today's business plan, whether written as an operational guide or financial proposal, demands unprecedented accuracy in detail and documentation. The role and resources of the local library have emerged as contemporary tools. Business reference texts and databases have gained in usefulness and prestige as individuals search for efficient, inexpensive methods of information and data collection.

Business textbooks offer sample business plans with limited application. The language is cumbersome for the neophyte. The actual research process remains a complex and complicated mystery. The application of fact and formula is viewed as overwhelming and lacking a logical or consistent structure.

Business Plans Handbook offers a template of successful plans enabling the entrepreneur to "plug in" their respective data and act with a plan in hand.

The business plan process begins with a database search to determine whether or not the product is manufactured or the service offered, perhaps under another name, or with another application. This initial search may suggest a manufacturer or a successful company. Use of the U.S. Securities and Exchange Commission Filings can offer data on publicly held companies, while *Dun & Bradstreet Market Identifiers* will provide detail on some privately held companies. But this initial review only begins to scratch the surface.

No single document or press clipping will provide all the information that will be required to make the final decision regarding a proposed start-up. The idea is to locate and identify any and all information. Each piece potentially contributes to an informed decision on trends and possible market entry.

General resources for locating information on products, services or companies include federal and state agencies and their respective regulatory agencies; financial institutions; chambers of commerce; local development authorities; local courts; trade associations; think tanks; trade magazines; as well as suppliers and vendors. Free technical assistance is available through the programs of the U.S. Small Business Administration (SBA), including the Service Corps of Retired Executives (SCORE); the Small Business Institute (SBI); and the Small Business Development Centers (SBDC). Contact your local SBA office (blue pages of your phone book) for the programs located in your area.

The more resourceful the entrepreneur, the more he will begin to appreciate the value of the thousands of non-traditional information sources such as public documents and industry experts. On-line databases, especially the ones maintained by the federal government, provide quick access to information on all types of companies.

Jeffry Timmons, an outspoken advocate and critic of the entrepreneurial movement in his text, *New Venture Creation: Entrepreneurship in the 1990's* wrote:

> *"Planning is a way of thinking about the future of a venture; that is, of deciding where a firm needs to go and how fast, how to get there, and what to do along the way to reduce the uncertainty and to manage risk and change."* (p. 239)

The business plan, a critical but often overlooked document, has become a significant tool of the 20th century business owner. Banks, venture capitalists, and investors alike now ask the question: "Do you have a business plan?"

The construction of a useful plan is not an easy task. Not only is it helpful to know what comprises the required content, it is also important to understand the process as it relates to the finished product, the plan itself. The difficulty with many of the traditional approaches to developing a business plan is that they fail to assist the writer in the rudimentary process of fact finding. The results are often poorly constructed plans that cannot perform adequately for the entrepreneur.

Part II: The Anatomy of a Business Plan

A business plan may be defined as:

> **A written document that specifically articulates how an entrepreneur expects to seize the opportunity and execute a strategy he or she has identified.**

The plan enables the entrepreneur to anticipate the opportunities, costs, difficulties and requirements of starting a specific business. The significance of the planning process is that the entrepreneur is forced to build the venture on paper first. It is a vital tool! It forces the entrepreneur to think about what must be done and how to do it. It provides creditors and investors with information and documentation to help them decide whether or not to finance the entrepreneur and the venture. Experts agree that the plan begins with researching the market. The typical research process consists of four steps:

- ❑Defining the need
- ❑Fact finding to support the need
- ❑Analysis of the facts
- ❑Taking action

Look at the big picture, first. The *SIC (Standard Industrial Classification) Manual* is the first source to check when researching a product or industry. The *SIC Manual* assigns a four-digit code which is widely used in business literature. To be effective in starting a business or expanding a product or service line, the entrepreneur must have a thorough understanding of the industry. Initial market research should include the *Small Business Sourcebook,* which identifies the professional trade associations, suppliers, trade shows, start-up information, educational programs, along with reference and statistical works; the *Encyclopedia of Business Information Sources,* which introduces newsletters and other publications, together with directories and resources of interest; and, the *Encyclopedia of Associations,* which details the specific services of the association including the availability of local chapters and instructional material. Infotrac, UMI Periodical Abstracts and Wilson's *Business Periodicals Index* offer a significant baseline of popular and business periodicals. The industrious entrepreneur will continue this search with several of the newspaper indexes including the National Newspaper Index and the Wall Street Journal Annual Index.

The *U.S. Industrial Outlook* further documents this global picture of the industry providing five year projections, background information, statistics, trends and forecasts. At this point it would be preferable to gather information on the application of the venture at the local or regional level that the business is intended to serve. Review the local scene as depicted in area or regional newspapers and business journals.

In defining a market niche, a thorough knowledge of the competition is necessary. Libraries offer a substantial number of other reference sources, including Moody's Manuals, which offer comprehensive information on the companies listed on the U.S. Stock Exchanges, including corporate history, income statements and balance sheets; *Standard & Poor's Industry Surveys*; the *Predicasts Basebook*, which gives historical economic data from 1960 on 16,000 industrial statistical series; *Statistical Abstract of the United States* extracting data from the Censuses and many other statistical sources with excellent reference citations; and the Economic Censuses. With diligence and the skillful eye of a detective, trends and forecasts of your industry, as well as contemporary issues, will emerge.

To add supporting evidence to the market research plan, specific company information should be gathered. Companies are either publicly or privately held. There is no one perfect source of information, however, *Dun's Million Dollar Directory* provides the best national source for identifying companies by SIC code and geographic location; or, the *Thomas Register* lists data on more than 100,000 manufacturing companies by type of product, a company name index, and product catalogs of many firms.

Local and regional company directories may include: *MacRae's State Industrial Directory* with product/service, SIC and company name indexes arranged geographically by county and city; the *State Directory of Manufacturers*; the *State Employer Directory*; the *Macmillan Directory of Leading Private Companies* indexing more than 12,500 companies; the *Dun's Directory of Service Companies* Other other regional purchasing guides may also provide excellent starting points.

These reference texts and directories offer answers or insight that the entrepreneur might address thoroughly in the narrative section of the business plan. This first section of the plan must discuss in detail, with as much supporting evidence as possible, the opportunity, the intended market, the marketing approach, existing competition and proposed market niche, location, pricing formula, management and personnel needs.

When looking for specific help, for example, when establishing pricing formula, do not overlook the popular college and university textbooks on small business management, together with the recommended retail price guidelines available from the manufacturer or distributors.

If the purpose of the plan is to serve as a financial proposal, an additional section entitled "Application and Expected Effect of the Investment" or "Investor Participation" is also required. The critical issues include: Will the cash infusion make a difference in growth? Will the revenues be sufficient to service this new debt? The content must "grab" the attention of the reader to go on to the other sections.

Throughout the narrative of this plan the entrepreneur must answer the questions of intention. Can the new company's business functions be properly managed? Are goals identified and measurable? Can these goals be reached? Can the product be produced efficiently? Can it be marketed effectively? What are the future trends and expectations? There is no one way to structure a business plan, and experts agree it is not an easy task, but standard, acceptable models do serve as a dependable starting point.

It is often of value to include the entrepreneur's mission statement. This is accompanied by the short-term strategic plan which simply delineates the entrepreneur's specific objectives for the initial twelve month period, providing the timeline and budget for each. The opportunities and threats of each objective are also discussed in detail. The detail of the strategic plan must tie back to the cash flow presentation.

The financials include a current balance sheet, together with pro-forma income and cash flow statements for a three year period beginning with the implementation of the plan. The income and cash flow statements are prepared on a monthly basis for year one, and by quarter for the second and third year. Existing companies mustalso submit a budget deviation analysis covering the previous years activity. Once again, the business reference section of the library can be an invaluable resource in identifying most of the information on industry averages and financial data. The *Dun and Bradstreet's Key Business Ratios* provides common-size percentages for the 14 key business ratios, representing over 800 different liens of business as defined by SIC code; or the *RMA Annual Statement Studies* provides comparative financial data and ratios in broad industrial categories. Troy's *Almanac of Business and Industrial Financial Ratios* offers the entrepreneur valuable information enabling a review of proposed numbers against industry norms. It also answers many basic concerns, for example, what is an appropriate budget for advertising or bad debt, rent or officer compensation?

Part III: The Optimum Plan

When compiling and writing a business plan, keep in mind these recommendations from the lending community:

- ❑No two business plans are exactly alike. Do not expect to copy a textbook model and have it suffice. It must be tailored to meet your specific needs.

- ❑Keep in mind the reader of the finished plan. If this document is to be reviewed by a loancommittee, take the time necessary to compile relevant data. It is helpful to have met with the reader/reviewer/ presenter, prior to writing the finished plan. Ask the important questions, for example: What is your lending policy? Must this plan reflect a capital infusion on the part of the owner? If "yes" how much? What are the terms of the loan(s)? Under what conditions?

❑Avoid technical jargon. It may make the plan difficult to read and comprehend, and as a result you may lose your reader's interest and commitment.

❑Do not make reference to any unnamed people. If it is your intention to have an accountant, have referenced them in your plan.

❑Be realistic. Most new ventures do not break even in the first year.

❑As you take notes in the data collection process, make photocopies of census material or industry trends, identifying each with the name of the publication, date and page number.

❑If the plan has been developed to assist in assessing the purchase of an existing business do our homework and learn as much as possible about why the business is for sale. If you are considering a franchise, take the time to meet with other franchisees as listed in the Franchise Disclosure Statement. With your accountant, carefully review the company's financials to arrive at your baseline purchase price as your starting point. If the business is going downhill, why? Can you reasonably expect to make the venture profitable?

❑Finally, if the business plan is serving as a financial proposal, this 40-50 page document will address only the purpose of the funds, the debt service schedule, and the impact of this capital infusion in the growth of the business. On the other hand, a plan that is serving as the organization's operational guide must include complete detail of all facets of the venture, including the quality control manual (if a manufacturer), the employee handbook, as well as contracts, leases, guidelines for quotes/estimates, credit reports, letters of reference, letters of intent, sampleproposals, warranties, credit policy, etc.

REMEMBER: Unless you have clearly explained to the contrary, the merit of your plan will be evaluated against existing industry standards. These are the *Dun & Bradstreet Key Business Ratios* or the *RMA Annual Statement Studies*. Every exception to the acceptable range should be explained in what the accounting industry describes as "Notes of Explanation." Using professionals as an active part of the review process can be invaluable.

In the past, developing and writing a business plan was in itself, a formidable task, often "given the lowest priority" in the planning cycle. The danger has been and continues to be that the owner, lacking control over the sources of information and fearing the demands of the research process, overlook the facts in favor of a quick fix alternative. These deceptions often lead to failure.

Work? Yes. Worth it? Definitely. Professionals believe the planning process is invaluable. These guidelines will help entrepreneurs identify expectations and plan for internal and external risks, some of which they may not be able to control, but all of which need to be taken into consideration.

Patricia A. Peacock, Ed.D.
Rutgers University - Camden
School of Business
Regional Small Business Development Center

Business Plans

ACCOUNTING MANAGEMENT SYSTEMS

2584 Chesswick Ave., Ste. 3
Calgary, Alberta , Canada G3J 1K9

October 14, 1992

Accounting Management Systems provides consulting services to assist small- and medium-sized businesses in choosing and implementing microcomputer accounting systems. This plan reviews current markets, competition, and the skills and equipment needed to successfully build a business of this kind.

ACCOUNTING CONSULTING BUSINESS PLAN

EXECUTIVE SUMMARY

The Purpose of the Plan

This document outlines a proposed microcomputer consulting service and will help in identifying requirements for starting and operating the business outlined here. In order to do this, the report will review the market or markets that might exist, determine what competition exists in those markets and identify the skills and equipment needed. Financial performance is projected and funding requirements are considered.

The information contained in this report will serve two main purposes: to determine the viability of the proposed business and to measure its ongoing operations.

The Company

Market Needs to be Met

Accounting Management Systems (AMS) will provide consulting services to small and medium sized businesses to assist in selecting and implementing available microcomputer accounting systems.

Many smaller and medium-sized businesses today need to implement or upgrade their accounting and business reporting systems. These businesses seldom have the necessary skills available to meet these needs in a successful or timely fashion. They simply want a solution that will meet their needs, works when it is supposed to, and is cost effective to implement.

Competitive Advantages

Accounting Management Systems will offer four and a half years of experience in the selecting and implementation of off-the-shelf micro-computer accounting programs. Other specific advantages include:

- ❑ Experience with proven microcomputer equipment and software.
- ❑ An existing network of contacts among resellers and other consultants.
- ❑ Formal training and practical experience in business management and operations.
- ❑ Polished communications skills.
- ❑ Low overhead costs.

Competitive Weaknesses

As a start-up, Accounting Management Systems will be faced with a number disadvantages:

- Dependent on one person.
- Will not possess all specialized skills required in every situation.
- The lack of formal offices for meetings.
- The lack of a professional image.

Products and Services

Accounting Management Systems will provide consulting services to small and medium-sized businesses that wish to implement or upgrade microcomputer-based accounting systems using off-the-shelf programs. These systems will vary from a single computer to small computer networks at several sites linked via telecommunications equipment.

A typical engagement would include some combination of the following services:

- A thorough needs analysis.
- An objective assessment of thc wide variety of accounting software available, and how each one meets the needs determined, with a recommendation and alternatives.
- Accurate documentation of existing procedures. Application of these procedures to the selected new system and documentation of the new procedures.
- Installation and configuration of the selected programs and required hard ware.
- Training of staff in the use of the new systems.
- Ongoing support for the new programs.

These services will be billed at an hourly rate between $40 and $70. The rate charged will depend on the size of each engagement, anticipated future activity with the client and the opportunity to develop or acquire new skills during the engagement.

Market Analysis

Target Market Characteristics

A typical business that might hire Accounting Management Systems is expected to be:

- Smaller in size, up to $5million or 100 employee.
- Local or regional in scope.
- In the service, retail, wholesale or light manufacturing sectors.

Target Market Size

The vast majority of businesses in Canada are small, as defined above. Approximately 6,700 businesses in Calgary in 1991 met all of these characteristics. That many exist outside Calgary in the southern Alberta area, for a total of about 13,500. At least 10% of that number begin as new businesses each year.

Marketing and Sales Activities

Marketing Strategy

Marketing activities will initially concentrate on networking in the following areas:

- ❑ Computer dealers.
- ❑ Accounting software vendors.
- ❑ Other consultants.
- ❑ Accountants and other personal service professionals.
- ❑ Participation in trade shows and industry seminars.
- ❑ Referrals from past or existing clients.
- ❑ Participation in electronic forums dedicated to the target market and to consulting.

Media advertising does not appear to offer any significant return at this point. Possible marketing opportunities include:

- ❑ Direct mailings.
- ❑ Cooperative advertising with computer dealers and accounting software vendors.
- ❑ Direct participation in seminars and trade shows in partnership with dealers or vendors.
- ❑ Paper and electronic bulletin board postings.

Sales Strategy

An initial meeting with prospective clients will be performed at no charge. This meeting will confirm the existence of needs for change. The prospective client must come away from the meeting with some trust or confidence in the consultant and his ability to implement a solution to the client's needs.

Operations

Accounting Management Systems will operate from a home office for much of its first year. Necessary equipment, including a phone, answering machine, fax capability, file storage and computer equipment will be kept in that office.

Most of the actual consulting services and meetings with clients will be performed at the client's place of business. Some configuration of equipment and software and the writing of proposals and documentation will be performed in the home office.

All significant engagements will be initiated with an informal meeting where the prospective client's needs are discussed and confirmed to exist. This first meeting will be followed by a written proposal and a contractual engagement letter to be signed by the client before further work is performed.

Records of existing systems and procedures, alternatives and recommendations, hardware and software purchases and configurations will be kept. Records of the billable time spent on each engagement will also be kept.

Meetings with the client staff will be held at important points during each engagement to ensure that everyone involved is aware of the progress and the work that remains to be done. In most engagements, it is expected that client staff will perform some of the configuration work.

Management and Ownership

Accounting Management Systems is organized as a sole proprietorship with Richard L. Sawinski as its owner, manager and only consultant.

Financial Data: Funds Required and Uses of Funds

The initial requirements for capital are between $10,000 and $12,000. Approximately half of this amount would be raised through debt financing, the rest would be met through cash flow. These funds will be used as follows:

- ❑ $5,000 to $6,000 for computer equipment.
- ❑ $2,500 to $3,000 for licensing agreements with several vendors.
- ❑ $2,000 for computer software purchases.

COMPANY DESCRIPTION

Nature of the Business

Who is Accounting Management Systems?

Accounting Management Systems is a sole proprietorship operated by Richard L. Sawinski. His resume available upon request. This company will provide consulting services to small and medium-sized businesses. Its primary services are to assist in selecting and implementing microcomputer accounting systems. Secondary services would include implementation of related business programs and hardware and possibly sales of specific hardware and software. Retail sales are not the focus of this business.

What marketplace needs will AMS meet?

All businesses need to be managed. The basic process of management is to: collect information about the business, its day to day operations, its customers and its environment; to compare the information with past information, projections and information about competitors; and to make decisions about the business's activities. A sound accounting/management system using readily available computer technology can collect data accurately, minimizing chances for human error. It can also analyze the report on the data quickly and communicate the information to staff, customers and associated businesses. Because the accounting/management system is central to any business, managers also have needs beyond the mechanics of the system itself, including obtaining a solution on a timely basis, cost effective implementation and operation of the system, and confidence in the abilities of the service provider.

Who has the needs for my service?

All businesses have these needs. Owners and managers are faced with more and more information with which to make decisions about their operations. They see current computer technology every day in newspapers, department stores and in other businesses. This technology promises to help them do more work in less time with better results.

Most of the skills will not be needed on an ongoing basis, sohiring or training staff cannot usually be justified. The business simply wants a solution that will meet their needs, one that works when it is supposed to, and is cost effective to implement and operate.

Accounting Management Competitive Advantages

Account Management Systems offers four and a half years of direct experience in the selection and implementation of off-the-shelf microcomputer accounting programs.

Formal training and nine years combined experience in both the management and operation of a variety of different business will help to provide a ready understanding of the specific needs in each client situation.

Polished communications skills will quickly and accurately document the client's needs, the alternatives and recommendations for change.

Direct experience with various mini- and microcomputer equipment, current knowledge of the latest PC technology and existing contacts among resellers and other consultants will help to ensure up-to-date solutions and smooth transitions.

Low overhead costs will help with profitability in the first few years.

Competitive Weaknesses

Reliance on a single person is a drawback. Only so many hours are available to perform chargeable services, prospect for new clients, manage the business and maintain or learn new skills. This is also the source of considerable flexibility in choosing with services to offer and which skills to obtain.

Some engagements will require specific skills that are not possessed and cannot be learned quickly. Through contacts in the consulting and computer sales industry these functions will have to be sub-contracted or referred to other parties.

During a typical engagement some functions are more labour intensive, such as installing cable and the physical installation of other equipment. In order to maximize chargeable time and profit, these functions may be sub-contracted to third parties with whom Accounting Management Systems has dealt in the past.

Initially, a lack of formal offices and a professional image will pose problems. Meeting space has already been secured with several computer dealers and office management contacts on an as-needed basis. Options for rented space and a leased vehicle are examined in detail in the body of this report.

Answering services are being met initially with a computerized voice mail box system. A cellular telephone is also an option that is being considered.

PRODUCTS AND SERVICES

Detailed Description

Accounting Management Systems will provide consulting services to small and medium-sized businesses that wish to implement or upgrade microcomputer-based accounting systems using off-the-shelf programs. These systems will vary from a single computer and program to small computer networks to several sites linked via telecommunications equipment. The systems will be chosen to meet the specific sites linked via telecommunications equipment. The systems will be chosen to meet the specific client needs, primarily to provide greater management reporting and control for the client businesses along with improved operating efficiency.

Specific services will typically be combined during a single engagement. However, each of these services can be offered individually, depending on the client's needs. The services will include:

- ❑ A thorough needs analysis.
- ❑ An objective assessment of the wide variety of accounting software available, and how each one meets the needs determined, with a recommendation and alternatives.
- ❑ Assistance in sourcing and obtaining the selected programs and equipment.
- ❑ Accurate documentation of existing procedures and application of these procedures to the selected new system with documentation of new procedures.
- ❑ Installation and configuration of the selected programs and required hardware.
- ❑ Conversion of existing data from paper records or previous systems to the new system.
- ❑ Training of staff in the use of the new systems.
- ❑ Ongoing support for the new programs.

The range of computer programs supported include:

- ❑Accounting programs: General Ledger, A/P, A/R, cheque writing, bank reconciliation.
- ❑Operations programs: Order Entry, retail Point of Sale, Inventory and Purchasing.
- ❑Management support programs: Property Management and Contact Management.
- ❑Fully integrated electronic data interchange (EDI).
- ❑Integration with other basic office programs such as local area networks, electronic mail,word processing, spreadsheets and databases.

Specific benefits of services

Businesses may already use computer equipment to conduct and manage their operations. Increasingly, smaller and medium-sized businesses are taking advantage of newer computer technology to increase their efficiency and competitiveness.

The new systems often require changes to existing procedures and can impact many related areas of a business operations. If the effects are anticipated and carefully considered, efficiency might be improved in these areas as well. If these effects are ignored there may well be unnecessary frustration and delay in the implementation. A consultant experienced in implementing new systems and anticipating the required changes will return the investment in his wages by increasing the benefits and decreasing the frustrations.

Wherever possible, the new systems will be integrated with existing computer systems and business operations. In some cases the new accounting systems will be required because of changes to business operations. In other cases the new systems will act as a catalyst for changes to their procedures and computer systems. In both cases there is an opportunity to provide greater efficiency; in the operations of the client businesses.

Legal agreements that could affect AMS

A consulting and sales agreement is being negotiated with Management Systems Inc. (MSI) of Georgia and Manitoba. This agreement will provide for referrals to Accounting Management Systems from MSI marketing and support activities. The sales aspect of the agreement is required because MSI does not sell its products through retail channels. The range of products available run from small business accounting software to management systems for medium-sized businesses and carry list prices from $225 to $15,000.

A similar agreement is being sought with International Computer of Alberta and New York. This agreement would involve only the consulting and support services for their line of Accounting Plus accounting programs.

Discussions have been held with Imagine Corporation of Oregon with respect to their ClearAccount 1 and 2 products. Although they do not have any formal consulting programs they have provided evaluation copies of all of their software.

Imagine and the other firms above provide an electronic forum where customers from all over North America who are using the products can request assistance and services.

MARKET ANALYSIS

Industry Description and Outlook

Description of primary industry

Most statistics available for the computer consulting industry are based on a broad category of computer services, including rental/leasing of computer systems, time sharing systems, programmers, support and help desk providers, as well as consultants for everything from large networks to publishing of CD-ROMs.

Consultants dealing specifically with accounting software are a small subset of this group. Many computer dealers or resellers are drawn to the market, but few have or acquire any specific accounting skills or an understanding of accounting and management systems.

Public accountants are more likely to offer competent skills in selecting and implementing this type of computer system.Whether they do or not typically depends on their size and management style.

Independent consultants who concentrate on the accounting software market are still rare.

Size of the industry

Currently

According to Statistics Canada the number of computer service providers in Canada, as defined above, grew from 9,380 in 1988 to 9,694 in 1989. The number of such firms with employees decreased from 6,560 in 1989 to 5,682 in 1991.

This does not likely indicate that the industry is shrinking or consolidating, but more likely reflects the trend towards self employment in Canada.

The number of such businesses in Calgary is approximately 3 to 4% of the total, or 300 to 400 businesses. Perhaps half of this number are involved in financial systems. However, the number that concentrate specifically on accounting systems is likely on 2 1/2 to 5% of this number, or between 8 and 20 firms.

In Five Years

A growth rate of 2.5% from 1988 to 1989 would translate into an additional 50 to 100 computer service firms in Calgary in five years.

Industry characteristics and trends

Historically

Computerized accounting and management systems consulting among smaller and medium-sized businesses is a new market that has existed only for the past 10 to 12 years, since the personal computer has allowed smaller companies to computerize.

It is becoming an established industry, but it is constantly evolving. The nature of any computer service business is that change is constant.

Currently

The industry is in growth phase as a result of the recent drop in price of 80/486 PC's and the move towards graphic user interfaces such as Microsoft's Windows.

In the future

The move towards graphic user interfaces in accounting software is just starting. Other future considerations include Electronic Banking (i.e. Direct Debit) and fully integrated business sstems between trading partners (EDI).

Target Markets

Distinguishing characteristics of primary target markets

Small businesses, under $5 million annual sales, fewer than 100 employees.

- ❑Local or regional in scope.
- ❑Involved in the service, retail, wholesale or light manufacturing sectors.
- ❑Located in the Calgary or southern Alberta geographic area.
- ❑Considering a new or upgraded computer accounting system.
- ❑Lack the skills needed to properly implement a computer accounting system.

Primary target overall market size

6,700 such businesses exist in Calgary, a total of 13,500 in southern Alberta. Computer Services, as defined by Revenue Canada generated $299 million in revenue in Alberta during 1989. Anticipated market growth for service sector and light manufacturing is 5% annually.

Market penetration

An average of 1 major engagement per week would represent approximately 40 new clients each year, with perhaps 50% of those as ongoing support clients. This would be a 100% maximum client load a single person could carry. 40 clients represents 0.3% of the total market annually.

Pricing levels

Anticipated sales price for consulting services is between $40 and $70 per hour. A typical implementation engagement would generate about 25 hours of chargeable time. This represents $25,000 to $35,000 in annual revenue. A support client would average 8 hours annually. Projecting an initial number of support clients at 20 represents $8,000 to $11,000 additional revenue. Sales of software and hardware are projected at less than $8,000 annually, representing software for two typical implementations and the hardware for one implementation.

Methods by which specific members of target market were identified

- ❑Directories of businesses in Calgary and area are available through the
- ❑Calgary Economic Development Authority and several private providers.
- ❑The Calgary Herald newspaper publishes a list of new business start-ups each Monday.
- ❑Some accounting software vendors make referrals from inquiries to therr own marketing efforts.

Media through which I communicate with specific members of my target market

- ❑Publication of advertisements for consulting services is not expected to be a primary source of new clients. Neither is advertising on radio or television. Space in the yellow pages will be considered, but not in the first year of operation.
- ❑Direct mail to lists of new businesses obtained from sources above could result in significant new client leads.
- ❑Participation in product and industry forums or trade shows has been effective for many consultants in this and in many other fields.
- ❑Networking is expected to be the largest source of new client leads. This includes referrals from other consultants, computer resellers, business acquaintances and existing clients.
- ❑Referrals are anticipated from accounting software companies, as discussed in the Legal Agreements section.

Trends and anticipated changes within primary target market

Many clients are looking for smaller, less expensive accounting software. Most clients do not understand initially that the cost of software is usually the smallest component of a computer system, and that hardware requirements, consulting fees and training costs each represent larger costs. The trend towards graphic user interfaces and computer programs integrated with each other are now strong factors even among smaller businesses. Many software firms are no longer offering free technical support. Technical support by telephone has certain limitations by nature. Consulting services at reasonable prices have been scarce in the accounting systems market.

Secondary target markets

Some specialized accounting software and computer hardware is not readily available or not available at all through traditional resale markets. Such products are sold exclusively through implementors, or Value Added Integrators. Such products include voice mail systems, integrated workgroup systems, EDI or Electronic Data Interchange systems. Each of these can overlap with accounting or management systems and represent potential sources of revenue. Computer training services by themselves represent a very large market, although generally not profitable for small providers. It can represent a source of additional cash flow, especially on a contract basis where consulting work could be scheduled flexibly. Ongoing support of accounting systems clients will likely grow into a considerable time commitment if past clients are retained for periods of a year or more. This would represent a need to either hire additional staff or scale back other secondary markets.

Market Test Results/Preliminary Contacts in Target Market

Market test procedures

During the months of December 1993 to March 1994, twelve potential customers were contacted regarding accounting systems consulting work. Visits were made to 10 of these potential customers for the purpose of an initial needs analysis.

Reaction of potential customers

Work was actually performed for 5 of these potential customers. Four of these engagements were for support work only, one was an implementation engagement that has generated 12 hours to date.

Two other potential customers have appreciated the initial meeting and expressed an interest in pursuing the recommended changes at a future date. The remaining three were appreciative but did not feel a need for any services at this time.

Test group's willingness to purchase services at various price levels

None of the potential customers were concerned about the rates charged for the services, all between $40 and $50 per hour. This indicates that the rate is reasonable and could be increased, especially for larger implementation engagements.

Competition

Identification

A number of direct competitors exist, as well as a wide array of indirect competitors. A partial list of competition and its market share is available upon request.

Competitor	Direct/Indirect	Market Share
KPMG Peat Marwick Thorne	Indirect	5.0%
Arthur Andersen Consulting	Indirect	4.0%
Ernst & Young	Indirect	2.0%
Deloitte & Touche	Indirect	1.5%
Collins Barrow	Direct	0.3%
Compleat Business Solutions	Direct	2.5%
C.A.T.S. Computer Inc.	Direct	0.3%
PJ Business Services Ltd.	Direct	0.3%
Gordon B. Lipon, C.M.A.	Direct	0.2%
C.S.B. Systems	Direct	1.0%
Bottom Line Solutions	Direct	0.5%
Cal-Mour Consultants	Direct	0.5%
Channel Systems Ltd.	Direct	0.7%
Retail Management Systems	Direct	1.2%
Quasar Business Solutions Inc.	Direct	0.5%
Roberts & Company	Direct	0.8%
Axiom Business Mgmt Systems	Indirect	?
A.G.W. Computer Consultants	Indirect	?
CompuTouch Ltd.	Indirect	?
Dun & Bradstreet Software Services	Indirect	?
Timesavers Information Technology	Indirect	?
P C Management Consulting	Indirect	?

Strengths of competitors

Larger competitors have a broader base of skill to draw on internally. Many of these competitors have as much or more experience than AMS. In addition, larger firms have larger capital bases to obtain new skills, arrange licensing agreements, work with advanced technology.

Weaknesses of competitors

Many of these competitors are larger organizations that must charge between $70 and $120 per hour for their services. Also, these larger organizations (speaking as an ex-employee of one of the above) are less flexible in meeting client needs and slower in adapting to changes in their markets. In fact, most of the indirect competition is more concerned with actual sales of software or hardware than with understanding and meeting client needs. Furthermore, almost all of the competitors have office space and salary costs resulting in higher overhead that must be met through higher volume (client needs vs. cash flow) or higher rates.

What is the competitor's target market?

Most of the larger firms pursue larger and medium-sized businesses than can justify high charge rates and require more specialized software and systems.

Barriers to entry into market

Capital costs do not represent a significant barrier to entry in this market, but time requirements to maintain skills and pursue potential clients are high, as with most professional consulting work. Technology is a key component and represents most of the capital costs. Without very current hardware a computer consultant is working at a disadvantage because he or she cannot be as efficient as the competition and is not familiar with what most of his/her clients will be using. Additionally, there are no regulatory restrictions to providing computer consulting services, which is in my favor.

MARKETING AND SALES ACTIVITIES

Overall Marketing Strategy

What are specific plans in marketing service?

- Networking among past and current customers, other consultants and other business acquaintances is at the top of my list for marketing my business.
- Posting notices at community bulletin boards, in community newspapers and on electronic bulletin board will also be pursued.
- Participation in accounting software forums is already in progress. Some of these forums are ongoing in electronic form, while others are less frequent.
- Participation in industry seminars and trade shows will be limited to attendance at this point. As a reputation is built, it may be possible to be invited to speak at some of these events. This will require a high degree of expertise and credibility and some political work efforts.

What are the expected costs of these activities?

- Networking will cost no more than the occasional lunch.
- Posting notices will cost nothing, until the larger circulation community papers are approached.
- Participation in various electronic forums adds to the cost of bulletin board system (BBS) subscription, but the incremental cost is averaging about $10 to $15 per month.
- Industry seminars quite often charge an admission of $5 to $20. This is expected to cost less than $300 per year. Any speaking engagements will not occur in the first year and travel costs are usually met in those cases.

How does AMS plan to grow?

In the first years the goal is to establish a reputation in the field and survive while doing so. The ultimate goal here is to become busier than a single person can handle. The aim at this point is to have a handful of associates with which work is shared. In the future, if the business is successful, it will become necessary to hire staff or contract out more of the support and hands on implementation work. After four or five years the ideal would be to have one or two salaried staff.

Sales Strategy

The actual delivery of the service will be carried out by Richard L. Sawinski, the owner of Accounting Management Systems. The process of making a sale is as follows:

- ❑Identify a potential client.
- ❑Meet with the client to determine whether specific needs exist and what they are. This meeting will be free of charge. Care must be taken that the client is not allowed to ask a million questions and then perform the implementation him or herself.
- ❑Sell the potential client on the reputation and capabilities of my business (myself).
- ❑Perform the actual services.

OPERATIONS

Service Delivery Procedures

Once an engagement has been agreed to the following steps will be performed:

❶ A formal engagement letter and contract is written and delivered to the client which:

- ❑Spells out the nature of the work to be performed
- ❑Recommends an initial schedule for providing the services
- ❑Details any hardware and software purchases that will be required
- ❑Highlights the client's responsibilities during implementation
- ❑Estimates the number of hours and approximate total cost
- ❑Contains legal recourse instructions and limitations

❷ The engagement letter is delivered to the potential client and when signed, constitutes an initial contract for the services. Any changes to the agreement that the client requests are considered at this time.

❸ The actual services are delivered according to the agreed on schedule.

❹ The engagement is reviewed periodically by AMS and the client to ensure that the goals are being met.

❺ Once the engagement is complete, billing is finalized. There may have been partial billings during the course of a particularly large engagement.

❻ A number of follow up calls are made to the client over the next two months to ensure that the new system is working properly and inquiring into any support services required.

❼ Mailings regarding upgrades will be sent to each past client unless they indicate they do not wish to receive them.

Operating Competitive Advantages

Techniques

The operations described above are proven techniques similar to those used while performing similar consulting work during the course of my employment with a local accounting firm. Some changes have been made to recognize market realities, but the structured approach serves to meet the client needs in most cases without overlooking minor needs or legal loopholes.

Experience

Most of the direct competition identified will have similar or greater experience in working with accounting information, computer systems and procedural analysis. Most of the indirect competitors do not possess the same experience. Economics of scale and direct costs of production do not exist for this service work.

Supplier Relationships

Suppliers of specific hardware or software are a concern only in secondary markets that Accounting Management Systems might enter. However, in providing consulting services, relations with the software vendors are important. Proper vendor relations offer:

- ❑ Advance notice of changes and upgrades.
- ❑ Access to program fixes and undocumented techniques.
- ❑ Potential referral of clients.
- ❑ Access to new versions of programs at reduced or nominal cost.

Care must also be taken when working with several vendors products. A certain rivalry can exist between vendors and this can threaten most of the above benefits to consultants.

Operating Conditions

Location

Operations for Accounting Management Systems are based in home office in Calgary. Some configuration and most of the writing of proposals and documentation will be performed in the home office. Most of the actual consulting services and meetings with clients will be performed at the client's place of business.

Hours of operation/availability

Hours of operation are expected to be from 7:30 AM to 6:00 PM Monday to Friday. Work on new implementations will routinely be done outside of these hours. Any support work not related to new implementations that is requested outside of normal hours will be charged at a 50% premium to the normal rate for that service or client.

MANAGEMENT AND OWNERSHIP

Organization Structure

Accounting Management Systems is currently organized as a sole proprietorship. Revenue during the first year or two is not expected to need sheltering from personal tax. In addition, there are no large start-up costs to capitalize and no special protection from liability that incorporation offers that cannot be incorporated into an engagement contract. If the business growth were to meet the projections contained in this report, then the business would likely be incorporated during its fourth year.

FUNDS REQUIRED AND THEIR USES

Current Funding Requirements

Approximately $6000 of initial funding is required in order to purchase initial computer hardware and software and to establish licensing agreements with several software vendors. Beyond these needs, most initial costs are expected to be met from the cash flow of the business.

This funding will be required within the first few months of operation. The funds will take the form of either bank or private borrowing at current rates and will likely be amortized over a three-year period.

Funding Requirements over the Next Five Years

Additional funding requirements over the next five years are related to acquiring additional computer equipment either for the business itself or for salaried staff.

Use of Funds

- ❑ Capital expenditures.
- ❑ Working capital needs will be met from personal finances or from cash flow.
- ❑ Debt retirement is limited to the initial capital funding and will be met from cash flow.
- ❑ Acquisitions are not seen as an issue, although opportunities for acquisition may arise and will be investigated at the time that incorporation becomes an issue.

FINANCIAL DATA: HISTORICAL

Current financial statements for Accounting Management Systems from November, 1993 to March, 1994 are available on request. These represent work primarily in the secondary market of formal training and should be interpreted as such.

Aerospace Supplier

BUSINESS PLAN

FLATLAND MANUFACTURING, INC.

Principals

Mr. Jon Jones

Ms. Mary Smith

Mr. Doug Douglas

Prepared with the assistance of

Tennessee Small Business Development Center
College of Business
East Tennessee State University
P.O. Box 70,698
Johnson City, TN 37614-0698
(615)929-5630

AEROSPACE SUPPLIER BUSINESS PLAN

DESCRIPTION OF COMPANY

This is an expanding company created for the purpose of owning and operating enterprises that manufacture gizmos and gadgets for the aerospace industry.

The firm was established in 1982 as a sole proprietorship by Mr. Jon Jones. The business was operated for three years out of Mr. Jones' garage on Q Street, Flatland, Kansas. During this period, the business' revenue grew at an annual rate of 27 percent. In March of 1984, Mr. Jones merged his business with a primary raw materials supplier. This firm was owned by Ms. Mary Smith, located in Smithville, Arkansas. A partnership was formed and Mr. Jones moved his manufacturing operation to Smithville. The partnership existed from this time through June 1989. The partnership continued to show moderate sales increases, but significantly better net income increases due to economies of scale that the merger created. The owners knew that additional revenue could be generated from expanding government contracts. In 1989, Mr. Douglas joined the firm as a principal and government contract specialist. The partnership was dissolved, a corporation was established and the plant was moved to Tennessee. Mr. Jones and Ms. Smith each own 40 percent of the stock and Mr. Douglas owns the remaining 20 percent.

As a result of Mr. Douglas' knowledge of government contracting procedures, revenue increased 253 percent annually until 1991. Since that time sales growth is approximately 23 percent. Total annual revenue for 1991 was $9,600,000.

Services and Products

The firm's primary products are electrical components for military aircraft. The descriptions of these component parts are classified Top Secret by the Department of Defense, and therefore cannot be identified. Additional component parts are manufactured for the domestic aircraft industry. These components are sold directly to the aircraft manufacturers. The firm also makes a line of "after-market" avionics for the private pilot.

As a manufacturer, we have no local competition. Our primary competitors are located throughout the United States. We face global competition for the aircraft after-market industry.

Location

The business is expanding to new facilities located in the newly developing Tristate Industrial Park. The facility will include 10,000 square feet of manufacturing space, 5,000 square feet of office complex to include drafting and graphic arts, and 250,000 square feet of warehousing space. The facility is located on 1,000 acres with rail access. This site was selected due to its zoning which permits a heliport and automatic weapons firing range.

MARKET FACTORS

The information in this section is derived from the Marketing Questionnaire, prepared by Smith Brothers. Please refer to the Support Documents section of this plan for details about obtaining the complete analysis.

Market Need for the Business

There are currently two major aircraft manufacturers in the United States. Total component part sales to these firms accounts for a total of $25,000,000 in purchases of the parts and components that we manufacture. As the air fleet ages, the demand for replacement parts increases. This market is expected to top $50,000,000 by the year 2000.

The end of the "Cold War", and the resulting "Peace Dividend" has dropped revenue from the Department of Defense contracts by 60 percent. However, some of this funding is being shifted to NASA for the development of the space station project.

This business is within a 50 mile radius of a major regional airport and 6 smaller local airports. There are about 700 locally owned and registered private aircraft. Thirty percent of the firm's manufactured products are related to the aircraft after-market. Approximately 150,000 square feet of the warehouse facility will be devoted to a Manufacturers Outlet Mall for aircraft enthusiasts.

Local Market Characteristics

Economic

Local air traffic at the Tri-state airport has been steadily increasing at a rate of 13 percent per year. Plans are in the works to expand the facility to two runways and to add two additional air carriers. This being done, air traffic should increase by another 27 percent. These additions would permit the establishment of a secondary air maintenance facility at the airport. This would increase the local demand for this firm's products.

Demographics

Two local schools, one a community college, the other adult vocational education, have added private pilot training to their curriculum. This will increase the flight hours logged on existing aircraft and increase the sales of new aircraft. Both of these situations will increase the demand for the firm's replacement parts and after-market components.

OWNERSHIP AND MANAGEMENT

This firm is owned by Mr. Jon Jones (40%), Ms. Mary Smith (40%), and Mr. Doug Douglas (20%). Mr. Jones is the CEO and president. Ms. Smith is the secretary-treasurer. Mr. Douglas handles government bidding and all estimating functions. The firm has two outside directors: Mr. Black and Ms. White. These directors have no ownership interest. They were selected due to their knowledge of business finance (Mr. Black) and corporate management (Ms. White). Mr. Black and Ms. White act as arbitrators in case of disputes. Each of the five directors have one vote on corporate matters. The outside directors, in accordance with corporate by-laws, are selected by unanimous vote of the stockholders.

Mr. Jones also oversees production operations as the firm's general manager. Ms. Smith is the firms purchasing director. She manages the daily business operations. Mr. Douglas works closely with the firm's CPA firm, Banks, Yür, Monnie & Runns Associates, in the area of cost accounting and pricing.

Personal financial statements and resumes of the three principals are available upon request.

IMPLEMENTATION PLAN

Facility

The newly constructed facility will consist of 265,000 square feet of office, manufacturing, warehouse and retail space. Information concerning preliminary construction plans is located in the Supporting Documents section. An environmental impact assessment has been conducted and the property received a clean bill of health from Greene Fields, Consulting Environmental Engineer, 1224 E St., Getty, TN 37290. The analysis and results are available from this office upon request.

The building is designed in accordance with standards set forth in the Americans With Disabilities Act and other laws and regulations pertinent to government contractors, local zoning requirements and pollution (air, noise, and water) abatement programs.

Equipment

The firm uses a mixture of high technology equipment and routine machine tools. A list of equipment to be purchased is available upon request. Approximately $850,000 of equipment has been provided by the Department of Defense. This equipment remains the property of the U.S. Government and is not pledged as collateral for this loan. The firm currently owns $250,000 in fully depreciated, paid-in-full equipment. A list of this equipment is also available upon request.

Inventory

The firm maintains an approximate 45 day supply of raw materials inventory for manufactured military aircraft component parts. These parts are manufactured under the Just-In-Time inventory system of the prime contractor. A 60 day supply of raw materials is maintained to comply with the Just-In-Time inventory system of the major airline manufacturers. The firm maintains an approximate 15 day finished goods inventory for the aircraft after-market.

Raw materials inventory is accounted for using the LIFO method, while finished goods inventory is accounted for using the FIFO method. The firm uses a fully integrated accounting package which permits a perpetual inventory. A physical inventory is taken at the end of each government contract, with appropriate adjustments made at that time. For non-government contract inventory items, a physical inventory is taken semi-annually in April and October.

Quality Control

The firm is implementing ISO 9000 standards for all non-government work. For government contracts, Military Inspection Requirements MIL-I-45208A and Military Quality Program Requirements MIL-Q-9858A continue to apply as quality standards.

The firm has implemented a Quality Control/Zero Defects program. Floor employees are provided financial and non-financial incentives for exceeding goals set for reducing rejects and re-works. Administrative employees are offered cost reduction incentives equal to 25 percent of cost savings for suggestions resulting in savings of $25,000 or more.

Labor Force

Employment at this firm falls into five categories. Table 1 shows current employment and the three year projection of employment increases due to expansion. The source of skilled employees is area high school vocational education and community college graduates from two-year programs. Professional and technical employees require a four year college degree. Local colleges and universities offer some, but not all, of the required degree programs. All educational specialties are to be found in Tennessee's university system.

Employment Trends

Employment Category	Current	Year 1	Year 2	Year 3
Management	2	2	2	3
Professional/Technical	5	6	6	8
Skilled	15	20	23	27
Unskilled	27	25	23	21
Clerical	3	3	4	4
Total	52	56	58	63

Training

This firm uses a variety of training methods. New skilled and unskilled laborers are trained as needed using Job Training Partnership Act programs. These training programs are available through the Alliance For Business and Training. This includes both classroom training and OJT. Newly hired professional and technical employees are tested at the time of employment with the expectation that they are fully trained and competent at the time of their employment.

The firm also offers a variety of continuing skill improvement programs. Managerial, professional, and technical employees are expected to attend at least one seminar, conference, or continuing education program per year. A tuition reimbursement program is offered to all employees. The firm pays 100 percent of tuition for employees receiving an "A", 80 percent for a "B", 50 percent for a "C", and 20 percent for a "D". No reimbursement is received for a failing grade.

PERSONNEL POLICIES

Employees will be paid at a competitive market rate.

Compensation

Management personnel will be paid a base salary, plus an annual bonus based on the net pre-tax profit of the firm, as established by the Board of Directors.

Skilled, unskilled, and clerical personnel will receive an hourly wage with time and a half for all hours over 40 hours per week.

Skilled, unskilled, and clerical employees will receive shift differentials of 10 percent of their hourly wage for second shift and 20 percent of their hourly wage for third shift.

Hours of Operation

Normal Office Hours (Monday - Friday) .... 8 am- 5 pm
First shift .... 6 am- 2 pm
Second shift 2pm-10pm
Third shift (when needed) .... 10pm- 8 am

Holidays

- New Year's Day
- Memorial Day
- July 4th (observed)
- Labor Day
- Opening day of deer season
- Thanksgiving Day
- Christmas Eve
- Christmas Day

Vacation and Other Time Off

Sick leave Sick leave is accrued at a rate of one half day per month. It shall be accumulated during the entire length of employment. Sick leave is a benefit to the employee for illness only, it will not be "cashed out" upon termination of employment. To reduce absenteeism and abuse of the sick leave benefit, employees not using sick leave during a twelve month period ending on their anniversary date will be given two additional days of vacation and a $100 bonus.

Vacation Managerial, professional, and technical employees will receive three weeks vacation per year. Skilled, unskilled, and clerical employees will receive two weeks vacation per year. At 5 years employment, each employee will receive two additional days vacation. At ten years of service, employees will receive an additional three days vacation.

Insurance The firm offers a group major medical policy for all employees. Coverage for the employee's spouse and family is optional and paid by the employee. The firm offers life insurance for managerial, professional, and technical personnel in the amount of one and a half annual base salary. Additional life insurance is available in $5,000 increments to be paid for by the employee. Key person life insurance is carried on the principals, industrial engineer, and chief accountant.

MARKETING PLAN

As a manufacturer, marketing choices are limited. The U.S. Small Business Administration sponsors Government Procurement Marketplace programs in several regions. Knowing the location of the major prime contractors for our products, we participate in these programs seeking additional government contracts. The Commerce Business Daily is used by the our Government Contracting Section to locate new sources of contracts.

We have designated one sales person to serve the private aircraft market. This individual will establish regular calling schedules for our primary customers.

A two-pronged approach will be taken with our aircraft after-market product line. First, a Manufacturers Outlet Mall will be established in our new warehouse facility. Since this is a retail store, "retail advertising" will be undertaken. Second, the firm shall become a member of the American Aircraft Owners Association. Print advertising will be used every quarter in the AAOA's magazine, Fly or Die. The firm will also purchase the membership roster of the AAOA and known flying clubs. These lists will be used to develop direct mail advertising.

A key to the marketing of our products will be the direct involvement of the principals in establishing sound business relationships and the selling of our products.

Pricing of our "retail" products will be competitive. However, we feel that the quality of our products compared to that of our competition demands a 10 percent price premium. Therefore, we shall price our products slightly ahead of the competition.

PRE-OPENING SCHEDULE OFEVENTS

❑**November-December**

- ■Review Articles of Incorporation and Corporate By-laws.
- ■Complete preliminary business plan.
- ■Select and engage outside professional assistance, CPA, attorney, architect and builder.
- ■Begin search for suitable site.

❑**January**

- ■Execute legal agreement with architect.
- ■Begin search for financing sources.
- ■Continue search for site.

PRE-OPENING SCHEDULE OF EVENTS...*continued*

❑**February**

- ■Finalize plans for the facility.
- ■Begin preliminary negotiations with the builder.

❑**May-June**

- ■Reach agreement with property owner and purchase the site.
- ■Complete financing plans and prepare loan request.
- ■Complete negotiations with contractor.
- ■Initiate discussions with equipment suppliers and manufacturers.
- ■ Begin negotiations to upgrade employee insurance plans.

❑**July**

- ■Obtain site approval from city and county.
- ■Complete detailed business plan and construction plan.
- ■Submit financing package to lending group.

❑**August**

- ■Obtain final financing approval.
- ■Complete site purchase.
- ■Begin construction.

FINANCIAL INFORMATION

Financial Pro-Forma Statements

The pro-forma financial statements are based upon the historical financial performance of this firm. Methods of operation make direct comparison to competitor performance unrealistic. Based upon knowledge of the market, the following revenue growth rates are projected.

Commercial aircraft components	+27%	$1,300,000
Commercial aircraft market share	19%*	
	22% **	
Military aircraft components	-60%	$2,750,000
NASA contracts (none now)		$1,900,000
Aircraft After-market wholesale	+75%	$750,000
Aircraft After-market retail (none now)		$1,000,000

**currently*
***end of year one*

Other Financial Statements and Projections

Current financial statements and financial projections for the first three years of operation have been prepared. Additionally, annual and monthly balance sheets, historical financial statments, and a break even analysis have been prepared. These documents are available from Banks, Yür, Monnie, & Runns Associates, 293 Adams Rd., Springhill, TN 37998.

STRENGTHS AND WEAKNESSES

Strengths

This firm has many strengths. Chief among them is the varied backgrounds of the principals. Each owner has at least 15 years experience in this industry. The skills and backgrounds of the principals are also varied. One has 25 years manufacturing experience; one has 22 years government procurement experience; and the third 15 years experience in purchasing and materials management.

Our dedication to our work force through established training and financial incentive programs insures that we have a productive and efficient work force.

Weaknesses

The main weakness of this firm is the market in which it operates. Our main contracts are "political footballs." Defense contracts are subject to sudden cancellation. NASA contracts have, in the past, been canceled without advanced warning. These are extremely profitable contracts, but unstable. As a result, our firm is limiting government contracts to no more than one-third of our production capacity. The remaining capacity will provide for a break-even operation until such time as additional contracts can be secured.

EXPANSION

This firm is always looking for ways to expand its revenue and market share within the existing market. Plans are being formulated to add a catalog to its retail operation. This will permit us to expand the sales territory of our after-market products to a national level. Once established, consideration will be given to international distribution of the catalog.

There are similarities in the production of avionic electronics to high quality consumer electronics. This firm is looking at several possibilities at this time. The company has sixty percent of the equipment needed to manufacture High Definition Television (HDTV) components. This firm has not ruled out the possibility of further mergers and acquisitions to enter this market.

SUPPORTING DOCUMENTS

Marketing Questionnaire

To obtain the comprehensive analysis and results of the Marketing Questionnaire, please contact Jerold Smith, of Smith Brothers, at 728 Downy St., Suite 59A, Springhill, TN 37987. The questionnaire offers detailed information concerning company product line, including percentage of total sales and gross margin; primary market; five largest customers, ranked by percentage of sales; customer terms; marketing strategy; industrial information; largest suppliers; market planning.

Construction Plans

Several construction plans have been designed by Athens Architects, Inc., 24 East Ave., Brownie, TN 37984. These drawings are available upon request.

Bed and Breakfast

BUSINESS PLAN

RED BARRON BED AND BREAKFAST

824 Springhill Dr.
Los Amos, CA 77385

April 27, 1990

The Gothic-styled Red Barron Bed and Breakfast currently supports five guest suites in the main house featuring a number of amenities. The proprietors hope to expand their operation to include three guest cottages, as business conditions allow. This plan presents a variety of specifics on crafting a successful B&B with comfort and charm.

- STATEMENT OF PURPOSE
- SUMMARY
- DESCRIPTION OF BUSINESS
- INDUSTRY ANALYSIS
- MARKETING STRATEGY
- PROMOTION AND ADVERTISING
- COMPETITIVE ANALYSIS
- PERSONNEL
- RENOVATION AND EXPANSION PLANS
- FINANCIAL DATA
- SUPPORTING DOCUMENTS

BED & BREAKFAST BUSINESS PLAN

STATEMENT OF PURPOSE

This plan will be used as an Operating and Policy Guide for the Red Barron Bed and Breakfast and to obtain necessary financing.

The business will be structured as a sole proprietorship. The principal, Margaret A. Barron, seeks loans totaling $525,000 to:

- Refinance property
- Perform necessary renovations and improvements
- Purchase furnishings and inventory
- Maintain adequate cash reserves for successful start up

This sum, together with an additional $95,000 provided by the principal, will finance start up of a five room inn.

SUMMARY

The property located at 824 Springhill Drive, Los Amos, CA is intended for use as a Bed and Breakfast. Situated in an historic neighborhood recognized as a popular tourist and visitor destination, it is well suited for this use.

A large house, three cottages, and a six car garage are situated on approximately one-half acre of landscaped grounds. The house is a Los Amos City Landmark and has been nominated for the National Register of Historic Places.

The B & B will initially be limited to the main house, with the cottages remaining as monthly rentals. The cottages will be added one at a time as business conditions allow. A Use Permit for eight rooms has already been granted by the City of Los Amos.

Occupancy, revenue, and room rate projections are validated by extensive research conducted over a three year period. The research includes professional survey data, information obtained through state and national industry associations, and the owner's private market analysis.

The research process played a vital role in the determination of features and amenities that will be provided by the Red Barron. Whirlpool tubs and in-room fireplaces were selected based on what B & B guests want, what they are willing to pay top of the market prices to utilize, and which items provide the highest return on investment.

Expense control measures have also been identified through industry affiliations. Through these affiliations, the inn will be able to take advantage of savings not otherwise available to a small purchaser. These range from reduced pricing on towels and linens to credit card processing.

The owner's 20 years of business experience will be a strong asset, particularly in the areas of sales and marketing. To strengthen the operations side of the business, personnel experienced in the hospitality industry are being utilized in the critical first year of operation.

An expansion plan is also in place that will allow the B & B to diversify its customer mix and increase revenues. By adding the three rental cottages, the Red Barron will be able to increase the number of guest accommodations available and market to the growing family and business traveler segments.

DESCRIPTION OF BUSINESS

Nature of the Business

The property is intended for use as a Bed and Breakfast Inn, to be called the Red Barron.

Requests for an eight room Bed and Breakfast Use Permit and a building permit for proposed renovations have been approved by the City of Los Amos. Construction bids were submitted by three licensed General Contractors. Bayside Construction has been selected to perform the necessary renovations and improvements. Based on the scope of work, construction is expected to take five to six months. Adding some time for contingencies and start-up preparations, and taking into account the expected slow down of tourism in the latter part of the calendar year, the inn is expected to open for business in January, 1995.

The property was selected based on a variety of factors, including:

- Appropriately zoned for B & B use
- Prime location in an older neighborhood already well into gentrification
- Location in a popular, scenic, and recreational destination, with a proven track record of attracting travelers, tourists and special event visitors
- Architecturally significant house that is already a City Landmark and has the potential for placement on the National Register of Historic Places
- Excellent floor plan in main house that will easily provide spacious guest rooms, private baths, and ample common areas
- Private, well landscaped back yard
- Ample off-street parking
- Three cottages that can provide either monthly rental revenue or income as part of the B & B

Initially, only the main house will be part of the Bed & Breakfast, providing 5 guest rooms. The 3 cottages will continue to provide monthly income until the (inn) business can support their inclusion. The inn will ultimately include eight guest accommodations.

Inn patrons can enjoy ample common areas, including a parlor, sunroom, large dining room downstairs, and a sitting room with window seat upstairs. Quality

Nature of the Business
...continued

furnishings and furniture, including many antiques and hand-stitched needlework items, will help create a warm and inviting environment. Features of the common areas include two fireplaces, a baby grand piano, and a varied selection of reading material and games. Sitting areas will be comfortable and well lighted.

Guests will also be able to enjoy outdoor seating, either on a deck adjoining the sunroom or in the secluded backyard. In addition to providing a pleasant spot to relax or dine outdoors, the deck will also provide an aesthetically pleasing solution to the required wheelchair ramp.

Each of the 5 guest rooms will have a private bath with shower. Three rooms will also have a whirlpool tub, two rooms will feature a fireplace, and two will have a private deck. One will also have a sitting room and private entrance. As described in some detail in the Industry Analysis and Marketing Strategy sections of this plan, these are increasingly popular features. One guest room and bath, located on the ground floor, will also be handicap accessible.

A full breakfast will be served and included in the room rate. Turn down service, evening refreshments, and an array of special services, including wine for purchase, will also be available. A Beer and Wine License will be obtained to accomplish the latter.

In addition to ample street parking on both Springhill Drive and Sun Lane, guest parking will also be available on the property. There are six existing garage spaces and three uncovered spaces will be added, including one handicap and one compact.

Proposed rates and policies are outlined in the Marketing Strategy Section.

Physical Description of Buildings and Property

Located at 824 Springhill Drive, the house and adjacent structures are on a prominent corner lot in an historic residential neighborhood of Los Amos with compatible Victorian homes representing the various styles of that era. Present on the approximately one half acre parcel are a large two story house, three single story cottages, and a six-car garage.

The main house was built prior to 1870 and is an excellent example of the Gothic Revival style popular in the United States in the 1850s to 1870s. It is on the Master List of the State Historic Resource Inventory and has been designated as a City Landmark. It has also been placed in nomination for the National Register of Historic Places, however, the house has been temporarily removed from consideration by the owner until exterior renovations have been completed.

Although no famous personage was born or resided in the house, it has many of the characteristics of the Gothic Revival style popularized in such books as Andrew Jackson Dowing's The Architecture of Country Houses. The Chief Officer of the State Office of Historic Preservation has deemed this house architecturally significant because it is such a good example of this popular style and retains the integrity of the original design. Also notable is the fact that the house was continuously owned and occupied for nearly 100 years by the descendants of an early Los Amos resident, Clyde Hawthorn, who purchased the property in 1895.

The house consists of five bedrooms, parlor, dining room, two sunrooms, kitchen, and large study. The interior is accented by such features as a built-in desk and display case, two fireplaces, a curved stairway, and hardwood floors.

Also on the property are three cottages, one studio and two one- bedroom units. These dwellings were built in the late 1930s and early 1940s as extended family living quarters. Like the main house, the cottages have hardwood floors and interior features such as built-in corner cupboards.

Landscaping is well established and includes holly, persimmon, fig, and tulip trees, as well as numerous rose and camellia bushes. Also on the grounds are a stone and mortar patio with a path leading around the main house, connecting the patio to the front walk. Shading the patio is a wooden arbor graced by tea roses planted by the early owner, Clyde Hawthorn.

Location

The property is located in the city of Los Amos, in the Paris Valley wine region. The Paris Valley runs southeast-northwest and is approximately 29 miles long and 4 miles across at its widest point.

The Paris Valley consists of approximately 32,000 acres of planted vineyards. In this valley alone there are over 200 wineries. Most of these wineries are visitor oriented, offering tours of their facilities and complimentary or nominal fee wine tasting. Some feature restaurants and art galleries or schedule music concerts, cooking schools, and other wine-related events.

The area is also one of the state's foremost tourist regions. The city of Los Amos typically receives 2 million visitors each year, with at least as many visitors to be found in the valley on any given weekend during the harvest season as in Southern California's Disneyland.

Only a little over an hour's drive from the Metropolitan area, city-weary guests looking for overnight or weekend get-aways are also attracted to this beautiful and peaceful area.

The county has scores of excellent restaurants, several notable galleries and gift shops, and an array of recreational facilities. Add to this the four distinct and desirable seasons, and you have an excellent foundation for a year-round tourist-based business.

Area Attractions

Points of Interest

- Over 200 wineries
- Numerous spas and hot springs
- The Wharf Marina
- Lake Sunfish
- Sumner's Dunes
- Thorne-Spring State Parks
- George Silver Blockhouse
- Terrance Museum
- Hawthorn Wine Museum
- Sharps Museum

Historical Landmarks

- Bale Grist Mill
- Robert Louis Stevenson Park
- Reading Railroad
- Old Calistine Depot
- Krammer Winery
- Charles Benning Winery
- Davis Wine Train

Recreational Activities

- Paris Valley Riverboat
- Tours by air, including glider, biplane, Cessna, helicopter, and hot air balloon
- Bicycle routes
- Hiking trails
- Horseback riding
- Golf
- Tennis

Seasonal Events

March & April
Great Chefs Series (Robert Price Winery)

June
Concours d'Elegance
Monday Night Concerts (Domanique Silano Winery)
Robert Price Summer Festival
Paris Valley Wine Auction

July
Paris County Fair
Fourth of July celebrations
Bastille Day celebration (Domanique Silano Winery)

August
Paris Town & Country Fair

September
Antique Show
Chesterfield Art Exhibit

October
OctoberFest
Silverville Days Festival
Great Chefs Series (Park Winery)

November
Paris Valley Wine Festival
Great Chefs Series (Georgia Cleo Winery)

INDUSTRY ANALYSIS

Travel Trends

Given the current condition of the U.S. economy, attention has been given to the impact of a recession on the travel industry. Information obtained from the U.S. Data Center was studied to get a better perspective on how the industry fared and how consumer behavior changed during past economic recessions.

The 1989-90 Economic Review of Travel in the United States revealed that the travel industry endures recessionary periods relatively well. In fact, when dealing specifically with volume, the first eight months of 1990 showed an increase of 3% over the previous year. Although the last quarter was expected to post a downturn, the Center cites past consumer performance, as measured during the 1981-82 recession, as hopefully being able to predict individual trends.

During 1982, travelers combined vacation trips with business trips and appeared to explore other ways to continue an activity that had become an integral part of their lifestyle. The lodging industry maintained relative success and despite sluggish growth in receipts during the last recession, industry employment outperformed overall employment in creating new jobs during the 1981-85 period. Since 1982, travel industry employment has grown 55% faster than jobs in the overall economy.

The Center's data says that vacation travel recovered more quickly than other types of travel after the 1981-82 recession and projects the same for this recessionary period.

The Paris Valley has numerous features that make it attractive to travelers, even in an economic downturn. It's close proximity to the Metropolitan area makes it an ideal getaway for both local consumers wanting a quick and easy escape from the stresses of everyday life and visitors looking for something to round out their Metropolitan experience. As business and conference travelers look for ways to combine business and personal travel, the Paris Valley is an ideal locale. Neither the year-round appeal of the Valley's weather nor the close proximity to the Metropolitan area should be underestimated.

Characteristics of Bed and Breakfast Guests

The following information about why guests stay at bed and breakfast inns and the characteristics that influence their selection was provided by a variety of experts in the bed and breakfast industry. Statistics were excerpted from two independent survey sources: the 1988 and 1990 "Bed and Breakfast Industry Survey and Analysis" and the 1989 "Market Analysis of Bed and Breakfast Guests".

■The personal touch of a bed and breakfast and the charm of the building are ranked as the most important reason for staying at a bed and breakfast.

■The three most popular information sources are:

- Recommendations from friends and family
- Inn's brochure
- Guidebooks

■Location and availability of amenities are the most important features or characteristics influencing the selection of an inn.

■Smoking permitted and pets allowed are the least important features in selecting a bed and breakfast.

■Pleasure is the primary purpose for frequenting a bed and breakfast inn. In each survey, the largest percentage of guests are "tourists." Respondents also cited special occasions, visiting family, and business travel.

■The average age of the bed and breakfast guest is 39.6 years. Over three-fourths of bed and breakfast guests are between the ages of 20 and 49 years.

■The typical bed and breakfast party consists of two people. The 1990 survey indicates nearly 80% are "couples," sometimes traveling with children or another couple. The number of families traveling to inns is also growing, with an increase from 7% to 10% in 1989.

■The typical bed and breakfast guest is well educated, a business professional, and in the upper percentile for annual income.

- •Nearly 90% of 1990 respondents and their spouses/partners have a college degree, some graduate school, or an advanced degree.
- •The most common occupations are professional, business, sales, banking, health, engineering, computer, and education.
- •Over 50% of respondents reported a 1989 household income of $50,000. (This is a national average).

■Discretionary funds for travel and leisure for individuals in this category are higher than the norm: The typical "upscale" couple frequents bed and breakfast inns for anniversaries, birthdays, and romantic get-aways an average of four times a year.

Amenity and Feature Data

1990 Inngoers Amenities Survey

This information was obtained from a survey conducted by Innsider magazine. A list of basic amenities was provided and readers were asked to rate their importance on a scale of 1 to 5. The results were based on 3500 responses. Respondents were also allowed to comment on other items of great importance to them or those not specifically mentioned.

- •Mattress Quality 87%
- •Towels 85%
- •Linens 81%
- •Washcloths 77%
- •Glasses 62%
- •Bath Mats 62%
- •Reading Lights 58%
- •Soap 56%
- •Phones (in room) 30%
- •Shampoo 23%
- •Books and magazines 20%
- •Wine or cordials (in room) 17%
- •Mints on pillow 13%
- •Hair conditioner 12%
- •Bath gel 11%
- •Comment Book 11%

Some of the additional comments included wanting a small table or place to set toiletries, a comfortable chair with a good reading lamp, good mirror lighting, a table on each side of the bed, luggage rack(s), clothes hangers, plenty of hot water, and extra pillows.

Authors of Innsider note repeated comments about comfortable beds and adequate lighting.

1988 Inngoers Qualities Survey

A survey conducted by the Yellow Brick Road industry newsletter disclosed bed and breakfast qualities considered very important by guests. Although conducted several years ago, current research indicates that those qualities deemed most important have not changed dramatically. Bed and Breakfast guests are becoming more sophisticated and have higher expectations. As an example, private baths are becoming the expected standard, with fewer guests willing to share. More guests are also seeking "luxury" features such as in-room fireplaces and spas, and they are willing to pay a premium for them.

Qualities considered very important by guests:

- Warmth of innkeeper 79.8%
- Private Bath 68.5%
- Breakfast 66.3%
- Owner-operated 37.1%
- Fireplace in Room 29.8%
- Afternoon/Evening Refreshments 18.3%
- Antiques 16.2%
- Historic Building 15.9%
- Spa in Room 6.1%

Other qualities guests like (based on comments): Privacy, gardens, cleanliness, ambience, charm, quiet, and decor.

Occupancy Data

Information obtained from the 1988 and 1990 PAII Bed and Breakfast and Country Inn Surveys indicates that overall occupancy increased over the four year period studied.

Overall:

1986 .... 51%
1987 .... 54%
1988 .... 65%
1989 .... 66%

It should be noted that these are national figures. Traditionally, establishments located in the West enjoy a higher occupancy percentage than the norm, particularly those considered a "destination." The Paris Valley clearly qualifies as a "destination" because most visitors are coming specifically to the area, rather than passing through on their way elsewhere.

The Professional Association of Innkeepers estimates that inns in the Wine Country (including DeLand and Quaal Counties) average an annual occupancy rate of 75%.

Based on information obtained from industry associations, a new inn can expect a first year occupancy of about 50-55% of the area average, with a minimum annual increase of 10%. Using an average of 75% for inns located in the Paris Valley, one could project an occupancy of about 38% to 41% in year one. This would increase to 51% in year two and 61% in year three.

Occupancy figures obtained through real estate records show actual first year rates of 44% for two new inns located in Deland and Quaal respectively.

Pricing Data

According to the 1990 Bed and Breakfast and Country Inn Survey, room prices have more than kept pace with inflation.

Average Daily Room Rate:

1986 .... $78
1987 .... $83
1988 .... $92
1989 .... $102
1990 .... $106
Corporate Rate $85

A few generalizations:

- The older the property, the higher the prices.
- Rates in the West are higher than the South and Northeast by $8-20.
- Urban prices tend to be the lowest, yet their corporate rate is the highest.

Feature Valuations

1990 survey results indicate just how much people will pay for in-room features:

Average Value of Special Room Features
(in addition to basic room priced at $80)

Private Bath .... $ 12 - 34
Fireplace .... $ 13 - 46
Whirlpool Tub .... $ 14 - 63
Extra space (balcony, deck, patio) .... $ 17

MARKETING STRATEGY

Positioning

The Red Barron will be positioned as a bed and breakfast offering a romantic experience with comfortable surroundings. There will be a strong emphasis on attention to detail and customer service. It will cater to the aesthetic tastes and expectations of the discerning and affluent traveler.

In the hospitality business, small inns have the unique ability to deliver personal and personalized services. This advantage will be exploited by offering individualized guidance in personal, recreational, and entertainment needs. An environment will be created to enhance each guest's experience by drawing on the innkeeper's heritage of "Southern hospitality."

The building, grounds, and decor play such an important role in the consumer's choice of a particular bed and breakfast. The inn must be luxurious, comfortable, and conducive to relaxation and romance. Those amenities most desired by guests, including private baths, whirlpool tubs, fireplaces, and private decks, will be provided.

Image

Image consists of many components and the Red Barron is being carefully planned to ensure that each of these elements has been considered and appropriately addressed.

Friendly and polite telephone and on-site presence:
Calls will be answered promptly, and all inquiries handled in a pleasant and professional manner. For those times when calls cannot be answered, an answering machine will be used. The messages will be checked frequently and calls returned as soon as possible.

Owner's personality, hospitality, manner, and business actions:
Recognizing that an owner-innkeeper on the premises and the warmth of that individual are two qualities that B & B guests look for, this will be a high priority. Attitude, appearance, and professionalism are key goals.

Cleanliness of bedrooms, baths, and public areas and dining facility:
The inn will be maintained in a manner befitting a first calss lodging establishment.

Amenities, features and unique services

The Red Barron will excel in its delivery of amenities, features, and special serevices. For clarification, an amenity referes to an extra service or product offered free to every guest that does not directly affect price. Sweet-smelling soaps, fluffy towels, and making dinner reservations will be available to all guests, while in-room whirlpools, fireplace, and private decks are features for which an additional charge is directly extracted. A special fruit and cheese tray or bottle of wine with room delivery is an example of a special service for which there will be an additional charge.

Each guest rom and bath will contain the following amenities:

- •King or Queen-sized bed
- •High quality mattress
- •At least 2 comfortable chairs and a table or desk
- •Good reading light
- •Closet or armoire
- •Luggage racks
- •Storage space in bath (plus tubs in four)
- •Luxurious towels and guest robes

Feature found in individual guest rooms are detailed below.

Name, Logo and Decor of the Inn

The name Red Barron was chosen because it will be easy to remember and it contains a marketing "hook" (i.e. the owner's last name, and a reference to a famous fictional character).

A logo was designed that will subliminally promote the four seasons concept due to the year-round attractiveness of the area to visitors. This scheme is further reinforced by naming guest rooms for the seasons and even decorating each one in the colors and accessories appropriate to that time of year. The fifth guest room will appropriately be called the Fifth Season.

The entire house will be furnished in antiques collected by the owner over many years; however, beds will be new to accommodate today's standards of size and comfort. The bed will be the room's focal point, selected with the "theme" of that room in mind. The Winter Room, for example, will feature a Sleigh Bed. A brief description of the features found in each room follows:

- ♦Autumn (#1) - Queen Bed with Private Bath (Whirlpool Tub),Fireplace,Bay window
- ♦Winter (#2) - Queen Bed with Private Bath (Whirlpool Tub), Fireplace
- ♦Spring (#3) - Queen Bed with Private Bath (Shower)
- ♦Summer (#4) - Queen Bed with Private Bath (Tub & Shower), Private Deck
- ♦Fifth Season (#5) - King Bed with Private Bath (WhirlpoolTub), Sitting Room w/extra bed, Private Entrance, Private Deck

In keeping with the Victorian farmhouse style, furnishings will be less formal than those found in the more ornate mansions. Although furnishings will appropriately reflect the Victorian era, chairs and sofas will be comfortable and rooms light and airy. A variety of color schemes will be used, with a balance of masculine and feminine schemes.

PROMOTION AND ADVERTISING

Public Relations and Personal Selling Program

Building strong credibility within the community is always helpful. Guests needing accommodations will be referred by people living in the area. The inn's location in a residential neighborhood will also generate activity from friends and relatives looking for accomodations in close proximity.

PROMOTION AND ADVERTISING...*continued*

Community public relations will include the following:

❑Support community programs by becoming a member of the Chamber of Commerce, Better Business Bureau, and Convention & Visitors Bureau. The inn will also be made available as a meeting place, as it includes not only a large dining room, but a parlor that can be closed off.

❑Working with community and state support groups to develop tourism. This includes membership in the local and Northern California Bed & Breakfast Innkeeper Associations, through which the owner will have the opportunity for joint publicity and advertising. These associations will also provide overflow referrals from other member inns.

❑Marketing the inn through local media. This will also extend to regional, state, and national coverage. A freelance writer has already expressed interest in developing a series of articles about the inn as it progresses. This writer has been published in a number of national magazines, including Sunset and Victoria.

❑Cooperating with area business. Personal calls will be made on area businesses, especially restaurants, other inns, wineries and recreational facilities. Each visit will be followed up with a letter.

❑Contacting private citizens. The immediate neighborhood will be notified via flyer. The flyer will announce the arrival of the inn and promote it as an alternative to hotels for visiting friends or relatives.

❑Answering inquiries promptly. People who make inquiries are the most promising potential customers. All inquiries will be handled promptly and with the information requested.

❑Use of Travel-Freelance-Guidebook Writer Lists and Media Kit

A media kit will be developed that contains the following basic materials:

- Pen and ink drawing of the inn and grounds
- Photographs of the exterior and interior of the inn
- Brief history of the property
- Detailed description of the house and rooms
- Copy of brochure and rate/policy cards
- Information on things to do in the area

A list of travel writers, guidebook authors, and other appropriate press members will be maintained. The list will include information on publication deadlines, special interests of the authors, and writers that visit properties and/or charge listing fees.

Brochure

An attractive brochure is an important tool for any marketing program. There has been a lot of attention given to the selection of images and copy that will represent the Red Barron in an accurate and inviting manner. A graphic artist was hired to design the inn's logo (see Supporting Documents). A tri-fold brochure, with a separate rate and policy card, is being developed for mailing purposes and rate displays. The owner's experience in the area of collateral development will help keep costs down without sacrificing quality or effectiveness.

The brochure will be distributed locally to the Visitors Center, Chamber of Commerce, and Reservation Services. B & B associations and Travel Agent services, of which the inn is a member, will also receive brochures.

Business Cards and Other Promotional Items

A relatively inexpensive way to promote the bed and breakfast is to incorporate the name and logo of the inn on business cards, stationery, envelopes, and rate/policy cards. Professional looking business cards can help establish credibility and create interest in the business.

The name and logo of the inn will also be used on note cards, featuring a pen and ink or water color drawing of the inn and grounds. These cards will be packaged and available for sale.

Also being considered as a means of heightening the inn's visibility is using its name and logo on polo-style shirts. This would help guests remember the inn, create interest outside the Metropolitan area, and generate additional income.

Reservation Services and Travel Agents

B&B Reservation Services will be an invaluable asset during the start-up months. There are several in Paris Valley which will, for a membership fee and commission on rooms booked, screen guests, handle deposits, and provide some publicity. One of these agencies has submitted a proposal where they will, in addition to providing these services at no charge for six months, also act as consultants and part time innkeepers (see Personnel Section).

Travel Agents are an additional resource that will help attract guests from outside the state. The inn will be listed in INNVIEWS, The Travel Agent's Guide to Unique Accommodations. This guide for agents includes a geographically arranged section that provides a detailed description of each inn, including rates and policies, and highlights local points of interest.

The inn will also be listed with INNRES, a Travel Agent's Reservation Service that includes a toll-free number and features personalized bookings, rather than use of an airline reservation system.

These services will be necessary during the first year of operation to compensate for limited word-of-mouth referrals and guidebook activity. After the first year, each service will be carefully reviewed to determine which, if any, will be continued.

Listing in Yellow Pages and Guidebooks

The inn will be listed in the yellow pages under the categories of Bed & Breakfasts and Hotels. The number of guidebooks in which the inn can be listed will vary depending on publication dates and availability of their writers. There are currently over 195 Bed & Breakfast and Country Inn guidebooks in print and fewer than 20% charge for a listing.

Using a current list of guidebooks whose publication deadlines can be met, the inn's media kit will be distributed to approximately 12 books before the inn opens. Additional books will be added to the initial list as new publication dates are published. Promotional information will also be sent to a current list of over 300 travel editors and freelance magazine and newspaper travel writers.

Special Promotions

There will be a variety of special promotions offered throughout the year, with an emphasis on those aimed at attracting guests during the off-season. All promotions will be monitored to determine those attracting the greatest number of guests and delivering the highest return on investment. In addition to tracking special promotions, all phone callers will be asked how they heard about the inn and the information will be recorded.

An example of a year round promotion will include packages that contain an activity such as hot-air ballooning or a trip on the Wine Train. Special events will also be planned for each season of the year, with local merchants encouraged to co-sponsor and promote some events. An example of a merchant sponsored promotion would be a wine tasting and a non-sponsored promotion might be a Murder Mystery weekend.

Gift Certificates will also be promoted as an ideal business or personal gift.

COMPETITIVE ANALYSIS

Competitive Differences

There are several factors differentiating the Red Barron from hotels and other Bed and Breakfast Inns.

The overwhelming advantage of a Bed and Breakfast over a hotel is its personalized service, individualized decor, and delivery of an "experience" rather than simply a room for the night. The Bed and Breakfast will appeal to the aesthetic tastes and expectations of the discerning, affluent traveler looking for a higher standard of attentive, personalized service and amenities. Delivery of these services will justify top of the market rates.

In comparison with other inns in the area, the Red Barron will stand out in its delivery of amenities and features. Using information obtained through extensive market research, including independently conducted surveys and the owner's own travel experiences, those amenities that guests most desire are being provided.

As outlined in the Competitive Section of this Plan, the Red Barron is also above average in its added features, such as in-room whirlpool baths, fireplaces, and The inn's location in a quiet and safe neighborhood surrounded by fine examples of Victorian architecture, it's secluded backyard and deck, and the spacious common room areas will also compare well to other inns.

The Red Barron will also have handicap accessibility, which is not available in most other inns in the area.

The property is a City Landmark and should be accepted to the National Register of Historic Places. Even without landmark status, the Gothic Revival home is a style not abundantly present. The Victorian "farmhouse" style will offer guests an alternative to the more formal Victorian mansions and contemporary styles offered by other inns.

Breakfast is another way to set one inn apart from another. The Red Barron will incorporate southern-style specialties into both its breakfast and evening refreshment service.

The inn will be positioned as a "full service" bed and breakfast, offering a variety of services for its guests. This will range from assisting guests with restaurant reservations to providing food trays, wine, and flowers for special occasions.

Competition: DeLand County

A competition chart has been drawn up comparing 24 inns with total of 108 guest rooms located in DeLand County. Comparisons were made in the following nine categories: number of rooms, prices, extra person rates, bed size, meals, amenities, policies, check-in/out times, and accepted credit cards. The complete chart is available through Anson Computers. Notable observations appear below.

If the Claymore Hotel with 18 rooms and the Blue Skies Inn with 22 rooms and three suites are excluded, there are 65 rooms. The average number of rooms, excluding the two mentioned above, is three.

Unlike DeLand, where the majority of B&B's are in Victorian styled homes, most of the inns in Paris Valley are contemporary structures ranging from Swiss chalets to French Country and ranch homes.

Eight inns have at least one room with a fireplace, one offers an in-room whirlpool, two others provide a hot tub on the premises, two offer a room with a private balcony, three mention air conditioning, four have a pool, and seven of the inns feature private baths.

Rates range from $55-$275. Half of the inns offer "off season lower rates." The specific discount is not publicized, nor is it known if the reduction applies to the weekend, weekday, or both. Four inns specifically mention "off season lower midweek rates" and one offers "midweek" lower rates.

Competition: Quaal County

A second competition chart was developed for the four inns located in Quaal County. This chart was compiled using the same nine categories mentioned above and it is also available through Anson Computers. An analysis of the data reveals the following observations:

All four inns are listed in the AAA Bed and Breakfast Guide and/or Chamber of Commerce. The inns contain a total of 21 rooms. One inn, Crossing Railway, has ten rooms.

Two inns have at least one guest room with a fireplace, one inn offers one room with a whirlpool, one provides a room with a private entrance, two others offer balconies or patio/decks, and one offers a pool and spa. Every inn provides private baths.

Rates range from $95-$140. None of the inns refer to the availability of lower rates weekdays or off season.

Proposed Rates

In Season (April-Nov.) Weekends/Weekdays		Off Season (Dec.-March) Weekends/Weekdays	
$175	$170	$160	$155
$170	$165	$155	$150
$105	$100	$90	$85
$120	$115	$105	$100
$170	$165	$155	$150

Average:

$148	$143	$133	$128
($145.50)		($130.50)	

Note: Rates were determined by reviewing local Bed & Breakfast rates and average valuations of special room features. Valuations were provided by the PAII survey of U.S. inns and can be found in the Industry Analysis Section of this Plan.

Proposed Policies

- ❑A deposit of one night's stay will be required to guarantee a reservation, either by credit card or receipt of funds seven days prior to check in.

- ❑Deposits, less $10, will be refunded. A cancellation fee will be charged if the cancellation occurs three days prior to scheduled check in.

❑There will be a two night minimum stay on seasonal weekends and all holidays.

❑Several credit cards will be accepted, at minimum Mastercard and Visa, as well as checks and cash.

❑Smoking will not be allowed in the house.

❑Pets will not be allowed.

❑Check in will be between 4 and 6 p.m., unless arrangements for late arrival have been made in advance.

❑Check out will be 11 a.m.

PERSONNEL

Personnel Requirements

The services of a part time innkeeper and part time housekeeper will be used during the first year of operation. A two person team, currently operating a Paris Valley reservation service, will be used as needed during the week to accept reservations, check guests in and out, supervise the housekeeper, and prepare and serve meals. It is estimated that innkeeping services will be required approximately two days a week during the months of January through June, November and December and three days a week July through October. A proposal is attached detailing services and rates, as well as a resume of the individuals to be hired.

The employment of these individuals will allow the owner to retain her current marketing position at full salary. The duties they perform during the week will be handled by the owner on weekends. In addition to providing basic innkeeping services, these individuals will provide vital knowledge about Bed and Breakfast operations. By using experienced personnel during the critical start up months, the owner can gain experience herself and build a solid business foundation.

A housekeeper will also be used part time to clean the inn and do laundry. This individual will be used as needed. The housekeeper will work weekdays only during the slower months, while some weekends may also be required during the busy season. It is estimated that housekeeping services will be required two days a week for three hours per day during the period of January through June, November and December and increased to three days a week for three hours a day from July through October. It is further estimated that the hourly rate for this individual will be $6 per hour. No fringe benefits or health insurance is planned.

When business conditions permit, the owner plans to operate the inn full time. This is currently projected to occur in the second year. Full time status will eliminate the need for innkeeper services, except as needed to relieve the owner and prevent burn out. Housekeeping services will increase as occupancyincreases. Some assistance in food service may also be required on a limited basis during the third year.

No full time employees are planned in the first three years of operation.

Innkeeping and Consulting Proposal : *Wine Country Reservations*

1. The fee for services provided under this agreement shall be $50 per day, due and payable on the first and fifteenth of each month.
2. This fee does not include a housekeeper to clean the rooms. We can suggest one. It is recommended that the individual come out twice a week.However,she may be needed more frequently during the busy season.
3. In addition to the $50 per day fee, there is a 5% commission paid for each room reserved (booked) the day the inn-sitting services are rendered.However,this fee will be waived for a six month period for the purposes of building up this new business and to show good will.
4. The owner of the inn understands that it takes about two to three years to establish a bed and breakfast.
5. In addition to the above mentioned fees, a 10% commission is charged for any future reservations (bookings) that are made while inn-sitting.This commission will be waived for six months, except during the months of July, August, September, and October. However, reservations that are made through any other reservation service will be subject to the 10% commission fee.
6. The owner will provide a cash fund for groceries and other innkeeping supplies.
7. It is suggested that the owner establish a Visa and Mastercard service to protect herself against no shows and from cancellations that are within the cancellation policy
8. Wine Country Reservations assumes no liability for accidents or no shows.

Proposal submitted by Mary S. Jones

Owner/Operator Resume

The objective of this resume is to outine business experience and qualifications relevant to the operation of a bed and breakfast inn.

Relevant Experience

Marketing

- ♦Market Research
- ♦Market Sizing/Revenue Forecasting
- ♦Competitive Analysis
- ♦Business Plan Development
- ♦Product Pricing
- ♦Collateral Development
- ♦Advertising/Promotional Campaigns
- ♦Sales Training/Tool Development

Management

- ♦Program/Product Management
- ♦Personnel Management

Sales

- ♦Product and Service Sales
- ♦Telemarketing Sales
- ♦Sales Management

Administration

- ♦Policy Analysis
- ♦Contract Negotiation
- ♦Policy/Process Development
- ♦Business Writing

Finance

- ♦Financial Analysis
- ♦Budget Development/Management
- ♦Revenue Forecasting
- ♦Compensation Planning

Innkeeping

- ♦Food Preparation & Service
- ♦Guest Registration
- ♦Housekeeping
- ♦Room Layout Design

Note: Experience gained in the first five categories was the result of full time employment over a period of 20 years at the corporations listed on the following page. Experience in the hospitality industry was obtained part time over the past two years at an 8-room inn located in Camino, California.

Personal History

Employment

ANSON COMPUTERS (1989 - Present)

Marketing Programs Manager
Responsible for identifying,developing and launching new support products and programs to enhance company's market position.

Senior Marketing Analyst
Responsible for identifying support issues impacting company's market position and strategic direction and developing program solutions.

DESIGNS INCORPORATED (1973 - 1989)

Western Division Service Sales Manager
Responsible for planning, organizing and managing sales efforts of five Service Sales Representatives within a 13-state territory.

Western Division Marketing Manager
Responsible for identifying market requirements within 15-state territory, developing and introducing non-standard service programs and alternate market channels.

Western Area Supervisor of Administration
Responsible for development, implementation and maintenance of administrative policies and procedures within 6-state territory.

PEOPLE'S CORPORATION (1972 - 1973)

Assistant Complex Manager
Responsible for leasing, public relations, advertising, and management of housekeeping/maintenance personnel for 150 unit apartment complex.

Design Consultant
Coordinated interior layout and design for 100 unit apartment complex.

Education
BA Degree in English/Journalism
University of North Carolina, Chapel Hill

Personal
Single,excellent health. Professional parents who operated successful small business for over 30 years.

Strengths
Strong planning and organizational abilities;solid interpersonal skills and a customer service orientation;self motivated, resourceful and creative; excellent analytical and critical thinking skills; effective oral and written communication skills.

Consultants and Other Resources

Professional

- ♦Member of Professional Association of Innkeepers International (PAII)
- ♦Workshops/Conferences
    - •PAII sponsored "Workshop for Aspiring Innkeepers", April, 1990
    - •Bay Area Innkeepers of Northern California (BBINC) Conference and Workshops, January, 1991

Research

- ♦Industry Reference Publications
    - •*1988 and 1990 Bed and Breakfast Inns Industry Survey and Analysis*
    - •*So, You Want to be an Innkeeper*, by P. Hardy, J. Bell, M. Davies
    - •*How to Open and Operate a Bed and Breakfast Home*, by J. Stankus

- ♦Special Reports compiled by PAII on
    - •Insurance
    - •Staffing
    - •Marketing
    - •Computer Software Packages
    - •Political Negotiations

- ♦Industry Periodicals
    - •Innkeeping
    - •Innsider
    - •Inn Review
    - •Country Inns

Consultants

Consulted with the Small Business Administration, California Office of Tourism, Los Amos Small Business Division, American Association of Bed and Breakfast Inns, Bed and Breakfast Innkeepers of Northern California and the Professional Association of Innkeepers International. Accounting and legal professionals familiar with the lodging industry regulations have also been consulted.

In addition to interviewing numerous owners and/or innkeepers from a variety of inns in northern and southern California, marketing assistance was provided for a new inn in Camino, California in exchange for on-the-job training and experience in the hospitality industry. The inn, known as Sand Castle Estates, is owned and operated by Joel Best and Chris Brown.

RENOVATION AND EXPANSION PLANS

Explanation of Renovations

Renovations fall into two basic categories:

1. Renovations required to satisfy city, state, federal or similar governmental ordinances or regulations.

2.Renovations necessary to meet standards set by the Bed and Breakfast industry and/or differentiate the Inn on Springhill Drive from its competition.

Renovations in the first category, which include but are not limited to fire sprinklers and handicap accessibility, are primarily conditions set forth by the City of Los Amos Bed and Breakfast Use Permit.

Items contained in the latter category are selected based on extensive market and competitive research, with an emphasis on identifying those features capable of providing the greatest return on investment. Included in this category are items such as whirlpool tubs and fireplaces.

Alterations required for health or safety reasons have been exploited wherever possible. The backyard deck, for example, was designed to meet wheelchair accessibility standards without altering the structure in a manner that would be unacceptable to the Cultural Heritage Commission or National Register of Historic Places. The deck will also serve as a positive differentiator for the inn by providing a quiet and private outdoor area for guests. Although a General Contractor has been hired to oversee construction and ensure that all work is performed in a timely, cost efficient, and correct manner, the owner will remain closely involved in the entire renovation process.

Expansion Plans

The three rental cottages will be added to the Bed & Breakfast one at a time, as business conditions permit. Based on current revenue projections, conversions are not scheduled to begin until 1996.

Addition of the cottages to the business will allow for a broader and more diverse target audience, specifically including families and the business traveler.

Research indicates that a growing number of families are interested in pursuing the B & B experience; however, the number of inns that encourage or even allow children is extremely limited. A cottage will provide accommodations spacious enough for a family, with the surroundings and personalized services particular to a B & B, but without infringing on the solitude and privacy of other guests.

The number of business travelers frequenting Bed and Breakfast inns is also increasing. The business traveler is becoming more demanding of personalized service and he/she is more likely to combine personal vacations with business travel. In addition to its close proximity to the Metropolitan area, the Paris Valley itself is becoming more attractive to the business community. The need for overnight accommodations and meeting space increases as more corporations move into the area.

Renovation requirements and pricing will be determined at a later date, based on then-current market need and availability of funds.

FINANCIAL DATA

Projected Renovation and Improvement Costs

Includes construction costs provided by Bayside Construction and owner supplied products and services.

Permits & Fees	$11,000
Grading/Paving/Foundation	$15,300
Carpentry - Rough	$16,590
Plumbing - Rough (incl. Fire Sprinklers)	$40,955
Electrical- Rough	$10,361
Misc. Steel/Hardware	$1,120
Roofing	$14,280
Sheet Metal	$12,300
Windows/Glass	$2,572
Interior Siding	$1,560
Painting (Interior)	$1,100
Insulation	$4,180
Sheetrock/Drywall	$18,600
Doors - Exterior & Interior	$980
Stairs - Exterior & Interior	$4,320
Heating	$12,825
Carpet	$1,200
Vinyl	$2,406
Fireplaces	$5,100
Bathroom Fixtures & Accessories	$6,000
Eletrical Fixtures - Ext. & Int.	$1,500
Bathroom Tile/Surrounds	$2,500
Appliances	$2,200
Misc. Electrical (includes fire alarm)	$1,943
Lumber - Finish	$5,500
Carpentry - Finish	$15,571
Landscaping/Fencing	$500
Clean up	$5,500
Concrete Flat Work	$1,000
Overhead	$27,878
Total	$243,620

FINANCIAL DATA
...continued

Note: To aid in controlling costs, the owner will take responsibility for supplying items such as gas fireplaces, bath fixtures, appliances and electrical fixtures. The contractor has included installation allowances for the appliances and bath and electrical fixtures. The owner will supervise installation of the fireplaces, which will be performed by manufacturer authorized personnel. The owner will also assume responsibility for supervision of certain other tasks, such as interior painting and landscaping.

Projected Start-up Costs

Following are start-up expenses not otherwise covered in the breakdown of renovation and improvement costs.

Marketing
(Promotions & Advertising) $1,200

Furnishings
(Includes furniture; window coverings; rugs) $7,000

Bedding inventory
(Includes mattress sets; pads; comforters;
skirts; shams; pillows; blankets; sheet sets) $2,900

Bath inventory
(Includes assorted towels & washcloths;
shower curtains; liners, rings; bath mats) $1,100

Room/Housekeeping Inventory
(Includes guest amenities (shampoo, etc.); cleaning
& laundry products; operating items (light bulbs, etc.)) $450

Total $12,650

Occupancy and Income Projections

Occupancy & Revenue Projection Summary
Years One, Two, and Three

	Occupancy %	Rooms Rented	Gross Revenue
Year One	41%	746	$104,779
Year Two	52%	946	$138,845
Year Three	61%	1113	$171,920

Occupancy and Income Projections..continued

Occupancy/Revenue Projection by Month, Year One

Month	Num Days	Rms. Avail.	Occupancy %	Rms.	Avg. Rate	Gross Income
Jan.	31	155	20	31	$130.50	$4,046
Feb	28	140	20	28	$130.50	$3,654
Mar	31	155	25	39	$130.50	$5,090
Apr	30	150	35	53	$143.00	$7,579
May	31	155	40	60	$143.00	$8,580
Jun	30	150	45	68	$143.00	$9,724
Jul	31	155	50	78	$143.00	$11,154
Aug	31	155	55	85	$143.00	$12,155
Sept	30	150	60	90	$143.00	$12,870
Oct	31	155	55	85	$143.00	$12,155
Nov	30	150	50	75	$143.00	$10,725
Dec	31	155	35	54	$130.50	$7,047
Total	365	1825	41%	746		$104,779

Occupancy & Revenue Projection by Quarter, Years Two and Three

YEAR TWO

	Occ. %	#Rms Rntd	Avg Rate	Gross Revenue
Q1	37%	165	$137	$22,605
Q2	50%	228	$150	$34,200
Q3	65%	299	$150	$44,850
Q4	55%	254	2 mos. @ $150 1 mo. @ $137	$37,190
Annual	52%	946		$138,845

YEAR THREE

	Occ %	#Rms Rntd	Avg Rate	Gross Revenue
Q1	45%	203	$144	$29,232
Q2	60%	273	$158	$43,134
Q3	75%	345	$158	$54,510
Q4	63%	292	2 mos. @ $158 1 mo. @ $144	$45,044
Annual	61%	1113		$171,920

Note: Average rates in the second and third years reflect a 5% annual price increase.

FINANCIAL DATA
...continued

Break Even Analysis #1

Year One

$ 69,702
$ 253,413 = 27.5% Occupancy Needed

Year Two

$ 72,950
$ 265,885 = 27.4% Occupancy Needed

Year Three

$ 79,706
$ 279,880 = 28.4% Occupancy Needed

Note: Figures based on inn operating expenses, interest expense less rental income, and revenue at 100% occupancy.

Break Even Analysis #2

Year One

$ 73,218
$ 253,413 = 28.8% Occupancy Needed

Year Two

$ 76,634
$ 265,885 = 28.8% Occupancy Needed

Year Three

$ 83,574
$ 279,880 = 29.8% Occupancy Needed

Note: Figures based on both inn and cottage operating expenses, interest expense less rental income,and revenue at 100% occupancy.

Projected Profit and Loss Summary for the first three years

All figures are based on a 25 year loan of $525,000 at 9.25% interest. These figures do not include taxes or depreciation.

Year One

Total revenue projected for the first year is $190,799. Operating expenditures, including marketing, office supplies, business fees and permits, utilities, and salaries, total $39,573. If the cottages are available for use, the operating expenditure would increase by $3,516 bringing the total operating expense to $43,089. Loan interest would create an additional expense of $53,952 for a grand total of $97,041. Given these expenses, the net profit and loss for the first business year is $94,181.

Year Two

In the second year, revenue is expected to decrease to $159,182. This is a drop of $71,617 from the first year's projected revenue total of $190,799. The inn's total operating expenses, including the operation and maintenance of the cottages, will be $47,694. Loan interest adds $53,952 to the total. The net profit and loss figure for the second year is $57,536.

Year Three

The third year establishes total revenue gain over the first two years with a figure of $199,788. Total operating expenses, including cottage expenses and loan interest, are $55,890. The net profit and loss figure for the third year is $89,946.

Revenue and Expense Notes

Revenue

Rental revenues are based on a 5% annual increase.

Expenses

Fixed costs such as insurance and taxes have been evenly distributed across the calendar year. Variable costs, those that are directly affected by occupancy, have been distributed accordingly.

Property Taxes and Insurance are calculated in the inn's operating expenses and include the three cottages.

Wherever possible, cost projections were based on current price lists or quotations; otherwise, information obtained through professional associations, market research and expense records for operating inns of similar size was used. Inflation has also been taken into account for Years Two and Three (postage, for example, was calculated using a rate of .30).

Year One capital includes a 6-month inventory of room and housekeeping supplies, towels and linens, and brochures and rate cards. Repairs and maintenance costs should also be relatively low, since renovations will have been completed just prior to opening.

Several programs or services have been identified which will help keep expenses down; they include, but are not limited to, the following:

❑Agreement with AT&T to function under their Multi-Location Pro Wats Program for a $5 monthly charge, with long distance service discounted up to 31%.

❑Agreement with AT&T to receive their Language Line service, at no additional charge, to provide instant access to interpreters in 140 languages. This service is part of a larger agreement to receive Guest Line, where the inn is paid a .30 per call commission on operator assisted, collect, third party billed and 0+ calling card calls (the commission is NOT added to the guest's phone bill and the guest pays regular AT&T rates).

❑Insurance coverage with a full service agency that pays dividends to bed & breakfast and country inns. In 1990, member inns received a 37% dividend on premiums paid in the previous policy year.

❑Discounts on a variety of products from telephone security devices and computer software to bath, bedding and guest amenities.

❑Agreement with National Bancard Corporation (NaBANCO) to receive a 2.10% merchant fee on credit card authorizations. There are no per-transaction fees and all major credit cards are electronically authorized.

Detail of Operating Expense Accounts

Marketing (Advertising & Promotion)
Brochures,magazine/newspaper ads, printing, direct mail, guidebooks

Commissions
Agent commissions, referral services, etc.

Bank Fees
Check charges, merchant credit card services

Office Supplies
Letterhead, office equipment rental, pens, etc.

Postage
Costs for non-promotional mailings

Dues & Subscriptions
Association dues and subscriptions to services, newspapers, magazines

Maintenance, Repairs, Fixtures
Materials for maintenance and repairs. Also includes miscellaneous purchases under $300 for appliances and fixtures

Insurance
Non-payroll insurance such as fire, theft, liability

Legal & Accounting Fees

Business Fees
Excludes sales, bed and income taxes

Property Taxes
Taxes on Land and Buildings

Food
Food and liquor for the Inn

Utilities
Includes trash, gas, electric, water

Telephone
Telephone and related expenses

Room & Housekeeping Supplies
Supply items such as soap, toilet paper, light bulbs, cleaning supplies, laundry soap, notions, toiletries, etc.

Towels & Linens
Purchase price of towels, linens, blankets, pillows, bathrobes, etc.

Auto
Gas, repairs and maintenance

Travel & Entertainment
Travel related expenses & business entertainment

Outside Services
Services such as gardening, etc.

Miscellaneous
Expense items not belonging to any account

SUPPORTING DOCUMENTS

The following documents are available upon request:

- Contractor Resume
- Innkeeper Resume
- Owner's Financial Statement
- Plot Plan
- Inn Logo
- Income Tax Statements
- Explanation of Operating Expense Accounts

Biscotti Bakery

BUSINESS PLAN

THE ITALIAN EATERY

2700 W. 45th Ave., Ste. 5B
Madison, OR 97002

June 23, 1993

The Italian Eatery seeks funding to introduce a product capaitalizing on Amercans' desire for products with a European flavor. Different from the typical American confection, Biscotti Rosa will be manufactured by a young enterprise seeking to reach a national market. This plan will offer an example of initiating a venture based on an innovative food concept.

BISCOTTI BAKERY BUSINESS PLAN

"Cookies, steel, car dealerships and laundromats can produce as much profit and growth as computers and biotechnology."

Thomas Peters, co-author
In Search of Excellence

STATEMENT OF PURPOSE

The name of this business is The Italian Eatery. It is a young business initiated in February, 1993. Currently, the business is a sole proprietorship engaged in the production, wholesale sales and distribution of Biscotti Rosa (cookies). This plan has been written as a business operating guide and a finance proposal for investors.

PRODUCTS

Biscotti Rosa are twice-baked Italian-style cookies. Each cookie measures 4.5-5 inches long, one inch wide, 5/8 of an inch high, and weighs between .75 and 1.25 ounces. There are four varieties: the original almond, hazelnut dipped in bittersweet chocolate, chocolate almond, and anise. Biscotti made with white or red wine is currently being developed.

The ingredients include unbleached flour, sweet butter, whole fresh eggs, pure cane sugar, whole almonds or hazelnuts, Dutch cocoa, Callebaut bittersweet chocolate, anise seeds, fresh lemon peel, aluminum-free baking powder, pure Madagascar bourbon vanilla, organic anise oil and vitamin E. They qualify as all natural products with no preservatives, although the addition of vitamin E, which acts as an anti-oxidant for the butter and nuts, does prolong the shelf life by approximately six months.

Biscotti Rosa packaging has consisted of two biscotti facing one another in a bio-degradable cellulose bag. The package is heat-sealed to preserve crispness, with a hole-punched, recycled stock label stapled to the top of the bag. (See Exhibit I.) Recently, a Consumer Survey revealed that customers want to select cookies from a jar, so jars need to be purchased and provided for current outlets that desire them. In most cases, retailers are willing to purchase the jars, so the cost to the company is negligible. Large labels, identifying the variety of biscotti and the ingredients, would be attached to the jars for a minimal cost. Single or double biscotti could be bagged without labels, significantly lowering the cost of sales and labor, and sent out in crush-proof cartons for refilling the jars. Also planned are packages of twelve biscotti, with a net weight of 9-15 ounces depending on the variety, and packages of twenty-four biscotti, with a net weight of 18-30 ounces. Exhibit II is an estimate of design costs for these packages.

MARKETING

Initial sales efforts have been concentrated in the Amarna Valley primarily because of the ease of handling direct distribution. The next immediate step is to facilitate shipping. Biodegradable shipping containers and packing materials will be used to ship all sizes of packages. The costs incurred, from $.40 to $1.83, will be passed on to the recipient as a handling charge. This is a standard industry procedure.

The distinction between biscotti and American cookies is noteworthy, since biscotti are a new faction in the established U.S. cookie industry. Using the universal appeal of cookies, biscotti has the potential for a nonexclusive target market. Five years ago, biscotti were known only to Italian-American communities in larger cities. Now, they tend to be purchased by up-scale urbanites and suburbanites because of the price. (Compare Choco-Wafers at $2.99 per pound with biscotti at $9.95 per pound).

The retail placement of biscotti among gourmet items and the Italian name assumes a certain worldliness of its consumers. Biscotti Rosa is a premium product, competitively priced. It is the only biscotti on the market packaged with an appropriately Italian-style label that announces the name of the product in larger type than the name of the company. This advertising attracts both the uninitiated consumer and biscotti aficionados alike.

Lighter and less sweet than typical American cookies, biscotti appeal to the growing demand for healthier, higher quality food products. Introducing them immediately into the national market is essential to achieving prominence in the growing biscotti industry. Arnold Brothers, a large chain of one hundred twenty-five gourmet stores and catalog company with a growing distribution of over forty million, has requested the twelve-pack biscotti package to test market response in some of their stores. They are now awaiting a prototype of the packaging.

After a successful introduction of Biscotti Rosa into the Arnold Brothers stores, it will be included in their future catalogues. Although the twelve pack boxes must be sold to them at a 21% discount, the resulting "free" marketing through their catalogues would be more than sufficient compensation.

Additional advertising strategy will be to seek free publicity from various printed media through the distribution of a press release. The response to small local businesses which have been featured in local newspapers and magazines has been dramatic in terms of increased sales. Purchasing booth space in specialty food trade shows is another possibility, but only after a following has been established with Arnold Brothers. It is estimated that an average of fifteen pounds of biscotti, with a wholesale value of $65-132, would be given away monthly as samples for in-store demonstrations and charitable donations.

COMPETITION

It is partially the success of the competition which has stimulated the formation of The Italian Eatery. The most widely distributed product of similarity is Valentino Biscotti. In 1987, after four years of operation, Gianelli Co. was producing 16,000 biscotti daily. The company is now making 40,000 confections a day. In 1989, Gianelli Co. became a $3.6 million business. The market for biscotti in America has been firmly documented.

Valentino Biscotti are hard, meringue-like cookies. They are difficult to chew, unless dipped in a beverage to soften them. Biscotti Rosa are softer cookies with a buttery consistency. These cookies will hold their shape if dipped, but are easily chewed without dipping. This will encourage the choice of Biscotti Rosa by youngsters and senior citizens who may have difficulty with biscotti, and by others who prefer Biscotti Rosa's richer flavor.

Other competitors include The Marsella Baking Company, with a hard textured biscotti. The Marsella Baking Company is known for their savory toasts, not their biscotti. Two local companies, The Sweetery and Heart's Delight sell a harder and heavier version of the Biscotti Rosa. There are several Italian commercial imports, but none with the texture and taste of Biscotti Rosa.

The Biscotti Rosa single pack is priced at $.33-.42 which compares favorably to Gianelli's single package at an average of $.41 each. The standard cost of goods margin in the food manufacturing industry is 22-23%. In this price range, The Italian Eatery's margin averages 23%.

Although Gianelli Co. occupies a primary position in the market, the distinct differences in taste and presentation of Biscotti Rosa should allow an equally favorable status for The Italian Eatery. The initial advantage of Biscotti Rosa over Valentino Biscotti will be its captivating packaging. The ultimate advantage will be its more widely acceptable and addictive taste.

OPERATIONS

The current production facility is a licensed commercial kitchen space rented in Portland, Oregon. The monthly rental for the kitchen is $1,200 per month. Presently, the kitchen is being shared at a cost of only $300 per month. It is estimated that production will increase in October of 1995 and monthly rent payments of $600 will be required. By January of 1996, an entire kitchen will be needed for projected production.

Initially UPS will be used for shipping as they have an office within two blocks of the kitchen. Other means of distribution are being researched. A low-mileage Nissan truck is being purchased for $2,000 to be used to pick up supplies, make sales calls, and deliveries.

The Amarna Valley has a good supply of minimum wage workers. Financing advantages are available through the Business Industrial Development Corporation if low-income minority workers are hired. There is also the availability of handicapped workers as well as Amarna Valley College students. Some small equipment must be purchased before hiring any personnel. Other operational costs are listed in the capital spending plan (Exhibit III). The current kitchen facility includes the minimum in large equipment, estimated to be adequate with moderate removable improvements for the next three years of operation. Permanent industrial locations are available for a current average of $.70 per square foot. The Italian Eatery would need 1,500 square feet for a monthly rental of $1,050. At that time, a bank loan could be secured to finance purchase or lease of necessary equipment.

In order to meet the demands for chocolate-dipped biscotti, a chocolate tempering machine would need to be purchased at a cost of $1,000. This purchase should be made well in advance of the 1995 holiday season. The design of a biscotti-cutting machine has been located and the designer estimates a cost of $10,000 to have the machine fabricated. Since it would multiply production at the cutting stage thirty times, its cost can be justified by the savings in labor. This machine could be ordered now and ready for use by January 1996.

MANAGEMENT

My passion for food was intensified during an 18-month sabbatical in Italy from 1976-1978. Upon my return, I spent two years working for an award-winning food service consulting firm. I gained a thorough understanding of the proper commercial kitchen layout and equipment. In 1980, I returned to Italy on behalf of Arnold Brothers to study the successful European franchise of Il Palio. Returning to Portland after two months, I orchestrated the American pilot, Il Palio Bakery, from three months of preparation through the first six months of operation. This provided me with comprehensive knowledge of every detail required for efficient management of a quality bakery. I acquired additional management experience with my participation in the start-up of Pasta Tante Bella, a stylish Italian deli/restaurant/catering service. A complete resume is available upon request.

As the sole proprietor of The Italian Eatery, I am presently responsible for production, packaging, sales, distribution and bookkeeping. My energy level is high and my confidence in Biscotti Rosa is backed by consumer and retailer response. I have exercised control over all aspects of the business, which has allowed me to monitor mistakes and streamline operations.

My collective expertise has prepared me for introducing The Italian Eatery into the market. Presently, I plan to continue managing all aspects of the business. However, since my strongest skills are in marketing and sales, the hiring of a part-time production assistant and an employee to handle packaging will free me to focus on increasing the market share.

APPLICATION OF INVESTMENT

This plan reveals the importance of immediate capital to increase sales by: 1) the designing of twelve-pack boxes for distribution by Arnold Brothers and eventually other outlets; 2) the development of twenty-four pack boxes for the holiday gift market; 3) the hiring of personnel to increase volume of production; 4) the purchase of labor-saving equipment; and 5) purchasing shipping containers to service current outlets more efficiently and to increase market share at the state and national levels. The amount needed for this, as detailed in the capital spending plan, Exhibit III, is $87,000.

Although some assumptions were made, most projections are based on real production capabilities, actual expenses, and estimates from professionals. With persistence, it is realistic to expect annual sales of one million dollars within five years, guaranteeing a generous return on the capital investment.

EXHIBIT I

Enclosed with this plan is the original packaging for Biscotti Rosa. (Not available for publication.)

EXHIBIT II

DATE: July 4

TO: Amy's Design Shop
824 Main St., Suite 1222
Salem, OR 97000

ATTN: Packaging of Biscotti Rosa

JOB NUMBER: 123

JOB TITLE: The Italian Eatery: Biscotti Rosa Packaging
Revised Estimate

Concept, art direction, and design for four finished comps: $4,250

- Single package Biscotti
- Twelve pack Biscotti
- Twenty four pack Biscotti
- Display box for single package Biscotti

This includes application and camera-ready art for logotype.

Typesetting/Photocopies	$ 480
Color Transfers/Comp Materials	$ 550

USAGE: The design solutions produced for comprehensives are the property of Amy's Design Shop and will remain the property of Amy's Design Shop until full payment is received with the release of approved final mechanical art.

NOTE: The above estimate does not include delivery charges or any state and local taxes.

APPROVED BY:_______________________________ DATE:__________

PAYMENTTERMS:

QUOTATION: *A quotation not accepted within thirty (30) days is subject to review.*
ALTERATIONS: *Alterations represent work performed in addition to the original specifications. Such additional work shall be charged the hourly rate plus expenses. All alterations must be in writing, except that invoice may include and client shall be obligated to pay, fees or expenses verbally authorized in order to process the work properly.*
TERMS: *Payment shall be net cash fifteen (15) days from the date of invoice or in accordance with payment schedule outlined on estimate.*

EXHIBIT III

Capital Spending Plan, August 1994

Custom-built biscotti slicing machine	$10,000
Packaging:	
Design fee	$4,950
Printing, 15K twelve-pack boxes	$11,700
Printing, 15K twenty-four-pack boxes	$16,350
Cellulose bags for interior packaging	$5,000
Macintosh PC system	$4,000
Purchase and installation of business phone	$500
Shipping containers (billed out as handling charge):	
5K @ $.40	$2,000*
5K @ $1.15	$5,750*
5K @ $1.84	$9,200*
Small kitchen equipment (stainless steel bowls, spatulas, knives ingredient bins, scales, etc.)	$1,000
Working capital (office supplies, gas, telephone, etc.)	$2,000
Subtotal	$72,450
20% error factor	$14,490
Total	$86,940

**The sum of these investments, $16,950, would be gradually recuperated as handling charges are collected.*

Business Consulting

BUSINESS PLAN

BLAKE & ASSOCIATES

5456 Universal Ave.
Cleveland, OH 76891

October 17, 1992

Blake & Associates offers numerous consulting and advisory services to primarily smaller businesses. It will specialize in advice on business planning. Inasmuch as this is an example of the very document on which it hopes others will ask their advice, it should serve to effectively highlight the general approach.

BUSINESS CONSULTING BUSINESS PLAN

EXECUTIVE SUMMARY

Blake & Associates provide several consulting and advisory services to the business community, with particular emphasis on small businesses of 25 to 175 employees. These services include: seminars and workshops on writing business plans, as well as complete business plan development and writing; financial analysis and balance sheet restructuring; business valuations for purchase, sale or buy/sell agreements; cash flow analysis; computer software and hardware analysis; installation and training; and workshops on upgrading computer hardware and software, among others.

The company is currently a sole proprietorship with a small staff of specialized individuals who are well suited to providing our services to small to medium sized companies and, in some instances, to the general public. In addition to the above mentioned services, we are creating video tapes on such subjects as business plan writing and upgrading a personal computer. The tapes will be sold through direct mail, magazine advertisements, and at our company sponsored workshop.

Blake & Associates has an opportunity to fill a need in the business community and become profitable in its first year. A loan of $65,000 will be a sufficient operating account to start the business, along with approximately $17,000 in existing capital assets and grants.

The first year should see total revenues of just over $288,000 and a net after tax loss of ($6,143), or -2.13%. The second year, we anticipate revenues of just over $970,000 with profits of nearly $110,000. The third year, we estimate revenues will be nearly $1,950,000, with a profit of over $260,000. The high profit margin in the third year reflects the results of building the organization in the first two years and developing a demand for higher attendance at the seminars and workshops, as well as greater demand for the books and audio and video tapes.

Objectives

In the first year, we will achieve revenues of approximately $290,000 while returning a net, after tax loss of ($6,143), or a 2.13% profit margin.

We are targeting growth of over 100% in the second year, based on the development of our strategic alliances and our access to the public and small businesses through our seminars and workshops. By focusing on the seminars and workshops, books, and video and audio tapes, we can increase revenues to over $1,900,000 by the third year and show a net after-tax profit of 13.7% or $266,183, on growth of nearly 30%.

The key to growth and profitability is to develop the marketing of the seminars, workshops, and the tools (i.e. video tapes, audio tapes and booklets). We expect these services to provide as much as 50% of our total revenues in the first year and approximately 70% by the third year. Using the workshops and seminars as a marketing vehicle for our services, we will see an increase in our consulting revenues and our seminar and workshop revenues.

Mission

To improve the performance and efficiency of small businesses and their chances of survival in a highly competitive, expanding, and unpredictable political and economic business environments.

COMPANY

Blake & Associates is a sole proprietorship, with a small staff of specialized individuals who are well suited to providing our services to small- and medium-sized companies and, in some instances, to the general public. Our services include: analysis and development of business plans; business valuations; cash flow analysis; demographic research for marketing plans; microcomputer hardware and software analysis, installation, and training; and consultation and workshops on sales management and sales staff motivation. In addition, we are creating video tapes on such subjects as business plan writing and upgrading a personal computer.

Company Ownership

Blake & Associates is a sole proprietorship, owned by John Doe. In the future, the company will be incorporated - most likely as an "S" corporation and, at that time, there will be other stockholders. Further, it is expected that, should any future funding for this venture come from an investor, the investor will require (and be entitled to) a percentage of ownership.

Company History

Blake & Associates is a start-up company, beginning its operation on September 1, 1992; however, most of the time during the first few months was spent developing the feasibility research. Some services were offered in the fall of 1992 and although clients were billed for services no revenues were generated. These projects did help in the research process and much of that research will be evident in the body of this plan.

Services & Products

We will provide numerous services to businesses, including: assistance in writing effective and concise business plans and financial analysis; conducting demographic market research; providing business valuations; and conduct workshops and seminars on these same subjects. We will also provide consulting services and conduct workshops and seminars on microcomputer software and hardware analysis, installation and training.

Company Locations and Facilities

The company has not made final arrangements for its office location John Doe is conducting business from his home, at the present time, but the conditions are unsuitable for business operations. To obtain the most effective amount of space, at the lowest possible price, we have concluded that our best choice would be shared office type facilities. These facilities provide private offices, secretarial support, copiers, faxes, reception, telephone equipment and answering services and so on. The prices range from $500 to $850 per month for each room, plus a cost for phones and furniture. We already have furnishings and the phones range from $75 to $125 per month, per room, depending on how many lines were needed. The least expensive facility we have found is Troy Commons. Two offices with two telephone lines would cost a total of $1,025 per month. This facility provides minimal space for meetings (eight people, maximum), no storage space, no audio/visual support and no training space. The most feasible location, for the first few months, would provide conference facilities for 10 to 12, audio/video, overhead and slide capabilities, and an extensive array of additional services, including color copies and color printing of computer disks. Although we would be using the shared office concept for the first year to 18 months, the business plan reflects the cost of a private facility from the first day of the second year of operation. Our concern with the shared office concept is the exceedingly high cost of ancillary services and the lack of conference, training, and storage space. For instance, an incoming fax is $1.00 per page while outgoing faxes are $2.00 per page plus phone time, copies are $.15 each. In our business, this could cost us as much as $500 per month or more in additional fees. On the other hand, it saves us as much as $1,500 per month in salaries (for clerical help) and another $300 to $500 per month in equipment rental and lease.

When we are ready for our own offices, our facilities will require six specific areas including a conference/training room, reception area, storage and equipment room, marketing office, operations office and administrative offices. The total space requirement would be between 2,000 and 2,500 square feet and we would enter into a lease of five years, negotiating for lower lease payments in the first three to six months of the lease. A chart of the office options available can be provided.

PRODUCTS AND SERVICES

Blake & Associates provide a number of necessary services and products to the business community and to the public. Although the products and services seem complex, they can be summed up in two areas - business finance services and business computer services. Our business finance services include business plan workshops, consulting and writing, financial and cash flow analysis, planning and restructuring, business valuation for purchases or sales, or for the structuring of a buy/sell agreement, demographic market studies, microcomputer hardware and software analysis, installation and training. In addition, we conduct seminars and workshops on such topics as sales and sales management, motivation, starting a business, developing vision in the staff and so on. Our business computer services include workshops on upgrading an existing microcomputer, increasing efficiency by upgrading software and so on. Many of these same topics would be of interest to the general public. We also provide consulting services to businesses on their hardware and software needs.

Product and Service Description

Our business planning services include: assisting companies with the research and structuring of comprehensive, written, business plans; conducting workshops and seminars on business plan writing; and providing a written business plan package, which delivers a complete, detailed business plan to the client, specifically designed to meet their needs, i.e. venture capital search, bank loans,

Product and Service Description
...continued

SBA 7(a) packages, SBA direct loans, restructuring, new product development, expansion market, and so on. In many cases, businesses of 25 to 175 employees consider next year's budget an acceptable business plan. Any investor or banker will disagree and insist on much more information prior to making a financial decision regarding funding a business. We want to provide the opportunity for businesses who have potential to receive the funding that would help them become solid employers and corporate taxpayers in their communities. Other services included in Business Planning are:

❑ Business valuations for the purpose of establishing a value on a business that is being bought or sold, as well as establishing a value for buy/sell agreements for partnerships and other business entities who wish to insure against the premature death of a principal in the business.

❑ Cash flow analysis that allows a company to anticipate lulls in production or sales, due to seasonal, political, or economic market adjustments that would cause unanticipated drains on "cash on hand" and the cash surplus. It is our observation that a company can borrow monies to cover an anticipated depression in cash flow much easier than trying to borrow monies to get out of a negative situation.

❑ Demographic information that can help a company decide the best location for expansion or product introduction, based on retail sales, per capita income, competition, real estate values and lease rates, union vs. nonunion labor, population, and so on. Many times a company sees an opportunity for growth or the introduction of a new product through "rose colored glasses." We help them realize the realities of the endeavor and provide guidance that would allow them to find a better location, reconsider their timing, or any other alternative that might exist.

Management Information Systems Consulting provides much needed assistance to the smaller companies who must be careful of every dollar spent on potentially "unnecessary" computer hardware or software. Hundreds of software packages are sold every day to unsuspecting buyers who think the software will perform a specific task for them, only to find that it won't. Furthermore, businesses and individuals alike spend thousands of dollars to buy computers and peripheral components to improve their efficiency and work environment only to find out that the system they got was too much, too little, or the totally wrong kind and incompatible with what their colleagues are using. We will assist these individuals and businesses with the proper decision on software and hardware. We will evaluate dozens of software packages for ease of operation, extent of benefits, learning time, and levels and cost. We will then be able to properly advise our clients as to what software package will do their task at the least cost and with the least amount of start-up time. As for hardware we can analyze the system needs of the client and advise them of upgrades which might be available for their current system, without going to the expense of replacing an entire computer. On the other hand, we can advise the client on just how much upgrading might need to be done. One client might simply need a new video board, while another needs an entirely new system.

Important Features and Comparison

Although there are a number of attorneys and accountants who profess to writing or assisting in the writing of business plans, the reality is that these professionals provide invaluable services in the areas in which they are best, but lack the imagination to write a comprehensive and effective business plan. The attorneys tend to dwell on the legal aspects and contractual arrangements while accountants sweat over the balance sheet, cash flow statements, product costs and income statements. Additionally, these vitally necessary professionals cannot afford to spend the many hours necessary to work on a business plan when they could be earning $90 to $200 per hour concentrating on their particular field of expertise.

Our expertise lies in the ability to listen to a business owner and perceive their vision for their company over the next few years. We can envision what the business person is looking for in the future, then put it in writing and at a cost they can live with.

As for computer consulting, there are literally hundreds of companies and individuals who provide "consulting" services to businesses. However, as in the case of the business plan writing area, most of them are too wrapped up in "their" ideas and opinions to hear what the client really needs. Further, many of these "consultants" are re-sellers of software and are less objective than they otherwise might be. We want the needs of the client to be the most important thing to us, so we will not be a re-seller of software or hardware. We will continually research the market so we can advise the clients as to where they can find the software and hardware they need at the most reasonable prices.

Finally, we are offering workshops and seminars where the knowledge we have gained can be shared with the smallest of businesses without costing them hundreds of dollars. The average business planning seminar will have a ticket price of $35 and the workshop, where participants will actually be able to write a business plan with the tools and information provided, will have a price of $90. Our computer hardware and software evaluation seminars will have an average ticket price of $35 and the attendee will be able to make decisions as to what software or hardware might be best for their situation. The computer assembly workshop will teach the small business person, or individual how to assemble, upgrade or trouble shoot a personal computer and will have a ticket price of $75. Even the smallest of businesses can afford these prices, as can the individual seeking this information. However, the greatest of seminars and workshops cannot give anyone ALL necessary information. Ultimately, our seminars and workshops become one of our most effective marketing tools, causing the attendees to come to us for further information (at our hourly rate of $50 to $90) or to have us write the plan, do the evaluation, upgrade the computer, install the software...any number of reasons. None of our competitors are doing this.

Sales Literature

Our literature is being designed by Graphics Inc. Kevin Johnson, the owner and graphic designer, has extensive experience in graphic design. Our literature will consist of a pocket folder, which will allow us to custom design the type of package needed for each client, an 8 1/2 x 11, bi-fold "mailable" brochure, which is designed to sell the need for service (rather than explain the services offered) and inserts for the folder that will detail the various services offered by the firm.

The copy is being written by Laurie Metcalf. She has an equally impressive list of clients and has written countless business and technical pieces for *The Post Dispatch*, *The St. Louis Business Journal* and several national publications. She has also co-authored several technical manuals, novels and text books. Her expertise is in taking the most complicated ideas and making them simple to understand.

A printer has been chosen to provide us a high quality printing job and a very reasonable price and, as in every case, we are using a locally based small shop which is known for its integrity and quality. The entire literature package should be completed by the second week of January. Rough draft examples of the materials are available on request.

Future Products and Services

In putting the company together, we have attempted to offer enough services to allow us to always be in demand by our clients. However, politics has provided us with a new era of opportunities for the small business person in which we can only guess at the needs.

David Mullins, Vice Chairman of the Federal Reserve Bank, is urging a major overhaul of the bank lending practices for small businesses (Wall Street Journal, December 15, 1992). Over the past several years, with the destruction of the Savings and Loan industry, the leading practices of banks have become almost nonexistent for the small business person. Now, we have the possibility of money being loosened for the small business people and that means there will be a substantial increase in the number of loan applications being filed with lenders and thus an increase in the number of business plans and business valuations needed and the software to run them. This provides additional business for virtually every area of business services we provide.

As we become more accustomed to the fall of communism in Russia and the demise of the Soviet Union, we continue to downsize our military. With this downsizing comes the release of thousands of highly trained, educated, and motivated individuals who have nowhere to go for jobs. Both military and civilian defense workers are finding themselves faced with unemployment. Statistics tell us that approximately 4 out of 10 of these individuals will start their own company within one year of being released from service. In that area alone, this will account for nearly 800 new small businesses starting between July 1, 1993 and June 30, 1994. All of the events of today create the need for new ideas and direction. It is our intention to offer ourselves, on a contractual basis as consultants to governmental agencies and corporations who are "downsizing," to work with their employees who might be receiving a "lump sum" severance package. It would be in the best interest of the employer to help these individuals instead of trying to live off the money until it runs out. These consulting contracts would allow us the opportunity to provide a service to the employer and their former employee and we could receive a fee from both. The employer would hire us to help the former employee wishing to start a business of their own find the best type of business for them, considering the amount of severance compensation they are provided. The former employee would pay us to help develop a business plan, analyze software needs, identify proper computer hardware, file for SBA or bank loans and so on.

MARKET ANALYSIS

According to Inc. magazine, during the 1980s, the number of businesses in the United States grew by approximately 53%. During that same time, the population grew by 10%. As major industry continues to "down size," more and more talented, educated, and experienced people are finding themselves going into business. Many of these people will ply their trade out of the basement of their homes, while others will open offices, hire staff and begin manufacturing, assembling or selling products or services. Each and every one of these individuals will need some sort of support we are providing. However, it is a mixed bag and the common thread we have found which would provide us with access to these new (as well as the existing) businesses is their need for an attorney, an accountant, and a banker. Therefore, we will concentrate our marketing efforts on these professionals, relying on them, and later our clients, for referrals.

Industry Analysis

It is impossible to measure an industry which expands every day. In recent times (the past 15 years), we have seen more independent businesses open than any other time prior to the original development of this country. In fact, according to statistics issued by the United States Commerce Commission, by the year 2000 we will be very near to reaching the same percentage of entrepreneurial businesses as existed prior to the industrial revolution. Major corporations are downsizing and leaving people stranded. These are educated, motivated people who strike out on their own by buying a franchise, an existing business, or developing their own ideas into an enterprise. The vast majority of these businesses will not succeed, due to a failure to properly evaluate the opportunity. In fact, 52,078 businesses failed in 1984 while 1991 saw 87,404 businesses closing their doors. As of June 30, 1992, the year had already seen the failure of 50,532 business. Many of them charged forth - mostly on emotion - and failed to see danger signals that an impartial advisor could have alerted them to. The opportunity they wish to take advantage of could be a sound one, with certain adjustments made. Unfortunately, the cost of such advice has, historically, been out of reach (or perceived to be out of reach) of the small business owner. Their entrepreneurial spirit tells them to "do it yourself," not recognizing that "self" tends to look at the beautiful mountain peaks in the distance - unaware that a grizzly bear is ten feet behind them. They must plan for the future, but manage today.

Participants

Since our target market covers companies of 25 to 175 employees, the participants in this market are difficult to number. Each day sees new entries into the business world and, therefore new prospects for our services.

Market Segmentation

The most likely types of businesses to require our services would include:

- New businesses seeking investment or start-up capital
- Existing companies who are expanding or introducing a new product or service
- New and existing companies who need to upgrade their MIS hardware or software
- Individuals and businesses who want to learn more about computers
- Employers looking for fresh approaches to goal setting andtechnique
- Governmental agencies assisting displaced or disabled individuals find employment

As mentioned, our target market is businesses of 25 to 175 employees, but we will be providing services to many entities of greater or lesser numbers. In doing the research for this plan, 390 businesses were contacted which met our target size. Of those, only 26 have current business plans. More importantly, 310 of them said their banker or investor group wanted an updated business plan. Of the 310, 160 of them said they would be willing to attend, or send a representative, to a workshop on business planning and over 200 were interested in seminars and workshops on computer hardware and software. Additionally, 351 of the companies are using computers and 285 said they were "less than satisfied" with either the hardware or software they were currently using.

Competitive Forces and Buying Patterns

The most important factor in this market is the quality of the service. Most of the companies we spoke with said the price they paid for services was not as important as the quality and availability. The majority of the companies said they were not satisfied with the current condition of their planning efforts, because their accountant was unfamiliar with the fundamentals of their business and they were less satisfied with the quality of the "computer experts" they had hired to improve their productivity. Hence, quality service will command a fair price.

Main Competitors

There are 122 companies operating in the metropolitan area who classify themselves as "business consultants." However, upon contacting these organizations, it appears that the majority of these companies are bookkeeping services, out-placement services, finance companies and medical practice counselling. There are some companies that provide services similar to those offered by us and that is good. The competition should keep us awake and appreciative. There are three companies who seem to parallel our services. Each of these companies offers business plan writing. Some offer computer services, some offer services to small and start-up businesses. However, none of them provide all these services and most of them are one- or two-man shops.

Keys to Success

We never want to forget the fact that we are a small business and the mainstay of our business comes from small businesses. We want to provide our services to our clients as though we were friends. We want to always be available when a client needs our help or has a question and we always want to make certain that we are giving our clients advice that will help them operate efficiently and effectively. We offer a background in consulting with the Small Business Development Center and our management and speaking expertise services, writing business plans and conducting seminars and workshops. One co-founder has operated his own computer business for two years and has been writing computer programs for software development companies even longer. His friendly ways and extensive knowledge of computer hardware and software give him a distinct advantage and workshops will give us access to people we might otherwise lose because they feel that they already have "advisors" in their attorneys or accountants.

Market Forecast

With the easing of bank lending to small businesses and with the continual "downsizing" of U.S. industry, our market can only get larger. We have estimated the projected revenues of the various products and services we will offer. This information is available upon request.

BUSINESS STRATEGY AND IMPLEMENTATION

We do not want to compete with attorneys and CPAs. We want them as allies. We intend to show them how we can be of value to them by freeing their time up and still being paid for services through our firm. We also want to work with the commercial and business loan officer of the numerous banks throughout neighboring areas and states, showing them how we can assist their clients and applicants with SBA loan packages, direct bank loans and other services, making the loan officer's job easier and more effective. By developing relationships with these professionals, we can develop a referral system which could keep us supplied with enough business to be profitable. In addition, our seminars and workshops will create business and provide one avenue for the sale of books and video and audio tapes on the topics we are presenting.

Marketing Strategy

Our strategy calls for the development of relationships with attorneys, accountants, and bankers to support our business with referrals. Interviews with commercial loan officers have indicated that there is a serious need for a firm like ours to help their clients develop comprehensive, concise business plans. We have already received permission from one financial institution to place our literature in their commercial loan lobby and they have agreed to mail several of the pieces to recent business applicants who don't have business plans. This same type of referral can come from the attorneys and accounts with whom we have developed relationships. Our consulting work and advertising will generate business for our computer services section, including service contracts with some of the law and accounting firms from whom we receive referrals.

Target Markets and Market Segments

Our target market is small business of 25 to 175 employees. The industry they are involved in has little relevance. We are able to work equally well with manufacturing, sales, service, assembly and business. All types of businesses need to know where they are headed and there is hardly any business in operation today that does not use a computer and software. Furthermore, there are many 1- to 4-person shops, such as ourselves in the initial stages, who still need help in identifying where they want to go and how they want to get there. For these types of "micro companies," our seminars and workshops are ideal. The workshops will cause them to think the process through and develop their own plans of action.

Pricing Strategy

For our hourly services, we must make ourselves profitable, but be competitive. For business consulting, we will charge an hourly rate of $90. Our hourly fee for computer consulting is $50 to $75, depending on the task. If it simply involves research and advice on software, the $50 would apply. However, if the client is wanting us to evaluate, upgrade and service a network of computers, the rate would be $75. Finally, our seminars will have an average fee of $35 and our workshops will average $85 per attendee. All of these rates are highly competitive with the industry and, in some cases are far less (i.e. Peat Marwick charges $190 per hour for business plan preparation).

Marketing Programs and Strategies

We will be instituting a regular schedule of telemarketing and direct mail solicitations to our target market. Every two months, there will be a mailing to a section of our market, with follow-up calls made to confirm that the information arrived. Then, those leads will be followed up on over the next few weeks by the Research or MIS Associates. There will be frequent visits to our strategic alliances, including lawyers, accountants, and bankers. These will be face to face discussions of our services and upcoming seminars and workshops. Graphic Design is developing a comprehensive package of materials we can use to promote the company, including small brochures of a mailable size and a larger folder, which will allow us to build a "customized" package containing information pertinent to a particular customer.

Sales Forecast

Charts and tables representing our forecast of sales for the first twelve months of operation, by product, have been prepared.

Strategic Alliances

Our strategic alliances are also part of our marketing strategy. As outlined earlier, our existing and anticipated relationships with legal and accounting firms, as well as bank lending officers, will provide us with the strong referral base we will need. In most cases, it will not be easy to win these groups over. Some will resist because they are offering some abbreviated form of one or more of our services now. However, if we can show them how we can do the work and still provide them a fee opportunity, it should appeal to them. We have already developed relationships with a local bank and law firm. They will provide us with much of the credibility we will need to access other professional and financial organizations.

ORGANIZATION

An Organizational Chart is available upon request.

Organization Structure

The company, simply because of its small size, will function more as a partnership than a corporate organization, in the early stages. With such a small group, it will be simple to communicate with and support one another. As the company grows, there will be more structure to the organization, with new hires being assigned a supervisor or subordinates. When the company is at its full staff potential, it will operate as any closely held corporation, but maintain the personal interest in each employee's personal and family welfare and their contributions to the business.

Management Team

A complete resume for each of the management staff is available upon request.

Management Team Gaps

There are three positions that we will need to fill in the first six months of operation. although two of the roles are not considered a part of the management team, they are integral to the fulfillment of the plan. The first vacancy to be filled is a Business Planning Associate to assist the owner in the writing of business plans and the presentation of seminars and workshops. This person could allow the company to nearly double the volume of business plans written by conducting the preliminary client interviews and performing research on competition and market.

The second person needed is a Marketing Director. This person will be responsible for keeping us on target with our seminars and workshops, as well as defining the specific marketing objectives of clients who hire us to write their business plans. Further, this person would work with our outside consultants on public relations, publicity and advertising and, in some cases conduct seminars and workshops on marketing plans and studies. Until this person is hired, these responsibilities will be handled by the owner with the help of the rest of the staff. We anticipate hiring this person near the end of the first year.

The third person needed is an MIS Associate, who would perform similar tasks to the Business Planning Associate. That is, to assist in conducting research into client needs, analyze software products for usability and learning curve, interview clients to obtain information on the daily usage of computers and software to evaluate needed upgrades or replacement, assist in conducting seminars and workshops on upgrading computers, and usage of software.

Personnel Plan

We do not intend to be a large corporation or "top heavy." We want the company to stay lean and flexible so that we can respond to a client's needs quickly. To do this, we will use outside consultants whose fees, in most cases, will be passed on to the client, indirectly, through our fees. A personnel forecast by both month and year has been prepared.

FINANCIAL ANALYSIS

Blake & Associates has an opportunity to fill a need in the business community and become profitable in the first year. $65,000 will be a sufficient operating account to see the business through the start-up phase and beyond break-even. In addition to the $65,000 loan, the company comes to the table with approximately $15,000 in assets, including $10,000 in a computer system and other equipment provided by the Department of Social Services, Rehabilitation Services for the Blind.

The first year should see total revenues of just over $288,000 and a net, after tax loss of ($6,143). The second year, we anticipate revenues of just over $970,000 with profits of nearly $110,000. The third year, we estimate revenues will be nearly $1,950,000, with a profit of over $265,000. The high profit margin in the third year reflects the results of building the organization in the first two years and developing a demand for and therefore, higher attendance at the seminars and workshops, as well as greater demand for the books and audio and video tapes. In other words, the third year will allow us to do twice the business with virtually the same number of people and a small increase in expenses.

Financial Plan

To put the operation into full swing, we require $65,000 of operating capital, which will cover payroll, rent, telephones and other general expenses for at least six months, assuming no revenues were received during that same period. It is expected that there will be no more funds needed, after this initial infusion of capital. It is our intent to repay the loan in the first three years of operation, with principle and interest payments beginning in the third month. The company has no plans to "go public." It is our intent to keep the organization small, efficient and closely held. However, it is possible that the company, or a portion, could be sold to another consulting firm, attorney, CPA, or the like. If such an offer is made, the decision to sell will be made at that time.

First Twelve Months: Pro Forma Income Statement

The Income Statement reflects three larger expenditures in the first 90 days. These expenses include:

- $5,500 for Video, Audio, and Book Production
- $9,250 for Advertising and Promotion
- $3,500 for Legal and Accounting

The first of these items is the cost to produce the Audio and Video tapes we will sell at seminars and through advertisements. $3,000 is for the video taping, including equipment, filming, editing and so on. The audio tapes can be produced from the sound track on the video except for a few special tapes we want to include. The remaining $2,500 is for the initial production of the business plan writing guideline, which accompanies the audio or video tapes, and the packaging of the audio and video tapes, as well as the printing and binding of the first order of books. After this initial investment, we have calculated a monthly expenditure which will cover the replacement of those products which were sold.

FINANCIAL ANALYSIS
...continued

The second major expense item is Advertising and Promotion. Included in this $9,250 is the cost of newspaper and magazine advertising to announce the opening of the company for business. We have calculated a monthly advertising budget that will allow us to keep our name before the public and advertise our seminars and workshops. With these budgeted amounts, we will be able to buy our advertising in advance and receive as much as a 50% discount from standard rates in local publications. The advertising budget grows to $56,000 in the second year and $93,000 in the third, with the expansion of the company to a larger geographic service area.

The third large item is the expense for legal and accounting. The $3,500 is sufficient to cover the cost of incorporation, contracts and agreements and setting up the general journal and general ledger.

In the first year, we expect gross sales of $288,640 and cost of sales to be $106,707, for a gross margin of $181,843 or 63%. Profit before taxes and interest expense are projected to be ($6,143). With interest expense of $5,623 and taxes of ($1,733), the company will show a net loss, in the first year of ($6,143). This is an acceptable result, considering the start-up time and expenses incurred during the first year.

The second and third years, FY95 and FY96, show gross sales of $972,228 and $1,941,285, respectively. Unit cost of sales are $307,676 for FY95 and $575,874 for FY96. The second year net, after-tax profit is projected to be $109,758. The third year net, after-tax profit is estimated at $266,183.

Financial Ratios and Break-Even Analysis

Ratio analyses, including profitability ratios, activity ratios, debt ratios, liquidity ratios, and others have been forecasted through 1996 and are available upon request.

It is our opinion that we can exceed the "usual and customary" ratios through the combination of services we are offering. Nearly half of the revenues, in the third year, will come from the mail order sales of books, videos and audio tapes. These products require little staffing and overhead and generate excellent profits, once the initial cost of production is absorbed.

Charts representing the sales revenues, personnel needs, expenses, and profit for the next three years have been prepared. Each chart reflects genuine estimates of the company's capabilities and the achievement of these results is totally dependent upon the $65,000 loan.

Spreadsheets to accompany financial projections as well as examples of advertising layouts and marketing materials are available upon request. These include: general assumptions; sales forecasts; personnel plan; the Pro Forma Income Statement, Cash Flow Statement, and Balance Sheet; ratio analyses; and advertising.

Business Consulting

BUSINESS PLAN

KOSHU

2275 Timberview, Ste. 4
Tucson, AZ 49787

June 15, 1994

Koshu is a one-person management consulting firm serving companies of all sizes in all industries. The company plans to "productize" its methods and the results of its services as software packages and manuals. The following plan outlines the ways that additional funding will help Koshu continue to fulfill its aim of providing visionary and quality work at lower costs than its competitors.

EXECUTIVE SUMMARY

Koshu is a unique management consultancy incorporated in Tucson, Arizona. The company provides strategic planning and technology management services to companies of all sizes in all industries, and plans to "productize" the results of its work and its methodologies into mass marketable software packages and manuals.

Koshu employs one professional, Kevin Vaartinna, but maintains affiliations with other independent consultants and small firms around the world. These entities work together as a kind of virtual consulting firm, utilizing modern communications technologies such as fax machines and electronic mail to complete projects without ever meeting each other.

The business began as a sole proprietorship more than one year ago, and was profitable in its first year of existence. Management expects to double revenues and profits this year, and to expand the product line.

The market is limited only by the ability of the company to market itself to other businesses; capacity is constrained by the number of hours in the day and the number of employees. Koshu is in the unique position of its competitors often turning into its customers, and feels that this is a strategic advantage.

The company prides itself on its technical ability, its value-added services at unbeatable rates, its high standards of quality, its technologically superior equipment and its adaptability to changes in the market and in the methods of its practice.

The professionals who make up Koshu value this phrase more than any other: "I think."

BUSINESS HISTORY

Koshu was founded as a sole proprietorship in 1992 in the name of Kevin Vaartinna. Mr. Vaartinna had prior experience as a market specialist for the New York Port Authority in Tokyo, Japan, and as an Asia specialist with the firm of Braxton Associates, the strategic consulting division of Deloitte Touche Tohmatsu.

After an extended tour in Korea, Mr. Vaartinna left the firm and moved to New Mexico. Although Mr. Vaartinna had no plans to continue consulting, the managing partner of Braxton referred a local client requested Mr. Vaartinna's involvement on another team for four more months. Concurrently, a subsidiary of the client contracted Mr. Vaartinna for a brief engagement. Former associates called and inquired about availability. A national special interest group requested a competitive analysis. An acquaintance of a former colleague employed Mr. Vaartinna for two pieces of work for a major client in Arizona. By the end of 1993, at approximately 40% utilization, the unintentional business had grossed approximately the average annual salary of a "Big 6" analyst.

In the late 1993 Mr. Vaartinna worked with Terry Kackman, a consultant and entrepreneur in Tucson. Mr. Kackman offered to purchase 75% of Mr. Vaartinna's time for the next year if he would relocate to Arizona. The original client in New Mexico continued to requisition small engagements, and other companies were making inquiries. Mr. Vaartinna relocated to Tucson and incorporated in early January 1994 as an S corporation under the name of Koshu. At that time, the company issued 10,000 shares of its available one million shares to Mr. Vaartinna for $1,000 paid-in capital. Koshu rents workspace from and utilizes the personnel of the Kelsey group, a management consultancy owned and operated by Mr. Kackman.

(Less than two weeks after incorporating, the business made a successful loan presentation to Tri-Star Bank and obtained it's first financing. The funds from this loan purchased the current assets of the company, primarily a laptop computer and relevant business software. The loan is collateralized with Mr. Vaartinna's personal assets and Koshu's assets.)

COMPANY CONCEPT

Koshu provides management consulting services to companies in all industries. Clients range in size from $50,000 to $500 million in annual revenues. The company intends to "productize" the methodologies and results of its services as computer software and manuals that can be sold and distributed independently or in conjunction with the services offered.

Koshu's image is that of efficient, visionary, technologically advanced and quality work. The company will compete in a lower price range than its competitors, with professional rates of $75 to $125 per hour.

Koshu fills a market need that seeks temporary action-oriented white-collar staff with interdisciplinary backgrounds, highly creative thinking and superior analytical techniques. Koshu is unique in that it maintains a synergistic existence with its competitors, which are often its customers. The company is also unique in the low level of cost associated with its high level of service.

The actual services that Koshu provides include, but are not limited to:

- ❑ Financial performance assessment and improvement
- ❑ Competitive analysis
- ❑ Market and customer research and segmentation
- ❑ Best demonstrated practice reviews
- ❑ Joint venture analysis and due diligence
- ❑ Strategic planning at the corporate, business unit, and product line levels

COMPANY CONCEPT
...continued

- ❑Macro and micro economic forecasting and scenario building
- ❑Information search and retrieval
- ❑Product conceptualization and development
- ❑Training in planning and analysis techniques, and technology utilization
- ❑ Technology recommendations and computer network administration
- ❑Ad hoc problem solving / solution building / catalysis and imple mentation

MARKETING PLAN

The General Market

The market for management consulting services is the entire business community. Any size firm in any industry can utilize good thinkers. Traditionally, companies in high-growth industries employ consultants to manage the growth and to compete most effectively. Companies in stagnant markets will often utilize consultants to improve performance or to discover new markets. The latter are more common than the former, although the fees commanded in servicing the high-growth industries are normally higher than those in low-growth to stagnant markets.

Client Geography

Currently, Koshu clients are primarily in the American southwest--California, Arizona, and New Mexico. The company intends to develop its Asia practice, due to the recent interest in the southwest in relationships with Pacific rim countries.

Client Industries

Koshu's current direct and indirect clients are involved in the industries of:

- ❑Healthcare
- ❑Health and Beauty Aids
- ❑Management Consulting
- ❑Publishing

Previous client industries include:

- ❑Telecommunications
- ❑Aerospace
- ❑Petrochemicals
- ❑Raw lumber and wood products
- ❑Specialty Steel

A particular niche that the company intends to market to is that of the sole practitioner senior management consultant or small firm. Typically, a more senior consultant will leave his or her position at a large firm or will begin practicing directly after exiting an industry. These consultants often lack the analytical skills, current techniques, and basic technological "horsepower" that Koshu has at its disposal. Larger firms are a smaller target market; these consultancies tend to employ their own staff analysts. Occasionally, however, these firms sell above their capacity or are in need of particular skills, and will outsource work.

The Consulting Purchase Decision and Critical Service Characteristics

Normally, Koshu works with executive-level clients, and it is at this level that the purchasing decision is made. The company customarily works at the executive level with Presidents, and Vice Presidents of Strategy, Planning, Operations, Information Systems and Quality Control, and their respective staffs. The priority that these executives place on the purchase of consulting services usually depends on the exigency of the issues facing them at the moment, and their lack of adequate skills or staff to combat these issues. While bids and proposals are occasionally solicited, customers are more often obtained through personal relationships and referrals. A consultant's value is based on his experience, knowledge, availability, personal compatibility with the staff of the client, and price.

Seasonality

Companies are less likely to engage consultants in December or in April, due to the calendar and tax year closings. The summer months are traditionally slower for consultants; the primary seasons of engagement are spring, fall, and early winter. These observations apply to the *securing* of contracts; an appropriate strategy to combat seasonality is to secure long-term contracts during favorable engagement sales periods that will run through the less favorable ones. Absolute volume and growth, therefore, are constrained more by Koshu's own ability to network and promote itself by any external factors: the industry has been argued to be both cyclical and countercyclical with the economy.

Compensation

The company currently receives monetary payment in exchange for the services it provides. The professional rates are between $75-$125 per hour, depending on the client. This price is 25-250% lower than most independent consultants charge for their services, primarily because the professionals of Koshu are between 25-30 years old, while most independent consultants are between 40-60 years old. The price is highly competitive with large firm rates: a consultant with commensurate experience would be billed out at 2-3 times Koshu's going rate. Because the professionals of Koshu were trained at these larger firms, customers receive the same level of quality and service at one third the price. Billing is performed on a monthly basis; payment is expected within ten working days of receipt of invoice.

Management intends in the future to provide its services for an equity stake in its clients, and and to eventually use the corporate identity to provide full-time executive management for developing companies with which it is involved.

Competition

Koshu's niche market of outsourced analytical work transforms its competitors into potential customers. There are tens of thousands of small and large firms in the national market. McKinsey & Company, the Boston Consulting Group, Bain & Company, Monitor, and Andersen Consulting are the prominent large national firms; each of the Big 6 accounting firms has one or more consulting practices as well. Research shows approximately one hundred small to medium-size potential customer/competitor firms in the local Tucson market.

The larger firms are successful due to several factors:

- ❑Prestige image is aided by the employment of a young prestige-school MBA staff.
- ❑Customer base provided by partners who are former industry executives with large contact bases.
- ❑Efficient networking and communication is encouraged and provides a large and rapidly growing knowledge base.
- ❑Publication of research findings and case studies enhance the company image.

Customers will choose Koshu over its competitors because they want the same quality work, but are price-sensitive. Competitors will engage Koshu because its quality matches their own, and they turn a profit even with the utilization of Koshu professionals.

Koshu does not expect to gain a large share in its current market of consulting services. As its methodology is productized, however, the packages will be unique enough to gain a large share of their particular niches.

Location Analysis

Arizona is the fourth fastest growing state by population. Consumer and commercial real estate sales are up, and Tucson's publicly traded companies yield a higher rate of return on investment than any other group of securities when judged by geographic area. Overall, the city is an ideal location.

The actual location of the offices is in premier real estate at the Tuscon Center. The company sub-leases space from and is provided office staff by The Kelsey group. The Kelsey group, have contracted almost 75% of Koshu's capacity for 1994, is the company's largest client, and the tenancy is therefore ideal for both parties. If Koshu takes on additional employees, it will be forced to find additional offices.

Marketing Approach

Because of the personal nature of the purchase decision in the engagement of consulting services, the company must utilize "high-touch" networking as its primary mode of customer acquisition. Channels most suitable for this purpose are:

- ❑High involvement in local professional activities and
    - •Chambers of Commerce
    - •World Trade Center
    - •Leads Clubs
    - •Entrepreneur's clubs and seminars
    - •Small Business Administration workshops
    - •Service organizations (Rotary, Lions)
    - •Asia-related clubs and activities

- ❑Personal acquaintances
- ❑Referrals by current and former clients
- ❑Former Braxton colleagues
- ❑Cornell/Kyoto alumnae
- ❑Athletic and religious organizations

In addition, the company intends to promote its services through periodic mailers to potential clients that will be followed up with personal interviews. If these promotional attempts fail, they will be discontinued.

As the company develops hard products, it will utilize more standard channels of distribution for software packages and books.

MANAGEMENT PLAN

Management Team

The sole employee of Koshu is Kevin Vaartina, whose complete resume is available upon request. However, the company maintains affiliations with other independent consultants and small consulting firms in Boston, Bethesda, Minneapolis, Seattle, San Francisco, Tokuo, and Sydney. Most of these consultants have five to ten years experience and prestige-school backgrounds. Many are interconnected through commercial electronic mail services, whereby communication and work product flow in a "virtual office" environment.

Employees

Koshu currently has no plans to take on additional employees, and will instead outsource work to independent contractors as the need arises.

Operational Controls

Capacity is constrained by the number of qualified affiliates and by the billable hours in a day. Koshu bills on a ten hour day, although twelve to eighteen hour daily peaks are occasionally reached. The ability and willingness to put in almost double the normal working hours of a standard employee is an obvious operational advantage.

The optimization of utilization and efficiency are critical to success of Koshu. If Koshu can achieve 120% utilization, complete all the work and maintain its high standards of quality, the company will be deemed successful. Once the level is achieved, the company will be ready to raise its prices, add employees, or diversify.

FINANCIAL PLAN

Start Up Costs

Start up costs are estimated to be approximately $8,000 dollars, as follows:

$5,000	Computer hardware and software
$1,000	Professional services (Legal and Accounting)
$1,000	Corporate identity system materials (Logo, stationery, marketing materials, supplies)
$ 500	Miscellaneous office equipment
$ 500	Miscellaneous licenses, subscriptions, etc.

These expenses were paid in the following way:

$1,000	Kevin Vaartinna paid-in capital for 10,000 shares
$4,000	Fees for services rendered (past due and current)
$3,000	Loan from bank

Less than two weeks after incorporating, the business made a successful loan presentation to Tri-Star Bank and obtained its first financing--a $10,000 six-month loan. $1,500 of this loan is payable in three months, and the balance is due at the end of another three. $7,000 of this loan was put into a certificate of deposit with the bank, and is therefore secured. The remaining $3,000 is collateralized with Mr. Vaartinna's personal assets and Koshu's assets. Excess funds were borrowed in order to establish a reasonable line of credit for the business. Funds were borrowed in order to obtain a lower rate of interest, and again, to establish a line of credit for the business.

Financial Projections Summary

Company financials are included in this report. In summary:

- The company earned $50,000 in revenues last year as a sole proprietorship, and netted 70% of this amount.

- On a worst case basis, the company will increase its revenues to $61,000 this year (a 22% increase), and will net approximately $40,000 (a 14% gain from the previous year).

- On a best case basis, the company will increase its revenues to $100,000 this year (a 100% increase), and will experience a corresponding rise in net profits.

KOSHU PRO FORMA

Actual & Projected : Q1 1993 - Q4 1994
DBA Kevin Vaartinna

	Q1 1993	Q2 1993	Q3 1993	Q4 1993
Revenues	$14,288	$12,091	$14,448	$10,552
Expenses	1,551	1,399	1,783	3,833
EBIT	12,737	10,692	12,665	6,719
Taxes	0	0	1,214	1,277
Net Income	$12,737	$10,692	$11,451	$5,442

	Q1 1994	Q2 1994	Q3 1994	Q4 1994
Revenue	$20,000	$18,000	$18,000	$18,000
Expenses	8,500	2,500	2,500	2,500
EBIT	12,250	15,500	15,500	15,500
Taxes	1,888	2,375	2,375	2,375
Net Income	$10,363	$13,125	$13,125	$13,125

BALANCE SHEET: BUSINESS & PERSONAL

Assets, Koshu

Business

Cash	$6,700
Accounts Receivable	$1,200
Computer	$3,500
Software	$1,000
Printer	$250
Misc. Office	$550
Total Business Assets	$13,200

Assets, Kevin Vaartinna

Personal

Cash	$850
Auto	$5,000
Music Equip.	$1,250
IRA	$4,000
Misc.	$1,000
Total Personal Assets	$12,100
Cash & Receivables	$8,750

BALANCE SHEET BUSINESS & PERSONAL

...continued

Liabilities, Koshu

Business		
Creditors Due	$6,217	
Total Business Liabilities		$6,217

Liabilities, Kevin Vaartinna

Personal		
Rent Liability	$550	
Creditors Due	$1,471	
Total Personal Liabilities		$2,021

Shareholder's Equity, Koshu

Business		
10,000 Shares Issued to RM	$6,983	
Total Business Value		$6,983

Net Worth, Kevin Vaartinna

Personal		
Net Worth (Minus Business)	$10,079	
Total Personal Net Worth		$10,079

Cash & Receivables	$8,750
Liabilities	
Personal	
Creditors Due	$1,471
Rent Liability	$550
Personal Due	$2,021
Business	
Creditors Due	$6,217
Paid-In Capital Due	$1,000
Optimal Working Capital	$1,000
Optimal IRA Contribution	$350
Optimal Salaries (Personal Due Plus $1000)	$11,588
Deficit Between Actual and Optimal	($2,838)

REASON FOR LOAN REQUEST

FINANCING OPTIONS

❑ Pay non-revolving credit with personal revolving credit and service minimum required

- ♦ High interest
- ♦ Business obtains no credit

❑ Obtain minimal loan for exact needs

- ♦ Lower Interest
- ♦ Business obtains some credit

❑ Obtain excessive loan (deposit excess in CD)

- ♦ Lower interest
- ♦ Business obtains higher credit
- ♦ Better deal for bank (higher collected interest, same risk)

Car Wash

BUSINESS PLAN

THE DIRT BUSTER

11535 Cornish Blvd.
Detroit, MI 46778

March 15, 1993

The Dirt Buster was designed by entrepreneurs wishing to provide a high quality car wash service in a virtually untapped market. Because new construction is necessary, a large amount of initial capital is required for this venture.

EXECUTIVE SUMMARY

Description of Business

Nature of Service

The Dirt Buster is to be a full-service car wash facility comprised of the following features: a one hundred-twenty foot, fully automatic tunnel; four high pressure wand self-service bays; and six vacuum stations complete with fragrance and carpet shampoo dispensing machines. In an effort to optimize our position as premium car care specialists, we will offer our customers the opportunity to purchase quality car care products in our reception area. The full service operation will offer three basic wash packages: a $7.50 Basic wash, a $9.50 Deluxe wash and a $12.50 Super wash.

All full-service wash packages will include an interior cleaning service, which consists of carpet vacuuming, window and dash cleaning, and a preservation treatment. Our coin-operated, self-service bays will cost $1.50 per 4.5 minute cycle. Additionally, all customers will have access to vacuum islands which will cost $.50 per 4.5 minute cycle. Fragrance and shampoo dispensing machines will also be offered, and will range in price from $1.00 to $2.50 per cycle.

Unique Features of Service

The property on which The Dirt Buster is to be located was the site of a car wash approximately ten years ago. For reasons external to the business itself, the owners decided to terminate operations. The existing tunnel structure is ideally suited to house our tunnel operation. The original tunnel's one hundred-twenty foot length, versus today's standard ninety foot tunnel length, provides a significant service advantage over other car washes in the area. Very simply, the longer the tunnel, the more wash and drip space is available and the better an automobile is cleaned and dried during each cycle. Unfortunately, most car wash operators know it is possible to provide reasonably good service utilizing just ninety feet of tunnel space. This reduces the initial construction costs by approximately 25 percent (based on a tunnel structure of 90' x 25' versus 120' X 25' at construction costs of $100/sq.ft.). The bottom line is that most car wash operators sacrifice service to minimize costs. The Dirt Buster's unique position of not having to sacrifice service to lower costs will allow us to provide superior service at a competitive price.

Our market area is characterized by wide ethnic and economic diversity. To capitalize on these demographic factors and concentrate on the unique demands each group asks of the market, our facility will incorporate both a full-service tunnel operation (for those who wish to allow our service team to clean their car) and a self-service facility (for those who wish to take a more active role in their car's maintenance). This type of car wash operation will be one of only three such facilities in the area. Additionally, we plan to provide an automatic dryer for each self-service bay, which will increase customer satisfaction by eliminating the need to hand dry an automobile after washing. Automatic dryers are a new and effective market innovation which currently exist in only one other car wash operation in our region.

Objectives

After in-depth analysis of our specific market area, national statistics on the car wash industry, and detailed evaluation of nine car wash operations in the area, we expect to generate sales revenues of $667,508 in the first year of operation. We believe our initial customer base will substantially increase as the community becomes aware of our existence, our reputation for excellent service, and our active involvement in community affairs. We then expect our growth to mirror the community's projected market growth, which is approximately 3.5 percent to 5 percent per year. Because there are no other car wash operations within a four mile radius of our site location, we feel confident our predicted growth will, at a minimum, follow industry trends. Therefore, we expect to have a 100 percent market share of our target market for at least the short term.

Strategic Direction

Stage of Business

A start-up business designed to fill a service void which was created ten years ago after the last full-service tunnel wash facility in this market area terminated its operations. Again, the last full-service tunnel terminated its operations for reasons external to the business itself.

Long Range Direction

We are dedicated to establishing and maintaining the finest car wash operation in the area, specifically known for the quality of service provided and the management's commitment to the betterment of the community.

MARKET/MARKETING

Market Segment Sought

We are extremely fortunate our service is not limited to a specific segment or group of the market. In fact, The Dirt Buster's sole limiting factor is the small segment of its specific market which is without an automobile. In our market area alone, there are approximately 400,000 automobiles, or .8 automobiles per person.

Benefits of Service to the Market Segment

We will provide the only full service facility within our market area. Additionally, our water reclamation system will provide an environmentally safe means for our customers to clean their automobiles. This differs from residential car washing, where untreated wash water fills storm drains and ultimately empties into our waterways.

Summary of Advertising and Pricing Policies

Our Basic, full-service tunnel wash will cost $7.50. It will entail a full exterior vehicle wash, as well as an interior service to include vacuuming, window cleaning, and dashboard cleaning. Our Deluxe Wash will cost $9.50 and will include all the Basic Wash services as well as an undercarriage wash, a rust inhibitor, and a wheel brightener. The Super Wash will cost $12.50 and will include all Deluxe Wash services as well as a polishing wax and a wax sealant.

We have investigated all available advertising mediums. After in-depth consultations with a myriad of car wash operators in the area, we have decided to utilize the advantages of a variety of mediums. Initially, we will utilize cable television and radio spots, in conjunction with newspaper advertisements, to announce our Grand Opening. We will also use direct mail coupons to increase consumer awareness of our existence. Additionally, we will work cross promotions with businesses in the area as a means to tap the client base they have established. Already, several existing businesses have expressed a desire to do so.

Sales Projections

We expect to wash 63,700 cars in the full-service operation and 29,440 cars in the self-service operation during The Dirt Buster's first year of business.

Management

Backgrounds

The principal owners will be the full-time managers. Both individuals have served in the United States Army as commissioned officers since graduation from college 12 and 10 years ago, respectively. They have vast experience in the management of finances, personnel, and equipment. While in the Army, both individuals successfully completed two years of company command, which closely parallels the running of a small business; it requires the managing of all associated personnel, budgetary, and operational situations. In addition, one manager is currently working as the assistant manager for a local car wash. This experience has provided invaluable insight into the operational aspects of managing and maintaining a car wash.

Responsibilities

One manager will focus on daily operations, including employee hiring, building maintenance, property maintenance, and equipment maintenance. The other manager will focus on marketing, advertising, and community relations, as well as all fiscal matters, including employee pay and benefits, taxes, payables, and receivables. Other members of the management team will provide support to the owners with regard to their specific areas of expertise.

Financial Features

Projections:

	Year 1	Year 2	Year 3
Revenues	$667,508	$746,518	$885,771
Net Income	$163,144	$180,405	$208,765
Assets	$789,389	$872,906	$1,010,126
Liabilities	$581,644	$480,288	$378,932
Net Worth	$207,745	$392,618	$631,194

Capital Needed

The capital needed to underwrite this proposal will be utilized to renovate the existing tunnel structure, construct four self service bays and one equipment room, and institute site improvements, including landscaping, asphalt repair, night light installation, and installing signs. Additionally, the capital would be used to purchase both full-service and self-service equipment, a water reclamation system, administrative equipment and supplies, the chemical inventory, and to provide operating capital to maintain the operation through its first four months.

Financial Arrangements/Exit

Expected Annual Return for Investor

Given an investment of $683,000, an investor could expect a total return of 20%. This is calculated by dividing net profit by total investment, where net profit does not make a provision for taxes, and includes expense depreciation.

Number of Investors/Minimum Investment

One investor is preferable. However, we have made a conscience decision not to limit the number of investors that may invest in order to retain financial flexibility. Ideally, we would prefer that no investment be less than $50,000, which would purchase a 4 percent equity position. It is our desire that all equity partners be limited partners.

How Investors will Get their Money

Each investor who purchases an equity position will receive their equity share of the net profit at the close of each business year. It is our intention to repurchase all equity stock within seven years, offering a balloon payment.

Summary of Financing

	Amount Needed	Current Amount
Debt	$400,000	$0
Equity	$200,000	$0
Bond	$83,000	$0

Our objective is to obtain the financing necessary to bring our concept to fruition. The aforementioned financing package merely outlines one possible financing option. We understand there are a myriad of ways to structure financing, and we welcome the opportunity to explore additional alternatives.

BACKGROUND AND PURPOSE

History

The Dirt Buster concept was born from the frustration we experienced when trying to find a car wash in the vicinity of our homes. Our frustration lead us to investigate the possibility of building a car wash facility. Twenty months of exhaustive research revealed three facts that propelled us forward in our pursuit to build a car wash. First, there is an enormous demand for a car wash in the area. Second, there are no car wash competitors in the area. Third, we were able to negotiate a lease for property ideally suited for a car wash; the traffic count, a key element in predicting a car wash's success, is twice the national average.

Current Conditions

Description of Products/Services

The Dirt Buster is designed to be a complete car care facility. The operation is comprised of two complementary systems: a full-service system for those customers who wish to allow our service team to clean their car and a self-service facility for those who wish to take a more active role in their car's maintenance. Both systems will be outfitted with the most technologically advanced equipment available, thereby providing our customers with the best service possible. The Dirt Buster's unique operational concept of combining a full-service tunnel operation with a self-service operation provides our customers with service flexibility unmatched by any other car wash facility within a twenty mile radius. Additionally, within our market area, which is determined by the industry to be a 3.5 mile radius from our site location, we have absolutely no competition.

Unique Aspects of our Strategy

We plan to market our car wash utilizing four primary mediums: Discount coupon mailings to selected ZIP Codes, radio and cable television spots, and cross promotions with local area merchants which will allow us to tap into their firmly established customer bases. Additionally, we will approach apartment and condominium management offices, asking them to include promotional coupons in their monthly newsletters.

Overall Objectives

Objectives

To develop a highly successful, profitable car wash business which provides our community with a much needed service.

Long-Range Goal

To clear The Dirt Buster of accrued debt and develop it into a $1,000,000 per year operation that is respected as a hallmark of successful customer service.

Specific Objectives

Revenues/Sales

Our first year's objective is to realize a gross profit of $667,508 based upon an expected service volume of 113,748 vehicles. The full-service tunnel operation will account for 85 percent of revenue on 56 percent of the sales. The self-service operation will account for approximately 12 percent of the revenue on 26 percent of the sales. The vacuum operation will account for approximately 3 percent of the revenue on 18 percent of the sales.

Profitability

Based on one year's revenue of $667,508 and one year's fixed, variable, and depreciation expenses of $504,364, we expect a net profit, before income taxes and interest payment, of $163,144. This computes to a 24 percent return on a $683,000 investment.

Market Standing

There are no car wash facilities within our target market area, which is defined as a 3.5 mile radius from the location. The closest car wash facility to our proposed location is 4.5 miles away. Therefore, we have no direct competition within our target market area.

Product/Service Quality

Providing our customers the very best possible service is our primary objective. We will achieve this by equipping our full- and self-service facilities with the finest equipment available, supporting our superior technological foundation with the region's best service to cost price package, and by insisting upon a highly trained and motivated service staff.

Management Development

Our objective is to cultivate our managers from within the organization. This practice is essential to ensuring that our business philosophy and management style remain consistent. Additionally, by adhering to this objective, we possess a means in which to reward employees who continually perform in an outstanding manner.

Social Responsibility

Our objective is to become an active and solid member of the business community in Hampton County. Additionally, we believe that we should provide an employment opportunity for members of our community.

MARKET ANALYSIS

Overall Market

Nationally, the car wash industry experienced a downturn in sales volume and an upturn in gross profit per car washed in 1990 and 1991. Specifically, between 1990 and 1991, sales volume declined 3.1 percent and gross profit per car increased by 7.9 percent. Thus, on the average, car washes experienced a small increase in gross profit. Industry experts blame the sluggish economy and unusual national weather patterns for the decrease in sales volume and predict volume will rebound to pre-1990 levels as the economy improves.

Specific Market

Location

The location is the most important aspect in predicting a car wash's success. Ideally, a car wash should be situated on a thoroughfare which possesses a heavy volume of traffic, often referred to as "traffic count." The wash location should have readily accessible ingress and egress routes. The target market's population should be at least 30,000 people. A majority of the target market should reside in apartments, townhouses, and/or condominiums.

Our location is easily accessible from two major roads. The population within a three mile radius of our location is 206,909. According to the 1990 survey, our target market is expected to grow at a rate of approximately 3.5 percent per year. Industry studies state a car wash will capture .06 percent to 1.5 percent of the daily traffic which passes its location; thus, the higher the traffic count the better the business's chance of success. Industry studies also reveal the average car wash location's daily traffic count is 24,000 cars. According to the 1990 survey,the daily traffic count in front of the proposed location is 50,000. This translates to between 300 and 750 cars washed per day. It is projected the traffic count in front of the proposed location will grow at an approximate rate of 5 percent per year. This projection bodes exceptionally well for The Dirt Buster.

Trends

A recent demographic study predicts a slow, but steady, increase in our target area's population over the next 10 years. Additionally, this study predicts the number of cars registered in our target area will also show a slow, but steady, increase over the next ten years.

Characteristics

Our target market is the most densely populated area in the city and is comprised of a diverse mixture of ethnic and economic groups. This diverse economic and ethnic make-up supports our view that there is a strong demand in our market area for a complete car wash facility that possesses both full-service and self-service facilities. Industry surveys reveal that young people between the ages of 18-25 (11% of the target market), blue collar workers of all ages, and those with little disposable income will patronize a self-service facility. Individuals over 25 (72% of the target market), white collar workers, and those with disposal incomes will patronize full-service facilities.

Buying Habits of Customers

In talking with hundreds of people in our target area over the past eighteen months, we have determined there is an enormous need for a car wash facility in this area. Currently, there is not a car wash facility within a 4.5 mile radius of the proposed location, and our proposal has received enormous support from both civic and government groups in our target market.

Companies in Specific Target Market

There are no car wash facilities within our target market area, which is defined as a 3.5 mile radius from the location. The closest car wash facility is 4.5 miles away. However, there are a number of car wash facilities located in the suburbs, most of which we have made contact with during our investigation into the industry, but who are not competitors due to their distance from our site.

It is virtually impossible to ascertain the industry's sales in the Hampton County and Monroe County areas, as there is no regional association which binds the individual businesses together and maintains such figures. The only way to obtain an active car wash's figures is to ask individual owners. Because this business is a cash business, many operators would not share their revenue figures with us. However, we were fortunate enough to obtain the actual annual financial operating figures from four car wash operations. We were given these figures in confidence and asked not to repeat them. We did, however, use these figures as a gauge to measure the validity of the calculations presented in our pro-forma financial statements. We believe our revenue calculations are extremely conservative, and our expense calculations are as accurately portrayed as possible.

Competitive Factors

Assessment of Leading Competitors

Overview

In our target market area we have no direct competition. There are cases where car wash owners have built their business in an area which put them into direct competition with another car wash operation. Business logic dictates that unnecessary competition benefits neither operation.

Current Business Focus

The Dirt Buster's focus in this service-dependent business is to provide the highest quality service, at the fairest price, to the largest percentage of the target market population as possible. This will foster a repeat customer base.

Annual Revenues

In a cash business, such as a car wash, it is difficult to obtain accurate annual revenue figures for the industry as a whole, and especially for individual operations. However, a number of the car wash owners in the city shared their general revenue figures with us and four car wash operations we studied in depth gave us detailed monthly and yearly revenue and expense break-outs.

Of the four car wash operations we studied extensively, three are just one-year-old and the fourth is thirty-years-old. Two of the operations are exterior wash conveyor system washes, one is a self-service wash, and one of the operations is a full-service conveyor system wash. Additionally, one operation combines an exterior wash conveyor system with a five bay self-service facility. We point out these operational and facility configurations because different operation and configuration arrangements drastically affect revenues. For example, revenue produced by an exterior wash conveyor system will be substantially less than a full-service wash facility, given operations with similar traffic count and population figures. Similarly, car washes which combine conveyor wash operations with a self-service operation will, under normal circumstances, produce more revenue than either the full-service conveyor wash operation or the self-service wash facility by themselves. Therefore, the optimum configuration for revenue maximization is a facility which incorporates both a self-service wash facility and a full-service conveyor wash facility. This is The Dirt Buster's operational concept.

Each car wash facility we studied produced a profit, including the two newer facilities. The full-service facility's annual revenues total $432,000. The self-service facility's annual revenues total $121,000. The exterior wash facility with the self-service facility's annual revenues total $522,000 and the exterior wash facility, which is thirty-years-old and possesses the best demographic figures of the washes we studied, generates $687,486 in annual revenues.

Market Share

Two of the four operations studied possessed a 100 percent market share of their target markets. The other two share their markets equally. However, there is no doubt the close proximity, one mile, of the two washes has adversely affected their profit margins.

Profitability

All four car wash operations are profitable. However, as could be expected, the oldest car wash enjoys the most lucrative profit picture as it no longer experiences debt retirement concerns. Equipment purchase, construction of building and land, and debt retirement, based upon the averages given, is expected to be approximately 20 percent of gross profit. Fixed and variable expenses, on the average, are approximately 60 percent of gross profit.

Other Factors

In careful examination of the car industry as a whole, the most important factor in an operation's profitability is location. Those that possess superior location produce sound financial pictures 99 percent of the time. Additionally, not enough can be said about a strong clientele base which, because of good service, continues coming back again and again. The chosen location of The Dirt Buster is indeed superior, and our excellent service will guarantee the development of a strong clientele base.

Advantage Over Competitors

Price

To arrive at our price listing for each car wash package, we carefully examined fifteen car wash facilities in the state. We analyzed each facility's wash packages and then compared the price of the package to its service contents to make a qualitative determination on the quality of service provided versus the cost of the service. Unfortunately, what we discovered was that, in most cases, the service provided did not warrant the higher price charged to the customer. The customer was not receiving any significant increase in the service received. Therefore, we carefully constructed our wash packages to ensure that our customers received the best possible service for the price charged.

Performance

Our research repeatedly indicated that the wash's performance is directly proportional to the type and make of equipment used. Therefore, in keeping with our business objective of providing the highest quality service possible, we've decided to purchase the most technologically advanced conveyor and self-service equipment available. This technologically advanced equipment will provide us with a qualitative edge over all the car wash facilities within a 20 mile radius of our location.

Advantages of Competitors Over Us

We believe there are only two temporary advantages a competitor could have over The Dirt Buster.

Customer base We will need time to firmly establish a sturdy customer base.

Business experience We lack daily experience in the industry, which our competitors have garnered over time. However, we believe our work at two separate car wash facilities over the last seven months greatly reduces this initial experience advantage.

Description and Assessment of Potential Competitors

We do not believe it likely we will face any competition in the near future. Quite simply, there are only a few pieces of property available which are zoned for and large enough to support a car washing operation in our target market area. The few available are also extremely expensive. Additionally, the majority of the available property we examined during our location search are much too diminutive to host a conveyor system. Thus, any potential competition would be limited to a self-service-only facility which cannot generate sufficient income throughout the business year to render it a profitable venture.

Other Market Features

Impact of the following:

Economic Factors

While the sluggish economy of the last few years has had a slightly negative impact on the car wash industry as a whole, more than half of the car wash owners surveyed by the International Car Wash Association Survey in 1990 and 1991 experienced an increase in levels of profitability. While not completely recession proof, the industry has retained a very strong financial picture through difficult economic times created by the prevailing economic downturn, even managing to increase revenues by 10 percent in each of the last three years.

Governmental Influences

The governmental influence on our business is not extensive. One government mandated facility-design feature is the installation of a water reclamation system. This design feature is one that we would have added to the facility even if not mandated by the county. It greatly reduces our fresh water consumption, which in turn reduces our water bill. In the future, governmental efforts to purify the area's bodies of water may result in legislation eliminating the release of soap, oil, waxes and other contaminants into storm drains by people washing their cars at home. Obviously, legislation of this kind would only enhance our business position.

Social/Demographic Factors

These factors are critical when selecting a car wash location and determining the type of facility to build. Obviously, the larger the population base in the market area, the better the chance of the business succeeding. Industry surveys indicate that the average car wash operation shares a population base in its target market of 118,000 people with four other competitors. We are in the unique position of having a 100 percent market share of the 206,909 people who make-up our target market. Research in the industry reveals specific types of car wash facilities appeal to different social groups. Eighteen to twenty-five year olds, regardless of ethnic group, blue collar workers, and minority groups tend to make the most use of self-service facilities. Twenty-six to sixty-five year olds, white collar workers, and mothers with children utilize conveyor facilities. Therefore, the makeup of a target area influences the design of the car wash facility. Our target area is a diverse mix of ethnic and social groups. We feel it is the most advantageous to build a facility which would cater to all groups in our target market. This is our rationale for developing an operation incorporating both a self-service facility and a conveyor facility.

Seasonal Fluctuations

Seasonal fluctuations, as defined by changes in the weather, directly impact a car wash's business volume. Contrary to logic, the winter months are the peak months for full-service volume, while the self-service volume remains constant throughout the year, with a slight decrease occurring in the November to February time frame. It is not uncommon for a car wash to generate enough sales volume from November through February to underwrite its expenses and debt load throughout the remainder of the year.

MARKETING

Marketing Philosophy

Our marketing philosophy is to present our company as an independent, service-oriented small business, which is genuinely concerned with providing high-quality service at a reasonable price.

Marketing Strategy

Environmental Opportunities

An issue of great concern in the area is water pollution. Efforts are being coordinated state-wide to stop the dumping of untreated sewage into the Bay. Car washing, in an uncontrolled environment, such as at one's home, directly contributes to the pollution of the bay by allowing soap, waxes, dirt, oil, and grime to flow untreated into the neighborhood storm sewer systems which in turn flows directly into area waterways. The Dirt Buster will utilize only biodegradable chemicals which will be cycled through the purification component of our water reclamation system prior to being released into the county sewer system. Once in the county's system, the water will be sent to the sewage facility for recycling and purification. Additionally, 30 percent less water is required to clean an automobile at a commercial car wash than at an individual's home. This helps conserve a precious, and often scarce, natural resource.

Company Strengths

One obvious strength of our company is market share. Since no competition exists in our target market, we will possess a 100 percent market share the day we open for business. Another strength is the management team. Both owners possess vast experience in budgetary, equipment, events, and personnel management. Finally, the superior quality of our equipment, in terms of efficiency and effectiveness, allows us to provide a superior quality service to our customer at a cost below that of the regional average.

Overall Marketing Strategy

Our marketing strategy is two-fold. First, we must develop a loyal customer base on which to build our business. Second, we must cultivate and expand this customer base to ensure a long lasting and solid relationship with our repeat customers and continued vitality of the business with the addition of new customers.

Image We Want to Portray

The entire foundation of our business rests on our pledge to provide quality service at a reasonable price. We will portray our business in such a manner. Additionally, we are genuinely interested in the positive development and quality of our market area's business community.

Pricing Strategy

List Prices

After careful analysis of this region's car wash operator's pricing practices, we crafted a pricing strategy that we believe more closely aligns service with price. Our system incorporates a three tier pricing scheme. In accordance with our pricing strategy, our Basic Wash will cost $7.50, our Advanced Wash will cost $9.50, and our Deluxe Wash package will cost $12.50. Additionally, we will provide customers the option to build their own wash package from a list of individual service options offered. These options will range in price from $1.00 to $3.00. We plan to charge $1.50 per 4.5 minute cycle in our self-service facility, and $.50 per 4.5 minute cycle for the vacuum service, which is in line with the prices that are currently being charged by the majority of the region's self-service facility operators.

Profit Margins

Calculating profit margin based upon the projected year-end financial figures is relatively clear cut and yields a profit margin of 40 percent. This percentage was determined by calculating the percentage of gross revenue that both expenses and debt retirement figures yielded, and subtracting that figure from 100 percent. [100% - (percentage of gross revenue expense + debt retirement) = profit margin]. For example, based upon industry averages, our variable expenses represent 45 percent of our gross revenue, while fixed expenses represent 20 percent of our gross revenue and debt retirement represents 15 percent of our gross revenue. These figures added together and then subtracted from 100 percent leaves a figure of 20 percent, which represents the overall businesses profit margin. Individually, our full-service package yields a profit margin of 8 percent, our Advanced Wash package yields a profit margin of 34 percent, our Deluxe Wash package yields a profit margin of 45 percent, our self-service wash yields a profit margin of 67 percent, and our vacuum service yields a profit margin of 87 percent.

Discount Prices

As part of our marketing strategy, we will at various times offer discounts on selected wash packages. Discounts will vary from a $1 to $3 reduction of the standard price.

Competitors' Prices

Although we do not have any competitors in our target market to use as a guide for establishing our pricing system, we did evaluate several pricing schemes to assist us in developing one appropriate for The Dirt Buster.

Advertising/Promotion

During eighteen months of research and hundreds of conversations with owners of regional car wash operations, two points became very apparent. First, older, established car washes do little to no advertising. Second, new, upstart car washes advertise extensively in an attempt to establish themselves in the community. We found no middle ground in the industry with respect to advertising, and most car wash owners who do advertise believe their best results have come from utilizing direct ZIP Code mailings, local cable TV spots, and cross-promotions done in conjunction with other local businesses.

During our first month of business, we plan to conduct a drawing to giveaway a big screen TV and two plane tickets to the Bahamas. The drawing will take place over the first month we are open for business. To enter, a customer will fill out an entry card with name, address, and make and year of car. The entry form will then be deposited into a central repository until the official drawing on the last day of our first month of operation. Customers need not be present to win; we will notify the winners by mail. The drawing will enable us to build a customer mailing list, to be used in future direct mailing promotions, from the entry cards, and gain initial exposure by bringing customers into the wash.

We plan on advertising our Grand Opening in all advertising mediums, including radio, television, news print, and direct ZIP Code mailings. During our first year of business, we will be actively involved in developing customer awareness of our business through extensive use of the radio, television, promotional giveaways, and direct mailings. We plan to dedicate 7 percent of our monthly gross revenues to advertising and promotions. At the end of each quarter, we will assess the effectiveness of our advertising campaign and make any adjustments necessary to provide us with the most positive community exposure.

Additionally, adjacent to our car wash facility is a 13,000 square foot building. Our plans are to lease the building to a business which operates within our industry, thereby allowing us maximum flexibility in developing cross-promotional plans. Tentative arrangements have been made to lease the property as a detailing shop when The Dirt Buster opens for business.

To build a solid repeat customer base, we will offer bonus services. On a customer's first visit we will provide them with a book to keep track of visits. On a customer's ninth visit to the car wash, he or she will receive a free basic wash. To build return customer traffic, we will also randomly hang scented discount wash coupons on each customer's rearview mirror which are redeemable on the customer's next visit to the car wash. Additionally, as a means to assess adherence to our primary goal of providing exceptional service, we will provide each customer with a postage paid comment card.

Cost of Advertising

Regional Cable TV Advertisements

It will cost $1,260 per month to purchase seven daily ads, four before 4 p.m. and three after 4 p.m., 7 days per week on CNN, ESPN, and TNT.

Radio

It will cost approximately $1,500 a week for twenty radio spots per radio station. This medium will only be used for the initial advertising campaign as a means to obtain mass market exposure. Cost would not justify extended use.

Direct Mailing

Direct mail will cost $350 per 10,000 pieces sent. It is the most effective means to reach specific target market patrons, as it offers the most bang for the buck.

Cross-Promotion

The cost of cross-promotion is minimal, and it will allow us to tap into an established customer base.

Initial Giveaways

One big screen TV will cost $1,000. Two plane tickets to the Bahamas will cost $500.

Comment Cards

Comment cards will be computer generated at minimal cost.

Fragrance Discount Coupons

The coupons will be computer generated and the scent applied by the car wash. Again, there will be only a minimal cost.

FINANCIAL DATA

Current Financial Position

In developing our projected financial statements, projected revenues and expenses were calculated, both fixed and variable, by using statistical reference data provided by the industry's national association, the International Car Wash Association (ICA). We coupled the information received from ICA with regionally specific data provided by regional car wash operators and government agencies. In constructing our financial pro forma statements in this manner, we hope to portray as accurately as possible the revenues and expenses we can expect to see. Any errors should be to the high side of expenses and to the low side of revenues; all projections are extremely conservative.

For example, to calculate our projected revenue, we used the industry's capture ratio of the percent of traffic count in any given 24 hour period which a business could expect to utilize its facilities. We then multiplied that figure by the cost of our projected revenue per car, $9. The ICA states that a car wash owner can expect to capture .6 of 1% to 1.5 of 1% of the traffic count on the road on which the car wash is situated. According to government officials, the traffic count passing in front of our site is 55,823 cars a day. Armed with the statistical data needed to project the revenue figures, we examined various car wash operations in the county to gain an appreciation for the validity of the capture ratio. Our investigation showed that, in this region, the capture ratio was an accurate gauge on which to project the business a car wash operation can expect based upon its location.

The car wash industry is cyclical in nature, with the highest point of revenue occurring during the winter months and the low revenue point occurring during the summer months. Our revenue projections reflect that trend. Conservatively, over the course of the first business year, we predicted that, on the average, we will capture .39% of the 50,000 cars that travel pass our location daily. Keep in mind, our projected capture ratio is .21% less than the industry's worst case capture ratio.

To calculate fixed and variable expenses, we used ICA's national statistical information as a guide and spoke with local car wash operators in order to achieve actual monthly expense figures. We then compared these sources of information and developed our own expense analysis ratios. Our fixed expense figures are based upon actual figures gathered from local operators and our variable expenses are based upon a combination of industrial statistical averages and local operator figures. The only expense not strictly in keeping with both national and local operator figures is our advertising expense. We have decided that it is extremely important for us to make our target market realize our presence from day one, so we decided to budget 7.5% of our gross revenue to advertising versus the 4.5% of gross revenue recommended by the ICA.

Start-up Cost

We calculated our total start-up costs to be $683,000. This figure includes $135,000 for operating capital and a contingency fund.

Profit and Loss Statement

Our pro forma profit and loss statement projects the first year's operating profit to be $163,144.

Cash Flow Analysis

Our pro forma statement of cash projects a positive cash flow starting in month one. At the end of the first year of business, we project a closing cash balance of $281,989.

Balance Sheet

Our pro forma balance sheet projects our net worth to be $207,745 at the conclusion of the first year of operations.

Cost Control

All fiscal control and accountability will rest with the management, who will be responsible for insuring that daily receipts are properly accounted for, properly documented, and deposited with a financial institution. In conjunction with the CPA, management will prepare the monthly, quarterly, and yearly financial statements.

Break-even Analysis

Units

Break-even Estimates:

Our break-even figure in automobiles washed in the full-service operation is 47,154 and, in the self-service operation, including vacuum figures, it is 36,516. These figures represent a 26 percent reduction in automobile wash volume.

Dollars

The total gross revenue generated with respect to the break-even analysis is $493,470, with $424,386 coming from the full-service operation, and $69,084 coming from the self-service operation, including vacuum figures.

Financial Ratios

Liquidity

Current Ratio

Current assets and current liabilities are 281,899 to 101,356, respectively. This is a 2.78 to 1 ratio.

Implications of Liquidity Ratios

Liquidity ratios provide insight into a business's ability to meet all financial obligations incurred during the course of the business year. Normally, financial ratios are used as analytical tools to compare one business to another within a specific industry. Because the ICA has not established any industry ratios, there are none available to compare to the ratios generated in this business plan. However, according to most business analysts, a good target ratio for most upstart businesses is 2 to 1. Therefore, our liquidity ratio of 2.78 to 1 further supports our financial analysis, which suggests The Dirt Buster will meet all liabilities incurred during our first year of operation.

Profitability/Implications

Our gross profit margin is defined as our gross profit divided by our total assets, where gross profit does not include taxes, interest, or the reintroduction of depreciation. Our figures show a margin of 21 percent (163,144/789,389=21%).

For our purposes, return on equity and return on investment are defined without figuring depreciation or taxes into the net profit. Our return on equity, using the formula net profit/total owner's equity, works out to 14 percent (96,336/683,000=14%). Our return on investment, or net profit/total assets, works out to 12 percent (96,336/789,389=12%).

Profitability ratios provide insight into a business's ability to make money. As previously stated, financial ratios are used as analytical tools to compare one business to another within a specific industry. Because the car wash industry has not established any industry ratios, there are none available to compare to the ratios generated in this business plan. The examination of our profitability ratios supports our financial analysis which suggests The Dirt Buster will experience a profit at the conclusion of the first year of operations.

Financial Projections

Assumptions

We assumed that the interest rate applied to the purchase of our assets would be 10 percent. Additionally, we assumed the useful life of the service equipment and office equipment to be ten years and that of the building and grounds to be fifteen years.

Financial Statement Highlights

The financial figures presented in our pro forma statements are extremely encouraging in that a monthly positive cash flow is predicted. This in turn leads to an expected positive net income and an increase in owner's equity at the year's end.

It is important to note that during the preparation of our financial statements, we endeavored to be conservative in our revenue calculations and liberal in our expense calculations. This approach was intentionally adopted to ensure we maintained a cautious, if not slightly pessimistic, approach to the evaluation of The Dirt Buster's liability.

ORGANIZATION AND MANAGEMENT

Key Personnel

Executive Team

The executive team consists of the company's two owners, one of which will be located on-site during each normal business day to oversee operations. The managers will divide the duties necessary to maintain the business, which include employee hiring; building, property and equipment maintenance; marketing; advertising; community relations; fiscal matters; employee pay and benefits; taxes; payables; and receivables. Military experience has provided both owners with a vast reservoir of knowledge in the management of personnel, equipment, events, and budgets. While in the military, both were schooled and promoted ahead of their contemporaries and assigned the Army's most challenging jobs. To enhance their professional knowledge of the car wash industry, as well as to gain a greater appreciation for the intricacies of owning and operating a car wash, both are currently working for different car washes in the tri-state area.

Compensation

Each owner/manager will receive a salary of $2,500 per month. In the event a net profit is accrued at the conclusion of the fiscal year, it will be equally divided amongst the owners.

Key Managers Needed

Initially, the company will be run solely by its owners. However, during the second year an assistant manager may be hired to assist with the day to day operations and maintenance. Our goal is to develop management from within the company, thereby insuring that positive management policies and practices are continued. Additionally, our policy of hiring from within provides us a means to recognize outstanding work performance and to develop a cohesive management team critical to The Dirt Buster's success.

Other Personnel

Employees Hired

Proposed

We plan to hire eleven full-time and seven part-time employees. Sixteen of the employees will constitute our operational personnel, while the other two employees will constitute our sales staff. The sales staff will be responsible for operation of the cash register and the accessory sales area.

Skilled Versus Unskilled

No special skills are required of our operations personnel. Sales staff must possess basic mathematical skills, be able to operate a cash register, and diplomatically interact with the general public.

Compensation

Our operational employees will receive a beginning salary of $5.00 per hour and will be offered an opportunity to increase their hourly pay in $.50 increments. Our sales employees will receive $5.50 per hour initially, with the same opportunity for the incremental $.50 per hour raise. All raises in base salary are dependent upon performance and the company's financial success. Additionally, the employees will, at the conclusion of each business day, receive their fair share of the collected tips.

Staffing/Training

Staff size is dependent upon time of day, day of the week, and weather conditions. During traditional peak wash periods, twelve operational employees and one sales employee will be scheduled to work. During traditional off-peak times we will schedule eight operational employees and one sales employee. We will remain flexible in our staffing policy in order to best meet customer demands and most efficiently utilize our employees. Our employee handbook will ensure that each employee understands the importance and applicability of a varied and flexible scheduling process. Our plan is to ensure that each employee receives the training necessary to be proficient in their assigned tasks. Our training program will focus on improving the employees' operational knowledge of the business as well as their interpersonal skills. The program is designed to ensure that our employee-customer interactions are as positive as possible.

MISCELLANEOUS ISSUES

The Dirt Buster's employees will be given the opportunity to participate in a health insurance program.

OWNERSHIP

Financing/Equity Considerations

Financial Features

4,001 shares of common stock have been issued. The total value of shares of common stock is $4,001. Presently, 100 percent of the common stock is controlled by two people, who therefore control the operational direction of the business. However, limited partners will be considered in exchange for financing.

Financing Arrangement

Collateral for Debt Issuance

All equipment will be used as collateral for debt issuances, as well as the lease to the site location. If we are unable to meet our business obligations, the lending institution controlling assets and the land lease could sell the lease to another business group. They would assume operational control of what would, in essence, be a turnkey operation.

Amount of Equity to be Relinquished in Exchange for Funding

We would consider an equity-limited partner in exchange for financing. The amount of equity to be exchanged for financing would be negotiated on an individual basis.

Expected Annual Return for Investor

The expected annual return for an investor depends on the type of investment arranged. Expected annual return for debt financing is approximately 15 percent. The expected annual return for equity financing is approximately 18 percent.

Number of Investors Sought

We have not set a limit on the number of investors we will accept. However, for accounting purposes, a minimal number of investors is the most appealing option.

Minimum Investment Required by Each Investor

Again, we will not set a bottom limit on the size of investments. However, our preference is a $50,000 or greater investment.

How Investors Will Get Their Money Out of the Investment

Each investor will receive a yearly return on their investment based upon the investment contract negotiated. It is the intention of the original partners to buy back all outstanding shares of stock within seven years.

CRITICAL RISKS AND PROBLEMS: DESCRIPTION

Sales Projections Not Attained

Based upon the extremely conservative figures used throughout our financial calculations, it is possible, although improbable, that we will not meet our projected sales goals. To demonstrate this point, we used the bottom end of the capture ratio the industry experts say a business ought to achieve, and reduced that figure by two full percentage points. We then used that number to calculate the project revenue we can expect to generate during our first year of business.

Unforeseen Industry Trends

Presently, the car wash industry is not expected to undergo drastic changes. Future industrial efforts are focused upon improving the quality of existing methods and machinery.

Competitive Price Cutting

Because we have no direct competition, we are semi-insulated from price cutting schemes. However, we realize we do not operate in a vacuum, and pricing schemes offered by area car wash operators do impact us. In light of this, we've developed our pricing scheme by examining eighteen separate car washes in the tri-state area. We then highlighted the best qualities of each package and built our own unique pricing scale, which we believe fairly balances quality and price.

Unforeseen Economic, Political, Social, and Technological Developments

Two critical environmental issues which concern everyone are the cleanliness and conservation of our finite water resources. Unlike waste water generated from residential car washing, which is discharged directly into storm sewers carrying contaminants directly into our local water ways, the wash water generated at The Dirt Buster will be recycled through a reclamation system. This will cleanse the water prior to its being discharged into the community water sewage treatment plant for further purification. Additionally, the chemicals used by the washing process are specifically engineered to be completely biodegradable and environmentally safe. It is also important to note that residential car washing, on the average, uses 200 gallons of water per wash. Self-service car wash customers use approximately 50 gallons per wash, resulting in a 75 percent water savings in comparison to residential automobile washing. Full-service car wash customers use approximately 84 gallons per wash, resulting in a 58 percent water savings in comparison to residential automobile washing.

Cyclical Fluctuations

The car wash industry does experience cyclical fluctuations in business volume. Peak months correspond to winter months and off-peak months correspond to summer months. It is during these known off-peak months that car wash owners carefully manipulate and orchestrate operations to insure peak efficiency is achieved. Also, during the off-peak period variable expenses decrease by approximately 40 percent of gross expenses as they are directly tied to business volume.

Other Risks

Perhaps the most critical risk we face is that of the establishment of a competitive wash in our target market. While it seems unlikely this will happen due to the cost of obtaining the land necessary to build a car wash facility, it is possible. One very real way we foresee competition presenting itself is in the form of an adjunct wash built onto an existing full-service gas station. While these adjunct washes will not compare to our facility in service or quality, they are less expensive and at times more convenient.

SUMMARY OF UNIQUE FEATURES AND BENEFITS

An extremely important feature of our business is its location. Without the proper location, the chances of succeeding are drastically reduced, although not impossible. It is interesting to note that, for the last five years, a regional car wash corporation with eight locations in the tri-state area has actively pursued the property owner to sell so they could establish a car wash on it. For personal reasons, the land owner refused to sell. Such a successful company would not have so vigorously pursued the site if they did not feel the land had enormous potential. We share their enthusiasm.

Our operation will incorporate the newest and most technologically advanced wash equipment in the industry. This will enable us to provide our customers with the best possible service at the best possible price. It will also allow us to ensure that the environmental concerns of the community are respected and acted upon. Additionally, we believe the strongest point in our business is our management team. Both owners possess vast knowledge, gained from operational, budgetary, and personnel experience, from which to direct the business and provide for outstanding customer service.

OVERALL STRATEGIC DIRECTION

We are determined to establish a business known for its high quality service at a reasonable price. We see ourselves playing an important part in community activities. We will provide employment opportunities for area residents, as well as a much needed service to the community which protects and conserves our finite water resources.

AVAILABLE MATERIALS

The following materials are available upon request:

- ❑ International Car Wash Association Industry Survey
- ❑ Traffic Volume Survey
- ❑ Market Survey
- ❑ Capture Ratio Calculations
- ❑ Break Even Analysis
- ❑ Organizational Structure and Concept
- ❑ Funding Timeline
- ❑ Start-up Costs
- ❑ Income Statement
- ❑ Cash Projections
- ❑ Balance Sheet
- ❑ Owner's Financial Statements
- ❑ Owner's Resumes

Crane Service

BUSINESS PLAN

CHESTERFIELD CRANE SERVICES

9055 S. Main
Moroco, ID 48181

August 2, 1993

Chesterfield Crane Service is seeking a capital infusion in order to expand its operation. It intends to increase its workload by adding a 50-ton capacity crane to its equipment line. The following plan provides an example of a business plan used to substantiate the need for additional equipment.

CRANE SERVICE BUSINESS PLAN

PURPOSE/OBJECTIVE

This is a request for a $200,000 loan (SBA guaranteed if required).
The purpose is to expand CHESTERFIELD CRANE SERVICES which has been in business since August 1989 serving hoisting needs with an 18 ton capacity crane.

The loan proceeds will be used for:

- Acquisition of a 50 ton crane (model TMS 475 50 ton Grove Hydraulic Crane),
- Approximately 4 months of working capital to place it in service and penetrate the higher hoisting capacity market serviced by 50 ton cranes.

This acquisition of a 50 ton crane, added to the current capacity of the company's existing 18 ton crane, is intended to take advantage of additional work frequently requested by customers who have the need for both 18 and 50 ton crane capacity to meet their job requirements. Having a variety of cranes opens a new market of customers who frequently use cranes and desire to use one company for all of their hoisting needs. The second crane will also bring in additional work for the currently owned 18 ton crane. The capacities of both an 18 ton and a 50 ton crane will enable the company to serve up to 80% of the hoisting market in the geographic region that the company serves.

BUSINESS BACKGROUND

Owner Background

Mr. Louis W. Chesterfield has been in the crane business since April 1979, starting out as an apprentice crane operator whose duties included crane operating, maintenance, job acquisition and coordination, and account collection for a Northern Idaho steel company, C. C. Iron Company. Mr. Chesterfield joined the union, went through the apprenticeship program and obtained union journeyman crane operator status while at C. C. Iron Company operating this steel company's 18 ton crane and 18 to 45 ton cranes which the company bare leased (leased without an operator). In 1988, Mr. Chesterfield achieved journeyman 10 year status with the union. Ten year status meant that either he was able to solicit his own work or interested companies could call for his services directly without picking the next available person in rotation from the list in the union hall. In 1989, Mr. Chesterfield then moved on to journeyman crane operator with Pikel Crane Services —Northwest Rigging, in Boise, Idaho (an affiliate company of Pikel Financial Corporation), the largest crane service company in the Northwest, operating 18 to 80 ton cranes, and then started CHESTERFIELD CRANE SERVICES on August 1, 1989 with the acquisition of an 18 ton crane. (A resume of Louis W. Chesterfield has been prepared and is available upon request.)

Start-Up, History and Management of Chesterfield Crane Services

In August 1989, CHESTERFIELD CRANE SERVICES commenced operations as a sole proprietorship upon the acquisition of an 18 ton TMS 180 Grov Hydraulic crane.

Management

Management responsibility for the company, both financially and day to day operations, rests with Mr. Louis Chesterfield. (See Owner Background above.)

For day to day bookkeeping requirements, the Company utilizes Wellborn Bookkeeping Services of Boise, Idaho. Further accounting and tax matters are handled through the Accounting Office of Sarah Thomas, CPA, 555 Marla St., Boise, Idaho 89448, phone (555) 577-1999. Legal counsel for the Company is Bob L. Meyer, 372 East 2nd Street, Boise, Idaho, 89702, phone (555) 572-8079. CHESTERFIELD CRANE SERVICES provides, at hourly rates, a compact crane, a professional operator, and any associated services needed to fulfill the hoisting requirements of the job.

Currently, Mr. Chesterfield is the sole operator. Upon acquisition of a second crane, it is anticipated that Mr. Chesterfield will be the primary crane operator over 90% of the time. When jobs dictate the utilization of both cranes simultaneously, an additional experienced 10 year status journeyman union crane operator will be retained from the union hall on an hourly basis. At this time such additional hourly personnel are paid at the rate of $33.00 per hour (includes wage and union fringe benefits). The crane operator's time is directly related to time that the crane is on the job and on the billing meter.

Except for major engine and major hydraulic repairs, Mr. Chesterfield performs all mechanical, maintenance, and crane repairs.

Initially, presently, and in the foreseeable future, the company services all of Idaho including Boise and surrounding areas.

In addition to steel erection and general hoisting, specialty services include crane services utilized in commercial construction, public works construction, highway construction, heavy equipment installation and removal for the mining and manufacturing industries, custom housing, residential and commercial roof and truss installation, and log home erection.

Initially, the success of CHESTERFIELD CRANE SERVICES was based on three factors:

BUSINESS DESCRIPTION

- ❑Mr. Chesterfield's established reputation and experience as one of the most competent crane operators in the local area for competence, safety practices, reliability, dependability, and cost effectiveness in performing jobs.

- ❑Customer service.
- ❑The niche filled by a small 18 ton crane.

The competence and customer service factors are closely related. Providing timely job estimates and bids are a standard necessity to success in the construction field. But CHESTERFIELD CRANE goes a step further in customer service by providing free preliminary job site checks.

The job site check is, in part, defining the hoists required by the job (loads, placement, distances, heights, crane placement site, crane rigging requirements, load placement methods, and safety considerations). This phase of the job site check is defining, with the customer, what the crane will be doing and how. The next phase of the job site check is defining with the customer the planning and coordination of the customer's resources needed to efficiently work in conjunction with the crane. This includes the scheduling of the customer's equipment, material deliveries, and labor, and their tasks to be performed upon arrival of the crane. Having all of these matters discussed, planned, and coordinated beforehand through the preliminary job site check results in efficient all around job performance for the customer by avoiding costly delay and stand by time of labor, trucked deliveries, and crane services.

Because the preliminary job site checks result in all around cost efficient job performance for the customer, CHESTERFIELD CRANE obtains a substantial amount of repeat business. In comparison, much of the competition simply take a call, and dispatch a crane to the job site to encounter whatever coordinated, or uncoordinated, conditions exist at the job site, billing all of the crane's time, whether it be actual hoisting time or stand-by time. Through that extra step of customer service in providing the preliminary job site checks, the customer base of CHESTERFIELD CRANE SERVICES has come to appreciate that more work gets done in less time with CHESTERFIELD CRANE.

Unmet Needs Operating Current Niche

The Company's reputation has resulted not only in steady repeat business for 18 ton capacity crane services, but has also resulted in consistent customer demand for the Company to provide 50 ton capacity crane services. One common example occurred in November 1991 on the construction of the new Idaho State Library project in Boise, Idaho. CHESTERFIELD CRANE SERVICES was on this job at one point hoisting steel for a subcontractor, Garth Iron Works, utilizing the current 18 ton crane. Later, the general contractor for the project, Owen Construction, having earlier observed CHESTERFIELD CRANE'S performance in steel erection for Garth Iron and being impressed with the performance they saw, requested CHESTERFIELD CRANE'S services to finish the general hoisting needs on the job including roofing materials. These needs, however, all required load and reach capacities of a 50 ton crane and were beyond the capacity of CHESTERFIELD CRANE SERVICES' currently owned 18 ton crane. CHESTERFIELD CRANE SERVICES is on many of the larger projects utilizing its currently owned 18 ton crane but frequently in the position of having to refuse work on these same projects requiring 50 ton crane capacity. Reference is made to the Market and Forecast sections for further analysis of the amount and dollar volume of 50 ton crane capacity needs for CHESTERFIELD CRANE to service.

BUSINESS OBJECTIVES AND GOALS

Immediate goals

- To continue to maintain and improve service and revenue based upon the company's existing niche in the compact crane category with existing equipment — 18 ton crane work.
- To generate additional revenue and profit by moving into the next higher niche served by the medium-high hydraulic crane category utilizing a 5O ton crane.
- To attain the equipment mix (a small compact 18 ton crane and a medium 50 ton crane) to enable the company to obtain both the light and medium hoisting work common on most construction projects.

Expected Results

These goals should result, within 2 years, of a doubling of income and net profit without the need for incurring additional full time personnel costs.

Intermediate goals

- To further increase market share, revenue, and net profit in hoisting services in the 18 to 50-ton crane capacity market.
- To further increase revenue and net profit from by 12% by 12/31/96.
- To add office staff, yard operations, equipment, and crane operators as hoisting demand and profit levels dictate.

Expected Results

To be a hoisting services company with a mix of 3 to 5 cranes, employing 2 to 4 competent crane operators, able to handle 90% (all but the largest projects requiring heavy capacity cranes) of the hoisting work within a 150 mile radius of Boise, Idaho, with a $150,000 cash reserve for contingencies, generating gross annual revenues of at least $500,000 and net profits of at least $100,000.

The long term (10 years) goals are to become a medium sized company, generating $2,500,000 in annual revenue, $500,000 annual profit, 7 to 10 cranes of various capacities with the ability to handle 80% of the market's hoisting needs, with 7 to 15 employees.

THE MARKET AND THE COMPETITION

Perspective/Overview

The crane business, as a whole, operates with hoisting capacities of 8 to 300 tons, and boom (reaching) capacities of 30 feet to in excess of 300 feet.

8 to 15 ton cranes generally service hoisting requirements for heating and air conditioning units, wood trusses for housing, and other general, small, light duty work.

18 to 25 ton cranes generally service general hoisting needs such as trusses, custom homes, smaller commercial, material unloading from trucks, and setting concrete barrier rails for highway construction. These cranes have a higher capacity than the smaller cranes, but are still compact and mobile enough to operate in tight working spaces common on most construction sites. They set up fast and transport quickly from the home base site to the job site. That is important to the contractor customers because they are charged from the time the crane leaves its base site to its return, portal to portal.

30 to 50 ton cranes are used for situations requiring a longer reach. These cranes are usually on the job site for longer periods of time and perform heavier hoists, placed higher and further out from the crane's center of gravity. For example, most steel erection requires crane hoists of several different sizes and weights of steel beams from inventory stacks of beams placed on the ground at various locations on the job site and placed into various parts of the building as it is constructed with the crane remaining in a fixed location.

Cranes of 80 ton capacity and over are used for very heavy hoisting needs such as concrete tilt-up building construction, high rise steel construction, train derailments, drag line and clam shell work.

Equipment Mix

As demonstrated in the Boise State Library job above (in the Business Background, Niche section), many construction projects require various hoisting capacities. Thus most hoisting companies in the market have a mix of cranes to be able to capture all of the hoisting work required on any given project.

Cranes are used in all phases of the building project lifting main structural members, materials for all trades, setting machinery, setting rooftop heating and air conditioning units. The weight of the object to be lifted and the distance from the crane that the object will be placed, determine what size crane is needed to do the job.

The Competition

Described below are the 5 primary competitors in this geographic area within a 150 mile radius of Boise, Idaho.

Pikel Crane and Rigging

Mr. Chesterfield worked for Pikel as a crane operator, truck driver, and oiler from 1/15/89 to 7/1/89. Pikel Crane is very large, owning close to 200 cranes and a trucking company, with offices in Boise, Meredith, and Gella. In the Northern Idaho area, they primarily serve a 150 mile radius with approximately 20 cranes with 10 to 300 ton capacities. David Sheldon is Pikel Crane's Boise office manager and salesman. Pikel Crane is very professional due to the union operators they utilize — some having 40 years experience. These are the top crane operators which customers want. Pikel Crane feels that they have a monopoly and treat customers as such. Adding costs after the crane is on the job is very common. Most commercial construction is union, so being union brings them these jobs. Having union wages brings them the top operators.

Stansell Construction

This company is owned by Harry Stansell. Stansell does some work in Boise, but primarily does non-union commercial jobs in Smithson, Idaho. Harry's son, Mike Stansell, handles the equipment for the company. Stansell has cranes from 12 ton to 150 tons primarily used for their own construction needs. Stansell is also in the crane rental business. Being non-union eliminates a large part of the market from them. Further, paying low wages for operators gets them inexperienced operators that scare off a lot of customers. In addition, non-union contractors do not want to use Stansell's crane services because Stansell, also being a general non-union contractor, is in direct competition with their potential crane rental customers. These rental customers are also non-union general contractors engaging in commercial construction. Stansell's main crane rental customers are the mining industry, Capital Power Company, subcontractors who primarily install heating units, and truss companies.

Falbo Crane

The owner of this company is Bob Falbo with his main office in Meredith, Idaho. His son, Tony Falbo, operates the Reno office. The Meredith office operates on very little overhead. Falbo Crane's Meredith operations have 3 cranes ranging from 18 to 30 tons. They employ 1 union operator. Tony does not operate the cranes. They are a very low key outfit with a few regular customers. They do not try to get much work beyond their regular customers. Falbo Crane appears to specialize in machinery moving and millwright work — the placing of boilers and heavy piping. Mr. Chesterfield has operated Falbo Crane's rigs on a bare rental basis during his employment with C. C. Iron.

A & BC Crane

This company is competitive in both union and non-union jobs. This company, out of Sparks, Idaho, is owned by Bob James and son Chris James. They, in my opinion, aggressively engage in "cut- throat" competitive practices. This firm started in 1983 or 1984 with one 25 ton crane and now operate four cranes ranging in capacity from 8 to 80 ton capacities.

Calamari Crane

Owner is Craig Blewski who has one 18 ton crane that he bare leases.

The Market

One of Chesterfield Crane Service's main customers, Slovum Steel, (formerly C.C. Iron) employed Mr. Chesterfield for 11 years. Jim Slovum, the owner of this company, gave Mr. Chesterfield a chance to start CHESTERFIELD CRANE by giving him his current 18 ton crane in the good faith expectation that he would be paid $35,000 after CHESTERFIELD CRANE got established and financing was obtained.

His goal was to help a former employee start what he felt was a needed service for him and other businesses in the area. Chesterfield Crane Service is the first to be called when they need 18 ton crane hoisting services. In addition, Blue Mountain Steel does a lot of commercial construction requiring 50 ton crane capacity. Because of their close relationship, Chesterfield Crane Services will continue to have the opportunity to provide Blue Mountain Steel's hoisting needs. A chart of the opportunities lost in 1991 due to Chesterfield Crane Services lacking 50 ton crane capacity for this single company has been prepared and is available upon request.

Confidential

In addition, a personal friend of Mr. Chesterfield's, a sales manager in Boise, allowed him to review his crane rental sales for the 4th quarter 1991. His support and thoughts towards CHESTERFIELD CRANE expanding into the 50 ton capacity class were positive and unexpected. When Mr. Chesterfield first met this individual, he was a salesman for American Equipment in Meredith. American Equipment is a Grove Crane dealer and services center. They discussed effective market depreciation on the 1980 TMS 475 50 ton Grove. His thoughts were that this model is twice the crane as compared to the newer models and that the TMS 475 is likely to appreciate rather than depreciate. The company that he works for has two 50 ton Grove cranes, a 1981 Model 475, and a 1991 Model 700.

According to the 4th quarter crane rental sales for this company, 42% of total gross crane rental revenue for one quarter was derived from 50 ton crane capacity. This is in a full service crane company having a full range of crane capacity from 12 ton to 150 ton. For one quarter, this company rented its 50 ton cranes for 584 hours

This non-union company's operators are paid approximately $11.00 per hour. This appears to be the major factor in their ability to charge only $125 per hour for their 50 ton crane services. Slovum Steel purchases 50 ton crane services for $150 per hour. Currently, Pikel Crane of Reno charges their 50 ton cranes out at $150 per hour. CHESTERFIELD CRANE SERVICES should remain competitive in this market charging $125 to $150 per hour for 50 ton crane capacity. Charts have been created outlining the above figures and are available upon request.

The financial forecasts herein are based upon CHESTERFIELD CRANE SERVICES charging $135 per hour for 50 ton crane capacity.

CHESTERFIELD CRANE SERVICES will be an effective competitor in the 50 ton capacity crane market. Even with the additional loan costs, overhead will remain contained such that the Company still has the pricing flexibility to charge between the lowest, $125 per hour, and the highest, $150 per hour, rates in the market. Immediate further business from Slovum Steel is highly likely due to the close business relationship that exists. Additional workload will come from accounts established over the last three years due to this Company's reputation. Mr. Chesterfield also has family members in the steel business (Chris Bennett, superintendent; Scott Bennett, general manager; Tom Bennett, structural steel erection foreman; Ray Bennett, foreman). These family members have at various times worked for steel companies such as Marvin Iron Works (Boise, Idaho). This relationship allowed the reputation of CHESTERFIELD CRANE SERVICES to spread quickly and created the opportunity for Mr. Chesterfield to provide hoisting services to Marvin Iron Works. Other foremen he has worked with over the years while at C.C. Iron are spread throughout other steel companies in the area. Those who contacted Mr. Chesterfield show interest in CHESTERFIELD CRANE obtaining larger cranes. In the past two and a half years CHESTERFIELD CRANE was not awarded larger jobs due to the lack of 50 ton capacity. This customer base will be personally contacted and informed that this Company can now handle those needs. Further, these customers and the size and amount of their hoisting needs are growing.

Additional advertising includes the yellow pages, promotional hats, plastic telephone book covers, and ads in the Boise Builder. Business is conducted in a professional manner as thorough attention is paid to customer service through job site checks. Cranes and trucks are always clean, sharply painted, and professionally lettered. All of this has led to strong first impressions backed up by cost efficient and safe performance. This company will continue to be successful operating in Idaho, a state that is rapidly growing in terms of business and construction. These factors, tied together, require crane services with a variety of capacities and thus makes the purchase of larger cranes essential to stay competitive.

EXPANSION

As CHESTERFIELD CRANE grows and expands, its operational needs will also expand. Additional yard space and shop size will be needed along with additional equipment and staff (crane operators, mechanics, office help). These additions will be added gradually as needed and business dictates. The same customer service factors that Mr. Chesterfield believes in will have to be shared by his employees. This is very important because these beliefs and values are what established CHESTERFIELD CRANE and made it successful and in demand. Safety, basic crane operation principles, and the job at hand must be priority in their minds at all times.

FINANCIAL DOCUMENTS

The following information regarding CHESTERFIELD CRANE SERVICES has been prepared and is available upon request:

- •Statement of Sources and Uses of Funds
- •Projected Income and Cash Flow Statements for worst, middle and best case scenarios
- •Actual Income Statements
- •Financial information for the past three years, including balance sheets, statements of income and verification of such numbers.
- •Tax returns for the last three years.
- •Appraisal on home.
- •Letters of intent from colleagues.
- •Photographs of an 18-ton crane.

Diaper Delivery

BUSINESS PLAN

DIAPERS 'N MORE

Betty and Barney Smith
555 Granite Ave.
Bedrock, IL 60614

April 17, 1993

Offering the area's only diaper delivery service, this new business seeks to reach the developing market demanding a more environmentally safe and less expensive option than traditional cloth diapers. This plan offers an example of how to attract a larger customer base by capitalizing on society's changing views.

DIAPER DELIVERY BUSINESS PLAN

STATEMENT OF PURPOSE

Diapers 'N More is seeking a loan of $25,000 to purchase equipment and inventory, purchase chemicals and softeners, purchase saturation advertising, maintain sufficient cash reserves and provide adequate working capital to run a diaper delivery and pickup service. This sum, together with the $6,500 equity investment of the principals, will be sufficient to finance transition through the beginning phases of the business and support a profitable enterprise.

DESCRIPTION OF BUSINESS

Diapers 'N More will be a diaper service delivering fresh clean diapers to northeastern Maine. Diapers 'N More plans on offering two sizes of diapers, an infant and a toddler size. The customer will have the added option to buy diaper wraps at an additional cost. Delivery to the various households will occur once a week at which time any used diapers will be picked up and returned to the laundry mat to be cleaned. A premium service will also be offered for those customers who wish to have the same set of diapers they used be returned to them. In essence they will pay extra for the guarantee that no one else has used their diapers. Deliveries will be made Monday through Saturday, official holidays excluded.

THE MARKET

Our goal is to provide cloth diapers that are less expensive and more environmentally safe than the currently used disposable diapers. This market has a total population of 3,200 households with babies under age 2. Currently 80% of these use disposable diapers and the remaining 20% use cloth. Of the amount using cloth we conservatively estimate that 20-30% will subscribe to the diaper service. At present birth rates and the above percentages this will give us a customer base of 130 to 200 households (excerpt on population reports and projections available). However, we feel with the changing viewpoints on waste disposal and the environment that a larger percentage of the people with children under 2 will switch to using cloth diapers. Customers will be attracted by

- A local radio advertising campaign
- Fliers placed in care packages to new mothers
- Pamphlets placed with OB/GYNs and Pediatricians' offices
- Promotions done in pre-natal and birthing classes
- Direct phone solicitation
- Door hangers
- Word-of-mouth advertising

THE COMPETITION

Currently there are no known diaper delivery services in northeastern Maine and the surrounding areas. Clean Babies Inc., part of the General Health Services Corporation, is the only diaper service serving the southeastern area of Maine and has no present plans to deliver in the northeastern Maine area. In fact, Don

Taylor, their main diaper salesman gave us a tour of their operation and offered us help on any questions we might have in beginning our business.

LOCATION

Diapers 'N More will operate from Laundry Inc. located at 254 Main St. The rent for the laundromat is $340 per month, with total square footage of 2,250 feet. The diaper service will occupy approximately 700 square feet, thus contributing to 1/3 of the rent or $115. The water district covering this area is district 9 and has one of the lowest water rates in the region. There will be no charge for sewage as the system is furnished by the building owner. The electric is furnished by Maine Electric Cooperative. The facility is approximately 1/4 a mile from an easy access to the Interstate.

MANAGEMENT AND MAINTENANCE

Barney Smith was born July 10, 1959. He was a journeyman electrician in Bangor for two years. He has 140 hours of college in areas of electrical and computer engineering. He currently owns and operates a company specializing in commercial refrigeration, heating and air conditioning repair. He is also a member of the Maine Army National Guard, 1/128 HHB Field Artillery Battalion. After 4 years service he has obtained the rank of Sergeant (E-5). He presently is a subcontractor. He has extensive long-term knowledge in pickup and delivery service in the and surrounding areas. His mechanical expertise is the real cost savings to this project. Mechanical repairs tend to be one of the most variable and highly unpredictable costs to a business of this sort. Barney has enough knowledge and experience to handle just about any breakdown that may occur, whether it be with the machinery or with the trucks.

Betty Smith was born on February 14, 1962. She graduated from UMC in 1984 with her Bachelor of Arts degree in honors Economics. She then pursued and obtained a masters degree in Economics and is currently working on her Ph.D. in the same field. She is an instructor for University of Maine in the evening program. Classes taught include basic Micro and Macro Economics, Theory of the Firm, Money and Banking, Real Estate, Corporate Finance and Investment Management. Betty handles the books of MGL Service and Maintenance with the help of a personal IBM compatible computer and DACEASY, an accounting program. She is the mother of two children, Abbey, age three and one half and Jack, age one and one half. Both children were raised in cloth diapers from birth and Jack is still using them.

Barney will be responsible primarily for set up of the routes, delivery and maintenance of equipment. Betty will be responsible for the cleaning and packaging of the diapers, customer consultations, inventory control and the basic accounting. In order to augment their skills, they have enlisted the help of a CPA who currently handles the tax accounting for MGL Service and Maintenance and the Smith's personal finances.

SALARIES

Betty will be earning a salary from MGL Service and the University of Maine, and Barney will be earning a salary from the Maine National Guard, his present employer, and profit from his existing business. This money coupled with the earnings from their real estate and the laundromat will enable them to support their family with very little help from the diaper service. At the end of the first fiscal year any net profit will be retained and invested in the diaper service to further enhance future earnings. In future years approximately 50% of the net profits will be drawn to pay the salaries of Mr. and Mrs. Smith. The remaining half will be retained to either continue expansion or accelerate payoff of the SBA note in an effort to improve the financial position of the company.

APPLICATION AND EXPECTED EFFECT OF LOAN

The $25,000 will be used as follows:

Purchases:

Diapers, infant and toddler size (Diapers last approximately 3 years w/150+ washes)	$7,500
Hampers	$500
Diaper wraps	$840
Plastic Bags	$420
Diaper wraps (to replenish inventory in month 9)	$420

Supplies:

3 months supply of salt	$120
Chemicals, approximately 1 year's supply	$650

Advertising:

Door hangers	$200
Radio for first week	$500

Equipment:

Washer/dryer (NADS (National Association of Diaper Services) approved)	$9,000
Setup charges	$400
Shelving	$400
Water softener (used, four years old)	$1,500
Reserve (not disbursed)	$2,550
Total	$25,000

The reserve will be held in an interest bearing account at the bank to be used to take advantage of special opportunities or to meet any unforeseen expenses not mentioned above. The setup charge will be for parts and material used in installing the washing machine and dryer as Mr. Smith will furnish the labor involved. Chemicals needed included 400 lb. drums of detergent and bleach, 100 lb. drums of fabric softener/bactericide and sours. Washing machine will be a Unimac Uniwash 50 (4 speed) 50 lb. washer. This carries a 5 year warranty. Dryer will be a 75 lb. Hibbs Commercial Dryer.

Small Business Development Program

We wish to thank the University of Maine Small Business Development Program for all of their help in preparing this proposal and for their general overall good advice. Special thanks are extended to Lydia Ferris for her time, dedication and hard work.

SUMMARY

Diapers 'N More will be a diaper delivery service covering the northeastern Maine area. We offer an alternative to the popular but often environmentally harmful disposable diapers and convenience for those household currently handling their own cloth diapers. The owners are seeking a $25,000 loan to help begin and maintain this potentially profitable venture. Careful analysis of the potential market shows an unfilled and growing demand for cloth diapers. We feel that the time is right for entry of this type of business. The city landfill has approximately 2-3 years of life left and the landfill problem has reached such proportions that they have resorted to charging "by the bag," for trash in an effort to encourage recycling. Several states in the Northeastern area of the country are severely restricting if not completely eliminating the use of disposable diapers and other such products. This trend will most likely penetrate to other parts of the United States and carries the possibility of an expanding market for our particular area. Possible further markets include entrance into the geriatric field of cloth diapers to handle the urinary incontinence that affects millions of the elderly in America. This type of service is a major part of the Rockport General Diaper's business. Several of the nursing care facilities and hospitals (including Tri-County and Maine Regional) have expressed an interest in this type of service and would entertain a bid at some later date.

CASH FLOW PROJECTION

A monthly cash flow projection worksheet has been prepared.

Notes and Explanations for Diapers 'N More
Monthly Cash Flow Projections

- ❑ Cash sales: Estimate 50 customers x $9/week = $37 per month, which comes out to a total of $1,800 for month 1; month 2, 55 customers; month 3, 60 customers; month 4, 65 customers etc.

- ❑ Supplies include $40 in salt per month for water softener and a $500 expenditure to replenish chemical supplies in month 12.

- ❑ Advertising includes $200 for door hangers and fliers each month.

- ❑ Maintenance is only $20 per month because the business is renting the facilities and part is for laundry.

- ❑ Car & Travel is $500 per month and will stay about the same even when more customers are added because of the route layout. However, in month 10 an additional $20 is added to compensate for extra gas that may be used do to the increase in customer stops.

CASH FLOW PROJECTION
...continued

❑Accounting & Legal: The accounting is based on a quarterly retainer.

❑Telephone & Utilities: Based upon the knowledge of laundry business.

❑Insurance: Insurance quote from Morgan Mutual.

❑Interest and Loan Payment: based upon a $25,000 loan, 12.5% interest for 7 years.

INCOME PROJECTION 3 YEAR SUMMARY

Pro Forma Profit & Loss

	Year I	Year II	Year III
Sales	$37,080	$64,800	$86,400
Purchases	420	840	1,680
Gross Margin	37,500	43,060	84,720
Operating Expenses:			
Supplies	980	1,180	1,500
Maintenance	240	240	240
Advertising	2,400	2,400	2,400
Car	6,060	6,240	6,240
Acct & Legal	400	400	400
Rent	1,380	1,380	1,380
Telephone	960	960	960
Utilities	1,800	2,200	2,750
Insurance	1,800	1,800	1,800
Other Expenses:			
Interest	2,991	2,888	2,558
Loan payment	2,348	2,488	2,817
Total	21,846	22,176	23,985
Net Profit pre-tax	15,234	20,884	60,735
Salaries	0	10,442	30,367.50

INCOME PROJECTION
...continued

Notes and Explanations for Income Projections

Sales: year 2 based upon a constant 150 customers per month; year 3 based upon a constant 200 customers per month.

- Purchases: based upon the percentage change of customer sales.
- Supplies: based upon the percentage change of customer sales.
- Maintenance should remain relatively constant.
- Car & Travel is $520 per month and will stay about the same even when more customers are added because of the route layout.
- Rent will stay constant since the building is leased for 5 years.
- Utilities are increased based upon percentage of additional customers.
- Insurance should remain constant since the quote is based on a gross of $100,000 a year.

POPULATION PROJECTIONS

A table of actual and projected births through 2005 for the northeastern Maine region has been prepared and is available.

FLOOR PLAN

A floor plan of the laundromat from which we propose to do business is available upon request.

Editorial Services

BUSINESS PLAN

HILTON & ASSOCIATES

7200 West Mackinac Island Blvd., Suite 17
Denver, CO 80222

May 7, 1990

Hilton & Associates offers writing and other editorial services, including training. The company's founder is seeking additional capital for a rejuvenated marketing campaign, an increase in staffing, and a stronger base for future goals, such as production of documentation and related materials and franchising. This plan is being used to substantiate a request for debt refinancing.

EXECUTIVE SUMMARY

Hilton & Associates (H&A) provides editing, writing, and training services to companies, government agencies, and a wide range of public and private organizations and individuals. This assistance is provided on a fee-for-service basis, and is billed hourly.

The firm's founder and president, William J. Hilton, has been a freelance writer and consultant for over 20 years. He is a versatile writer of both fiction and non-fiction documents, and has published extensively.

Three concepts define the unique character of this venture:

❑ **Use of Subcontractors for Staffing Flexibility.** Mr Hilton's client base has expanded beyond the point at which he alone can provide service of the quality required, in a timely and cost-effective manner. As a result, he began experimenting with the use of subcontractors to help him fulfill his clients' requirements, and has learned that, through the careful selection of self-motivated professional writers, he can serve a much larger and more diverse audience of clients.

There are many talented freelance writers and trainers with their own offices and modern text editing equipment who are willing to augment the H&A staff of a subcontractual basis. These subcontractor relationships will be transparent to H&A's clients, since the firm's permanent staff will handle all client negotiations, and will oversee all client accounts. The primary advantage to be derived from using subcontractors will be to allow the firm optimal flexibility in managing a variable client load.

❑ **A Manufacturing Component.** Long-term, this company expects to manufacture a variety of documentation and training products, for licensing, sale and distribution worldwide. A particular emphasis will be placed upon the design and deployment of self-paced, industry-specific training materials for use by the customers of H&A business clients.

❑ **Eventual Franchising of the Concept.** The firm's leadership expects that, once the procedures essential in establishing and maintaining the H&A service concept have been refined through broader experience, this kind of service can be franchised in major population centers across the nation and around the world.

Mr. Hilton's wife, Mildred Freeney-Hilton, is the Vice President of the company. Mrs. Freeney-Hilton is a sociologist, and a professional trainer with extensive education and experience in the human resources, adult education and personnel development fields. She will head up the training component of the company.

H&A already owns an extensive inventory of computers, printers and software to support this venture. Limited debt financing in the amount of $15,000 is needed to finance the acquisition of specialized telephone and other communications equipment, to upgrade existing computing and printing equipment, and to finance the marketing campaign described in the "Marketing Plan" section of this document.

The three-year projections developed in support of this business plan clearly demonstrate that the profit potential of this business far exceeds its start-up and maintenance costs.

ABOUT THE BUSINESS

The Demand for Writing Services

Despite our increasing dependence on electronic media for instant communications, the written word continues to be a primary means of exchanging information and ideas worldwide.

Existing and start-up businesses in Colorado alone spend millions of dollars each year in the preparation of business plans, proposals, reports, marketing brochures, and other written communications materials. Smaller firms are particularly handicapped because their available expertise is usually limited to whatever skills are needed to maintain their businesses, and that usually *doesn't* include writing effective communications materials.

Most of Colorado's 40,000 businesses are small businesses, 90% of which employ fewer than ten people. Except for those firms that are themselves in the communications business, virtually all of these organizations need *affordable* editing, writing and training services.

The demand for writing services is so pervasive that it is difficult to get a meaningful "handle" on the universe of demand for such services. No meaningful figures are available concerning the demand for writing services among businesses, government agencies, and countless public and private agencies, associations, and other organizations. However, annual revenues for this small company have ranged from $35,000 to $60,000 over the past three years, without the advantage of the expanded marketing and subcontractor support called for in this plan.

Particularly in today's competitive markets, every industry has a need for effective writing services in the preparation of business plans, reports, proposals, internal training aids, press materials, speeches, brochures and other business communications materials.

Written materials must often be mass-produced, made as readable as possible for a general audience, and packaged in an eye-appealing manner to attract the attention of readers. Such packaging may require the involvement of graphics designers and photographers. These types of skilled professionals will be included among H&A's subcontractors, as will printers who can handle print

The Demand for Writing Services
...continued

runs of any magnitude.

The demand for writing services is being met in a variety of ways. Most segments of the consuming public rely on non-professional writers to meet their sporadic needs for important internal and external documents. Organizations that have a more frequent need for highly visible, written documents usually hire their own professional writers.

But a growing number of organizations that are not primarily in the documentation business are seeking every available opportunity to streamline their operating costs so that they can be more competitive in a world market. These firms are turning to outside writing organizations to fulfill their documentation needs.

Because they are not permanent employees, contract writers do not represent a long-term expense for the hiring first. They can be called in only when needed, and do not become part of the employee benefits burden carried by most companies.

While the physical act of writing is essentially the same for everyone, the types of products written are as diverse in purpose, content, and design as the clients who need them. This diversity is reflected in the labels given to various types of writers. There are journalists, copywriters, speechwriters, scriptwriters, novelists, poets, technical writers, financial writers, legislative analysts, critics, academicians, and business writers, to name a few, generally recognized categories. Each distinguishable field of writing requires a particular industry perspective, research strategy, and writing style. (In many industries, the styles are strictly governed by published standards, called *style guides*.)

The better able a writing support organization is to respond to a diversity of writing needs, the broader will be its market of potential clients. H&A has deliberately structured its service to encompass the preparation of such high-demand products as:

Proposals Includes grant proposals, bid responses, and client sales proposals of the type commonly used by service companies (like advertising and public relations firms) in building their businesses.

Business Plans For businesses and corporations of all sizes.

Reports Includes corporate annual reports, financial reports, and research reports.

Marketing Materials Includes marketing plans, brochures, newsletters, press releases, press kits, direct mail promotional materials, audio/visual aids, product catalogs, etc.

Technical Documentation Includes technical and procedures manuals, hardware and software installation guides, and user guides.

Training Courses and Training Aids Emphasis on job-related, self-paced instructional resources, and end user training materials designed to promote the sale and proper use of new products and services.

The firm's leadership also has experience and expertise in writing speeches, articles, book-length manuscripts on a wide variety of subjects, and published proceedings from major conferences.

The Demand for Training Services

Phrases like "adult and continuing education" and "lifelong learning" were very much in the limelight about five years ago, when the press was enamored with the idea, and the federal government was spending millions of dollars to promote it. People don't *talk* about it as much today, but they are still *doing* it, in increasing numbers. Associated services, in the areas of adult counseling and career planning, are also being used to an increasing extent, especially whenever those services are financed by employers.

The ever-changing realities of our technological age make lifelong learning more a necessity than a luxury. Americans are pursuing both formal and informal learning opportunities, in a broader range of subjects, in greater numbers than at any time in the history of this country. Except where costs are prohibitive--which is a growing problem for parents of private school youth--most of the formal learning opportunities are still being provided in our national school and college systems. Among adult learners, however, and particularly among employed persons who may be taking courses part-time, there is a wide variety of public and private providers of instructional services.

Among adult learners, the most popular training services are those that:

- ❑ Relate most directly and immediately to income-producing activity (i.e., job- or career-related training)
- ❑ Are being financed by someone other than the learner (i.e., employers or social service organizations that guarantee payment of all or part of the required tuition)
- ❑ Are self-paced instructional opportunities that don't require participation in formal classes, and that allow learners to acquire the knowledge and skills they need on their own terms, at places, times, and in ways that are most effective for them.

H&A's overall strategy in its training component will be to develop products and services that are compatible with these primary interests. Many of the firm's subcontractors will be experienced adult educators with in-depth knowledge in curriculum design, course content in job-related areas, and course delivery methodologies. The writing resources of the firm will be closely coordinated with the training resources in the production of useful, attractive, and salable printed

The Demand for Training Services...*continued*

and audio/visual training aids.

As in the documentation community, training is being provided either on an individual, freelance basis, or by established training firms. Individual trainers are prospective subcontractors to H&A, while training firms are *at least potentially* direct competitors, but only to the extent that they are offering the same kinds of training as H&A.

Most training firms are specialized, i.e., they offer training on specified topics. Hence, these firms rely heavily on pre-designed training curricula, instead of working with clients to develop customized courses and programs. H&A intends to offer *customized training that meets the specific requirements of the firm's clients.* Hence, H&A will design and develop the training the firm delivers, and will not rely solely on "canned," pre-designed programs.

The concept of training is highly adaptable to a variety of settings and circumstances. Certain principles underlie the design of training courses and programs for virtually any purpose. H&A will employ persons with substantial education in and experience with these principles in meeting the needs of its clients.

Training involves three categories of activities:

Training Design Involves assessing the needs (down to the level of individual knowledge and skill sets) required to perform a job; defining an approach toward imparting the required knowledge and skill sets; and devising an appropriate "filter" to determine who can, and cannot benefit from the proposed training. (The filter is designed to screen out persons whose attitudes and skill levels would frustrate the goals of the training experience, or who lack the intellectual capacity to benefit from a particular training experience.)

Training Development Training manuals, printed job aids, and audio visual aids are produced for use in support of the training experience.

Training Delivery Concerned with the actual conduct of the training, based on the design and using the supporting manuals and aids that have been developed.

H&A recognizes that many of the fields in which training is most needed are underserved, primarily because of the emphasis within the industry upon "group" training experiences. Hence, if all the salespeople in a store need to be trained, they must all be off the sales floor during the course of the training, or they must be brought in on an overtime basis to receive the training. The problem of making training *convenient* is often just as important as making training *effective* and *affordable*.

H&A will address this problem by placing a special emphasis upon the development of self-instructional materials that don't require formal "classes" or substantial time commitments by groups of trainees. H&A will design and develop these materials to the specifications of the client, using programmed instruction and other appropriate self-paced learning strategies.

How the Company Will Function

Role of the Permanent Staff

The permanent staff of the firm will work to further the goals of the company by:

❑Aggressively marketing the firm's capabilities among clients who need the editing, writing, and training services being delivered. The details of the firm's marketing plan are described in "Marketing Plan."

❑Negotiating work contracts with clients.

❑Coordinating the efforts of subcontractors in the execution of client contracts. H&A permanent staff and subcontractors will be organized into project teams in handling all client contracts, and permanent staff will have the primary responsibility for managing those teams. Under this approach, permanent staff members are always responsible for ensuring a qualitative and timely response to client needs.

❑Selecting and evaluating subcontractors. Just as the firm will make a special effort to recruit clients, it will make the same kind of effort to recruit quality subcontractors.

❑Handling administrative support details, including accounting, client billing, and payroll for permanent staff and subcontractors, in addition to serving as a single point of contact for clients and subcontractors. The permanent staff will also be responsible--with the advice and assistance of the Professional Advisory Committee (PAC)--for formulating a range of legally binding contracts that will govern H&A relationships with clients, subcontractors and suppliers.

❑Handling all logistics in connection with training activities, including scheduling meeting facilities, orienting trainers, handling registration, generating invitations, and evaluating the training.

❑Providing professional development opportunities for permanent staff members and subcontractors. Partly because quality service to clients demands that the firm keep abreast of technological changes, and partly as an inducement to high-quality, freelance writers and trainers, H&A will sponsor professional seminars and workshops throughout the year for the members of its subcontractor network.

Relationship with Clients

Selling any kind of *service* poses certain accountability problems from the outset, and these must be anticipated and effectively addressed. When people are buying tangible *things* (fruit, cans of soup, yards of cloth) they can see and

Relationship with Clients...*continued*

feel in advance exactly what they are getting. The chances for disappointment after the product has been paid for are greatly reduced.

When clients order writing services, they must trust that the job will be done satisfactorily until they actually see at least an early draft of it. If that draft doesn't meet with their expectations, the time and effort invested in its production will have been wasted.

Hence, early negotiations with clients must be handled carefully, and these will only be conducted by permanent staff members who have been specially trained for this purpose by the firm's leadership. (Initial consultations with prospective clients are offered at no charge.)

Whenever appropriate, and always on major projects, special "mock ups" will be produced to show clients, to the extent possible, how final products will be organized and appear. Clients will be required to "sign off" on each stage of development, including the mock ups. Clients will also be asked to provide examples of the kind of work they want produced before any assignments begin, to further minimize the chances for miscommunication.

As a further step toward ensuring a generally smooth operation, H&A reserves the right to accept or reject prospective clients. Persons who, for any reason, refuse to sign a client contract; whose ability to pay for the services rendered is questionable; or who exhibit attitudes and behaviors that could be disruptive to a professional working relationship, will not be accepted as clients.

Many of H&A's clients will be entrusting the firm, and its subcontractors, with proprietary information. H&A will sign reasonable non-disclosure agreements designed to protect the interests of the client, after such agreements have been approved by the firm's attorney. In general, highly confidential assignments will only be handled by a permanent staff member, unless the client requests or agrees to some other arrangement.

Following each initial consultation on a new project, and with the prior approval of the firm's leadership, H&A staff will prepare a written proposal defining the rationale, proposed scope of work, and budget for the project. These proposals typically run 3-5 pages in length, and must be approved by the president or vice president of the firm before they are released.

Because the preparation of client proposals takes time (and the cost of this activity is absorbed by the firm), every effort is made during the initial consultation to ensure that this proposal-writing step has a high probability of resulting in a new account, or additional business from an existing account.

During this initial consultation H&A staff members make every effort to determine:

- ❑ Who is the audience for the particular writing or training product?

Relationship with Clients...*continued*

❑What is it that the client hopes to see happen because this product was provided? (What should be the consequences of making the product available?)

❑How much is the client willing to pay for the product?

❑What kinds of payment terms are most acceptable to the client (30-day terms, scheduled installments, weekly billings, etc.).

❑What are the terms and conditions under which the product is to be provided? For example, if completing the project will be a shared responsibility involving the client and a team of vendors, which team members will be responsible for which aspects of the job? How will the team members coordinate their respective roles and responsibilities?

❑What types of information and expertise will be required by H&A in order to fulfill its project obligations? (This information is essential, since the company may have to arrange to subcontract for the necessary talent.)

❑What are some possible "hooks" that can be built into H&A's proposal? (Hooks are attractive fringe benefits that can make the difference between success and failure in a competitive bid situation. Hence, H&A might offer to throw in free printing up to a certain quantity, or to maintain a mailing list at no additional cost to the client.)

❑What is the *ultimate* deadline for completion of the project? (Depending on the magnitude of the project, H&A staff will negotiate a series of draft deadlines leading up to the "ultimate" deadline for project completion.)

In evaluating a new project opportunity, H&A staff will also be alert to new or ancillary business opportunities that might derive from the current contract opportunity. These additional opportunities might not be acknowledged in writing in the client proposal, but H&A personnel will be trained to be on the alert for them anyhow. Indeed, preference will be given to accepting contracts that offer a great deal of potential for future business.

Eventually, client proposals are incorporated into a mutually binding contract defining the relationship between H&A and its clients. Prior to the signing of that contract, several drafts of the proposal may be reviewed, discussed, and modified by either H&A or the client.

A major goal of the client proposal is to prevent future problems in the relationship between the company and its clients.

Each client proposal concludes with a commitment of a follow-up call, within a specified time, by the staff member who handled the initial consultation. H&A maintains a computerized calendar to help ensure that follow-up commitments are not overlooked.

The Role of the Subcontractors

H&A's leadership recognizes the importance of treating subcontractors strictly as subcontractors, rather than as employees, so as to minimize the firm's overhead and thus help ensure its competitive position in the marketplace. The use of subcontractors also provides the firm with the king of elasticity in staffing resources that is so essential in responding to fluctuations in the demand for its services.

Subcontractors will be *carefully* selected, and internal work flows, as well as the pace of the company's overall growth, will be controlled to ensure that commitments to clients never exceed the availability of competent staff.

For the purposes of this venture, the ideal subcontractor will be someone who:

❑Has demonstrable interest, experience, and talent in the areas of editing, writing, or training required by H&A's clients.

❑Owns his or her text-editing equipment.

❑Maintains his or her own separate place of business.

❑Is able to provide at least 20 hours of service each month to H&A's clients.

As a condition of their acceptance as H&A subcontractors, these individuals will be required to sign two critical agreements:

❑A non-compete agreement, prohibiting them from competing directly with the company for the company's established clients. The agreement will apply for one year after they cease to be associated with H&A.

❑An employment agreement that binds them to the nondisclosure of the proprietary information of H&A and the firm's clients.

The credentials of prospective new subcontractors will be carefully evaluated before they are "registered" into the network. Applicants must submit resumes, and a recent writing sample, or provide evidence of experience supporting their claims of expertise. Prospective subcontractors will also be visited in their worksites (homes or offices), so that a permanent staff member can confirm first-hand that these individuals are suitably equipped to handle work assignments from the company.

Once selected for inclusion in H&A's subcontractor network, these individuals will be asked to complete a survey questionnaire that details information about the kinds of writing they do, the hardware and software they use, and other work resources that may be available to them.

As the firm's permanent staff is expanded, priority consideration will be given to hiring the most loyal and qualified subcontractors in H&A's network.

Productivity Aids

H&A is being designed from the ground up to be a high-volume, creative services enterprise. The firm therefore makes optimal use of the latest communications technologies, not only in servicing its clients, but also to ensure maximum efficiency in its internal operations.

Accordingly, the following tools and procedures will be used to ensure that the firm can keep abreast of the demand for its services, without having to invest substantially in manual support systems:

- A series of software programs have been developed by Mr. Hilton, and are his exclusive property, to facilitate making projections on the amount of time (and therefore the expense) of producing documents and training courses of varying lengths. These so called *Calendaring Programs* are Dbase III + applications that automatically generate production deadlines and cost estimates, based on the length of the document or training course that is to be delivered. The programs have been tried and tested, with positive results, in the Documentation and Training department of U S West Advanced Technologies.

- By specializing in a finite number of documents, of a particular type, H&A is able to develop and maintain re-usable templates and boilerplate that will make it easier to produce documents of a particular type in the future. A soft-copy template is the outline of a particular type of document that can be given to a writer in a diskette file. The writer can then modify that template where appropriate, and use it as a guide in preparing other documents of the same type.

Boilerplate is standard text that can be re-used repeatedly to prevent the expense of repetitive typing. Hence, historical information about a client firm for which numerous grant proposals are being written can be merged into each new proposal in far less time than it would take to reconceptualize and re-write those details.

Because of the firm's use of templates and boilerplate, clients who make frequent use of H&A services will find that, in the long run, their costs will actually *decrease* because it will take less time for the company to prepare professional documents of a routine nature. This point will be emphasized in the firm's marketing activities.

- H&A's staff use and own a wide variety of software products, including word processors, database programs, spreadsheets, project management software, desktop publishing/page layout software, and other productivity tools. Hence, the firm can accept client information in electronic form, work with it using the same applications that the client uses, and return it to the client in a form in which the client can easily manipulate that data.

- Under the present request for expansion funding, H&A will acquire a FAX machine for the speedy exchange of documents between and among clients and subcontractors, and a scanner that will allow the firm to convert a client's original typed material into a computer disk file for easier manipulation and professional publication.

Product Development

While a primary focus of H&A will always be upon the provision of writing and training *services*, the firm expects to gradually evolve a manufacturing component in which a wide range of printed and audio/visual communications aids will be sold to clients and to the general public.

The types of products that are likely to be developed are expected to be as simple, as functional and as popular as 3M's Post-Its (notepads with gummed sheets that allow consumers to stick handwritten messages anywhere). Following are three examples of the types of products the firm will be developing for sale:

Business Planning Support (BPS) Program

This strategy for helping start-up and small firms successfully complete the business planning process centers around the development of a training course for selected intermediaries (e.g., local chambers of commerce and other business support organizations, financial planners, investment bankers, venture capitalists, etc.). These intermediaries will be trained to assist local entrepreneurs who want to start their own businesses, using a series of orientation tools and questionnaires that have been developed by H&A. Local entrepreneurs will use these tools, and the advice that their intermediaries are trained to give them to assemble the essential facts of their business and will submit that information to H&A. H&A will then use the information to produce top-quality, professional-looking business plans. Clients complete the needed research and pay for the service in installments, over a period of months. The option of making installment payments is expected to make this opportunity particularly attractive to small, start-up firms that are operating on limited budgets.

Writing Development Service (WDS)

A personal, correspondence service that is useful in teaching individuals how to strengthen their written communications skills. Based on the principle that practice makes perfect, the service will use a proprietary, computerized database application that automatically generates a variety of practice exercises designed to eliminate the writing flaws reflected in writing samples received from program participants. This confidential service can be subscribed to by individuals or groups (i.e., a corporation might enroll certain managers or classes of employees).

Customized Quick Reference Guides

A series of job aids that are industry-specific and can be used to help quickly orient employees to the jargon, policies, and practices within those industries. Hence, a law office employee can be given a primer on the nature and functioning of the law office, the most common legal terminology, and a summary of the steps involved in completing certain procedures in support of the firm's partners.

Over time, we expect that certain of the industry-specific training materials we develop will be re-usable for a wide variety of clients, and may be published as products. Hence, H&A will retain ownership of all training designs, and will, in effect, license the use of the materials by the clients for which they were developed. The materials will be archived and cataloged, and will be available for use on the broadest possible scale within each industry to which they apply.

For each new product initiative, H&A will develop a business plan to determine the feasibility, marketability, and profitability of the venture before R&D funds are dedicated to its design and development.

Copyrights will be obtained on all products. The firm's policy will be to retain ownership of innovative products, procedures, and approaches, and to license the use of same to others whenever possible and appropriate.

No special physical plant will be necessary for H&A product development, due to the nature of the types of products to be developed.

Items produced by H&A will be conceived, designed, prototype, and tested in-house. Subcontractors (usually printers, designers, and audio visual experts) will be retained as necessary to finalize the development and deployment of those products.

The firm will retain a list of backup suppliers for any raw materials or essential services required in this aspect of the firm's operations.

Overview of Funding Requirements and Intended Uses of Funds

Hilton & Associates is seeking debt financing in the amount of $15,000 to support the launching of this innovative business concept. Those funds will be used for the following purposes:

- To finance an aggressive, multifaceted marketing campaign designed to establish the firm's presence in major local markets.

- To finance RAM and mass storage upgrades for the more than $20,000 worth of computers and printers already owned by the company.

- To finance the acquisition of specialized telecommunications and text-editing equipment for use by H&A permanent staff and subcontractors. That equipment will include dedicated business phone lines (supported by voice messaging and teleconferencing capabilities), a photocopier, a FAX machine, a scanner, one printer, and two microcomputers (a high-performance IBM or compatible, and an Apple Macintosh).

MANAGEMENT AND ORGANIZATION

Legal Structure of the Firm

Hilton & Associates will continue to function as a sole proprietorship, and will rely heavily on its contracting arrangements with clients, suppliers, and subcontractors to minimize operation-related liabilities. Since there is no expectation that public funding will ever be needed in support of this venture, there are no plans to incorporate at this time.

Internal Structure

A graphic overview of the internal structure of the company is available upon request "H & A Organization Chart." (Appendix A)That structure includes the following components:

❑H&A's management team, which includes the President, Vice President, an Operations Manager, and an Administrative Assistant. Appendix B contains the resume and publications list of William J. Hilton, the firm's founder and president.

♦ Appendix C contains the resume of Mildred Freeney-Hilton, Vice President.

♦ Appendix D describes the role and responsibilities of all manage ment team members.

❑A Professional Advisory Committee (PAC), comprised of legal, accounting, and technical experts who will be convened at least six times each year to review the progress of the firm, and to make recommendations regarding its future directions. Investor representation is also welcomed on this committee. No more than eight persons will serve on the PAC in any year, and all will serve for one-year, renewable terms. Core staff members and H&A subcontractors also qualify to serve on the PAC.

♦ Appendix E lists the current appointees to the PAC. As of this writing, the firm is still seeking committee representation in the fields of accounting and insurance. The following knowledge and skill sets will be represented on the PAC. (This list will be amended as experience and new products and services dictate.)

♦ The PAC will be able to offer advice and assistance concerning:

- Desktop publishing equipment, methods, and procedures
- Staff management and supervision
- Consultative selling techniques
- Federal, state and local tax laws
- Financial accounting procedures and requirements
- The management of documentation projects
- The management of training projects
- Trends in the computer graphics industry
- Printing methods and options
- Trends in the use of microcomputer hardware and software for text editing and related purposes.

❑Subcontractors to H&A who will be called upon to augment the efforts of the permanent staff. A roster of the individuals already identified, and a brief description of their backgrounds, appears in Appendix F.

Note: Appendices mentioned herein are available upon request and were not included at the time of submission

As the firm grows, the management team functioning will, of necessity, become more specialized. A Human Resources professional will be added to the team and, in anticipation of future expansion, a Franchise Manager will eventually be hired to spearhead the deployment of this concept into other major cities across the nation.

Exit Strategy

H&A will consider the sale of the firm, but only after the concept has been established and franchised in major urban areas throughout the United States. The leadership of the firm expects to retain all foreign rights to proprietary products, services, and licensable procedures.

COMPETITIVE ANALYSIS

Who Are the Firm's Competitors?

An important distinction must be made at the outset among the various sources of commercial writing and training services that operate in the Colorado marketplace. Among the organizations that must be excluded from H&A's competition immediately are the temporary clerical help firms that offer "clerical support services" to clients on a contractual basis. Leaders in that industry include Kelly Services, Manpower, The Job Store, and Norrell. These are *not* H&A's competitors.

H&A staff *edit and write materials* for clients, and in the process, documents get typed, and even mass produced, but that is incidental to the creative support that the company provides to its clients. H&A is *not* a clerical support service.

H&A has made an aggressive search for objective information about its competitors. During April, 1990, two H&A associates conducted two telephone surveys for the purpose of gathering information about the nature and scope of the firm's competition, and about consumer demands for writing and training services.

One telephone survey was addressed to 71 writing and training services providers; the other to 48 potential corporate clients, all from high tech firms. Because of the sensitive nature of the information being sought, and the firm's presumption that particularly the service providers would be understandably reluctant to cooperate with a competitor, some subterfuge was used in the phone survey that was directed to providers. The interviewer who called the providers pretended to be a client seeking writing and training assistance.

The interviewer who called prospective clients frankly confessed to doing market research for a new company planning to offer such services and seeking consumer feedback on the demand for those services.

The two surveys revealed the following:

❑ Among the providers who participated in the survey, all but three firms (called herein "creative writing support organizations") are primarily in the business of providing technical writing services. In all but a few cases, those services were

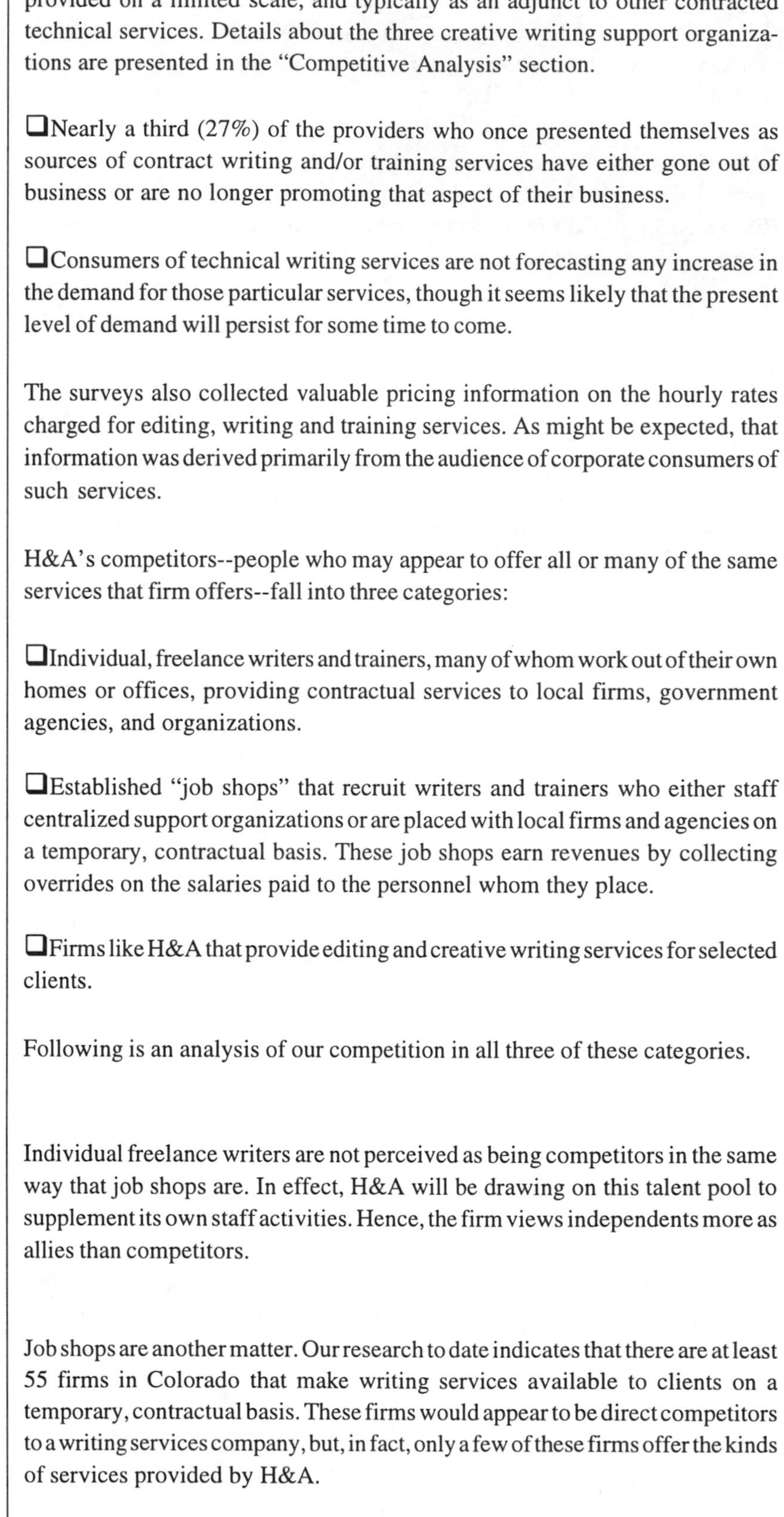

provided on a limited scale, and typically as an adjunct to other contracted technical services. Details about the three creative writing support organizations are presented in the "Competitive Analysis" section.

❑Nearly a third (27%) of the providers who once presented themselves as sources of contract writing and/or training services have either gone out of business or are no longer promoting that aspect of their business.

❑Consumers of technical writing services are not forecasting any increase in the demand for those particular services, though it seems likely that the present level of demand will persist for some time to come.

The surveys also collected valuable pricing information on the hourly rates charged for editing, writing and training services. As might be expected, that information was derived primarily from the audience of corporate consumers of such services.

H&A's competitors--people who may appear to offer all or many of the same services that firm offers--fall into three categories:

❑Individual, freelance writers and trainers, many of whom work out of their own homes or offices, providing contractual services to local firms, government agencies, and organizations.

❑Established "job shops" that recruit writers and trainers who either staff centralized support organizations or are placed with local firms and agencies on a temporary, contractual basis. These job shops earn revenues by collecting overrides on the salaries paid to the personnel whom they place.

❑Firms like H&A that provide editing and creative writing services for selected clients.

Following is an analysis of our competition in all three of these categories.

Individual Freelance Writers

Individual freelance writers are not perceived as being competitors in the same way that job shops are. In effect, H&A will be drawing on this talent pool to supplement its own staff activities. Hence, the firm views independents more as allies than competitors.

Job Shops

Job shops are another matter. Our research to date indicates that there are at least 55 firms in Colorado that make writing services available to clients on a temporary, contractual basis. These firms would appear to be direct competitors to a writing services company, but, in fact, only a few of these firms offer the kinds of services provided by H&A.

The vast majority of these firms place only *technical writers*, or directly provide *technical writing services* to high tech clients. Often these services are provided only as an adjunct to other contractual services these firms offer their clients. Most of these firms primarily subcontract computer programmers, engineers, draftsmen, and other technical professionals. Some also subcontract project management personnel in technical fields. They do not, for the most part, aggressively promote non-technical writing services.

While H&A staff will pursue technical writing opportunities, in direct competition with these job shops, that aspect of the business represents only part of the firm's repertoire, so that job shops are not perceived at this time to be major direct competitors.

Creative Writing Support Organizations

Original ideas are the stock-in-trade of creative writing support organizations, Job shops provide writing services that are primarily geared toward documenting what exists; while creative writing organizations are called upon to give form and substance to the ideas they document, and to write materials that are pedagogically sound in their approach and persuasive--as well as factual--in their contents.

A technical manual may document the features and benefits of a particular hardware or software product, but a business plan--especially for a start-up firm requires documenting processes and procedures that are not yet in place. The writer of such plans must bring to that task certain knowledge about the practical requirements of owning and operating a business, along with an appreciation for the kinds of information that should be included in a plan to satisfy the informational requirements of prospective funders, suppliers, and the entrepreneurs themselves.

The proper preparation of an *effective* business plan, or proposal, or sales presentation, or speech is a far more creative exercise than is generally recognized, and few companies currently exist that are staffed to provide this kind of service.

To the universe of potential H&A clients, three Colorado firms will "appear" to offer the same services, and are therefore being treated here as direct competitors to H&A. They are all small businesses, located in the Denver metropolitan area.

Those firms are:

- ❑ Infinite Energy
- ❑ TIA/Technical Information Associates, Inc.
- ❑ Edutech, Inc.

Following is additional background information on each of these firms.

Infinite Energy: A Marketing and Communications Consultancy

Rebecca Vories, the founder and owner of Infinite Energy, comes out of an energy research and development background. She built her business primarily by applying marketing communications techniques to the needs of clients in the energy industry, in which she has many long-standing contacts and a national reputation for her research and analytical expertise. The firm is currently working to diversify its client base, but its credentials, expertise and experience appear strongest in the energy industry.

The firm employs fewer than five permanent staff, and uses subcontractors to extend its capabilities when needed. It has been in business for three years.

Infinite Energy offers a wide range of traditional marketing communications services, including:

- Market research
- The design and development of marketing plans
- Advertising (including the development of ad copy and graphics, brochures, and direct mail materials)
- Public relations
- Business plan development (excluding the preparation of financial projections)
- Writing and editing of technical materials
- Evaluation services (assisting government agencies in assessing the impact of their activities)
- Policy analysis
- Training services (specifically, the design and development of in-house workshops, train-the-trainer experiences, and the organiza tion and promotion of conferences)

The firm also offers what Ms. Vories calls "coaching" to help her clients evaluate their own current and proposed marketing strategies.

The firm's pricing is negotiable, but clients are typically billed at a $65.00 per hour rate.

Infinite Energy's strong ties to a particular industry--and to an industry that has seen better days!--clearly puts it at a competitive disadvantage in today's market. The firm doesn't offer the range of products offered by H&A, and does not appear to have the adult learning theoretical and practical background so essential in the design and delivery of training services.

TIA/Technical Information Associates

This firm has been in business since 1987, and currently employs five individuals, including its president and founder, Ms. Doann Houghton-Alico. Subcontracted employees are used to extend staff capabilities when needed.

The firm has established relationships with several leading companies, including Kaiser Permanente, Citicorps' Diners Club, Aspect Telecommunications,

Eastman Kodak, and Meredith/Burda. Its services include the following:

- ♦Designing and producing information materials such as business plans, proposals and policy/procedure manuals.
- ♦Developing training materials, conducting end-user training and staffing train-the-trainer workshops.
- ♦Reviewing, critiquing and editing client drafts.
- ♦Creating a project- or company-specific design plan and style guide.

The firm's writing and production services include help in the preparation of technical manuals, reports, sales guides, and standards manuals. Its training services include the preparation of user guides, quick reference guides and audio/visual materials. TIA will also conduct workshops for its clients, and uses a project team approach in working with its clients to address their communications support needs.

TIA boasts expertise in cognitive processing, adult learning and ergonomics, all of which are fundamental to the effective design of training materials and aids. It also reports that 80% of its business is repeat business.

The firm prices its services either by project, or on an hourly basis, to be negotiated with its clients. Specific pricing parameters were not available for this analysis.

TIA comes closer to H&A than any of its other direct competitors in the expertise it offers, in its breadth of experience and in the diversity of its client base. However, H&A offers more high demand services to a broader potential client base. There is no indication, for example, that TIA has any experience in the areas of writing speeches or press materials.

The firm publishes a newsletter (*Documenter*) among current and prospective clients, and uses that communications vehicle to tout its expertise and to announce new and current services.

Edutech, Inc.

This firm opened its doors in 1984 and now employs 6-10 people. Alfred C. Loya is the president of Edutech.

The firm specializes in providing the following services, mainly to high tech companies like AT&T and Bell Labs:

- ♦Customer Presentations
- ♦Sales Training
- ♦Equipment Demonstrations
- ♦Market Research
- ♦Competitive Product Analyses
- ♦Marketing Strategies Development
- ♦Due Diligence Services (re: personnel or company capabilities)

The firm boasts experience in working in international markets, and exceptional graphics design and production capabilities (none of which were evident in its own promotional literature). Writing services are available in the production of technical manuals, business plans, reports and brochures, but the company's primary emphasis is upon the design and delivery of pre-packaged and customized training experiences.

Like H&A, this firm uses both permanent and subcontracted staff resources in serving its clients. It is clear that pricing is negotiated on a contractual basis, but the specific pricing parameters were not available for including in this analysis.

Edutech's focus differs from that of H&A in the following ways:

- ♦Edutech specializes in serving high tech companies, and seems to have a substantial installed client base in that arena.
- ♦Edutech's primary focus is on training.
- ♦While Edutech acknowledges the significance of self-paced training materials in its brochure, that is not a primary focus of the firm's t raining activities at this time.
- ♦There is no evidence of substantial adult education training in Edutech, as there is in H&A.

In reality, the nature of the communications business is such that *every* organization with demonstrable expertise in writing and training can provide a wide range of services, both to clients and--on a subcontractual basis--to each other. Indeed, H&A anticipates that its expertise will be tapped by many of its direct competitors over the coming months. The joint venture marketing strategy described later represents a conscious effort of the part of H&A's leadership to capitalize upon that reality.

Basis for Competition

A well-written, beautifully produced document that accomplishes a client's communications goals is a job to behold, regardless of who produced it. There is nothing H&A can do to improve upon the concept of quality writing and training products--except to make them more affordable to a broader base of clients.

Hence, H&A will compete primarily on the bases of price and quality. The firm expects to enjoy a major advantage in the market place because of its expertise in this area of service, its marketing acumen, and its low overhead.

Lower prices, combined with H&A's joint venturing strategy (see Market Penetration Method), virtually assure our success in the firm's chosen markets.

Because of the range of products and services offered by H&A, the concept of "market share" presents a special challenge. Contract writing services can be desegregated into many different types of writing, each of which has its own potential "market." Similarly, H&A's training products appeal to diverse markets. Any attempt to assess the dimensions of a *global* market share would be difficult and, ultimately, meaningless. Knowing that Colorado firms spend $10 million a year on contract writing services doesn't help H&A unless the firm knows exactly what type of writing services are being sold most often, or most profitably.

It was primarily because of the firm's need for clearer guidance in the design and implementation of is marketing strategy that H&A undertook the telephone surveys of prospective clients and competitors, which is discussed in the "Marketing Plan" section.

PRICING

H&A expects to derive revenues from five activities, and its financial projections reflect these revenue sources. Following is an overview of these activities and a more detailed explanation of each.

Activity	Cost/Hours	Price/Hours
Edits/Rewrites	28.00	35.00
Original Writing & Research	40.00	50.00
Data Processing Support	20.00	25.00
Training Services	32.00	40.00
Other Income	Varies	

Note that for both documentation and training services the "Cost/Hours" figure is the salary paid to subcontractors on an hourly basis, and the "Price/Hours" figure is the amount charged to the client. On the projections that are appended to this plan, subcontractor costs are distinguished from permanent staff costs for accounting and control purposes.

These activities are defined as follows:

Edits/Rewrites
H&A staff and subcontractors work from clients' preliminary drafts, without further research, and produce quality documents.

Original Writing and Research
H&A interview clients in detailabout their requirements, conduct the necessary research, and produce quality documents.

Data Processing Support
H&A uses electronic spreadsheets to produce budget printouts, and database software to maintain mailing lists. H&A can also generate customized form

letters to clients' target audiences, on clients' stationery.

Training Services

H&A will design, develop, and deliver courses to client specifications. Budgets are projected based on the length of the course, using a 10/1 ratio. Hence, a 4-hour course requires 40 hours of effort, at the $40.00 per hour rate.

Other Income

This option is left in H&A's projections to allow for the possibility of income derived from such activities as leasing equipment to subcontractors, the liquidation of company assets, etc.

OPERATING AND CONTROL SYSTEM

H&A's leadership recognizes the need for at least three types of internal controls to ensure efficient and cost-effective operation of this venture:

- ❑ Accounting Controls
- ❑ Marketing Controls
- ❑ Performance Controls

Accounting Controls

For accounting purposes, H&A currently uses a Client Time and Billing Program that was written by Mr. Hilton. That program:

❑ Stores transaction data for tax accounting purposes. It permits the storage, manipulation and retrieval of travel and "Other" expenses, as well as hourly billings.

❑ Automatically calculates bills and generates individual invoices.

❑ Allows the firm to apply discounts to bills.

❑ Generates a series of reports reflecting: all invoices by client; all payments by client; and a summary of billings minus payments by client.

Despite its usefulness at the present time, the program is not well-suited for the level of expanded activities that H&A anticipates. There is no payroll component, and day-to-day expenses must be stored in a separate program designed for managing state and federal tax accounting.

Because of the variety of accounting software features and capabilities on the market today, a careful analysis will be made of the firm's record-keeping and reporting requirements before a suitable computerized system is acquired. Final recommendations in that regard will be approved in advance by the PAC. The firm will offer customers 30-day terms, and will bill in monthly installments. A discount of 3-5% will be offered for prompt payment of invoices. Preferred customers will also be offered 30-day terms, and credit will be extended selectively.

Marketing Controls

Marketing controls are simply measures of the firm's success in making prospective clients aware of its capabilities. A variety of outreach strategies are included in H&A's overall marketing plan. Marketing controls derive from the firm's consciousness of the need to know:

❑ Which strategies are most effective in reaching target markets?

❑ Which strategies are most cost-effective (i.e., have the greatest impact for the least expense)?

Periodic assessments of these strategies will be made by interviewing clients ("How did you hear about our company?"), and by comparing the internal costs of alternative marketing strategies in relation to their outcomes, as a basis for future decision making.

Many of the parameters for H&A's marketing controls will be derived during its survey of prospective clients, which will be discussed in greater detail in the "Marketing Plan."

Performance Controls

While the firm will not deliberately conceal that reality, the fact that H&A's subcontractors are themselves independent business persons will be transparent to the firm's clients. Both permanent staff and subcontractors will be expected to respond to client's needs, and the quality of that response will lay the foundation for future business.

The permanent staff members will have the primary responsibility for evaluating the performance of subcontractors. A file will be maintained on each permanent employee and subcontractor, and formal performance reviews will be conducted for each employee every six months.

Clients will also be asked to provide brief and candid evaluations of company personnel at the end of each project, and all of the feedback gathered will be factored into H&A's bonus awards strategy.

MARKETING PLAN

Marketing Needs Assessment

Hilton & Associates subscribes to the view that if you don't know where you're going, you're likely to wind up somewhere else!

That is why H&A has invested considerable time and energy into carefully researching its current and potential markets in order to chart a course for the future growth and profitability of the firm. H&A's market planning effort began with a multi-faceted needs assessment designed to answer the following questions:

❑ Who are the other providers of editing, writing and training services, and how do their offerings compare with those of H&A?

❑ What kinds and how many clients in the Denver market are likely to be most receptive to the kinds of services offered by H&A?

The answer to the first question is presented in the "Competitive Analysis" section of this plan. That section summarizes the results of two telephone surveys that were conducted by H&A associates during April, 1990.

The second key question--relating to the demand for a more creative range of writing services--has not yet been the subject of direct telephone surveys, though such surveys are contemplated over the coming weeks. For H&A's immediate planning purposes, library research was done in support of a needs assessment schema that involved the following elements:

❑ A finite number of editing, writing and training services in which the company has, or can acquire expertise were identified. This effort resulted in the following list of high-demand communications products: proposals, business plans, reports, marketing materials, technical documents, training courses, speeches, books/booklets and published proceedings from major conferences.

❑ The universe of people and organizations in the Denver area who might use these services was then classified into three groups:

Clients Potential public and private sector end users of H&A services.
Referral Sources Companies and organizations that can refer clients to H&A, once they have been oriented to the goals and capabilities of the company.
Joint Venture Partners Business support organizations (including other creative writing firms) that might be willing to subcontract work to H&A as an adjunct to other services they provide to their clients.

❑ An analysis was made of the numbers of businesses and other organizations in the Denver metropolitan area that fall into the categories of potential clients, referral sources, and joint venture partners. Appendix G, "Potential Demand for H&A Services," shows a breakout of the numbers of firms and organizations in each of the three categories that are likely to require any of the H&A products being offered. The statistics on firms and organizations were taken from the 1989 edition of *Contacts Influential*, a leading Rocky Mountain business reference.

The firm recognizes that this schema is imperfect since any given firm might qualify as a client, a referral source, and a joint venture partner. Even so, the scheme is a helpful starting point for organizing and prioritizing a multifaceted marketing effort.

During the next and final phase of this needs assessment, H&A will establish detailed marketing strategies for approaching clients, referral sources, and joint venture partners. Priorities will be established with each of these categories, and the marketing strategies will be implemented in priority sequence. The members of the PAC will be involved in reviewing both this overall process and the conclusions and decisions made as a result of it.

The remaining sections of this marketing plan highlight, in a general way, many of the strategies that have been anticipated for reaching out to the many markets available to H&A.

Specific Marketing Strategies

H&A's marketing plan encompasses the following specific strategies, each of which will be discussed in greater detail below:

- The development of Marketing Tools
- Building an identity within the firm's target markets
- Selective advertising
- Direct Mail Campaigns
- Trade show exposure
- Fostering repeat business
- Maintaining a sales-oriented organization
- Monitoring the marketing strategies of competitors.

Each of these strategies will be discussed in greater detail below.

Development of Marketing Tools

H&A will develop the usual tools to ensure that it projects a professional image in its various markets. These will include:

- Business cards and matching stationery
- An identifiable logomark
- A very professional-looking, easy-to-mail brochure that also serves as a printed capability statement
- A quarterly newsletter, which will be published as a key means of maintaining communications with and among current and prospective clients.

Building An Identity Within Target Markets

H&A will begin by identifying its target markets, and by isolating the most profitable of these. Those target markets will be represented in the upcoming telephone surveys, which will be designed to provide the firm with precise feedback on how best to promote its services in those markets.

Selective Advertising

H&A will run ads in selected trade journals for the purpose of establishing its visibility among potential clients.

There are no plans at this time for radio or television advertising. A display ad will be obtained in the *Yellow Pages*.

The firm will make a conscious effort to garner as much favorable publicity as possible in the general press, in order to optimize its visibility among its target markets.

In connection with the paid advertising campaigns, H&A will offer "freebie" publications, such as booklets on how to write a business plan, or how to write an annual report, primarily as a means of expanding its direct mail lists of firms that might need technical assistance in the communications area.

Direct Mail Campaigns

Hilton & Associates will maintain a variety of computerized databases, both for its own use and the use of its clients. Certain of those databases will be indispensable to the firm's marketing efforts, and those include:

❑ All news media in the state and nation, as well as foreign printed and electronic media in markets where the firm's products are available for sale.

❑ A list of contacts for conferences and meetings at which H&A will have trade show representation.

❑ Economic development organizations in Colorado and elsewhere that are committed to assisting small businesses in the sale and distribution of their products and services.

❑ International trade contacts who can offer assistance and advice in the area of foreign sales and marketing.

❑ Lists of active and prospective clients, referral sources, and joint venture partners.

Other lists will be added to the database as experience and the requirements of business dictate.

Trade Show Participation

H&A will exploit every available opportunity to highlight its services at trade shows attended by a substantial representation from its primary target markets. The Denver Convention and Tourism agency, and similar entities for other major cities, are recognized as a primary source of information about upcoming trade shows.

Fostering Repeat Business

H&A already has a list of satisfied clients who have a first-hand familiarity with the quality of the services provided by the company. The company will actively solicit new business referrals from its existing customer base.

Testimonials about the services provided by H&A will be actively solicited and this information will be summarized, where appropriate, in brochures and other promotional materials developed and distributed by the company.

Maintaining a Sales-Oriented Organization

To ensure the success of a small business, *everyone* in the company must be a salesperson. H&A permanent staff and subcontractors will receive special training designed to teach them how best to "grow the business" while they are in the field.

Monitoring the Marketing Strategies of Competitors

H&A will maintain a constant vigil over the marketing activities of its competitors so that it can respond appropriately to strategies that may jeopardize its ability to realize its optimal market share.

SCHEDULE

H&A's first year schedule and plans are summarized in this section, but a five-year narrative reflecting the future growth of the venture is presented in the "Financial Data" section.

H&A will use the June-September, 1990 timeframe to acquire and upgradc equipment, train staff and subcontractors, and develop the database and other resources needed to support its marketing initiatives. The firm will also recruit new accounts all during this period.

During the fall of 1990, an aggressive kickoff campaign will be conducted. Funds set aside for selective advertising will be committed in support of that campaign.

H&A will maintain a home-based office during the rest of 1990, with substantial, dedicated office space and telephone service devoted entirely to this enterprise. During that period, client training classes will be conducted either on client premises, or at rented hotel accommodations.

FINANCIAL DATA

The Income and Expense projections for Hilton & Associates reflect the fact that the company is being vamped up from a one-man, part-time operation to a full-time venture that will ultimately employ dozens of workers nationwide. Hence, projected revenues rise slowly in 1990. A fall, 1990 marketing campaign will cause a substantial growth in the company's client base, and that growth will continue at a significant pace during 1991 and 1992, fueled by a sustained level of marketing, the performance of the venture, and the outcomes of the firm's R&D efforts.

Three years of detailed projections are provided (1990-1992), but five years (1990-1994) of expected trends are presented in narrative form in the section entitled "Annual Summary of Projections."

Assumptions

In this industry, inflation-related increases in income are negotiated as often as possible, while inflation-related costs are driven by general economic trends.

The hourly rates charged to customers in the 1990 projection are lower than the rates that appear on H&A's price list, but reflect what H&A expects will be the true average hourly income for the year. Likewise, costs have been adjusted to reflect a true average for the year.

Beginning in 1991, H&A's charges and costs will be as advertised.

Structure of the Projections

The projections for each of the next three years list the income sources that are detailed in the "Pricing" section. Those sources are:

- Edits/Rewrites
- Original Writing and Research
- Training Design, Development, and Delivery
- Data Processing Support
- Other Income

Except for "Other Income," these revenue sources derive from hourly rates that are listed in the "Parameters" section of each projection. The income projections are based on a reasonable estimate of the total number of project hours the company will handle each year. The percentages of revenue derived from each source are then adjusted to reflect seasonal shifts, which are modest in this industry.

Under "Expenses," the total number of hours to be subcontracted each year is presented. (The expectation is that H&A's Management Team, and any permanent writers and trainers employed by the firm, will handle all jobs that aren't subcontracted.)

The "Non-Personnel" expenses for 1990 reflect less than a year of full-time operating costs, to allow for the reality that the business is evolving from a part-time to a full-time status. The normal seasonal patterns of the business have been adjusted to ensure a more realistic reflection of cash flow for this year.

Annual Summary of Projections

Briefly, the Income and Expense projections reflect the following trends and expectations with regard to the development of this business.

1990

A gradual ramp-up of the business to full-time status will occur. Heavy expenses are expected in upgrading existing text editing equipment, acquiring new equipment, and implementing the firm's marketing plan.

The revenue projection for the year is conservative, showing only a 43% gain over 1989, when Mr. Hilton staffed the company single-handedly. Business activity is loaded heavily toward the last half of the year, during which time the marketing campaign will be fully underway. It is projected that 30% (1,050 hours) of the business developed during that period will be subcontracted.

Initial recruitment of a subcontractor staff of twelve (12) writers and trainers has already been completed. An extensive marketing survey was recently completed, and the results were used in the formulation of H&A's plan. That survey solicited feedback from potential competitors and clients, and was very helpful to the firm in defining the most effective, and cost-effective strategies for promoting its services.

A new and improved accounting system will be put into service, and all of the required, basic operating contracts and agreements will be formulated this year, causing higher than usual accounting and legal fees.

A business telephone, supported by voice messaging and other appropriate voice and data communications capabilities, will be installed at the headquarters site of the company.

1991

The Administrative Assistant will be employed full-time, and, by the end of the year, a modest, three-person office will be opened in a location that affords easy access to many of H&A's prospective business clients. (For example, the firm might be located in a downtown high rise, or a Denver Tech Center site.)

The business is projected to grow three-fold over the 1990 growth rate, which is not unusual considering the fact that it will be a full-time operation for the first time, and will be staffed by three FTEs (two writers and the Administrative Assistant).

A total of 10,500 project hours are projected, and 62% of that workload will be subcontracted.

The company will acquire a vehicle used exclusively in making deliveries and for other business travel.

R&D activities will be undertaken in earnest. One half-time marketer will be hired to assist the president in promoting the company.

1992

All of the management team members will be employed full-time, including the President, Vice President, Operations Manager, and Administrative Assistant.

The total number of projected project hours for this year is 15,000, 73% of which will be subcontracted. The balance of work is expected to shift somewhat, with editing dropping to 15% of the business, and writing services increasing to 65% of the business.

The central office accommodations will be expanded to include one training room (that can also function as a conference room); desk space for two more, full-time employees; a professional library; and storage space.

Plans for franchising the concept in major population centers will be completed this year.

R&D activities will begin to produce income, reflected in the projection under "Other Income."

1993

A part-time Franchise Manager will be hired. The first franchise effort will be launched in Chicago, and the foundation will be laid for similar efforts in Atlanta, Los Angeles, New York, and San Francisco.

A second company vehicle will be purchased.

Central office space will be increased 50%, and branch offices may be established elsewhere along the Front Range, and throughout the Rocky Mountain region.

R&D activities will be in full bloom, and will represent a major profit center for the company.

1994

The Chicago franchise will be launched with a full-time director, a full-time secretary, and a carefully selected cadre of 20 subcontractors.

A separate business plan and projections will have been developed for the first year of the Chicago Office.

R&D products will be an even greater revenue source for the company, and products will also be marketed and sold out of the Chicago office, causing a 50% increase over the 1993 revenue stream from this source.

Elder Care

BUSINESS PLAN

SUMMER GARDENS RESIDENTIAL CARE FACILITY FOR THE AMBULATORY ELDERLY

472 Gull Flight Ave.
Freemont Hills, CA 56789

February 14, 1993

Summer Gardens is a living facility providing food preparation, laundry, housekeeping, and personal care services to its senior residents. Run by a professional nurse, the facility hopes to provide an alternative to traditional nursing homes.

- PRODUCT PROFILE
- MARKET
- LOCATION
- COMPETITION
- DISTRIBUTION
- SALES
- KEY PERSONNEL
- ORGANIZATION
- REFERENCE LIST
- ADDENDA
- FLOOR PLAN
- CASH FLOW STATEMENT

PRODUCT PROFILE

According to an article published in the Executive Female, "Companies offering alternatives to the nursing home are taking off." Residential Care Facilities for the Elderly (RCFE) are a recognized, cost-effective alternative to the nursing home. Summer Gardens Residential Care Facility for the Ambulatory Elderly will be a community-based living and care giving facility established to serve the needs of our rapidly increasing elderly population.

Residential care facilities have existed in various forms for decades. Over the past twenty years, most states have developed licensure requirements as a means of standardizing the quality of these facilities. RCFE's operating in the state of California must be licensed and must operate under the comprehensive Code of California Regulations.

Summer Gardens will comply with all licensure and Title 22 requirements. The facility will focus on providing services which promote independence in a safe and pleasant environment. As the elderly struggle to stay out of nursing homes and hospitals, they seek help with food preparation, laundry, and housekeeping. As an alternative to nursing home placement, Summer Gardens will provide housing and assistance to its residents, including meal preparation (general and special diets), laundry, linen, housekeeping, and personal care. Appropriate staff will assist in recreational activities. Staff will also arrange physician appointments and coordinate transportation.

Elderly men and women frequently express a desire for basic companionship or the need for assistance, but prefer not to impose on family members. Concerned family members may be forced to acknowledge that it has become increasingly difficult for loved ones to take care of themselves and their homes. Summer Gardens will provide needed services to adults 60 years of age and older who require assistance to remain safely independent. Summer Gardens will be able to accommodate eight residents, 24 hours a day, seven days a week. The facility will be staffed 24 hours a day with qualified employees who are trained to respect the individuality and promote the dignity of every resident.

While there are other residential care facilities in the area, Summer Gardens is the only one owned and operated by a Masters-prepared Registered Professional Nurse. My fifteen years of nursing experience include the start-up and management of a Medicare-certified home health agency, and the management of a private home health services branch office. Additionally, I have been on the staff of Andrews Hospice as an on-call advisory nurse for two years. Both relatives and residents will feel confident that the appropriate level of care will be provided, along with monitoring and supervision. As a professional nurse, I am a credible and competent link to the physician. I am qualified to make nursing assessments and able to communicate findings to physicians as appropriate.

The elderly population in this country is increasing. In Aaron County, the population aged 62 and older has increased from 8% of the population in 1980 to 14.9% in 1990 (See Addendum A). The elderly are living longer and requiring alternative living arrangements. RCFE's are fulfilling a need. Qualified owner/ administrators of care facilities are in demand.

A loan in the amount of $25,000 will facilitate the acquisition of property to house this community-based RCFE. The loan will also provide beginning capital for lease deposit, leasehold improvements, insurance and furniture.

MARKET

The residents at Summer Gardens and their families will live in the San Francisco Bay area; most will live in Aaron County. The Aaron County location chosen for Summer Gardens is important because the elderly will want to continue to live in an area familiar to them and families will want their loved ones close enough to visit regularly.

The primary users of residential care services are men and women who cannot live safely in their own homes, but do not require the full-time skilled nursing care provided by convalescent hospitals. The targeted client market for the services provided at Summer Gardens RCFE is comprised of people who are 60 years of age and older. According to the Continuing Care Resources newsletter, the average age of residents of RCFE's is mid-to-late eighties. Of the 34,240 people in Aaron county aged 62 and older, 6,177 are already aged 80 and older, with the other 28,063 nearing age 80. Many of these elderly adults are single or widowed individuals who may have outlived other relatives and friends. If they are left alone at home, confusion or forgetfulness may render them unsafe and may affect their ability to care for themselves. However, with supervision and minimal assistance, these elderly will be able to maintain dignity, remain safe and independent, and conserve needed funds for future medical care. In addition, state and federal funds need not be used to provide care for these elderly at a level much higher and much more costly then they require.

According to a 1989 report from the Association of Bay Area Governments, 60% of the heads of households in Aaron County aged 65 and older had an annual income of $25,000 or more. Less than 25% of the heads of households had an annual income of less than $15,000. Of the market targeted as potential residents of Summer Gardens, at least 60% will be able to afford the services offered and less than 25% will be dependent solely on SSI (see Addendum B).

The cost of a semi-private room at Summer Gardens will be $2500 per month, or $83.00 per day (less than the cost of a hotel room). Future residents and families who investigate available options will find that the cost of the average semi-private room in a convalescent or nursing home in Aaron County is $105 to $150 per day, and the cost to hire 24-hour unskilled home care is $205 per day (see Addendum C).

MARKET...*continued*

Residents and families who choose Summer Gardens will do so because of:

- The nursing experience and expertise of the owner
- The high quality of care provided
- The safe, comfortable, and home-like environment
- The locality, which makes visitation easy
- The peace of mind which comes from keeping loved ones out of nursing homes

Presently, the 36 residential care facilities located in the Aaron County area cannot meet the needs of that portion of the 34,240 elderly residents who are already age 62 or above and in need of some degree of assistance. There are waiting lists at most of these facilities. Reports from the County Conservator, Rehabilitation Hospital, and Acute Care Hospital discharge planners show that there are not enough residential options for people who are unable to live alone but not ready for convalescent home care.

LOCATION

Summer Gardens RCFE will be located in Freemont Hills, California. It is important that the facility be located in Aaron County because of its reputation for beauty, relative safety, affluence and proximity to desired clients and their families. The city of Freemont Hills was chosen because property is less expensive than any other city in Aaron County and has less restrictions (e.g. use of water).

Summer Gardens will be located in a large home in a quiet residential area of the city. Residents will be able to sit safely on the patio or take short walks in the neighborhood. The house itself will be built on one level. It will be large enough to accommodate 8 adults comfortably and will be brought into compliance with all state and local safety regulations. (See Floor Plan).

COMPETITION

There are six (6) other RCFE's located in Freemont Hills. Five (5) are of similar size and offer similar services. According to the California Code of Regulations, RCFE facilities cannot be located within 300 feet of another RCFE. The names and locations of the RCFE facilities located in Freemont Hills are:

Riverview Terrace
Administrator: Lee Smith
123 Bay St.
Freemont Hills, CA 56789

Seaside Residential Care
Administrator: Donna Jones
234 Mason Ave.
Freemont Hills, CA 56780

Pine Acres
Administrator: Thomas Beech
345 Pollyanna
Freemont Hills, CA 56789

Lyle B. Morton Care Facility
Administrator: Andrea Morton
4567 J St.
Freemont Hills, CA 56789

Shady Arbor
Administrator: Diane Brown
56789 Irving Lane
Freemont Hills, CA 56780

The similarities between RCFE facilities is due to the California Code of Regulations, Title 22, Division 6, Chapter 8. All facilities offering services to the elderly are strictly supervised and mandated by this Code. Despite the inherent similarities, I do not expect to need to take clients away from my competitors because of the growing elderly population. These businesses are very profitable and many owners (e.g. Andrea Morton) subsequently opened second and third facilities. Once eight residents are found, it may be 1-5 years before an opening exists for another resident.

DISTRIBUTION

I intend to contact individuals who will use my facility through professionals in the community who find appropriate accommodations for the elderly. These referral sources include the county conservators, hospital discharge planners, rehabilitation center discharge planners, day care centers, senior citizen centers, home care agencies, and independent case managers. I plan to mail a brochure describing Summer Gardens along with a cover letter announcing the opening of the new facility. I will follow up with a phone call and a request for referrals. I plan to place a continuous ad in the local "senior" newspaper and advertise in the yellow pages. I will gain access to many referral sources by taking advantage of the contacts made when I was in an administrative position at Miller Health Care Services, which was located in Aaron County.

SALES

I plan to open with one resident in January 1994, and expect to increase to three residents by February, six residents by March, and a full census of eight residents in April. Based on these projections, end of the year assets will be $83,728.

I have considered what could go wrong with this plan. The condition of the economy could affect the ability of the elderly to pay for their care with private funds. Regardless of the economy, there will be an elderly population. If funds run out and the elderly are placed on SSI, or if I would need to admit some residents whose only source of income was SSI, I would be guaranteed some payment from the State. In the unlikely event that this would occur to some of my clients, it would decrease the amount of profit, but would not result in a negative income.

KEY PERSONNEL

As the owner of Summer Gardens, I will be in charge of the business operations (See Resume for qualifications). I will have three employee care givers: two regular employees and one on-call or back-up person to handle sick calls, vacations, and holidays. Tracy Stevens and Samuel Jackson will be regular employees and Lucy Johnson will be on-call as needed.

Tracy Stevens is a Registered Nurse with five years experience in home care, hospice, and rehabilitation hospitals. Samuel Jackson is a Certified Home Health Care Aide with six years experience in acute care hospitals, convalescent hospitals, rehabilitationhospitals, and home care. Lucy Johnson is a Nurse Assistantwith six years experience working with the elderly in their own homes. She has also worked in acute care hospitals and convalescent hospitals.

Employees will be responsible for providing personal care and related services for residents, providing companionship, and promoting mental alertness and physical well being. Please contact Marian Currey, the owner, for complete descriptions of employee qualifications and comprehensive job descriptions.

ORGANIZATION

This organization will be a sole proprietorship owned by Marian Currey. My short term goals are: 1) to open Summer Gardens RCFE in January 1994, 2) to have 8 residents by April 1994, and 3) to show a small profit by March 1994.

My long term goals are to purchase the leased property in January 1995 and to begin the process of opening a second RCFE in 1996.

REFERENCE LIST

- *Between Home and Nursing Home*, Down and Schnurr, Buffalo NY, 1992
- "More for Your Money," Inc. Magazine, September, 1992
- "Where the jobs are," Executive Female, July/August, 1991
- "Tips for Venture-Capital Seekers," Executive Female, July/August, 1992
- "The Weekly Cash Flow Planner," Inc. Magazine, June, 1992
- "How Much Should I Pay Myself," Inc. Magazine, June, 1992
- "How to Improve America's Medical Care," Mona Magazine, April, 1992
- "Your Business Starting It Growing It," Executive Female, March/April, 1992
- "Health Care Fraud," U.S. News and World Report, February 24, 1992
- "Banking and Capital," Inc. Magazine, June, 1991

- ♦"How to Write a Personnel Manual," Small Business Success, June, 1991
- ♦"How to Write a Business Plan," Small Business Success, June, 1991
- ♦Summary Volume of the Aaron County Cities and CVP 1990
- ♦Association of Bay Area Governments, Oakland, CA
- ♦Aaron County Conservators Office
- ♦Department of Social Services - Community Care Licensing Division

ADDENDUM A

Census of Aaron County

Age	1980	1990
62-64	5,278	6,071
65-74	13,193	
65-69		99,596
75-84	6,141	
70-74		7,142
75-79		5,252
80-84		3,358
85>	2,168	2,819
Population over age 62	26,780	34,240
Total Population	222,568	230,096

ADDENDUM B

Annual Income of Aaron County 1989

Total number of householders aged 65 and up: *18,574*

Income	Householders
<5,000	474
5,000-9,000	1,964
10,000-14,999	1,796
15,000-24,999	3,245
25,000-34,999	2,682
35,000-49,000	2,821
50,000-74,999	2,805
75,000-99,999	1,296
100,000>	1,491

ADDENDUM C

Daily Rates

Convalescent Hospital/Nursing Home	Private	Semi-Private
Murphy Convalescent Hospital	130-140	95
Rosewood Convalescent Hospital	220	110
Ellworth Convalescent Hospital	215	120
Ivy Terrace Convalescent Hospital	NA	96
St. Mary's Convalescent Hospital	180	125

Daily Rates

24 Hour Live-In:

Jenson Home Care	205
Alert Nursing Service	175-195
Guardian	160-185
Desmond Home Care	180-200
Martin Critical Care	185-195
Certified Home Care	175-195

FLOOR PLAN

A floor plan of the Summer Gardens facility is available through Simon Architecture, Inc., 100 Diamond Ave., Fremont Hills, CA 56780.

CASH FLOW STATEMENT

The Tribunal Accounting Firm has developed a spreadsheet to illustrate cash flow for Summer Gardens during the first year of operation. The statement includes data on cash receipts, investments, capital expenditures, operating expenses, loan payments, taxes, sales, and administrative tasks.

RESUME

A personal resume and references are available upon request.

Equipment Rental

BUSINESS PLAN

RICH RENTALS

777 W. Langley Ave.
Bradenton, Florida 89201

February 1992

Rich Rentals is an equipment rental business providing a wide variety of tools and machinery for the Do-it-Yourselfer. This family-owned venture seeks to provide a competitive service to its customers and secure a long-term financial opportunity and livelihood in which the entire family can participate.

EQUIPMENT RENTAL BUSINESS PLAN

OVERVIEW

Since 1988, our business has suffered from cash constraints. We have used the services of University of Southern Florida's Business Analyst Program, Small Business Development Center, and our accountant to analyze the problem. Our large number of assets and varied services have made our situation difficult to analyze. However, we now know the basis for our cash shortages, and they are as follows:

- The addition of small gas engine repair to our services.
- Increase in our labor force to accomplish the above.
- Financing the needed small gas engine parts inventory through existing cash flow and accounts payable.
- The age of some key rental equipment.
- Our low equity position.

This plan specifically addresses several methods that we will use to correct the cash flow, profitability, and equity deficiencies.

We have already initiated several changes that have had positive results. The future changes fall into two categories: Management and Financial. When these changes have all been implemented, the company will be within industry norms in two years, as will be shown later in the plan.

Business Objectives

In the summer of 1983, my wife and I began discussing the possibility of relocating to Bradenton, Florida and starting a family business. We were attracted to Bradenton because of its proximity to family, the lifestyle, and the ability to raise our children in a more controlled environment. After months of discussion, market studies, and reviewing several different potential business opportunities, we decided on the equipment rental business. The equipment being rented by the existing equipment rental business was in very poor condition and they had recently filed Chapter 11 Bankruptcy. We spent time evaluating their particular circumstances and determined that their failure was primarily related to overextension financially, brought on by the tremendous drop in oil prices significantly hurting this area, as well as an absentee owner.

The salient points in our consideration were as follows:

- To provide our family with long-term financial opportunity and to provide an adequate standard of living.
- To have a business where competition could and would be limited.
- Long term, we wanted a business that was in a growth industry with greater opportunities for the entire area.
- To open a family-owned business in which our children would later have the opportunity to participate and learn just how important small business is to the future of our country.

The equipment rental business met all of our needs.

PRODUCT AND SERVICE

Our primary product/service mix is:

❑The Rental of Tools and Equipment. If you have a job to do, we have a tool to make it easier and quicker. Service to our customers, both professional and "Do-It-Yourselfers," is a primary part of our daily operation.

- We must FIRST provide equipment that is in good working condition.
- We must provide the equipment when it is needed.
- When necessary we will provide our equipment at a competitive price, BUT ALWAYS at a profit.
- We provide complete written "HOW TO" information on all of our equipment and detailed verbal or visual explanations when needed.
- We provide pickup and delivery for a fee.
- Last but far from least, when our customers have a problem, we go to them.The completion of their job becomes our No. 1 priority.

Also...

We also provide, for sale or rent, most accessories needed to use our tools and equipment.

We provide "damage waiver" to create a worry-free environment for our customers and ourselves by charging a ten percent mandatory fee. This has been very successful in our operation.

❑We are a Ryder Truck Rental Agent. In that capacity, we are able to provide consumers with a complete range of moving needs, from trucks to dollies of all kinds, pads, trailers, towing equipment, boxes, and related supplies.

❑We are a Kubota Consumer Products Dealer with the ability to sell parts for the complete Kubota Tractor line. The bulk of our profit and sales is directly related to Bilt Contract Co. and the mines in our area.

❑We are a Western Union Agent with the capability to send and receive money, mailgrams, and telegrams. They provide an IBM Computer which we also use to run the business.

❑ In addition we are a Briggs & Stratton Service Dealer. However, we have decided as of March 1, 1993 we will no longer provide small engine repair service to walk-in trade. We will limit this end of our business to the more lucrative commercial trade which will also reduce our manpower requirements and make it easier to schedule the work around our needs. We will no longer allow outside repair work to conflict with the needs of our rental business.

MARKET POTENTIAL AND COMPETITION

Rich Rentals has been in business now for almost eight years and we have maintained detailed financial information since the beginning. Our projections for 1992 are included in this business plan and are based on historical data, and augmented with the latest charges that are outlined in this plan. In addition we have maintained records of most requests for equipment that we were unable to fill for whatever reason, and thereby have an accurate estimation of demand.

When we opened our business in 1984, unemployment in Bradenton was at one of its highest levels and the mines were doing poorly. Because of this, we and experts from Quick Rentals performed detailed market analysis prior to making our final decision. Quick Rentals provided regional and community market and site location analysis and start-up aid. Bob Shafer who owned Quick Rentals, and his family had extensive experience in this industry, having opened over 150 stores through Quick Rentals. The potential for success was here especially with the Bilk Contract Co. construction just beginning. In addition, the size of the community and our knowledge of the existing rental store indicated that we could soon be the only equipment rental business in Bradenton. Since 1988 we have been the only rental equipment business in this market area.

We know the current market potential for Bradenton is only partially reflected in our historically-based financial projections. Certain rental equipment additions and planned construction for 1992-1993 will enhance our revenues for the near future. Further information on the local economy, including recent newspaper articles are available upon request.

REVIEW OF FINANCIALS: 1990 VERSUS 1991

Revenues are up substantially: (Balance Sheets and income statements outlining this have been prepared and are available upon request.)

- ❑Rental is up $8,059.00 or 4 percent before implementation of Damage Waiver.
- ❑Rental & Sales Combined are up $34,274.00 or 13 percent.
- ❑Gross Profit is up $32,363.00 or 17 percent.
- ❑Total Income is up $29,307.00 or 13 percent.
- ❑Rental Revenue/Equipment Cost is up from .95 to 1.06
- ❑Rental Revenue/Net Rental Equipment is up from 1.39 to 1.69 or an 18 percent improvement.

These improvements reflect our rate increases beginning in October 1990, which made up for no real rate increase since 1987. As a result our return on equipment investment in Bradenton has improved substantially. THE POTENTIAL IS HERE.

Expenses went up as well: Wages paid to employees were up $13,952.00 or 33 percent and equipment repair costs were up $14,610.00 or 72 percent. Wages were up because, we increased our labor force by one full-time individual in early 1991. Prior to that we had added a third full-time person in 1988. This was to provide the necessary personnel required for the additional repair volume created by adding the Kubota and Briggs & Stratton line. Due to the nature of our business our efficiency per man hour decreased proportionally making the addition of outside service work not profitable. This fact had escaped our analysis because all of our personnel shared responsibilities and duties. Service was also the only area where we encountered substantial competition.

The results of adding manpower are clear. We slightly increased our profit from "LABOR AND DELIVER" plus "NET SALES INCOME" by $559.00 over 1991. However, when you subtract the increase in total wages paid over previous years, you can see all we did was create a deficit of <$13,393>.

In addition our increase in "Equipment Repair Expenses" are two-fold in nature. First, because of the manner of accounting (non-cost), we are unable to track all items to the proper department. Therefore, the shown expense account is higher than it should be, by about $3,218.00 or 47 percent over 1990. Much of this expense is related to customer repair work and not rental maintenance. Secondly, we have had excessive repair costs on some of our large equipment (Skid Steer Loader, Trencher/Backhoe, Tractor, and one Compressor) of approximately $6,952.00. The current management goals will reduce and contain these costs.

In 1991 we could have shown additional income of about $8,459.26. This was a paper loss on a John Deere Tractor and a Kubota Riding Lawn Mower that were sold primarily because they were beginning to cost us a lot more in repairs than they could possibly earn. This adjustment should be noted when comparing 1991 to previous years. This comparison indicates an improvement in our revenue over previous years related to the addition of Damage Waiver and our aggressive rate increases beginning in 1990.

REVIEW CONCLUSIONS

Even before the end of 1991 it became apparent that several changes were still needed to improve our financial situation. Our analysis merely highlighted much of what we already believed. Even though our revenues were up in 1991 we still did not have the strong financial showing possible primarily due to higher labor and equipment repair costs. As a result of this information, we have made certain decisions and established some long and short range remedies as follows

GOALS AND PROJECTIONS FOR 1992

Management

First, we have already DECREASED OUR WORKFORCE by two employees and will maintain this level, except for possibly temporary workers during peak periods.

We will be CONCENTRATING ON STRICTLY THE RENTAL BUSINESS and EXTENSIVELY LIMITING OUR REPAIR BUSINESS to commercial accounts. This should decrease scheduling problems we have had with homeowners and other individuals.

WE WILL TERMINATE our Kubota and/or our Briggs & Stratton agreement IF ASKED TO INVEST ADDITIONAL TIME OR MONEY. Currently our inventories are more than sufficient to support our rental business. Our analysis has shown service work to be a loser.

Review the potential for Total Quality Management in the business.

Financial

We have REDUCED OUR PERSONAL INCOME.

We are practicing COST CONTAINMENT on a daily basis.

We have REFINANCED BOTH OF OUR COMPANY VEHICLE NOTES.

- Bradenton National Bank, 1988 pickup, from $356/month to $262/ month, a $94/month savings.
- NFCU, 1987 Van, from $383/month to $215/month, a $168/month savings.

We are requesting that G.E. Capital assist us in one of the two options listed below in our efforts to upgrade our equipment and to realign our cash position as follows:

- To finance a new Ditch Witch 3500 and 1020 Trencher through our G.E. Capital line if possible, and to reamortize the lease at close to the current payment amount. The net purchase amount would be about $28,500 after trade-ins.
- Restructure our existing lease to provide the necessary cash flow to finance the trenchers through another source.

    1. Extend our lease approximately one year or extend it sufficiently to reduce our payment by about $700/month March through November.
    2. Change our reduced payment months to December, January, and February to match our needs.
    3. Release the Ditch Witch 2310 trencher and A220 Backhoe to be used as a trade. This will allow us to upgrade critical equipment and reduce maintenance cost. This combination unit is now five years old and the engine is now bored to .040 over. If not traded soon this machine combination,which creates substantial rental revenue, will become a liability.

We are requesting that SBA reamortize our loan to allow for four months without payments starting in June. We would like the maturity date to remain the same. This would result in an accumulation of $9408 in operating capital.

We have purchased a new Skid Steer Loader from Case. This was necessary because:

- Our previous unit was giving us constant problems and we were unable to keep it on a good long-term commercial rental. Maintenance costs were running very high.
- There is a real need for a good small loader with optional pallet forks in our rental fleet. The demand is there from a broad range of customers. Our cash flow would be enhanced by at least $161/month, over the new payment amount based on historical information available.
- We used our old unit as a $2,000 trade-in.

We renegotiated a long-term rental we have had with Biringer effective January 1, 1993, from a previous level of $750/month to $920/month. This is a contract we have had for over two years and it should go for about two more.

Summary

THE CHANGES WE HAVE INITIATED SHOULD SAVE AN ANNUAL COST OF $23,436 PER MONTH. (A chart outlining this information has been prepared and is available upon request.)

MARKET ANALYSIS

Rich Rentals has several areas where we maintain a sustainable competitive advantage from the standpoint of being the only service provider in town for the areas of equipment rental; Kubota sales, parts, and service; and Bostitch and Interchange Air Tools and Fasteners. Areas of limited competition are Western Union (one competitor) and Ryder Truck rentals (one competitor; U-Haul).

Marketing Strategy

It is our goal to extend the very best service and equipment to our customers at a competitive price. Our prices must remain competitive to prevent competition in the rental business from within Bradenton and the surrounding areas.

Target Market and Market Share

Our target markets for rental equipment has been and will continue to be:

- ❑ Small contractor - 45 percent of total
- ❑ Industrial sector - 25 percent of total
- ❑ Homeowner - 30 percent of total

They are listed in order of profitability. Since we are currently getting all of the small contractor and industrial rentals we can fill, we most exploit the homeowner segment to a greater degree than in the past.

Target Markets and Market Share...*continued*

Our target markets for Ryder truck rentals are:

- People moving out of town - 70 percent of market
- In town moves - 20 percent of market
- Commercial moves - 10 percent of market

They are listed in order of priority. Ryder Truck Rental has estimated our share of the truck rental business at 52 percent of the local market. As of April, we became a zone leader for the distribution of Ryder trucks. This will be a revenue enhancer from the standpoint of having additional trucks to rent when needed.

Our target market for Kubota sales is as follows:

- Industrial sales - 40 percent of market
- Institutions and business - 20 percent of market
- Upper middle-class homeowner - 40 percent of market

Western Union is a service we provide because:

- They provide a computer and software that can be used in other areas of the business.
- To increase walk-in trade with other revenue potential.

SALES PLAN

Rental

We plan to enhance our rental income by selectively targeting the homeowner market. Our goal in the coming years is to continually increase the homeowner segment of our rental business by eight percent over the previous comparable period. We will continue our existing efforts directed at the contractors and industrial areas.

Ryder

We will target the realtors as a vehicle to promote greater usage of our trucks and trailers. In addition, Michelle's Moving will also enhance the sales and rentals in this area. Our goal is to increase this area by a factor of six percent on an ongoing basis. Ryder has some discretionary co-op advertising that we will avail ourselves of when possible.

Kubota

We will continue our sales in this area. Promotion will be minimal because of the excessive labor demands it creates for our service. We have backed off outside service since we have determined that to be a loss area.

Michelle's Moving

Since this area is a contract with Biringer, it will require no promotion. However, if it appears to be profitable after this one-year contract period, we will entertain moving into the local moving business as a separate venture. There is only one existing business providing the service in Bradenton at this time.

PROMOTIONAL

The primary thrust of our promotion program in 1992 will be in the form of "DIRECT MAIL" and "DOOR TO DOOR" flyers directed at the "HOMEOWNER" market in hopes of expanding our rental business. In the past we depended primarily on radio and newspaper. Most of our potential customers in this trade area are aware of "WHERE WE ARE" and "WHO WE ARE", but not "WHAT WE HAVE" and "HOW THEY CAN USE US TO THEIR ADVANTAGE".

- ❑ Our mailing list can be directed to individual neighborhoods and we will tie discounts and promotions to each mailing to determine their effectiveness.
- ❑ Thank you letters with additional promotional information and a ten percent discount on their next rental will be a key part of our direct mail campaign.
- ❑ Our mailings will highlight individual tools, how to properly use them for maximum results, and new ideas. We will stress our concept of personal service and just how "rich" we can make their rental experience.
- ❑ We will be utilizing DOOR TO DOOR on a trial basis.

We will begin promoting our equipment rentals by using retail outlets of related merchandise.

- ❑ Automotive equipment, pullers, transmission jacks, hoists, torque wrenches, impacts, timing light, etc. We will provide a coupon worth $2 off any equipment rental at the counter of outlets such as Kmart, Walmart, American Auto, Wilsons, etc.
- ❑ Ryder trucks, moving equipment ad related supplies, such as boxes and tape. In a joint effort with Ryder, we will provide a coupon worth $5 on any local rental and $15.00 on any one-way rental to every real estate agent in Bradenton. We are considering a promotional incentive for the referring agent courtesy of Ryder.

We will continue to use some radio and a minimum newspaper contract of 240" annually, coordinating those mediums with our direct mail campaign.

A detailed outline of our "1992 ANNUAL CAMPAIGN" will be completed by the end of May as follows:

- ❑ It will be budgeted by type of advertising.
- ❑ It will be itemized by type of equipment and/or service by promotional period.

To help promote the business and provide a higher level of service we will also be setting up an answering machine to give basic after-hours information and emergency numbers for our customers who call after hours and weekends.

ORGANIZATIONAL

Michelle's Moving could become our biggest move in 1992. We will begin in May 1992 providing contract moving services between offices for Biringer Bradenton, Florida. In the fall of 1991 we were approached by Biringer Purchasing to bid on these moving services. This basically consists of providing one full-time employee in a supervisory/labor capacity with assistance from day labor as needed, a Ryder truck, and any necessary moving equipment, about five to six days per month on average. Advance notice will be provided by Biringer to allow us sufficient time to schedule our manpower.

In the past this service had been provided by a local moving company but was not satisfactory. Our long-time relationship with and the availability of all the necessary moving equipment was what brought them to us. This service concept tied in well with our goals to expand our revenues by offering additional services forBiringer that complimented what we were already doing. The basic service contract should be very profitable and will increase the sale of moving boxes which is also very profitable. In addition, it does not require us to invest in any new equipment to provide the service.

For better control of equipment repair costs we will improve our record keeping to include all costs as well as information. In addition, we will return to keeping track of rental revenues by equipment. This information when combined, will give us better data when buying new equipment. We have implemented weekly and monthly P&L Statements as a management tool.

Until further notice any manpower requirements over the basic two employees will be strictly on an as-needed, temporary basis. We are in the process of building financial models to use as a management tool to provide keys for when we must cut back on manpower or other expenditures.

OPERATIONS

Location

This business is centrally located in Bradenton, Florida at 777 W. Langley Ave. The business is situated on a lot 101 feet by 165 feet, with a 2,450 square foot metal building built by us in 1984. One third of the building is the showroom display area. The Ryder trucks are parked in the front area of the business and across the street in a parking lot.

Equipment

The business currently has all of the equipment that it needs to operate except for the following replacements and/or additions required:

Ditch Witch 1020 Walk Behind
Trench Net After Trade of Our Current C99 010 .... $2,530
Small equipment, such as transmission
jack,scaffolding, and small roto-tillers $1,560
Ditch Witch 3500 Riding trencher (replacement
for our 2310/A220 Combination Unit) $25,930

Total $30,020

Labor Force

Our labor force consists of the owners, Jim and Michelle Griffith and two employees, Dave Weager and Donald Carp

Dave Weager is 29 years old, married with two children, and has 11 years experience as a mechanic. He was hired by us September 5,1988 and is currently our Shop Foreman with an hourly wage of $9.25.

Donald Carp is 30 years old, married with two children, and was hired on August 18,1988. He had previously operated his own lawn service business. He is currently a Rental Clerk and primarily responsible for equipment maintenance and service. He is also our parts man with an hourly wage of $6.25. Both employees are Bradenton natives with extensive local knowledge and contacts. A resume outlining the qualifications and experience of Jim Griffith has been prepared and is available upon request

TIMING

Management Calendar

Regular Activities

10th of Month Evaluate marketing program, financial goals, and major management decisions for previous month.
20th of Month Define specific marketing objectives for following month. (i.e. door-to-door, direct mail, etc.)
Weekly P&L and cash flow analysis of performance vs. goals.

Short Term Schedule of Events

May 7th Start Michelle's Moving contract with Biringer
May 10th Initiate door-to-door campaign (evaluate on 10th).
May 10th Schedule newspaper and radio ads for peak summer and fall seasons.
May 20th New lease agreement from G.E. Capital.
May 20th Initiate coupon campaign (Section 2 A & B of promotional section).
May 22nd Purchase new Trencher.
May 30th Initiate direct mail campaign.

FINANCIAL PROJECTIONS

It is the goal of management through this plan to maximize cash and profitability. This is being accomplished as follows:

- ❑Cost containment through ongoing analysis and aggressive daily management.
- ❑Revenue enhancement through the marketing plan and ongoing evaluation and adjustment of our rental rates.
- ❑Cash Management

The monthly P&L Statements reflect our success to date, in terms of increased profitability over the same period a year ago. These are available upon request.

Our goal for this coming year is to accumulate $15,000 in cash for operating and emergency purposes. This will be accomplished via operations. A 12-month cash forecast has been prepared and is available upon request. It projects an accumulated cash balance at year end of $16,142. This will be accomplished via:

- ❑Reduction in our labor force
- ❑Reduction in owner's draw from previous years
- ❑Refinancing our two vehicle notes
- ❑Recapitalization of G.E. Capital note
- ❑Four-month SBA payment waiver
- ❑Upgrading our trencher and loader to reduce maintenance cost and enhance revenue

Pro-forma statements have been prepared and are available upon request. Assumptions based on these are as follows:

Income Statement

Revenue

- ■An increase in rental revenue is projected from 1991, based on the local construction activity, and generally a solid local economy. (Aforementioned newspaper articles support this)
- ■Michelle's Moving revenue is projected at 50 percent of the unofficial estimate from the Biringer Procurement office. Therefore, these projections may be very conservative.
- ■Sale projections were reduced because we are no longer promoting sales, which are marginally profitable when compared to rental revenue and we are discouraging service work. A most recent financial comparison based on the first two months of 1991 versus 1992 has been prepared and is available upon request.
- ■Current financial statements are also available.

Expenses

■The labor projection represents one less full-time position and one less temporary from 1991.
■The moving insurance is additional workman's compensation due to the inclusion of Michelle's Moving.
■Equipment repair is reduced because of the projected purchase of two new large items that replaced older ones in poor condition.
■Also, the deletion of the small gas engine area impacts here. We have already rebuilt two of our three larger diesel air compressors.
■The finance charges should be reduced due to more available cash and reduced payables.
■The SBA interest payable assumes the four-month waiver.
■The G.E. capital interest also assumes a recapitalization. Although this is technically a lease purchase, we have always shown the debt on our balance sheet as a financed purchase to more accurately project our equity position in the equipment.

The current pro-forma income statement shows a before tax profit of $73,434. The pro-forma balance sheets have been adjusted for changes in accounts payable and debt service from year to year. The ALP are reduced to $8,500 within three years and are maintained at that level. This reduction is accomplished solely through operations and assumes the SBA Waiver and the G.E. Capital request for 1992. The May 1994 balance sheets show a $50,000 equipment purchase that will be necessary to maintain our rental equipment inventory.

Replacement vehicles are scheduled in 1993 and 1994. Their respective value and debts are shown. The loader and trencher are scheduled for June 1992, and are included in the May statement for analysis purposes. All of these statements are available upon request.

Income Statement *...continued*

Framing/Antiques Store

BUSINESS PLAN

FLORA'S FRAMES & ANTIQUES

2600 Richardson Turnpike
Nanton, CT 02170

November 21, 1993

This family-owned business, whose proprietors have experience in the picture framing and antiques field, have designed a combination venture that they believe will cater to an untapped market. The following plan outlines the factors that are crucial to consider when launching a new business.

PLAN OBJECTIVE

The purpose of this document is to provide operating policies and budgetary guidelines for Flora's Frames & Antiques - a family operated retail establishment located in Nanton, CT. The financial projections and objectives contained herein are intended to serve as benchmarks for measuring and evaluating company performance and growth. They were derived from industry standards and have been adjusted to reflect the particular strengths and weaknesses of Flora's Frames & Antiques. Actual financial performance will be tracked closely and adjusted when necessary to ensure that full profit potential is realized.

BUSINESS PROFILE

Flora's Frames & Antiques will be a privately-owned, family operated retail operation specializing in quality custom frames, framed art and antiques. It will be incorporated under the laws of Connecticut and will be located in Nanton, Connecticut. The business will be in close proximity to other retail and specialty shops including: Kitchen Supplies, Wrap & Ship, and Super Video Chain, all of which have name recognition and draw high traffic volumes. Flora's Frames & Antiques will open for business on December 1, 1993 and will maintain the following business hours:

- ❑Monday through: Wednesday10 to 6
- ❑Thursday: 10 to 8
- ❑Friday, Saturday: 10 to 6
- ❑Sunday: Closed

In the profitable and growing picture framing market, Flora's Frames & Antiques will stand out as a leader in customer service and quality craftsmanship. A strong customer focus, an accessible location and a broad product line will enable the establishment to slowly and steadily develop a loyal customer base. Sales are expected to reach $200,000 within the first year and to grow at a conservative rate of six to eight percent during the next two to five years. To stimulate growth Flora will introduce new products and services including: home consultations, instructional workshops and an expanded product line that includes international acquisitions. The specific products and services added will depend on consumer trends, projected profit margins, customer draw and overall company direction. The initial product and service line for Flora's Frames & Antiques will include:

- •Museum-quality, premium-priced custom frames and framing
- •Same-day custom framing (for certain items)
- •One-hour custom framing (for certain items)
- •Discounted "Frame your own" service
- •Consignment art and antiques
- •Dry mounting
- •Ready-made, photo and standard size frames
- •Prints, oils, mirrors, textiles, local artists' works
- •Antiques (includes furniture, artwork, decorative objects and jewelry)

The antique selection will draw customers who are not currently in the market for frames, but whose interest in quality decorations and generally higher incomes make them perfect targets for Flora's more premium priced services. Once they are aware of the quality of Flora's work, they will return to fulfill all of their art and framing needs as they arise. The business will be indexedunder "antiques" in the yellow pages, as well as under "picture framing services" to ensure that people are aware of this product offering. In addition to drawing customers, the antiques on display will generate ambiance for the business making it pleasant to browse. As a result, customers in general will spend more time in the store and will be more likely to make a purchase, recommend the store to others, or return at a later time.

MARKET PROFILE

Industry

Total industry sales for 1992 were estimated at $6 billion. However, this figure is expected to increase, as picture frames/framing is a growth industry. According to The Professional Picture Framer's Association (PPFA), The Weekly Home Furnishings Newspaper, and the Journal of Commercial Bank Lending, growth of the picture framing industry began in the seventies, reached double digit figures in the eighties, is currently in the five to eight percent range and is expected to continue at this rate for the next few years. Several environmental factors have spurred industry growth:

- ❑A recent boom in amateur photography has increased demand for photo frames.

- ❑The recession has required people to seek more affordable options for decorating and gift giving.

- ❑A rise in the number of frame shops and franchises has increased overall customer awareness of and demand for frames and framing services.

- ❑Expanded product lines at the manufacturer level (trendier styles of ready-made frames, moldings and mats) has opened the door for retailers to establish niche markets and provide more variety in their product offerings.

Customers

According to a study conducted by the Professional Picture Framer's Association (PPFA) the target customer for custom framing services is female, twenty five to twenty nine years old, well educated, lives with her family in a home that she owns and has family income of $30,000 to $45,000. Experience has shown that on average, customers are willing to drive up to thirty minutes for custom framing jobs, which would mean that the target market lives within ten to fifteen miles of Nanton. Eighty percent of the customers will be individuals and twenty percent will be businesses including interior decorators, restaurants, and professional photographers.

U.S. Census data shows that the number of twenty five to twenty nine year old females who live within a fifteen mile radius of Nanton is approximately 100,000. Average incomes for residents of Nanton and surrounding towns fall either within or above the target income range. Competition is stiff, with over fifty-seven other custom framers within fifteen miles of Flora's Frames & Antiques. Factoring in mass merchants and other competitors (identified below) it would be reasonable to expect Flora's Frames & Antiques to capture 1.5% of the market - which comes to 1500 people.

Studies by an independent contractor for Intercraft Corp., and by the Professional Picture Framer's Association (PPFA) show that the average customer purchases between one and five frames per year. Based on an average of three purchases per customer per year, there are 4500 opportunities a year for Flora to sell her merchandise to the target market. In addition, some non-target individuals will be expected to make purchases, and additional sales will be generated by business customers. Given an average customer ticket of about $65.00, the break even for Flora's Frames & Antiques can be calculated at $118,855 per year, or just under 2000 sales per year (see calculation sheet). This breaks down to an average of six sales per day which is highly feasible given the size of the framing market and Flora's expected share.

COMPETITION PROFILE

The competition for custom framing services comes mainly from other small custom framing shops and professional photography studios. The list of competitors for ready-made frames is longer and includes: mass merchants, department stores, drug stores, variety stores, art & craft stores, camera stores, card & gift shops, supermarkets, women's apparel chains, bath & linen chains, housewares chains, home office superstores and catalog showrooms.There are over 200 frame shops and photography studios listed under the "picture frames-dealers" section of the Nanton Yellow pages which covers the city of Nanaton as well as thirty-six nearby towns. Fifty seven shops are listed in towns located within fifteen miles of Nanton, and twenty-six of the shops listed are located within five miles. The closest competitors are The Framing Workshop, a custom framing establishment specializing in self-service framing and Ready Photo, a film developing franchise which has a very limited selection of ready-made frames. Both The Framing Workshop and Ready Photo are within one quarter mile of Flora's Frames & Antiques. Neither offers the combination of quality, service, broad product line, and affordable prices that Flora's Frames & Antiques will. In fact, customer reports and experience show that framers in general, and The Framing Workshop in particular are especially weak in the area of customer service. Customers who shop around for quality are sure to find the products, service, and prices at Flora's Frames & Antiques superior to those at competitors' stores.

The framing industry is very fragmented with each small frame shop acting in isolation. No single shop, franchise or group of competitors has enough market share, resources or influence in the industry to react strongly to new entrants. Local shops may increase advertising, however, only thirteen percent of customers find shops through advertising and Flora's Frames & Antiques plans to match their efforts in this area. Some of the larger franchises have more resources upon which to draw, however there are none of these located close to the business.

Prices

Prices will be based on a combination of past experience, industry figures and manufacturers' suggestions. Flora has been setting prices for over five years and her close contact with customers will allow her to react quickly to changes in demand. Custom framing services and framed art on display will be priced at a premium to reflect the value added by Flora. However prices for these items will be slightly lower than industry average for items of comparable quality. Custom framing is a high margin business so Flora can afford to keep prices slightly lower than the competition without compromising quality or losing unnecessary profits. Custom framing is Flora's core business so it will be important to maintain competitive advantage in this area.

Prices for ready-made frames, mats, glass and self-service framing materials will be virtually the same as the competition. Generally there is an industry standard for pricing these items. Although significantly lower than the prices for customized frames, the prices for standard size and ready-made frames will be comparable, to slightly higher than, average prices set by mass merchandisers for similar items. The purpose will be to maintain the quality image of the business. Prices for consignment items will be set by the sellers, though Flora will assist with the pricing if requested. Flora will earn ten percent of the purchase price of all consignment items that are sold. For large orders and preferred customers (i.e. business customers and people who make frequent purchases) Flora will negotiate fair, discounted prices.

Quality

Inc. Magazine reports that quality is the most important consideration for customers buying frames. Flora's Frames & Antiques will stand out among the competition as a leader in quality for the following reasons:

- ❑Materials used to construct custom frames will be of high quality.
- ❑Seventeen years of combined framing and art design experience will be applied toward every framing job.
- ❑Only unique and high quality ready-made frames and artworks will be carried in the store.
- ❑Close customer contact will allow Flora to determine not only how her customers define quality, but also whether or not her products are meeting those standards.
- ❑Customers will be encouraged to return, exchange, or modify items with which do not meet quality standards.

Previous experience has shown that customers are impressed by the quality of Flora's work. Customers do return to Flora for additional framing and they do recommend her to others. This history is significant considering that seventy-six percent of all framing business comes from repeat buyers.

Service

Outstanding customer service will give Flora's Frames & Antiques an additional edge in the competitive local framing market. Fast, friendly, professional service as well as customer convenience will be top priority for the business. Flora's sales and framing experience, her dynamic personality, and her artistic talents make it possible for her help customers' find or create exactly what they want. She is expert at assessing customers' needs / preferences and can provide them with information or advice they request.

Free delivery for extra large items (within a fifteen mile radius) and choice of payment options will also contribute to the superior service package. Master Card, Visa and personal checks will be accepted. On average for the framing industry, credit card purchases comprise twenty percent of sales. The goodwill gained from offering this convenience will outweigh the five percent commissions charged by credit card companies.

All purchases will be guaranteed. Customers will be able to purchase items on a trial basis to ensure they are pleased with the effect they generate in their homes. Returns, exchanges, and modifications will be honored within one month of purchase. Longer grace periods will be allowed for preferred customers. Modifications will be made either at no cost (i.e. exchange mat for different color) or for the cost of the new materials (i.e. more expensive frame). Flora will also modify items that are on display for customers who wish to match particular home or office decor. A policy of satisfaction guaranteed is crucial considering that for the custom picture framing industry, customer recommendations are the most important factor in establishing and maintaining a broad customer base.

Advertising

Flora's Frames & Antiques will rely heavily on the recommendations of satisfied customers and decorative window displays as means of attracting customers away from the competition. According to a survey by the PPFA, these are the two avenues through which the majority of framing customers find framing establishments. Past experience has also proven that many customers come on the recommendations of others.

Although word-of-mouth is an effective way of increasing market share, it is also extremely slow. To accelerate the process of expanding the customer base, the business will maintain an advertising budget of $7000 for the first year, which is a full percentage point above the industry average. The bulk of this budget will be spent on listings in the Nanton yellow pages, advertisements in local newspapers, and direct mailings to preferred customers. These are the three most popular media used by picture framers, and they will all reach the target market for Flora's Frames & Antiques. For the second and third years, advertising will be cut back to the industry average of 2.5% of total sales.

LOCATION AND FACILITIES

Flora's Frames & Antiques will be located in the KMC Plaza in Nanton, CT. The plaza is situated on a busy turnpike just minutes from interstates 91 and 84. It borders a large parking lot which is shared by all the businesses therein. The location will be advantageous because:

- ❑The business is both easy to locate and accessible to a number of upscale communities.
- ❑High volumes of traffic driving by the business will increase the chances that new customers will spot the store and stop on their way past.
- ❑Active shoppers who see the listing in the Yellow Pages will recognize the location immediately.
- ❑Plentiful parking and nearby retail establishments draw volumes of people.

Flora's Frames & Antiques signed a three year lease for a 2400 square foot space. The cost is very reasonable at $5/ sq. foot which is well below the industry average of $8-10/ square foot. There is more than enough room to house the equipment, set up displays, and allow customers to browse. Renovations are being done by Andrew Lucas, an experienced architect and builder at an estimated cost of $4300.

The Wall Street Journal ranked Connecticut eleventh out of the fifty US states as a place to start a new business. It ranked this state ninth in the country in terms of availability of resources for assisting small businesses and start-ups. Included among these resources are the following, listed in The Hartford Courant: Small Business Development Centers, Business Outreach Centers, Service Corps of Retired Executives, and The Entrepreneurial Center for Women / Hartford College for Women. Finally, Connecticut was ranked eighth in terms of economic climate and business development capacity.

MANAGEMENT AND PERSONNEL PROFILE

Flora Lucas, Co-Owner and General Manager, will manage all aspects of the business with the support and assistance of her family and Co-Owner John Grande. Flora's background includes an education at the European School of Art, nine years experience in picture framing, and ten years experience in decorative rug design. She has worked for the past seven years in a custom framing shop similar in size and purpose to Flora's Frames & Antiques and has acquired the following relevant experience:

Custom framing

- •Designed and constructed thousands of customized frames
- •Framed unique and hard-to-frame items
- •Created frames and framed-art displays for shop window and display areas
- •Trained assistant in custom framing techniques

MANAGEMENT AND PERSONNEL PROFILE
...continued

Customer service
•Assisted customers with self-service framing
•Assessed customer needs and tastes
•Greeted customers, answered questions, handled complaints

Sales / Operations
•Bought and sold frames and artwork
•Executed sales transactions
•Developed pricing schemes
•Tracked inventories and purchased supplies
•Trained employees in selling techniques

Co-Owner John Grande, a local entrepreneur, will be providing the start-up capital for the business. Mr. Grande became aware of Flora's artistic abilities and professional skills when she framed several pieces of artwork for him while working for her previous employer. Mr. Grande serves as ongoing business advisor to the corporation. He is awell respected business professional; he is the founder and director of a successful charitable organization; and he serves on the boards of several large organizations. In additional to being the primary investor, Mr. Grande is an ongoing source of motivation and inspiration for everyone involved in the business. He also has extensive personal and professional networks which he will tap into to further expand the customer base for the business.

Flora's husband Andrew Lucas will work for the business twenty to thirty hours a week handling general office management, bookkeeping, renovations, vehicle maintenance and occasional deliveries. Andrew is an internationally active businessman with a broad experience base that includes architectural design, import / export brokering, consulting and business negotiating. During busy periods he will assist Flora with operational tasks including purchasing supplies, tracking inventories, and modifying displays. As the business grows, he will utilize his international experience to buy and sell art and antiques abroad. For the first year Andrew will work for $10 per hour. The second and third years he will work for $12 per hour and $14 per hour, respectively. For these two years he will work only twenty hours a week as an assistant will be hired to help Flora during busy periods.

During vacations, summers and some weekends, Andrew and Flora's daughter Anna will return from the University of Connecticut where she is currently pursuing a degree in business, to assist with framing and help with administrative duties. Anna will work for a salary of $6.00 per hour. Within twelve to eighteen months after opening, Flora's Frames & Antiques will hire an Assistant Framer to replace Anna who will be leaving to pursue full-time career in business. The new assistant's duties will include framing, customer assistance, and limited administrative work. The position will require twenty hours per week for the first eighteen to twenty four months and forty hours per week after that. It will carry a salary of $8.50 per hour for the first year (year two of the business) and $10.00 per hour for the second year. This employee's work schedule will be adjusted so that more hours are worked during busy months and less are worked during slow months.

Other family members who will be providing support and assistance include: Flora's son Joseph, an engineering doctoral student in New York who is not available to assist with the business on a regular bases, but is very supportive of the family's efforts; and a close family friend, Karen Coskren, an MBA candidate who has experience consulting to small businesses and has offered advice and assistance, primarily in the areas of marketing and financial management.

The attorney for Flora's Frames & Antiques will be Nan A. Morrison, Esq. He is well established in his field and works at a reasonable rate. He will be advising the business on both legal and insurance matters. Flora is currently in the process of obtaining an accountant through the Community Accounting Aid Service which works closely with Connecticut Small Business Development Centers.

START-UP EXPENSES

Beginning Inventory	$11,740
Supplies	$500
Opening Advertising Expense	$3,000
Accounting/Legal Expenses	$800
Miscellaneous	$327
Rent Deposits	$2,000
Renovations (Leasehold Improvements)	$4,300
Telephone Deposits and Installation Charges	$350
Ulitily Deposits	$600
Capital Equipment	$6,991
Delivery Van (Used)	$5,700
Total Start up Expenses	$36,308

CAPITAL EQUIPMENT LIST

Major Equipment Cost		
Mat Cutter	$900	
Glass Cutter	$900	
Dry Mount Machine	$1,300	
Heat Dry Mount Machine	$500	
Frame Cutter	$900	
Underpinner	$1,600	
Total Major Equipment		$6,100
Minor Equipment		
Filler Cutter	$250	
Misc. Tools (Screwdriver, Etc)	$200	
Catalog W/ Displayer	$50	
2 Paper Support Racks (18" & 36")	$49	
3 Tape Guns @ $25/Each	$75	
Nail Gun	$27	
Screw Gun	$40	
Total Minor Equipment		$691
Other Equipment		
Cash Register	$200	
Total Other Equipment		$200
Total Capital Equipment		$6,991

INVENTORY LIST

Molding	$3800
Ready-Made Frames	$1000
Art/Antique	$3400
Mats	$1000
Backing	$500
Glass	$500
Fasteners (Nails, Screws)	$300
Frame Nails	$140
Glue, Double Tape	$100
Frame Corners	$200
Mat Corners	$100
Art Displays	$300
Wire	$200
Dry Mount Spray	$200
Total	$11,740

BALANCE SHEET AFTER ONE YEAR OF BUSINESS

Assets		
Current Assets		
Cash	$43,353	
Inventory	$11,740	
Supplies	$500	
Rent & utility deposits	$2,950	
Total Current Assets		$58,543
Fixed Assets		
Equipment (including van)	$12,691	
(less depreciation)	$1813	
net	$10,878	
Renovations - start up expenses	$4,300	
(less amortization)	$860	
net	$3,440	
Total Fixed Assets	$12,691	
Total Assets		$71,234
Liabilities		
Current Liabilities		
Notes Payable	$0	
Accrued Taxes Payable	$5,503	
Total Current Liabilities		$5,503
Owner's Capital		
Owner's capital	$45,000	
Retained Earnings	$20,731	
Total owner's capital	$65,731	
Total Liabilities & Owner's Capital		$71,234

BALANCE SHEET AT THE START OF BUSINESS

Assets		
Current Assets		
Cash	8,719	
Inventory	11,740	
Supplies	500	
Prepaid expenses	4,100	
Rent & utility deposits	2,950	
Total Current Assets		28,009
Fixed Assets		
Equipment (including van)	12,691	
less depreciation	0	
net	12,691	
Renovations - start up expenses	4,300	
less amortization	0	
net	4,300	
Total Fixed Assets		16,991
Total Assets		$45,000
Liabilities		
Current Liabilities		
Notes Payable	0	
Total Current Liabilities		0
Owner's Capital		
Owner's Capital	$45,000	
Retained Earnings	0	
Total Owner's Capital		$45,000
Total Liabilities & Owner's Capital		$45,000

BREAK EVEN ANALYSIS

Fixed Costs	
Manager Salaries	25,000
Employee Salaries	14,304
Payroll Taxes	5,503
Accounting/Legal	1,800
Rent	12,000
Utilities	3,600
Telephone	2,200
Insurance	2,600
Property Taxes	1,395
Depreciation	1,813
Amortization	860
Total Fixed Costs	$71,075

Break Even ➔	Fixed Costs / Gross Profit as % of Sales	➔	$71,075 / 59.80%	➔	$118,855 Per Year
Feasibility ➔	Break Even / Business Days/Year	➔	$118,855 / 312	➔	$ 381 Per Day
	Sales/ Day / Average Sale Amount	➔	381 / $65	➔	6 Sales/ Day

Import Boutique

BUSINESS PLAN

BELLISIMO IMPORTS, INC.

891 Henrietta
Jacksonville, MI 48009

May 3, 1993

Bellisimo Imports is a unique place for shoppers seeking imported Mexican handcrafts, including furniture, decorations, and other home accessories. This plan will provide details on how to approach the design of an import boutique.

IMPORT BOUTIQUE BUSINESS PLAN

STATEMENT OF PURPOSE

Bellisimo Imports, Inc. seeks loans totalling $75,000. The proceeds from this loan will be used to purchase equipment and inventory, obtain store space in Jacksonville, Michigan, perform necessary renovations and improvements, and maintain adequate working capital cash reserves needed to open a Mexican Import retail store. The owner and operator of Bellisimo Imports, Inc., Diane Smith, has pledged as collateral $90,000 of assets in the form of personal stocks, bonds and savings.

DESCRIPTION OF THE BUSINESS

Bellisimo Imports, Inc., is a furniture and accessory store specializing in selling unique Mexican Imports to Jacksonville- area retail customers. At the onset, 100 percent of the store's sales will be retail. Bellisimo Imports, Inc. plans to pursue the interior design community working on a cost plus basis to specifiers in the future. Although margins are lower selling to the design trade, profits are higher due to lower personnel costs and faster inventory turnover.

Bellisimo Imports, Inc., plans to open for business during July, 1993. The store will be open Monday, Tuesday, Wednesday, and Saturday from 10:00 a.m. to 6:00 p.m. and Thursday and Friday from 10:00 a.m. to 8:00 p.m. and occasional Sundays during special events in downtown Jacksonville.

The retail demand for home furnishings and accessories is seasonal and business in Jacksonville fluctuates according to the weather. I feel that Bellisimo Imports, Inc. would atttract business during seasonally slow months due to the uniqueness of the products and competitive pricing. There is no direct competition in the area. I feel that Bellisimo will offer products that will be well-received by the market.

DESCRIPTION OF THE MARKET

Bellisimo Imports, Inc., will provide imported Mexican products not yet available from a single source in the metro area. Our goal is to sell interesting furniture and accessories through a knowledgeable and professional sales staff. Our inviting atmosphere will make customers want to return to the store.

Customers will be attracted by:

- ❑ Our convenient downtown location where ample parking is available.
- ❑ A local newspaper and magazine campaign.
- ❑ Word of mouth advertising from local designers and past customers.

DESCRIPTION OF LOCATION

Bellisimo Imports, Inc., intends to lease 800 square feet of retail space in a two story, brick building located at 327 Maplewood Ave., in Jacksonville, Michigan. The monthly rental cost of this leased space will be $1,400. Included in the lease is approximately 500 square feet of furnished office and storage space along with two bathrooms in the basement. The space adjacent to Bellisimo has been occupied for six years by All the Comforts of Home, a reputable home furnishing store. Bellisimo intends to perform minor leasehold improvements, such the installation of pine board flooring, a sales counter, and window signage. These leasehold improvements are currently being negotiated into the lease.

DESCRIPTION OF THE COMPETITION

Americana Antiques A creative retail store specializing in one-of-a-kind antique furnishings. It's showroom is inviting and similar in size to Bellisimo Imports, Inc. It is located on Chicago Ave. in the art gallery district of Jacksonville.

Exclamations A large franchise furniture showroom specializing in upholstered furniture located downtown. Exclamations is well-financed and uses an extensive advertizing campaign. The Exclamations shopper is primarily looking for larger household items that have to be custom ordered. However, it offers a large array of mass produced accessories for sale from it's retail floor.

Arte Latino Americana Located in downtown Birch City, Arte Latino Americana specializes in Latin American handcrafts. The store has been in business several years and it's staff is friendly and knowledgeable. There will be some duplication of items between our stores, but Arte Latino Americana only carries smaller ticket items.

There are several stores that attract shoppers to the downtown area for home furnishings. All of them, however, specialize in European and American antiques.

DESCRIPTION OF MANAGEMENT

Diane Smith was born in Jacksonville, Michigan and has lived in the area all of her life, with the exception of her college years. While studying for a degree in Interior Design she had the opportunity to study abroad on two different occasions and has traveled extensively throughout Europe and Mexico. Since graduating from Michigan State University in 1988, she successfully utilized her interior design and selling skills as an account executive/design consultant in both residential and commercial furniture sales. She currently lives in Jacksonville, Michigan and is unmarried.

Ms. Smith is young and energetic. She believes that her determination along with product knowledge and selling skills will help make Bellisimo a success. Ms. Smith knows several designers in the area and is an active member of the community. Ms. Smith will be responsible for all major operating duties of the store.

Ms. Smith's salary will be $27,000 during the first year of the store's operations to enable the business to pay off start-up costs. She currently rents a two bedroom flat with a roommate and has the opportunity to move into her parents' home should her personal expenditures become overly burdensome. During the store's second year of operation, Ms. Smith will be paid a salary of $30,000, with any profits returned to the business.

In order to augment her skills, Ms. Smith has enlisted the assistance of Shawn Doran (J.D., C.P.A.), Paul Timmons of Timmons, Clancy (J.D.), and Dr. T.A. Armstrong to help in making business decisions.

DESCRIPTION OF PERSONNEL

Bellisimo Imports, Inc., will hire one part-time employee in approximately five months to work with retail customers and to re-stock the showroom. He or she will be paid $6.50/hr. to start for evening and weekend hours; no fringe benefits or overtime are anticipated. During the second year of the store's operations, one full-time employee will be hired on a salary plus commission basis.

APPLICATON AND ANTICIPATED EFFECT OF BUSINESS LOAN

The $75,000 loan will be used as follows:

Location

Inventory	$40,000
Deposit on Maplewood store	$2,800
Interior Renovations	$2,820

Equipment

Computer	$1,500
Phone/Fax	$450
Sales/Display Counter	$ 800
Window Signage	$120
Graphics Package, Paper Produucts	$600
Phone Install/Security Deposit	$310
Utility hook up	$20
Miscellaneous	$350
Working Capital	$18,000
Cash Reserves	$7,230
Total	$75,000

The inventory will be purchased initially by the truckload to lower the cost of importing and to maintain a well-stocked showroom.

The renovations will involve: installation of natural pine flooring in the retail showroom and application of a faux paint finish to the walls and ceiling to provide a Mexican ambience to the store.

The equipment to be purchased will enable the store to operate efficiently on a daily basis.

The working capital will enable Bellisimo Imports, Inc. to meet current expenses, offset negative cash flows in the beginning (as shown in the Income Projection sheet), and to insure growth of the business.

Royal Crest Bank will hold the reserve line of credit that will be used to take advantage of special opportunities and to meet emergency needs.

SUMMARY

Bellisimo Imports, Inc. is a retail store in Jacksonville, Michigan specializing in furniture and accessories made in Mexico. Diane Smith, the owner and operator, will borrow $75,000 to lease space at 327 Maplewood Ave., perform necessary renovations and improvements to the space, maintain a cash reserve, and provide adequate working capital for anticipated expansion of the business. This amouunt will be sufficient to Bellisimo throughout the start-up phase so that the business can operate on a professional and successful level.

VALUE OF COLLATERAL

AT&T	$4,500
Ameritech	$2,240
Bell Atlantic	$2,079
Bell South	$1,680
Nynex	$1,691
Pactel	$1,951
Southwest Bell	$2,240
U.S. West	$1,653
Ford Motor Company	$1,036
Bond Fund	$8,449
Cash Management	$154
Carolina Telephone	$5,000
Southern Company	$43,049
Prudential Growth Fund	$12,509
Standard Federal and other Savings Accounts	$93
	$1,300
	$1,200
Total	$90,824

Inn/Resort

BUSINESS PLAN

THE LIGHTHOUSE INN

333 Pine Rd.
Lakeland, FL 22255

May 19, 1993

The Lighthouse Inn is a resort with a variety of recreational facilities. The Inn seeks to provide lodging for both families and business travelers. This plan describes the ways the owners will expand advertising, offer a variety of pricing packages, promote recreational activities, and renovate rooms to attract more guests.

- TYPE OF BUSINESS, PRODUCT, AND SERVICE
- HISTORY
- LOCATION AND SIZE
- PERSONNEL
- ECONOMICS AND ACCOUNTING
- INVENTORY, SUPPLIES, SUPPLIERS, AND EQUIPMENT
- LEGAL ISSUES
- FUTURE PLANS
- MARKET ANALYSIS
- CUSTOMERS
- ENVIRONMENT
- COMPETITION
- COMPETITIVE ADVANTAGES AND DISADVANTAGES
- PROJECTIONS
- MARKET STRATEGY: SALES AND PROMOTIONS
- PERSONAL QUALIFICATIONS AND MANAGEMENT POLICY

INN/RESORT BUSINESS PLAN

TYPE OF BUSINESS, PRODUCT, AND SERVICE

The Lighthouse Inn is a resort offering lodging for vacations, weekends, and over-night trips. There are ten units each furnished with a kitchenette, refrigerator, stove, dishes, a color television, and an air-conditioner. Guests have access to a private beach, a swimming pool, and boat docks. The eighteen docks are reserved for our clients who wish to leave their boat by the week or month. We also have small fishing boats, ski boats, and Waverunners (jet skis) available for rent. There is a store, located on the premises, offering some personal items as well as souvenirs and small gifts.

We are a retail service business providing a place of lodging and relaxation for both the general public and business travelers. Our goal is to provide the best service, cleanliness, and enjoyable atmosphere for all of our clients.

Our most prominent advertising is a highway sign depicting a clean and inviting look. We also advertise in the yellow pages, a local newspaper, the Lake County Visitor Information Center, brochures sent to several travel agents, and through word of mouth. We plan to expand our advertising to include the AAA tour book, a travel magazine entitled Sunset, and large circulation newspapers such as the Lakeland Bee and the Tampa Chronicle.

Our current rates are $45 to $85 per night. There is also a standard fee of $10 for each additional adult and $5 for each additional child aged 3-15 years old. These fees will be assessed at check-in. A special promotion will be running from May 1 through October 15 which will lower the base rates to $37.50 and $65, with only a $5 charge per night for each additional adult. All children, under the age of 15, can stay for free.

HISTORY

The business was under prior ownership. It was run by a family who used 30% of the units for personal use. This arrangement lasted for seven years. All requests for the previous history of sales have been denied. We obtained ownership as of November 2, 1993 with the objective of creating a family oriented operation by using the maximum capacity of the business to its fullest potential.

The previous owners chose to have an off-site manager run the business. At this stage, I do not feel that this type of situation would best suit the development of the inn's potential. Therefore, I intend to live on the premises in order to solely operate the business 24 hours a day, year round.

LOCATION AND SIZE

The Lighthouse Inn is located at 333 Pine Road, Lakeland, FL 22255. This area is know for its lakes and national park sites. It is approximately one and one half hours from the Tampa Bay area.

The sizes of buildings are as follows: Units 1, 2, and 3 are each 360 square feet, Units 4, 5, and 6 are each 267 square feet, Units 7, 8, and 9 are each 352 square feet, and Unit 10 is 485 square feet. There is a total of 3,609 square feet in the rental units. There is also a total of 562 square feet of storage area, 186 square feet of office/store space, a laundry area of 420 square feet, and living quarters containing 908 square feet. The grand total for all buildings, storage, and living quarters is 5,685 square feet. The business is located on four lots each measuring 50 x 128 feet for a total of 25,600 square feet.

We are currently refurbishing the interiors and exteriors of each building. This includes the replacement or addition of linens, bedding, drapes, wallpaper, carpeting/rugs, paint, and new landscaping in front of all parking spaces and recreational areas.

The business is conveniently located at Exit 4 off of Highway 150. A well-marked driveway leads into a parking lot that can accommodate 16 vehicles. There is a storage area at the south end of Units 7, 8, 9, and 10 that can accommodate six boat trailers. Additional points of access include: our beach area between the main building and residence/office building; the marina area and boat docks located to the north between the residence/office building and Unit 7; and the lake which is accessed using our marina area and boat docks. There is a restaurant located to the south approximately 150 feet from the residence/office building.

PERSONNEL

At the present time, the only employees are my wife and myself. If additional help is needed, employees would be sought on a contractual basis or placement would be found through the Bay Area Employment Office.

ECONOMICS AND ACCOUNTING

The business generates its income through the rental of housing units, fishing boats, Jet skis, and the sale of various sundries and souvenirs to the general public. I have set the prices after surveying the competition and figuring the cost of miscellaneous items from our suppliers based on a fair mark-up.

INVENTORY, SUPPLIES, SUPPLIERS, AND EQUIPMENT

Our inventory consists of T-shirts, hats, laundry soap, bleach, fabric softener, sheets, towels, wash cloths, blankets, hand soap, toilet paper, dish soap, and various sundries (tooth paste, charcoal, razors, etc.).

The Inn's equipment would consist of one ski boat in very good condition, two fishing boats also in good condition, one sail boat in fair condition, and two new Waverunners (jet skis that seat two people). Total value of approximately $13,500 based on the Waverunner receipts and the list prices on boats of comparable size and type.

LEGAL ISSUES

This is a sole proprietorship in my name only, thus there is no need to file a fictitious name.

I have obtained the Transient Occupancy Registration Certificate, No. 610 from the Bay Area Better Business Bureau and a Sellers Permit, No. SR JHE 27 832235 from the State Board of Equalization.

All required business insurance has been obtained from McGregor Business Insurance Company, 890 Trenton, Tampa, FL 22435. For a complete description of coverage or copies of the policies, please contact the main office.

FUTURE PLANS

We would like to expand our advertising, especially in St. Petersburg, East Bay, Clearwater, and the area south of Tampa Bay. These areas constitute approximately 85% to 90% of our current clientele.

We plan to continue the complete refurbishing and upgrading of all rooms, docking facilities, and recreation areas (new decks, lawn, lounging chairs, and barbecues). We also plan to expand the office and sales area.

A game room and lounging area is scheduled to be built during the first year of operation. This would give guests a place to relax and provide a play area for the children. The facility could also be used for such activities as the Thanksgiving Dinner, and special events such as Christmas, New Year's Eve, Super Bowl parties, etc.

We are painting all buildings with a new paint scheme. At present, the project is approximately 65% complete. The entrance to the business is scheduled for new paving by Dura-Pave.

Our schedule is to increase business by at least 20% next year. We will be offering specials and contacting all previous guests through our computerized directory. The future increases will continue by 5% to 10% each year during the summer season, with an expected occupancy rate of 75% to 85%. During the off-season, a 25% to 35% occupancy rate will be achieved. This will be accomplished by clean facilities and courteous service, which have already been established. The general response to these services has been very favorable. The main service goal is to provide a homey and friendly atmosphere.

Our current sales of souvenirs and the rental of boats and sporting equipment is approximately 250% over expectations. We will be increasing inventory of sundries, souvenirs, and additional sporting equipment.

MARKET ANALYSIS

A market analysis for the Lighthouse Inn has been prepared by Goodman Consultants, 4823 Ryan Drive, Suite 3A, Tampa, FL 22435. It explores several areas which have the potential to impact finances. The five market categories are as follows: customers, environment, competition, competitive advantages and disadvantages, and projections. This analysis is available upon request.

CUSTOMERS

Our market consists of families, business travelers, and tourists. We extend to our customers an old fashioned code of hospitality and service. We provide a wholesome environment, clean rooms, and friendly and polite hosts. We also provide various types of lake recreation such as fishing, swimming, waterskiing, jet skiing, and sailing.

The average customers would be middle-class couples and families, with an annual income of $20,000 to $50,000. These people will spend between $250 and $1,500 per year for getaway weekends and vacations.

We are targeting Lakeland, St. Petersburg, areas south of Fort Meade, and all of the bay area from Temple to Bradenton for a total of approximately 1 million customers.

ENVIRONMENT

The weather in the winter and extended periods of rain are factors that effect business. Winter temperatures will tend to diminish swimming and water sports, but should not have much effect on fishing. The summer months are usually better because most families and groups plan their vacations at this time. This is due to warmer weather and children being out of school.

Other things that can have a negative impact are the business not possessing a clean and inviting look, extreme weather, including fires or other natural disasters, and low level or poor quality lake water.

COMPETITION

Our competition consists primarily of other resorts in our immediate area and those located along Highway 150 that face the water. These establishments draw a large amount of the business in the area, especially during the summer months. Our immediate competitors are Sand Castles, located downtown; Ocean Cove, a few hundred yards down the road from the Lighthouse Inn; The Blue Fish Motel, approximately one-half mile to the south of the Lighthouse; and Barry King's Resort, one-quarter mile to the west of the Lighthouse.

Sand Castles has been in business for three to four years and benefits from being the first or last lodging that the customer will see when traveling through Lakeland. Ocean Cove has new owners who are quickly renovating to build a reputation as an accommodating resort offering all the amenities of a four star hotel. The Blue Fish Motel has been in business for several years and enjoys a large clientele, with an established reputation among fisherman. Barry King's Resort has also been in operation for quite some time and attracts the family vacationers. The other resorts in the area draw business from small segments of society and, as a result, offer only fragmented competition.

Sand Castles, 100 Main St., Lakeland, FL, is located in the downtown area. The Inn offers large sleeping rooms and rooms with kitchens. This appeals to people who want to stay in a more populated area or those who wish to have use of a kitchen.

COMPETITION...*continued*

Ocean Cove, 250 Sea Coast Dr., Lakeland, FL, offers seven rooms, six with kitchens and one sleeping room. There are only two units facing the water, but Ocean Cove provides large grass areas for lounging or barbecuing. There are limited dock facilities, a small boat launch, a small beach area, and a fishing pier. Ocean Cove has two Waverunners and two fishing boats available for guest rental.

The Blue Fish Motel, 725 E. Turtle Rd., Lakeland, FL, has approximately fifteen rooms, several with kitchen facilities. Only one room has a lake view. The Blue Fish has limited boat docking, with no beach area. The attraction of the resort is a nice fishing pier. The owners have supplied one Waverunner and one Jet Ski for rental.

Barry King's Resort, 464 East Wharf, Lakeland, FL, offers rooms with kitchens, barbecue areas, a nice boat launch, boat docking, boat fuel on the lake, and some rentals.

Most of the resorts in the area do not appear to have any aggressive promotional or advertising methods. Many do not even have advertisements in the yellow pages, other than their regular listings. They appear to rely on the Information Center, the Chamber of Commerce, word-of-mouth, and the passerby.

One of the main services offered in this area is recreation. This is one of the key areas to be exploited if we are to gain a competitive edge over the other facilities.

COMPETITIVE ADVANTAGES AND DISADVANTAGES

We try to maintain a friendly, helpful attitude in every thing that we do. Our rooms are clean and comfortable, with full service kitchens. Seven of our ten units overlook the water, with balconies for relaxation and viewing the lake. We have nineteen boat slips and one hundred feet of clear beach for swimming and other water sport recreation. We have areas for barbecuing and picnics, a gazebo with a view of the lake, and fishing from our many docks.

PROJECTIONS

We feel that there will be a 20% increase over present business next summer. The coming months are difficult to predict because the business was closed last winter due to a fire. However, the feeling is that sales should continue to increase through the winter months. Customers are supporting us by renting rooms for fishing and special events. We currently have deposits on several rooms for the first two weeks in October, and we have deposits for 60% of our rooms for the Thanksgiving week promotion. We are working on other special promotions for Christmas, New Year's Eve, and Valentine's Day.

MARKET STRATEGY: SALES AND PROMOTIONS

I feel that the key to obtaining the edge on our competitors, in the quest for new customers as well as retaining our present clientele, will be to offer the very best in friendly, clean, and prompt service. We are also offering specials, including group discounts and unit packages. A group discount will require a reservation for several rooms and an immediate deposit. The unit packages will be available during holiday seasons or popular vacation periods. An example of a unit package is the Thanksgiving Week Special, where we will be offering an open check-in time on the Wednesday before Thanksgiving, staying through to Sunday, and invite each of the guests to have Thanksgiving dinner with us. Additional unit promotions will be held on the Fourth of July, Valentine's Day, and for the Super Bowl.

We have already contracted with two radio stations for promotions. One promotion is starting in October to attract the winter customers in the northern part of the state. This advertisement will reach approximately 300,000 homes. It will emphasize the warmer climate which makes this area ideal for fishing and relaxation. The other station, located in Tampa with a listener potential of 2,500,000, has scheduled a promotional advertisement in the spring. These promotions will be running simultaneously with a mass mailing project to all of our past and present customers as well as my prior business clients.

Future promotions will directly target dissatisfied customers who previously spent their vacations at Lake Minnette, where the water levels are still extremely low, winter vacationers in Orlando and the Keys, and college students looking for spring break vacation spots. We will be offering special discounts with these promotions.

Other areas that we have explored for promotional opportunities, include the expansion of our yellow page advertisements, the addition of a toll-free number that covers all of Florida, maintaining a working relationship with Bay Area Visitor Information Center, which promotes the lake for the good of the whole community, and the Chamber of Commerce.

PERSONAL QUALIFICATIONS AND MANAGEMENT POLICY

The reasons that I chose this type of business are the enjoyment of being my own boss and having control over the management of the establishment. I enjoy working with the general public and prefer working in a smaller community.

I have worked in fields that service the general public for the past 24 years. My educational background includes three years of college course work in Business Management, as well as a degree from the Life Underwriter Training Council.

I intend to live on the premises year round to operate, promote, and enhance the business. The Lighthouse Inn will be my sole source of income. In the future, I foresee hiring additional help to increase my free time for other endeavors, but I will always have the final word on how the business will be run.

Ladder Company

BUSINESS PLAN

JACK'S LADDER INC.

1212 Valley Rd.
Pemberton, CA 45831

December, 13, 1991

Jack's Ladder is a maker of aluminum and fiberglass ladders and step stools. The company supplies specialty products for niche markets, such as orchards. The following plan explains the need for an expansion and describes ways to help Jack's retail distributors increase their sales.

LADDER COMPANY BUSINESS PLAN

INFORMATION ON THE BUSINESS

Owner--A California Corporation with Two Stockholders

Type of Business and Product

Jack's Ladder Inc. is a manufacturing business in California that makes aluminum and fiberglass ladders and stepstools. The goal of Jack's is to manufacture and sell throughout the United States high quality specialty ladders to the extent that, in the specialty market, the name Jack's becomes synonymous with quality.

Products currently produced are: aluminum tripod orchard ladders, aluminum "straight" orchard ladders, aluminum and fiberglass double sided stepladders for the construction industry, aluminum and fiberglass posting ladders for the billboard advertising industry, and various aluminum stepstools and maintenance stands for the automotive and truck detailing and maintenance industry. Jack's also manufactures custom ladders.

Ladders are currently sold primarily to retailers, who in turn sell them to the consumer/user. Some agricultural ladders are sold direct from the factory in areas that are not near dealers. A few stepstools are sold to a wholesaler, who sells to retailers, who sell to consumers. Most orders come over the phone directly; others come by facsimile.

Jack's delivers agricultural ladders wherever it is economical to do so. Most large ladders are shipped via common carrier truck line, while most step stools are shipped via UPS. Local customers pick their ladders up at the manufacturing plant.

Most of the ladders manufactured at Jack's are industrial quality (type 1) or extra heavy duty industrial (type 1A) ladders, designed for constant industrial or agricultural use. The material is high quality, and the quality of workmanship is medium to high. The average price of most of the products is comparable to similar type ladders on the market.

History

In the early 1960's, John Smith, a local pear grower and building contractor, didn't like the aluminum orchard ladders that were available. He decided to use his mechanical engineering background and his knowledge of aircraft assembly to make his own brand of ladders. He set up his first orchard ladder jig tables in his garage, and, with the help of seasonal employees, began making ladders. In 1966, he incorporated his business as John Smith's Ladders Incorporated, set up a small shop on the corner of his pear orchard, and built ladders there. Jack Dunn, another local pear farmer, joined the firm, bought some stock, and began handling the sales end of the business, taking the orchard ladder to various orchard equipment shows in California. Sales increased throughout California, Oregon, and Washington. In 1974, Henry Dunn was hired to set up a small manufacturing division in Washington state.

Upon John Smith's death in 1977, Jack and Henry Dunn took over all daily operations. In 1984, they purchased all of the stock in John Smith's Ladders Incorporated and changed the name to Jack's Ladders Inc.

Jack's Ladders Inc. has a good reputation in the agricultural community across the United States. It is known for making a good, heavy duty aluminum orchard ladder that will last. It is also well thought of locally for its aluminum industrial stepladder, which is used by many building contractors. Jack's Ladders Inc.'s general image is one of quality, and although the prices are higher than those of other ladders sold in stores, the feeling, generally, is that the extra price is worth paying.

The company has four salaried employees, including two part-time bookkeepers. Its hourly work force varies seasonally between three and eight employees, with the largest number needed during the summer. In 1991, the sales volume was about $650,000, down about 10% from 1990, with a profit of about $40,000.

One factor that has affected the firm's development is the product liability lawsuit situation. Since the mid 1970's, the company has been named in eight suits. Although Jack's has never lost a case in court, it has paid an estimated $400,000 in product liability insurance premiums, legal fees, and settlements.

Office and Plant

Jack's Ladders Inc. is located at 1212 Valley Rd., 2 miles west of Orrville. It is situated at the corner of a pear orchard, and has cattle pasture land to the south and to the east. The building and about three acres of land is leased from Barb Smith, widow of John Smith. The lease is for five years and expires on August 31, 1994. It is a square corrugated metal building of about 3600 square feet, with a concrete slab floor. There are two small wood frame offices inside. An old farm equipment shed just west of the main building is used to store a small amount of aluminum and some shipping cartons. Besides another small amount of raw material which is stored inside the main building, all other raw material and finished product is stored outside, to the north of the main building.

There is parking for employees along Valley Road outside the fenced raw material storage area. Customers must park in front of the building. There is not much room for customer parking, but most of the business is phone ordered. Freight trucks, inbound and out, must park on Valley Rd., as there is no room inside the fenced area for trucks to turn around, or to maneuver forklifts and raw material.

Business hours are from 8:00 a.m. to 5:00 p.m. Monday through Friday. Most hourly employees work from 7:00 to 3:30 in the winter, and 6:00 to 2:30 in the summer. Only one shift is worked.

Personnel

Jack's Ladders Inc. currently employs four salaried and four hourly people. The salaried personnel are the owners, who are the managers, and the owners' wives, who are the bookkeepers. The hourly employees are semi-skilled, and have been trained on the job. All but one of the hourly employees are Hispanic. Employees have, for the most part, been found by word of mouth through current employees. During the spring/summer season, three or four more employees are usually hired, sometimes including an occasional high school student. These employees are usually laid off, due to lack of work, beginning in September. One or two of these seasonal employees are sometimes kept until November or December, depending upon the amount of work available.

Current employees have been with Jack's for or three or four years. Most are relatively well trained, friendly and cooperative, although there are reports of increased amounts of goofing-off when management is not present. All hourly employees are at the maximum wage level, and are becoming dissatisfied with that fact. Motivation other than wage is needed to keep them interested. There is currently no lead man, foreman, or other type of middle management. This type of position will become necessary in the near future as management spends more time traveling, selling, and handling administrative tasks.

Economic/Accounting

Jack's Ladders Inc. makes its money primarily by selling aluminum and fiberglass ladders and stepstools. It also repairs aluminum orchard ladders, sells aluminum ladder parts to the two other plants that now manufacture Jack's ladders, and receives a royalty from third plant that manufactures and sells Jack's ladders under its own corporation.

Prices are determined by calculating material and labor for each product, marking it up a certain percentage, then comparing that to competition and modifying the price accordingly.

All financial records are kept in one of the offices at the manufacturing plant. The day to day bookkeeping is done by the two part-time staff hired for that purpose. The accounting books are sent quarterly to a CPA who then prepares a balance sheet and some accompanying reports and support schedules. Payroll is done by the staff bookkeepers. Tax returns are prepared by the CPA who prepared quarterly reports.

Inventory, Supplies, and Equipment

The company uses, and keeps an inventory of, various extruded aluminum shapes needed for its variety of ladders, along with fiberglass side rails for its fiberglass ladders. It also uses and inventories all the rivets, bolts, and other various fasteners used to assemble ladders. A finished product inventory is kept also, the size of which depends upon the time of year and anticipated demand. An attempt is made to keep just a large enough inventory to meet expected immediate demand in the most frequently sold ladders. Sales literature, business cards, copier paper, and various office supplies are also kept.

It has been relatively easy to obtain supplies. Prices of aluminum have fluctuated greatly since it became a commodity a few years ago. Jack's maintains the prices of its products based upon the upper end of the price fluctuation range, while watching competition for any price drops.

Most equipment used by the company is in fair to good condition. However, there are a few items which need work in the near future, including the Ruvo chop saw, the ladder jig table, and the air delivery system.

Legal

Jack's Ladders Inc. is a California corporation, formed in 1978. It has a Federal ID number, a state ID number, and a state resale permit and number. It is located in an area that is zoned for agriculture, but is grandfathered into the present facility.

The company carries the required workman's compensation insurance through State Compensation Insurance Fund. It carries insurance on its automobiles through State Farm. Its general liability and products liability insurance is through Allied Insurance Brokers.

Building codes were complied with when the facility was built in the mid-to-late 1960's. Known health codes are complied with, although the code has not been checked recently. The company has partially satisfied OSHA and Cal OSHA regulations, but more work needs to be done in this area. Jack's is also in the process of writing and implementing an Illness and Injury Prevention program, which is required by the state.

The lease on the building and property is a five year lease which expires on August 31, 1994. A subsequent lease has not yet been negotiated. It is a Standard Industrial Lease, printed by the American Industrial Real Estate Association. It requires the company to carry insurance against loss of the premises at replacement value. The lessor is required to supply water to the premises.

There are no trademarks, patents, licenses, or copyrights held by Jack's Ladder Inc.

The company has, as its corporate attorney, Bob Bailey of Smith and Brown to handle questions of a business nature. The company's Product Liability Insurance carrier appoints an attorney for each such case the company is involved in.

Future Plans

Plans for Jack's Ladder Inc. are for controlled expansion, to increase sales by increasing market area for existing products, and to find new products to manufacture and sell. Currently, there are no plans for expansion to levels that would require year round multi-shift manufacturing.

MARKET ANALYSIS

Customers

The market is divided into two segments: agricultural and industrial. Our agricultural customers are primarily retailers across the United States, but concentrated in Northern and Central California, and in the northeastern US. Many, if not most of these retailers are farm supply stores. Our industrial customers currently are retailers in Northern California, with the exception of one catalog sales customer that is nationwide, and a few retailers that are out of state.

Both the agricultural and industrial markets need high quality, durable, safe aluminum and fiberglass ladders. There are many climbing-type accidents caused by people using over-stressed, under-built ladders and stools. Also, a lack of confidence in climbing equipment causes workers to be inefficient and less productive in their jobs. Jack's seeks to sell climbing products that, because of the way they are designed and built, promote safety and confidence in the worker, and thereby reduce accidents and increase productivity.

The agricultural market will need our ladder as long as people want fresh fruit, and as long as there is a labor force to pick it. And because of the increasing awareness and emphasis on safety, high quality ladders will be in demand. The same is true of the industrial specialty ladder market. As long as people need to get off the ground, whether it is 6 feet or more, they will need a safe way to do it. In both markets, some technological advances are bound to reduce market size, but for a company our size, it will still be large enough.

Our average agricultural ladder customer is the semi-successful to successful farmer, who sees a potential for success in farming, and plans for longevity in business. Currently, most customers are in California, although there are a growing number on the East Coast.

Our average current industrial ladder customer is a male mechanic or construction contractor in Northern California who wants a safe, stable product, even if it costs more than what is generally found in hardware stores. The potential market for step stools is nationwide; every auto mechanic shop and auto detailing shop represents a possible sale.

Customers like the quality and detail of the ladders we make. The weight of the material we use is heavier than in other ladders and offers greater durability and safety. The design of the ladders themselves is usually much better than the minimums for OSHA and ANSI specifications. This means the customer has a ladder that can be counted on to provide safety for employees, and which will satisfy insurance and OSHA inspectors. Complaints we get from customers are usually related to price and/or shipping costs, although some of our agricultural customers would like to see steps which provide more traction when wet.

The number of customers in the agricultural market is estimated to be 300 retailers, and 4,000 tree fruit growers. An estimated $2 million will be spent on orchard ladders in 1992. The number of customers in the industrial market is estimated to be 2,000 retailers, and 1 million consumers, with an estimated $20 million spent on our products, or similar products, yearly.

Environment

The extended drought in California, along with the generally poor agricultural economy, will have a negative effect on our agricultural market, at least in the short term. A generally slow economy will also have the same effect on the industrial market. An increase in the amount of workplace safety legislation passed could have a positive effect. However, the legal climate, specifically products liability litigation, is poor as viewed from the ladder manufacturer standpoint. More lawsuits and higher insurance costs will drive prices up on domestic products, possibly causing customers to purchase imported goods.

Competition

Competitors in the agricultural market number about 12 nationwide. These are firms that manufacture orchard ladders. Eight of these are on the West Coast, with four in California. All but two are the same size as Jack's or smaller. The two larger firms manufacture and sell a larger number of other types of ladders than we do. Half these firms are older than Jack's, and half are younger, with the newest coming in only a year ago. Two of these firms are making our ladder, with one of them paying a royalty for its sales.

Brown Ladder in Billings, Montana offers an inferior product at a lower price. They probably sell about 2500 to 3000 orchard ladders per year. They like to sell in truckload quantities, and have been willing to haul from Montana to New Mexico at no cost. The low cost is appealing to growers feeling the economic pinch. Brown likes to sell direct, although they have some retailers representing them. Their direct sales/retail sales strategy has put them at odds, at times, with the retailers. They sometimes exhibit at farm shows.

Overhead Ladders, although they manufacture the Jack's ladder, would have to be listed as a competitor because Jack's Ladder Inc. receives no income from the ladders they sell. They are located in Oregon, and sell in that state and in Michigan and states to the east. The ladders, even though they are Jack's, are priced lower, primarily because of a lower overhead, and the fact that it is not the principle's only source of income. They are able to be quite competitive not only because of price, but because they are in a more favorable freight location, and can ship ladders to the East less expensively. They attend a few farm shows, and advertise in a trade journal. They sell an estimated 2500 to 3000 ladders per year.

Tall Tree Ladders, in Washington state, makes a good quality orchard ladder which is priced somewhat lower than the Jack's. They sell an estimated 3500 to 5000 ladders per year in California, Oregon, Washington, and the East. Because they do not have the extensive retailer network in California that Jack's does, they sell a number of ladders directly to the consumer, at a significantly lower price. They claim to have interchangeable parts with their ladders built 30

Competition...*continued*

years ago. They attend nearly all farm shows Jack's attends, and advertise in the same trade journals. They are also on a more favorable freight route, both into California, and to the Eastern U.S.

Reach Ladder, who makes Jack's ladders, is listed as a competitor only because they sell into the same areas as we do. While we are paid a royalty for these sales, it reduces the number of ladders sold directly. They are also located in California, and have the advantage of being in the center of the large citrus industry in California. Freight is an advantage there, because their published FOB prices are the same as ours. They also have a freight advantage to the south and east. They advertise sparingly in a trade journal, and attend one agricultural show, sharing a booth with Jack's. Their advantage is their proximity to their market.

Hanson Ladder, located in Northern California, makes an inferior ladder which is higher priced than Jack's. Not much is known about their sales volume in the agricultural market, but it is believed that they sell some in Southern California. They are a firm about as old as Jack's and manufacture other types of ladders also. They advertise in the same trade journal as does Jack's, and also in the Thomas Register. They have a freight advantage to the East Coast, which could overcome some of the ladder price differential.

Sampson Ladder Co. of California makes a somewhat inferior ladder which is much higher priced than the Jack's. It makes other types of ladders which are also high priced. They are about as old as Jack's. Their agricultural ladder sales volume is unknown, but they sell some to the government, and some to landscape people. They have not been seen by Jack's at any equipment shows. However, they do advertise in the Thomas Register and have a freight advantage when shipping to the East Coast, as well as when exporting.

Best Products of California is a new ladder company which copied some of the parts of the Jack's ladder. It's product would probably be rated as a medium-to-good ladder, with listed prices about the same as a Jack's ladder, although they have been known to sell directly to the consumer at lower-than-list prices, with no delivery charge. Their volume this year is estimated to be about 1,500 ladders, but they are growing and aggressive. They also manufacture fruit picking bags, and the two go together well. Their reputation in the bag industry has been that of a cutthroat, doing anything to outsell the competition. However, the ownership changed last year, and the new ownership's strategy is still in question. They advertise in a few trade journals, and attend one of the same ag shows as Jack's. Competition from them is expected to be fierce, especially in Southern California, but probably on the East Coast as well.

Skyreach Ladder Inc. of California used to be located in Washington state, but was purchased two years ago by Cloud Nine Ladders of Sunnyvale. In Washington, Skyreach made medium quality orchard ladders with medium prices. When Cloud Nine bought them, they immediately obtained national distribution because of the existing sales network of Cloud Nine Ladder. Their advantage is price and distribution. Their disadvantage is quality of material and workmanship, which will become even worse since the Cloud Nine deal. Cloud

Nine sells largely in the homeowner's market. Sales volume is unknown, but could be 2,000 to 4,000 ladders per year.

There are three or four ladder manufacturers on the East Coast which make agricultural ladders, only one of which is aluminum. It is Meany Ladder in Vermont. It is an overpriced, inferior ladder sold in the New England states through a well known farm supply catalog. Nothing is known of their volume or their marketing strategy. The other manufacturers are making wooden orchard ladders, and must be supplying the East Coast with ladders. They are probably selling a total of 2000 to 4000 ladders per year total. They have freight advantages from being located in New England, and wooden ladder prices have been historically lower than aluminum. However, the number of growers using wood ladders is declining, especially as wood becomes scarce and prices become more equitable. Some of these companies are old companies and have a loyal following among farmers.

In the industrial ladder market, there are large companies making industrial stepladders, both in aluminum and fiberglass. They have both distribution and price advantages over Jack's. And while they do not specialize in double-sided, type 1A ladders, as Jack's does, they do make that ladder, and many do a good job of it. Small stepstools are made by a number of companies also, but, again, they do not specialize in them. In most cases, their prices are higher than Jack's, but they have better distribution. A few of these companies have warehouses in different locations across the United States. No advertising has been seen on any of these, except in the Thomas Register, and then not specifically related to step stools.

In the next year, an estimated 15,000 agricultural ladders and 2 million industrial type ladders will be provided by all the competition.

Competitive Advantages and Disadvantages

Jack's Ladder Inc. meets market needs by supplying high quality, safe climbing products. Most of the agricultural competition is inferior. In this market, demand is being met by supply, making competition high. Our emphasis, then, is on quality and reliability. In the industrial ladder market, there is much competition, but there appears to be room for a small company which can specialize. Our disadvantage appears to be price and distribution among the prominent orchard ladder and industrial ladder manufacturers. Our advantage is that we make a superior product. We also provide repair parts and advice. In the stepstool market, it appears that there is not much emphasis on advertising or pushing this product among our competitors. As we have a good product here, it appears we can compete for awhile. However, because the product is so easy to build, competition could arise in a short time and dilute the market.

Projections

It is expected that, in the short term, the number of agricultural ladders sold will remain the same or decline some, as will the number of agricultural ladder customers. In the long term, the number of both will remain about the same, depending upon how many new manufacturers get into the act. In the industrial market, it is projected that the number of customers, and therefore sales, will increase 25% to 50%, tempered by the economy.

MARKET STRATEGY

Sales Strategy

In the agricultural ladder market, the strategy will be to educate existing retailers and their sales forces as to what the advantages of Jack's ladders are. Also, we will continue advertising nationwide, but will emphasize follow-up as the advertisements go to consumers, asking for names of potential retailers in various areas, thereby increasing the number of dealers. Efforts will be made to locate and establish retailers in areas not currently covered, with emphasis on personal contact by phone. Participation in farm equipment shows will emphasize the advantages of our ladder over the others, with an emphasis on service of already owned products.

In the industrial ladder market, the strategy will be to increase our area of distribution by increasing the number of retailers. Getting to them first will be our edge. In this, we will have to demonstrate the value of the product and provide quick service in shipping.

Promotion Strategy

In the agricultural market, word-of-mouth at the agricultural equipment shows, along with nationwide trade magazine advertising with intensive follow-up, will be the strategy.

In the industrial market, locating new retailers by current customer inquiries, and by getting specific customer lists, will be followed by phone contacts, and then by direct mail. In the direct mail, testimonials by others in the same business will be sought and used. In the direct mail, we will emphasize our longevity, our good service, our friendliness, and the quality of the product. We want to project knowledge, quality, and ability to deliver. We already have an out-of-state toll-free number. We will seriously consider the advantages of an in-state one also.

Management

I am in this business because it allows me the freedom to be my own boss while using my engineering background to fill a need to make safe, high quality ladders. Personal freedom is a premium because of the time I want to spend with my family at school activities and at home. However, I have been and plan to continue to be a full-time manager of the business. I have prepared a resume and personal financial statement, both of which are available upon request.

FINANCIAL INFORMATION

Sources and Uses

The project to be financed is a leasehold improvement project. Phase 1 is to erect a raw material storage building. Phase 2 is to enlarge the current manufacturing facility and to do some remodeling and renovating.

Jack's Ladder Inc. currently has a line of credit with a 16th National Bank for the amount of $60,000, which is used for working capital and inventory. The line was used sparingly in 1990, and not at all in 1991, because the company was able to supply enough of its own capital. We would seek project capital from 16th National Bank.

Statements—Historical and Projected

Historical - Business Tax Returns and Financial Statements
Projected - Projected Financial Statements

Both statements are available upon request.

Magazine Publisher

BUSINESS PLAN

GRAPEVINE MAGAZINE

555 Main St.
Ashland, FL 50945

November 25, 1990

GRAPEVINE is a demographically well-positioned magazine catering to a growing segment of the population. Due to developing circumstances and a changing business climate, it is looking for a capital infusion to maintain and further encourage already strong sales. Recent events have created the need to review all aspects of operation.

MAGAZINE PUBLISHER BUSINESS PLAN

MISSION STATEMENT

GRAPEVINE Magazine needs an infusion of capital of approximately $150,000-200,000.

Nationally known for high quality and its current key position in its market, this company has opportunities beyond the bridge requirement for short-term cash.

Long-term convertible debentures can be retired, probably at substantial discount, opening a major equity position at multiples far below industry average. Current record sales and long-term contracts, coupled with '92 pro forma projections, clearly show investment worthiness.

Recent circumstance of events, completely removed from any connection associated to the publication's operations, has created an unprecedented opportunity for participation in a company where industry profits historically grow in excess of 20%.

This is a clean operation and due diligence can be accomplished.

EXECUTIVE SUMMARY

Business Description

GRAPEVINE is a national specialty magazine with highly targeted demographics, designed to reach the top 7% of its market. Through a research driven, "benchmark" system of circulation, it has achieved, and maintains, the second largest advertising market share in its industry and is recognized as one of the four major "sources" in its market.

Business History

Established in November 1978 as a community newspaper distributed by bulk drop-off, it had a circulation of only 7,000. By 1988 through a carefully created network distribution concept, the publication had developed an audited circulation of 233,000. The magazine became the largest consumer lifestyle publication in the state. Impacted by its limited cash and a change in state tax laws, the magazine was bought out in May of 1988 by a public company that took the publication national, as a visible entity to its various subsidiaries. The public company experienced financial difficulties, and the Publication's management took the magazine back in July 1990. In the process of raising cash, convertible debenture financing was secured along investor's communication vehicles. A $2 million contract was signed with a hotel chain to provide paid circulation for the publication and meet cash flow requirements for the bimonthly circulation of over 400,000. The hotel chain has breached its contract. Simultaneously, a second-class postage application was filed and not approved for 15 months, creating a $135,000 security deposit for the publication's current investors, who, like the hotel, ended joint-venture operations. These combined series of events have created a cash crunch, in spite of record sales and a new multi-million dollar contract. The publication must either retire its existing long-term debts under new partnership arrangements, or obtain short-term bridge financing to counteract its drastic decrease in cash flow.

Business Highlights

Product

7-3/4" x 10-3/4", saddle-stitched, web offset printed, 4-color, consumer lifestyle magazine. Produced on 34/36 lb. enamel-coated stock, full body text and 60 lb. coated cover stock, the magazine is an award-winning editorial product.

Market

The publication is one of the four major leaders in the industry and serves a highly targeted niche. It has been reported to reach the top 7% of the market place. The publication is considered for quality rather than quantity reached and is positioned specifically in the fast growing segment of the market.

Customer Base

The magazine has the unique stature of being the only publication to have a qualified paid audited circulation in its industry. Qualified paid means the specific demographics are guaranteed to be reached by the publication's circulation. The methodology of its "benchwork" approach to the demographics of its readers has launched its circulation to be the most sought-after marketing approach in the industry.

Sales

The company's sales have grown from $1,000,235 in 1981 to $2,708,080 in 1990 with projected growth in excess of $3.3 million in 1992, and net profits in excess of $450,000.

Management

The management team is made up of those who have been recognized as authorities in their emerging market. The company has a secondary management team that provides uninterrupted continuance. The top management team is in place and hopes to remain.

Potential

Not only does the magazine serve the fastest growing market in the country, it has developed over its tenure a "franchise" into the advertising community. Further, the concept of contract printing as a new revenue stream is being addressed with one contract just being started and two pending.

OVERVIEW

Established in 1978, GRAPEVINE Magazine uniquely serves that segment of the huge and growing senior consumer base that has the following highly targeted characteristics:

- ❑ Female
- ❑ Between 50 and 64 years old
- ❑ Household income $40,000 plus
- ❑ College educated

In short, the publication serves an active, involved readership whose numbers

OVERVIEW...*continued*

are going to continue to grow for some time as the "baby boom" generation matures. There are now over 63 million people in the over 50 age group with discretionary spending power of over $78 billion. GRAPEVINE has positioned itself to serve the "Optimal Target Prospect", which is the core of the market as characterized above and defined by Yankelovich Clancy Shulman. A dramatic shift is occurring in the population as the over 50 age group assumes a larger and larger portion of the population.

The importance of this market is best illustrated by the increasing number of publishers who are approaching it and the quality of its industry leaders. In addition to GRAPEVINE, there are MODERN MATURITY, a benefit of membership publication of the American Association of Retired Persons; NEW CHOICES published by the Reader's Digest; and MATURE OUTLOOK published, under contract, by Meredith for Sears Roebuck's Allstate Enterprises' Mature Outlook Club, as a benefit of membership. Other publishers that are attempting to cover the market through the creation of special demographic sections are not direct competition for GRAPEVINE, although they do serve to focus the marketing community on the value and the huge potential of the emerging senior consumer. In fact, Ken Dychwald, president of Age Wave Inc., a research firm, has identified "over 200 newspapers, magazines, and tabloid-styled publications" serving the market in various degrees. According to the Patterson Advertising Lineage report, however, GRAPEVINE maintains the second largest market share by ad page count as of their February '91 quarterly.

Grapevine Senior News, Inc., was acquired by John and Jane Doe in December of 1980. At that time GRAPEVINE was a newspaper having a circulation in London County, Florida of just 7,000. Today the magazine as a national circulation of 400,000. It has enjoyed steady growth in advertising revenue since it was acquired and has developed a unique, targeted circulation marketing program utilizing research that differentiates the title from the rapidly growing field of competitors, and positions the magazine to deliver the top 7% of the entire senior consumer base--"The Optimal Target Prospect".

Having achieved the largest circulation in Florida, the 1988/1989 period was an important time for GRAPEVINE Magazine. The publishers had seen the national advertising revenue base opportunities grow substantially. The title was already attracting national advertising accounts who were seeking to reach the critically important bellwether Florida market, which has a large concentration of seniors. Management felt that the next step in the development of the title would be to take GRAPEVINE to the national market by extending the circulation coverage and building a stronger base to attract more national advertising dollars. The publishers were able to obtain an interim financial partner to accelerate the growth of the title to the national level. This objective has been accomplished.

To augment the advertising revenue stream, circulation driven, long-term, contract-printing contracts were developed to provide GRAPEVINE Magazine a "Qualified Paid" group subscription magazine for Day's Inn of America's

September Day's Club beginning January 1990. A wholesale publishing division was set up in February of 1990 that included corresponding contracts with September Day's Club to produce its 32-page insert; new contracts with Pioneer Financial Services, Inc. to produce two additional magazines for their associations, providing paid circulation revenue and vastly improving, via terms, cash flow; plus a long term corresponding contract with Humana Hospital Corporation.

Current two year contracts are valued at $1,906,999.

The title is forecast to generate net operating revenues of $484,470 during the fiscal year December 31, 1992. Revenue growth is expected to accelerate sharply FY 1991 as a result of the company's new, profitable paid, contract circulation revenue streams, the removal of non-profitable contracts created for cash flow benefits, and the increase in national advertising as a result of the company's steadfast "key" position in the market place.

FINANCIAL SUMMARY

FY 1989 - FY 1992

	12/89 Act	12/90 Act	12/91 Act	12/92 Est
Gross Ad Revenue	$1,832	$1,502	$1,672	$1,809
Circulation Revenue	195	564	737	1,323
Other Revenue	6	642	86	176
Gross Revenue	$2,0338	$2,708	$2,495	$3,051
Less: Agency comm. &disc.	295	268	258	257
Net Revenue	$1,738	$2,440	$2,237	$3,051
Less: Op. Exps.	$1,853	$2,397	$2,266	$2,567
Op. Profit/ (Loss)	$(115)	$ 43	$ (29)	$ 484

Management's advisors believe that GRAPEVINE represents an exceptionally attractive strategic acquisition or investment opportunity for the following reasons:

GRAPEVINE serves one of the largest and most important emerging markets--the affluent senior market.

GRAPEVINE has established a national presence in the advertising community, and has earned top market share.

GRAPEVINE has established a unique audited circulation strategy that effectively differentiates the title from its competition and positions it as delivering the top 7% of the market with an industry exclusive "qualified paid circulation". This is a niche that empowers the magazine and aligns it with quality rather than with quantity.

FINANCIAL SUMMARY
...continued

The publication is poised for dramatic revenue increases, having made substantial investment expenditures during the three-year national launch periods. (The work is done.)

Operating profits should be able to be enhanced by a number of sales actions not currently employed by management due to lack of resources.

The title has an ongoing development programs to extend its reach into new distribution areas and into additional contract-publishing, revenue-stream opportunities.

The award-winning editorial product is attuned to the market and is recognized as one of the four leading national publications serving the over-50 adult.

GRAPEVINE is the only independent magazine serving its market. National advertising sales are low in '91 due to the recession and war. In spite of the restriction within the advertising industry and compared to the competition, high growth potential in revenues is evidenced by the publication's continued record-breaking revenue issues.

According to Patterson's Advertising's Par Report, GRAPEVINE maintains the second largest market share of advertising lineage in the industry even though its current circulation is the smallest amongst the other three major publications.

Circulation opportunities have only begun to be exploited by management, creating new and inherently profitable sources of revenue. Contract Publishing: 3 contracts pending (not budgeted).

The management team of GRAPEVINE is and has been recognized as national authorities in this emerging Mature Market Industry for over 11 years and has a tremendous appreciation of the market and the advertising and revenue base potentials.

GRAPEVINE represents an ideal opportunity to get into an emerging market, with a nationally accepted quality product having a national advertising "franchise" already in place. The potential of a strong return on investment is assured.

GRAPEVINE is a federally registered magazine trademark.

The company is located at 555 Main St., Ashland, Florida 50945. Ashland is on the west coast of Florida. The offices occupy roughly 1800 square feet and the magazine pays rent of about $12.88/ sqft. The building, a historic site, is owned by the Doe's and leased back to the company at higher than market value in an arm's length transaction. The company has regional sales and support personnel who operate out of rented facilities. These sales offices are in Florida. All operations are handled out of the Fish, Florida headquarters, including editorial, production, marketing and administration.

PERSONNEL

The company employs 15 people as of July 13, 1991. The company offers all normal benefits to employees (except retirement or 401K plans). The following list identifies the employees by position:

Editorial

Doe, Jane .... Editor-in-Chief/President
Fore, Liza .... Managing Editor
Pun, Audra .... Asst. to Editor

Production

Gill, Gilbert .... Art Director
Strange, Keith .... Production Asst./Typesetter

Sales

House

Stick, Susan .... Acct. Exec.--Midwest and Florida
Leaf, Barry .... Acct. Exec.--East
Reaves, Chris .... Acct. Exec.--Dir. Resp. plus New England

Contract Representation

Kent, Clark .... Northeast--Tri-city area
Bart Group .... West Coast

Administration

Doe, John .... Publisher/CEO and Corporate Secretary
Dawson, Geoff .... Executive Asst. to Publisher
Lind, Paul .... Bookkeeper
Turn, Lauren .... Data Processing/Programmer
Brushe, Marie .... Secretary (Sarasota Sales Office)
Pitcher, Sue ..... Accounts Receivable/Sec. to Sales Department

As in many entrepreneurial companies, the staff of GRAPEVINE Magazine performs in multiple roles, and the above titles indicate only the primary responsibilities of the individuals.

KEY MANAGEMENT INFORMATION

John Doe--Publisher, CEO, & Corporate Secretary

Role in Company

Responsible for Marketing & Sales, Finance, Administration and Profitability.

Specialty

Marketing & Sales, Business Management. Good motivator with excellent people skills. A visionary with good business acumen.

Background

President (CEO) for several years of a wholly owned subsidiary of a 1/4 billion dollar public conglomerate. He took the company from sales of $2.9 million with a negative bottom line to sales of $7.4 million with an after-tax profit of 6.7% within 5 years. He had total sales, operations, and P&L responsibility. The company employed 75 people.

Executive Vice President/Director of Marketing for a toy manufacturer; a position he held for several years prior to his assignment to head up the above subsidiary.

Sales Administrator, National Sales Manager, and Assistant to the President of a large juvenille furniture and T.V. toy manufacturer. These positions ultimately led to the assignment of heading up the acquired subsidiary.

Started working at a young age in his family's retail chain business and did so for six years prior to entering private industry.

Education
American University - Bachelor of Business Administration/Marketing
Richardson Valley Technical Institute - Accounting and Business law

Jane Doe--Editor in Chief & President

Role in Company
Responsible for Editorial Content, Art and Design of Magazine. Functions as a business partner. Personnel Manager.

Specialties
Award-winning editorial talent. Great business acumen. Excellent organizational and leadership skills. Has exceptional insight and understanding of peoples' attitudes and feelings, which complements the task of writing and editing for the magazine's audiences. Intuitively in tune with the market's needs and interests.

Background
Successfully organized and started a company, which she ran for many years, that provided substitute Registered Dental Hygienists to dentists. Supervised a staff of twelve hygienists serving over 100 clients. Prior to this, she was a Registered Dental Hygienist for several years.

Education
Florida University - Working on Masters--Health Counseling
Rochester University - Bachelor of Arts
New York City Technical College - Dental Hygiene
Scotch Plains University - Nutrition
Bergen Community College - Counseling Certification
Montclair University - Psychology

EDITORIAL OVERVIEW

GRAPEVINE Magazine is edited for a target audience that is described as the top 7% of all senior consumers. It is that portion of the market between the ages of 50 and 64, well educated, with household incomes over $40,000. This is a group that represents the new attitude towards the senior years by focusing on quality of life rather than years of age. The magazine is editorially tuned to this new sensibility and provides important information to its readers.

The magazine takes a complete lifestyle and psychology of aging approach, with a special award-winning editorial emphasis on the need and interests of the inter-generational adult reader. While addressing the important quality of life areas that make living fun, the additional award-winning design format of the magazine sets a tone of professionalism throughout its pages.

GRAPEVINE has differentiated itself from its competition's editorial in a number of ways. The personality cover concept of GRAPEVINE is a good illustration of this differentiation and industry distinction. Every issue has on the cover a famous role model--an over 50 personality, well-known for accomplishments in entertainment or public life. The editors fellow the cover exposure with a feature story inside the issue. The focus of the story is not the glamour that may surround the individual, but the variety of interests that he/she may have and his/her attitude on aging, serving as a public role model for its readers.

They utilize Pulitzer Prize-winning columnists, such as Jane Bryant Quinn, to write authoritatively about subjects that are of importance to the GRAPEVINE reader. When required, expert technological information is disseminated.

One indication of the quality level is the fact that the magazine continually wins awards for its editorial excellence.

CIRCULATION AND MARKETING STRATEGY

The following commentary by management provides background on the history of circulation development for GRAPEVINE, as well as the current operational steps being taken by the title. In brief, management has identified, through cellular analysis, the optimal target prospect. The "key" segment of the over-50 adult market that has proven to be the most desirable marketing target for the advertising community, and thus has created a very valuable, exclusive market niche.

History

When GRAPEVINE was born in November of 1978, it had a circulation of 7,000 in Brewer County, Florida. The method of circulation was bulk drop-off at areas of senior concentration. By December, 1982, there were five regional editions of GRAPEVINE, basically covering the central corridor of Florida. By networking with the biggest businesses in Florida, who also recognized the importance of the 50+ adult, it created a massive distribution network through the Wesley Drug Store chain and Monopoly Supermarkets. Its association with these retailing giants helped to build GRAPEVINE into Florida's largest, statewide, consumer lifestyle publication. By January, 1988, it had a verified audited circulation (VAC) of233,000.

Marketing Strategy

In preparation for the 1989 roll-out of GRAPEVINE from a regional publication into a national entity, it retained Yankelovich Clancy Shulman to help create, through "cellular analysis," the "optimal target prospect" for its clients. It designed circulation to accomplish a very special marketing plan, not to build "rate base." As you know, in the industry the norm is to acquire subscribers, usually at high first-year premium costs, in order to develop "rate base" (the basis used to establish advertising rates). Not only did the publishers find this to be backwards, but the advertising client was not correctly being served. Their goal was to deliver only the best prospects not "tons" of anybody. Once Yankelovich defined whom the client base identified as its "ideal prospect" (predominantly women, between the ages of 50 and 64, having household incomes of $40,000 or better), GRAPEVINE simply had to deliver that reader and in so doing it created the uniquely simplified approach to lasered, target marketing. The system, according to Yankelovich, is "benchmark" for the industry and delivers "the top 7% of the entire senior consumer base." Once GRAPEVINE had the methodology of circulation designed, it brought in BPA and asked it to identify those list houses whose acquisition of names had been approved and audited by BPA. Once identified (TRW and R.R. Donnelley), it simply went out and purchased 400,000 names having the specific criteria of the clients' "ideal prospect." (The database of the national perspective of this specific criteria is 18.3 million.) It then began the process of converting the controlled database into "qualified control requested." This was important, as it gave GRAPEVINE the "requested subscriber" status.

After one and a half years of continual efforts to convert to "qualified requested" subscribers and then to make the second phase of conversion from "controlled requested" to "qualified paid," the circulation has proven to be a marketing tool unique to the magazine industry, exclusive among its competitors and an important marketing edge for our clients.

GRAPEVINE has successfully completed the conversion of its national circulation of 407,513. (282,821 are Qualified Paid, 65,384 are "Qualified Requested," 10,739 are non-qualified paid, and the balance goes to doctors' offices as reception area copies. This additional exposure was carefully incorporated to take advantage of a huge 10 to 15 times "pass-along" opportunity.)

June 27, 1990, BPA completed its audit process--the report audits our circulation and exclusive demographics. GRAPEVINE is the only Senior Publication that has a national "qualified paid" circulation. GRAPEVINE's circulation strategy is to be the best, NOT the biggest. Delivering the "creme de la creme" of the senior market is the unique and exclusive niche it has carved for itself.

A circulation of 407,513 cannot (in many cases) carry the entire media buy. But being able to guarantee that our qualified circulation is delivered to the top 7%

of the entire senior consumer base reinforces the business intelligence to be sure it is, at least, included in the media buy.

Since being the biggest is virtually impossible to duplicate, creating the ability to deliver the MOST important segment of the market NOT only filled the void, but it also created a publication with outstanding response factors. Being dramatically different and credible is how management is building GRAPEVINE.

ADVERTISING

Competition

Direct Competition

There is a growing number of publications serving this developing market; however, only a few are currently significant, important competition for GRAPEVINE. These are titles with a proven track record and/or major corporate ownership. It is clear that the advertising community has a number of choices in reaching this market, and each of the titles, except GRAPEVINE, is generic in positioning. What is important to note is that while GRAPEVINE has had national circulation only since February, 1989, its unique positioning--on quality, not quantity--places GRAPEVINE in the select group of primary media properties. As evidenced by its top market share rating over all others, GRAPEVINE maintains a unique key niche in its industry. The oldest and largest title serving the market is MODERN MATURITY. Founded in 1958, MODERN MATURITY is a bimonthly publication distributed to members of The American Association of Retired Persons (AARP) as a "member benefit" communication vehicle, and currently has the largest circulation of any magazine in the U.S. with 22 million member copies distributed. The editorial content is broad general interest with a focus on the interests and activities of AARP members. The average age of the MODERN MATURITY reader is 67.1. While the current marketing focus is to bring the age down to adults over 50, it nonetheless addresses the oldest, limited spectrum of the demographic. The large readership creates a broad demographic profile which requires that the editorial be edited to an "average" reader. The advertising volume is limited by the advertiser's size as the large circulation creates a one-time 4/c page rate of over $207,000.

NEW CHOICES (formerly 50 PLUS) was established in 1960 and recently purchased by Readers Digest Association. This is a monthly publication with a circulation of 594,807. It is a paid consumer publication sold primarily through subscriptions, both individuals and bulk to corporations. Editorial content is very good and is directed towards the younger end of the demographic who also have better education and higher income/net worth. It is also a good publication and a formidable competitor. Its 4/c page rate is $20,490. The current marketing shift of the publication is to produce a reader between the 45-64 age group.

MATURE OUTLOOK is a bimonthly publication produced by Meredith Corporation for Sears Roebuck. It has a circulation of 729,254. Like MODERN MATURITY, MATURE OUTLOOK is a member benefit, in this case of the

Competition *...continued*

Allstate Enterprises' Mature Outlook Club. The editorial is general interest, skewed toward a male reader, and carries heavy "House" editorial and advertising for the Sears operation. It is fast becoming a "House Organ" for Sears after its attempts to serve the senior market as an editorial product. This title was established in 1984. Its 4/c page rate its $17,300.

GRAPEVINE's 400,000 national circulation is edited for the "ideal target prospect," a very carefully defined segment of the over 50 demographic. The publication is designed to reach the top 7% of the entire consumer base. This positions the magazine into the niche that affords its clients a competitive advantage, separates it clearly from the older less desirable reach of MODERN MATURITY, and aligns it closely to its best competitor, NEW CHOICES. (MATURE OUTLOOK, by virtue of its predominantly male audience and the publication's marketing strategies to move more in tune with Sears' needs, is removed from close comparison.) GRAPEVINE 4/c page rate is $15,290.

Depending on Budget Size the "media buy" is:

Full Market Coverage .... NEW CHOICES
MODERN MATURITY
Top of Market .... GRAPEVINE NEW CHOICES
Reach or Older Skew .... MODERN MATURITY
Opportunity Buy .... NEW CHOICES, GRAPEVINE
Bargain Price/Male .... MATURE OUTLOOK

Indirect Competition

There are always new launches that are also claiming to reach the senior market. McCALL's magazine, one of the "seven sisters," introduced a demographic edition, McCALL's SILVER, which is edited for the woman 50-64. Like most demographic editions, McCALL's SILVER, a 4-8 page supplement, is inserted in the regular edition of the magazine and delivered to one million age-selected subscribers. There is little that is new and/or specific for the reader that she wasn't already getting from the national edition. So far, the impact this title has had on the advertising market is not a factor.

Advertising Lineage Data

Advertising lineage information for all titles serving the senior market is not readily available from an independent tracking source. Only the four major titles are tracked for market share and provide some insight into their market standings.

Advertising Sales Background

GRAPEVINE has grown from a small regional publication to a national industry leading title in just 11 years. In the process, it has expanded both its advertising base, its forms of revenue streams, and its sales organization. The unique ability of the publication to go from carrying local real estate advertising and services for the reader to carrying major national advertising, such as General Foods, GEICO, Coca-Cola, Chrysler, Jockey, and Anacin, as well as advertising, is a testament to the importance and the credibility that GRAPEVINE has established in delivering the most sought after segment of the market. The advertising growth of the title has been impressive.

OPERATING PLAN EXPLANATION

Introduction

The following explanations are written to clarify the logic of the financial projections in the BUSINESS PLAN. Many notes and schedules have been included along with the numbers, when appropriate. However, this section is meant to serve the reader as a reference tool rather than a plan summary.

This Business Plan is designed to provide GRAPEVINE Magazine, with an operating road map. The one and one half years of projections are presented as actual "operating budgets." (Available on request.)

We have tried to envision reality in great detail for the projection period. On the revenue side, it is thought that projections are realistic and ad sales projections are supported by trend-line. While on the expense side, we have gone to great effort to make sure all expenses are included. Therefore, we feel the cash flows and projected profits should be achievable.

Revenue

The format for projecting advertising revenue is based upon the "average page rate method." This means that the projected ad pages are multiplied by the estimated average page rate. Projecting revenue by pages (units) helps keep in line the related variable printing and production costs.

Circulation Revenue is centered primarily around two programs: regular subscriptions and contract bulk sales. Detailed explanations of these are found in the circulation section of the Business Plan and on circulation schedules in the financial section.

Agency Commissions

Advertising agencies charge 15% commission for all ad sales they place for the magazine. Historically, agency sales have represented 79.4% of all sales in the magazine.

Production Expenses

Determining total pages in the magazines is the key to calculating production expenses. Total pages are derived from applying the appropriate editorial/advertising ratio to projected ad pages. The ratio will vary according to the mix of national ads and Florida ads. However, generally the overall ad percentage is running around 45%-50%.

Since printing is the biggest single expense of the company and is based on total pages printed, the ad/editorial ratio is a key factor in publishing economics. The ratio will vary a few percentage points because changes in the number of total pages have to be adjusted in jumps of eight pages--press requirements.

The projections of total pages and related production and printing costs are enumerated in a special schedule in the Operating Plan.

Sales Expenses

Sales expense projections are enumerated on a special schedule in each year's plan. Most of the account titles adequately explain the project expense. The following are a few accounts needing explanation:

Sales Commissions
Are based on an account executive making his/her quota. Each AE receives 10% commission (in addition to base pay) on all sales over their quota. The current quota per sales person is $48,000 each per issue.

Sales Aids
Mostly media kits and related materials.

Travel & Entertainment
Primarily N.Y. ad agency sales by Publisher.

Telephone Expense
Heavy use of telephone -- this is a telemarketing business.

Postage (Marketing & Sales)
Mailing of media kits and promotional materials, much of which is overnight mail. Support of dynamic telemarketing program.

Postage (Magazine Distribution)
Second class postage. 19 cents per copy for the operating plan period.

Label Maintenance
Outside service to handle mail list, mail labels, etc.

General & Administrative

Most G & A expenses are self explanatory. Accounting expenses are for a year end "audit" and tax returns by a "big six accounting" firm. GRAPEVINE has had an accounting "review" for the past several years. Consulting fees are for a financial consultant who serves the proper amounts of liability insurance. Equipment leases are for personal computers, copy and fax machines. Auto leases are two cars assigned to the Publisher and the Editor.

Payroll & Related

Each year's plan contains the details of payroll projections. These projections include strategies to adjust personnel appropriately as the business expands as well as specific pay increases to each employee for the entire operating plan period.

Cash Flow Projections

All numbers in the cash flow model come directly from the Operating Plan, except for balance sheet items for July, 1991, when the projections of cash begin.

The method used to project cash is as follows:

❶ Initially, "expected cash receipts" are determined by applying the expected collection percentages (Issue Month, 30, 60, 90 days) to sales projections. It is anticipated that 5% will be collected in the issue month,45% will be collected in 30 days; 40% in 60 days; and 10% in 90 days. Net sales is defined in the operating plan as gross sales less agency commissions and bad debt expenses.

❷ Next, subtract "expected deductions" from "planned expenses." Production expenses are expected to be paid in 60 days. The bulk of this expense is for printing. Payroll, payroll taxes, and postage expenses ar paid in the month they are incurred. All other expenses will be paid 30 to 45 days, dependents upon specific arrangements with the vendor or the penalty/reward system relating to timing of payments.

❸ Depreciation expense is added back since this is a non-cash item.

❹Then, "cash from operations" is derived. The accumulated negative cash balance indicates the amount of cash needed to fund working capital.

Online Consulting

BUSINESS PLAN

BORDERLINE TRANSMISSIONS, INC.

5012 Seymore Rd.
San Jose, CA 60342

January 31, 1994

Due to the rapidly changing landscape of online communications, this newly formed online computer service company maps out its strategy for the early stages of its development. Services to be provided, future goals, and financial status (current and projected) are a few of the issues explored in this plan.

- EXECUTIVE SUMMARY
- BACKGROUND
- BUSINESS CONCEPT
- MARKET ANALYSIS
- OBJECTIVES AND STRATEGIES
- COMPANY ORGANIZATION
- APPENDICES

ONLINE CONSULTING BUSINESS PLAN

EXECUTIVE SUMMARY

The use of online technology to obtain business information, which has for several years been the sole domain of large corporations, has become viable for businesses of all sizes--and even individuals--in the mid-1990s. At the same time the technology to provide such information, inexpensively and on a global scale, has come into its own. But the complexity and fast-changing nature of online communications continue to make it hard for the average small- or medium-sized business to reap the full benefit of these new possibilities.

This situation has created the opportunity for a consulting service devoted to helping businesses gain, and optimally benefit from online technology, to go into business. Borderline Transmissions, Inc. (BTI) a sole proprietorship located in San Jose, California was formed in January 1994 to take advantage of this opportunity.

BTI will initially target, as clients, small- and medium-sized service businesses in the San Francisco Area. Services provided will include an assessment of the advantages that online access offers to the client, plus help in establishing and maintaining online capability.

This document comprises the start-up business plan for Borderline Transmissions.

BACKGROUND

In the past eighteen months, several interrelated market factors have made the use of online information services much more appealing to small and medium-sized US businesses than in the past. These are:

❑ The rapid and sustained growth in personal computer and modem ownership is a result of substantial performance improvements with concurrent reductions in price.

❑ The explosive growth in the availability and usage of online information resources, especially the worldwide Internet.

❑ The introduction of user-friendly client software which means for the first time, the average business person need not have advanced computer skills to use online resources effectively.

❑ Increased media attention given to online services and, in particular, to the Internet.

All of these trends are likely to continue for at least the next 5-8 years.

While the business benefits of online information are fast coming into focus, the process of going online remains difficult. This is because:

❑ The online environment is growing and changing very rapidly.
❑ The amount of available information, as well as the options for gaining access to it, can be overwhelming.
❑ There are currently no turnkey online access solutions for businesses. They must negotiate a maze of hardware, software, connectivity solutions, and service providers to gain the full benefit that online services have to offer. Moreover, there are few consultancies or service providers with expertise to guide them through this process.

Even without the above factors, many businesses are too occupied with their own operations to spend a significant amount of time pursuing the benefits of online resources.

BUSINESS CONCEPT

BTI will offer the following services to its clients:

Online Needs Evaluation Research and present to the client a description and cost analysis of the various online resources that would benefit the client's business--from both the user and provider perspectives.

Online Provider Recommendation If the client decides to use or provide any online services, identify the service providers that offer the best value to the client.

Service Implementation Make all necessary arrangements to:

For Online Users Install the services that the client selects, including hardware and software acquisition, service establishment, system configuration, training, and documentation.

For Online Providers Set up an online marketing program for the client, including development of marketing materials and service establishment, training, and documentation.

Post-Implementation Support Provide ongoing consulting support to the client as needed.

Borderline Transmissions, Inc. will also develop the following as secondary profit centers:

- Referral Services
- Online Service Resources

MARKET ANALYSIS

Market Research

BTI will market its services mainly to businesses that fit the following profile:

Location The counties of San Jose/San Francisco/Santa Cruz, and Monterey.

Industries Business-to-business services, especially (a) those with international operations (e.g. import/export firms, travel agencies, freight forwarders) and (b) other information-intensive services (e.g. law, accounting, and consulting practices, financial services, brokers).

Size 50 to 5,000 employees

Equipment Microcomputer users (primarily Macintosh, secondarily IBM-compatible).

An estimated 1,600 businesses fit this profile. According to an industry magazine, only 30 percent of businesses with microcomputers have "online capability" (i.e. are equipped with a modern and telecommunications software). This implies a total market of 1,120 businesses (70 percent of 1,600) with no online capability, and an additional 480 businesses (30 percent) that have online capability. but may or may not be using it to their full advantage. It is the latter 30 percent that have the highest potential as BTI customers.

Competitive Factors

Several firms currently offer the same, or similar services to those planned by BTI. None of these firms are seen as a significant barrier to the success of BTI because, as stated previously, the overall market comprises nearly every service business in the country. In fact, some of these organizations may be potential alliance partners to BTI.

OBJECTIVES AND STRATEGIES

This section outlines how BTI will do business in general and in the specific areas of marketing, operations, financial management, risk management, and company organization.

General

Mission

The mission of BTI is to help organizations and individuals make the best use of the online information resources available to them.

Objectives

Develop a consulting service that:

- ❑Helps organizations link to the online environments that are most beneficial to their business, as easily as possible.
- ❑Provides "one-stop shopping" for clients' online service needs
- ❑Always uses and provides the best available resources

Strategy

❑Operate as a general project manager in a "virtual corporation," outsourcing work to alliance partners when expertise is needed in the following areas:

- Connectivity to External Networks
- Data Security
- Hardware
- Local Area Networks
- Software
- Training and Documentation

❑Remain small, but portray the image of a large corporation through superior service and marketing, and the use of computer and telecommunications technology

❑Develop a network of alliance partners who have similar business goals and philosophies to that of Borderline Transmissions, Inc.

Marketing

Objective

Build a client base large enough to support BTI's financial objectives, but small enough to be effectively serviced within the means of a single-person company.

Strategy

Target Market During its first year of operation, BTI will target as clients, business for the profile described elsewhere in this document. The custom of other businesses, as well as individuals, will be encouraged, but this group will not be the subject of an active marketing effort during the startup phase.

Marketing Plan BTI will use the following means to market its services:

❑A high-quality paper marketing brochure that highlights the company and its services

❑An electronic marketing brochure

❑A generic online sales presentation, including a demo, that can be customized to the interests of a potential client

❑Participation in the following networking activities:

- Online discussion groups
- Trade shows
- Local chamber of commerce events

❑Arrangements to barter services with vendors where feasible

❑Development of secondary profit centers, including written articles and seminars about online services

Strategy ...continued

Service Pricing Services will be priced based on the following rates:

Businesses

Online Needs Evaluation $400

Service includes: Presentation to the client of a description and cost analysis of the various online resources that would benefit the client's business from both the user and provider perspectives.

Network Provider Recommendation .... FREE

Service includes: list of 3-5 network providers, commercial services, and other server providers that offer the best value to the client.

Implementation (User) $600/Day

Service includes: installation of all services that the client has selected, including hardware and software acquisition (passed on at cost), system configuration, network establishment, training, and documentation. 1-Day Min. Expenses addl.

Implementation (Provider) $600/Day

Service includes: establishment of an online marketing program for the client, including development of marketing materials, application design, development, and installation, server design and installation, network establishment, training, and documentation. 1-Day Min. Expenses addl.

Post-Implementation Support $75/Hour

Service includes: Providing ongoing consulting support to the client as needed. 1-Hour Min.

Individuals

Online service connection for Macintosh or Windows $200

Service includes: software installation and configuration for Internet, one commercial online service, and arrangement with telephone company and/or network provider.

Services will be provided on either a fixed-price or hourly basis,as appropriate to the situation.

Operations

Objective

Build client loyalty by offering superior service and keeping all verbal and written commitments.

Strategy

Operate as a "virtual corporation" by developing a network of alliance partners that offer expertise, local geographical coverage, or additional consulting resources. Subcontract work to alliance partners when appropriate, and offer reciprocal services.

Specialize in Apple Macintosh technology and develop a secondary specialization in IBM-PC technology.

Financial

Objective

Generate gross sales of $90,000 in the first year of operation.

Strategy

Follow the stated general, marketing, operations, and risk management strategies to maximize sales. Practice sound financial management by maintaining awareness of expenditures and costs at all times. Incorporate during the first year of operation to gain liability and tax benefits.

Risk Management

Objective

Identify, and act to minimize, any substantial risks to BTI assets, operations, reputation, and to its general viability as a business.

Strategy

Address the specific issues.

COMPANY ORGANIZATION

Ownership

BTI will begin business as a sole proprietorship under the ownership of Samucl H. Palmer, a resident of San Jose, California. The possibility of incorporation will be pursued during the first year of operation.

Management

The business will be managed and operated solely by the owner, with work subcontracted to Sunnyside Inc. where appropriate.

Coverage for the owner's vacation, sick time, should this occur during a client project, will be arranged in advance with one or more individuals from Sunnyside Inc.

Location

Borderline Transmissions, Inc. is located at the following address.

5012 Seymore Rd.
San Jose, CA 60342
(802)555-1212 (voice)
(802)555-1212 (fax/data)

APPENDICES

Issues List

Issue

While the owner has significant management experience in a medium-sized corporation, he has no experience as a business owner.

Solution

(1) Use the services of experienced consultants during the startup phase, and thereafter where appropriate.
(2) When possible and prudent during the startup phase of the business, create learning opportunities by performing work directly that might in the future be subcontracted.
(3) Read industry publications and take pertinent training courses on a regular basis.
(4) For the long term, identify potential equity partners in the business whose strengths complement the owner's weakness.

Issue

The proposed business concept is unproven because the combination of services that Borderline Transmissions plans to offer have rarely, if ever, been offered as the single specialty of a consulting business.

Solution

Owner's intuition says otherwise.

Issue

It may take longer than anticipated to build a sufficient income stream to support the owner

Solution

Owner has sufficient financial resources to devote full time efforts to Borderline Transmissions through October, 1994. If this problem extends beyond that time, the owner may need to pursue other income opportunities.

Issue

Borderline Transmissions will, at least initially, be a single-person company. Situations may arise where this resource is overextended due to project demands

Solution

(1) Limit the number of projects undertaken at any given time.

(2) Arrange contingency coverage with Alliance partners in advance of each major project.

Issue

The most valuable assets of Borderline Transmissions are its computer equipment, and the data stored on that equipment. These are subject to damage or loss.

Solution

(1) Obtain insurance for all computer and telecommunications equipment.
(2) Obtain and install a backup hard disk for the Quadra 660AV, and backup all business data each day. Also backup vital data once a month and store it offsite.

Sample Language for Marketing Brochure

Why Online?

In the mid-1990s, online access has come into its own as a business communications tool. Companies (and their customers) are going online in record numbers. Many consider it indispensable and are turning it into a competitive advantage. Why? Because they know that online access puts some very powerful tools onto your desktop (or laptop, or palmtop):

•Electronic mail and fax capability, so you can instantly exchange messages and files with co-workers, customers, and vendors--across the hall or across the globe.
•Admission to the electronic marketplace, where products and services are traded in the fast-growing online community of over 20 million people.
•A key to the online data banks that provide--on demand--almost any type of business information.

The best thing about going online is that it frees you from the old limitations of time and location. Online, you can do business at any time of the day or night, anywhere in the world.

Why Now?

Why wait? Getting connected now is a smart move for companies of any size that use or provide information. That's because:

It's affordable. Today's communications hardware, software, and network services are within the reach of most company budgets, and they keep coming down in price.

It's easy. Most online resources are accessible with simple, point-and-click graphical software--the kind that's familiar to any Macintosh or Windows user.

Your competition is probably doing it.

By the way, you don't even need your own connection to advertise online--you can put your ad on rented disk space at of the many electronic shopping centers that have sprung up. But because communication is a two-way street, and because communicating online is the wave of the future, we recommend a direct connection for your business.

The Race for Cyberspace is on!

Why Borderline Transmissions?

Going online is the right move, but preparing a business for its launch into cyberspace can be an ordeal--even for experienced computer users. You have to negotiate a maze of tasks and issues, like:

Strategic direction. What specific online activities will support your business objectives? How can you best leverage your connection to increase sales and cut costs?

•Choosing from among the hundreds of available hardware, software, connection, and service options.
•Installing, configuring, and testing your system. Training your staff. Writing the user manual.
•Once online, navigating through cyberspace so you find what you need--and avoid information overload.

To get set up, you have two choices--you can do it yourself, or get help from an expert. If you decide to go it alone you can expect many hours of effort and frustration, and maybe some costly mistakes. If, on the other hand, you decide you can use some help--that's what Borderline Transmissions is for.

Current Balance Sheet

Borderline Transmissions Balance Sheet as of 7/15/94

Assets

Cash and Bank Accounts	$5,500	
Total Cash and Bank Accounts		$5,500
Other Assets Accounts Receivable	$250	
Total Other Assets		$250
Total Assets		$5,750

Liabilities & Equity

Liabilities

Credit Cards	$545	
Total Credit Cards	$545	
Total Liabilities		$545
Equity		$5,205
Total Liabilities & Equity		$5,750

Income Statement

Borderline Transmissions
Income and Expenses: 1/1/94 through 7/15/94

Expenses		
Advertising		$94
Bank Charges		$157
Miscellaneous		
Conferences	$275	
Training	$110	
Online Charges	$409	
Publications	$287	
Total Miscellaneous		$1,081
Office Expense		
Hardware	$582	
Postage	$32	
Software	$1,140	
Total Office Expense		$1,754
Supplies		$153
Taxes		
City	$35	
County	$44	
Total Taxes		$79
Utilities		
Telephone	$333	
Total Utilities		$333
Total Expenses		$3,882
Total Income		$0
Total Income/Expense		($3,882)

Startup Costs

Borderline Transmissions
Startup Costs (Expenditure for 1993 & 1994 YTD & Estimate through 9/94)

Advertising		$1,094
Bank Charges		$157
Miscellaneous		
Conferences	$275	
Training	$110	
Online Charges	$559	
Publications	$287	
Total Miscellaneous		
		$1,231
Office Expense:		
Hardware	$5,700	
Postage	$232	
Software	$1,140	
Total Office Expense		$7,072
Supplies		$153
Taxes:		
City	$35	
County	$44	
Total Taxes		$79
Utilities:		
Telephone	$453	
Total Utilities		$453
Total Estimated Startup Costs		$10,470

Glossary

Following are definitions of the ex-dictionary terms used in this business plan.

BBS
Bulletin Board Service. A single-location Online Service (could be either commercial or non-commercial).

Commercial Service
One of the following: America Online, BIX, CompuServe, Delphi, Eworld, Exec PC, GEnie, MCIMail, NVN, or Prodigy.

Database Service
One of the following: CAN/OLE, Chemical Information System, Data-Star, DataTimes, Dialog, Info Globe Online, Lexis, Nexis, NewsNet, OCLC, Orbit,

Questel, STN International, or Westlaw.

Internet
A global, non-commercial online network.

ISDN
Integrated Services Digital Network, a high-speed data communications technology employed over standard telephone lines.

Internet Provider
An organization providing Internet Access to the public.

Online Technology
The use of to modems (or more advanced connective technology) with communications software to allow computers to communicate with other computers.

World Wide Web
A hypermedia system for searching the Internet.

About the Owner

Samuel H. Palmer's long-time interest in personal computers began in 1979 when his parents bought a new Apple II and he spent many hours tinkering with it. He has never been the same since.

Palmer, 34, is a thirteen-year resident of San Jose, California by way of St. Louis, Missouri; London, England; and Eugene, Oregon. He holds a Bachelor of Arts degree in International Relations from San Jose State University. Before starting Borderline Transmissions he worked for eleven years in the international banking industry, much of that time involved in the development of CashNet, an online financial data transmission network. Away from business pursuits he keeps himself occupied traveling, writing, playing the keyboard, and spending time with his two sons, ages 5 and 7.

Printing Company

BUSINESS PLAN

MASTER PRINTER AND PARTNERS PRINTING

52 James St.
Grace, NM 84753

6924 Auburn Dr.
Grace, NM 84753

June 23, 1990

This business plan outlines a two-store operation offering a full range of printing services and supplies. The joint enterprise will improve efficiency through the use of Total Quality Management (TQM). Following is a description of the ways in which the companies will employ extensive use of strategic, operational, and financial planning, as well as ways they intend to incorporate TQM methods into their businesses.

PRINTING COMPANY BUSINESS PLAN

EXECUTIVE SUMMARY

There are two components to this company: Master Printer of Grace and Partners Printing of Theadora. Master Printer has been owned, all or in part, by Shawn Russell since 1981. Ms. Russell started Partners in 1990 to increase market share and penetrate the Theadora market. The firm lost a major contract in 1991. This experience caused the first major loss in eight years. It is our goal to diversify the sales to the extent that we will never be dependent on one customer to that degree again. In addition, we will improve our efficiency and effectiveness through the implementation of Total Quality Management (TQM).

The two stores offer a full range of printing services and supplies. We have the ability to operate as a "quick printer" when necessary. A full list of services is included in the Business Description section.

The market is divided into commercial taxable and nontaxable accounts. We are currently identifying the number of potential accounts. The main competition is Charter Stationary, Langston Printing, and Monroe's Print Shop in Grace, and Penny Printing and Paper Supplies and Priceless Printing in Theadora. Our company will emphasize service, quality, price, and speed of service to compete in the market place. The printing industry is growing at a rate of 8 to 11 percent a year. We estimate our market share to be 34.2 percent and plan to increase that to 44.4 percent in five years through the implementation and annual revision of this plan.

Master and Partners have the ability to offer full-line printing services. The labor force consists of 13 people who have 150 combined years of printing and/or sales experience. We will use a delivery service to get the products to our customers in the outlying areas and for customers who need rush service.

We presently have a need for the following funds:

Payoff existing loans/notes	$161,000
Accounts Payable	64,000
Operating Capital	25,000
TOTAL	$250,000

We would like to have this loan over a 12-year term at 8.34 percent interest.

This business plan makes extensive and exhaustive use of strategic, operational, and financial planning. An essential element of this plan is the installation of the TQM method.

BUSINESS DESCRIPTION

Master Printer and Partners Printing offer a range of services, including:

- ◆ Offset printing
- ◆ Limited in-house full-color
- ◆ Job out balance of full-color
- ◆ Forms
- ◆ Books, manuals, brochures
- ◆ Programs
- ◆ Checks
- ◆ Computer typesetting with Apple MacIntosh and Varitype
- ◆ Letter press

At the current time our regular customers are:

- √Percy's Restaurant
- √Jim's Video Arcade
- √Grace School System
- √PineAcres Rest Home
- √First Bank
- √Government Printing Facility
- √Sarah's Stitchery
- √Others

In addition to the few accounts listed above, we have approximately 100 accounts not listed (i.e., churches, businesses, clubs, etc.).

COMPANY HISTORY

Master Printer is a local commercial printing company that has recently expanded to Theadora, New Mexico. Master was established in Grace, New Mexico in 1889 as a local newspaper printer, along with a job print shop. It was created to meet the printing needs of the local community.

After a period of time, the job print shop was sold as a commercial print shop. It was owned and operated as Grace Printing Company by Mrs. Dorothy Simmons.

In 1935, an employee, Drake Master, purchased Grace Printing Company and changed the name to Master Printer. During 1945, Mr. Master had a building erected at 52 James Street. This site remains the location of the present shop.

Master Printer was operated by Mr. and Mrs. Master until 1972. A few years after the death of Mr. Master, the shop again changed hands. It was sold to Mrs. Jane Appleton, who had been an employee of the company for 20 years.

In January 1981, Ms. Appleton sold Master Printer to two employees, Arthur Banes and Jack Wilson. Annie Reese became a junior partner.

Master Printer operated under this general partnership until it was dissolved in October of 1984. It was during this time that Shawn Russell became the sole proprietor of Master Printer.

In October of 1990, Shawn Russell expanded to Theadora, New Mexico. She opened a print shop under the name of Partners Printing. The two locations are full service printing companies and offer a wide range of printing products and services.

MARKET ANALYSIS

Potential Customers:

In addition to our current customers, I have identified the following businesses that will help diversify our revenue base:

√Tandy Toy Store
√Wednesday's
√Thomas, Bailey, & Hardy
√Jamie's Boutique
√Ralph White's Hardware

Small customers that have been overlooked in the past, such as physicians, young professionals, nonprofit organizations, and small businesses in our market area will be identified by next December.

Estimated Printing Market Size and Competition:

Competitive Company	**Revenue**	**Revenue %**	**Advantage**
Charter Stationary	$500,000	25.5	1,2,3,4,8
Langston Printing	$120,000	6.1	6,7
Monroe's Print Shop	$120,000	6.1	1,2,4,5
Penny Printing & Paper	$250,000	12.8	4,5
Priceless Printing	$350,000	17.9	1,2,4,7,8
Partners Printing	$120,000	6.1	2,3,5,6,7
Master Printer	$500,000	25.5	2,3,5,6,8
Total:	$1,960,000	100%	

Legend

①Location
②Service
③Quality
④Selection of Service
⑤Price
⑥Speed
⑦New Business
⑧Equity

The threats within the local market are:

- ❑New print shop(s)
- ❑Price wars
- ❑Lawsuits
- ❑New and better copiers, for in-house do-it-yourselfers
- ❑Brokers

These are only potential threats, so no plan of action is necessary at this time. It is important to recognize and monitor these items for future strategy.

MARKETING STRATEGY

Target Markets

We are going to strengthen our local market by concentrating on increasing our smaller business accounts, as mentioned above. We estimate that by concentrating on maintaining our existing accounts and securing new accounts, our market share will increase as follows:

Master and Partners Combined

	1993-94	1994-95	1995-96	1996-97
Est Sales	$811,000	$924,000	$906,000	$1,033,000
Market Share	35.7%	37.2%	39.8%	44.4%
Growth Rate	10%	14%	-2%	14%

We intend to price our services and products just below or equal to our competition. The goal is to accomplish this while maintaining superior service over our competitors. We can accomplish this through efficiency, company training sessions, and by concentrating on quality control.

We will emphasize our perceived competitive advantage of service, quality, and price, to penetrate the market. To accomplish this, our promotion plan will include:

Public Relations

We intend to have periodic meetings and training sessions teaching employees how to communicate effectively with customers on the phone, and in person. One of our aims, in hopes of satisfying our customers, is to demonstrate alternative ways to do their printing. This should, in many cases, save them time and money. These training sessions are scheduled on the master calendar. (See Supplemental Documents section for information about the company calendar).

Advertising and Sales Incentives

We will develop a series of radio commercials that will be effective in exposing both companies to our market areas. We plan to have periodic promotions offering discounts or specials on various printing items (i.e. business cards, envelopes, letterheads, etc.). We will be able to determine what means of advertising will be most effective for our companies by utilizing these promotions at different intervals on various types of media. Campaigns will be initiated at the monthly Marketing Evaluation Meeting as scheduled on the monthly calendar.

Outside Sales

Outside sales has been a weak area. It has been targeted as a major area of emphasis. We are presently utilizing certain employees who we feel are qualified to work in outside sales. By readjusting production and work schedules, we are certain that the volume of business should noticeably increase for both companies.

Surveys

We will survey present customers and potential customers in an effort to find the weak and strong areas of our products and services. This will be accomplished by utilizing outside sales people and the mail service. Through this survey, we should be able to gain valuable information giving us a competitive edge over our competition. Surveys are also scheduled on the master calendar. A sample survey has been provided in the Supplemental Documents section.

If the marketing goals, as outlined above, are not within 25 percent of projection by February 1, 1994, then the following strategy will be implemented immediately:

- ♦ Additional emphasis will be placed on outside sales by doubling our sales efforts.
- ♦ A 25 percent increase in radio advertising will be initiated.
- ♦ Additional promotional incentives will be implemented.
- ♦ A conference will be held with our accountant and banker.

If the marketing goals are still not met by July 1, then a marketing consultant with proven experience in the printing industry will be hired to implement a successful strategy.

OPERATIONS

The printing plants are located at 52 James Street for Master Printer and 6924 Auburn Drive in Theadora for Partners Printing. The combined labor cost for both companies is $121 per hour. Our operations consist of the following procedures:

First, the customer places the order. The employee taking the order should get as much information from the customer as possible (filling out the job worksheet should be sufficient). Also, at the time the employee receives the order a reasonable time should be determined for completing the job. The customer should be notified of any changes occurring with the order.

JOB FLOW DESCRIPTION

Second, the job ticket with all the information should be completed and documented in the job log book. The typesetter should be notified if typesetting is needing or the job should be taken directly to layout if all of the information is camera-ready. If the job is a repeal order, it should also be taken to layout.

Third, the typesetter should typeset any required copy as specified by the customer. Questions or problems should be directed to the person who took the order. No work should leave the typesetter until it has been properly proofed by two or more employees.

Fourth, every time typesetting is done for a customer, the customer must see a proof before printing is done. Therefore, the client is to be called in for proofing and they should sign a proof slip after reviewing the completed work. A customer who is proofing the typesetting that we have done should be encouraged to check spelling, phone numbers, etc. for accuracy.

It is a good idea, and should be a regular practice, for an employee to go over the proofing process with the customer and review the printing specifications as they are printed on the job ticket. Take nothing for granted and never ASSUME anything.

Fifth, after the proofing and correction stage, the job should go to layout, where logos and art work are added, an original is made, and a plate is prepared for printing.

Sixth, the plate is taken to a pressman. The pressman's job is to pull the stock required for the job and then print it to the specifications on the ticket. Again, the pressman should not assume anything. If there is any question or doubt as to the specifications of printing the job, the pressman should take the questions to the shop foreman for clarification.

Seventh, the job is printed and then goes to the bindery for any bindery work needed (i.e. collating, numbering, padding, cutting, gathering, packaging, etc.). When all bindery work is done and the job is complete, it should either be delivered or taken to the front office for pick-up.

Eighth, the delivery person or the front office employee should get a signed delivery receipt and/or a signed invoice when the job is picked-up. The delivery receipt should then be placed in the job envelope and the envelope filed in the completed box. The invoice also has its assigned place and should be filed there without fail.

Personnel in each department should be aware of the delivery dates requested by customers. The work schedules should ensure that these dates are met. Should a job be held up in a department that will affect the delivery dates, the customer should be notified to help maintain proper public relations.

Also, it is the responsibility of the bookkeeper to make sure that all customers are invoiced weekly and that statements are in the mail at the proper time. Any time an invoice can be delivered with the job, it should be, as this will eliminate unnecessary postage and work load in the front office.

MANAGEMENT AND ORGANIZATION

Managers

The managers' duties are quite encompassing, as they oversee all shop employees. Therefore, this job requires knowledge of operational procedures, people skills, and a very broad knowledge of shop equipment maintenance. Further duties and responsibilities are:

- Management of each department supervisor
- Ordering supplies and all paper stock
- Overseeing the completion of jobs and ensuring quality control
- Maintaining schedules
- Cost controlling and waste management which requires shop personnel to use stock that is cut and left from previous jobs, instead of cutting down new stock
- Responsible for monitoring job flow and ensuring that each order is on schedule
- Taking job orders, answering the phone if the front office needs help, and waiting on customers

A listing of all management goals that have been derived as a result of this plan are listed in the Supplemental Documents section.

When the previous months financial statements are received, these procedures will be reevaluated and appropriate changes will be made. If the cost containment measures are not effective, then changes will be made. Financial reviews are scheduled on the monthly calendar.

Target percentages for the line items that will be monitored for containment are:

Cost of Sales	35%
Auto Expense	1%
Telephone	0.8%
Maintenance and Repairs	0.5%

TQM will be instituted after management is educated on the benefits and short comings of the process. TQM has been scheduled on the master calendar.

GOALS AND OBJECTIVES

Management Goals

- ❑Recapitalize through loan proceeds.
- ❑Initiate a plan of action to create a better working atmosphere.
- ❑Reduce cost and increase profits.
- ❑Through new formats and procedures, increase profitability.
- ❑Strengthen present customer base and expand customer base to outside areas (Rosemond, Alareado, Mansfield, etc.).
- ❑Update equipment to expand into more specialized areas of the printing market.
- ❑Increase employee benefits.

Operational Goals

Cost Containment

- ❑Contain all costs within FRA guidelines where applicable.
- ❑Establish a regular insurance audit to determine needs and reduce cost where applicable.
- ❑Install TQM in phases as indicated on the master calendar.
- ❑Examine costs on a regular basis during monthly financial review.

Implement the following accounting changes:

❑Capital Expenditures

These items are projected to be purchased in the following time frame:

February 1994 equipment improvements approximately $5,000
July 1995 additional equipment purchases
(typesetting equipment, presses) $30,000

Productivity/Efficiency Goals

- ❑Contain waste through regular management meetings, at the present time and through TQM methods in the long-run.
- ❑Install employee suggestion box with cash incentives for suggestion that result in cost savings on increased productivity. This will lead to a team based presentation program through TQM in the long-run.
- ❑Outline Quality Control Procedures. (See subsection on Production and Quality Control).

Timing

Business Plan complete - September 21st
Loan Funded - October 2nd

A management calendar has been developed to indicate projection dates for reaching strategic decision goals. It is also used to schedule strategic planning sessions, evaluations, and general meetings.

HISTORICAL FINANCIAL ANALYSIS AND OPERATIONAL GOALS

Information about obtaining the comprehensive historical income statements can be found in the Supplemental Documents section. The following text is a summarized version of these statements.

An analysis of the 12-year trend indicates an increase in revenue for 11 of the past 12 years. The year, 1981, is the exception to this trend.

In 1981, Shawn Russell was adjusting to making management decisions, while continuing her work as a presswoman. The work force consisted of the two general partners, one junior partner, one full-time employee, and occasional part-time help. The high number of employees resulted in lower salaries and wages for that year.

In 1982, there was a considerable salary increase without a corresponding increase in sales or gross profit. The difficulties experienced in the partnership limited sound management decisions. This salary increase, along with the absence of an active sales force, contributed to a decrease in gross profits for the company by 1984.

In August of 1984, the partnership realized that it needed to disband. It was dissolved in October of 1984. After the dissolution of the partnership, the shop has realized steady growth.

Several expense line items have been analyzed and have provided opportunities for cost containment.

Cost of Goods

This item appears to have been out of proportion at certain periods. To remedy this, several steps have been and will be taken.

- ❑ Procedures are being taken to monitor material waste. Waste due to errors can be considerably reduced by implementing and enforcing policies on quality control.

- ❑ Pricing updates will be made more often to reflect price increases on papers and supplies. Price lists have recently been updated and modified to simplify pricing procedures for employees. This will be a major help in eliminating pricing errors.

- ❑ Each department will be responsible for recording time spent on each job. This will show what types of printing jobs are more or less profitable, and indicate what measures should be taken to increase profitability.

Wages (including owners)

Wages have averaged 28.6 percent over the 12 year history. Current labor expense is high, 37.3 percent of gross sales, due to the loss of the Hillman Equipment contracts. The figures are 1/2 actual and 1/2 projection. One employee has been terminated and one employee quit. As a result, this percentage should be lower by year end. The FRA (Financial Research Association) comparison for a like-size business indicates a 35.98 average. Therefore, Master Printer and Partners Printing are only 1.32 percent above this industry average. Increases in productivity brought about through the implementation of this plan will bring this figure to below the industry average.

Payroll Taxes

Payroll taxes have increased from .7 percent in 1981 to 3.7 percent in 1992. However, this line item is only controllable indirectly through total labor.

Advertising

Advertising is .7 percent on average and is above the FRA average of .39 percent for small-sized businesses. In order to increase our penetration in the market, this item will have to remain above this average for a short time. However, we do feel that by utilizing an effective advertising strategy, our advertising dollars will yield a greater return than in the past.

Auto Expense

Auto expense was .8 percent in 1982, and 1.9 in 1992, or a 237 percent increase. There are no industry averages for this line item, but it is deemed to be high.

The increase is contributed primarily to the frequent trips and distance from Grace to Theadora. These trips should be less frequent due to the loss of certain Hillman contracts. Therefore, this expense should decrease without an action plan.

Bad Debts

Bad debts have not been a significant problem in the past, but we will continue to monitor accounts receivable to avoid developing any problems in this area.

Insurance

Insurance costs have escalated from .4 percent of gross to 1.2 percent and are in line with the FRA industry average of 1.78 percent.

Interest

Interest has moved from 2.3 percent of gross to 2.8 percent in 1991, which is a 21.7 percent increase in 11 years. We hope to reduce our interest expense by obtaining a loan at lower interest rates than we are presently paying.

Lease Expense

Lease expense has fluctuated over the years, starting at 4.6 percent in 1981 and decreasing to 2.3 percent in 1991. We hope to reduce this expense even further by purchasing equipment, rather than acquiring it on lease options.The purchases will be evaluated with our accountant to determine what items will be most advantageous at the time.

Repairs and Maintenance

Repairs and maintenance increased significantly from 1981 through 1988. This was due in part to service agreements on new equipment. From 1988, however, this expense has significantly decreased from .77 percent of revenues to .37 percent.

FINANCIAL INFORMATION

Pro-forma income statement projections and balance sheets are available from the main office of Harris, Ridder, & Manny, Inc., 6734 Desert Drive, Grace, NM 84753. The following is a summary of their findings and recommendations.

Two pro-forma income statements were constructed for the purpose of analysis. One is based on the current debt structure and the other focuses on a capital restructuring program. The first indicates a net cash position of $18,348 at year end, while the second reveals a new cash position of $25,016. The capital restructuring program is as follows:

Payoff existing loans/notes	$161,000
Accounts Payable	$64,000
Operating Capital	$25,000
TOTAL	$250,000

Of the $25,000 in operating costs, $10,000 will be placed in a money market account and marked for emergency use only. This account will be built to a level of $26,000, which is ten percent of gross profit. It will be maintained at that level in accordance with the gross profit figures.

Historical growth has occurred at 15 percent over the last 11 years. However, for purposes of this analysis, the growth rate was held to ten percent. The actual year to year growth rate varies in accordance with the ebb and flow of the local economy. The 1995-1996 fiscal year shows an actual decrease in sales, something the company has experienced only once in the past 11 years.

Owing to greater efficiencies and economies of scale, the net cash available grows from $25,223 in 1993-1994 to $80,404 in 1994-1995.
A FMV balance sheet was constructed because of the extensive depreciation the company currently has on the books. A market analysis was obtained from the company (See Supplemental Documents) to establish the value of the real property. The value of the equipment was estimated using replacement costs, instead of new costs, as a guideline. Value was given to the leased equipment only if it was projected to pay out in less than six months. The owners' equity in FMV terms is 34.5 percent.

Cash was used as a plug figure from the income statements. Accounts receivable and inventory were increased at five percent per year, and this amount was subtracted from cash because no allocation was made in the pro-forma income statements. The capital purchases were also subtracted from cash. Depreciation was estimated at the current rate for the life of the projection. After the current period, the payables were reduced to $1,000.

Since the business has a substantial amount of equipment depreciated out or almost out, the net worth figure was modified by adding the FMV net to arrive at an adjusted figure.

BALANCE SHEET

ASSETS

	FMV	%
Current Assets:		
Cash	$3,240	0.9%
Cash Equivalents	$0	0.0%
Accounts Receivable	$54,563	15.6%
Inventory	$15,322	4.4%
Salary Advances	$642	0.2%
Prepaid Interest	$7,194	2.1%
Prepaid Loan Costs	$754	0.2%
Total Current Assets	$81,715	23.4%
Long Term Assets:		
Partners Printing	$65,000	
Master Printer	$65,000	18.6%
Machinery & Equipment	$126,510	36.2%
Leasehold Value	$5,800	1.7%
1-P/U; 1-VAN	$10,000	2.9%
Rental Property	$60,000	17.2%
Total Fixed Assets	$267,310	76.6%
Total Assets	$349,025	100%

BALANCE SHEET
...continued

LIABILITIES

Current Liabilities:		
Accounts Payable	$60,000	17.2%
All Current - Notes	$42,332	12.1%
Current - Notes Payable	$0	0.0%
Current Portion - Long Term	$0	0.0%
Total Current Liabilities	$102,332	29.3%
Long Term Liabilities:		
Mortgage Payable	$0	0.0%
All Long Term Balance	$0	0.0%
Other Long Term Liabilities	$126,361	
Total Long Term Liabilities	$126,361	36.2%
Total Liabilities	$228,693	65.6%
NET WORTH	$120,333	34.5%

Major Assumptions

⇨Economy of Grace and Theadora remain relatively the same.

⇨No "significant" new competition.

⇨No large capital purchases within two years.

⇨TQM will be implemented within one year, with resultant efficiencies.

SUPPLEMENTAL DOCUMENTS

Company Calendar

The Master Calendar is a long range planning tool for company managers. It is a five year record of management meetings and programs. Some of the items included on this calendar are: Insurance Audits, Financial Review Sessions, Policy and Procedure Meetings, a schedule for implementation of the TQM Program, and Quarterly Management Summary Meetings.

A copy of the Master Calendar can be obtained from the Master Printer office.

Organizational Chart and Management Resumes

A chart illustrating the management hierarchy has been prepared by the owner, Shawn Russell. Please contact Ms. Russell for a copy.

Management resumes and references are available upon request.

Financial Documents

Tables containing sales figures, gross profit, operating expenses, other income, and net income over the past 12 years have been prepared by Harris, Ridder, & Manny, Inc., 6734 Desert Dr., Grace, NM 84753.

The firm of Harris, et al has also compiled additional financial statements and supplementary schedules including: a proprietorship balance sheet; a table illustrating the proprietor's capital for the one month and eight month period that ended in August of 1993; and other related statements of income. Please contact the main office, at the address listed above, for copies of these financial documents.

Market Analysis

A Market Analysis of local properties has been completed by the Benchman Company, 7483 Riverside Dr., Grace, NM 84753. The report revealed the estimated market value of both single family dwellings and retail office space. The homes ranged from $45,000 to $105,00 and the office facilities were between $9,500 to $70,000. A copy of the full analysis is available upon request.

Employee Guidelines and Production and Quality Control

Production and Quality Control is everyone's responsibility.

Dealing with Customers

Be polite and cordial

A prerequisite and requirement to taking orders is being friendly and cordial, regardless of how bad a day you may have had. Make each customer feel he or she is important and welcome. Every customer is important, so be careful not to be rude or brash.

When a customer arrives, know in advance who is going to deal with their order. Wait on customers immediately. DO NOT keep them waiting. If more than one customer comes in get someone in the back to help.

Receiving Jobs or Information
(in person or on the phone)

Write everything down (use the work order form)
1. Record person's NAME, TIME of call, and DATE.
2. Get the address and phone number if possible.
3. Get a complete and detailed description of what the customer's request. This includes:

Employee Guidelines and Production and Quality Control
...continued

- •Type, color, and weight of stock
- •Size or sizes of stock
- •Color or colors of ink
- •Types of bindery required (if necessary)
- •Job due date
- •Question information that is vague
- •Quantity or quantities of order
- •Record price quoted if possible

4. Do not quote the customer a price unless you are sure of it. Double check the price with someone if possible.

5. When receiving information concerning jobs already in production, write down the change and send it immediately to the appropriate department. Make sure that the change is recorded on the job ticket.

6. Watch for Obvious Errors: Always check name, dates, and phone numbers.

Follow-Up

❑Job Orders

After information on Page One has been obtained and recorded, the old job ticket should be pulled and a new ticket should be filled out. Someone other than the person taking the job should call the customer to verify information recorded, including the price.

❑Proofs

After a proof is ready, with respect to the due date, the customer will be contacted, or proof will be delivered to the customer. If proof has not been picked up or OK'd in a reasonable time, with respect to the due date, a follow-up call needs to be made to the customer.

The same shall apply to completed jobs waiting to be picked up by the customer.

❑Supplies

If supplies that have been ordered have not arrived in a reasonable amount of time, a follow-up call is to be made to the company. This also applies to orders shipped outside of the print shop.

Errors

❑If it is clear where the fault lies, due to carelessness or negligence, the cost of the job may be charged to the person or persons responsible for the error.

Employee Guidelines and Production and Quality Control *...continued*

❑The majority of errors can be eliminated by follow a few simple guidelines:

1. Communicate effectively
2. Work together
3. Keep your mind and thoughts on your job

Reducing Expenses

❑Reducing Waste

1. Utilized supplies efficiently
2. Avoid cutting too much stock
3. Be conservative when using supplies. Use only what is needed.
4. Designated persons will be responsible for cutting papers and stocks for each job prior to printing
5. Each job ticket will be attached to a production control sheet. Each person and department will be responsible for recording the time the project was started and the time it was completed.

❑ Production Time

1. Quality Time
   a. Utilize time efficiently
   b. Strive to produce 8 hours of quality production daily
2. Overtime
   a. Work overtime only when necessary
   b. Overtime is encouraged when the level of production justifies it.
   c. Inform the front office when you are making up time or working comp-time or overtime.

❑Maintenance & Neatness

Equipment

1. Regular Maintenance on equipment is required:
   Equipment will be lubricated on a regular basis. Operators of each piece of equipment will set up a regular maintenance schedule for each piece of equipment. These schedules will be submitted and reviewed at the end of each month.
2. Equipment will be cleaned and kept clean daily.

Work Areas

1. Each person will be responsible for keeping his or her immediate work area neat and organized
2. An organized work space will create a more efficient work environment

It is in everyone's best interest to be efficient and to reduce costs as much as possible. If you see something that needs to be done, inquire about it, and see that it gets done. Each person working at this company is a valuable and important part of our success.

CUSTOMER SURVEY FORM FOR MASTER PRINTER

Thank you for taking a few moments to complete this Survey. It is designed to ensure that our company provides the best possible quality of products and services.

Date__________________ Phone Number (___)__________________

FAX (___)____________________________

CustomerName______________________________________

Address____

How would you rate Master Printer in the following areas:

	Excellent	Good	Fair	Poor	Not Sure
Prices	❑	❑	❑	❑	❑
Phone Courtesy	❑	❑	❑	❑	❑
Friendliness	❑	❑	❑	❑	❑
Product Quality	❑	❑	❑	❑	❑
Communication with Customer	❑	❑	❑	❑	❑
Promptness of Product Delivery	❑	❑	❑	❑	❑

Please comment on how we might better serve you and your company or organization with printing needs and service.

____

____

____

____

____

Name of person authorized to complete this survey

____

For completing and returning this survey, you will receive a coupon for 10% off on your next printing order. When placing your next order, attach the coupon to the order form to receive your discount.

THANK YOU

Printing Company

BUSINESS PLAN

PRINTER PERFECT

7521 Hwy. 59
Baton Rouge, LA 26390

March 9, 1993

Printer Perfect is a new venture specializing in full-color, sheet-fed printing. It caters to short and medium runs. The following start-up plan provides an approach to new business planning and describes how the company will keep ahead of its competition.

SEC NOTICE

The information contained in this presentation is confidential and intended for the private use of those parties selected by the Officers of Printer Perfect pursuant to the needs of Printer Perfect and has been issued to those parties in good faith and under this pretence. This presentation is not intended as an offer to purchase stock in Printer Perfect nor is such an offer being made, implied, or otherwise stated by the Officers of Printer Perfect.

Any and all selected parties who may share the views of Printer Perfect, regarding the potential for growth and financial prosperity, and who may desire to become financially involved with the Officers of Printer Perfect, with regards to such potential, are assumed to be of a "Sophisticated Investor" class, as described in the codes of the Securities Exchange Commission.

Printer Perfect is a new start-up venture organized and chartered as a corporation in the State of Louisiana. Its Officers are listed later in this presentation. Printer Perfect is a Sub-Chapter S Corporation, capitalized at $1,000, with 1,000 shares, and no par value stock issued. Printer Perfect will build its home base of operations in Baton Rouge, Louisiana.

Printer Perfect is seeking financial assistance to commence its operations. The amount needed to begin operation is a fifty-thousand dollar ($50,000) line of credit.

OFFER

The Officers of Printer Perfect realize the necessity to offer an attractive incentive for the use of an Investor's credit lines. In an effort to be realistic and fair from the viewpoint of the potential Investor, the Officers of Printer Perfect have elected to offer a simple and totally realistic profit plan for the Investor, based solely on gross sales.

Printer Perfect will deposit five percent (5%) of all gross receipts from all sales of Printer Perfect in an escrow account with National Bank, Baton Rouge, LA, until such funds in said account amount to a total of twenty-five thousand dollars ($25,000). The proceeds of this account will be made available to the Investors upon the release of the lines of credit by Printer Perfect. The total length of time for the use of the Investor's credit lines shall not exceed two years from date of investment. This twenty-five thousand dollar ($25,000) profit represents a net gain of fifty percent (50%) in two years or less.

Printer Perfect agrees to make quarterly financial statements available to all Investors until such time as escrow funds attain the twenty-five thousand dollar ($25,000) maximum. All accounts of Printer Perfect will be audited on an annual basis by Cooper and Schornack, PC, New Orleans, LA. The findings of these audits will also be made available to the Investors until such time as escrow funds reach the twenty-five thousand dollar ($25,000) maximum.

The debts incurred, as a result of the use of the Investor's credit lines, will be repaid in the following manner: A ten thousand dollar ($10,000) limit will be placed on the general fund account of Printer Perfect. Any and all deposited funds which exceed the ten thousand dollar ($10,000) limit will be swept out and automatically applied to any outstanding debts resulting from the use of borrowed funds. This sweep account method of repayment will allow Printer Perfect to use the available credit lines in a more efficient and cost effective manner than regular thirty, sixty or ninety day notes.

It is understood that all assets of Printer Perfect will be pledged toward repayment of any and all unpaid debts resultant from the use of the Investor's credit lines, until such time as all said debts have been fully repaid. Furthermore, the Officers of Printer Perfect will pledge to make personal restitution for any and all unpaid debts resultant from use of the funds of Investor's credit lines, should Printer Perfect default in such-indebtedness.

CONCEPT

The basic concept of any printing company is to put ink on paper for a profit. The primary difference between a large printing company, such as Random House, and a small printing company, is how much ink they can place on how much paper for how much profit. This simple concept allows for major differences in the degree of sophistication by which ink is applied to paper, the types of paper to which ink is applied, what is done with the paper once the ink has been applied, and the amount of profit to be made. This brings us to where Printer Perfect will fit in the overall picture of the printing industry. Printer Perfect will be a short-to-medium run, sheet-fed, full-color printing company, which specializes in affordable, pleasing color printing. Short-to-medium runs means jobs of 1,000 to 100,000 copies. Sheet-fed means that the equipment prints individual sheets of paper, rather than continuous roll stock paper. Full-color means that the end product is a printed image like a color photograph. Pleasing color means that the color printed images produced are reasonably close to the colors of the original from which they were taken, and are clear and pleasing to the eye. In layman's terms, Printer Perfect will specialize in producing the type of color printing which accounts for seventy-five percent of all color printing that is produced in America today.

In Baton Rouge there is only one company classified as a full-color printing company, Print 1. This company has become specialized as a short-to-medium run color publication company, with long-term contracts for monthly publications. Print 1 does not solicit general color printing. The market in the Baton Rouge area is wide-open for an aggressive, full-color printing company. Printer Perfect intends to aggressively serve this market.

As our nation grows, it becomes more sophisticated. Due to the technological revolution which is being waged, small companies are demanding more of their printers than they did ten years ago. Today's printing clients demand perfection. They want smart, good-looking color pieces for their products and advertising. They want it, they can afford it, and they deserve to get it. To survive in any business today a company must zero in on a market in which it wants to compete, be capable of producing the type of work which that market demands, be well organized and capable of producing its product cost-effectively, and be sales oriented and aggressive. Printing is no different. No longer can a printing company simply hang out a "Print Shop" sign and expect the world to come running.

Printing can be a very lucrative business venture. However, to be profitable in today's competitive market one must become specialized. If a company can only produce short run, simple printing profitably, then this is the market it must aggressively pursue. A full-color printing company simply cannot produce 250 business cards profitably. Conversely, a small single-color print shop cannot produce 50,000 full-color brochures profitably. Specialization is here.

No printing company can compete in a '90s high-speed, full-color world with slow '50s equipment and skills. The ones who try will fail. Any printing company, large or small, which refuses to expand, upgrade its equipment, and increase its skill levels, will slowly lose its profitability and eventually vanish. The days of the local "Print Shop" that could print everything its customers wanted have drawn to a close.

Printer Perfect will start with an edge over its local competitors because of its equipment choices and skilled people. It will remain a leader because of the vision and determination of its officers.

Today's full-color printing companies require extensive and sophisticated equipment, skilled personnel, and a good client base for survival and growth. Printer Perfect can lease the equipment, it has the key personnel in place, and has instant access to a broad client base. All that is needed to make this new company a thriving Baton Rouge industry is a small financial "Jump Start." Printer Perfect needs your assistance. Today IS the future and Printer Perfect is for today.

MARKET

Within a forty mile radius of Printer Perfect there are over fifty large national and international manufacturing companies. Each of these companies uses the services of full color printing companies. Printer Perfect will aggressively seek out these accounts to produce their printing. One advantage Printer Perfect will have over the printing companies in New Orleans will be the ability to produce the end product at a more competitive cost. As earlier stated, we are living in a computer world. By selecting new state-of-the-art equipment, the production costs will be lowered because of the speed of the equipment and the lower skill level requirements. By being a "new" company, Printer Perfect will not be concerned with recovering its investment in slower, "old style" equipment which has many good years of service left.

Full-color printing will be the specialty of Printer Perfect. However, simple single and two-color work will also be solicited. The same sophisticated equipment that prints four colors of ink on one side of a sheet of paper is also capable of printing two colors of ink on one side of the paper, reversing the paper, and printing two additional colors on the other side. This is an obvious advantage over simple single-color equipment. Although the equipment may cost more initially, the speed at which the work may be accomplished will easily offset these costs and make the end product better and less expensive for the client.

In the immediate Baton Rouge area, there are over two hundred smaller accounts which are now being serviced by the local "print shops." These accounts will be easily serviced by Printer Perfect simply because of the ability to provide a better product, at the same or even lower costs, than the local "print shops."

INITIAL START-UP COST

It would be sheer folly to think that all building improvements, equipment purchases, inventory, and operational expenses for six months of operation could be covered for $50,000. However, we will start the operation in a conservative and cost effective manner that will allow growth at a financially solid pace.

The building, described later, will need a few internal improvements to make operation feasible. Two restrooms must be added to accommodate the production employees, a camera room must be built, and electrical current for equipment must be run from the main source. The labor for these improvements will be done by the officers and staff of Printer Perfect. The plumbing for the additional restrooms will be the responsibility of the landlord. There are several small used pieces of equipment that will be purchased, rather than leased. The offices must be furnished and made presentable.

Listed below are the budgeted figures for these start up costs.

Initial lease payment	$1,229
Initial utility services	$600
Internal improvements	$2,000
Small equipment purchases	$15,000
Office furnishings equipment & supplies	$2,500
Initial printing supplies	$1,500
Total	$22,829

LEASE EQUIPMENT

There are four major pieces of equipment which will be acquired during the first year of operation. These four pieces are:

- ❑ 30" Challenge auto-spacer program paper cutter (or its equivalent)
  Approximate cost: $13,500 (new)
- ❑ 19" x 25" Omni Adast two-color perfector offset printing press
  Approximate cost: $165,000 (new)
- ❑ McCain nine-pocket collator/saddle binder with three knife trimmer
  Approximate cost: $24,000 (used)
- ❑ Merganthaler/Linotronic typesetting machine
  Approximate cost: $35,000 (new)

All of the above equipment will be acquired on lease/purchase plans which are available through the respective manufacturers. Total lease payments for all of the above equipment will not exceed $4,000.00 monthly. No lease/purchase will be entered into until such time as a positive cash flow has been established.

LOCATION

One of the pitfalls of any new business is the poor choice of a location. Printer Perfect has circumvented this potential problem by selecting an excellent location for its operation. Printer Perfect will be located at US Hwy. 59 at SR 51. This location is a short three minute drive from the west side of Baton Rouge, and is located in an area which shows the greatest potential for growth in Baton Rouge. The building is a 13,520 sq.ft. metal structure with a solid concrete base capable of handling the weight of any massive printing equipment. It has a loading dock for paper and equipment deliveries, ample employee parking, and a 1,000 sq.ft. brick veneer office.

Many printing companies opt to select more prestigious locations under the false pretense that clients will seek them out. In many instances, a small printing company will locate in a more retail traffic-oriented building, thinking that walk-in traffic will offset the additional costs of the more sophisticated environment. This has proven to be a false concept over and over again. Printing clients are not the general public, but rather, business executives who make their selections of printers based on performance, quality and costs, rather than location of the printing company. Printer Perfect has opted to put its financial investment in space, rather than prestige.

The following factors have been carefully considered in selecting this location for Printer Perfect.

Proximity to clients

Since the printing industry demands personal one-on-one service, most of the clients will be served by sales/ management personnel at their respective businesses. However, should a client desire to visit the printing facility in person, the selected location will be easy to find. It will be clearly identifiable, as a stand-alone structure facing US Hwy. 59, not hidden in a maze of look-a-like offices in some discrete industrial complex.

Potential for expansion

This one factor is probably the largest deterrent to growth that any new business faces. Printing companies are complex with many large pieces of equipment. They require highly skilled, industrial moving companies to relocate. Moves are very costly in actual dollars spent and loss of revenue from production down-time. There have been thousands of instances where printing companies elected to stay small simply because the cost of relocation was too great. Printer Perfect is fortunate to have this location available. Through negotiations with the lessor, Printer Perfect will be able to secure a portion of the entire building for the first three years, with an option for the balance of the building after the first three years. This will allow a great potential for growth. Based on national averages for the printing industry, a company with 13,000 sq.ft. of production area, when properly managed and staffed, should be able to produce approximately twelve million dollars in annual gross sales. This potential should be sufficient for ten to twelve years of operation of Printer Perfect. Once a printing company reaches this level of production, an alternate production facility is usually chosen over a plant expansion or relocation.

Cost

Obviously, any company must consider the cost of the location. Printer Perfect is fortunate that the chosen location will be available at realistic costs. For the first three years, the lease will be on an accelerating scale, beginning at $0.13 (thirteen cents) per sq.ft. occupied space and ending at $0.20 (twenty cents) per sq.ft. This will give the company an opportunity to recover start-up costs and build a solid financial foundation prior to accepting responsibility for the larger monthly rent expenditures. The officers of Printer Perfect have negotiated to begin operation in the east portion of the building, which encompasses 9,460 sq.ft. of the total 13,520 sq.ft. This translates into a monthly expenditure of $1,229.80 ($0.13 x 9,460 sq.ft.) for the first year, $1,513.60 ($0.16 x 9,460) for the second year, and a maximum of $1,982.00 ($0.10 x 9,460) beginning the third year and continuing for six additional years thereafter. First option for the entire 13,520 sq.ft. building, at the end of the first three years, at the $0.20 per sq.ft. rate, has also been agreed upon by the lessor.

ASSUMPTIONS

Gross Profit

Using a formula developed and tested over a lengthy period of time, we found the average gross profit to be 67.67% of sales price. We will be using 68% as a gross profit figure in making the projections for the potential profitability of Printer Perfect. The average price per impression was $.05.

Efficiency

Using a similarly tested formula, we found the total number of impressions (applying ink to one piece of 8 1/2 x 11 inch paper) possible in an eight hour day will be 1,032,000. This is a 100% efficiency rate. No company can possibly attain this figure. However, based on the experience of the officers of Printer Perfect, efficiency ratios of 45% to 65% are attainable. We will use the efficiency factor of 50% in making projections regarding the addition of more equipment or an additional shift of workers.

Typesetting

Typesetting will not be figured in this presentation. Typesetting is a separate entity in printing and must be treated as such. Printer Perfect will have typesetting facilities by the sixth month of operation. However, the cost and profits from this phase of the operation are not included in the projections. Any and all profits from the typesetting department will be included in all financial reports and dividend payments, since such reports and payments are based on the gross sales of the entire operation.

Existing Economic Conditions

It will be assumed that the economic conditions that currently exist in Louisiana will continue. The officers of Printer Perfect cannot control these factors. Should extreme negative economic conditions befall the Louisiana area, these adverse conditions could effect the projections made in this presentation.

FIXED MONTHLY EXPENSES

The first six months of operation are probably the most crucial for any new business. The Officers of Printer Perfect are fully prepared to guide this new venture through this difficult stage of operation. Every effort will be made to maintain a low fixed monthly expenditure level during this time period.

Tables for projected fixed monthly expenditures for the first six months, the first year, and the second year have been prepared.

OFFICERS

Mr. Paulie Perlman, President. Mr. Perlman's experience in color printing spans a twenty year period. His in-depth printing knowledge and skills assure Printer Perfect of a foundation from which to build an exceptional color printing company. Mr. Perlman has served in virtually every phase of the printing industry. He began his printing career during his high school years in the late 1950s. By 1968, he had become a journeyman color pressman. Mr. Perlman entered management in 1970, and by 1976 had risen to the position of General Manager of Copy Quickly, a major New Orleans printing company employing over 75 skilled people. In 1975, he was asked to join the staff at New Orleans Junior College, where he taught evening classes in Advanced Color Printing. Mr. Perlman also served as Advisor to the Board of the Printing Industry Association in 1977. In late 1979, Mr. Perlman left the printing industry to become self-employed as president of Bayou Building Trades, a New Orleans-based, offshore model construction company. Under his leadership, BBT grew to become the most respected and well-known offshore model construction company on the Gulf Coast. Due to negative economic conditions that existed in New Orleans during late 1987, Mr. Perlman was unable to continue operation of BBT and, in mid-summer 1988, he elected to relocate to Baton Rouge. He is currently employed as General Manager of Vidalia Imports in Baton Rouge. Mr. Perlman is a man of vision and wisdom. He is enthusiastic, with sharp business skills and a vast knowledge of color printing. Mr. Perlman gives Printer Perfect an enviable edge over any of its competitors, both present and future. Mr. Perlman is 49 years old, married, and lives in Baton Rouge.

Mr. Mark Benjamin, Vice President. Mr. Benjamin comes to Printer Perfect with 12 years of solid, "hands on" printing experience. Mr. Benjamin began his printing career here in the Baton Rouge area while under the employ of Louisiana State Insurance Company. In 1979, he joined the staff at Vidalia Imports, where he currently serves as production manager. Mr. Benjamin has a unique ability to bridge the "gap" between the desires of the customer and the production necessary to meet those desires. Mr. Benjamin is constantly seeking ways to increase efficiency and lower costs, while maintaining high standards of quality for the client. He is a very capable manager of production employees and has an extensive knowledge of printing equipment. Over his ten year tenure with

OFFICERS...*continued*

Vidalia Imports, Mr. Benjamin has become well-known for his promptness with delivery schedules, as well as for working with clients. Mr. Benjamin is driven by his desire to improve the quality of printing services in Baton Rouge. He is stalwart of energy and strength for the long, laborious hours so necessary in building a new company. Mr. Benjamin is 38 years old, married, and lives in Baton Rouge.

Mr. Gregory May, Secretary/Treasurer. Printer Perfect is indeed fortunate to secure the services of such an outstanding professional as Mr. May. Mr. May began his professional career with the Louisiana State Insurance Company in New Orleans. While under the employ of LSIC, Mr. May managed the largest single Premium Payment Department in the LSIC state office. He was honored several times with efficiency awards and quickly rose to division manager for the LSIC State Premium Payment Department. In 1979, Mr. May joined the National Bay Bank in New Orleans as assistant bookkeeper. In three years, Mr. May had risen to Assistant Head Teller of that same bank. In 1983, Mr. May joined the staff of Gulf State Bank, also in New Orleans, as manager of Drive-Thru Operations, where he became solely responsible for the 21-lane Drive-Thru. His efficiency and excellent management skills were awarded upon two occasions as "Employee of the Month" for the entire GSB system, encompassing 17 branch banks and the third largest downtown bank in New Orleans. This is most impressive when one considers that his competition was over 6,000 fellow employees and managers. In 1988, Mr. May relocated to Baton Rouge and is currently serving as Accounts Manager for AABAA, a Third Party Administrator for the Louisiana School Systems. His primary duty, under this employ, is the management of over 5,000 individual payroll deducation accounts for teachers and other school officials. Mr. May is well-versed in computer skills and has mastered the use of all of the popular database and financial computer software programs used in business today. Mr. May is a very personable and talented individual. He is driven by his desire for perfection and efficiency. His financial background with the banking industry, plus his ability to control and manage massive amounts of data, will provide Printer Perfect with financial and office management second to none. Mr. May is 44 years old, married, and lives in a suburb of Baton Rouge.

Publisher

BUSINESS PLAN

INFOGUIDE INC.

118 Wilson Ct.
Paramus, N.J. 12204

February 12, 1992

Infoguide Inc. is a reference publisher. This plan provides details on how it intends to utilize additional funding to purchase, market, and support the continued production of a title it will purchase from a larger publisher.

EXECUTIVE SUMMARY

The Bakers Bread Guide, completed and first introduced in April 1991, is the only updated source of bread laws reporting instructions for every state, county, city, town and parish in the U.S. - some 4300 jurisdictions. It is an annual subscription service priced at over $500 per year. More than 200 grocery stores and bakeries already subscribe to the Guide: annual subscriptions are over $90,000 today.

Able Bakery Publications has agreed to sell the Guide to me for its balance sheet book value, about $131,000, because the Guide is not significant enough as a new product within their new business strategy.

Initial Financing

I have established a company, Infoguide, Inc., a New Jersey Corporation, which will be capitalized at $200,000, for the purpose of producing and marketing the Guide. The company will be owned 2/3 by me jointly with my wife and 1/3 by my wife's mother. $75,000 will show as common stock; $125,000 will be a subordinated five-year balloon note.

This financing is adequate to meet the needs of the expected forecast for cash needs to operate and market the Guide successfully.

Five-Year Goal

Most of the purchase price will be allocated to 750 sets of the Guide which are held in inventory ready for distribution. The initial goal and total focus of the company will be to get these 750 sets into the hands of power users, the grocery stores and bakeries which do a national business.

At the anticipated sales rate of 240 sets per year, the 1000 subscriber level will be accomplished in 1996.

Once all 1000 sets originally printed are subscribed, annual sales will exceed $500,000 while production and fulfillment costs will be less than $200,000. In other words, the products will become a cash cow.

Excess cash will be invested in related products and services and/or acquisitions, leveraging the company into a position to sell out or go public.

Marketing/Sales Strategy

I have access to a number of lists of prospective subscribers, including continuing access to Guide clients under the acquisition agreement. The markets are very highly targetable: total penetration will be about 3000 sets worth almost $2 million in annual sales.

The most effective sales approach to the target markets is telephone sales. I have identified two successful salespeople to work as independent contractors selling the Guide to firms I will identify.

Additional Financing

I intend to obtain another $100,000 in term financing in order to sell the 1000 sets more quickly and to reduce production costs significantly.

PRESENT SITUATION

The marketplace has a genuine need for the Bread Laws Guide as demonstrated by the fact that five of the top ten grocery stores in the U.S. are already subscribers. However, markets are still mostly untapped because the present owner of the service is unwilling to commit adequate resources to direct marketing.

I am poised now to get to the target markets with adequate resources and effective selling propositions.

Products and Services

At its present stage, the Bread Laws Guide is fully developed as an annual subscription print service. It is the only updated service of its kind. It was introduced initially in April 1991 with a quarterly update cycle. Since then, three updates have been completed.

Product Life Cycle

The current service is early in its life cycle, with total sales of 200 in a market estimated at 3000 potential users. There is little likelihood that the need for such a service will diminish because the bread statutes are law in all 50 states.

During the next few years, the objective of the company will be to increase the subscription level to 1000. At that point, sufficient funds will be available from operations to extend the product line to include ancillary services, such as online access, a call-in service, a newsletter, and Bread Laws forms sales.

Pricing and Profitability

Current prices may be too high at $595 per year for initial penetration marketing; this will be reviewed as soon as the Guide is acquired. There is significant leeway in pricing because of the economics of this type of annual subscription publication.

Profitability is, in a real sense, controllable because the most substantial cost is for marketing/sales rather than for production, fulfillment, and administration. At the targeted 1000 subscription level, in any event, the service is solidly profitable with positive cash flow.

Why Is Able Bakery Publications Selling?

First, the division responsible for the Guide was restructured in 1991 for many reasons, one of which was that many of the companies had become unprofitable. Second, the Guide produced an accounting loss of $137,000 in fiscal 1991 and was expected to show a loss of $50,000-100,000 in fiscal 1992.

The combination of these three factors led Able Bakery Publications to consider my purchase offer at their book value because it solved short term problems for them, that is,

- ❑No further worry about producing the publication.
- ❑No further operating losses during development.
- ❑No writedown in the disposition.

Customers

Current customers are using the service daily in preparing their Bread Laws reportings. They are reportedly enthusiastic about the usefulness and quality of the service.

Management and Staffing

Management is in place. Initially, staffing will consist of family members and independent contractors who are familiar with the Bread Laws marketplace and services. Printing, storage and fulfillment are done under contract by Brown Printing, a major, quality printing firm in Rochester, N.Y. An independent direct response marketing firm may also be utilized if cost-effective.

Financial Resources

After acquisition and startup costs of $150,000, an additional $50,000 has been allocated initially to marketing/sales activities.

The current annual sales of $90,000 are adequate to cover most operational cash needs during the first year because operating costs will be kept to a minimum.

OBJECTIVES

The primary objectives of Infoguide, Inc. are to:

- ❑Establish and maintain a unique position among Bread Laws publications as the only reference work of its type.
- ❑Generate significant profits and cash flow after the second year of operation.
- ❑Develop related products and services through internal creation and by acquisition.
- ❑Position the company for a public offering or acquisition by a major publisher within five years.

Business Goals

Profits...Annual profits will approach initial investment by year five
Products...Focus on serving the Bread Laws market niche will be maintained
Customers... Company motto is "Love Thy Subscriber"
Quality...Products and services will set a standard for quality
...“Gold Stripe” Service
People...After the initial investment phase, a professional organization will be built
Growth... Cash flow will be reinvested first into expanded market penetration and then into ancillary products/services

Compared to past performance of the Bread Laws Guide in its first year of publication (April 1991-March 1992) under Able Bakery Publications, I intend to be both more creative in marketing and more aggressive in selling in order to penetrate the marketplace more effectively, as detailed below.

Rationale

To understand the potential of the Bread Laws Guide, I looked at a sister publication service provided by Able Bakery Publications, called The Cookie Service. That publication sells for over $900 per year and has over 3000 subscribers. It is the only publication that provides an up-to-date compendium of cookie laws for all fifty states. Each year the price is raised and the renewal rate is over 90%. I estimate that its production and fulfillment costs are no more than $200 per subscriber per year.

Like The Cookie Service, the Bread Laws Guide is also unique in its niche.

One of the markets of the Bread Laws Guide is the same grocery stores that purchase The Cookie Service. Therefore the key to matching the success of The Cookie Service is to get the Bread Laws Guide into the hands of these firms: this is the key element of my marketing strategy. In addition, the costs of production and fulfillment will be less than those for The Cookie Service, making the breakeven point very low and marginal profits after that high.

Return on Investment/Financial Objectives

Based on a 31% market share for the Bread Laws Guide by 1996, I estimate the return on investment to be 83% in 1996 alone. In summary, here are the figures in thousands of dollars:

Year	1992	1993	1994	1995	1996
Sales	179	266	335	397	452
Accounting Profit	(61)	3	73	124	166
% Margin	(34)	1	22	31	37
Share of Market (%)	13	2	23	27	31
ROI					
Annual	(33)	12	37	62	83
Cumulative	(31)	(29)	8	70	153

Position for Growth

The initial focus of the company will be on the core subscription service, concentrating on basic activities and priorities in sales, production, etc. with a goal of adding 240 subscriptions per year, for a total of 1000 by the end of 1996.

At that point, options of acquiring other related products, selling the company or going public can be considered.

Potential Products/Services

Once this growth pattern is realized, the company will expand beyond the core service. Various new product ideas are noted in this presentation.

PRODUCT/SERVICE DESCRIPTION

The Bread Laws Reporting Guide (Bread Laws Guide for short) is the only comprehensive publication related to Bread Laws.

Physically it is a five volume loose leaf set containing approximately 6000 pages of text organized by state for each of the 50 states plus Washington, D.C. The pages contain information as follows:

- 4300 jurisdictions reporting/searching information
- An introductory section
- The Bread Laws code for each state, notated for non-conformance with the model act
- Illustrations of the forms acceptable in each state

The set is presently updated quarterly based upon a questionnaire distributed to all the reporting jurisdictions and upon information gathered regarding new and revised legislation and regulations in each of the states. The first three updates were as follows:

- July 1991--600 pages
- October 1991--1200 pages
- January 1992--1200 pages

Subscribers may order the entire set or individual states. Pricing is set so that a subscriber with a need for more than 5-6 states would order the entire set. A facsimile service is also offered: a client may call for a specific jurisdiction and receive a copy of the current Guide page immediately by facsimile.

Development of other ancillary products/services is in progress and future products/services are planned to be introduced as cash flow allows. The first of these will be a facsimile newsletter, which will be sent out whenever there is a significant change going into effect in any state.

Unique Selling Proposition

As noted, the Bread Laws Guide is not a look-alike directory so frequently produced by publishers. It is rather, the only frequently updated guide to Bread Laws reporting and the only one with specific information aboutthe local (4200) reporting jurisdictions.

Proprietary Technology

The product is protected in the following ways:

The publication itself is copyrighted and carries an ISBN number. "Bread Laws Guide" and similar expressions will be trademarked at the federal level.

The information for the 4300 jurisdictions is maintained on a computer database that may be loaded to an online system for immediate access as a future product. The database presently makes communication with the jurisdictions inexpensive.

Pay Back Benefits

For most subscribers, the Bread Laws Guide will pay for itself in terms of cost and reject savings within a few months for the following reasons:

- ❑15-25% of Bread Laws reportings are rejected by every jurisdiction because of preparation errors (e.g., use of wrong ink) or wrong fees, which use of the Guide eliminates.
- ❑Ease of lookup in the Guide cuts down on Bread Laws reporting preparation time and expense: all the information for a jurisdiction is on one easy-to-read page.
- ❑Experience just in 1991 indicates that almost half the states will change their Laws, regulations or fees during a typical 12 month period.
- ❑Professionals who file under the Bread Laws cannot afford touse out-of-date information because and bad bread can lead to million dollar lawsuits.

Useful Purpose

The Bread Laws Guide does not purport to be a legal text. There are other services and publications which fill this requirement. Rather, the Guide is for the professional who needs to do a reporting now and who understands the law itself. It is a practical working tool in other words.

Features Highlights

There is no other source of this up-to-date reporting information.

The Bread Laws Guide is extremely easy to use because:

- ❑It is sorted by reporting jurisdiction name alphabetically within each state.
- ❑Each state section begins with overall information about that state, including a list of cities to assist the user in determining where to file.
- ❑Each state section contains the actual law for the state highlighted with differences from the model law which appears in the introductory section.

The combination of quarterly updates with the planned newsletter keeps the publication current (and will keep the service before its audience in each firm continually). The nearest competitor issues an annual paperback that is out of date before it is published.

Economies of Scale

As sales ramp up, the profitability of this publication surges because of the characteristics of an annual subscription service, summarized as follows:

- Product cost in the initial year of subscription includes five binders and all 6000 pages (about $150); product cost of updates in the second and later years is about half that.
- Marketing cost per initial subscription is high (estimated $200); marketing cost to keep an existing subscriber is maybe one-quarter as much.
- The cost of maintaining the information annually is fixed.
- The cost of printing pages decreases as subscription levels increase because of the fixed cost component of composition, etc.

Product/Service Life Cycle

The Bread Laws were first enacted in the 1970's. They cover the sale, leasing, and financing of commercial bread manufacturing establishments. Each state has enacted its own version of the model act recommended by the American Bakers Association. Even the model act has been altered a few times over the years. Therefore major inconsistencies exist from state to state in the law and regulations, including reporting fees.

Most states have some form of local reporting, which requires reporting two forms, one at the state level and one at the local level. The local level also varies depending upon the state, and may be a town, city, county or parish.

Over the years, there has been continuing discussion of the possibility of federalizing the law, that is, centralizing all reportings at the federal level. This is as likely as the federalization of corporate law.

Planned Products/Services

The company plans to develop new products and enhance existing products. New products/services that are to be developed in the near future include a facsimile newsletter, paperback semiannual summary guides, and reporting services.

Concepts for follow-on (next generation) products or services include an online version of the service (on Lexis, Westlaw) and a CD-ROM version.

Just as important as my own vision of the future, I and my staff will be listening carefully to the subscribers in order to determine their future needs which the company can meet.

MARKET ANALYSIS

Key points in defining the market segment for the Bread Laws Guide are by service type, user type, and geographic location.

In the service type dimension, the service is unique. The only other publications are an annual paperback put out by Charlie Baker, the leading Bread Laws forms provider in the U.S., and a small, general booklet from Bread Reporting Services. The user type dimension is critical to targeting. The significant user types are as follows:

Type	Total Size	Practical Potential
Grocery stores	45,000	1,000
Bakeries	12,000	900
Other Bakers	3,000	500
Bread Companies	3,000	500
Bread Reporting Cos.	1,000	100
Totals	64,000	3,000

Geographic location is also considered a market dimension because of the obvious disparity in the size of states. Clearly New York and California are not only the largest states, but also are the baking centers where the national bakers are located. Therefore any marketing plan will focus especially on these two states.

Currently, the only market distribution information available is from: Charlie Baker, which reports that it has over 7,000 subscribers to its annual paperback; and Warren Gorham Lamont, which sells a number of Bread Laws related publications, has 30,000 names on its subscriber mailing list (which I will use for leads). These figures do confirm that the estimated market potential for the Bread Laws Guide (3000 subscribers) is within reason.

Of course, the current recession has seen the reduction in both grocery stores and bakeries, as well as greater difficulty in selling publications because of budget constraints. However, these short-term trends will not have that much impact on long-term potential for the Guide since the total market size is so large. The key to marketing is to get the Guide into the right user hands.

Strengths

The Bread Laws Guide has several distinct advantages over the potential competition, of which the top six are listed here.

- ❑ It is an advantage to be the first up-to-date service. To the extent that the Guide gets into firms before any competing service comes along, barriers to any other entrant will be too high to overcome.
- ❑ The comprehensiveness and depth of information in the Guide makes it the most complete possible source, with a full page of information about every reporting jurisdiction in the U.S. It is presented by jurisdiction within state for easy, efficient access.
- ❑ Since the information is maintained on a computer database, other forms of publications and non-print access will be easy to create as ancillary products.

❑My own experience in and knowledge of these markets is a key strength because I know precisely where to focus marketing efforts for the Guide.
❑The Guide is the only product of the company. Therefore, there will be no confusion about where the priorities of the company should be directed. All efforts, resources and imagination will aim at just this one target: get the Guide in as many hands as possible.
❑The initial investment of $200,000 constitutes a key financial strength. Although the company is small, a budget of $200,000 which essentially can be dedicated to marketing the Guide over the first two years represents a major investment even by comparison to a large professional information publisher.

Weaknesses

There are two distinct handicaps inherent in the product today, which I will focus on remedying as noted below.

❑Promotional activities since the inception of the product by Able Bakery Publications have not been sufficient to establish the level of demand. In fact, direct response mailings have been mishandled, follow-up by telemarketing has been nonexistent, and too little funds have been allocated to target marketing. Because of this, the marketplace does not yet appreciate how significant this new tool is. Promotional efforts will be extended to my contacts in the states, in the American Bakers Association, and in other associations to get the word out better. I will mount a major, focused marketing effort ($50,000) to the target markets, including mail telemarketing and in-person visits where necessary, in order to get all 1000 copies of the Guide out of inventory and into the hands of potential long-term subscribers.
❑Product updates are too slow in getting out, and some of the initially designed subscriber communication vehicles (fax update, newsletter to users) have not been implemented. Within two months I will have these important marketing tools in place to maintain and increase interest of current subscribers, thereby protecting renewal rates.
❑I am also considering inhouse printing and fulfillment to replace the outside printer in order to get sets out faster while saving expenses.

Opportunities

The upside potential for the Bread Laws Guide within these target markets over the next five years may well be greater than the 1000 sets forecast based upon the money allocated to marketing under the conditions introduced in the Present Situation and Strengths/Weaknesses analysis.

In addition to the product extensions discussed elsewhere in this presentation, an altogether new application for this type of product/service would be tapping environmental related markets. Since this field is so new, the kinds of procedures that have been standardized over 20 years for the Bread Laws are hardly in place for searching or reporting environmental-related records. I am working on a "Bible" on how to deal with environmental agencies around the U.S. (state and federal) to assist the same markets the Guide is sold in now.

Further opportunity for product extensions depend upon generating funds from the Guide itself.

Still another possibility for development involves Bread Laws reporting and search services. However, this direction would involve a commitment to compete with Able Bakery Publications, which I hesitate to do for a number of compelling business reasons.

COMPETITION

Direct Competition

The only complementary products/service already in use by these customers is the Charlie Baker Guide, a paperback which is published once a year around December at a price of $15.95. It goes out of date very quickly and only includes state level information.

Other publications that contain general Bread Laws information include:

- Bread Reporting Handbook, $9.95, contains brief descriptions of state reporting information.
- NBI subscription service, $665.00 annually, covers the law but not the fees, addresses, etc.

The latter publication is for the legal researcher, whereas the Bread Laws Guide is for the person who actually has to report under the law.

As noted, the print competition is not in the same category as the Bread Laws Guide because the Guide is in fact unique.

The question for the future is whether anyone will decide to enter the market with a comparable product. On the one hand, a prospective competitor could use the Bread Laws Guide to get a head start on its data collection. On the other, it is unlikely that another publisher will chance such an entry when the niche is so small. For comparison, The Cookie Service on Able Bakery Publications and the NBI Bread Laws Law Service have no competitors.

See the marketing plan for information about how I intend to keep any competition out of the market.

Indirect Competition

A source of indirect competition must be considered: service companies that prepare reportings for attorneys and bakeries. As already explained, hundreds of these companies are located in state capitals around the country. Although most are primarily local to their own state, many also do a significant national business. Since these companies will purchase the Guide themselves to handle their own clients, those same clients may not need the Guide.

The impact of this competition is not anticipated to be all that great because 90% of Bread Laws reportings are traditionally prepared by the institution or its attorneys.

RISKS

This table shows how I evaluate the risks involved in the development of the Guide today. It allows a comparison of exposure, given various assumptions.

I have weighted each element according to its importance to the success of the Guide and listed them in descending order.

Elements	Degree of Riskof Risk				
	Low	Med	High	Weight	Total
Maturity			10	.25	2.50
Strategy		5		.20	1.00
Competition	1			.15	0.15
Industry	1			.10	0.10
Management	1			.10	0.10
Past Prfrmnc.		5		.10	0.50
Economy		5		.10	0.50
Overall Risk				1.00	4.85

Rationale

Maturity In this initial stage, gaining subscriber confidence is critical. Therefore, both weight and risk factor must be considered high.

Strategy Effective product/service, price distribution, promotion strategies are critical. Therefore strategy is highly weighted. Risk is only medium because I am able to take advantage of lessons learned over the past year.

Competitive Position The market is wide open with few competitors today.

Industry: Company must stay competitive as business matures. Company must keep out any direct competitors. Risk is low because good products/services have loyal long term followings in these markets.

Management Careful planning, clear objectives and experienced leadership are in place.

Past Performance Medium risk because results to date could have been better except that resources were not applied.

Economy The economy must be considered because the current recession has significantly slowed service company sales and Bread Laws reportings, and represents some risk. However, capitalization of the company will take it through this period and the company is prepared with its inventory to take advantage of the next upswing in the economy.

Conclusion

These risks clearly point to the need for focus in the marketing plan to place the Guide in as many potential subscriber offices as possible as soon as possible. This strategy is the key to addressing almost all the risks, as discussed below.

MARKETING STRATEGY

The marketing strategy of the company may be summarized in two statements:

- ❑Focus on the logical buyers of new subscriptions and attack them in every effective way.
- ❑Once the initial sale is made, "Love Thy Subscriber" with "Gold Stripe" Service.

Comprehensive Plan

The overall marketing plan for the Bread Laws Guide is based on the following fundamentals:

- ❑The Guide is not just a publication. It is a unique, essential service for all power Bread Laws reporters. As an entirely new concept, however, it cannot sell itself.
- ❑The target market segments are well known, but it is sometimes difficult to determine the decision makers within individual firms.
- ❑Direct sales methods are best for the service because it demands personal contact with the prospect and subscriber to assure that it is used effectively.
- ❑Selling never stops. Renewals are just as important as new sales, and depend upon satisfied subscribers who understand how to use the service effectively.
- ❑Users, decision makers, and librarians all need to be sold.

To prove the value of The Guide, the marketing strategy will focus on benefits of use, including efficiency improvements, cost savings, and elimination of rejects. This can be done not only by the typical brochures, cover letters and telesales scripts, but through personal professional contacts I have developed, references by satisfied subscribers, etc.

Product Strategy

The Bread Laws Guide will be treated as a long-lived product/service, which will be improved only in small ways beyond the basic service concept. No frills are needed to sell successfully, as long as a basic focus on top grocery stores and financial institutions is maintained.

Positioning

Because of the special characteristics of these markets, the strategy must incorporate a strong message that the Bread Laws Guide and its publisher are the experts in the field.

This position will be enforced through the ancillary products/ services, such as the facsimile newsletter for instant updates on significant changes as well as through a continuing dialogue with the top people in the field.

The Guide is seen in this light by many of the current subscribers, but more promotion is obviously needed to get the publication into the minds of the entire target markets.

Its unique characteristics can be exploited to arrive at a winning position in the consumer's mind. In terms of market segmentation advantages, I will use the satisfied subscribers more effectively.

"Love Thy Subscriber"

Since the long-term success of the Guide depends upon renewals, annual, constant, effective, and positive contact with subscribers must be maintained. Most publishers do not seem to recognize who the actual subscribers are; they are not just the person or department that pays for the service.

I define a subscriber as anyone who uses the Guide. Therefore, contact must be established with paralegals who use copies in their libraries and documentation specialists in bakeries who prepare Bread Laws reportings. One account may have dozens of users.

They will be identified through telephone surveys, questionnaires and the like, and will then be kept informed about the Guide.

"Gold Stripe" Service

In order to produce a consistent identity, I will introduce "Gold Stripe" Service to the subscribers. It will include thefollowing features, plus others to be added in the future in order to maintain the highest possible renewal rate:

- ❑Next day shipping of all orders.
- ❑No hassle return policy: anytime you are not satisfied, your Guide subscription may be canceled.
- ❑Fax Newsletter: news of important changes in reporting requirements sent directly to all users in the subscriber firm.
- ❑Whatever payment plan is most convenient for the subscriber, including monthly, quarterly, annual and even longer.
- ❑A free annual jurisdiction name/address/telephone directory.

The name "Gold Stripe" has been chosen for a very specific reason. After the acquisition, the Guide is not allowed to continue to use the name Able Bakery Publications, leaving me with 6000 binders costing $6.00 each, which has already been embossed on its spine with the name Able Bakery Publications. Not wishing to throw away $36,000, I came up with the idea of obtaining a high quality, gold-leaf or brass overlay that can be firmly glued over the Able Bakery Publications name: thus, "Gold Stripe" becomes the logo of the company.

Critical Mass

The concept of critical mass is important to understanding the selling tactics which will be utilized initially (Stage One) and how these tactics will change over time (Stage Two). Stage One tactics are discussed in the Selling Tactics Section, and Stage Two is discussed in the Advertising Section.

A product/service has reached critical mass when it has gained enough market penetration to become a sort of household word in its industry. In other words, once critical mass in a market is reached, a significant percentage of sales will come from more indirect marketing, and tactics such as advertising and public relations make sense to keep the product name before the customers. Before critical mass is reached, however, such indirect marketing is a waste of money because there is little name recognition to start with in the market.

Therefore, the Stage One sales plan will be focused on obtaining critical mass status for the Bread Laws Guide. This will be accomplished by directing all marketing resources into the telesales channel with a goal of placing the first 1000 sets of the Guide in the top 500 grocery stores, bakeries, etc. I estimate that the Guide will reach its critical mass once these 1000 sets are in place, at which time the marketing strategy will be adjusted to Stage Two.

Next Steps

Based on this strategic plan, I am presently pursuing the following tasks:

- ❑ Put together prospect lists for telesales.
- ❑ Identify telesales personnel.
- ❑ Identify printer for brochures, etc.
- ❑ Review and adjust fulfillment procedures with Brown Printing.

PRICING AND PROFITABILITY

The prices for the products/services are determined first and foremost by value to the subscribers. Since pricing is not constrained by direct competitive pressures, the approach taken is to test various levels of prices, volume discounts, for cash, package deals, etc. in order to find the best price-volume mix in each market.

Experience so far confirms that the current pricing is not excessively high, but further testing is needed to determine whether lower prices can expand demand (Is there any price elasticity?). Testing will be done continuously as part of the direct response and telemarketing programs.

The other annual subscription services mentioned in this plan are priced for $665 to $900 per year, and the only Bread Laws-related newsletter is priced at $395 per year. The Bread Laws Guide retail price of $595 per year again appears to be in the right range from these comparatives.

I feel that customers will pay in the $400-700 per year based upon the perceived values discussed in the Description Section (Payback) and in the Strategy

Section. To reiterate, potential subscribers must be convinced of these values through the correct marketing strategy.

The current price structure appears in the Exhibits. The volume discounts, which previously applied only if the purchase order came from one place in a company, will now be extended to all locations from one company, even under separate purchase orders.

Also, the Bread Laws Guide can be examined and returned for full credit within 30 days of receipt if the customer is not 100% satisfied. Experience so far indicates less than a 10% return rate.

Margin Structure and Long-Term Economics

Profitability in the long run is not so much a function of the initial price cost relationship as of the number of years a customer renews the subscription. Consider the following:

Subscriber for	Sales @ $500	Cost @200	Profit	Cost @400	Profit
1 year	500	200	300	400	100
5 years	2500	Lost		2000	500
10 years	5000			4000	1000

The lesson of this example is that lower cost (or for that matter, higher initial price) does not equal more profits in the annual subscription business. If as a result of costs being twice as high subscribers renew for 5 years versus one year, profits are significantly higher and they get even better in 10 years. Thus, as the marketing strategy explains, the Bread Laws Guide philosophy will be "Love Thy Subscriber, " and significant resources are allocated to obtain and maintain each subscriber.

This analysis does not mean that I am cavalier about costs: just the opposite, in fact. Non-marketing expenses, including personnel, printing and other costs will be watched severely so that maximum resources can be committed on a continuing basis to obtain new subscribers and keep existing ones.

The costs and expenses, as detailed in the financials, are as follows per subscription per year:

	New Subscribers	**Renewal Subscribers**
Product Cost	$250	$100
Production Expenses	149-74	149 decreasing to 74
Marketing Expenses	200	165 decreasing to 37
Total (Max)	599	414
Total (1996)	524	211

Experience to date has indicated that the cost of obtaining a new subscriber is relatively high ($200) because of price and market characteristics. Although I will be examining ways to increase the efficacy of each marketing dollar, I feel it is only fair to use this figure in the forecasts. Any productivity improvements will only improve results further.

Initially, therefore, I plan to lose $99 on each new subscriber the first year based upon an average net sales yield per set of $500, and to earn $86 on each renewal subscription.

The wisdom of this approach becomes clear over time: while new subscriptions will continue to cost more to obtain than renewals, costs will decrease significantly as the subscriber base rises, leading to 60% margins ($300 profit on $500 sale) on renewal business by 1996.

It should be noted that the 6% delivery charge is inherently very profitable ($300 of sales versus $6 for postage).

Discounts

All estimates are based upon experience to date. For example, the $500 average sales price was determined from the sales of the first 200 sets, some at full price of $595, some at the introductory price of $545 and some at multiples of $75 for individual states. The reason the average of $415 on the sales worksheet for 1991 is lower than the forecast is that 30 sets were given to Able Bakery Publications offices at $215 per set. Per the acquisition agreement, Able Bakery Publications will pay over $400 per set starting in 1992.

Discounts will continue to be offered to subscribers as an inducement for:

- ❑ Early payment of new subscriptions
- ❑ Early payment of renewal subscriptions
- ❑ Multiple sets in the same firm
- ❑ Upgrade from a few states to a full set
- ❑ Special deals for association members

SELLING TACTICS

Three selling approaches have been used by Able Bakery publications, with mixed results:

Direct Mail

Over 25,000 pieces have been sent out, resulting in about 60 sales. At a cost of $1.00 per piece, this approach has cost over $400 per subscription. However, the best of mailings, from the Warren Gorham Lamont list, showed a .5% sale rate, for a cost per subscription of $200.

Telesales

The 20 Able Bakery Publications telesales people "mention" the Guide in their presentations to Bread Laws search prospects and clients as part of their overall sales pitch. Very few sales arise from this source.

Outside Sales

The 20 outside sales people were instructed each to sell 5 sets in the July-august period of 1991. Actual sales achieved were about 3 per person,which accounts for the sales bulge in thoseshown on the sales worksheet. Since that time there has been little focus on this product and fewerthan 5 sales per month come from this source.

The remainder of sales to date come from word of mouth and fromcalls to other service companies.

A little advertising was done and a public relations piece wasput out, both with little effect. Some complimentary sets were sent to important figures in the American Bakers Association and other recognized national Bread Laws experts, but recently these people were insulted by being asked to pay for updates.

None of these approaches have yielded satisfactory results as far as I am concerned.

Stage One Planned Sales Method: New Subscribers

These experiences lead to the conclusion that a more focused sales approach is necessary in order to grow sales at a faster rate and/or at a lower unit cost, as follows:

- ❑Combine targeted lists of high potential prospective subscribers to obtain master lists of individual users within each firm.
- ❑Develop specific telephone scripts for each market segment. Develop sales materials specifically to support telephone sales.
- ❑Contract independent, experienced telephone sales people to contact the individuals on the master lists.
- ❑Spend no money on indirect sales methods, such as advertising, although creative, low-cost ideas will be pursued.
- ❑800 number support line.

The following sections discuss each of these steps in more detail.

Many specific sources of Bread Laws reporting firms are available to me, including,

- ❑Client lists are available as part of the acquisition agreement.
- ❑I have developed lists of all bakeries who report liens in the major states (NY, CA, IL, TX, PA). These lists are particularly valuable because they can be crossmatched to find multistate filers who are the most qualified prospects for the Guide.
- ❑Warren Gorham Lamont's list of publication buyers (30,000) names is the best commercially available mailing list. National Commercial Finance Association list includes most large asset based bakeries.
- ❑The Charlie Baker Guide, mentioned in this presentation a number of times,

is owned by two brilliant men in St. Louis, MO. I have contacted them to obtain a list of their 7000 subscribers. Their initial response was to allow me to have this list. I will be following up with them once the acquisition is complete.

All these lists are just raw material, of course. I have developed logic and programs to match and combine these lists for use by the telephone sales people.

The resulting combined file will contain multiple individual names and multiple locations for each significant national grocery store chain.

Telephone Scripts

The combined lists will provide more than one access to each targeted subscriber, which in turn will allow multiple scripting for different kinds of contacts, such as:

- ❑ Ask the librarian who utilizes the NBI Bread Laws law service since those people will be interested in reporting also.
- ❑ Ask the librarian for names of paralegals in the baking or M&A sections of the grocery store.
- ❑ Ask the client who is responsible for preparing Bread Law reportings and how many states the firm files in.

In other words, the telephone will be used for initial contact with an objective of identifying the people in each firm with the greatest need for the Guide. When these people are identified, they will be approached with a specific script focusing on the benefits of the Guide:

- ❑ Did you know there is a new and only source of accurate reporting information to help you file more efficiently?
- ❑ Did you know that there is a way to reduce rejects of Bread Laws reportings to almost none?

The close of this call will usually be to send the prospect more information (the sales material) about the Guide, or even better, to get a commitment to try the Guide on a trial basis.

The follow-up call will review the material and ask for the order.

Of course, if this particular prospect does not agree to purchase, the sales person will call another user in the firm. There is always another user in each firm who will listen.

Once a trial is assured, the telesales person will ask for the names of other users in the firm and will notify them that the Guide is available. The more people who use the Guide, the easier it will be to keep it in the firm year after year.

Sales Materials

Sales material is designed specifically to support the telephone sale, that is, to address the questions of the user and to help convince that person to find it in the budget to purchase the Guide.

Materials will include:

- Brochure explaining the contents of the Guide and showing what each jurisdiction page contains.
- Question and answer sheet.
- Note from the Publisher showing that I am an expert in the field.
- Actual jurisdiction sheets. (Use up old sheets that have been replaced. Each will be stamped "Out of date; do not use.")
- How to use the Guide sheet to be sent to each user when the Guide is delivered.

Experienced Sales People

Some of the sales people who worked for me on past projects are now available to work for the Guide as independent contractors, and I will contract with two of them, one in the East and one in the West. They have the following characteristics in common:

- Knowledgeable in Bread Laws law and products/services.
- Knowledgeable on how attorneys, paralegals and baking think, and how they differ from one another from a selling perspective.
- Client oriented. They listen to what the client wants and pass all suggestions on for response.
- Incentive motivated.
- Comfortable on the telephone and in person.
- Well-dressed.
- Used to working with me.

In other words, I am assembling a mature sales force whom I am confident will achieve my sales goals of 240 sets per year.

Compensation will consist of commissions based upon paid sales with additional incentives for achieving sales over my targets. The company will pay for all sales materials, telephone calls, mailing lists and travel expenses.

These people will also be the feedback loop between the product and the customer. They continually ask for suggestions and improvement ideas as well as addressing any complaints. In fact, these sales people will be fully empowered to address any subscriber need, including flexibility to price the Guide creatively in order to get the order and to maintain the renewal subscription.

Low Cost Ideas - No Frills

As discussed in the Marketing Strategy Section, advertising and other forms of indirect or pull marketing do little good for a product such as the Guide that has not reached critical mass in its market penetration. Therefore, these costly frills will be avoided until Stage Two.

I will, however, implement two indirect sales plans that will cost the company virtually nothing and which will produce an extra 30-100 subscription sales per year, as follows:

❑Able Bakery Publications will continue to sell the Guide through its 40 person sales force. I will pay a small 10% commission on these sales, which I expect to total about 30 sets per year.

❑I will offer a special price for members to the two major associations in the industry, NBA and AAEL, if they will promote the Guide on behalf of the company. Promotion could take the form of direct response marketing by them or merely an endorsement of the product. This is an experiment, but it is worth a shot as a separate sales channel.

Support Line

The Guide will, as part of the acquisition package keep in place its distinct 800 number: 800-4-BREAD. This number is used by subscribers to place orders, to ask for information including the fax order service, and to contact the Guide for any other reason. It is also used by jurisdictions to let the Guide know about impending changes in regulations, procedures, etc.

The number will ring in the Paramus headquarters, and any messages for the sales people will be forwarded to them by voice mail. The phone will be answered in person from 8-5 Eastern time.

PRODUCTION AND FULFILLMENT

Production

The Guide has been in production since April 1991. As noted above, it has already gone through three update cycles. At present this cycle is quarterly. Updates are based upon information from the following sources:

❑Quarterly, all 4300 jurisdictions are surveyed by mail. The survey repeats the information that appears in the Guide and includes a return envelope for changes, additions or deletions. The survey is easy to produce because the mailing information is kept in a computer database. Over 80 percent of jurisdictions have responded to the survey, because they appreciate how the Guide helps to eliminate rejects. In the future, I will ask the jurisdictions for their help in identifying filers who have high reject rates as a source of leads.

❑Other services are searched continually.

❑Through the International Association of Bread Law Adminstrators,which the company will support through sponsorship of their annual convention. I maintain personal relations with many of the Bread Laws administrators in each state. I will enlist their aid to send me all proposed changes in each state in order to have more up-to-date information.

As information arrives, it is entered immediately into the jurisdiction database so that the most current information will be available for call-in customers (and later for immediate updating of an online database). Then, once a quarter, the altered pages are printed and distributed by Brown Printing.

I contemplate three significant improvements in this process:

❑ The quarterly cycle is arbitrary. Most subscription services of this type send updates whenever anything significant happens, which may often be on a monthlybasis. Certainly, changes are more likely in the fall than in the summer because of legislative schedules. Also, if a state has substantial changes (over 60% of pages), the whole state section will be reprinted to save subscribers the trouble of replacing individual pages.

❑ No matter how fast changes are printed and sent out, any change to reporting requirements that is not known immediately by a filer my cause a reject. The goal of the Guide is of course to eliminate all rejects. Therefore, I will demand that all critical changes in jurisdiction information be faxed to users in time to assure reportings are not made in error. Critical changes are if fees are changed or acceptable reporting form changed.

❑ The costs of composition and printing are expected to rise from $40,000 per year to $80,000 by 1996 as the subscriber base expands. Of this amount, almost half the cost is for composition because the press runs are so short (1000). One use of term loan funds being requested will be to obtain a desktop publishing PC system with a high quality laser printer (total cost - $20,000) which will be utilized to do composition in-house. Savings will be invested in additional marketing/sales.

Fulfillment

Brown Printing not only prints the Guide and its updates, it also inventories sets; fulfills orders for new sets; packages and delivers updates; and updates the sets in inventory. The company will continue to use Brown for fulfillment services because they have a fine reputation for service, accuracy and timeliness.

I will make only two changes to the fulfillment process:

❑ New sets are sent out by courier, which will continue. However, I am designing a new, permanent courier package in the form of a briefcase for deliveries. The package will be returned to the company by the subscriber once the set has been accepted. This packaging will protect the sets better from dents and the like, while making a statement that this service is a premier subscription like no other. One other benefit is that a subscriber who wants to return a set must call the company in order to get a package to return it, giving the company a chance to save the account.

❑ Brown charges $10-12 per set to update the ones in inventory. The total cost can amount to over $15,000 per year because so many sets are still in inventory. This cost will be eliminated by having my family do the updates.

ASSUMPTIONS: BASE CASE

The base case is what I consider the most likely scenario for sales, costs, and growth. The next section examines worst and best cases as well.

General

Inflation is not considered in the forecasts and estimates because prices for this kind of subscription service typically can be raised to offset cost increases.

The column entitle "Factor" on some of the worksheets contains cost per unit or growth factors used in the forecasts.

Sales

The sales forecast is based upon experience to date. 1992 sales are for 10 months, on the assumption of a March 1 purchase date.

Note that sales tax will only be charged in New Jersey because the new company has no other locations.

Cost of Sales

New sets include 5 binders at $6 each. 6000 pages of test, tabs and the like. 750 sets were purchased as part of the acquisition.

Update costs are computed at 2400 pages per year per set at $.04 per page.

Production/Editorial Expense

Management fees, such as a salary for me, are not included in the estimates, as my compensation will depend upon results and available cash flow.

Editor fee is estimated based upon prior results.

Postage is for new sets and update delivery, newsletters and faxes.

Telephone is for administrative and jurisdiction calls.

Jurisdiction mail is estimated at 4300 pieces of mail four times a year at $.75 per letter, including return postage.

Production coordinator is a part-time position that will be contracted out.

Subscriptions and supplies are needed for research and general operations.

Amortization of startup expenses is taken over three years.

Interest is calculated at 6% on the subordinated debt of $125,000.

Royalties at 6% of sales are due to Able Bakery Publications as part of the acquisition agreement.

Marketing/Sales Expense

Mailing list costs are primarily for the Warren Gorham Lamont list.

Brochures include the cost of about 20,000 direct mail pieces utilized by the telephone sales people at $.80 per set of sales materials.

Postage includes direct mail and delivery of new sets and updates.

Telephone is estimated at 80 calls per day/$1.00 per call.

Commissions are estimated at $100 per new subscription sold.

Cash Flow Projection

See balance sheet assumptions for most cash flow items.

Cost of sales for new sets is not a cash expense because of the 750 sets purchased in the acquisition, until 1995 when the present inventory has been depleted. At that time, 500 more full sets (New Inventory) will be printed and packaged at a cost of $150 per set.

Note that withdrawals for management fees and to pay taxes on earnings by stockholders (subchapter S corporation) are not included in this presentation.

The initial stockholder investment of $200,000 is allocated as follows:

- 750 sets of the Guide in inventory at $150 per set.
- Startup expenses include attorney fees of $10,000 and development fees taken over on the acquisition of $26,000.
- Unearned income represents the remainder of each paid 12 month subscription, net of set costs, as of acquisition date. I have chosen not to use this accounting method for the forecasts in order to keep the presentation simple. However, for tax purposes, I intend to use the unearned subscription approach to defer taxes on corporate profits.

Balance Sheet Detail

Receivables are estimated at 60 days sales outstanding.

No fixed assets are shown because the computer equipment obtained in the acquisition is expensed. No other capital assets are required to operate the business.

To be conservative, no payables are assumed.

CASH FLOW PROJECTION (1992-1996)

Beginning Cash Note A	65000	17000	50200	155300	227520
Accounting Profit	-61250	3200	73100	124220	165764
Add: Non-Cash Outlays					
Cost of Sales - New	32250	36000	36000	36000	36000
A/P Balance	0	0	0	0	0
Amortization	12000	12000	12000		
Less:					
A/R Outstdg. Chg.	-31000	-18000	-16000	-13000	-13000
New Inventory				-75000	
Net Cash Flow this Year	-48000	33200	105100	72220	188764
Ending Cash	17000	50200	155300	227520	416284

Note A:
Capital Contributions of $200,000
Less Purchase Price of $125,000. Which Is Primarily 750 New Sets
Less $10,000 Legal and Other Startup Costs

BEST AND WORST CASE ANALYSIS

Best Case: Schedules

A term loan of $100,000 is added to the balance sheet to be used as follows:

Purchase computer publishing equipment	$20,000
Double marketing/sales expenditures	$70,000
Increased production expenses	$10,000

As a result of the increased investment in sales, the number of new sets sold is doubled to 40 per month, and the cost of updates is decreased by utilizing advanced computer methods.

By 1996, sales will rise to $799,000 because of the compounding effect of renewal sales, 77% more than base case sales of $452,000.

Expenses reflect both the interest on the term debt and the depreciation over 5 years of the computer equipment.

Although cash flow appears to be less advantageous than the base case, in fact this is only due to the continued discretionary increased marketing/sales expenditure levels. Profits before these discretionary expenses in 1996 are $414,000 vs $239,000 in the basecase. In other words, the company has a lot more to spend on future growth because of the additional impetus provided by the term loan funds.

Worst Case: Schedules

The worst case scenario continues expense projections at the base case rate while sales decrease to only 10 sets per month, or half the base case rate.

It is significant to note that even without a cutback in market/sales expenses, a cash shortfall of only $5500 is generated. Renewal sales still put the company into positive cash flow over the 5 year period.

Best Case Cash Flow Projection (1992-1996)

Beginning Cash Note A	165000	45000	-400	-16540	20624
Accounting Profit	-137250	-63400	84860	202164	274522
Add-Non-Cash Outlays					
Cost of Sales-New	32250	72000	20000	0	0
Amortization	12000	12000	12000		
A/P Balance	0	0	0	0	0
Depreciation	4000	4000	4000	4000	4000
Less:					
A/R Outstanding	-31000	-70000	-104000	-136000	-164000
Repay Term Loan			-33000	-33000	-34000
Cash Flow this Year	-120000	-45400	-16140	37164	80522
Ending Cash	45000	-400	-16540	20624	101146

Note A:
Starts with capital contributions of $200,000
Less purchase price of $125,000, which is primarily 750 new sets
Less $10,000 legal and other startup costs
Plus a term loan of $100,000 repayable in years 3-5

Worst Case Cash Flow Projection (1992-1996)

Beginning Cash Note A	65000	5000	-5500	12600	53820
Accounting Profit	-70000	-31500	-4900	29220	38764
Add: Non-Cash Outlays					
Cost of Sales-New	18000	18000	18000	18000	18000
Amortization	12000	12000	12000		
A/P Balance	0	0	0	0	0
Less: A/R Outstanding	-20000	-9000	-7000	-6000	-6000
Cash Flow this Year	-60000	-10500	18100	41220	50764
Ending Cash	5000	-5500	12600	53820	104584

Note A:
Capital contributions of $200,000
Less purchase price of $125,000, which is primarily 750 new sets
Less $10,000 legal and other startup costs

Restaurant

BUSINESS PLAN

AMERICAN DINER

5409 Lapel St.
Timbuktu, UT 48224

January 4, 1993

Adopting a 1950s theme, the American Diner intends to serve traditional foods, such as fruit pies and cobblers, freshly baked breads, pot pies, and other "home-cooking" with an eye toward health. The two proprietors, both experienced restauranteurs, intend to draw on their extensive food service backgrounds as they launch their new business. The following plan outlines the strategy the Diner will develop to cater to the growing Timbuktu community in the face of strong competition.

- EXECUTIVE SUMMARY
- INTRODUCTION
- MENU
- MARKET DESCRIPTION
- COMPETITION
- MARKETING STRATEGIES
- MANAGEMENT TEAM
- FINANCIAL PROJECTIONS
- APPENDICES

RESTAURANT BUSINESS PLAN

EXECUTIVE SUMMARY

Founders

John Doe has worked in food service for over 17 years. In 1984, he established the popular and successful downtown restaurant, Paris Cafe, and as owner, was involved in all aspects of its business for six years until its sale in 1990.

Jane Smith was instrumental in the planning and start-up of The Watering Hole one of Timbuktu's most popular bar/restaurants. She has worked in food service/ food retailing since 1980 and has extensive managerial experience.

Type of Business

Diner, structured as a limited liability business.

Company Concept

American Diner will create a community atmosphere as a good, old-fashioned neighborhood cafe in thriving downtown Timbuktu.

Financial Goals

To acquire $107,000 needed to capitalize the American Diner project, with an estimated payback in five years.

INTRODUCTION

American Diner is designed to create a community atmosphere as a good, old-fashioned, friendly, neighborhood cafe. The location at 5409 Lapel St. puts the diner in the heart of lively, downtown Timbuktu.

A priority of American Diner will be serving fresh, healthful fare with all selections made on the premises from "scratch." To keep food costs down, the menu will be simple, yet creative with many interchangeable ingredients. Foods will come from local and regional suppliers whenever possible, with a preference for organically grown products. Emphasis will be placed on the bakery which will feature old-world breads baked daily. A deli counter, fine coffees, and a fresh juice bar will also be showcased.

Setting the mood of a '50s diner with decor, American Diner will be a simple 50-seat cafe with neon signage, checkered tile floors, grey booths with formica/ chrome tables, a refurbished pressed-tin ceiling with ceiling fans, and a lunch counter (with the look of an old soda fountain) to match the tables. Only counter service will be offered to keep labor costs low. This will also keep the dining costs reasonable for consumers--self-service with no tipping expenses.

Most of the menu will revolve around baked goods, e.g. pot pies with fresh, flaky crusts, freshly baked breads, pies and cobblers. The deli will offer a choice of fresh mini-loaves for sandwiches. As learned from her experience with the downtown Timbuktu restaurant, Paris Care, a strong need exists for quick, diverse (vegetarian and non-vegetarian), and well-organized carry-out food for the downtown labor force as well as for downtown shoppers. In increasing numbers of single households and dual earner households with limited time for food preparation, many consumers are seeking fast, nutritious meals. College students, another large group of consumers for American Diner, are well-known for their appetite for quickly prepared good food.

Future plans include expanding the bakery line, increasing over-the-counter sales (e.g., packaged loaves of bread and whole pies), possible downtown and university delivery, and a continuing effort to become more proficient in carry-out operations.

Based on projections by the Institute for Public Policy and Business Research at the University of Timbuktu, the Timbuktu population is expected to grow 5-7% in the next five years. during that time, downtown Timbuktu will continue to provide a unique, vibrant, shopping and entertainment center for this region.

MENU

To keep food and labor costs low, priority is being placed upon a menu with interchangeable ingredients. For example, today's vegetable special will be in tomorrow's pot pie. The limited menu will be based on "comfort" foods at reasonable prices (Mom's cooking made better).

Imagine:

A pot pie made with fresh, flaky crust with a variety of meat or vegetable fillings.

A deli with a variety of meats, cheeses, and spreads (chicken salad, vegetarian) with a choice of herb or plain French mini-loaves.

The deli will also offer creative versions of traditional side salads: potato salad, cole slaw, bean salads and tossed salad.

"Pocket" breads are known in virtually every culture, e.g., Mexican burritos, Greek spanokopita, chinese eggrolls, Indian somosas. American Diner will emulate the German version of the pocket bread--the bierock--which traditionally includes ground beef, onions, and sour cream wrapped in a flavorful dough. The ingredients of American Diner's bierock will vary to satisfy vegetarians as well as meat-eaters.

To round out meals of pot pie or bierocks and side salads, will be soup-of-the-day and desserts of freshly baked cobbler-of-the-day, cheesecake, baked maple custard and seasonal fruit pies.

Breakfast will emphasize baked goods with a European style breakfast that includes a bread basket with fruit and cheese. Also featured will be freshly baked scones and muffins.

To top it all off, beverages offered will include freshly brewed organically grown coffees (with choices of espresso or cappuccino), hot or iced sun tea, freshly squeezed citrus and vegetable juices, as well as limeades, lemonades and smoothies (blended fruit drinks).

On Sundays, in addition to the regular menu, whole grain waffles (ginger pumpkin) will be offered.

The menu offers a variety of healthful choices--note that there are no fried foods. An advantage of not having fried foods is the savings in operating and service costs that exist with the use of deep fryers.

MARKET DESCRIPTION

Timbuktu is the fifth largest city in Utah with a population of 65,000 (80% of the total population for Buck County). The city lies almost mid-way between Capital City and Middleton and Buck County is ranked sixteenth in the U.S. for young adults. Almost a third of the population in Buck County is aged 18 to 24, compared with the U.S. average of 10.8%. Studies have shown that members of this age group are heavy consumers of restaurant fare.

The presence of two institutions of higher learning in Timbuktu provide the area with a progressive-minded clientele. Sporting events, particularly football and basketball, bring visitors from throughout the region. The recent addition of Timbuktu's Mall and the unique downtown shopping area draw people heavily from neighboring cities as well as from out of state. In addition, Buck County and Timbuktu are serving as hosts for an increasing number of conferences and conventions. Downtown Timbuktu is the focus for entertainment with movie theatres, historic Timbuktu Hall (concerts, plays, etc.), a brew pub, an historic hotel, and several successful restaurants. This clustering effect of features creates a large customer base from which to draw.

COMPETITION

Although many restaurants exist in Timbuktu, the majority are "fast food." The demand for high quality, sit-down restaurants is evident by the amount of time spent waiting to be seated at most downtown cafes. Upon entering the American Diner, the decor conjures up the feeling of an old-fashioned comfortable diner. The food service concept is a cross between a deli and a coffeehouse, with a full-service bakery, emphasizing an organized, efficient carry-out operation. With this combination of atmosphere, "comfort" food menu, service and carry-out, the American Diner will be unique.

American Diner's strengths relative to the competition lie in the controlled labor and food costs. The simple menu with interchangeable ingredients is designed to keep food costs low. To keep labor costs down, plans include hiring an experienced, versatile staff that is able to both work in the kitchen and out front. As stated earlier, table service will not be offered; strictly counter service will be utilized. This feature will eliminate a number of employees that increase personnel costs in other restaurants. With the growing concern over health and smoking, the cafe will be smoke-free. Another strength for the American Diner is location--the heart of downtown Timbuktu.

MARKETING STRATEGIES

Advertising costs will be 1-2% of sales. Believing that radio and print ads are not cost effective, American Diner will spend ad dollars in other creative ways:

- ❑ Selling t-shirts and coffee mugs with American Diner logo
- ❑ Postcards of the storefront in an old-fashioned airbrushed style illustration
- ❑ Carry-out bags featuring the printed logo with menu stuff-in
- ❑ Menus will be distributed to downtown businesses and the university campus
- ❑ Sponsoring various community projects and events to help with name recognition

Ultimately, the best advertising for the American Diner will be the word-of-mouth from satisfied customers.

MANAGEMENT TEAM

The business will be a 50/50 partnership in terms of management. John Doe will oversee the front end and Jane Smith will oversee the bakery/kitchen. All policies will be decided between these two. John and Jane will be involved in every aspect of the business, including the design, menu, food preparation, service and management. The team will hire an experienced manager to oversee the operation when they are not there. Major medical insurance will be provided for John and Jane. After one year of employment, full-time staff will be eligible for insurance.

Since he was a boy in western Utah John Doe has worked in food service in a variety of capacities. Starting out peeling potatoes and graduating to dishwashing at eight years old, he fulfilled a life-long dream when he opened his own restaurant in downtown Timbuktu, the Paris Cafe. The Paris Cafe is still a wildly popular and thriving business at 1 Block St. The restaurant expanded in 1987, doubling its size and adding a bar. At the time of its sale in 1989, Paris Cafe was grossing $1,040,000 per year and employed a staff of 67. John Doe was involved in all aspects of the operation from 1984 up to 1990: managed day-to-day operations, oversaw financial and personnel matters, planned restaurant public relations, and more. John Doe's track record in the restaurant business has illustrated only success.

Jane Smith also comes into this project with a strong food service background. She was instrumental in the planning and start up of Paris Cafe, which is now one of Timbuktu's most popular bar/restaurants. In charge of creating a scheduling system for the staff, she also hired and trained the wait, host and bar staff, dishwashers and buspeople; and worked closely with the kitchen manager to oversee equipment/food purchases and menu worked as a host/waitress/ bartender. Jane Smith's other restaurant experience includes work as baker, waitperson, and hosting at the Paris Cafe as well as baking biscuits, quick breads, danish and desserts as needed daily. A co-manager of Natural Foods from 1981-1985, Jane Smith is again a co-manager at this store. She is a full-time staff member spending half her time as a floor manager and the other half as a supplements/ personal care products buyers. During her time as a buyer, sales for her departments have risen significantly. She has a good understanding of food distribution, which will be valuable in her role at the American Diner. To a large degree the success of any food service venture depends on ordering and inventory skills.

FINANCIAL PROJECTIONS

The following projections are based on past experience with downtown business in Timbuktu. The equipment and leasehold improvement figures come from estimates given to the management team by suppliers and contractors.

- Most Conservative Projection of $420,000/year in sales is based on approximately 245 customers per day (360 days/year) with an average guest check of $4.75 (available upon request).

- Middle Projection of $540,000/year in sales is based on approximately 315 people per day (360 days/year) with average guest check of $4.75 (available upon request).

- Most Optimistic Projection of $720,000/year in sales is based on approximately 420 customers per day (360 days/year) with an average guest check of $4.75 (available upon request).

- Inventory Purchases are based on 40% of sales, which is admittedly high--the goal is to reduce this area to around 33%.

- Labor Costs are based on prevailing wages for necessary employees, hours and duties based on similar operations. Current government tax rates and insurance quotes are the basis for the payroll taxes and benefit package.

- Growth in sales is figured at a 17% increase per year.

See appendix for a complete breakdown of equipment and start-up costs.

Plans include the purchase of a computer with a software package to do payroll and weekly inventory. The cash register system will track sales by category. An accountant will be hired to take care of quarterly payroll and business taxes.

Income Statement and Balance Sheet

Middle Projection : Year 1

INCOME STATEMENT (Feb. 93-Jan. 94)

Net Sales	$540,000
Less: Cost of Sales	$220,000
Gross Profit	$320,000
Less: Operating Expenses	$306,774
Operating Profit	$13,226
Less: Other Expenses (net)	$0
Profit Before Taxes	$13,226

BALANCE SHEET (As of Jan. 31, 1994)

Current Assets:	
Cash	$120,226
Accounts Receivable	$0
Inventory	$4,000
Other Current Assets	$0
Total Current Assets	$124,226
Noncurrent Assets:	
Equipment Less Depreciation	$28,000
Intangible Assets (net)	$0
Other Noncurrent Assets	$0
Total Noncurrent Assets	$28,000
Total Assets	$152,226

LIABILITES AND EQUITY

Current Liabilities:	
Accounts Payable	$0
Currently Maturing LTD	$18,540
Other Current Liabilities	$0
Total Current Liabilities	$18,540
Noncurrent Liabilities:	
Long Term Debt	$55,620
Other Noncurrent Liabilities	$0
Total Noncurrent Liabilities	$55,620
Equity:	
Owners Equity	$78,066
Retained Earnings	$0
Total Equity	$78,066
Total Liabilities and Equity	$152,226

APPENDIX A: RESUMES

John Doe

123 Maple St.
Timbuktu, UT, 00000
(505)555-1212

EDUCATION

Graduate, Northwest High School, Morgan, Utah, 1974.

Graduate, University of Michigan, 1978, Bachelor of General Studies in Liberal Arts.

WORK EXPERIENCE

November, 1989
to Present: Shift Manager/Supplement and Personal Care Buyer, Save-On Drugs: staff supervision, customer service, inventory control, receiving shipments, pricing and stocking shelves, and marketing the departments.

May, 1989,
to May, 1991: Host, Waiter, Joe's Deli.

October, 1988
to April 1989: Manager, Paris Cafe. Duties: supervised the start-up of the restaurant/bar operation, hired and trained the staff, negotiated with suppliers about equipment, helped develop menu, worked as host and bartender.

July, 1985
to April, 1986: Advertising Coordinator, Advertising U.S.A. Duties; coordinated advertising material for two publications and worked as a telemarketer for one of the publications, part of show management team for the Natural Foods Expo (the Industry's largest trade show).

July, 1981
to June, 1985: Co-Manager, Loon River Saloon. Duties: staff supervision, inventory control, day-to-day store operation and coordination of promotional events.

WORK RELATED ACTIVITIES September, 1984 to June, 1985: Board Member, Board of Directors of Cooperative Warehouse, Timbuktu, Utah, a distributor of natural foods.

References available upon request.

Jane Smith

555 N. Main St.
Timbuktu, UT, 00000
(505)555-1213

EDUCATION Graduate, High School, Salt Lake City, Utah. 1968, University of Michigan, 1969-1972, Studies in Liberal Arts.

WORK EXPERIENCE

June 5, 1992
to June 30, 1992: Head Cook, Morgan Elementary. Duties: manager of kitchen and head cook for sixty grade school children as well as ten staff members.

November, 1984
to May. 1990: Owner, Manager, The Watering Hold, Timbuktu, Utah. Duties: founded business, managed day-to-day operations, involved in all aspects of business, including financial, personnel, public relations and more.

August, 1970
to May, 1971: Kitchen Worker, Oceana Restaurant. Duties: worked in kitchen as well as in food serving line.

June, 1963
to May, 1968: Food Service Worker, Meats-N-Things: dishwasher, hostess, waitress, cashier.

References available upon request.

APPENDIX B: MASTER COST LIST

Contract Work	$43,500.00
Start-Up Wages (based on eight weeks start up time)	$8,000.00
Blodgett Stack Oven	$1,300.00
Opening Food Inventory	$4,000.00
Booths, Tables	$4,500.00
Neon Signs	$3,500.00
Deli Case	$2,100.00
Refrigerator Reach-In	$1,650.00
Computer System & Cash Register	$2,500.00
Hobart Mixer (60 qt.)	$3,000.00
Hobart Mixer (20 qt.)	$1,400.00
Misc. Supplies/Pans, Utensils	$2,000.00
Six Burner Range Oven	$1,850.00
Freezer Reach-In	$600.00
Sandwich Unit	$1,360.00
Proofer	$550.00
Glassware, Silverware	$300.00
Plates, Etc. (100 settings)	$1,000.00
Berkel Chopper	$750.00
Bzerba Slicer	$2,150.00
Business Structure Fee	$800.00
Three Compartment Sink	$600.00
Coffee Machine w/pots--three burner	$500.00
Stereo System	$500.00
Steamtable (two compartment)	$450.00
Work Tables (three)	$450.00
Microwave	$300.00
Hobart Coffee Grinder	$385.00
Blenders (two)	$230.00
Ingredient Bins w/wheels	$100.00
Toaster	$200.00
Time Clock	$200.00
Business Insurance	$500.00
Window Shades (storefront)	$200.00
Chairs (for tables)	$150.00
Cutting Boards	$100.00
Table Accessories (salt and pepper shakers, etc.)	$100.00
Menus	$100.00
Bus Tubs	$50.00
Pick-Up Window Heat Lamp	$50.00
Ticket Wheel	$20.00
Rent	$5,775.00
T-Shirts/Mugs	$600.00
Advertising Package	$1,000.00
Utilities	$1,000.00
Payroll Taxes	$1,300.00
Total	$101,670.00
Cash reserve of	$5,330.00
Total	$107,000.00

Restaurant

BUSINESS PLAN

PEACH BLOSSOM DINER

1 Congaree Battery Drive
Columbia, SC 34345

January 17, 1993

The Peach Blossom Diner is an authentically restored diner featuring period paraphernalia from the 1920s through the 1950s. This plan includes details on how to create an establishment with a nostalgic atmosphere and discusses issues relevant to the genesis of any new restaurant.

The Opening of America's Most Authentic Restored Diner on the Banks of the Congaree River at the Gervais Street Bridge

Presenting the restoration of America's largest and most authentic diner with a nostalgic overview of life from the 1930's into the future. The menu will offer contrasting health conscious foods with an international flavor. The Diner will be in a special setting on the Congaree River.

Contact: David Jones

BUSINESS DESCRIPTION

Overall Purpose

The Peach Blossom Diner, situated on the banks of the Congaree River, will become a South Carolina landmark. The Peach Blossom Diner will be the largest and most authentically restored diner in America.

Specific Purpose

To offer the authenticity of a true Diner as a backdrop to a nostalgic overview of life from the 1930s to the present.

Features

The Diner will feature paraphernalia of different time periods. There will be a collection of salt and pepper dispensers from the 1950s, miniature table "juke boxes" from the 1940s, and a private dining room from the 1920s. The contrasting menu is somewhat futuristic in that it offers a wide variety of health conscious foods with an international flavor. Jonathon Perry, co-owner of Shadows Tavern, will coordinate the international menu. This menu, combined with the ambiance of the Diner, the Congaree River, a public park, a boardwalk, and a view of Columbia's skyline will provide several advantages. The Diner will be the catalyst to the long awaited Congaree River development. It will be used to promote the revitalization of our inner Tri-Cities.

Peach Blossom Diner was the original name of the establishment. This name promotes the intrigue associated with Southern culture and hospitality. It typifies the deep south and clearly expresses authenticity and nostalgia.

Brief History

The Peach Blossom Diner was built in 1952 by the Mountain Ridge Company of Lowell, New Jersey. The style and grace of this Diner exemplifies the era of Diners. This is an authentic Mountain Ridge Streamliner. The Streamliner was an extremely popular design. It was called "America's fastest selling Diner" by the diner industry.

Diners became obsolete during the upsurge of the fast food era. Now, less than 50 of these rare diners are in existence. It is unusual to find one in the deep south due to high transportation costs. This particular diner was moved to Beacon, South Carolina in 1957 where it was operated for 26 years. Around 1983, the owners built a new restaurant on the site and the original diner was placed in a field.

The Diner was purchased by David Jones in 1989 and moved to Columbia, South Carolina. It was then fully restored and two matching sections were built at the Campton Department of Corrections on Willow Road. Photographs of the restoration process are available upon request.

Marketing Strategy

The partners, David Jones and Jonathon Perry, wanted to put the Diner in a place that would ensure a competitive advantage in the downtown market. The chosen site should make the Peach Blossom Diner an attraction that would draw both local residents and tourists. The combination of the Peach Blossom Diner and Columbia's strongest untapped amenity, the Congaree River, will be an attraction worth visiting.

The site of the Peach Blossom Diner is adjacent to the Gervais Street Bridge. It is part of a 16 acre tract between the Gervais and Blossom Street Bridge on the West Bank. David Jones has developed a plan for the area and a model has been prepared to illustrate the development of this plan. A photograph of the model is available upon request.

This plan will include the owners of the land, Dr. Leslie Smith and Benjamin Taylor, deeding approximately 1 1/2 acres to the Bellshire County Parks and Recreation Department for a park, boardwalk, and public road along the Congaree River. This plan is in progress. West Chester City Council has passed a 100% vote of approval. The West Chester Planning Commission has approved the plan and validated the local zoning. The Metro Chamber Board has also passed a 100% vote of approval and is working with the SCDDA to assist in the JEDA financial package. Bellshire County engineers have designed the road and the administrator of Bellshire County Parks and Recreation is working on the funds for the park and boardwalk.

The new road along the river front will be given the name Congaree Battery Drive. The Peach Blossom Diner will be located at 1 Congaree Battery Drive at the Gervais Street Bridge. The many attractions being created along Congaree Battery Drive complement, and will be complemented by, the authenticity and ambiance of the diner.

This nostalgic diner, combined with a contrasting upscale international menu, will be a marketed as a VIP box seat for the enchanting view of the Columbia Skyline, the enticing park and boardwalk, and the captivating backdrop melody of cool water splashing over the rocks of the Congaree River.

Food Preparation and Strategy

The food preparation will be based on the philosophy that has made Shadows Tavern so successful. Our kitchen motto will be "Freshness, consistency, and abundance."

The Chowder Shop will supply fresh seafood and meats for our varied menu. Fresh vegetables and produce will arrive daily from the Farmer's Market. Fresh sourdough rolls will be baked daily at the diner. Jonathon Perry's seasoned talents as a food buyer will be utilized to assure proper control of the inventory and turnover.

Management and Owners

The ownership of the Diner is presently in the form of a partnership. The President and Treasurer of the partnership, Jonathon Perry, controls 50% of the stock. The Vice-President, David Jones, and the Secretary, Janice Hanner, each own a 25% share of the business. The partnership will be incorporated prior to opening with the same percentages of stock. It will be called Peach Blossom Diner, Inc.

Jonathon Perry will operate and oversee the Diner. The manager of the Diner will be Tracy Wade. For the past two years, Ms. Wade has been working and training under Jonathon Perry as his assistant at Shadows Tavern. She will share in a percentage of the profit and participate in a stock earning plan. The stock plan will provide a return of up to 20% of the stock and net profits over a 5 year period. After construction is complete, it is not foreseen that Jonathon Perry or David Jones will continue to have any day to day activities involving the operation of the Diner.

Objectives

It is the owners' objective that the menu represent an exciting international flavor with a wide variety, yet it should not intimidate anyone. To ensure this, the Diner will also offer basic favorites, such as hamburgers and apple pie.

The nostalgia and ambiance of the old Diner will be an attraction that no other restaurant can offer. The original front section with the original counters will serve as both a bar and a dining area. One of the two counters has been modified with a large stainless steel ice tray where the fresh entrees of the day will be displayed. This setting will bring new people and new monetary gain to the city.

The Diner has wiring and plumbing to accommodate a bar on the large patio overlooking the river. This patio will be open on pleasant days to serve customers. Bar sales are expected to be excellent from both the inside and outside bar area, though the outside bar should produce higher sales in the Spring. Alfresco dining on the patio will allow 40 more people to be seated. The patio will be open about one-half the amount of days the Diner is opened, approximately 105 days per year.

The seasonability at Shadows Tavern illustrates that the low profit months are July and August. The best months are in the Spring and Fall.

The owners will have a viable option to test the market with an exciting breakfast menu similar to the one that has been so successful at the Seashore Cafe in Shellfish Isle. The price point will be about $1 more than a typical Columbia breakfast. However, the menu would offer some special touches, such as small slices of different fruits on the plate and beach water grits, with an optional sprinkle of New York cheddar cheese. A choice of low-fat, regular and honey butters will be available. There would also be homemade preserves (with no added fat) and a choice of three coffees. The private dining room, called the Hospitality Room, would also be available for breakfast meetings for up to 16 people.

The attendants will wear custom diner uniforms. Please contact David Jones for a photograph.

The Diner will house part of the World's largest known salt and pepper shaker collection. The parents of David Jones started the collection at their truck stop diner in Fayville, South Carolina. It was popular for the truckers to bring his parents salt and pepper shakers from their travels around America. The collection has been in storage since 1961.

Music from the 1930s and 1940s will be selected and played through miniature "juke boxes" on the tables. The decor and setting of the middle section dining area will be modeled after the 1930s and 1940s. The private dining room will have the flair of the 1930s.

MARKET DEFINITION

Customers

The primary market for the Peach Blossom Diner during lunch and the possible breakfast is the local work force. The work force in Bellshire County is the second highest in the State with 172,000 average workers per month. West Chester County has an average daily work force of 57,000 for a total daily work force of 229,000. The metropolitan area of Bellshire and West Chester counties is approximately 500,000 people. The busiest corner in Columbia is one block up Diamond Avenue at the corner of Diamond and Howard Street with over 65,000 cars per day. Over 23,000 of those cars cross the Gervais Street Bridge where the Diner is highly visible.

There are 2.5 million visitors to the metropolitan area each year. There is no information compiled to separate the business visitor from the tourist, but it is estimated that only 15% are true tourists. The area has 1,300,000 room nights. Of the total room nights, 455,000 are within the city limits of Columbia.

The State Museum is located diagonally across the river with over 400,000 visitors per year. The location and uniqueness of the Peach Blossom Diner will be an advantage in competing for local residents, the business travelers, and the tourists.

The location is also in the overall plan of the Congaree Vista. The Congaree Vista is 900 acres of the old historic district of Columbia. Strong efforts began almost ten years ago to revitalize the Congaree Vista. Recently, progress has become visible. The Congaree Vista has become an attraction that draws people back into the City. Congaree Battery Drive will be a focal point of the Congaree Vista.

In the Spring, the 4.3 million dollar beautification of Gervais Street, from the bridge to the Capitol Building, will begin construction. Congaree Battery Drive is at the beginning of Gervais Street at the Gervais Street Bridge.

The Five Points area was the primary draw for dining and socializing for years. The Congaree Vista is quickly taking over that position. The Vista exhibits a mature image and seems to be a fresh and appealing alternative.

Competition

The general downtown and surrounding area has a number of restaurants. Discussed below are the restaurants that will offer the most competition to the Peach Blossom Diner.

The first chain to realize the future of the Vista:

Monte's Steak House is located four blocks up on Blossom Street. The restaurant has been very successful and has an excellent customer return rate. The menu is limited to basic meat and potatoes.

The second chain to move into the Vista:

The Spaghetti Shop is located one block off Blossom Street on Raymond Avenue. It is in a renovated warehouse, with a trolley theme. The seating capacity is 440. Despite the size, this restaurant offers a family oriented approach, featuring low cost pasta meals. They have been well received in the downtown area.

Established competition located downtown:

Bountiful Seafood has been downtown for years. It is located next to Monte's Steak House. Bountiful Seafood is a very casual and informal dining experience. The cement floors and paper table cloths set the tone for a restaurant. The featured fare is oyster-shooters and beer. Bountiful does not experience the volume of the other two chains, but they do a very substantial business.

The closest neighbor, only one block away, is Arnie's Upstairs. The wonderful story of Arnie's begins with a young 18 year old boy. His father leased the upstairs of a building one block from the end of The Gervais Street Bridge. Young Arnie was then put in charge of creating a dream for himself. From Arnie's Upstairs, the view of the Columbia skyline is beautifully magical from sunset to evening's end. The menu is expensive and is at the highpoint of the scale. Northern Italian cuisine is featured. Arnie's Upstairs is one of the most successful restaurants in Columbia, with the exception of Shadows Tavern.

Athens On Highway 501, five miles away, another successful restaurant called Athens is very popular. This Greek restaurant is not in a prime location, but their food keeps the parking lot full for lunch and dinner.

Competitive Strengths

The Peach Blossom Diner will be the most authentic diner in America with a setting on the river and a wide range of international foods. No other restaurant offers all these features and attractions.

The menu will have a wide variety of appetizers, entrees and deserts, plus additional culinary choices such as Thai and Indian dishes. The price point of the menu will be situated below Arnie's Upstairs and slightly higher than Athens and Monte's Steak House. A daily "Blue Plate Special" will be offered for the frugal customer. When dining at the Peach Blossom, one may choose foods from around the world in various price ranges. There is also a patio overlooking the river where drinks and a wide choice of international appetizers may be enjoyed.

MARKETING PLAN: OVERVIEW

The Peach Blossom Diner will maintain an ambiance incomparable to any other place in the Midlands. The food and menu will be upscale, capturing the contrast of the old and the new.

The menu will feature culinary foods from around the world, but will still offer the choice of an American hamburger and apple pie. Diners have enjoyed a tremendous resurgence in the last few years and are constantly in national magazines and advertised on television. David Jones has maintained a clippings file of articles and advertisements. This file is available upon request.

The City Diner in San Francisco and Simone's Diner in West Chester enjoy great success. The following quote was found in a recent edition of Southern Entertainment and Travel:

> *... while in West Chester you must visit Simone's Diner and enjoy gourmet food in contrast with the old Diner. When the sun goes down, not only will you see other tourists, you will also meet the locals. However, you better call for reservations about two months ahead.*

The Peach Blossom Diner will also attract local residents, tourists, business travellers, and the media.

The backbone of the Peach Blossom Diner will be two basic and proven formulas of success. First, good food at reasonable prices. Second, a financial plan and sufficient equity investment to assure staying power.

Abundant research and detailed work has already gone into the building and authenticity of the Diner. People are seeking different, unique, and nostalgic things to do. Trolley Tours of Columbia provide daily evidence that people are intrigued and excited with the nostalgia of the old Trolleys. Nostalgia blended with the magnetism of the river will draw people into the city and ultimately to the site.

MARKETING PLAN: OVERVIEW...*continued*

The Peach Blossom Diner will draw from the existing work force and bring new dollars. People will visit the Diner and Congaree Battery Drive for special events. One special attraction will be to visit as the sun settles in the sky behind you. The city skyline glows with intensity and beauty.

However, we will not sit back and strictly depend on word-of-mouth and free media. Trolleys will be used to attract customers. Trolley Tours of Columbia is operated by David Jones. Trolley Tours will expand the present historic tours with a package that will include a trip to the waterfront and lunch at the Peach Blossom Diner. In the future, a trip to the River and Diner will be added as an option for birthday parties and senior citizen outings.

The Trolleys will reach out to areas such as Wooded Acres, South Chaplin, and business parks. The Trolleys will bring people into the city for dining and visiting the river front.

There have been numerous articles in the Sun Daily Newspaper and discussions on local radio and talk shows about the development of the River. This coverage, combined with the anticipation of a revitalized river, will attract local, regional, and national attention. This will bring people into the city from outlying areas.

As done with the Trolleys, inexpensive flyers will be printed and placed in motels, the visitor's center in town, and on interstate billboards. A special emphasis will be placed on special events in the park and boardwalk area.

The Trolley business works daily with the surrounding hotels, motels, and the Columbia Visitor's Center and Convention Bureau. The Bureau advises guests on the sites and events to discover and enjoy while in Columbia. When a guest is in town and asks that age-old question: "What do you recommend I do while I am in town?", the Visitors Center is going to be suggesting a visit to the riverfront and the Peach Blossom Diner.

The Peach Blossom Diner will epitomize the sights and sounds of the 1930s and 1940s, with progressive touches of contemporary style. From the moment customers approach the premises, the glow of days gone by will entice them toward the grace, charm, and magnetism of the big band era. The Diner will emit a captivating welcome mat of hospitality which will be even more evident upon entering the oval glass doors.

The attendants, donning authentic uniforms of the era, will spark a magic touch to the already superior event. They will present appetite pleasers for any palate.

As the customers enjoy their booth seats in the front section, attention will immediately be drawn to the enchanting replica juke boxes from the 1940s filled with delightful tracks from the same decade. The music will flow as charmingly romantic and high stepping as when it was played during the Great Depression, Prohibition, and the two World Wars. No matter where the eye is turned, this decade of elegance, high life, and patriotism will abound.

FINANCIAL

JEDA LOAN AND APPRAISAL

A loan was requested for $190,000, with a monthly payment plan of $1,150. The amortization is 20 years. The interest rate requested is 4.5%. The first payment should be due 150 days from closing to allow for a construction period. It was also requested that a condition be established to allow the partners to draw on the funds in six $30,000 increments as needed. The Peach Blossom Diner will be used as collateral. It has been appraised at $700,000. A copy of the JEDA loan request, including a detailed summary of project costs and proposed financing, and the Appraisal can be obtained at the South Carolina Development Office, 123 Main St., Columbia, SC 98765.

Equity and Effort

Original note to purchase and move the Diner was $47,000.

Balance of original note $25,000
Cash equity to date $170,000
Funds requested from JEDA to secure the
location,finish construction, and equip the Diner $190,000
Appraisal of the Diner $700,000

The original note is held by G&L Bank. The note is current and the principle amount is approximately $25,000. The note is on a five-year term with monthly payments of $1,000.

The land is to be purchased from Hank Verillae and Betty Dimagio. It is 202' x 164', approximately three fourths of an acre. There is also a cabana area of 40' x 50' on the river bank.

The price of the land is $232,000. There is a $16,000 downpayment required to close and take possession of the land. The balance will be $212,000, after Mr. Verillae and Ms. Dimagio pay $4,000 in clearing costs. The partners are paying the first $6,000 of the $16,000 downpayment. The final downpayment of $10,000 is due upon receiving the JEDA funds. Mr. Verillae and Ms. Dimagio have agreed to finance the property with interest only payments.

Monthly payments for the first year will be at 6%, the second year at 7%, and the third year at 7.5%. The terms stipulate a four month period without any payments, while the construction is completed. At the end of the 3 1/2 years of interest only payments, Mr. Verillae and Ms. Dimagio will finance the balance between 8% and 10% for five more years.

Use of JEDA Funds

All prices are estimates based on buying and selling experience. Some of the pieces will be used equipment.

Use of JEDA Funds *...continued*

PURCHASE OF EQUIPMENT

Chairs and tables	$4,000	
Glasses and silverware	$1,000	
Table items and napkins	$600	
Plates and cups	$1,500	
Busboy trays	$300	
Miscellaneous	$500	
Total Equipment		$ 7,900

KITCHEN EQUIPMENT

Stove	$1,500	
3 compartment bar sink	$900	
Oven	$1,000	
Deep fryer	$600	
3 compartment wash sink	$700	
1 refrigerator	$800	
1 freezer	$800	
Steam table	$1,500	
Cutting table	$300	
Dishwasher	$3,000	
Hot water booster	$300	
Hood system	$3,500	
Grill	$900	
Coffee makers	$750	
Bar coolers	$1,000	
Shelves and racks	$1,000	
Walk-in-cooler	$5,000	
Pans and pails	$500	
Utensils	$750	
Metal tables	$800	
Dessert display	$2,000	
Miscellaneous	$3,200	
Total Kitchen Equipment		$30,800

Use of JEDA Funds *...continued*

CONSTRUCTION

The construction period will be four months.
All cost numbers are estimates based on the actual numbers used in building the first phases of the Diner.

PREPARATION AND PLANNING OF THE LAND AND SITE

Survey fees	$400	
Engineering site and drainage plan	$1,500	
Elevation sighting	$500	
Grading and clearing	$3,000	
Paving and parking lot	$8,000	
Terracing of land and retainer walls	$2,500	
Engineering structural fee	$1,500	
Landscaping	$5,000	
Legal fees	$750	
Total Preparation		$23,150

GENERAL EXPENSES

Moving Diner to location and setting on foundation	$3,500	
Foundation, footing, and piers	$6,500	
Curtain wall	$1,500	
Porch	$5,500	
Licenses	$500	
Insurance	$1,000	
Telephone hook-up	$300	
Water and tap fee	$ 5,800	
Total General		$24,600

Use of JEDA Funds *...continued*

CONSTRUCTION OF DINER

General		
Steel for middle section		
and rear storage area	$3,935	
Labor for steel erection	$2,300	
Welding materials	$400	
Crane rental	$500	
Decking material	$1,745	
Concrete and rebar	$900	
Labor	$2,500	
Lumber, plywood, nails, paint, etc.	$5,200	
Labor for framing and finishing	$5,500	
Sheetrock	$800	
Labor for sheetrock	$1,500	
Total General		$25,280
Roof		
Galvanized metal	$ 1,100	
Labor for roof	$ 2,000	
Sealant	$400	
Glass	$750	
Total Roof		$4,250
Electrical		
Electrical supplies	$2,000	
Labor	$4,000	
Total Electrical		$6,000
Ceiling		
Material	$2,000	
Labor	$1,500	
Total Ceiling		$3,500
Floor		
Tile	$ 3,000	
Labor	$ 2,500	
Total Floor		$5,500

Use of JEDA Funds ***...continued***

Interior		
Back wall seating booth	$2,500	
Finish front section	$3,500	
Finish rear section	$4,000	
Private dining room	$2,000	
Lighting Fixtures	$1,800	
Finish doors	$1,200	
Materials	$800	
Labor	$3,500	
Total Interior		$19,300
Miscellaneous		
Misc. construction materials	$3,000	
HVAC	$6,000	
Misc. labor	$5,000	
Exterior odds and ends	$1,800	
Signage	$4,500	
Total Miscellaneous		$20,300
Labor Other		
One general laborer		
$350/week x 16 wks	$5,600	
David Jones - $400/wk.	$6,400	
General contractor - $500/wk.	$8,000	
Total Labor Other		$20,000
Subtotal		$190,580
Initial Food Invoentory		$5,000
Downpayment on Land		$10,000
GRAND TOTAL		$205,580

CREATION OF JOBS

Current plans are to operate two shifts which will offer new jobs as follows:

Hostesses Or Hosts	2	8.00 Per Hour
Cashiers	2	6.00 Per Hour
Wait Staff Hourly Rate	16	2.13, plus Tips
Cooks	4	8.00 Per Hour
Salad Persons	2	4.75 Per Hour
Cooks' Helpers	4	4.25 Per Hour
Dishwashers	6	4.25 Per Hour
Pot Washers	2	4.25 Per Hour
Clean Up Persons	2	4.25 Per Hour
Total	38	

FINANCIAL PLANNING

Operating Budgets

A Projected Operating Statement for the Diner's first two years of business has been prepared by Jameson's Small Business Center, 656 North West Street, Columbia, SC 96845. A brief summary of the financial figures is provided below.

Operating expenses incurred during the first year are expected to total $324,632. This figure will increase to $455,507 in the second year. During the first year, the net income, before taxes, is projected at $186,485. Net income will substantially increase in the second year to $267,295. Requests for the detailed document should be directed to Jameson's Small Business Center at the above address.

Monthly Sales and Cash Flows

These reports are also available upon request at Jameson's Small Business Center.

SUPPORTING DOCUMENTS

As mentioned throughout this proposal, photographs of the restoration process, articles concerning the resurgence of diners, and a model of the riverfront development are available upon request. Please contact David Jones, 345 Wellship Dr., Columbia, SC 96745.

Also available upon request are an Attorney's statement, the owners' resumes and personal finance statements, and a menu.

Restaurant (Nonprofit)

BUSINESS PLAN

McMurphy's Grill

St. Patrick's Center
1200 6th St.
St Louis, MO 63106
(314) 621-1283

April 26, 1994

This business plan has not been disguised in any way. References to locations, people, and products are real, not fictional. McMurphy's seeks to give job skills to mentally ill homeless people in order to help them get off the street. The contributor has asked that those interested in forming a business of this type contact St. Patrick's Center with their questions during regular business hours prior to instituting any of the suggestions in the plan. ***Note:*** *A number of Appendices to which the plan refers were deliberately excluded due to privacy considerations. Contact St. Patrick's Center with questions relating to those that were omitted.*

RESTAURANT (NONPROFIT) BUSINESS PLAN

EXECUTIVE SUMMARY

Opening its doors on December 3rd, 1990, McMurphy's Grill has brought a little bit of earth-quaking to the St. Louis community. While operating as a competitive restaurant, McMurphy's has set about the task of making people without homes, but with diagnostic psychiatric labels, into food servers and cooks. This business plan primarily focuses on the operational aspects of McMurphy's Grill, defining McMurphy's as two distinct, but interrelated functional organizational units: one being the restaurant business and the other being the employment training component. A strategic plan is presented for each component and the strategic direction which this operation as a whole should take to achieve growth will be outlined.

With an appealing product, both in terms of its mission and its fare, McMurphy's Grill certainly has an added advantage over its competitors. Located at Eleventh Street and Lucas in downtown St. Louis, McMurphy's, as a restaurant, has been favorably noted by restaurant critics and customers alike. Its mission, of training mentally ill homeless men and women, certainly sets it apart from any other competitive restaurant in the St. Louis area.

The success of this operation depends a great deal on the cohesiveness of the two functional organizational units as well as an aggressive marketing strategy. With this in place and a little "luck of the Irish", McMurphy's will likely reach its optimistic sales goals. If the Celebrity Hosts promotion, a newly initiated program, which will be described in more detail in the Strategic Plan, is any indication, a 30 percent increase in sales over fiscal year 1994 is not unrealistic.

Most of us can only imagine the obstacles people who are homeless and mentally ill must overcome to hold down a job, much less one in the restaurant business. Yet, this innovative employment training program has helped to ease the transition for many. From life on the streets to independence, McMurphy's goals are enthusiastic to say the least.

Perhaps the most compelling concern of this type of endeavor lies with the ability to balance both sides of the coin -- the mission and the business. An organization's focus on its prime business. The delicate balance of maintaining the effectiveness and success of each component requires extra care and effort. However, with a well defined strategic plan, the community support afforded St. Patrick Center, a myriad of volunteers, and a staff with a vision -- this tightrope can be successfully maneuvered.

THE COMPANY AND THE CONCEPT

While operating as a competitive establishment, McMurphy's prime focus is on teaching homeless individuals, many suffering from mental illness, skills in food preparation as well as the restaurant service.

THE COMPANY AND THE CONCEPT *...continued*

McMurphy's has enjoyed favorable reviews for both its food and its mission. The 80-seat restaurant provides its customers with wholesome, hearty meals and a comfortable, pleasant atmosphere,while its trainees learn on-the-job skills in self-sufficiency. Primarily drawing customers from the downtown lunch business crowd, McMurphy's has a unique advantage in that it also draws people from other areas because of its mission. To support its favorable status, in both categories, McMurphy's Grill is proud to have been the 1992 Winner of the Midwest Living Magazine Hometown Pride Award and Hospitality Awards finalist for the Restaurant of the Year -- Casual category sponsored by the Convention and Visitors Commission. In addition, McMurphy's Grill has been awarded grants from the Share Our Strength Foundation for its efforts in training for self-sufficiency.

Owned and operated by St. Patrick Center, a multi-service nonprofit agency providing a variety of services for homeless and low-income people in St. Louis, this innovation transitional employment program has provided an opportunity for sixty-seven men and women, thus far, to learn valuable employment skills. St. Patrick Center is located at 1200 North Sixth Street, on the near north side of downtown St. Louis. Dedicated in 1983, the Center provides opportunities for homeless and low-income persons to attain self-sufficiency and dignity through programs which effect permanent solutions, including education, counseling, job training, employment, housing assistance, and substance abuse rehabilitation. Special emphasis is placed on those who experience mental illness or chemical dependency.

The concept of a restaurant operation stemmed from a restaurant in Rock Island, Illinois which is run by mentally ill employees. By owning their own business, which serves as a transitional training program, St. Patrick Center is able to provide the flexibility required to allow the clients to move at their own pace.

With a generous grant from McDonnell Douglas Employees Community Fund and the McDonnell Douglas foundation as well as contributions from other private and corporate sources, McMurphy's Grill became a reality. The Pasta House Company provided the management expertise and restaurant operations knowledge in addition to numerous donations of restaurant fixtures and supplies. Through the Neighborhood Assistance Program of the State Department of Economic Development, McMurphy's was able to receive free rent for much of its existence. In 1993, Paric Corporation, the owners of Lucas Place, the building which houses McMurphy's Grill, donated the entire 3-floor building to St. Patrick Center. The top two floors are constructed for office space. This innovative project is truly a community endeavor.

The operation of McMurphy's Grill has provided a challenge to St. Patrick Center, whose primary expertise has been in the social service arena. In addition, McMurphy's is only one of thirteen programs operated by St. Patrick Center and thus does not have the concentrated effort that many small restaurant operators employ. Changes in administration at St. Patrick Center, especially at the Executive Director's level, along with changes in the management at McMurphy's has significantly affected the operations of the restaurant.

Under the direction of St. Patrick Center's new Executive Director and the Center's Board of Directors, efforts are underway to develop a long-range strategic plan for the entire agency along with establishing better methods to measure program effectiveness. This business plan will provide the long-range strategic direction for this particular operation, providing target measurements and goals for the business component as well as the employment training component. In addition, this operational plan will help to define management responsibilities, controls and reporting expectations of each component. The strategic plan will also help ensure consistency of operation, despite personnel changes, within each component as well as for the entire McMurphy's Grill operation.

THE INDUSTRY AND MARKET ANALYSIS

McMurphy's Grill falls into two industry classifications. As a competitive restaurant, McMurphy's Grill falls into the foodservice industry. As a facility which provides employment and training for mentally ill homeless persons and those recovering from substance addictions, McMurphy's can also be classified among other vocational rehabilitation programs.

The Foodservice Industry

Description of Product Category

Restaurants are the largest part of the U.S. foodservice industry and according to the National Restaurant Association. They "had an estimated sales of $255 billion in 1992." Fuller-service stand alone restaurants, the category which would include McMurphy's, accounted for "32 percent of all foodservice sales in 1992."

The characteristics of most limited menu tableservice restaurants, of which McMurphy's is a part of, include:

- 62.7 percent of limited-menu tableservice restaurants are single units (independent).
- 46.3 percent of these restaurants have a sales volume under $500,000.
- Over 65 percent serve both food and beverage.
- The average check per person is usually under $10.00.
- The average daily seat turnover was 1.8.

The Size of the Market

The foodservice industry is highly fragmented, thus making it an extremely competitive industry. This industry continues to be dominated by small businesses as is evidenced by "average unit sales of $429,000 reported by tableservice restaurants..." McMurphy's Grill has experienced, thus far, a much lower unit sales volume than the average. This is in part due to the limited time

McMurphy's is open on a daily basis. Lack of a comprehensive marketing strategy has also had an impact upon sales.

The foodservice industry continues to experience healthy growth patterns. The National Restaurant Association forecasts an increase of 5.6 percent. Sales for Eating and Drinking places for the City of St. Louis are much higher than for the state as a whole. Total retail sales for the City of St. Louis, of which 18.7 percent are from Eating and Drinking establishments, is expected to increase 45.3 percent over 1992 sales by 1997. With this growth pattern, along with an aggressive marketing strategy, McMurphy's has the potential for significant increases in sales over the next three years.

McMurphy's is located in the extreme northwest section of the downtown core district. Thus, this geographic area represents a huge potential market for McMurphy's lunch business, box lunches, and business functions.

Consumer Attitudes and Demographics

Because McMurphy's is located in the core downtown business district, comprised mainly of white-collar professional persons, its ability to attract a lunch crowd is greater than for many other locations not in the downtown area. Thus, there is a significant potential market for McMurphy's services. It is also important to note that, "Consumers are spending 52 cents out of every dollar at restaurants and bars. This shift reflects the fact that there are more women in the work force and that convenience has become a major decision factor."

McMurphy's Grill has the added attribute in that dining at McMurphy's brings the satisfaction of helping people become self-sufficient. While fast-food operations are marketed as "value" deals, restaurants that are moderately priced, like McMurphy's, are more likely to be considered an overall value by the consumer.

The Competition

In terms of the business aspect, McMurphy's Grill certainly has a competitive edge that no other restaurant in the St. Louis community has. In addition to providing a quality meal and friendly service, this operation also offers its customer the satisfaction of knowing that they have contributed to helping someone achieve self-sufficiency. While other restaurant operations can compete more effectively by offering lower prices or boasting of quick service or providing a more elaborate atmosphere, none can compete directly with McMurphy's Grill's unique attribute -- its mission.

McMurphy's large bright dining area, appealing decor, warm atmosphere, friendly service and homey meals set it apart from many of its competitors. It is also the only restaurant with outside seating, an important consideration among office workers on warm days. After being cooped up in an office all morning, people look for ways to get outside and enjoy the fresh air. The management is making plans to develop the small plot of land in front of the restaurant into a garden, which will add to the attractiveness of eating outside. It is also the only one with celebrity hosts (to be described in the Marketing Plan).

In regard to the private function market, competition is also extremely tight. Eleven facilities, located in the downtown area, advertise under Banquets/ Catering in the Yellow pages. Seven are hotels, three are restaurants and one is a non-traditional facility which has a facility rental of $750.00. This non-traditional facility will be eliminated in the analysis because it competes in an entirely different arena. McMurphy's can compete very effectively in terms of price as it has one of the lowest priced facilities for both a sit down meal and open bar event. Free parking and the privacy of being the only ones in the establishment are other advantages afforded customers of McMurphy's evening functions. Its major limitation is in its capacity limits. It certainly cannot compete with the hotels in that regard. McMurphy's will need to highlight these attributes in its advertising and promotional programs.

McMurphy's is in the position to gain the support of many of its suppliers when promoting a special event or day. This is in large part because of McMurphy's overriding goal of employment and training for people working toward self-sufficiency. Unlike any of its competitors, McMurphy's Grill is a member of the following organizations which gives it credibility as a restaurant and networking capability:

- ❑ Downtown St. Louis, Inc.
- ❑ Missouri Restaurant Association
- ❑ St. Louis Convention & Visitors Commission

Only members of the St. Louis Convention and Visitors Commission will have direct access to scheduled conventions and can directly market to them. Thus McMurphy's can directly target any potentially large conventions through direct mail as well as publicly via material at the Convention Center.

Transitional Training/ Employment Industry

Description and Size of Industry

McMurphy's Grill does not focus on individuals only with mental illness, which alone complicates a person's ability to function independently within the community, but those who are also homeless. It is difficult to assess the number of people who are homeless and mentally-ill. According to the National Resource Center on Homelessness and Mental Illness, "an estimated one-third of single, homeless adults have severe and disabling mental illness, and that as many as half of homeless persons with mental illnesses also have alcohol and/ or drug problems." Many are unemployed and have few or no employment skills that will enable them to earn a living wage. Vocational Rehabilitation Programs and other related agencies tend to inhibit the participation of this population due to their many regulations and lack of models which meet the specific needs of this population.

The continuum of services provided by St. Patrick Center for individuals with mental illness and substance addictions, of which McMurphy's Grill is a key component, is consistent with the psychiatric rehabilitation model. Current research points to the success rate of psychiatric rehabilitation as an effective and cost-efficient treatment for persons with serious and persistent mental illness. The psychiatric rehabilitation model emphasizesactivities which are integrated into the normal life of the individual and the community.

Competition

In St. Louis, two other agencies are recognized for their efforts, at the community level, with people suffering from mental illness, Independence Center and Places For People also utilize this general psychiatric rehabilitation model. The need for psychiatric rehabilitation programs is far greater than what the existing programs in St. Louis can address. McMurphy's Grill has provided training and employment skills, along with the other supportive services offered by St. Patrick Center, for sixty-seven individuals since the inception of this program in December of 1990. Thirty percent have been employed in the community in a variety of positions. A total of 36 percent, which includes the 20 individuals employed, have moved into more stabilizing situations. Places for People reports that "21 percent of all clients surveyed worked at sometime during the year examined (July 1, 1992 through June 30, 1993)." Independence Center was not able to track clients beyond the initial supported work environment and so statistics are not available. Thus, from the available data, McMurphy's Grill appears to be the most effective in terms of permanent solutions.

In comparing the efficiency of McMurphy's Grill Employment Training component with other similar programs, in terms of the cost of the training program, McMurphy's is certainly competitive. The Fountain House program, of which Independence Center is a branch, reports that their cost of training is $30.00 per day, per client. McMurphy's Grill projections for 1995 indicate that the cost of training will be $21.00 per day, per client. By 1997, this number will be significantly reduced as a result of the operating profit from the restaurant business which will be used to offset the training portion of these costs. Appendix B presents this analysis.

There is very little competition among providers of programs for the mentally ill homeless. All providers agree that there is no competition for clients/members. In fact, most would agree that there are more clients than can be served by the existing programs. The two other providers work cooperatively with St. Patrick Center in an effort to deal more effectively with this population. Information and ideas are shared, and collaborative efforts are organized.

The only source of competition is in terms of funding. However, even here the competition is minimal. Independence Center and Places For People rely heavily on the State Department of Mental Health for some of their other programs,

McMurphy's Grill is strictly funded through corporate grants and private contributions. Except for Neighborhood Assistance Tax Credits through the State Department of Economic Development which has been used to offset rental costs at the outset and to help facilitate the contribution of the building which houses McMurphy's Grill, no government funds are used in the operation.

STRATEGIC PLAN

McMurphy's Grill houses two functional organizational units. Each is viewed as distinct, but interrelated. The Restaurant Business component operates to employ persons from the second functional unit, the Employment Training component.

Because of the distinct nature of each component, separate strategic plans have been developed. The close integration of these two units requires a third step which links the two and provides operational guidelines which assist in the efficient and effective management of McMurphy's Grill.

McMurphy's Grill: The Business Unit

Mission: To maintain a viable business operation in order to employ participants of the Employment Training Program.

Description of Product Services

Lunch Business

McMurphy's offers three primary services. First, McMurphy's Grill is a full-service limited menu restaurant located in downtown St. Louis. It is open from 11:00 a.m. to 3:00 p.m. and serves a hearty lunch of traditional American cuisine, with an Irish flair, at a modest price (prices on the menu range from $3.00 to $7.00). The menu, while limited, offers a wide range of soups, sandwiches, salads, entrees, plus daily specials. By offering moderate prices and reasonably quick service (a customer can be in and out within 60 minutes), McMurphy's is attractive to those individuals who like a home-cooked meal, but who are limited somewhat by time. In orderto attract more of the business community and improve on McMurphy's "value" image, the menu has been revised. The changes reflect both a surface change in terms of design, but also adds side dishes to some of the entrees. This makes the meals more appealing to the value-oriented consumer.

The same homey, tasty meals are available for carry-out as well, which can be phoned in or faxed prior to being picked up. Takeout remains the driving force behind industry growth and continues to offer expansion opportunities for foodservice operators. Thus, it is extremely important that the carry-outs continue to be emphasized in the marketing efforts since the trend in lunch traffic is away from long lunch hours.

Its appeals as a restaurant have been favorably noted by restaurant critics and customers alike. The large bright dining area, appealing decor, warm atmosphere and homey menu make McMurphy's a far superior dining experience than most of its nearest competition. Because McMurphy's Grill falls into the "moderate" price range, it is considered more of a value by the customer than fast-food operations or those establishments whose price per person is over $10.00.

Box Lunches

Box lunches are another service available from McMurphy's Grill. For a reasonable price of $6.50, McMurphy's box lunch menu offers a variety of sandwiches, salads and combo's for business and organizational meetings. The current box lunch menu has previously only included sandwiches. In order to be more attractive to the business community, McMurphy's box lunches now include more options. Recommendations for these changes came from people in the business community whose firms are potential customers. Delivery of both the box lunches and the carryouts is a must in this industry. McMurphy's currently delivers box lunch orders of 10 or more. In the near future, McMurphy's will need to establish a full delivery service for carryouts as well as box lunches.

Lunch sales, including box lunches, have represented approximately 80 percent of total sales. Box lunches have represented less than one percent of the total sales until in March of 1994 when sales for box lunches skyrocketed because of one very large order. For the first quarter of 1994, box lunch sales represented 5 percent of the total sales and lunch business represented 78 percent.

Private Functions

The restaurant is also available for private functions every evening and on weekends. Cocktail parties, hors d'oeuvres and full-service dinners are offered. Prices for a cocktail party range from $7.95 per person (for up to 3 hours of open bar) to $8.95 per person (for 4 hours or more). Hors d'oeuvres prices range from $4.95 per person to $8.95 per person, depending upon the selection of options. Full course meals range from $11.50 per person to $16.50 per person. Functions with personalized menu items are also welcomed, but prices will vary with items requested. For the first quarter of 1994, sales in this area represented approximately 17 percent of total sales.

Target Customer

The characteristics of McMurphy's customers differ whether we are discussing the lunch business, the boxed lunch business or the party business. Each has its own unique characteristics. However, they all encompass supporters of St. Patrick Center as well as individuals and groups who are unfamiliar with the restaurant's primary mission.

Marketing Plan

The overall goal of McMurphy's Grill marketing strategy is to increase the number of employment training opportunities in order to expand the number of clients participating in and moving through the program. In order to accomplish this goal, however, the restaurant component must be a viable operation so as to employ persons from the employment training component. The following objectives have been identified by management as targets:

- ❑Begin realizing an operating profit by the end of 1997 by:
- ❑Increasing lunch time customer traffic by 40 percent over a three year period.
- ❑Increasing the number of private functions and catering events by 2 1/2 times the current level over the next three years.
- ❑Increase dollar sales by:
    - ♦30 percent in Year 1 (1995)
    - ♦20 percent in Year 2 (1996)
    - ♦20 percent in Year 3 (1997)
- ❑Institute a motivational compensation program for the restaurant manager and the kitchen manager.
- ❑Increase public awareness of McMurphy's Grill and its mission.

The management of McMurphy's Grill has been busily making plans for marketing the various services offered by the restaurant (i.e. lunch, boxed lunches, and parties). At the same time, they have already begun making some changes in the environment to enhance the decor by changing the curtains and adding new tablecloths. In addition, the bar has been reorganized which has improved its appearance and helped the efficiency of the operation. Table groupings have been rearranged so as to increase the number of tables for two. In the past, most of the tables had been set up in groups of four. Since more customers arrive in groups of two, rearranging the tables helps to eliminate wasted space.

Future plans include both short term and long term efforts to assist the Restaurant in achieving its goals of increased sales.

Financial Plan

McMurphy's previous financial history can certainly leave one wondering about its future. Sales have decreased while costs have increased. However, there is much information gleamed from these results that can be channeled into a brighter future.

As one glances at the history and then at the future based on new sales results, it is obvious that much depends upon the level of sales an operation is able to achieve. Most of McMurphy's expenses are fixed, therefore the higher the sales level the better the bottom line.

To achieve the objectives outlined in the marketing plan, it is important to understand some of the financial data and assumptions which led to the arrival of these target levels. A 40 percent increase by the end of year three would increase the average number of customers to 97 per day. This is not unrealistic, considering that the management has made plans to reduce the size of the bar which would increase its capacity of 28 seats. The seating capacity would then be 108 instead of 80.

The current breakdown between lunch sales and sales from private functions is approximately 80 percent lunch and 20 percent parties.This certainly demonstrates the significance of the lunch business. However, growth in the lunch business is not as great as in the private function business, due in part to capacity limits as well as the time frame for lunch. Thus, the future sales breakdown is more likely to resemble: 70 percent lunch and 30 percent parties.

The increase in the number of parties and catering events is expected to more than double. This assumption is based on the fact that sales per party is averaging $750. At a sales level of $150,000, the sales from private functions is approximately $30,000 (maintaining our 80/20 breakdown as explained above). With the average sales per party at $750, the number of parties would be 40 per year. Transferring this analysis to the 1997 estimated sales level, but assuming a 70/30 breakdown, the sales from private functions would be $75,000. Assuming the average sales per party remains the same at $750, the number of parties would increase to 100. This is more than double the current level. Given the potential market of area firms, future convention traffic, and supporters of St. Patrick Center, management feels this is a feasible target. They also realize that a significant marketing effort must take place to achieve this goal.

The financial reports in the future will also reflect more detail. The current accounting procedure for St. Patrick Center will need to be adjusted in order to segregate out more detail,especially in terms of sales, various types of wages, and some operational expenses. The process should be in place for the start of the new fiscal year in July.

McMurphy's Grill: The Employment Training Unit

Mission: To select and assist appropriate clients in the process of attaining on-the-job skills that will assist them in becoming self-sufficient.

Description of Service

Along with other St. Patrick Center programs, McMurphy's Grill provides a continuum of services which moves the client from the street, receiving no services, to competitive employment and independence. The pre-training portion of this program begins with the selection of appropriate mentally ill homeless clients by counselors at Shamrock Club (one of St. Patrick Center's programs). These clients will complete a series of pre-training classes before placement at McMurphy's. Training includes, but is not limited to communication, self-esteem, personal hygiene, accepting criticism, coping with past problems, time management, and problem solving. Usually the first four classes (Self-Image; Behavior (Old and New); Making Choices; and Communication) are required before being placed at the restaurant. During the period in which the client is involved in the On-The-Job- Training portion of the program, the remaining four classes (Problem Solving: Saving Money/Goal Setting: Leisure Time Management/Personal Growth; and Budgeting Priorities) are offered once a week.

After the client has completed the first series of Pre-Employment Classes and before being placed into a position at the restaurant, an orientation is conducted by the Client Case Manager and individualized treatment plans are developed.

Clients are then assigned to an appropriate position at the restaurant and receive proper on-site training. This phase of training includes basic skills such as cleaning and mopping and can lead into more complex positions such as waiting. The client is encouraged to move on to competitive employment only when fully emotionally, psychologically, and socially ready to do so. The initial placement in the community will include careful monitoring by the Case Manager. Hopefully, independent employment is the end result.

Target Market

For the Employment Training component, the customer (or client trainee) is most often homeless and has symptoms of mental illness. Many also are recovering alcoholics or dealing with drug addictions. While most of our trainees are men, which is indicative of this population as a whole, there have been a few women in the program. They suffer from a variety of psychiatric illnesses and have been a part of The Shamrock Club, a day program for mentally ill homeless men and women, operated by St. Patrick Center.

While the prime target for this training program are persons who are homeless and mentally ill, if space is available clients from other programs offered by St. Patrick Center may also participate in this training program. Most are homeless, but without disabling psychiatric illnesses.

The following goals have been set in terms of the number of participants and the number who successfully become self-sufficient:

- ❑ 25 participants in 1995 with 10 successes
- ❑ 28 participants in 1996 with 12 successes
- ❑ 30 participants in 1997 with 14 successes

Financial Plan

The cost of the Employment Training component will be funded in part by the remaining corporate contributions as well as additional solicited funding. By 1997, profits from the restaurant business will help to defer a portion of these costs. Continued profits from the restaurant business segment will reduce these training costs, so that future expansion of this endeavor is likely.

Continued interest in this program from McDonnell Douglas Corporation has been received and the potential for further funding has been expressed. With this possible source of funding, coupled with St. Patrick Center's ability to raise funds, the employment training portion will be covered.

OPERATIONS AND MANAGEMENT

Perhaps the most important aspect of this strategic plan is in the operations and management of the endeavor. The management indirectly involved in the operating of the restaurant business component or the employment training component. It is vital that there be clear reporting relationships and expectations. It is also essential that both components work closely together to ensure the success of the client trainees.

As one of St. Patrick Center's programs, McMurphy's falls under the governance of the St. Patrick Center Board of Directors. The full board meets bimonthly and the executive committee of the board meets on the odd months when the full board does not meet.

Six task groups have been organized, made up of board and staff members, to look at important issues facing the center in the future:

- ❑ **Mission and Vision**: What should be our continuing mission and vision be for the next five years?
- ❑ **Programs**: What programs will best meet the client needs?
- ❑ **Organization and Staffing**: What are the ideal organization and staffing necessary to effectively serve our clients?
- ❑ **Facilities**: What facilities will be needed to house these services?
- ❑ **Revenue**: How will the revenue needs for the future be met?
- ❑ **Board**: What should be our board composition?

Chosen by the board of directors, the executive director of St. Patrick's Center reports directly to the board and is responsible for the budget of over $1.8 million, a full-time/part-time staff of over 50 people and the effective management of thirteen programs.

The Director of Programs (Mental Health) and the Client Case Manager are responsible for the selection of appropriate clients, conducting the pre-employment classes and the orientation session, preparing individual treatment plans with the client/trainee, and providing support services (budgeting, help with locating housing, clothing, transportation, etc.).

The Client Case Manager directly monitors client progress through the training program, assessing the clients ability to move on. This position reports directly to the Director of Programs (Mental Health).

The Director of Programs (Mental Health) reports directly to the executive director and is involved with selection of appropriate clients. The Director also supervises the Client Case Manager. A monthly report indicating client progress will be prepared for the executive director by the Director of Programs (Mental Health).

The Business Director is responsible for overseeing the operation of the restaurant business component of McMurphy's Grill. It is essential that this person have a significant background and experience in business. This person works very closely with the restaurant manager in the operation of the restaurant. This position, which reports directly to the executive director, also supervises the Marketing Consultant. Because the foodservice industry is so competitive, it is essential that the marketing effort by carefully monitored and progress noted.

The Restaurant Manager is responsible for the effective and efficient operation of the restaurant business component. This includes the training of client employees in their assigned restaurant positions, hiring other professional staff, as well as all that is involved in the daily operation of this facility. This position will report directly to the business director, who will work closely with the Restaurant Manager and his staff to ensure the viability of the operation.

Assisting the Restaurant Manager the Kitchen Manager. The Kitchen Manager is responsible for the efficient and effective operation of the kitchen facilities. Responsibilities include: ordering food and supplies, training client trainees at the various stations within the kitchen area, quality food preparation, suggesting new menu items, costing out menu items, and monitoring food waste. This position reports directly to the restaurant manager.

The Management Consultant coordinates activities with the restaurant manager and the business manager. The Management Consultant is directly responsible to the business director. Responsibilities include: preparation of a marketing plan along with an annual calendar of events; the organization, coordination and implementation of the marketing activities; establishing measurements to evaluate the effectiveness of various marketing efforts; and networking with various community organizations.

Operations

Weekly and Monthly management reports will be prepared and discussed at weekly and monthly staff meetings of those involved in this program. Problems will be identified and potential solutions discussed. Progress will be highlighted and noted for future plans. Currently, the staff meetings consist of the Restaurant Manager, the Kitchen Manager, the Director of Programs (Mental Health) and the Client Case Manager. In the future these meetings will also include the Business Director and the Marketing Consultant. This will assist in shoring up the fragmentation that exists and improving the communication process, which will help in assessing particular marketing efforts and keep everyone informed of future plans. All involved will have a better understanding of the performance of the entire operation, including the training process and the operations of the business. This will certainly improve the effectiveness and efficiency of the marketing efforts.

In addition, the following procedures need to be incorporated into the operations.

Inventory

Responsibility of the Restaurant Manager. Inventory should be taken on a weekly basis and maintained via computer so that prices can be updated regularly and will require less time each week. At this time there is not a computer at McMurphy's, but the Executive Director and Director of Development at St. Patrick Center will seek donations of computer equipment.

Meal Costing

Responsibility of the Kitchen Manager. A listing of each menu item and the ingredients needed for each, along with their costs needs to maintained and updated regularly. This will assist the management in determining prices as well as evaluating cost of sales margin.

Daily Receipts Report

Responsibility of the Restaurant Manager. To be completed on a daily basis and turned into the finance office at St. Patrick Center within two days. The receipts should be deposited daily as well.

Invoices

Responsibility of the Restaurant Manager and St. Patrick Center's Finance Office. To be checked against ordered items and then sent over to St. Patrick Center to be paid. Price changes should be noted on the inventory list and entered with the next weeks inventory.

Daily Report

Responsibility of the Restaurant Manager. In addition to the sales report, a report should be prepared summarizing the prime costs. A food statistic summary should also be maintained along with a summary of the daily productivity.

Management Reports and Variance Report

Responsibility of the Director of Finance/Administration. They include:

- ❑ **Customer Count** Comparisons with previous years and periods
- ❑ **Inventory Valuations and the determination of Gross Profit**
- ❑ **Income Statement** To include a breakdown of the various productsoffered (lunch business, box lunches, carry-out, and parties). It should also include comparisons with previous years and prior periods.
- ❑ **Annual Budget** To be compiled with the input of the restaurant manager, the kitchen manager, the Business Manager, and the Marketing Consultant.
- ❑ **Labor Costs** With this item being such a large percentage of the operating costs, this expense needs to be carefully monitored by the restaurant management on daily, weekly, and monthly reports which are to be prepared for the Restaurant Manager and Business Director by the Finance Office.

Calendar of Events

Responsibility of the Marketing Consultant and (indirectly) the Business Director. A plan that includes specific promotional events and advertising efforts by month. An estimated cost of each event and ad should be identified. The plan should be evaluated monthly by the project team along with the Marketing Consultant and revised as necessary. This will help reduce the fragmentation that has existed and served to assist management in the preparation of the annual budget.

McMurphy's Grill Operations Report

Responsibility of the Business Director; to be prepared for the Executive Director. A periodic written report (monthly or quarterly) of progress, problems, and potential solutions for the review and updating of the executive director. Problems that need immediate attention will be dealt with separately and in a timely manner. Variances in budget projections, marketing program expectations, client progress, and specific measurable results of advertising efforts should be included.

MAJOR COMPETITORS: LUNCH BUSINESS

Le Dejeuner Deli & Bakery

Located next door to McMurphy's Grill, this newly opened deli is open Monday through Friday from 7:00 a.m. to 2:30 p.m. This small operation provides a variety of menu items at a somewhat lower price. Services include dining in, carry-out, boxed lunches and catering. However, the dining environment is definitely lacking in appeal and does not seem to draw the professional business person. Its carry-out and boxed lunch business may detract from McMurphy's Grill. The atmosphere prevents a significant competitive threat. It is only the nearness of its location that identifies it as a competitor.

The Shell Cafe

Located at 1221 Locust on the Main Floor of the Shell Building, The Shell Cafe is within four blocks of McMurphy's Grill. Open primarily during the lunch period, the prices are similar. However, the menu items do not have the "homemade" appeal that is characteristic of McMurphy's Irish stew, meatloaf platter, or chicken and noodles. Menu items include dinners (steak, fish, pasta, ham, beef and gyros) and a variety of sandwiches and salads.

The Missouri Bar & Grill

Located on north Tucker (701 N. Tucker), a couple of blocks from McMurphy's Grill, has a menu selection and prices comparable to McMurphy's. It also has a full bar (open until 2 a.m.). The outside of the restaurant has an attractive big, bright red awning, which is visible from far away. While similar in some ways to McMurphy's, The Missouri Bar and Grill primarily attracts people interested in the bar. It has the largest sales volume of any of the competition.

The St. Louis Fish Company

Located 2 blocks from McMurphy's Grill on Locust, the St. Louis Fish Company (a new addition to the downtown area) offers a unique menu listing. Open from

10:30 a.m. until 10:00 p.m. (Monday through Friday), this establishment offers: a lunch buffet for $2.99 per pound, and "All You Can Eat" Special for $5.99, and a Lunch Box Special for $2.50 which includes choice of fish plus one side order. This is in addition to the regular menu. Service is similar to the St. Louis Bread Company and thus does not include the full-service provided at McMurphy's.

The St. Louis Bread Company

The Saint Louis Bread Co. is considered a bakery/cafe that offers authentic breads, as well as croissants, muffins and pastries. Their advertisements usually focus on their "fresh" bread and pastries. However, their menu also includes cold sandwiches, salads and soups. Prices for their sandwiches range from $4.00 to $6.00 and each restaurant has a fax number for ordering. Since their service is similar to that of a fast-food restaurant, they capitalize on the "alternative" to burgers and fries by focusing on a quick and healthy meal.

DEE DEE's Deli

DEE DEE's Deli is an interesting establishment. Located at the corner of 10th Street and Washington Ave, three blocks from McMurphy's, it appears to be a "hole in the wall" from its very unattractive exterior and the interior is very drab and dark. However, it is usually full every working day. What makes it successful is a reputation based on good food, friendly service and a great price. They differ from the Saint Louis Bread Company in that they offer items that come from the grill. Burgers and charbroiled chicken are listed among the hot and cold deli sandwiches. The service makeup is practically identical to the St. Louis Bread Company. An average customer orders from a display menu and pays the cashier. They are then given a number to take back to their table. When the order is ready, an employee will bring it to the table. Everything else, from condiments to utensils, are self-service.

All of these operations are fairly small and (except for The Missouri Bar & Grill), are only open for lunch. They all offer boxed lunches. While specific data is unavailable on these competitor's sales levels and market share, it is reasonable to assume that each possesses less than one percent of the market share and that their annual sales level is well under the industry average of $429,000 for a tableservice operation. It would be safe to assume that most of them realize between $100,000 and $300,000 in sales annually. The Missouri Bar and Grill might be higher because of its longer hours, yet it would be safe to estimate that it recognizes less than the industry average because it is not a high traffic area.

Lastly, but certainly not least among the competitive issues, are those firms which provide an inside cafeteria for their employees. The Post-Dispatch and Mercantile Bank both have international cafeterias available for their employees. This certainly detracts from business as both are large employers within walking distance of McMurphy's Grill. Management will need to reduce the impact by appealing to the employees desire for a home cooked meal and the satisfaction that they are helping someone at the same time.

EMPLOYMENT TRAINING COST ANALYSIS

Financial data for this analysis is taken from the Pro Forma Income Statement found in Appendix P. Using the bottom line figures, which include both the operational profit/loss as well as the training costs involved, a picture of the true training costs can begin to materialize.

1995: Loss of $49,118 divided by 260 days of operation divided by the number of clients per day (which for this analysis we will assume to be 10) would derive a cost per client day of: $18.89

Utilizing a similar analysis, by taking the loss of $49,118 and dividing it by the expected success rate of 10 (success rate = clients/trainees who have completed the program and have gone on to attain self-sufficiency through employment) would derive a cost for each success of: $4,912

Utilizing this same analysis, by taking the loss of $49,118 and dividing it by the number of participants expected for 1995, of 25 would derive a cost per trainee of:: $1,965

1996: Loss of $32,595 divided by 260 days of operation divided by 10 clients would derive a cost per client day of: $12.54

- Cost per success: $2,716 (based on 12 successes)
- Cost per trainee: $1,087 (based on 30 participants)

1997: Loss of $12,890 divided by 260 days of operation divided by 10 clients would derive a cost per client day of: $4.96

- Cost per success: $ 921 (based on 14 successes)
- Cost per trainee: $ 430 (based on 30 participants)

MENU

McMurphy's Grill is owned and operated by St. Patrick Center, a multi-service agency which addresses the needs of poor and homeless people in our community.

Through a generous grant from the McDonnell Douglas Foundation and the McDonnell Douglas Employees' Community Fund, along with theassistance and expertise of The Pasta House Company, McMurphy's Grill opened on Dec. 3, 1990. It serves as a training facility for homeless mentally ill individuals who wish to make positive changes in their lives.

Open Monday through Friday from 11 a.m. to 3 p.m., McMurphy's offers carry out service, box lunches, and private parties any evening or weekend. We invite you to become a part of this endeavor by visiting McMurphy's often and by telling others about us.

Thank you for your patronage.

MENU *...continued*

Soups (Cup/Bowl)

Irish Clam Chowder 1.75/2.50
Soup of the Day 1.50/2.25
Celtic Chili 1.95/2.95

Appetizers

Fried Mozzarella Sticks 3.95
Toasted Ravioli 2.95
Chicken Wings 3.95
Homemade Irish Chips 2.95
Handcut French Fries 1.25
Onion Rings 2.95

Salads
(Your Choice of Dressing)

Side Salad 1.25
House Salad (Mixed Greens) 2.25
Caesar Salad 3.50
Caesar Salad w/chicken 4.95
Chef Salad 4.50

Sandwiches

McMurphy's Deli 4.50
Charcoal Broiled Chicken 4.50
Hamburger 3.95
Cheeseburger 4.50
Sirloin Strip Steak 5.95
Corned Beef 4.50
Roast Beef 4.50
Breaded Fish 4.50

Specialties

Meat Loaf with Potatoes and Fresh Vegetables 5.95
Irish Stew (with Beef) served with Irish Soda Bread 4.95
Fresh Steamed Vegetables served with Garlic Butter 4.75

Soup and Salad

Bowl of the Soup of the Day w/House Salad 3.75
Cup of Soup of the Day & 1/2 Sandwich
Choice of Roast Beef or Deli 4.00
House Salad & 1/2 Sandwich
Choice of Roast Beef or Deli 4.25
Low-cal Chicken with Side Salad & Vegetables 6.25

Daily Specials

Ask about our Daily Specials and Light Entrees!

Desserts

Bailey's Irish Cream Cake 2.75

Ask about our Daily Dessert Specials!

TARGET CUSTOMER ANALYSIS

Lunch Business

The lunch customer tends to be a professional person, approximately equal distribution between men and women, who work within walking distance of McMurphy's Grill. Observation by the management points to the speculation that most are in mid-level management positions. Three factors support this observation. First, most are wearing business suits or dresses that reflect a professional position. Secondly, they have the leeway to enjoy a more leisurely lunch and are not bound by a time clock. Thirdly, their incomes or expense accounts seem to equate with mid-level positions since McMurphy's Grill is a medium-priced establishment. Numerous other nearby options, which are much lower priced, are available. While not in the direct vicinity, higher priced establishments that are equated with a higher status are also easily accessible from anywhere in the downtown arena and usually have better parking facilities.

A much smaller portion of the lunch business are customers who come to support St. Patrick Center and the Mission of McMurphy's Grill. This group includes professional people working in the area, employees of other nonprofit or religious organizations, and other individuals who are either downtown shopping or in the area for a business appointment.

McMurphy's carry-out service tends to draw mostly business workers in the local area. Usually, the order is for more than one person. It is a growing business segment and certainly consistent with the lunch time trend of shorter lunch periods. By offering free delivery and soliciting orders through a series of discount coupons, McMurphy's expects to significantly increase this portion of the lunch business. Previously, McMurphy's has not tracked this aspect of the lunch business, but will do so in the future.

Other groups and individuals that McMurphy's Grill hopes to target more effectively in the future include:

- ❑ Tour guides and their groups.
- ❑ People attending special events (i.e. St. Patrick Day parade, Olympic Festival and Cardinal Baseball games).
- ❑ Convention and Tourist Traffic. With the Cervantes Convention Center only two blocks away, this market seems to be a perfect opportunity to increase business. However, to be able to do this, McMurphy's Grill needs to be open when it is compatible with the particular convention's schedule. This may not be feasible or profitable for every convention.

Boxed Lunches

The boxed lunch business usually attracts the following groups:

- Nonprofit and other charitable organizations. Groups that have consistently ordered from McMurphy's Grill are United Way, Cardinal Glennon Hospital and the Girl Scouts of America.
- Religious organizations, including churches, religious congregations and schools.
- Business Meetings. An area that McMurphy's would like to increase.

The boxed lunch business needs to be more aggressively marketed to all of the above target markets, especially to the business community. Appendix F depicts a possible advertisement for the box lunches along with the revised menu which has been recommended. These revisions reflect additional options which make it more appealing to those in the business community as well as other organizational groups.

Private Parties

This particular segment of the operation has the most diverse customer base and realizes the largest contribution margin. McMurphy's Grill has been the site of wedding rehearsal parties, birthday parties, anniversaries, holiday parties (especially during the Christmas season), business meetings, art shows, fund raisers, and a variety of other gatherings. Customers learn about McMurphy's Grill from a variety of sources, most however are familiar with the restaurant's mission and desire to support its efforts. There have been other groups who were looking for space to have a party and have been steered to McMurphy's Grill by supporters or other people familiar with McMurphy's quality, service and lower cost. Management intends to focus more on this segment of its operation, recognizing that the private party business is the aspect of the business which will most help the operation research, or at least come much closer, to its break-even point.

MARKETING STRATEGY

Remodeling

In order to increase capacity, so as not to discourage those coming for lunch on days that the restaurant is full and to improve McMurphy's ability to attract lunch business meetings, McMurphy's Grill is planning to reduce the size of its bar. The bar business at McMurphy's is negligible during the lunch hour. By cutting the bar in half, which leaves sufficient space in which to service small group meetings, a new room could be created which would increase capacity by 28 seats. The benefits of this improvement, aside from those mentioned above, are additional party seating and/or cocktail area. Bar area will be easier to maintain and more inviting for customers to sit at. In addition, there is the potential for two groups to use McMurphy's Grill in the evening. The estimated cost for this, including reorganizing the serving area, would be $5,300. The restaurant manager has already solicited bids for some of the work.

Improvements to the kitchen area which would help to make the operation more efficient and the service better, include the addition of a six burner stove, a 48-inch grill, shelving, a salad window, and improvements to the dishwashing area. The cost of these changes would be approximately $1,850.

Note: The benefits are hard to estimate for items 1 & 2 above, however, in terms of the lunch business alone this increase in capacity could potentially realize a gross profit of $33,124 (based on an average check of $7.00 and full capacity every day). The assumption of full capacity is probably unreasonable considering that currently the restaurant is only filling, on the average, 69 seats per day or 86 percent of its current capacity. However, if other marketing efforts continue to improve the customer traffic, as has the Celebrity Hosts Program (sales are up 20 percent over 1993), then this assumption is not totally unrealistic.

Advertising

A large sign or printed awning that would better identify the location of McMurphy's Grill from Eleventh Street. Currently, the name is not visible until you have already passed the location. This issue is currently under consideration.

Marketing

Parking, which has been a headache from the beginning, has a significant impact upon sales. The Executive Director, the Board of Directors and the staff of this program have been working on this problem. Thus far, McMurphy's Grill has succeeded in getting the City of St. Louis to add additional parking meters along Eleventh and Lucas Streets. Management is in the process of talking with lot owners in the vicinity (of which there are several) and negotiating an arrangement whereby customers from McMurphy's can park at a reduced rate and that we can be guaranteed a particular number of parking spaces.

Develop a customer evaluation/survey for all of various services offered by McMurphy's. A recommended customer evaluation/survey for McMurphy's lunch business has been included in Appendix H. Request suggestions for improvements from customers or potential customers. Periodically invite members of the Board of Directors or other interested supporters to have lunch at McMurphy's to evaluate the quality of the food and service.

ADVERTISING AND PROMOTION RECOMMENDATIONS

McMurphy's Grill has had an added advantage in this area as the operation receives a lot of free coverage, which has been beneficial. From articles on the restaurant by the *Post-Dispatch* to being featured on local radio and television McMurphy's has received a lot of free publicity. The most recent coverage in the February 1994 edition of *St. Louis Commerce*, continues to keep St. Patrick

ADVERTISING AND PROMOTION RECOMMENDATIONS...*continued*

Center and McMurphy's Grill in the mind of the St. Louis community. These efforts certainly help to increase the scope of McMurphy's Market potential by educating people as to its mission and location.

McMurphy's has recently implemented a Celebrity Hosts Promotion strategy, which has been extremely successful. Various local and state celebrities are featured each Wednesday at McMurphy's where they become the Celebrity Host for the day. Each is asked to provide names of guests to whom we can send a special invitation. This has the added advantage of increasing the restaurants mailing list for all major promotional events.

It is important that McMurphy's continue to keep its name in the forefront, both in terms of getting the message of what its mission is all about and to dispel some of the myths that may surface when discussing a project that involves the homeless mentally ill. It also doesn't hurt the bottom line by encouraging people to participate in this endeavor.

However, McMurphy's Grill long ago realized that it would never survive based solely on this type of exposure and so has aggressively advertised from the beginning. Except for a period of time after the founding Executive Director left and until the arrival of the newest Executive Director, advertising and promotion of the restaurant business has been on the forefront.

McMurphy's advertises regularly in Downtown Dollars, which is a flyer with a distribution of over 20,000 published on a monthly basis. In addition, McMurphy's occasionally advertises in the *St. Louis Business Journal* and *St. Louis Commerce*. Sometimes these are complementary adds. As a member of the St. Louis Convention & Visitors Commission, McMurphy's Grill can promote the restaurant business directly to convention traffic and tourists. McMurphy's is also listed in the National Restaurant Association Membership directory as well as among the members of Downtown St. Louis., Inc. Occasionally, an ad is run in the *St. Louis Review*, the Catholic newspaper of the Archdiocese of St. Louis. Finally, but certainly not least, is that McMurphy's Grill is usually cited in the *St. Patrick Center Chronicles*, a publication of St. Patrick Center published three times a year.

Direct mail is often used to notify supporters or other people on our mailing list about various promotional events at McMurphy's Grill. The mailings often focus on businesses downtown, supporters of St. Patrick Center, nonprofit organizations and other patrons of McMurphy's Grill. Postcards were sent out, for instance, promoting the Celebrity Hosts program. Appendix I provides a sample of what was sent out.

Continue the Celebrity Hosts Program

This effort has increased sales by 20 percent over last year during the same period. The list of willing celebrities continues to grow with the addition of a nationally known St. Louis artist. Recently, we have begun to get phone calls from leaders in the community interested in becoming a celebrity host. And this is only after two months of operation.

Add to the list of Celebrity Hosts, CEOs of major firms located in downtown St. Louis.This can have a significant impact sales from the business community. By inviting the top executives, who are likely to invite other significant people within their organization as well as other employees, McMurphy's reputation as a quality restaurant will spread. The business community will become better informed as to what McMurphy's Grill is all about.

Reinstitute Lunch of the Month Club

Set up a calendar of events and identify advertising and promotional efforts needed. Appendix K is a sample of some recommendations for the next year.

Make personal contacts with key personnel at local firms that are within walking distance to invite them to McMurphy's Grill for lunch. Offer free menu items to motivate them. The best person to identify within these local organizations are the secretaries.

Offer Sales Promotions for Frequent Diners

Revise boxed lunch menu to offer an upscale version to groups seeking a higher quality boxed lunch and who are willing to pay for it.

Offer special promotions for Secretaries Day, Boss's Day, Birthday's, etc.

Promote the anniversary of McMurphy's Grill through specials on the menu, printed advertisement, articles in a local publication, and a featured article in the St. Patrick Center Chronicles.

Advertise the availability of McMurphy's Grill for private functions in the evening or on weekends, by focusing on various wedding supply places, churches, local publications, with musicians or mobile DJ's, membership organizations (such as fraternities and sororities) and business firms in the downtown area.

Continue Responding to Convention and Visitor Commission Leads

Continual evaluation and re-focusing of these efforts is a must. By regular monthly meeting with the Marketing Consultant and better communication efforts regarding the business side of the operation, these efforts should prove to be effective and more efficient than past efforts.

MCMURPHY'S GRILL INCOME STATEMENT:

Fiscal Years 1992 - 1994

	Final FY92	Final FY93	FY94 YTD
Sales:			
Food & Beverage	$167,369	$146,392	$88,203
Cost of Sales:			
Food & Beverage	65,1705	2,4223	4,175
% Of Sales	39%	36%	39%
Gross Profit Margin	102,199	93,970	54,028
Operating Expenses:			
Salaries	81,791	77,929	59,246
P/R Taxes/Benefits	21,948	20,732	13,611
Utilities/Bldg Exp	9,707	22,79	29,068
Telephone	1,857	1,910	1,468
Supplies	12,713	16,90	69,452
Postage	266	0	856
Stationery/Pstg	912	195	792
Equip Purchases	879	1,169	411
Depreciation	0	4,775	9,550
Repairs/Rent Equip	5,027	3,560	1,144
Local Transport	457	464	507
Advertising/Publicity	8,940	8,170	5,394
Business Svc's & Fees	7,820	13,845	3,985
Insurance	2,825	3,290	2,670
Membership Dues	125	325	275
Licenses & Permits	949	675	858
Aid to Individuals	0	250	20
Total Expenses	156,216	176,987	119,307
Net Profit(Loss)	($54,017)	($83,017)	($65,279)

CASH FLOW CALCULATIONS

Cash Flow: Designated Funds*

Balance as of 6/30/93	$142,648
Estimated loss for 1994	-97,919
Depreciation	+9,550
Balance as of 6/30/94	$54,279
Estimated loss for 1995	-49,118
Depreciation	+ 9,550
Balance as of 6/30/95	$14,711
Estimated loss for 1996	-43,095
Depreciation	+ 9,550
Balance as of 6/30/96	$(8,334)
Estimated loss for 1997	-25,390
Depreciation	+ 9,550
Balance as of 6/30/97	$(11,674)

**This assumes no increase in grant dollars.*

FINANCIAL ASSUMPTIONS AND ANALYSIS

Pricing Strategy

McMurphy's Grill has a twofold pricing strategy. First, since McMurphy's prime objectives is its training opportunities, the flow of customers through the restaurant is essential. Customer volume is also important to the bottom line. Thus, the price must remain reasonable in order to attract customers. Many restaurant patrons, according to the National Restaurant Association study, thought that medium priced restaurants provided the most value for their money. McMurphy's Grill falls into this category and thus is seen as a provider of value. It must also be competitive with other similar (limited menu tableservice) establishments.

Secondly, the prices must be at a level to cover variable operational costs as well as allow enough margin to cover fixed operational costs and help to defray the training costs involved. The training aspect incurs increases in personnel, employee benefits, food waste, and supply costs as a result of the learning curve -- which is likely to be higher than in other cases because of the turnover of trainees and their disability.

For the limited-menu tableservice establishment, the cost of food sold should be about 35 percent. The cost of food and beverage (wine, beer and other liquor) is usually around 29 to 32 percent. We can assume that 30 percent is a good average cost that McMurphy's should attempt to target. Reviewing the Income Statement for Fiscal Years 1992, 1993, 1994, which can be found in Appendix L, it can be seen that McMurphy's is higher than the average. Better inventory and waste control will assist with maintaining lower margins. The cost of sales will decrease as the party volume increases and more liquor is sold.

Thus, it is the goal of McMurphy's Grill to maintain a 30-32 percent cost of sales so that at least 68-70 percent of total sales goes toward operating expenses. Operating expenses, for foodservice establishments, tend to be rather high because of the amount of fixed assets involved. McMurphy's Grill is running high in this area, but management is in the process of assessing where the problems lie.

The kitchen manager and a volunteer at St. Patrick Center are also in the process of conducting a food cost analysis. Once this has been completed, it will be maintained and evaluated periodically with the restaurant manager. To facilitate this process, the analysis will be computerized so that it can be updated as prices change.

Sales

While sales levels have fallen since FY 1992, much can be attributed to the change in management at St. Patrick Center. Initially, the original Executive Director was heavily involved in marketing McMurphy's Grill and had become rather successful. After she moved from St. Louis, her predecessor was not very active in the marketing of the restaurant business. In fact, during his stay as Executive Director, very little marketing was done. The Marketing Consultant

Sales...*continued*

was rarely communicated with and at that time, the Executive Director was the only one who could direct her activity.

In addition, very little financial reporting or control was taking place. With the recent change in the Executive Director position, these areas are being highlighted more intensely. It is recommended that responsibility for the marketing and business aspect of McMurphy's Grill be handed to a newly defined position of Business Director. This will be a new position and is currently not filled, but the responsibility for the Restaurant business should fall to the Finance and Administration Department in the mean time. Such an approach reflects a more effective business approach, rather than laying the responsibility for running a business to a Director of Programs. Just as it would be inappropriate to assign the responsibility of coordinating the training program to the Director of Finance/Administration, so the current approach does not reflect a strategic orientation toward growth. This is a key consideration for implementing an effectivestrategic plan which will realize growth in the business component.

Since the start of the Celebrity Hosts promotion, sales for the past two months are higher, by 20 percent, than for the same two months of 1993. The increase in sales from January and February, as is depicted in Appendix M (Calendar Year 1994 Sales Breakdown), is also significant. It is obvious from this picture that liquor is not a priority item during the lunch period, but is a significant portion of the total sales of private parties.

The customer count is also a significant factor as is illustrated in both Appendix M and Appendix N (Calendar Year 1994 Customer Count). Appendix N is a little more detailed and shows that the average number of customers per day is under the 80-seat capacity that currently exists. For a restaurant like McMurphy's, the average daily seat turnover was 1.8 (this includes operations that are open for both lunch and dinner) and the median check was $6.48. McMurphy's daily seat turnover, using the data from the last two months, is .86 and the average check amount is $7.11. The large jump in the number of customers per day from January to February reflect growth as well. This picture also shows that Wednesday is by far the biggest day. This is not surprising as this is the day the celebrity hosts are with us. Thursdays and Fridays seem to also be good days. This is helpful information when considering other promotional activity.

Information such as in Appendix M and N are not available for the prior years so as to better make comparisons. In the future, however, this type of information will be maintained and reviewed on a regular basis. The usefulness of this information is beyond saying in making day-to-day decisions in any business environment.

Pro Forma projections of sales are based on the marketing goals of a 30 percent increase in the first year; a 20 percent increase in the second year; and a 20 percent increase in the third year. Also taken into consideration has been the breakeven point. For the 1995, 1996 and 1997 sales projections, the following breakeven points exist:

- 1995: $198,197
- 1996: $203,298
- 1997: $208,058

The variable costs used in calculating these breakeven points includes cost of sales, supplies and advertising. All other items are assumed to be fixed. The costs involved in the trainingcomponent have not been included in this analysis. It is anticipated that McMurphy's Grill will breakeven after year two (1996). It is well on its way to success. Refer to Appendix S for the complete Breakeven Analysis.

Cost of Sales

The Historical Income Statement reflects that McMurphy's Grill is achieving a 39 percent Cost of Sales, which is higher than the industry's average of about 35 percent. It must be noted that these numbers do not reflect inventory changes. For the past year and a half no inventory records have been kept and until very recently inventories had not been taken for some time. For many food operations this is a major issue. In the future, management will ensure that inventories are taken on a regular basis. Thus, in the future, it is reasonable to assume that McMurphy's Grill will be able to maintain the industry average of 35 percent cost of food and an overall cost of sales in the range of 30 percent.

Operating Expenses

It is rather obvious, when looking at Appendix L (Historical Income Statement), that the Operating Expenses are where much of the problem is. The high level of operating expenses can in part be attributed to the high salaries/wages. The number of employees working is far more than a regular operation would utilize. In fact, an operation the size of McMurphy's might have four people working in addition to the Manager and the Kitchen Manager. For McMurphy's, the number is usually around ten people. Thus, in the Pro Forma Income Statements (Appendix O and P) the cost of training has been deducted from the Operating Expenses and noted separately to give a better reflection of the restaurant operation's performance.

In reviewing some of the operating expenses for 1993 and 1994 it was obvious that expenses for the entire building had been charged to McMurphy's Grill. The building, which had been donated in 1993, has two other floors (one of which had been occupied for a part of 1993) which can be rented out for office space. This practice, of charging the entire building's expenses to McMurphy's, had been at the direction of the Executive Director. This practice has been reversed with the arrival of a new Executive Director and so for FY 1994 an attempt was made to deduct expenses, or a portion of them, that did not directly relate to the operation of the restaurant.

An attempt has also been made to better organize these categories for the sake of industry comparisons in the Pro Forma statements. In the preparation of the Pro Forma Income Statements, an attempt was also made to review expense items with industry averages and as a result reduce some line items. In the past, budgets have been prepared based solely on historical data without consideration for what might be reasonable for a restaurant operation the size of McMurphy's Grill. Appendix P depicts line items as a percentage of sales, which will be useful in making future decisions. For the most part, the Pro Forma Projections are in line with the industry averages or are at least heading that direction. Appendix P (Pro Forma Income Statements -- 3 year summary) highlights this point when looking at the Operating Expenses as a whole. As a percentage of sales, these expenses are decreasing significantly over the next three years. The industry average indicates that Operating Expenses usually average about 53.4 percent of sales. At least now, McMurphy's is heading in the right direction. It is recommended that management continue to review industry averages in the future for a better understanding of its performance and to stay ahead of its competition.

One last note, most of the fixed expense projections reflect an inflation rate of approximately 3.5 percent. Variable expenses are somewhat less that the expected changes in sales, but much higher than the 3.5 increase per year applied to most of the fixed expenses.

Income Taxes

Because McMurphy's Grill is a part of a nonprofit entity and any profit that is reaped will be channeled back into the program or into the programs at St. Patrick Center, no income taxes will need to be paid. This assumption flows throughout all the financial analysis.

Balance Sheet Cash Flow

Finally, a few notes about the Balance Sheet and a further explanation of McMurphy's Cash Flow assumptions. Appendix Q presents the Pro Forma Balance Sheet. Because McMurphy's Grill is categorized as a nonprofit operation, things are presented in a somewhat different manner. Fund Balances reflect what a for-profit organization would consider Owners Equity.

The Balance Sheet reflects very little activity because the accounting procedures for St. Patrick Center and McMurphy's Grill implement a cash-based system. While some of the parties are on a receivable basis, they are usually collected within a month. The same can be said about the payables. Invoices are paid as they are received. Cash flow is not a significant issue for St. Patrick Center or McMurphy's because of its large resource base and so the timing of receivables and payables is not a problem.

On the balance sheet, the cash reflects the balance of a grant received from McDonnell Douglas as well as other smaller contributions at the outset of this project. Further contributions will be solicited as these funds run out, primarily to cover the cost of training. The property and equipment line reflect a portion of the contribution of the Lucas Plaza building. Thus is seen as an asset for the restaurant as no rental payments must be paid out, thus it is important that it be documented. This valuation is one-third of the total value of the building, land and equipment that had been contributed. Depreciation has been deducted for the building and the equipment.

Balance Sheet Cash Flow
...continued

The cash flow, as seen in the cash line, takes into consideration the declining designated fund balance as a result of restaurant losses. Keep in mind that St. Patrick Center has been extremely successful at fund-raising and is confident that it can receive corporate support to cover the cost of training. However, because we have included depreciation in the expenses, which is not a cash item, it has been added back in to reflect a non-cash item. The loss which was used in this calculation was the Operating Loss and thus does not include the reduction of the loss by the amount of the training costs. Refer to Appendix R for a review of Cash Flow projections.

Retail Clothing

BUSINESS PLAN

CLOTHES AS ART INC.

49567 Main St.
Los Angeles, CA 55550

April 1, 1993

Clothes As Art offers a creative alternative in the retail clothing industry: customers create and then produce their own designs on garments. Faced with strong competition, this plan outlines several marketing strategies and provides insight into factors like location and demography when planning a clothing venture.

RETAIL CLOTHING BUSINESS PLAN

EXECUTIVE SUMMARY

Clothes As Art Inc. will be a wearable art retail store. Clothes As Art Inc. enables people, male or female, young or old, to design their own clothing whether they have any artistic abilities or not. It will be fashion art that's unique and original. Most of all they will be entertained while creating their own fashion art.

Clothes As Art will begin conservatively by offering T-shirts and sweatshirts as in-store inventory from which the customer can choose. In addition to blanks for the customers to design, Clothes As Art Inc. will have a moderate inventory (30% of projected sales) of pre-painted shirts and sweatshirts. This will tap into the market of those who like the clothing but are more spontaneous buyers. Any customer will be allowed to bring in pieces from their own wardrobe to paint. In addition, at the end of the day the spin drum is coated with a strip of the paint around the edge. This dries over night and becomes a durable, pliable material. This can be fashioned into belts, cut into earrings and other jewelry that will match all clothing produced by the artist. These will be offered as accessories at Clothes As Art.

Clothes As Art's products have two target markets. The first being female, 21 to 35 years of age, with household income of $35,000 per year or higher. The second target market is 50% male, 50% female, 5 to 16 years of age, with household income of $35,000 per year or higher. The only location that would be conducive to the sale of these products is in a small or similar location with very high walk-by traffic. Therefore, the location requirements are a high traffic, indoor mall.

Clothes As Art will have no true direct competition by another store in the area. Clothes As Art's edge will be its price. Of the existing indirect competition, there are few companies that will be able to compete with Clothes As Art's price.

Clothes As Art's financial statements have been compiled with the greatest degree of conservatism. Clothes As Art will require a loan of $179,077. The loan will comprise 31% up-front expenses and 69% working capital needs. Close analysis will show that Clothes As Art's gross profit margin is 77% before tax, return on investment is 20%, and time interest earned is 2.0 for the first year. According to Robert Morris and Associates' most recent studies, these ratios are at or above average for this type of company.

Please feel free to contact me if you have any questions.

Name of the Business

Clothes As Art Inc.

This is not the legal name as of yet. I wish to incorporate and trademark, which will give rise to legal costs.

Ownership

Owner: **Cathy Wood**

Form of Ownership to Be: Corporation

DESCRIPTION OF THE BUSINESS

(Pictures are available for a more visual demonstration of the product.)

Clothes as Art will be a wearable art and accessory retail store. Whether you consider the 1990's as the "me" generation or the "I" generation, consumers today want to do their own thing. Clothes As Art enables people, male or female, young or old, to design their own clothing whether they have any artistic abilities or not. It's fun, it's exciting, and it will be inexpensive for them. It will be fashion art that is unique and original. The consumer will be able to design any number of pieces to go with any other articles of clothing they own. Most of all they will be entertained while creating their own fashion art. In addition, accessories will be fabricated from the by-product of the artwork. Therefore, the accessories will complement any article sold in the store.

The service procedure of the store is quite simple. The customer enters the store and picks out an article of clothing they wish to paint on or they may bring in a piece of their own wardrobe (I will use "shirt" to identify the clothing article). The customer then takes a number to await a free work table at which they will paint. The customer then chooses 4 colors that they will paint with. The paints are applied with squeeze bottles full of bright colors. While they are choosing their colors their shirt will be clipped and stretched on a cardboard board the same size as the shirt. This prepares the shirt to be a canvas for the artist. The attendant will then give the customer brief instructions on how and where to paint on the shirt. The customer then paints on the shirt in any way they believe will look good when it is spun. When the customer is done he/she hands the shirt to the attendant who spins it. This is where the excitement begins. Spinning at about 450 RPM, the paint that was applied to the shirt quickly evolves into original art right before the eyes of the customer. (Pictures are available for a more visual demonstration of the product.) The centrifugal force caused by the spinning causes the paint to be drawn from the center of the shirt to the edges resulting in a star-burst (spin art) look to the design. The colors swirl together but don't blend into new colors. The original colors remain separate colors. while this is happening crowds gather to watch the artist and they quickly form a line to do their own thing. The shirt is then sent through a large belt drier that adheres the paint permanently to the shirt. when the shirt is done drying, the customer's number is called at the cash register and another happy artist is born. The finished product is a self-made piece of artwork that can be machine washed and dried for years along with the customer's regular clothing. The entire services process takes an average of only 20 minutes, so the turnover is great. This includes average time to paint 5 minutes, to spin 30 seconds, and to dry 15 minutes. There will be several tables at which to work. The drier can dry up to six shirts on a continuously moving conveyor belt.

Clothes As Art will begin conservatively by offering T-shirts and sweatshirts as in-store inventory. In addition to blanks for the customers to design, Clothes as Art will have moderate inventory (30% of projected sales) of pre-painted shirts and sweats. This will tap into the markets who like the clothing but are more spontaneous buyers. Any customer will be allowed to bring in pieces from their own wardrobe to paint. A caution will be given that the shop won't guarantee the results and no flammable materials will be allowed. When in-house inventory expansion is warranted, Clothes As Art will expand into jeans, jackets, women's casual suit coats, jean jackets, leggings, leather jackets, collared shirts, canvasses, placemats, more jewelry, sweatpants, ties, belts, and shoes. With respect to canvasses, Clothes As Art will have blank canvasses on which the customer can paint. Many people decorate their homes with certain color schemes. This will give the decorator the ability to create their own piece of artwork that the end of the day the spin drum is coated with a strip of the paint around the edge. This dries overnight and becomes durable rubber type material. This can be fashioned into the accessories such as belts, cut into earrings and other jewelry type articles that will match all clothing produced by the artist.

MARKET

Target Market

In accordance with the manufacturer and my own experience, Clothes As Art will be tapping primarily in to two separate markets.

- Target Market A:
  - Sex: Female
  - Type: Working woman who is fashion Conscious
  - Age: 21-35
  - Education: Some College or Degree Holders
  - Household Income: $35,000 +

- Target Market B:
  - Sex: 50% male, 50% female
  - Age: 5-16
  - Education: Grade School
  - Household Income: $35,000 +

As you will see in my biography (available upon request) I will have previously worked for a retail store of this nature. It has been my experience that this product's market is both sexless as well as ageless (age 5 to 50). I have also spoken with another shop owner who agrees that the product has this type of wide appeal. For analysis I will deal with these two target markets. My choice for location is the Shelby Corners Mall, which offers no traffic studies for their mall. According to their "Primary Trade Market, Neighborhood/Lifestyle Composition"Target Market A fits into those categories called Blue Blood Estates, Money and Brains, Urban Gold Coast and Young Influentials. This accounts for 81.8% of the 1.1 million in this mall trade market. Target Market B fits into the category called Furs and Station Wagons. This accounts for 2% of the 1.1 million in the trade market of the mall. With respect to Target Market B showing such a low market share of the trade area, please keep in mind that the mall offers no traffic studies. If you visit the mall you will see quite a few more children and teenagers than the mall market study shows. Therefore, the overall market with respect to children is very healthy.

Total Market

According to the Standard Industrial Classification Manual, Clothes As Art's Industry Group Number is 565 and the Industry Number is 5699, under which "Tee Shirts, Custom Printed - Retail" is listed.

According to the 1991 U.S. Industrial Outlook published by the U.S. Department of Commerce, the forecast for total retail sales increase is 6.5% in 1990. This is an increase of .8% over 1989's increase of 5.7%. According to most recent information (1989) apparel and accessory stores showed the largest gains of 7.1%.

In addition, Standard and Poor's Industry Surveys (1991) suggest that specialty retailing is the way to go. Their research indicates the general merchandiser is suffering by trying to meet everyone's needs at the same time. This publication states that by meeting the more specialized needs of people, a retailer will be in a better position to grow. Given Clothes As Art's ability to customize to any person's needs, it fits with this analysis very well.

COMPETITION

Direct Competition

According to Spin and Dry Inc., the manufacturers of the spinning and drying equipment, there is no other equipment-based store of this kind in the metropolitan area. Therefore, Clothes As Art would have no direct competition in the Los Angeles area.

Clothes As Art's toughest competition is Artwear, Custom Designs, and Clothes Etc. This is due mainly to the fact that their capital strength is greater than Clothes As Art, their prices will be competitive, and their lines will be more full.

Clothes As Art's main drawback will be a lack of capital necessary to compete with these stores. Clothes As Art can handle this drawback in one of two ways: either avoid them altogether or have a location that has a large enough market to handle all of the shops. The only way to avoid them is to choose another location; this would greatly affect our chances for success. Clothes As Art's location in the mall will have a large enough market for all of the shops. Currently the mall houses only two of our competitors. The expansion has added mainly high-end, high priced shops to the roster. Clothes As Art's main marketing device will be the low price of the goods; therefore, the new expansion has had little effect on the competition but it has increased the number of potential customers. Clothes As Art will bring a product to the market that each of these shops either do not carry or carry in small quantities. Most, with the exception of Clothes Etc., have prices that are quite a bit higher than Clothes As Art. We may not have the capital strength, but we also don't have the expenses that the other stores have to cover. We will be highly competitive with our prices.

Indirect Competition

The remaining T-shirt retailers are men's and women's sportswear stores and little shops that sell small proportions of T-shirts. Clothes As Art will be competing with them by giving the customer something that they don't offer. We will meet a market niche that is not being filled by the current stores.

Other T-shirt retailers are generally custom silk screeners. Clothes As Art is not going to directly compete with them by doing silk screening per se. We will be competing with them in that a proportion of Clothes As Art's sales will be to fraternities, sororities, church groups, etc. to supply their baseball jerseys, event T-shirts, etc.

MARKETING STRATEGY

Based on experience in this market, with respect to T-shirts, price sells. This will be the same case with Clothes As Art's sweats. The cost of a finished T-shirt at our store will be $14 and a sweatshirt will be $17.50. This will be the store's major selling point. Even with this low price the goal of profit and positive cash flow can be achieved. This price may even be able to be raised given the superiority of the location and relative price flexibility of the patrons of that mall.

In addition to my own advertising the mall does quite a bit of advertising itself and will be augmenting other advertising.

The greater proportion of Clothes As Art's advertising will be in give-a-ways to local groups such as high schools, fraternities, and church groups. This will be the best way to build local support in both target markets given that the product is relatively difficult to describe on the radio. In addition, this is a community-oriented advertising device that will help the respect of the store. In contacting local fund raising organizations, such as fraternities and church groups, they will be very apt to be return customers when their next fund raising drive comes around.

Another shop owner has commented that birthday parties are a very effective means of advertising. By bringing in a group of children (Target Market B) to paint, they will either return themselves or show others our product. This is achieved by advertising in small local newspapers and church leaflets.

Another marketing avenue we will explore is contacting the local art clubs at high schools and colleges. The object of an art club promotion will be to teach people how to use the process efficiently. That would in turn help to make repeat customers out of them. Once they have mastered the techniques they would now be in a position to create wearable art gifts or garments for themselves. They will also bring in their friends which they will attempt to teach. In addition, this would be a great method of getting artistically done pre-painted inventory for Clothes As Art for their work. This would be done with the understanding that all designs must be pre-approved. This could also give rise to a special "gallery" section of the store for local artist's work thus adding to the stature of Clothes As Art.

Clothes As Art will be advertising toward local schools. The store will bring in local art classes and charge a nominal fee if they bring their own shirts. The object will be to derive repeat customers out of the class and new customers out of the school. This is another avenue to exploit target market B.

Logo identification will be another advertising method. Garments can be manufactured for the local bowling groups, fraternities, restaurants, and companies. The logo can be screen printed and brought in for establishment or hand painted with the Clothes As Art system. Clothes As Art will attempt to exploit the local professional sports team's logos. The need for licensing agreements will be explored. It is my impression that as long Clothes As Art is not doing the initial screen printing, Clothes As Art will not have to incur the large costs of acquiring a licensing agreement. Clothes As Art can create shirts for special events such as Valentine's Day, Mother's Day, and Father's Day.

LOCATION

Clothes As Art will require very little space. The space needed is only 850 square feet so the rent will be lower than a regular retail store. T-shirts and sweatshirts can be stored in stacked cubicles which take up very little space while storing large amounts of inventory. The pre-painted inventory will constitute 30% of sales and will therefore require a small amount of space also. In using cubicles there will be a very little space needed in a storeroom to store other inventory.

Through my experience with this product, Clothes As Art must be located in a very high walk-by traffic mall with high visibility through a glass store front. A large selling point of this product is entertainment. Therefore, in addition to the above-mentioned marketing techniques, it is sold by one person watching another spin their shirt and then wanting to paint one themselves.

The mall affords the greatest visibility for Clothes As Art product. As mentioned earlier, the mall has no traffic studies but it is known as the most successful mall in the metro area. It also affords the greatest means of reaching Clothes As Art's two target markets. A simple trip through the mall shows overwhelming evidence that Clothes As Art's two target markets will be very effectively reached.

The costs associated with the mall are quite steep. The track record of the mall owners who own several plazas in the area of delivering a fruitful market to their renters has been shown conclusively by the longevity of and need for expansion of both the malls and plazas.

Clothes As Art's first choice would be a pre-built space where another was operating and is in a good location.

This would lower the store construction costs. The preconstructed space would have to be in a good location. It is the experience of the owners of the mall, that the shops that fail were in the worst positions; therefore, the chance of Clothes As Art finding an adequate, preconstructed space is very remote. To be as conservative as possible, financial statements are based on a few, not yet built, store site in the expanded section of the mall. The average cost per square foot is $25.

Analysis of the completion indicates that the Shelby Corners Mall is the best location to access our target markets, while avoiding locations that house direct competition.

MANAGEMENT

Owner: Cathy Wood earned a Master of Business Administration from St. Louis University in May of 1991. She completed her Bachelor of Science in Business Administration/Finance at St. Louis University in December of 1990.

Throughout her life she has been very involved in entrepreneurship. She has owned her own house cleaning business since she was in grade eight. During the summer of 1988 she completed and entrepreneurial internship in North Carolina with a retail store specializing in Clothes As Art's product. There she learned many aspects of the business from inventory control to cash management.

In addition, during the summer of 1989 she was an original partner in a car part retailing business register in the State of California as Core Enterprises. She has done work for the Small Business Institute as a small business counselor for Bellni Baby and Children's Furniture in Glenwood, California. She was also commissioned by South County Landscaping and Construction Company in Sacramento, California as a small business counselor. During her last year of her undergraduate work she was the founding Vice President of the Association of Collegiate Entrepreneurs (ACE). The Association was begun on campus to help students who aspire to become entrepreneurs get needed information and meet the necessary people. In this association she was responsible for promotion and scheduling of speakers and events.

This plan received an Honorable Mention from the Kennesaw State business plan competition. This competition is international in nature and highly competitive.

Currently Ms. Wood is employed as a business planner for Fox Associates. Fox Associates is an entertainment business in Los Angeles, which owns and operates the Bijou Theater (a local landmark) as one of its lines of business.

Manager

Clothes As Art will not have a manager in the first year of operation. The owner will perform the duties of a manager. When the time comes for the company to acquire a manager he or she will have to have two outstanding abilities. She or he will have to perform all the normal managerial duties such as scheduling, employee guidance and sales computing, and she or he will have to have adequate artistic abilities to lend in the sales process by giving advice to prospective customers.

Directors

The directors will include the owner Cathy Wood. Other directors will include people currently involved in local small business, the local artist community and the local financial community.

PERSONNEL

General Hiring Philosophy: Each employee of Clothes As Art will have to possess enough artistic ability to aid and advise the customers. We already know that Clothes As Art requires almost no artistic abilities to produce a shirt. Therefore, with respect to customer aid the employee's ability to give advice will need to be the strongest. They will have to be pleasant and sales-oriented. They will have to be able to emphasize the ease of the painting process and therefore sell the product effectively. In addition, to their duties to the customer, they will have to be able to design shirts for the pre-painted in-store inventory. With respect to pre-painted inventory their artistic abilities will need to be strong. They must be able to excel in design beyond the average customer.

FINANCIAL SECTION

Analyses and financial statements for projections and information concerning competition and location have been prepared and are available upon request.

The loan will be collateralized with inventory, equipment, and leasehold improvement. Clothes As Art will always have 8 weeks worth of inventory in the shop at all times. T-shirts and sweatshirts are a staple item for screen printers and will therefore have a high resale value in the event of default. In addition, the dryer is commonly used by screen printers; therefore, it is not considered specialized equipment like the spinner and has a high resale price. I will attempt to persuade the mall to take a subordinated position on the leasehold improvements as another form of collateral. It is my intention to use all available net cash flow to pay down the outstanding long term liabilities of Clothes As Art. In addition, the unused portion of the loan will be held in short-term certificates of deposit at the loaning bank.

Financial statements for year 1, as well as supporting documents have been prepared. Financial statements for years 2-5 consist of monthly income statements and year end balance sheet.

I have assumed a 20% growth in sales for years 2 and 3. This is due to the time it takes the product to take hold of its market. The sales then level off at a 15% growth rate for years 4 and 5. This is due to the fact that the store will be becoming an established business in the mall. I have assumed a 5% increase in the cost of my inventory. This is closely tied with the national inflation rate.

Retail Florist

BUSINESS PLAN

DESIGNS BY LINDA, INC.

378 Martin Luther King, Jr. Bldg.
Columbus, OH 74730

June 10, 1991

Designs by Linda is a full-service retail florist providing decorative planning for weddings and conventions, plant maintenance, and plantscaping. Designs is seeking funding to incorporate its new second location into its current successful enterprise. This plan details how funding would assist in the continued growth of the company.

RETAIL FLORIST BUSINESS PLAN

INTRODUCTION

The following is the proposed business plan designed to implement the continued growth of Designs by Linda, Inc. This plan was written by its president, Linda Irvin.

Statement of Purpose

The reason for developing this new business plan is to include our second store located in the Martin Luther King, Jr. Building in the University District area of Columbus. We have secured a lease, effective September 27, 1991, in the former location of Wilson & Burton Florist. This space, in the Martin Luther King, Jr. Building, has occupied a full-service retail florist since the building opened 63 years ago.

Our second location is an integral part of Designs by Linda, Inc. The expansion will give us over 1600 square feet of new retail space, 300 square feet of office space, and over 2000 square feet of production and storage. Currently, we have only 650 square feet of usable space in our Phoenix Center store.

We are also negotiating with the management company, Phoenix Center Venture, and with Guido Associates, a leasing company, for more suitable facilities within the Phoenix Center.

At this time, 1240 square feet of retail space on the promenade level, formally occupied by Henry's Horticulturals, should be available after the landlord completes legal proceedings to repossess the space.

Financing Sought

Designs by Linda, Inc. is seeking to secure financing of $100,000 comprising a $75,000 loan and a $25,000 line of credit. The $75,000 loan would be for five years and the money will be repaid from the proceeds of the Fisher building location and the Phoenix Center location. The $75,000 and the $25,000 line of credit will be spent on leasehold improvements, beginning inventory, and debt restructuring. These monies will supplement a cash allowance of $36,600 that Goble, the Martin Luther King, Jr. Building landlord, is supplying Designs by Linda, Inc. for leasehold improvements. A copy of the work letter detailing the cash allowance is enclosed in the appendices.

$45,000 of the loan and $20,000 of the line of credit, along with the $36,600 cash allowance, will give us over $100,000 to open the Martin Luther King, Jr. Building store. This store will enable Designs by Linda, Inc. to more than double our annual sales and will provide us with a facility capable of handling the future growth we plan to produce with our aggressive marketing strategy.

The remaining $30,000 loan and $5,000 line of credit will be used in leasehold improvements at the Phoenix Center location.

DESCRIPTION

Location

Designs by Linda, Inc. is located within the 100 Tower of the Phoenix Center in the former location of the Terra Viridis Plant Boutique.

Mission

Designs by Linda, Inc. strives to be one of Columbus's most innovative and unique florists. Our approach to floral design is pure and natural and it explores not only the character of flowers, individually and in combinations, but also the aesthetic relationship between flowers and the setting. We are determined to continue and enhance the tradition of flowers through innovative design, aggressive marketing, and most importantly, quality products and service.

Activities and Services

Designs by Linda, Inc. is a full-service retail florist selling cut flowers, fresh-cut arrangements, silk and dried arrangements, dish gardens, and green and blooming plants. We offer a variety of services such as:

- ❑Decorative planning (including a referral service for caterers and musicians) for conventions, corporate and private parties, weddings, cultural events, and holidays
- ❑Standing floral orders for offices and homes
- ❑Plant maintenance
- ❑Interior and exterior plantscaping
- ❑An AFS floral wire service for out-of-town orders.

Merchandise

In addition to a wide variety of fresh cut flowers and green and blooming plants, Designs by Linda, Inc. sells stuffed plush animals, gift wrapping, greeting cards, ceramics and pottery, crystal and glassware, baby novelties, balloons, and birthday products.

Staff

Designs by Linda, Inc. currently maintains eight full-time employees. We supplement regular staff with part-time help as needed for major holidays such as Christmas, Valentine's Day, Sweetest Day, and Secretaries' Week, and for local events such as the Columbus Grand Prix.

Experience

Designs by Linda, Inc.'s designers have many years of combined experience in the field of design. In addition to skills required in the floral industry, Designs by Linda, Inc.'s designers have experience in architecture, interior design, graphic design, the fine arts, and hospitality industries. The variety and quality of staff experience and skills strengthens Designs by Linda, Inc.'s ability to provide the customer with a variety of approaches--be it traditional or state of the art--and allows them the versatility to choose the style that fits their own individual tastes.

Hours of Operation

Designs by Linda, Inc.'s business hours are from 8:00 AM to 6:00 PM, Monday through Friday, and from 9:00 AM to 5:00 PM on Saturdays. However, we routinely keep the store open past our normal closing hours if there are customers in the shop.

Business History

Designs by Linda, Inc. is an S corporation and was chartered under the laws of the state of Ohio in September of 1989. Its 50,000 shares, with 500 shares outstanding, are owned by the president, Linda Irvin.

We assumed the existing lease and bought the assets of the Terra Viridis Plant Boutique for $8,000 in February of 1990. Terra Viridis is a plant maintenance company with over 900 accounts in the metropolitan area.

Designs by Linda, Inc. was established as the result of a combination of circumstances. Terra Viridis's owner, William Wilson, was highly motivated to relinquish his lease on the Plant Boutique after losing the Park Place Hotel plant maintenance contract which carried an annual value of $200,000. Without the Park Place contract and with the store's annual sales only totaling $80,000, the Phoenix Center location was not profitable and became a financial burden.

With my years of experience as a floral designer in the metropolitan area and my familiarity with downtown businesses, hotels, and restaurants, I knew my reputation was established and secure enough to support such a venture. In addition, the $8,000 price was very reasonable for a turnkey operation with such a favorable location. All of these factors--the situation of the previous tenant, the sound price, and my professional experience--contributed to the establishment of the store.

First Year Successes

In its first 12 months, Designs by Linda, Inc. brought in over $210,000 in sales, almost tripling the previous tenant's business.

Our projection of $320,000 in sales for the second twelve months, shows an additional increase of over 50 percent.

Future Needs

Although Designs by Linda, Inc. has nearly quadrupled the previous tenant's sales, we believe the existing facility has hampered potential growth. Our current location has no running water and does not have adequate cooler space for the volume of cut flowers we require. Inadequate refrigeration has also impeded our ability to create, display, and sell stock floral arrangements which, with the existing cooler space, we are unable to store. These floral arrangements are used throughout the industry as an important, proven sales tactic.

MARKETING

Designs by Linda, Inc.'s marketing program is geared toward enlarging our customer base, building up corporate accounts, increasing our special-occasion and "cash-and-carry" sales, and expanding our traditional holiday business.

Target Market

The Phoenix Center has over 10,000 people who work in the center and studies show an additional 4000 people, on average, visit the building daily. The Martin Luther King, Jr. Building quotes similar numbers by incorporating residents and visitors of the Martin Luther King, Jr. Building, the University District, Columbus Town Center, the Federal Building, and the Hotel St. Regis -- all of which are connected by skywalks and tunnels.

Designs by Linda, Inc.'s secondary market is any hotel, club, restaurant, or conference center in metropolitan Columbus. The expansion of our corporate client base is a priority because businesses generate a consistent sales flow which covers fixed costs.

MARKET STRATEGIES

National Marketing

Designs by Linda, Inc. is a member of the American Floral Marketing Council (AFMC), an independently funded committee of the Society of American Florists (SAF). AFMC's mission is to provide the industry with a marketing program that builds business between holidays when traditionally sales are slow. AFMC conducts a three-tiered program of advertising, merchandising, and public relations which covers the entire United States.

FTD, AFS, and other floral wire services offer national marketing using radio, television, and print media. In addition, these wire services have national spokespersons making public appearances on television talk shows to inform the public of new ways to purchase flowers and plants. These efforts stimulate consumer demand for flowers which translates into additional sales for our store. In order to boost our in-coming wire service orders and build our reputation outside of Ohio, Designs by Linda, Inc. has established an 800 number in our wire service advertisements to attract more business.

Local Marketing

Designs by Linda, Inc.'s local marketing program will utilize many of the national marketing tools, but will employ a more direct approach. By exploiting information gathered in our cash register (we track over eighty different items) and analyzing our sales figures, we identify our problems, take advantage of opportunities, and develop marketing objectives and strategies.

Current Situation

Designs by Linda, Inc. studies the current marketing situation on a daily and monthly basis to analyze trends and identify sources of business growth. Designs by Linda, Inc.'s owners are on hand daily to insure customer service. Our services include products of the highest quality and a prompt response to feedback from customers and clients. Our extensive and highly detailed financial statements, produced monthly, have enabled us to stay competitive and exploit presented opportunities. Copies of our financial statements are available upon request.

Marketing Budget

Our objective in setting a marketing budget has been to keep it between two and five percent of our estimated annual gross sales. Our main marketing "fixed costs" have come from our participation in AFMC and AFS. The remaining marketing programs have been more discretionary. Some examples are:

- ❑ Promotion expenses (free gifts for coming in the shop)
- ❑ Printed materials (pamphlets, fliers, postcards)
- ❑ Media advertisements (radio, newspapers, outdoors)
- ❑ Bartering (exchanging our products for ad placement)
- ❑ Product donations (door prizes, building promotions, charities)

Marketing Objectives

Our overall goal is to continue to offer excellent quality, service, and value.

Primary Objective

Increase corporate sales by fifteen percent.

Strategy We will use our metropolitan Columbus chamber of commerce to target prospective contacts. We will mail letters to each prospect describing our corporate services. We will follow-up with phone calls and product samples.

Second Objective

Increase standing orders for floral arrangements by 200 percent.

Strategy We will exploit our corporate and hotel contacts which will be our best source for new clients.

Third Objective

Increase overall sales by fifteen percent.

Strategy We will monitor our sales figures and data to confirm that products in demand are well-stocked and slow moving products are phased-out. We will improve telephone skills of employees to boost phone orders.

Fourth Objective

Increase sales for Mothers' Day by ten percent.

Strategy We will advertise with flyers, distributed throughout Phoenix Center offices, in an effort to capture more of the outgoing wire orders. We will decorate the shops early and promote specials.

Fifth Objective

Increase sales for Secretaries Week by twenty percent.

Strategy We will advertise through direct mail campaigns aimed at all offices in the Phoenix Center and in surrounding buildings. Free delivery to local offices will be offered. We will follow-up direct mail campaigns with phone calls to the larger offices. We will coordinate our efforts with The Phoenix Club and other downtown restaurants to promote the holiday.

Sixth Objective

Increase sales of our Christmas decorating services.

Strategy We will set up appointments with prospective clients and follow-up with product samples and photographs of past work.

Seventh Objective

Increase overall sales by 300 percent within a two year period by opening Martin Luther King, Jr. Building location and moving or remodeling Phoenix Center Location.

Strategy We will increase our market share by the tactics listed above. We will also increase our plant maintenance program in order to boost our overall sales. With our increased buying power, we expect to be in the position to offer discount prices on particular items which will, in return, encourage clients to buy more flowers more frequently.

Monitoring Marketing Results

Designs by Linda, Inc.'s financial statements will offer excellent data to track all phases of sales. These are available for review on a daily basis.

COMPETITION

Designs by Linda, Inc. has three main competitors: Alexander's Flowers, Blossoms Fresh Flower Market, and Flowers Plus. Our main downtown competition, Henry's Horticulturals, has recently gone out of business and their Westside Center location has been taken over by Alexander's Flowers.

Alexander's Flowers

Headquartered at: Trapper's Alley, Columbus, OH
Additional Locations at: Ashley's, Westside Center, Columbus, OH

Strengths Alexander's is run by a hands-on owner. Located in the University District for over ten years, the shop continues to do well even though Trapper's Alley has been struck particularly hard by the recession and has had difficulty keeping tenants.

Weaknesses With the recent establishment of their second location in the Westside Center (doing business as Ashley's), Alexander's could have over-extended itself. The Westside Center location, with its marginal success record, could prove itself a burden on the University District location.

Blossoms Fresh Flower Market

Owned by: Ron Silk and Dale Morgan
Headquartered at: 2338 Carpenter Highway, Dayton, OH
Additional Locations at: 154 W. Maple, Columbus, OH; 115 Kercheval, Columbus, OH

Strengths Blossoms, in business for over ten years, is well-known for their avant-garde design and imported products that are high in quality and originality. Their business is expanding and they are recognized for their high profile parties and weddings.

Weaknesses Because of Blossoms' concentration on lavish imported products, they have effectively priced themselves out of the downtown Columbus market. Although their business is expanding, it is growing mainly in the suburbs. They have failed to maintain a steady repeat business in the downtown area, a necessity in the floral industry, because along with their high quality comes extremely high prices. Their emphasis on imported flowers has been very successful for their suburban locations, but they have been unable to translate this success to the downtown area because they misunderstand the different type of customer. With the recent closing of their Westside Center store, the result of low sales, they are concentrating their efforts in the more affluent suburbs.

Flowers Plus

Headquartered at: Columbus Town Center, Columbus, OH
Additional Locations at: Algonquin Building, Columbus, OH

Strengths Flowers Plus is a well-managed operation that concentrates on providing products at reasonable prices.

Weaknesses Both stores operating under the Flowers Plus name are not owner-operated which impedes their ability to make decisions and results in a less personal approach to customer satisfaction. The recent closing of their store in the Columbus Dispatch Building illustrates the disadvantages of not having an owner on the premises.

Designs by Linda, Inc.

Our store has the aggressive sales strategy necessary to compete in the downtown market. We take the initiative to show clients, like The Phoenix Club, the Park Place Hotel, and the Dayton Inn, the type of work and the quality of service we can provide. In the few months since the closing of Henry's Horticulturals, Designs by Linda, Inc. has moved quickly to absorb several of their major accounts including the Park Place Hotel, the Columbus Athletic Club, and several corporate accounts located in the Phoenix Center.

Although there has been a general decline in the number of florists in the downtown area in the past few years, we have been successful in expanding our client base. Our business continues to grow because we concentrate on satisfying every patron, whether corporate or individual. We are determined that every customer will walk away happy regardless of their budget. We have found our customers appreciate having the owner on the premises taking an active part in every order. It is a guarantee that their business is important and will be given undivided attention and care.

Our sound business practices have resulted in credit accounts with every major Columbus wholesaler allowing us the flexibility to make wise and speedy purchases. All competitors cited within this report have a strict cash on delivery relationship with wholesalers impeding their ability to maintain a wide variety of products.

Although our competition may try to undercut our prices, we feel we will be able to meet their challenge because our reputation is both financially and artistically reliable. Growth in the Columbus floral industry during the 1990s will come from market share. Although the number of downtown florists has shrunk dramatically, the demand for flowers has not, making this the ideal time for Designs by Linda, Inc. to expand. Our clients and our suppliers trust that we will deliver.

LOCATION

Martin Luther King, Jr. Building Location: Designs by Linda, Inc. has been extremely fortunate to assume the former location of Wilson & Burton's within the Martin Luther King, Jr. Building. Taking over a location that has been identified as a flower shop for more than sixty years carries tremendous recognition value and almost certainly guarantees a secure client base.

The Martin Luther King, Jr. Building location will give Designs by Linda, Inc. 1600 square feet of sales space, over 300 feet of office space in the mezzanine level, and over 2000 feet of storage and production space directly accessible to the store. We have the option of expanding the storage and production space to over 5000 feet as business warrants.

Lease Agreement The Martin Luther King, Jr. Building is owned by Goble Properties, Inc. and terms of our lease are available.

RenovationsThe necessary renovations to the Martin Luther King, Jr. Building location are as follows:

- ❑ Installation of air-conditioning
- ❑ Structural repairs to marble cooler
- ❑ Construction of check-out and production counters
- ❑ New floor covering
- ❑ Updated lighting
- ❑ Painting and other general cosmetic repairs

Goble is giving us a cash allowance of $36,600. (A copy of the work letter detailing the cash allowance is available.) We believe in order to complete renovations, buy necessary fixtures, and purchase a beginning inventory, it will cost an additional $65,000. We are currently working with John Olgensen, A.I.A., P.C., and they have recently completed a set of drawing working within a budget of $40,000 or less.

Martin Luther King, Jr. Building Tenants: Major tenants of the Martin Luther King, Jr. Building include Unisys Corporation, Capitol City Communications, Alexander and Alexander of Ohio Inc., MLK Hospital, and the Columbus Theater. Connected to the Martin Luther King, Jr. Building by extensive skywalks and tunnels are Columbus Town Center, University District One, the Hotel St. Regis, and the Algonquin Building.

Parking Goble Management offers shoppers validated parking to encourage commerce.

Location Possibilities The Martin Luther King, Jr. Building location offers Designs by Linda, Inc. the latitude and space to meet our growing needs. Although over five times larger than our Phoenix Center location, the Martin Luther King, Jr. Building store has essentially the same operating costs. Given its sixty year history as a flower shop, the equitable lease and work allowance we negotiated with Goble Properties, and its well-balanced division of production, retail, and office space, we believe this location is the best possible option for Designs by Linda, Inc.

MANAGEMENT

Personal History

I have been working in the floral industry for over eight years, gaining personal knowledge and experience in all phases of the industry from horticulture to wholesale to retail. Prior to working in the floral industry, I worked in party stores gaining experience in running small businesses.

I have had college course work in business administration, banking and finance, investments, and commercial credit management. I have also attended several FTD management seminars.

Reasons for entering the business include the personal challenge.

Duties and Responsibilities: Currently, I handle all aspects of planning, purchasing, sales, personnel, promotion, and production. As the company grows, a more formal management hierarchy will be developed.

Financial growth is monitored by myself and by an accountant who completes monthly statements used to make sound management decisions. A "check and balance" system is in place and entails the cross-checking of daily receipts against the cash register tape and the accountant's review of bookkeeping for errors.

Salaries

I draw an annual salary of $60,000 from the business although most of this goes to repay loans to finance Designs by Linda, Inc.'s start-up costs. These loans will be paid-in-full by March of 1993. One additional fringe benefit is membership in The Phoenix Club, which is a business tool used to maintain a good working relationship with the Club (one of our larger clients) and its members.

Resources Available to the Business

- Accountant
  S.L. Schornack, P.C.
  26847 Grand River
  Redford, OH

- Attorney
  L.J. Bowden, P.C.
  2115 Livernois
  Troy, OH

- Insurance Broker
  D.C. Davis
  Florists' Mutual
  500 St. Aidan St.
  Edwardsville, IL

Additional Assistance

Floral wire services, such as FTD and AFS, and wholesale suppliers offer assistance in marketing, design, accounting, and management practices. In addition to FTD and AFS advice, Designs by Linda, Inc. is currently a member of the American Floral Marketing Council, the Ohio Floral Association, the Society of American Florists, and the National Association of the Self-Employed, all of which are professional associations designed to assist small businesses.

PERSONNEL

Designs by Linda, Inc.'s personnel structure is that of one company with two locations. Many of the employees will work at both stores depending on production needs. The office staff, located at the Martin Luther King, Jr. Building, will service both stores. Drivers will also serve both stores simultaneously.

Phoenix Center Location We currently employ eight full-time people. We supplement core staff with additional part-time help during holidays and special events. We expect to transfer some personnel to the Martin Luther King, Jr. Building location when the store opens.

Martin Luther King, Jr. Building Location We expect to employ four to six additional full-time people for this location. The Martin Luther King, Jr. Building store will function as the main facility for Designs by Linda, Inc. because it has over 2,000 square feet of production space. The Phoenix Center store does not have running water, sufficient storage space, adequate coolers, or enough design tables. The Martin Luther King, Jr. Building location was designed as a flower shop and has functioned as such for over 60 years. In addition, this location has over 300 square feet on the mezzanine level which will be used as our office.

Skills and Abilities Staff must have a high school education, be self-motivating, and have strong customer service skills. Previous experience in the floral industry is preferred.

Recruitment Designs by Linda, Inc. has found that local wholesalers and personal referrals are an excellent source for experienced designers and sales clerks. We have not had much success with published classified ads.

Training and Supervision Training is largely accomplished through hands-on experience with supplemental instruction given on more complicated design projects. Additional knowledge is gained through FTD and wholesaler design shows, and industry books, magazines, design manuals, and promotional materials. Designs by Linda, Inc. fosters professional development and independence in all phases of our business. Supervision is task-oriented and the quantity is dependent on the complexity of the job assignment. More experienced employees are responsible for managing certain aspects of production.

Salaries and Benefits Designs by Linda, Inc. pays from $5 to $15 an hour depending on experience. An employee discount of 30 to 50 percent on merchandise is offered. As business warrants, we hope to put together a benefit package that includes insurance, parking, and paid vacations.

APPLICATION AND EFFECT OF LOAN

The secured monies will be applied as detailed below and will enable Designs by Linda, Inc. to increase our overall sales to over one million dollars annually within the next two years.

APPLICATION AND EFFECT OF LOAN...*continued*

Martin Luther King, Jr. Building As stated earlier, the Martin Luther King, Jr. Building location, with its production and office space, gives Designs by Linda, Inc. the facilities to increase our market share in the downtown area.

Phoenix Center By moving our shop to the Promenade Level with its large walk-in cooler, running water, and greater production area, Designs by Linda, Inc. expects to gain efficiency, improve the store's image, and increase gross sales. An additional benefit is the guarantee of the Park Place Hotel's banquet contract (estimated sales worth $200,000 to $300,000 annually) which is a condition of the lease agreement. The expanded space and promise of a lucrative contract make this relocation a financially sound decision.

EquipmentPurchasing a computer with adequate software packages to satisty our accounting needs is a priority. We expect to set up a system for $5,000. Cash registers for the Martin Luther King, Jr. Building store, duplicates of the models currently used in the Phoenix Center, will cost $1,000. A zon machine (credit card data capture machine) costs approximately $300. The purchase and installation of telephones for the Martin Luther King, Jr. Building will cost at the most $5,000. We plan to purchase used office equipment to supplement our existing fixtures. We plan to spend no more than $4,000 for office equipment.

Leasehold Improvements The bulk of the load will go towards leasehold improvements at the Martin Luther King, Jr. Building store. These include:

- Air-conditioning
- Tile floorcovering
- New and upgraded lighting
- Structural repair to marble cooler
- General and specialty painting
- Check-out and design counters
- Other carpentry and metal work

We have asked our architect to work within the budget of $50 per square foot, or less, for these improvements not to exceed $80,000. Designs by Linda, Inc., along with Goble Management, are acting as general contractors and have begun to gather bids.

With the expected relocation of our current store in the Phoenix Center to the Promenade Level, certain leasehold improvements will be necessary including:

- Upgraded lighting
- New signs
- Repairs to work counters and cabinets
- Repairs to glass doors
- Wallcoverings
- Painting

A budget of $25 per square foot, not to exceed $30,000, is our starting point for this project as this space does not require the extensive repairs the Martin Luther

King, Jr. Building site does.

Operating Capital The remaining monies, comprising most of the line of credit, will cover:

- ❑Any cost overruns
- ❑Start-up costs
- ❑Moving expenses
- ❑Initial advertising and promotional costs associated with the move and opening
- ❑Additional tool purchases
- ❑Security deposits
- ❑FTD and AFS wire service fees and membership expenses
- ❑Additional insurance premiums.

SUMMARY

Designs by Linda, Inc. has experienced tremendous growth and success in its first two years of existence. We have outgrown our current facility in the Phoenix Center. Our production has expanded far beyond what our current facilities can handle and it has hampered our ability to deliver quality service. Our primary goal is to increase customer satisfaction by providing quality products and attentive service. Relocation is the only answer to our problems with production and storage space. We believe our new stores within the Phoenix Center and in the Martin Luther King, Jr. Building will satisfy current and future plans for expansion.

Both stores are located in areas where the demand for flowers has been proven. These locations have already established reputations as flower shops and, based on our experience with the Terra Viridis space, we know this is an advantage over an untried location.

Our recent successes have been, in part, a result of less competition. It is imperative that Designs by Linda, Inc. take advantage of this opportunity and move quickly to capture business left in a void by the recent closing of our main competitor, Henry's Horticulturals. We are better suited to do this than other downtown florists because of our key commercial accounts and the customer loyalty we have built over the last two years.

By expanding our production facilities and client base, Designs by Linda, Inc. will have positioned itself as the dominant florist in both the downtown and University District area. Because our reputation is established with the downtown work force (most of whom reside in the suburbs), we have an added edge over suburban florists because their business rarely overflows their neighborhoods. This lays the groundwork for potential future growth into the suburbs.

The Martin Luther King, Jr. Building location will provide us with ample production and office space as well as being a desirable retail space. It is also very reasonably priced.

SUMMARY...*continued*

By moving to the Promenade Level of the Park Place Hotel, we would be guaranteed the Hotel's Banquet business with an annual value of $200,000 to $300,000. The 1,200 square feet of retail space is enough to insure that this would not become a satellite shop to the Martin Luther King, Jr. Building, but will be a full-service flower shop capable of satisfying the majority of what this location generated in terms of business.

Designs by Linda, Inc.'s two years in business has eliminated the time needed to experiment and establish management techniques that work the best for our company. We are confident that our success can be translated to more than one store.

To finance our planned expansion, we are asking for $100,000 which comprises loans and lines of credit. We are open to suggestions as to the best way to secure this type of financing. We welcome the chance to meet and interview with any prospective party interested and willing to help us excel.

Supplemental Materials

The Martin Luther King, Jr. Building lease and work letter, letters of intent, and architectural drawings are available upon request.

Tobacco/Magazines

BUSINESS PLAN

STANDARD TOBACCO & NEWS

1170 Promenade Ave.
Traverse City, WA 43856

December 20, 1991

Standard Tobacco & News provides magazines, newspapers, tobacco products, and candy to upscale shoppers. Its proprietors intend to follow the successful formula, with amendments, created by their chief competitor. They outline the steps in the following plan, giving detailed consideration to each aspect of their business.

- THE COMPANY
- THE INDUSTRY PERSPECTIVE
- MARKET ANALYSIS
- MARKETING STRATEGIES
- MANAGEMENT AND OPERATING PLAN
- FINANCIAL INFORMATION

TOBACCO AND MAGAZINES BUSINESS PLAN

The Complete Source for Periodicals and Smoking Products

EXECUTIVE SUMMARY

Our Business

Standard Tobacco & News is a new retail store offering magazines, newspapers, tobacco products and a limited selection of candy. It is registered with the State of Washington Department of Commerce. This business is a partnership owned by Dwayne and Samantha Peters.

We will specialize in magazines and tobacco products so as to appeal to both female and male customers. We are targeting the upscale shopper who is looking for value in the products that they buy We will serve these customers by offering a broad selection of products at competitive prices while providing friendly service and attention to their special needs. In the longer term, we will seek to earn a premium for our higher level of service. It is our goal to become recognized as the premier news and tobacco store in the Traverse City Metro area.

To achieve this goal we have chosen to model ourselves after a large, successful competitor, Jeff's Cigar Store. Jeff's, that sells the same mix of products that we will offer and achieves annual sales in excess of $1,000,000. The successful track record of Jeff's has provided us with an ongoing validity check on the details of our business plan. However, we do not intend to blindly follow the formula employed by Jeff's. Our business plan details the actions we will take to improve upon this formula.

Our store will be located in the Town Center area, thus allowing us to draw upon the regional customer base that shops there. With only one tobacco competitor and no magazine competitors, North County represents an under-served market for a specialty retailer.

Our store will be designed using light colors and an uncluttered, open layout to provide a pleasant shopping environment. We will utilize personal computer technology and an integrated point-of-sale (POS) and accounting software program to provide us with a significant enhancement of our customer service as well as to improve the operational performance of our store. The system will allow us to track sales on a daily basis, thus enabling us to adjust inventory levels in response to demand and improve upon the operational performance of the store. This improved performance will be measured by higher than industry averages for stockturns and improved cashflow. The system will also enhance our ability to track our performance by providing financial reports on demand.

We established a management structure that will meet our

needs as we grow. This structure provides for an allocation of responsibilities and authority to the individual manager with appropriate oversight by the General Manager and Partners.

Management Team

Our General Manager will be responsible for managing the day-to-day affairs of the business. Reporting to the GM will be three managers: a Magazine Department Manager, a Tobacco Department Manager and a Systems Manager. The Department Managers will be responsible for the selection, ordering, pricing and sale of products. They will jointly act to hire, train, supervise and dismiss employees. The Systems Manager will be responsible for the selection, setup and maintenance of the support systems.

We will employ an experienced management team at standard. Samantha Peters will be the General Manager and Magazine Department Manager. She has over 19 years of bookkeeping experience, including the last five years at Rich's Cigar Store. Her work experience at Rich's included responsibility for all of the day-to-day bookkeeping, management of a successful mail order business and preparation of written operating procedures. Previous to this, she was a partner in a bookkeeping and tax preparation service. Most recently, she completed the Greenhouse Small Business Development Course offered by our community college.

Dwayne Peters will be our Tobacco Department Manager. He has 14 years of sales experience with over 11 years in tobacco shops. He has worked for his present employer for the past 10 years and has held successively higher levels of responsibility. Dwayne is currently the operations manager for three tobacco shops and is responsible for all aspects of the operation. Dwayne, while continuing in his present position as an application engineer with General Electric, will serve as the Systems Manager. He has worked for GE since 1974 and brings over 14 years of sales, marketing and engineering experience to bear on the issues facing Standard Tobacco & News.

MARKET OPPORTUNITY

The following table summarizes the size of the available market in the metro area for each of the products which we will offer. This represents the market located within 25 minutes driving time of our location.

Product	Estimated Available Retail Market
Tobacco	$66,530,000
Magazines	$13,125,000
Candy	$39,940,000

PROJECTED FINANCIAL SUCCESS AND NEEDS

The primary competitor we are modelling ourselves after is Jeff's Cigar Store. This business has annual sales of over $1.0 Million with sales split 63.2%/33.8%/2.5%/0.5% between tobacco, magazines, candy and miscellaneous. Based upon the previous calculations of metro market size, Rich's commands shares of 1.0%/2.7%/0.06% respectively.

Based upon our evaluation of the market and the success of Rich's, we are projecting the following sales goals and associated market shares. For our purposes, we are assuming constant 1991 dollars for the comparison.

Market Share

	Brkvn	Yr. 1	Yr.2	Yr.3	Yr.4	Yr.5
Tobacco	0.41	0.51	0.80	0.94	1.01	1.05
Magazines	1.11	1.37	2.14	2.51	2.70	2.82
Candy	0.03	0.03	0.05	0.06	0.06	0.07

We have projected that we will achieve monthly breakeven sales of $36,000 by the end of our fourth month in operation. Our losses during this period are expected to total $10,000. Projected first year profits are expected to be $32,000, excluding owners' draws. Projected profits for the following years are: Year 2-$136,000, Year 3-$174,000, Year 4-$183,000 and Year 5-$190,000. The partners will not take any draws from the business until the monthly income exceeds $3,400. The monthly draws will then be limited to $3,400 per month through the end of the first year.

We have established that the following are our financial needs:

Capital/Equipment Needs	$57,165
Leasehold Improvements	$26,250
Start-up Inventory	$61,672
Prepaid Expense & Deposits	$ 4,489
Loan & Lease Fees	$ 5,812
Miscellaneous Start-Up Costs	$ 7,005
Cash Reserve	$42,697
Total	$205,100

These financial needs will be met through a blend of bank loans, equipment leases and personal cash investment. At present, we anticipate that we will meet our capital/equipment needs by leasing $48,590 of equipment and fixtures. We will seek a startup capital loan in the amount of $96,500.

The loans and leases will be secured by the value of the capital equipment purchased, the value of the inventory. In addition, Dwayne will continue in his present position at GE thus providing a personal guarantee of payment. The remainder of the funds will come from a personal cash investment of $60,000.

SUMMARY

We are establishing a retail store that will become the premier tobacco and magazine store in the metro area. Our business plan shows that we have researched our market, have evaluated our competitors and recognize what we will need to do to break into these markets so as to take share away from these competitors. We have put together an experienced management team with the necessary retail, marketing and financial experience. Most importantly, we have the talent and vision necessary to make Standard Tobacco & News a success.

THE COMPANY

Introduction

Standard Tobacco & News will be a new retail store offering magazines, newspapers and tobacco products. Our specialization in magazines and tobacco products is intended to appeal to both female and male customers. We are targeting the upscale shopper who is looking for value in the products that they buy. We will serve these customers by offering a broad selection of products at competitive prices while providing friendly service and attention to their special needs. In the longer term, we will seek to earn a premium for our higher level of service. It is our goal to become recognized as the premier news and tobacco store in the metro area.

Standard will be located in the Promenade shopping mall in North County, the fastest growing area in the state. This area was selected because it is a relatively unserved market for both magazines and tobacco thus providing us with an excellent opportunity. Our strategy for success is to draw upon the existing base of southeast metro consumers by becoming recognized as "The" specialty store for these products. Our location near the Town Center will give us the opportunity to meet the needs of a much larger regional customer base. We can offer these customers a pleasant and attractive alternative to downtown-based competitors. Our growth will be driven by drawing upon this larger regional customer base.

Features

Layout

The store will feature an open floor plan and will use a blend of modern colors and natural wood finishes to create a convenient and attractive place to shop. The store layout features a separation of the tobacco products from the periodicals. This will serve to minimize the objections of the non-smoking shopper. Magazine selections will be displayed such that titles that might appeal to the smoker will be located near the smoking section while titles that appeal to the non-smoker will be located farthest away from the tobacco section.

Magazines and newspapers will be displayed in racks arranged in a "sawtooth" manner and mounted against the outside walls. This arrangement results in a succession of open alcoves in which a shopper can stand to browse the large selection of titles without being disturbed by other shoppers. This is in contrast to the typical magazine store that uses back to back racks with narrow aisles.

The tobacco products will be showcased though through the use of a serpentine display case arrangement that fronts a large 10 foot by 20 foot walk-in humidor. The humidor will feature private lockers that can be rented by our customers to store their cigars. The friendly service of our staff will be enhanced by providing a smoking area. This area will allow our customers the opportunity to sample new tobaccos or savor their latest purchase. The ventilation system will vent the air from this area directly outside.

Computer System

It is recognized that the operating efficiency of a retail establishment is key to long term profitability and success. Mass retailers and supermarkets have adopted the use of computerized point-of-sale systems and inventory management systems to improve their operating efficiency. Specialty retailers who sell magazines and tobacco products coexist with these large, low-price competitors by offering a broader range of products and a superior level of customer service. However, the specialty retailers have been slow to adopt the efficient methods of their larger competitors. Currently, none of the area retailers who specialize in magazines and tobacco use computerized point-of-sale systems.

Standard will make extensive use of a personal computer-based integrated accounting and point-of sale terminals and bar-coding of products. The system provides for real-time updating of all records, which will give us excellent control of inventory, reduce the time spent processing inventory, immediate updating of pricing, reduction in bookkeeping effort and faster training of employees. This will allow us to maximize profits by minimizing our costs through tight control of our inventory and improvements in our operational efficiency.

The system will also provide us with on demand reports of our financial status performance as all key reports are easily generated by the software. The system will help us to achieve a level of efficiency and profitability superior to that of our specialty store competitors and, most importantly, enhanced customer service.

Customer Service

The use of a computerized point-of-sale system is also intended to supplement the personalized service our staff will provide. This system will be unobtrusive and not detract from the appearance or atmosphere of the store. It will serve to enhance the knowledge and responsiveness of our staff. This will give us a competitive edge in satisfying our customers' needs.

The POS system will help us to quickly and efficiently serve the needs of our customers through on line support of our sales personnel. Product information will be available in the form of computer databases for our tobacco products and magazines. The tobacco database will include characteristics of tobaccos and cigars that we carry along with sources of supply for non-stocked items so that we can special order these items. Similarly, the magazine database will provide an easy way to identify which magazines, both stocked and non-stock, meet the special interests of our customers.

Special orders can be quickly processed through the POS system. If a customer chooses not to place an order, a record of the inquiry can be made thus providing immediate feedback on lost sales opportunities. Prompt action can be taken to assure that our customers' needs are met in the future by stocking requested items.

The POS system will further enhance customer service by allowing easy location of stocked items in the store. It will speed responses to customer telephone inquiries as to the current availability of any item. Rather than waste the customer's time while the employee searches the magazine racks, the POS system will provide for immediate checks on stock levels and allow us to quickly indicate when we can get a non-stocked item.

Goals

As was stated previously, our primary goal is to become recognized as the premier news and tobacco store in the metro area. As we seek to achieve this goal, there are a number of financial and operational measurements that will be key to meeting this goal. Among these are:

Our short term goal to achieve breakeven sales of $36,000 per month by the end of our fourth month in business. These breakeven sales do not include any draws by the owners. Our first year sales goal is $540,000. Achieving this first year sales goal will result in a gross margin of over $230,000 and net profit to the owners, exclusive of draws, of $32,000.

Our longer term goal (3 to 5 years) is to achieve sales of $1,115,000, which results in a gross margin of $482,000 and a net profit to the owners of $190,000. We will need to double our market share to achieve these goals.

The market shares necessary to support our sales goals are as follows:

Market	Breakeven	First Year	Long Term
Tobacco	0.41%	0.51%	1.00 to 1.05%
Magazines	1.11%	1.37%	2.70 to 2.80%
Candy	0.03%	0.03%	0.07%

The location of the store in a relatively unserved suburban market area will help to support these goals.

Another measure of our success will be to meet industry average turnovers for each of our product lines during our first year and improve on those values in succeeding years. Our three year goal will be to improve upon these averages by a minimum of 25%.

As we focus on our primary goal of becoming the premier news and tobacco store, our success will allow us the opportunity to seek out other unserved suburban markets in the metro area. Our long term goal is to achieve growth through expansion into these unserved markets.

Products and Services

Introduction

The sale of tobacco products and magazines in the same store is a retail marriage of two diverse and unrelated products that has a history of success. This combination provides us with an improved opportunity for success as we can tap into two established markets. The market demographics of each product are complementary to each other and will allow us to reach a broader base of consumers than would be possible with either market alone. The selection of products we offer in each market will appeal to the mid- to upper-income consumer. Quality and value will be emphasized in the products we offer.

We have targeted Jeff's Cigar Store as the example of a combined smokeshop and magazine store wish to emulate. This large downtown based competitor has annual sales of approximately $1,050,000. Of this, approximately $100,000 is out-of-state tobacco sales. Their product sales are split 63.2% tobacco, 33.8% magazines, 2.5% candy and 0.5% miscellaneous. The size of their store is 1850 square feet.

The size of our store will be 1875 square feet. We are entering an untapped market for a magazine specialty store. There is only one tobacco shop competitor within 5 miles of our location. Our market data shows that it is reasonable to expect that we can achieve the same product mix as Jeff's. For purposes of evaluating our expected performance, we are using a split of 63.8%/33.7%/2.5% for tobacco, magazines and candy, respectively. The market data also supports the potential to achieve an equivalent sales volume as Jeff's once we become established. Our anticipated gross margin for each product is 45%/31%/35% respectively with a composite gross margin of 39%. Detailed information on each product follows.

Tobacco

A wide variety of tobacco products will be carried to meet all the needs of the discriminating smoker. This will include imported and domestic cigarettes, cigars, bulk tobacco and pipes. Other smoking accessories will be offered such as humidors, lighters and pipe stands. Table 1 summarizes the mix of tobacco products we will offer and our anticipated gross margin. We have established expected levels based upon the industry averages and the actual mix for Rich's. This mix has further been adjusted to reflect actual experience in the North County market.

Table 1 - Tobacco Sales Mix and Gross Margin

	Jeff's	**Industry Averages**			
Tobacco Merchandise	*% of Sales*	*% of Sales*	*Gross Mrgn*	*% of Sales*	*Gross Mrgn*
Domestic Cigarettes	8.3	25.2	26%	18.0	30%
Imported Cigarettes	13.6	4.7	42%	12.0	40%
Cigars	38.0	31.0	39%	30.0	40%
Pipe Tobacco	14.5	11.6	59%	14.0	57%
Pipes	3.6	11.6	62%	11.0	60%
Tobacco Accessories	18.1	9.3	58%	9.0	60%
Lighters	3.8	4.7	55%	4.0	55%
Smokeless Tobacco	N/A	1.9	37%	2.0	30%
Composite			43%		45%

Source: Industry averages are from the "1991 Industry Report," *Smokeshop*, September/October, 1991.

Strong emphasis will be placed on the service aspects of tobacco salcs. Pipc cleaning services will be offered on a complementary basis. Private lockers in our humidor will be offered for lease to our patrons for storage of cigars. Smoking clubs will be established for cigar and pipe smokers that will allow these customers to gather together and sample new products. We will strive to become known as the complete source for this upscale and profitable segment of the tobacco market.

Unlike Jeff's, we are not projecting a high level of out-of-state mail order business during our initial year of operation. We do anticipate that we will establish a level of business comparable to that of Jeff's Cigar Store. This will tend to increase the respective shares of product sales for tobacco and cigar categories as these are the primary mail order items handled by tobacco stores.

Magazines and Newspapers

Standard Tobacco & News will carry over 1500 magazine titles. The selection includes the popular news, entertainment, sports, women's and business titles

Magazines and Newspapers...*continued*

normally carried by the mass retailers and supermarkets. This consists of a base of 250 to 400 titles upon which our list will build. We have expanded on this list to provide a much broader selection and variety of titles on each of these subjects. We will also carry the special interest magazines such as Fine Homebuilding, Architectural Digest, Harvard Business Review, and regional magazines not found at larger retailers and supermarkets. We will also offer a limited selection of foreign language magazines to meet the needs of the growing international community in the metro area. Our title list comprises 72% domestic and 23% foreign titles.

Attention will be focused on stocking magazines that meet the special interests of the geographic market we are serving. Emphasis will be placed on customers' requests. If we don't carry a magazine a customer is looking for we will make every effort to locate a copy for them. Surveys of customer interests will be conducted to provide guidance. Sales experience with our title list will be tracked and adjustments made accordingly. We anticipate that this list will be held constant for at least the first four months that we are in business and then adjustments will be made to this list as we gain experience.

In keeping with our image of an upscale retailer, we will not offer any of the magazines that feature nudity or sex (also known as "men's sophisticates"). Our decision to do so eliminates any need to provide a restricted access area for these magazines. We will also avoid offending the female customers we want to attract into our store.

The list of newspapers we will carry includes those papers which are easily found at other retailers, such as the New York Times, Wall Street Journal, Daily Journal of Commerce, etc., along with papers from regional centers such as Seattle, Spokane and Boise. We will also carry newspapers from the major national cities, such as the Washington Post, Los Angeles Times, Boston Globe and San Francisco Chronicle.

The gross margin that can be earned on magazines is a combination of the distributor discount and the publishers' retail display allowances (RDAs). The discount we will receive on domestic magazines ranges from 20% to 45% depending upon the distributor. With this wide range of discounts, the proper management of the title list and sourcing of the magazines will have a big impact on our bottom line. By sourcing as many titles as possible from the distributors offering the higher discounts, we expect to earn a gross margin of 31% on our domestic titles.

The discount we will receive on our foreign titles ranges from 20% to 35%. The market for these magazines, however, allows for mark-ups above the suggested retail. We will price all foreign titles with a 35% gross margin. This results in a composite gross margin of 32% for the magazines.

This margin can be increased by the collection of retail display allowances from the publishers. Typically, publishers will pay the retailer an RDA in return for featuring the publishers' titles through full-cover displays and by placement of the magazines in high-traffic areas. To collect the RDA, the retailer must sign a contract with the publisher. Typically, the RDA is equal to 10% of the cover price. In practice, they equal 7%. Not all publishers offer RDAs.

The collection of the RDAs is no small task as significant documentation is required by the publishers before they will pay the RDA. There are collection services available to assist the retailer in collecting the RDA. These firms will negotiate these contracts on behalf of the retailer and file the necessary paperwork with the publisher to collect the RDA. In return, the collection agency keeps 10% to 20% of the RDA. RDAs are typically paid quarterly with a 6-month time lag between the request for payment and receipt of the RDA.

Candy

Standard will also carry an assortment of specialty candy and popular brands to satisfy our customers sweet tooth. Although we do not anticipate that the sales of candy will be very large, candy represents a profitable retail product that generates sales without a lot of effort. Since it is primarily an impulse purchase item, sales will be supported by locating the candy near the cash registers.

Candy will be priced to provide a gross margin (GM) of 40%. This compares to the tobacco shop average of 34% and a GM of 39% for convenience stores. Efforts will be made to increase this level based upon consumer demand and our need to remain competitive.

THE INDUSTRY PERSPECTIVE

Tobacco

The Market

The market for tobacco products is a mature one with the 1980's being marked by a declining number of smokers. This decline can be attributed to increased public pressure against smoking in public and increased awareness of the potential health hazards. In spite of this, The Tobacco Institute reported in it's "Tobacco Industry Profile 1990" that sales of tobacco products reached an all-time high of $40.9 billion in 1989. This represents an increase of 8% over 1988. Most of this growth can be attributed to increased taxes and prices. Per capita consumption of cigarettes continued to decline to 2,926. This marks the 16th straight year of decline.

The decline in the number of smokers has led to a decline in the number of retailers. This has resulted in increased traffic flow for the remaining tobacco shops. The positive aspect for these shops is that they are primarily dependent upon the sales of higher margin tobacco products rather than domestic cigarettes. As reported in *Smokeshop*, these products provide a much higher gross margin (37%-62%) when compared to domestic cigarettes (25%). The lower margin on domestic cigarettes reflects the effects of competition from other outlets, while the higher margins on the other products reflects reduced competition, the emphasis on quality products and the personal service offered by these outlets.

It should be noted, however, that the margin earned by the tobacco shops on domestic cigarettes is much higher than that earned by the mass retailers (12%-17%) or the discount merchandisers (7%-14%), the major sellers of this product. These low margins reflect the fact that these outlets are high volume, low service suppliers.

The demographics of the tobacco products market has also demonstrated a slow but steady change. This includes a shift to more female customers at tobacco stores. In 1987 about 55% of all smokers were female, while only 30% of the tobacco store customers were female. Since then, the percentage of female customers has increased to 35%. This trend is expected to continue. Another reason for this increase is that women are purchasing tobacco products and accessories as gifts for their husband or friends. These gifts tend to be higher margin items.

The other significant demographic shift is the aging of the baby boomers. Historically, as smokers aged they have increased their pipe smoking. This is expected to result in a 14.7% increase in pipe tobacco users from 1988 to 2000 and an overall growth for tobacco products of over 9.5%.

These changes are expected to drive growth in premium cigars, cigarettes, pipe tobaccos and accessories. The successful tobacco retailer of the 90's will adapt to meet the needs of these customers, particularly the women. The retailer will do so by providing convenient shopping and excellent customer service in a clean, pleasant environment.

Social Environment and Trends

The smoking of tobacco is no longer socially acceptable. There are many restrictions on when and where people may smoke. These smoking restrictions are going to be expanded in the future. There have been restrictions for cigar and pipe smokers for several years, but now cigarette smokers are facing the same restrictions. We probably can gauge the response of the cigarette smokers by reviewing the previous experience of cigar and pipe smokers.

The restrictions on cigar and pipe smokers caused a few smokers to quit altogether, but the majority adapted and choose to continue to smoke. This required them, in many cases, to seek refuge in their home or to smoke out of doors if they were at work. Even at home, the cigar smoker did not find refuge as their wives would not allow cigar smoking inside the home, so the cigar smokers went out to the patio or garage to smoke. For many, they chose to become a recreational smoker by enjoying an occasional good cigar or pipe tobacco.

The hard-core cigarette smokers will find future restrictions difficult, but they will adapt as the cigar and pipe smokers already have. Some will quit altogether, but others will choose to continue smoking or become a recreational cigarette smoker; i.e., people who like to smoke an occasional cigarette and are willing to pay a premium price for a premium cigarette. For these smokers, price is not a deterrent because the cigarettes are only bought once in a while and are viewed as a reward or treat. Others will choose to switch to the occasional cigar or become a pipe smoker. In any case, the full service tobacco shop will benefit by the transition as they can meet the needs of the smokers who choose to continue to smoke, but change their habit from cigarettes to premium tobaccos.

It will be many years before America is a "smoke-free" society, if ever. It is unlikely that the current level of tobacco users (over 25% of the population) will ever decrease to zero. Industry projections are that the reduction in the overall percentage of the population that smokes will be offset by a real increase in the number of smokers. There will be additional restrictions placed on smoking in public, but the current view is that it is unlikely that a complete prohibition on smoking is possible. The core group of smokers teamed with the tobacco industry will organize against any such effort.

Economic Impacts

The recession coupled with the Mid-east war had significant impacts on the sales of tobacco in 1990. *Smokeshop* magazine prepares an annual report on the tobacco industry based on surveys of tobacco specialty shops. The 1990 Report, which reflected 1989 results, showed that the average tobacco store experienced an increase in tobacco product sales of 2.3%. The 1991 Report showed a decline in revenues for tobacco shops of over 20% for tobacco products. The biggest decrease came in the sales of domestic cigarettes and tobacco gift items. The bright spot in this report continued to be sales of imported cigarettes.

A closer examination of this Report shows that there are other factors involved in this report that may have caused the significant decrease. The Report shows that there was a significant shift in the makeup of the stores that responded to the survey. A total of 309 stores responded for 1990 with 52.7% (163) of them located in an urban setting and 46.3% (143) of them located in a suburban setting. This compares to a total of 208 stores responding for 1989 with only 28% (58) being urban while 63% (131) were suburban. The impact of the additional urban stores that reported was not evaluated in the report, but they probably had as much of an impact on the average per store sales as the economic climate did. A conversation with Chris Ebel, the author of the report, supported this viewpoint.

Government/Legal Issues

In 1991, the Washington Legislature enacted tougher laws and penalties for minors who possess tobacco products and for selling tobacco to minors. Uncontrolled purchases of cigarettes by minors was reduced with the elimination of vending machines. The laws require retail tobacco sellers to be as diligent in checking the identification of people buying tobacco products as a bartender is in checking the identification of a young person attempting to buy a drink in a tavern. Store clerks need to be trained to check identification and be made aware of the penalties for selling tobacco products to minors.

The rising cost of tobacco products resulting from new taxes has caused a decline in the number of cigarette smokers. The per capita consumption of cigarettes has shown a continued decline since 1974. However, 1989 sales of tobacco products hit an all-time high with an increase of 8% over 1988. A major portion of this increase can be attributed to increased taxes.

Both the Federal and state governments impose significant taxes on tobacco products. The Federal government collects a tax on tobacco based upon the weight of the product. This tax is paid by the distributor/producer prior to the product being shipped into the State, thus the retailer need not be concerned with paying this tax.

The State of Washington collects a tax on all tobacco products sold in the state. The cigarette tax is collected by selling stamps which are then affixed to the packs of cigarettes. The retailer can choose to buy pre-stamped cigarettes or stamp them himself. The state tax on cigars and bulk tobacco must be paid by the person or business that brings the tobacco into the state. It is based upon gross dollar value of the product brought into the state less discounts, returned merchandise and products shipped out-of-state. Credit is given for the taxes paid to the Federal Government.

The retailer's ability to avoid paying state taxes for products shipped out-of-state has helped to create mail order business for tobacco retailers in Washington. At present, the retailer is not required to collect sales or tobacco taxes due the state in which the product is being sold. The obligation to pay the state taxes rests solely with the purchaser. This right of the retailer has been established in court cases that have been decided by the U.S. Supreme Court. The Supreme Court has viewed the states' attempt to collect these taxes from the retailers as a restraint of interstate commerce. The states, which are in need of additional revenues, are continuing to challenge this right in the Federal Courts. The Supreme Court will once again be making a decision on this matter during the current court session. A decision in favor of the states will serve to eliminate most of this market, but would be offset by increased sales to in-state customers.

Technological Issues

While the retail sale of tobacco products and magazines in not "hi-tech", "hi-tech" tools to sell these products are available, specifically the use of computerized point-of-sale and accounting systems. The use of these systems supports the control of inventory and improves cashflow. These are key factors in improving the profitability of these stores if they are to survive in the long term. A visit to any of the tobacco or magazine stores in the metro area shows that these stores are typically "mom and pop" operations with little evidence of computerization.

This technology is already being used by the large retail outlets for tobacco and magazines. The supermarkets and mass retailers have been utilizing point of sale systems for a number of years. The volume of products sold by these stores has required that they invest in the costly systems that were available for NCR, Nixdorf and others. The adoption of Universal Pricing Codes has simplified the implementation of these systems.

The cost of these systems has been the primary barrier to the small retailer's adoption of this technology, even if they wanted to adopt such a system. The advent of personal computers and development of small business software now allows the small retailer to adopt this technology in a cost- effective manner. In spite of this, the local tobacco/magazine shops have not made any move to these systems.

We perceive that the main reason that these stores have not adopted point of sale technology in tobacco stores has been the outdated thinking of the owners. It seems to be a commonly held view of tobacco store owners in the Northwest that they have too many products and are too small to justify the expense and effort involved in implementing a point of sale system. However, the potential for increasing operating efficiencies by decreasing inventory and increasing product turns is too great to be ignored. An interview with the owner of a Seattle-based store that recently implemented a PC based inventory system was very revealing. He stated that he expects to increase his inventory turns from 3.75 to 4.25 turns each year with an attendant decrease in inventory. The net result expected by this individual is increased positive cashflow with less money tied up in inventory.

Magazines

The Market

The magazine market has also experienced relatively flat sales growth through the 80's, but was marked by an upturn (6% to 10%) '87-'89 period followed by a downturn (4% in 1990). The upturn was attributed to the increase in regional and special interest magazines. These magazines typically command a higher price than the mass market magazines and afford the opportunity for higher gross margins. Sales in the first half of 1990 were on track to continue the growth of '87-89, but fell apart in the second half of 1990. This downturn was attributed to the recession and the war fears.

Magazines are brought to market by two primary means; direct subscription sales and single copy retain sales. The president of the Periodicals Institute, John E. Fitzmaurice, estimates that direct subscription sales of magazines captures 70% of the physical volume. Due to discounting, this represents an estimated 58% of the sales dollars (see Section D, Market Analysis). Retail magazine sales for the U.S. market were $3.57 billion in 1990. This was a 0.43% decrease in sales from 1989.

The consumer's choice of one of these market paths over the other is driven by the perceived benefits of one outlet over the other. A recent study of the magazine market revealed that people are just as likely to buy magazines through retail outlets as they are through subscription sales-"59% buy both ways vs. 24 percent who buy magazines through subscription and 17 percent who only purchase single copies." Direct subscription is the least expensive (discounts of 35% to 65%) and most convenient means (direct mail) for the consumer to purchase magazines. On the other hand, retail purchasers of magazines believe that they are saving money because they can try out the magazine first before committing to a subscription. They also believe they can obtain the best value by buying only those magazines that have a story or feature that interests them.

The retail outlets for magazines include: mass retailers, grocery stores, convenience stores, discount stores, newsstands, smokeshops and magazine stores. The relative shares for each of these outlets are given in Table 2.

Table 2 - Magazine Market Sales Through Retail Outlets

Retail Outlet	**Market Share**
Supermarket	54%
News Stand	11%
Convenience Store	10%
Drug Store	9%
Bookstore	7%
Discount Dept. Store	2%
Other	7%

Source: *Periodicals Institute 1990 Databook*

Mass retailers, grocery stores and discount stores offer a limited selection (250-400 titles) with some discount (5% to 15%) and are primarily offering one stop shopping for the consumer. Convenience stores offer a much more limited selection (50-100 titles), typically do not discount and offer convenience for the impulse buyer. Newsstands, smokeshops and magazine stores will offer a much broader selection (1000-2000 titles), but typically do not discount. Their focus is on service.

Social Environment and Trends

The issues facing the magazine industry in the social arena are relatively minor when compared with the tobacco industry. The primary area of concern is the free speech issues surrounding men's sophisticate magazines. These magazines while being big sellers, are found to be offensive for a variety of reasons, including concerns for children who might see them and their exploitation of women. A vocal minority has expressed it's displeasure with these magazines by picketing and boycotting stores that carry them. The most notable case of this was the boycott of some local convenience stores. Picketing and the resultant loss of business contributed to the stores' financial problems which in turn led to the corporation filing for Chapter 11 bankruptcy. There has been some activism on this issue in the metro area.

Economic Impacts

The past year marked the most significant recession that the United States has experienced since the early 80's. The recession coupled with the Gulf War had significant impacts on the sales of magazines. 1990 magazine sales decreased, primarily in the second half of the year, by a little over 4% when compared with 1989. On the positive side, overall revenue growth for magazines in the 80's was over 7% compounded annually. This growth represents a positive trend for the magazine retailers in spite the slowdown in 1990.

As was the case for all communications media, magazine publishers experienced an accompanying slowdown in their advertising receipts. This slowdown has been reported in the popular press and has resulted in reduced profitability for the publishers. Some publishers have responded by raising the retail price for single copy sales of their magazines, while others have gone out of business. The impact of these actions on retail sales has yet to be determined, but one can envision a period of reduced retail magazine sales for the industry as a whole.

Technological Issues

The use of "high-tech" tools to sell magazines was covered in the discussion in a previous section. The use of a point-of-sales systems in tracking sales of magazines and in managing inventory can have significant impact on the profitability of the retailer.

In researching the current state of the magazine business, it has become apparent that the retailers, especially small stores, place a heavy reliance on the local distributor to select and manage the titles the stores carry. This appears to be true for all retailers, including the mass retailers. The adoption of a computerized inventory control system allows the retailer to control his own destiny. With these systems, market preferences can easily be identified thus allowing for shifts in the mix and quantity of magazines offered. This, in turn, will increase the profitability of the store as sales will be increased relative to inventory carried and the labor wasted on the processing of the unsold magazines will be reduced.

MARKET ANALYSIS

Tobacco

Demographics/Psychographics

A broad overview of the tobacco market shows that use of all categories of tobacco is fairly constant across all age groups with usage falling off among those people age 65 or older (see Table 3). The exception is among users of smokeless tobacco where the 18 to 25 year olds are the biggest users with usage dropping off to a constant percentage among users 45 and older. The 35 to 44 age group, the baby boomers, is the exception to this as their use of smokeless tobacco is 50% less than that of the next largest group of users.

Pipe tobacco represents the other significant variant from the pattern of constant use among all age groups. Pipe tobacco usage among those under age 35 is

Demographics/Psychographics
...continued

constant at 2% of that age group. Traditionally, the incidence of pipe smoking increases with age with an observable shift occurring at age 35. From this age on, the percentage of any population age group smoking pipes remains constant with a slight upturn at age 65. The aging of the baby boomers with their higher levels of disposable income bodes well for the pipe tobacco market with the growth in the number of users predicted to be the highest for any of the tobacco products. Along with this increased use in pipe tobacco comes an increase in sales of high margin pipes and smokers' accessories.

Tobacco Use by Age (In Percent of Population)

Product	18-24	25-34	35-44	45-54	55-64	>65	Total
Pipe tobacco	2.0	2.1	3.5	3.5	3.5	4.1	3.0
Cigarettes	10.1	12.4	14.6	14.5	13.2	5.3	11.7
Cigars	5.1	4.3	4.5	4.4	4.4	3.6	4.4
Cigarillos	2.0	2.3	1.5	2.1	1.5	1.3	1.8
Smokeless	11.0	7.1	2.6	5.7	6.2	5.1	6.3

Source: "What's Hot, What's Not," *Supermarket Business*, March, 1988

The demographics of the tobacco store customer shows a 2 to 1 split of male versus female customers. This is to be compared with the fact that approximately 55% of the smokers are female. The reasons for this difference can be traced to the products used by each group.

The products a typical tobacco shop offers are primarily used by men. The male smokers who frequent a tobacco shop are looking for a quality tobacco or cigar that suits their taste. They are typically willing to spend more than the average cigarette smoker to get the product that they want. Both cigar and pipe smokers tend to be loyal to a particular product, but in general, are willing to try something new. Both user groups also expect to receive a high level of customer service and expect attentive service from sales people. This requires that the sales personnel be knowledgeable of the tobacco products offered.

Another characteristic of the pipe smoker not readily apparent to the non-smoker is that they continue to purchase additional pipes over the years. The reasons for doing this may be as simple as "it feels good in my hand" to they just want to have a new pipe. This desire for a new pipe fuels an ongoing market that would not be justified if one were to simply look at the number of pipe smokers.

The tobacco products women tend to smoke are cigarettes, domestic and imports, with a few women smoking small cigars/cigarillos. These products are easily purchased at the stores where women shop regularly. They do not need to take time to stop at the local tobacco store. The tobacco store, while offering these products, is primarily focused on the higher price/value segment of the market. This includes cigars, bulk tobacco, pipes and accessories. Typically, women do not smoke pipes, while a small minority will smoke cigars. The majority of women customers who shop at tobacco shops do so to purchase gifts of tobacco products and accessories for their spouses or male friends.

The primary growth opportunity with women smokers is to focus on getting them to switch from domestic cigarettes to the "price/value" market of import cigarettes. It is unlikely that women will change to cigar or pipe smoking although this represents an intriguing approach to increasing sales of these items. This opportunity results in a focus on women who are age 25 to 50, with a household income of over $25,000. This age group is more likely to be interested in trying something different and they will have the disposable income to afford it.

The target market among men is much broader, with all male smokers from age 25 to 65+ being part of our primary market. This market can be narrowed down to those households with income of $25,000 or more as the products we will offer require that the household have more disposable income available.

Market Size

The research we have conducted reveals that there exists no direct measure of the metro tobacco, magazine and candy markets. There are two methods which can be used to give us an indication of the relative size of each of these markets. Briefly, they are as follows:

Method 1 - This approach uses the overall sales figures for the various retail outlets for the metro market and multiplies them by the industry average for percent of sales for each product by retail outlet. The result is an estimate of the sales of each product attributable to each retail sales channel. The sum of all sales channel figures gives an estimate of the total retail market for the metro area. Retail sales figures are reported in the "1987 Census of Retail Trade for Washington" and industry averages are reported in the "1990 Data Book".

Method 2 - This method estimates the available market by multiplying the average consumer unit expenditures for each product by the appropriate number of consumer units for our market area. Consumer expenditures are reported in the "Consumer Expenditure Survey, 1987." Information on numbers of consumer units in our market area is found in the "Market Data Report - Town Center Area."

Using Method 1, we arrive at a total metro tobacco market of $66,530,269. Method 2 gives us a total of $53,637,215. The two Methods provide values that match fairly well, thus giving a reasonable estimate of market size. A complete presentation of the market calculations are available upon request.

Competitors

Information on types of competitors was presented in under subsection **1. Tobacco** of **Section C. The Industry Perspective.** The following provides specific information for a representative sampling of the competitors.

Competitors *...continued*

Name: Jeff's Cigar Store
Type of Business:Tobacco Shop &Magazine Store
Location: Downtown/Northwest Store
Size:900Sq.Ft. (Northwest) - 400SF for tobacco & gifts.
1850 Sq. Ft. (Downtown) - 850SF for tobacco & gifts.

Strengths:
- ❑A well-established store.
- ❑Has more than one store in the metro area thus allowing for easy customer access.
- ❑Downtown location provides them with a steady flow of foot traffic.
- ❑Downtown location places them in the center of a large population base.
- ❑They have a large inventory of tobacco products and accessories.
- ❑They have an excellent tobacco mail order business.
- ❑Low prices for tobacco products.

Weaknesses:
- ❑Parking is limited resulting in a long walk to get to either store.
- ❑The layout of the downtown store is congested. It can be extremely difficult to get around in the store.
- ❑They are not automated.
- ❑Downtown location limits their appeal to suburban customers.
- ❑Competition is stiff with numerous competitors within 1 mile.

Name: Superway
Type of Businesss: Supermarket
Location:Various (chain)Store
Size:200 to 300 Square Feet (Tobacco Department)

Strengths:
- ❑They have low domestic cigarette prices due to volume sourcing.
- ❑Easy access when shopping for groceries.
- ❑Conveniently located.

Weaknesses:
- ❑They have a limited stock and selection of tobacco products.
- ❑Limited selection of smoker's accessories, and no imported cigarettes.
- ❑Limited level of customer service.
- ❑Except for cigarettes, tobacco products may be hard to find.

Name: Thompson's
Type of Business:Mass Retailer
Location: Various (Chain-One location is adjacent to our site)
Size: 200 to 300 Sq. Ft. (Tobacco Department)

Strengths:
- ❑Same as Supermarkets plus,Variety allows for one-stop shopping.

Weaknesses:
- ❑Same as for Supermarkets.

Magazines

Demographics/Psychographics

In 1990, Publishers Clearinghouse, in consultation with the Magazine Publishers of America, commissioned the first comprehensive study since 1976 of how and why magazines are purchased. "The Study of Magazine Buying Patterns," was conducted by Audits & Surveys, and provides significant insight into the market drivers. This survey forms the primary basis for our discussion of the demographics of the magazine market.

The magazine market represents a contrast to the tobacco market. While it can be viewed as one large segment of the communications market, it can be broken down into a number of special interest topics such as business/financial, cars, regional, general editorial, house and gardening, motorcycles, news, men's, women's, outdoor, entertainment, sports, teen/music, tabloids and social. It is this variety that provides this market with something for just about everyone.

The idea that magazines represent something for everyone is borne out by the fact that 81 percent of all adults buy magazines. Of these buyers, 27 percent are classified as being "Heavy Purchasers." "Heavy Purchasers" buy at least 7 magazines per month and accounted for 58 percent of all magazine purchases. Of the "Heavy Purchasers," 59% have household incomes of $35,000 or more. Of this group, over 61 percent of the chief wage earners attended college. A recent issue of Magazine & Bookseller summarized this report with the headline, "Magazine Readers Are Smarter and Richer."

The sales channels for magazines are retail sales and subscription sales. The typical retail magazine purchase is an impulse purchase (68% of sales), while the typical subscription purchase is planned (70% of sales). The swapping of buyers among these two categories is relatively stable with an equal number changing from one source to the other. This would indicate that this market is relatively mature with the sales approaches used by each channel having reached their maximum level of effectiveness. This may also indicate that this market is ripe for a new approach.

The following table and observations are excerpted from the study:

Demographics/Psychographics
...continued

Demographic Profiles of Subscription and Single-Copy Buyers

	% Subscriptions	% Single Copies	% Both
Sex			
Male	48	43	47
Female	52	57	53
Age			
18-34	28	50	52
35-54	33	35	30
55 and over	39	15	18
Household Income			
$35,000 or more	47	37	52
$15,000-$34,999	38	43	32
Less than $15,000	15	20	16
Education--*Chief Wage Earner*			
Some college or more	51	38	60
Completed high school	31	38	22
Some high school or less	18	24	18
Occupation--*Chief Wage Earner*			
Prof./Mgr/Owner	32	20	41
White-collar	12	14	9
Blue collar	24	47	33
Retired/not employed	31	19	17

Note: Households are classified as mainly subscription or single copy if 60% or more of total titles were bought by one channel.

Basis: Adults in Magazine Households Buying Mainly by Subscription (475), Single Copy (318) and Equally (167); Magazine Households Buying Mainly By Subscription (375), Single Copy (255), and Equally (131).

Demographics/Psychographics
...continued

Demographic Profiles Of Subscription and Single-Copy Buyers

"Subscription buyers tend to have higher socioeconomic levels than those who purchase single copy. These households have the life-style and economic position to commit to the regularity afforded by subscription magazines while single-copy purchasers are more apt to" begin subscribing with advancement in age, occupation and income.

"Subscribers are better-educated and more affluent than single-copy purchasers. In half of the subscriber households the chief wage earner is college-educated and the annual household income exceeds $35,000 (47%). Comparatively, single-copy buyers are younger - 50% between 18-34 years - and only one in five chief wage earners have reached the professional/managerial/owner occupational level."

"The households buying subscriptions and single copies in equal proportions may represent the most active and eager group of magazine purchasers. These dual purchasers buy the greatest number of magazine titles (7.5 per year) of any group and represent 21% of the magazine volume (Table 12)."

"Demographically, the dual-purchasing households enhance the quality characteristics of the subscription buyers while maintaining the youth factor of single-copy purchasers. Over half of these buyers are between the ages of 18-34, 60% are college educated, four out of ten have achieved professional/managerial occupational status, and 52% have household incomes exceeding $35,000."

A review of the data in Table 17 of the report, shows that split between female and male purchasers of magazines conforms closely to the split in the population as a whole.

Approximately 56% are women and 44% are male. The report does provide some additional information on female vs. male buying patterns that appears to contradict the data in Table 17. In a commentary on who made the purchasing decision, the report states "Females play a dominant role in the purchasing transaction of both subscriptions and single copies. Three out of every four single-copy titles are claimed to be bought by females and two of every three subscriptions are ordered by females. Males buy one-fourth of single-copy and subscription magazines." The report goes on to state that, "While 25% of all types of magazines are bought by men, 32% of single copies and over 40% of subscriptions are acquired <u>for</u> men."

The survey also provided insights into the interests of magazine buyers. The buyers of magazines are likely to be owners of electronic/video equipment. Among the heavy buyers of magazines, in excess of 80% own a VCR, over 71% have cable TV and 93% rent movies. In the same vein, 54% of all buyers have listened to records, audio tapes or CDs at home. Other activities that buyers indicated that they had engaged in the last twelve months include: 48% cooked or baked, 33% fixed or built things around the house, 45% went out to eat in a restaurant or cafe, 42% attended a religious service and 44% have read a book. Each of these interests provides vital insights that will be of significance when planning our advertising program.

A summary observation regarding the purchasers of single copies is that over 80% are between 18-54 and over 80% have household incomes in excess of $15,000 per year. The Consumer Expenditure Survey (see Table 4) shows that there are fairly uniform buying practices by all age groups within given income bands. Also, within all age groups, the amount expended on magazines increase with increasing household income.

Average Annual Expenditure per Consumer Unit With Reference Person by Age

Age	<25	25-34	35-4	445-54	55-74	<64
Income:						
$40,000 or More	73	116	136	128	137	178
$30,000 to 39,999	77	74	84	95	91	110
$20,000 to 29,999	47	63	79	71	73	92
$15,000 to 19,999	43	56	58	63	64	70
$10,000 to 14,999	30	41	44	43	54	61
$5,000 to 9,999	33	25	38	45	46	40
Under $5,000	19	32	46	53	38	27

Note:The CES provides data for the broad category of "Reading." The above table was derived by assuming 1/12 of the dollars spent on reading was spent on magazines.

Source: *Consumer Expenditure Survey, 1987*,U.S. Dept. of Labor, Bureau of Labor Statistics, June, 1990.

In summary, the mix of demographics means that the successful magazine retailer will offer a wide variety of titles to meet the varied interests of both men and women as well as all age groups. The target market will be both men and women with emphasis on women as they tend to buy more magazines. The target customer will be those household units that are likely to spend over $60 per year. This results in our focusing on all households with an income greater than $20,000 and the reference person being 25 and older. The magazine buyer will also be better educated with at least a high school diploma. College educated buyers should be the biggest purchasers. This encompasses the same market that we are focusing on for tobacco.

Market Size

Using Method 1 (see description of Method 1 under Tobacco) to calculate market size, we arrive at a total retail (single-copy sales) market of $13,124,945. Method 2 gives us a total magazine market (single-copy sales + subscription sales) is $27,514,812. While we are interested in the size of the total market, we are primarily interested in the retail portion of this market.

We can breakdown this second figure by sales channel by recognizingthat 1) 70% of the physical volume of magazine are sold through subscription sales and 2) subscription prices for each magazine are approximately 55% of the retail price. If we multiply the physical volume by the unit price we get an Equivalent Sales Volume (ESV) for each sales channel. Thus, the ESV for subscription sales is $0.385 (70% *$0.55) and the ESV for retail sales is $0.30 (30% *$1.00). The total market ESV is $0.685. Dividing the individual sales channel ESV by the total market ESV gives us a sales dollar percentage for each channel. Thus, subscription sales can be estimated to be 56% ($0.385/$0.685) of the total market sales dollars and retail sales represent 44% ($0.30/$0.685).

Multiplying the Method 2 figure by this percentage gives estimated retail sales of $12,062,000. This compares favorably with the Method 1 figure, thus validating our estimate of the retail magazine market in the metro area.

Competitors

General information on types of competitors was presented in under subsection **1. Tobacco** of section**C. The Industry Perspective**. Detailed information for a representative sampling of the competitors is as follows:

Name: Jeff's Cigar Store
Type of Business: Tobacco Shop & Magazine Store
Location: Downtown/Northwest
Size: 1850 Sq.l Ft. (Downtown) - 1000 SF for magazines
900 Sq. Ft. (Northwest) - 500 SF for magazines

Strengths:

- ❑A long time established store.
- ❑The have more than one store in the metro area thus allowing for easy customer access.
- ❑Their downtown location provides them with a steady flow of foot traffic.
- ❑Downtown location places them in the center of a large population base.
- ❑They carry approximately 2000 titles at the downtown store.

Weaknesses:

- ❑Parking is limited resulting in a long walk to get to either store.
- ❑The layout of the downtown store is congested. It can be extremely difficult to get around in the store.
- ❑The store has the appearance of being crammed full. It can be intimidating or aggravating depending upon your perspective.

Competitors...*continued*

- They are not automated.
- Downtown location limits their appeal to suburban customers.
- Competition is stiff with numerous competitors within 1 mile.

Name: 7-11 & Metro Mini-Mart
Type of Business: Convenience Store
Location: Various (chains)
Size: 2000 Sq. Ft. - 50SF for magazines

Strengths:
- They are conveniently located in neighborhoods.
- Parking is convenient.
- Magazine sales are primarily impulse purchases.

Weaknesses:
- Selections limited to approximately 200 to 250 titles.
- Customer service is extremely limited.
- No special orders.

Name: Superway
Type of Business: Supermarket
Location: Various (chain)
Size: 200 to 300 Sq. Ft. (Magazine Department)

Strengths:
- They discount their magazines by 10%
- Easy access when shopping for groceries.
- Conveniently located.

Weaknesses:
- Selections limited to 300 to 450 titles.
- Limited level of customer service.
- No special orders.

Name: Thompson's
Type of Business: Mass Retailer
Location: Various (Chain--One location is adjacent to our site)
Size: 200 to 300 Sq. Ft. (Magazine Department)

Strengths:
- Same as for Supermarkets plus,
- Variety allows for one stop shopping.

Weaknesses:
- Same as for Supermarkets.

Candy

Recognizing that candy sales will represent a minor part of oursales volume, we have not conducted as extensive analysis of this market segment. The following is a brief summary of the conditions for this market.

Demographics/psychographics

Over 90% of the population purchases candy at least once a month. This figure holds true for both males and females, and all age groups except adults aged 50 and over. The purchase of candy is split evenly between planned and spontaneous purchases. Candy's popularity is derived from it being a relatively inexpensive pleasure/reward, with 72% of the purchases being for $1.49 or less and 50% being for less than $1.00.

Market Size

Using Method 1, the metro retail candy market is estimated to be $39,939,000.

Competitors

Please refer to the information provided for the tobacco and magazine competitors.

Market Specifics

Location Selection

The establishment of a retail store that sells tobacco products, magazines and newspapers requires a review of the market opportunity. Suffice it to say that none of these products represents a high growth market when viewed within the context of the overall economy. Within the metro market, however, there are geographic areas experiencing rapid population growth and as such represent a growth opportunity. It is this opportunity that led to the selection of the location for

A review of the population growth statistics for the metro area shows that North County is one of the fastest growing areas in the state. The number of people living within 5 minutes travel time of Town Center is expected to increase by 30% from 67,000 to 87,000 people during the 1990-2005 period. This compares to a predicted growth of 20% for the overall metro area during the same period.

An evaluation of the retail outlets that serve this area reveals that there is only one major tobacco store in this area. The remaining tobacco stores are primarily located downtown. National averages reveal that one tobacco shop can be supported by a population base of 82,000. While the 5 minute travel time population base of 67,000 would not indicate that two stores could be supported, the 15 minute travel time population base of 484,000 will easily support two stores. The Regional draw of the area also supports the use of the 15 minute travel time population base.

As for magazine and newspaper sales in the metro area, the primary outlets are the book stores, mass retailers and grocery stores. Typically, these outlets offer a limited selection of 200 to 400 titles. There are a number of smokeshops and magazine stores downtown that offer upwards of 1800 titles. In North County, there is no outlet that offers the large selection of titles that we intend to, which leaves the market wide open to support such a specialty store.

Our stated goal to become recognized as the premier news and tobacco store in the metro area also influenced our site selection. The selection of a location in an area which is already established as a regional shopping center enhances our ability to fulfill this goal. Towards this goal, we have tentatively selected a location in the Promenade shopping mall. Promenade is adjacent to Town Center. Alternate locations were explored including various neighborhood malls as it offers us significantly better opportunity to meet our goal of becoming a regional presence. Further, the lease rates offered by Promenade are competitive with the neighborhood malls and will not place an undue burden on our business.

Area Demographics

A review of the demographics for the area shows that a population base of only 23,000 lives within two miles of this area. Clearly, this base is not large enough on its own to support the established retail base that exists in the area. The market demographics for the Town Center shopping mall shows that in 1988 the car count in the parking lot ranged from a low of 18,355 cars per day to a high of 31,285 cars per day. Traffic counts for the adjacent shows an average of 31,000 cars per day drive by the planned location of Standard Tobacco and News.

The area is recognized as a regional shopping center. Clearly, the traffic volume demonstrates that the area serves a regional market. An estimated 1,242,895 people comprising over 500,000 households are located within a 25 minute drive. Of these, approximately 40% are within a 15 minute drive. Locating the store in the area allows us to draw on the regional market that the area serves.

The location of the store in the Town Center area also places us approximately 15 minutes to 25 minutes travel time away from all of our major competitors except for one tobacco store located in the Town Center. The size of the tobacco market available within 25 minutes travel time is estimated to be $66,000,000. The magazine market for this same area is estimated to be $213,000,000. With only 0.4% of the tobacco market and 1.1% of the magazine market, we can achieve a breakeven sales level. It is our belief that market shares of 1.0%-1.05% of the tobacco market and 2.7%-2.8% of the magazine market are achievable in this market within 3 years of opening. The resulting monthly sales are projected at $67,000 to $85,000.

By comparison, Jeff's Cigar Store, one of the major downtowncompetitors, has monthly tobacco sales of $55,200 (1.0%), magazine sales of $29,400 (2.7%) and total sales of $84,600. This is based upon a store having a total of 1850 square feet of space. The space we have selected in Promenade had 1875 square feet of space. Assuming the same level of success, monthly sales as projected above are achievable.

Advantages

The selection of the location in the Promenade offers a number of significant advantages:

Transportation Freeway access to the location is excellent. Future traffic improvements will only serve to improve the accessibility.

Parking Parking is close to the store and it is free. This offers us a significant advantage over our downtown competitors. Further, the convenience of the parking and easy store access will help to draw customers from the tobacco store in Town Center.

Existing Market Base Local businesses include a large Hospital, three hotels, a community college and Washington Institute of Technology satellites, and the retail businesses of the area.

Growth While the immediate population base is small, it is growing fast. The immediate area represents a significant growth opportunity for the stores of the area.

Market Opportunity With only one tobacco competitor and no magazine competitors, the North County represents an under served market for a specialty retailer such as Standard. The demographics of the area support our target market of men and women over the age of 25 with incomes in excess of $25,000. Over 60% of the population within our market area is 25 years of age or older and approximately one half of the households earn over $25,000.

Complementary Business Our location in Promenade places us near a number of businesses that offer the activities that magazine readers are likely to engage in. These activities include dining out, renting video tapes and purchasing audio tapes or CDs. Our store will be located between two restaurants and three other restaurants are located within 500 feet of the store. Other complementary businesses include a store that sells audio and video tapes, and CDs and rents video tapes and a software retailer.

Sales Projections and Market Share

Previously we stated our goals and presented information on sales projections and market share. The primary competitor we are modeling ourselves after is Jeff's Cigar Store. This business has annual sales of over $1.0 million with sales split 63.2%/33.8%/2.5%/0.5% between tobacco, magazines, candy and miscellaneous. Based upon the previous calculations of the metromarket size, Jeff's commands shares of 1.0%/2.7%/0.06% respectively.

Tables 5 and 6 summarize our projected sales and market shares for breakeven sales and for the first five years that we are in business. For our purposes, we are assuming constant 1991 dollars for the comparison. Detailed projections are provided in the financial section.

Sales Projections and Market Share...*continued*

Sales Projections

Product	Breakeven	Year 1	Year 2
Tobacco	$275,600	$341,500	$532,800
Magazines	145,600	180,400	281,400
Candy	10,800	13,400	21,900
Total Sales	$432,000	$535,300	$835,100

Product	Year 3	Year 4	Year 5
Tobacco	$622,600	$670,000	$700,000
Magazines	329,000	354,000	370,000
Candy	24,400	26,000	27,000
Total Sales	$976,000	$1,050,000	$1,097,000

Market Share (%)

Product	Breakeven	Year 1	Year 2
Tobacco	0.41	0.51	0.80
Magazines	1.11	1.37	2.14
Candy	0.03	0.03	0.05

Product	Year 3	Year 4	Year 5
Tobacco	0.94	1.01	1.05
Magazines	2.51	2.70	2.82
Candy	0.06	0.06	0.07

Note: *Market shares are based upon 1987 dollars.*

MARKETING STRATEGIES

Market Approach

General

Standard will initially offer a wide variety of tobacco products and accessories, newspapers and magazines and specialty candy. It is our plan to add complementary gift products, such as steins or knives, at some later date. Our initial product offerings will be sourced from a variety of reputable suppliers. The following sections will provide additional detail on each of these product areas.

Our target market is households with income in excess of $25,000. We are targeting both men and women of all ages, with primary focus on those between the ages of 25 to 55. Our image is upscale as befits our location in a new suburban mall with significant effort being made to offer our products in an attractive environment. We will emphasize personalized customer service. The computerized point-of-sale system with product databases will support our service without intruding on the store setting.

Specific Thrusts

Our plan for meeting the needs of our customers and establishing a customer base are threefold. The first part is to have a good location from a customer viewpoint. Our proposed location, in the Promenade, provides an attractive alternative for the Southeast Metro purchaser of magazines and tobacco products. Once a customer decides to shop at our store, they will find that access is easy and convenient from the road. We are locatedonly 100 feet off of the street and 1/4 mile from the freeway exit. Our location near the entrance of the mall provides us with good visibility from the road. Upon arriving at the store, customers will find plenty of free parking with a short walk in to the store.

The second part of our plan is to provide a pleasant shopping environment. Visually, this will be accomplished by the use of light interior colors and woods to create a pleasing and inviting atmosphere. This is in contrast to most tobacco stores that use dark colors and woods. This is intended to draw in the female customers as well as males. On the practical side, the layout of the store will be open allowing for a traffic flow pattern that will make it very easy for the customer to shop without having to step over and around other customers.

Customer convenience will be enhanced by the separation of the magazines and tobacco sections. The magazines will be in front of the store and tobacco in the rear. This will allow our non-smoking magazine customers to avoid the tobacco section. Direct ventilation will be used in the tobacco section to carry any unwanted smoke directly outside.

The customer will find it easy to locate their favorite magazine title as the magazine and newspaper racks will have category signs above the different sections. The magazine racks are designed with a minimum depth so that the customer will be able to view all titles without crouching. The magazines will be

Specific Thrusts*...continued*

displayed individually with the full masthead or cover visible. Typically, magazine stores overlap the magazines in an attempt to squeeze in the largest number of titles possible. This tends to make it difficult to locate specific titles. We prefer to sacrifice the additional titles for the sake of customer convenience. We will also maintain the clean and neat appearance of the store by avoiding the stacking of magazines on the floor. Mobile magazine carts will be used on the days we are putting out new titles and pulling the old ones off of the shelves.

The tobacco section will be organized with our display cases devoted to particular products, i.e. one for pipes and pipe accessories, one for cigar and cigarette accessories. The cases will not be so crammed with merchandise that the customer is overwhelmed with options. The cases will front a large 10' by 20' walk-in humidor. The inside of the humidor will be visible from the main floor through windows.

The third part of our plan to create and keep our customers is service. We will place emphasis on employing a knowledgeable and pleasant staff. We will pay close attention to our customers needs by responding to special requests for both magazines and tobacco. We will always try and get the customer the item they are looking for even if we have to get it from our competition. We will enhance our tobacco selection by providing extra services such as the rental of lockers in our humidor for storage of the customer's favorite cigars and we will offer free pipe cleaning.

Our capable staff will be assisted in their duties by the use of our integrated computer system. The system will allow us to answer customers' questions quickly and efficiently. The system will help in locating stock, providing information on the availability of items, immediate ordering of new items and will even allow us to provide information on the products. Our product database will enable even the newest staff member to answer customer questions concerning our cigars and tobacco merchandise, such as it's characteristics, where it is made and what similar products are available. As with the tobacco products, a database will be maintained to assist in identifying magazines that are of special interest to our customers.

The system will also allow us to maintain an inventory which is responsive to the needs of our customers. We will be able to easily identify which titles are not selling and remove them from the shelves while replacing them with new titles of interest. Our goal of improving stockturns will allow us to maintain a magazine and tobacco inventory that is new and fresh thus maintaining customer interest.

We believe that our threefold plan will meet with the approval of our customers and will make us the premier magazine and tobacco store in the metro area.

Pricing

Products will be priced with moderate to premium margins. We will not attempt to be a low price discounter. A store of our size cannot afford to attempt to meet the loss leader levels offered on domestic cigarettes and magazines by the mass retailers and supermarkets. Our focus will be on those products the consumer cannot find in the limited tobacco and magazine departments of these competitors.

We do intend to be price competitive with the specialty tobacco and magazine stores in the area. We will use our computer based pricing to optimize our sourcing and will work to improve our turns so that we can achieve lower costs. This should allow us to improve upon the margins used in our financial projections. Specific information on price levels and margins can be found in **Section:** Management and Operating Plan.

Marketing Programs

We intend to implement a number of programs to keep our customers aware of us and to ensure that they are satisfied when they leave the store.

Tobacco Inventories We will use our inventory tracking system to monitor inventory levels of cigars or tobacco, project usage levels and adjust inventories to meet indicated trends. Improved stockturns will allow us to maintain a new and exciting inventory. This will entice pipe buyers and lighter aficionado to stop in and visit on a more frequent basis.

Magazine Title List We will use our POS system to monitor magazine & newspaper sales. Inventories will be adjusted to make certain that we stock a sufficient quantity of the titles that are of interest to our customers. Titles that do not sell will be removed from our buy list to make room for other titles that meet the interests of our customers.

Smoker's Clubs We will sponsor pipe and cigar smoker's clubs. This will consist of reserving special times for the clubs to meet and affording them the chance to sample new tobaccos and cigars. This will provide us with a unique opportunity to draw in these high-end customers as there are no such clubs in the metro area.

Newsletter A bi-monthly newsletter will be sent out to interested customers. This newsletter will provide details on new magazines and tobacco products as well as special promotions.

New Product Announcements Postcards announcing new additions and features will be mailed out to interested customers as a supplement to our newsletter.

Market Surveys We will conduct regular surveys of our customers to establish a database of information on demographics, interests and comments on our service. This information will be used to make improvements where necessary and insure that we continue to pay attention to the needs of our customers.

Marketing Programs...*continued*

Demographic data regarding customers will be routinely logged in to the computer as each sale is made. This will include sex and age of the customer. This will provide us with a database upon which we can draw as we tailor our advertising and future expansion plans.

Advertising A key factor in achieving our short term goals will be the initial phase of our advertising. During this phase we will strive to make our presence known on a regional basis. A multi-media campaign is planned that will include radio, newspaper and some direct mail to known tobacco consumers. The advertising plan will be developed and implemented by an outside advertising consultant.

Beyond the initial advertising program, we plan to have an on going advertising program to keep our name out in front of the regional consumer. This will include yellow page advertisements under 4 different classifications, occasional radio ads and ongoing newspaper ads rotated among local newspapers. This will include advertising in the county papers so as to draw Washington state residents shop in the area.

MANAGEMENT AND OPERATING PLAN

Structure & Personnel

Standard Tobacco & News is registered with the State of Washington Department of Commerce. This business is a partnership owned by Dwayne and Samantha Peters. The business will use a defined organization intended to support long term growth plans. This organization delegates authority to the lowest levels thus motivating our workforce to perform to the best of their ability.

The General Partners (GPs) will jointly direct the long term affairs of the business and establish general operating procedures. All purchasing and financing of capital equipment will require approval of the GPs. The GPs will also act upon items brought to them for review by the General Manager.

The day to day affairs of the business will be managed by the General Manager (GM). The GM is responsible for the maintenance of all financial records, approval of purchases of products and supplies, payment of bills, marketing programs and advertising, approval of hiring and firing of all employees with specific responsibility for office and support service employees, establishment of specific operating procedures and all other matters that do not require approval of the partners. The GM will also oversee the maintenance and upkeep of the store, computer systems and capital goods.

The position of Systems Manager (SM) will be established. The SM will report to the GM. The SM will be responsible for the selection, setup and maintenance of the support systems. This includes the computer hardware, computer software, and the telephone system. Dwayne Peters, while continuing in his present position with General Electric, will serve as the Systems Manager.

The store will have two department managers, a Tobacco Department Manager (TDM) and a Magazine Department Manager (MDM). The TDM and MDM will report to the GM. The TDM and MDM will have joint responsibility for the hiring and firing of employees. All hiring and firing actions must be approved by the GM.

The TDM will have responsibility and authority for the selection and sale of cigarettes, cigars, tobacco, pipes,lighters and other tobacco accessories. The TDM will have the authority to purchase and price tobacco goods within the limits defined by the GM. The TDM will have responsibility for the training and supervision of employees who work in the Tobacco Dept. The TDM will also be responsible for direction of all sales personnel when the TDM is on duty. Marianne Johnson will be the Tobacco Department Manager.

The MDM will have responsibility and authority for the selection and sale of magazines, newspapers, candy and other gift items. The MDM will have the authority to purchase and to price magazine goods within the limits defined by the GM. The MDM will have responsibility for the training and supervision of employees who work in the Magazine Dept. The MDM will have responsibility for the direction of all sales personnel when the TDM is not on duty. Ken Boardman will be the Magazine Department Manager.

Resumes

The following are abbreviated resumes for the principals.

Samantha Peters brings over 19 years of bookkeeping experience with various levels of responsibility to Standard. During the past 4 1/2 years, she worked as the bookkeeper at there Cigar Store. Her duties at Jeff's included all maintenance of financial records, payment of bills, and billing of customers.

During this period, her achievements included:

- ♦ Implementation of a new, comprehensive, bookkeeping system
- ♦ Development of mail order business
- ♦ Development of written operating procedures for employees
- ♦ Integration of the bookkeeping records for a new store

Through her position, she gained knowledge of products and suppliers that will be applied in the operation of Standard. She also gained an extensive understanding of the operation ofa smokeshop and magazine store and the duties of a general manager. Her position required her to answer customer telephone inquiries, process magazine returns and assist in taking inventory. She acted as an advisor to the owner of Jeff's and was a key contributor in the day-to-day operation of the store.

Resumes...*continued*

During 1991, she completed a Small Business Development course of study at the community college.

Dwayne Peters has worked for General Electric (GE) since graduation from college in 1974. He moved to this area in 1978, where he has held various positions with GE's Utility Sales Department. He is presently a Senior Application Engineer in Utility Sales with responsibility for applying electrical equipment in utility systems, system application engineering and economic and technical evaluations of equipment and financing alternatives. He has attended numerous General Electric Company courses including Sales Leadership, Managing Account Potential and Modern Marketing I.

Dwayne has also been involved with the implementation of personal computers (PC) at GE. This includes set up of equipment, installation of software and general troubleshooting of equipment and software problems. He has been an active member of a GE field sales PC work group that has advised management on problems and recommended solutions for implementation on a Division wide basis.

While continuing to work for GE, Dwayne will bring his considerable sales, marketing, financial and technical expertise to bear on the issues facing Standard.

Marianne Johnson 14 years of sales experience with over 11 years in tobacco shops. She has worked for her present employer for the past 10 years and has held successively higher levels of responsibility. She currently is the operations manager for three tobacco shops and is responsible for all aspects of the operation.

Her responsibilities as operations manager include the hiring and training of employees and store managers, selection and purchase of inventory and maintenance of the same. Marianne's experience allows her to effectively manage her employees as she knows what is required to be a successful retail sales person. She has extensive knowledge of all of the tobacco products. This knowledge and experience allows her toeffectively work the counter as well as train employees.

Ken Boardman also brings an established reputation with tobacco suppliers. This reputation coupled with his knowledge and experience will allow Standard to hit the ground running. He will provide instant credibility with suppliers and with knowledgeable customers. His extensive experience as a manager will make him a vital part of the management team at Standard His retail expertise and knowledge of tobacco products will be a key to our achieving the sales projections.

Labor Requirements

Standard Tobacco and News will require only one type of labor, namely sales clerks. We intend to source our clerks from the existing pool of retail clerks, but will consider hiring people with no prior experience as is necessary. Training of employees is the responsibility of the Department Managers. All employees will be expected to perform all tasks including cleaning. We do, however, expect to have some of our full time employees specialize in either tobacco or magazines. Specialized tasks, such as accepting delivery of goods and preparing returns of magazines will be assigned to specific employees. These tasks may be performed by other employees, but the work will be performed under the direction of the assigned employee.

We plan to establish a multilevel system for classifying our sales clerks. All beginning clerks will be classified as Assistants, a probationary position. They will be on probation for a minimum of 3 months to a maximum of 6 months. At the end of the probationary period they will either advance to the position of Sales Clerk or be terminated. Their promotion or termination will be based upon having demonstrated a basic working knowledge of the systems used at Standard, shown a capability for retail sales and consistently followed the work rules established by the Managers. The individual who continues in the position of sales clerk will have a similar opportunity for advancement to the position of Senior Sales Clerk based upon demonstrated performance. Of course, advancement to a higher level will result in a higher pay level.

We intend to use a blend of full time and part time workers to meet our staffing needs. We have established an employment level based upon achieving a target level of $160,000 of salesper employee. This compares to an estimated tobacco shop average of $90,000 convenience store average of $115,000 and supermarket average of $200,000.

Based upon our projected sales and target sales per employee, we arrive at the following 5 year estimate of our employment needs:

Projected Number of Employees

Employee Type	**Yr 1**	**Yr 2**	**Yr 3**	**Yr 4**	**Yr 5**
Magazine Dept. Mgr.	1	1	1	1	1
Tobacco Dept. Mgr.	1	1	1	1	1
Full Time Clerk	1	1.75	2	2.75	3
Part Time Clerk	1.2	1.5	2	1.7	1.8
Total # of Employees	4.2	5.25	6.0	6.4	6.8
Sales per Employee	$127,839	$159,068	$163,786	$161,031	$163,140

Accounting Plan & System

Accounting Plan

We will make use of an integrated accounting and point of sale software program operating on a network of personal computers. The use of a computerized system will enhance the operation of the store by automating all facets of inventory management and control, bookkeeping and financial reporting. This will allow us to have day to day oversight of our financial status.

Inventory management and control will be enhanced through the use of computer generated bar code stickers on all products. This code will include the stock number and source of each product. Levels of inventory will be monitored by tracking the flow of products from the time they are ordered, received, placed into stock and are removed from inventory by either being sold or returned to the supplier for credit. Updating of the cost of goods sold will automatically be translated into a new price for approval by the TDM or MDM.

The system will allow for multi-supplier sourcing that will enhance our ability to control costs. The TDM or MDM will be able to determine who the low cost supplier is, thus maximizing margins. Likewise, when items are sourced from two suppliers, such as with magazines, emphasis can be placed onmoving the items with the higher margins first so as to maximize profitability.

The system will allow for easy generation of purchase orders, receiving lists and pull lists for merchandise to be returned. Generation of purchase orders and return lists, payment of bills or receipt of payment, whether cash from a customer or a credit from a supplier, will result in the automatic updating of the appropriate accounting modules. The use of this system will reduce the time needed for bookkeeping, thus allowing the TDM, MDM and GM to concentrate on running the store.

The management of the goods carried, particularly the magazines, will be enhanced by the ability to generate sales history reports. Future stock levels can be adjusted upwards or downwards to reflect historical and seasonal trends. Items that don't sell can be eliminated. Ultimately, margins can be improved on the low margin, high volume magazines by using surplus cash to pay for direct subscriptions from the publishers.

Software

The program we have selected is called StoreWare(tm) Act Accounting Series from Cougar Mountain Software of Boise, Idaho. StoreWare(tm) includes:

- Point of Sale
- General Ledger
- Check Reconciliation
- Inventory
- Purchase Order
- Accounts Payable
- Payroll
- Invoicing
- Accounts Receivable
- LYNX (ASCII File Converter)

Cougar Mountain Software has been in business for nearly a decade and has supplied over 60,000 installations of the ACT series integrated accounting packages for businesses. The StoreWare software was introduced in the spring of 1991. It is one of the few truly integrated point of sale and accounting packages available at an affordable price to the small retail store. The software makes extensive use of pull down menus and online help screens to make the program easy to use.

Products, Pricing & Inventory Levels

Tobacco

Pricing

The pricing of the various types of tobacco products is a function of the competitive marketplace in which the tobacco shop competes. This results in a wide variation in the gross margin which can be earned on tobacco products. For example, the tobacco shop that sells domestic cigarettes and smokeless tobacco must compete against large competitors who are willing to earn a low margin on a large volume of these products. The successful tobacco shop will typically sell these items on a single pack/can basis. This allows the tobacco shop to charge a higher margin than the large competitors, typically 30% versus 7% to 17%. The marketplace for the other tobacco products is much more limited with other tobacco shops being the main competition. This allows the shops to earn a much higher margin of 45% to 60%, depending upon the product.

Inventory Levels

The establishment of the opening inventory levels is a key issue which a new tobacco store faces. The new store must balance the need for the broad selection of products, required to impress new customers with the capital needed to pay for the inventory. Careful attention must be paid to the selection of the products as cashflow will be restricted if too much start up capital is incorrectly spent on slower moving products. Our strategy is to open with a broad, but shallow selection of products.

Our computerized inventory tracking system will support this strategy by allowing us to monitor inventory levels, track sales levels and project the need to reorder stock on a daily basis. Our suppliers, who can deliver goods within 3 to 7 working days following placement of an order, will be relied upon to support this strategy.

Our strategy of maintaining a shallow level of inventory will allow us to support a much broader level of inventory than would otherwise be possible. The wholesale cost of our opening inventory will be $61,700. This level of inventory will support monthly sales of $32,000 based upon a compositestockturn of 4 to 4.5.

Due to the variety of tobacco products offered, multiple levels of pricing margins are required. The competitive environment establishes the Gross Margins that can be realized for any given product line. Domestic cigarettes are sold at the lowest levels, while the remainder of the products are priced at levels commensurate with the other smokeshops. A review of the prices of selected products at Jeff's Cigar Store shows that the industry average levels are appropriate for establishing our beginning price levels, as well as for use in our financial plans.

The following Table details the various products we will offer, sales splits by product, gross margin, expected stockturns and beginning inventory which will be required to support our first year sales target. As for the mix of products, we are using a level that is an average of the industry averages and the actual mix at Jeff's Cigar Store. This mix has further been adjusted by our TDM to reflect his experience in this market.

Projected Tobacco Sales and Beginning Inventory

				Beginning Inventory		
Tobacco Merchandise	*% of Total Sales*	*Target Retail Sales*	*Stock Turns*	*Retail Value*	*Margin*	*Cost*
Domestic Cigarettes	18.0	$55,700	26	$2,150	30	$1,500
Imported Cigarettes	12.0	50,000	20	2,500	40	1,500
Cigars	30.0	120,000	4	30,000	40	18,000
Pipe Tobacco	14.0	53,300	5	10,650	57	4,500
Pipes	11.0	37,500	2	18,750	60	7,500
Tobacco Accessories	9.0	30,000	4	7,500	60	3,000
Lighters	4.0	26,600	3	8,865	55	4,000
Smokeless Tobacco	2.0	7,400	26	285	30	200
Totals & Composites	100.0	$380,500	4.6	$80,700	45	$40,200

All of the major tobacco suppliers will require cash on delivery for the initial six months of operation. This will require that the beginning inventory be paid in full prior to opening of the store.

Suppliers

We have contacted all of the major tobacco suppliers as well as a number of the smaller suppliers. All have sent us price lists that have been entered into a computer database. The prices have been sorted and evaluated to determine who the low cost suppliers are. Our major suppliers and the products they will provide are listed below.

Suppliers...continued

Tobacco Suppliers

Type of Tobacco Products Offered:

Supplier	Cigars	Tobacco	Pipes	Accessories
International Cigar Hartford, FL	X	X	X	
Monroe Cigar Co. Carson Corners, NY	X		X	
Capital Tobacco Rockford, CA	X	X	X	X
Tobacco Unlimited Turnbridge, GA	X	X	X	X
Johnson & Fredericks Cigars Halstead, CA	X	X	X	X
Wyndham Int'l Ltd. Martin's Point, PA	X	X		

Detailed information on each of the above suppliers is available on request.

There are many other smaller suppliers for cigar and tobacco products and accessories we will use. Included among these are two local distributors, Stevenson Distribution and Kelly Tobacco Co. While both of these distributors carry many of the same products, comparison of their price lists shows that Stevenson Distribution has the best prices. A recent survey of local small retail outlets gave Stevenson the highest marks for service and consistent pricing policies.

The local distributors, along with wholesale outlets will be our primary sources for domestic cigarettes. A number ofsmaller suppliers will be our sources for import cigarettes. A key factor in one distributors favor is that they will stamp the import cigarettes with Washington cigarette stamps. We intend to purchase either unstamped or stamped cigarettes depending upon the cost savings offered by either approach.

Magazines & Newspapers

Pricing

The pricing of the mass market magazines is dictated by the level of competition and the exclusive distribution arrangements between the publishers and major local distributors. The local distributor typically sells magazines at 20% off suggested retail price. This is the discount offered to all retailers. National distributors offer discounts ranging from 25% to 45%. The wide range of discounts, the proper management of the title list and sourcing of the magazines will have a big impact on our bottom line. By sourcing as many titles as possible from the distributors offering the higher discounts, we expect to earn a gross margin of 31% on our domestic titles.

The discount we will receive on our foreign titles ranges from 20% to 35%. The market for these magazines, however, allows for mark-ups above the suggested retail. We will price all foreign titles with a 35% gross margin, except those titles that are competitively priced with a lower margin. This results in a composite gross margin of 312% for all magazines.

This margin can be increased by the collection of retail display allowances from the publishers. Typically, publishers will pay the retailer an RDA in return for featuring the publishers" titles through full cover displays and by placement of the magazines in high traffic areas. To collect the RDA, the retailer must sign a contract with the publisher. Typically, the RDA is equal to 10% of the cover price. The level of the margin is dependent upon the number of titles carried and how many of the titles receive full cover display.In practice, they equal 7%. Not all publishers offer RDAs. The design of our racks will allow for full cover display of over 35% of our titles and full masthead display for all remaining titles. This will allow us to maximize our RDA levels.

The collection of the RDAs is no small task as significant documentation is required by the publishers before they will pay the RDA. There are collection services available to assist the retailer in collecting the RDA. These firms will negotiate these contracts on behalf of the retailer and file the necessary paperwork with the publisher to collect the RDA. In return, the collection agency keeps 10% to 20% of the RDA. RDAs are typically paid quarterly with a 6 month time lag between request for payment and receipt of the RDA.

The terms of payment and return policy for the magazines are key elements in maximizing profits. Terms of payment are typically 30 days net, thus allowing the retailer the opportunity to generate cash flow to pay for the magazines. The distributors and publishers return policy allows the retailer to return unsold magazines for a credit so that in essence you are only paying for magazines. This allows the retailer to order sufficient copies to assure that sufficient stock is on hand to meet demand without having to be concerned with absorbing the cost of the extras.

It is imperative that the distributor's policies regarding returns are followed. The period allowed for returning outdated issues is limited and the length of this period varies by distributor. In addition, each distributor requires that you prove that the magazines did not sell. You do so by either returning the masthead, the cover or the whole magazine. Failure to properly follow the distributors requirements can result in rejection of your credit request. All of this requires effective management of the magazine inventory.

The return of the magazines and mastheads results in two other operational issues, shipping costs of returns and disposal of stripped magazines. Shipping costs are minimal since most distributors require the return of only the masthead. Disposal of the magazines can present an ongoing waste disposal cost issue if not properly handled. We will minimize this cost by recycling, when possible.

The management of the magazine inventory will be easilyimplemented through the use of the integrated accounting and point-of-sale software. This system will provide for swift processing of the magazines with identification of the source of supply via bar code labels. The system will insure that returns are properly handled on a timely basis. The system will also provide us with the ability to source our magazines from the most cost effective suppliers. The system will give us the ability to track the performance of suppliers and to establish sales histories for magazine titles so that stock levels can be adjusted to minimize costs while maintaining a high level of customer service.

Inventory Levels

The typical stockturn for magazines is 4 to 52 with 9.4 being our composite value. Approximately fifty percent of the magazines are typically returned for credit, although we will have a much higher level of returns during startup. To achieve our sales target of $200,000 in annual sales, we will carry a beginning inventory that supports monthly sales of $22,000. The retail value of this inventory is $29,300 and a wholesale cost of $20,000. Our ability to return unsold titles allows us to maintain a larger inventory than would otherwise be justified. In the longer term we will strive to improve the percentage of magazines sold from 50% to 75% through tight management of inventory levels. If we can achieve this goal, our initial level of inventory will be sufficient to support our long tcrm salcs goals, except for seasonal variations.

Suppliers

Traverse Bay News of Leland is the primary distributor for this area and serves the needs of all local magazine outlets. They offer the standard 20% discount off of the suggested list price. On the positive side, Bay provides local delivery. The negative aspects of dealing with Bay are 1) terms of payment are net 7 days, 2) they have a much shorter period for accepting returns 3) they are more likely to reject magazines as not being theirs and 4) their discounts are the lowest available. We will use Bay as our supplier for approximately 45% of our titles.

An alternative to Bay is to purchase magazines from large national distributors, such as Ingram Periodicals, International Periodicals Distributor, or Eastern News. These distributors offer many specialty titles that Bay does not carry along with a number ofmagazines that Bay does offer and at a discount off suggested retail of 25% to 40%. All of these distributors pay the cost of shipping the magazines. The positives of dealing with these distributors are 1) larger discounts, 2) terms of payment are net 30 days and 3) they are easier to deal with regarding returns. The negative aspect of dealing with the distributors is the time delay due to their remoteness. However, we will actively seek to use these distributors due to the significant increase in margins available to us and the superior terms.

Approximately 28% of our titles will be sourced from these distributors. The net result of this will be to increase our composite margin for domestic magazines to a respectable 31%, exclusive of RDA payments. We will also source a large selection of specialty titles from a number of small distributors and directly from publishers who are willing to deal directly with a retail shop. The discounts available, terms of payment and return policies for these sources are similar to those offered by Ingram, IPD and Eastern.

The remaining 27% of our titles will be foreign magazines and newspapers. We will price all foreign magazines with a minimum gross margin of 35%, thus assuring a decent level of profit on these titles.

Implementation Plan

Facilities

Standard will be located in a leased retail space in the Town Center area. We are presently negotiating lease arrangements for retail space in the Promenade. The space is located in Building 1, Space 1-K. The size of this space, 1,875 square feet supports the space requirements needed for a combined tobacco shop and full line magazine store.

The space will be provided as a standard vanilla shell. This includes finish of all outside interior walls with wallboard ready for final finish, suspended ceiling, electrical service, lighting (100 foot candle level at 4 feet above the floor), complete bathroom, and heating, ventilation and cooling system. In addition, the landlord will reimburse us for up to $2.00 per square foot of improvements.

The term of the proposed lease is five years. The proposed rentpayments are as follows:

Month 1:	$16.00 per square foot
Months 2, 3, and 13:	$ 0.00 per square foot
Months 4 through 12:	$16.00 per square foot
Months 14 through 18:	$16.00 per square foot
Months 19 through 36:	$16.50 per square foot
Months 37 through 60:	$17.00 per square foot

In addition, we must pay for all utilities consumed and our pro rata share of taxes, insurance costs, and common area maintenance. This cost is expected to be $2.75 per square foot for the first year of our lease.

Capital Requirements: Improvements

The improvements that we will need to make include:

Improvement	Estimated Cost
Interior paint finish of wallboard	$300
Carpeting	3,000
Slatwall display board (10 sheets)	1,000
Humidor (10' by 20')	20,000
Wall with door to back room	500
Special Lighting	1,000
Computer electrical outlets	1,000
Telephone lines (in building)	500
Computer cabling	500
Direct ventilation duct in tobacco department	500
Contingency	1,700
Total of Improvements	$30,000

Capital Requirements: Equipment/Fixtures

		Sourcing	
Equipment	**New/Used**	**Buy**	**Lease**
Magazine Racks	New		$20,000
Display Counters (10)-6'	Used		4,000
Merchandise Racks 50'	New		5,000
Storage shelvesNew/	Used		1,000
Humidor Cabinet	Used	1,000	
Newspaper Racks	New	750	
Magazine Stocking Racks	New	300	
POS Counters (3)	New		1,800
Computer & Printer	New		3,300
POS Terminals (3)	New		7,500
Point-Of-Sale Software	New	1,500	
Miscellaneous Software	New	500	
Outdoor Sign	New		4,500
Window Sign	New		1,500
Interior Signage	New	500	
Miscellaneous Tobacco	New	1,000	
Stools	New	100	
Desk	Used	150	
File Cabinet	Used	100	
SafeNew/	Used	175	
Phone System	Used	500	
Contingency	Used	2,000	
Total Capital/Equipment Needs		$8,575	$48,590

FINANCIAL

We believe that the initial funding of $205,100 will be sufficient to carry Standard Tobacco & News through to initial profitability. These financial needs will be met through a blend of bank loans, equipment leases and personal cash investment. The loans and leases will be secured by the value of the capital equipment purchased, the value of the inventory. In addition, Dwayne Peters will continue in his present position at GE thus providing a personal guarantee of payment.

We anticipate that we will be able to sustain a minimum gross margin of 39%. We will seek to increase this level through management of our inventory sourcing. We anticipate that, after our initial year of operation, we will be able to sustain a net return on sales of 16% to 17%.

Assumptions underlying our financial projections are:

- Partners contribute $60,000 cash during startup phase.

- Partners defer taking any draws until monthly income levels exceed $2,500.

- Loan term is five years with interest fixed at 12% per annum.

- Lease term is five years with an assumed cost of financing of 18% per annum.

- Depreciation is calculated on all equipment assuming a five year recovery period with the regular MACRS method and the half year convention.

- Receivables are not a major factor as all sales are cash sales. Credit card sales are assumed to be 10% of total sales and will be collected through immediate electronic credits. An allowance of 3% for the cost of credit sales.

- Payables are net cash for all tobacco products and candy. Magazines are net 7 days and net 30 days depending upon the supplier.

- The composite inventory turn is 4.8 time per year. The individual turns for each product are as stated in the business plan. Inventory calculations and cashflow requirements are based upon the individual turns figures, not the composite.

- Minimum cash on hand will be maintained at $20,000 although our projections do not show that we will reach this level. Arrangements have been made with a family member for a $15,000 line to provide for short term cash needs to maintain this balance.

Detailed budgets underlying the financial projections are available for further review and discussion.

APPENDIX I

Market Size

General

The research we have conducted reveals that there exists no direct measure of the metro tobacco and magazine market. There are two methods that can be used to give us an indication of the relative size of each of these markets. Briefly, they are as follows:

Method 1

This approach takes overall sales figures for the various retail outlets for the metro market and multiplies them by the industry average for percent of sales for each product by retail outlet. The result is an estimate of the sales of each product attributable to each retail sales channel. The sum of all sales channel figures gives an estimate of the total retail market for the metro areal. Retail sales figures are reported in the "1987 Census of Retail Trade for Washington" published by the Bureau of the Census, and industry averages are reported in the "1990 Data Book," published by the Periodicals Institute.

Method 2

This method estimates the available market by multiplying the average consumer unit expenditures for each product by the appropriate number of consumer units for our market area. Consumer expenditures are reported in the "Consumer Expenditure Survey, 1987" published by the Bureau of Labor Statistics. Information on numbers of consumer units in our market area was given in the "Market Data Report - Town Center Area" published by the North County Development Agency.

Tobacco

Method 1

The overall sales figures for various retail outlets can be found in the 1987 Census of Retail Trade for Washington, published by the U.S. Department of Commerce. This is the most recent issue of this publication. Industry averages for percent of sales for various retail outlets can be found in the "1990 Data Book" published by the Periodicals Institute. This Data book provides data on retail sales for magazines, paperbacks, candy and, indirectly, tobacco markets. The Periodicals Institute has compiled information from various industry publications and surveys.

The following Table details the estimated available sales for each market in which Standard will participate.

1987				
	Retail Market		**Tobacco Sales**	
SIC	**Category**	**Total Sales**	**% of Total**	**Dollars**
		A	B	A x B
531	Dept.Stores	$1,056,461,000	1.16	$12,254,948
541	Grocery Stores	1,316,392,000	3.25	42,782,740
549	Misc.food Stores	10,795,000	3.25	350,838
591	Drug Stores	139,012,000	6.20	8,618,744
5993	Tobacco stores	3,364,000	75.00	2,523,000
	Total Tobacco Sales			$66,530,269

Method 2

The "Consumer Expenditure Survey, 1987" published by the U.S. Department of Labor, Bureau of Labor Statistics in June, 1990, provides information on expenditures for various consumable and non-consumable products. These expenditures are provided in tabular form for various categories of consumer units. We have used the information provided in Table 2, "Average Annual Expenditures per Consumer Unit by Income Level." These are national averages that need to be adjusted to reflect the usage in our area. We can arrive at a "metro usage factor" by dividing the composite metro average consumer unit expenditure of $178 by the composite national average of $232. This gives us a "metro usage factor" of 0.77. The values given in the following table are the adjusted Portland average expenditures for each group of consumer units.

Information on the number of households within a given distance of the Town Center can be found in the "Market Data Report - Town Center Area," published by the North County Development Agency. For our purposes, we will use the figures for numbers of households within 10 miles of the Town Center. This roughly corresponds to the 25 minute travel time that was used in Method 1. The following table summarizes this data and shows the resultant calculation of market size.

Estimated Tobacco Sales in the Metro Market

	Avg. Ann. Expenditures/ Consumer Unit	# of Hshlds. w/in 10 Mi. of Town Ctr.	Total Sales/ Income
	A	**B**	**A x B**
Income			
$75,000 or more	$200.20	14,391	$2,881,033
$50,000 to 74,999	200.20	28,306	5,666,824
$35,000 to 49,999	214.83	48,078	10,328,653
$25,000 to 34,999	204.05	51,111	10,429,205
$15,000 to 24,999	177.87	63,2421	1,248,871
Under $15,000	141.94	92,172	13,082,629
Total Tobacco Sales			$53,637,215

Summary

The comparison of the values we have derived for the retail tobacco market in the metro area are consistent. Using Method 1, we arrive at a total of $66,530,269 while Method 2 gives us $53,637,215. These values compare favorably, thus validating our approaches. We will use the Method 1 estimate available tobacco market in our performance calculations.

Magazines

An estimate of the magazine market can be derived using the same Methods and information sources as for tobacco.

Candy

In the same manner as above, an estimate of the candy market can bederived.

BIBLIOGRAPHY

"1991 Industry Report," *Smokeshop*, September/October, 1991.

Tobacco Industry Profile 1990, The Tobacco Institute, Washington, D.C.

"The True Look of the Discount Industry," *Discount Merchandiser*, July, 1988.

"1990 Smokeshop Industry Report," *Smokeshop*, June/July, 1990.

Operating Results of Mass Retail Stores and the Mass Retailers' Merchandising Report, International Mass Retail Association, Washington, D.C., 1990.

"What's Hot, What's Not," *Supermarket Business*, March, 1989.

1990 Data Book, Periodicals Institute, Inc., West Caldwell, N.J., 1991.

The Study of Magazine Buying Patterns, Conducted by Audits & Surveys, Publishers Clearing House, 1991.

"The Realities and Myths of Marketing Sophisticates," *Magazine & Bookseller*, November, 1991.

Consumer Expenditure Survey, 1987, Bulletin 2354, U.S. Department of Labor, Bureau of Labor Statistics, June, 1990.

"Magazine Readers Are Smarter & Richer," *Magazine & Bookseller*, January, 1991.

"Dispelling Some RDA Myths," *Magazine & Bookseller*, January, 1991.

Salad Packaging

BUSINESS PLAN

LYONS & COYNE, INC.

11695 San Pedro Dr.
San Francisco, CA 87239

June 19, 1993

Salad Ready is a pre-packaged, ready-to-eat salad created by a company seeking to fill the market desire for foods that are both convenient and healthy. This plan is an example of a company attempting to make an innovative food product available to larger markets.

SALAD PACKAGING BUSINESS PLAN

COMPANY OBJECTIVES

The aim of Lyons & Coyne, Inc. is to manufacture and market an innovative food product: a fresh and ready-to-eat leaf lettuce salad package.

The product Salad Ready will have wide appeal to a large variety of market segments nationwide, from consumers to the hotel, restaurant, and institutional markets. The strategy of Lyons & Coyne, however, is to build a consumer brand in successively larger segments of the market, region by region, and to build sales to H/R/I markets at the same time.

Profitability will be demonstrated in the first year of operation: cash flow will be generated in amounts that will permit extension of existing operations, and new regional market entries, in the first five projected years.

The firm's financial objective is to reach a point where stock can be offered publicly. The factors that make this possible are the size of the market, lead time of the company over competitors, and its dedication to stay ahead through an aggressive marketing strategy and a solid R&D program.

PRODUCT

Product Description

Salad Ready is a consumer food product -- fresh, washed, bite-sized, detached leaves of leaf lettuce, contained in a sealed, transparent, polypropylene bag.

The product concept flows from the European culinary tradition of "salad" -- a tasteful selection of appetizing and eye-appealing green leafy lettuces. These lettuces include romaine, radicchio, mache, etc.

The packaged version of this concept places it in the rapidly growing group of high-quality, premium-priced, convenience-based products which fit with the emerging American family and lifestyle.

- ❑ Variety of salad greens eliminates need to buy heads of several kinds of lettuces, mix portions of those heads, and store the unused portions
- ❑ Sustained freshness for at least five days if bag is maintained at proper temperature
- ❑ Ready-to-use -- eliminates trimming, washing, drying and cutting the salad
- ❑ Pre-selection of highest quality green
- ❑ Maintenance of nutritional content through the retail cold-chain
- ❑ Hygienic protection of produce from dust, uncontrolled spraying spill-overs, or easy touching and tampering

Salad Ready is manufactured through an industrial process. The bag containing the lettuces is made of transparent polypropylene. Pressurized air is added to the pouch before sealing to allow vapor exchange and to protect leaves from being crushed or bruised.

The recommended shelf life varies between 5 and 20 days, depending on the quantity of lettuce involved, the combination of leaf lettuce types, and the quality of the customer's storage facilities.

The Salad Ready product line will include:

Contents

- The "combination" product (mixture of leaf lettuce types)
- The "single variety" product (single kind of leaf lettuce)

Sizes

- 1/2 lb. bag (11 x 9 inch bag) and 1/4 lb (8" x 6" bag) for the retail market
- 1 lb. and 5 lb. for the institutional market.

Proprietary Position

There is currently no similar product on the market in the U.S. Existing products that come closest to this product are quite different in content, containing compacted shredded vegetables or iceberg lettuce instead of loose-leaf vegetables. They also differ in appearance, sold in a cloudy package instead of transparent film.

Salad Ready-type products have been successfully marketed for five years in Switzerland, and were introduced only a year ago in France, where they have already taken one-third of the linear shelf space in the chain stores and supermarkets. (After only nine months of operation, the leading French company is currently under buyout negotiations for as much as four times its initial capitalization.)

The processing technology for Salad Ready, which was developed in Europe, falls in the realm of "trade secrets." Although there is no patent protection, the technology is proprietary and unique, based upon a combination of machines, including vegetable processing units as well as other food product processing units;a specific design for some of the machines;and a particular set of quality control methods.

However ingenious, the process remains relatively simple at first glance: raw material is trimmed and cored by hand; selected raw material is then mechanically and automatically cut, washed, rinsed, spin-dried, weighed and packaged. In fact, this proprietary process know-how is necessary to assure the distinctive high quality of the product and avoid production problems that lead to a deterioration of quality.

Lyons & Coyne, Inc. has secured the source of know-how via a license option granted by the leading French company manufacturing Salad Ready-type products.

Experience in Europe shows that Salad Ready know-how can be mastered only after a one-year learning curve. This will give the management of Lyons & Coyne, Inc. the time to close at least one one-to-two-year contract with a major chain store company before the competition comes in.

Product Potential

It is anticipated that as soon as operations begin, an R&D program will be instituted, conducting continuous consumer research to determine changes in public preference and market trends as they occur. Again, Salad Ready-type product experience in Europe shows that continuous product development is a necessity to stay ahead of competition and grow.

The relative simplicity of the technology and its production capacity flexibility permit quick and inexpensive adaptation of the process to new products. The product characteristics that could be modified in the course of business are:

Contents

- ❑ Mixture of lettuces
- ❑ Addition of other vegetables (radishes, mushrooms, olives, etc.)
- ❑ Addition of other loose ingredients (nuts, corn, etc.)
- ❑ Addition of other packaged products (salad dressing samples)

Packaging

- ❑ Dimensions
- ❑ Packaging material
- ❑ Graphics, labelling

Salad Ready has a high capacity for adaptation to regional differences, different market segmentation needs, and food consumption trends, because it can easily accommodate variations around its basic two-fold concept of freshness and convenience.

MARKET TRENDS AND POTENTIAL

Consumer Market Overview

All indications are that the U.S. market is poised for growth in the green, leafy lettuces category, and that salads are increasingly important as a component of everyday American diets.

Fresh fruits and vegetables are already the fastest growing category in U.S. supermarkets. This fact is propelled by the strong consumer trend to eat more fresh produce. Per capita fresh vegetable consumption in the United States (excluding potatoes) increased to a record 100.9 pounds in 1982, up from 89.1 pounds in 1972. According to the USDA, which tracks trends in the sale of specific vegetables, fresh lettuce consumption increased 28% between 1962 and 1982.

Most of this lettuce consumption takes place in the form of salads, although some is used as garnish on sandwiches. A study done for Progressive Grocer Magazine in 1984, by Leo J.Shapiro Associates, polled American consumers at random about their salad usage. The results, which are projectible to the population at large, were:

- ❑21% are serving more salads
- ❑72% are serving the same number of salads
- ❑7% are serving fewer salads

Overall Market Size for Lettuces

We estimate that the overall lettuce market, including both iceberg, or "head," lettuce and green leafy lettuces is a $2.5 billion market at retail, and a $1.03 billion market at farm level. Of this, green leafy lettuces comprise roughly 20% of the retail market on a weight and value basis. (These figures do not include the imports of exotic and specialty lettuces such as radicchio and mache, which have been increasing.)

Consumer and Demographic Trends

The major consumer and demographic trends which play a key role in selection of food products are as follows:

- ❑More women working outside of the home
- ❑Smaller households requiring packaging of smaller portions
- ❑Sophistication of consumers' eating habits (consumers are looking for high quality, more adventurous flavors, and new eating sensations)
- ❑Consumer concern about fitness and health

--Source: *Food Processing Magazine*, 8/86

We believe that these trends are favorable to the success of a high-quality, premium-priced, convenience-based product like Salad Ready.

Leaf Lettuce Usage and Trends

American consumers are demanding a greater percentage of leaf lettuces in their diets vis-à-vis the traditional iceberg lettuce usage.

In a 1984 study done for the California Iceberg Lettuce Commission, consumer researchers found that almost 5 percent of the American public used leaf lettuce exclusively.

Current Lettuce Usage

- ❑Leaf Lettuce Only-- 4%
- ❑Iceberg and Leaf Lettuce-- 35%
- ❑Iceberg only-- 61%

Although iceberg retains its strong hold in the supermarket basket, leaf lettuces already have loyal followers. We believe that this following is growing.

Type of Lettuce Most Preferred

- ❑Iceberg Lettuce-- 78%
- ❑Romaine-- 7%
- ❑Red Leaf-- 3%
- ❑Green Leaf-- 3%
- ❑Bibb-- 2%
- ❑Boston-- 2%
- ❑Butter-- 1%
- ❑Spinach-- 1%
- ❑Endive-- 1%
- ❑Don't Know/No Preference-- 2%

Demographics of Consumers and Purchasers

Although we believe that the demographics of leaf lettuce consumers are more up-scale than those of iceberg lettuce consumers, both are members of the "salad user" category.

Ninety-eight percent of all homes serve salads. "Heavy users" were identified in a 1984 study by the California Iceberg Lettuce Commission as differing from the household population in general by being middle aged, better educated, and more affluent.

Women represent four out of five daily salad consumers, and three out of four people who consume salad four to six times a week basis. In ethnic terms, whites are the heaviest salad consumers overall; 92% of those eating salads daily are white. Leaf lettuce purchasers are more upscale consumers than salad users as a whole.

Usage Patterns in Regional Markets

Higher salad consumption occurs in suburban and central city areas than in nonmetropolitan (rural) areas; this is a constant throughout our examination of regional markets.

Household usage of fresh lettuce is tracked by The Food Institute, which shows the following differences regionally:

Fresh Lettuce - Annual Average Household Usage
(Quantity per Household Per Week in Pounds)

- ❑Northeast-- 1.22
- ❑North Central-- 1.14
- ❑South-- 0.89
- ❑West-- 1.42

- ❑Total U.S.-- 1.13

--Source: *"Facts in Food Consumption"*
The Food Institute, 4/85

Percentage of Households Using Lettuce - Annual Average

- ❑Northeast-- 68.5%
- ❑North Central-- 66.5%
- ❑South-- 55.1%
- ❑West-- 75.4%

- ❑Total U.S.-- 65.1%

--Source: *Facts in Food Consumption*
The Food Institute, 4/85

It can be seen that the West and Northeast consistently rank highest in terms of both usage patterns; pounds consumed and percentage of households using.

This regional pattern holds true for the percentage of consumers who have prior purchase experience with leaf lettuce:

Percentage of Consumers who have Purchased Leaf Lettuce

- ❑Northeast-- 51.9%
- ❑North Central-- 45.0%
- ❑South-- 46.7%
- ❑West-- 70.0%

- ❑Total U.S.-- 51.8%

--Source: Vance Research/The Packer

Consumer attitude information by region is not currently available to us on salad or Salad Ready Products, but a working assumption is that consumers in the Northeast have more "refined palates" and sophisticated tastes than the nation as a whole, and that consumers in the Western states tend to enjoy fresh foods, particularly produce.

COMPETITION

DOLE Dole did some early testing in the prepared salad market, using their "Dole" label rather than "Bud." They test-marketed pre-cut vegetables in a plastic packet in the East and Northwest, but terminated the market tests. One product attempted was a salad mixture of primarily iceberg, with some added vegetables for color.

CAMPBELL Campbell entered the prepared salad market in 1984, with controlled-portion, pre-packaged salads of the pasta variety, under the brand "Fresh Chef Salads." These salads are sold in the dairy case; the product line includes 9 salads and 6 sauces. In March 1986, Campbell acquired Mrs. Giles Kitchens, Lynchburg, VA, a privately held company with 1985 sales of $18 million, generated from 35 varieties of salads. In the branded produce category, Campbell has recently tested two varieties of exotic mushrooms in the eastern U S. and

COMPETITION...*continued*

Chicago, and has also tested Campbell's Fresh brand asparagus in markets throughout the country.

KRAFT Kraft already has involvement in the salad business from the salad dressings category.

INTERHARVEST Interharvest reportedly entered retail markets in the East, Midwest, and West with a salad-bowl package containing an 8 oz. bowl of romaine, chicory, and a tomato on the top. To date we do not know whether this was a market test or a full-fledged continuing entry; however, consumers in the Western markets rejected this product.

ORVAL KENT Orval Kent Company, Wheeling, IL, is a $100 million company in the prepared salad (non-lettuce) category. It sells under its "Signature" label, and has 23 varieties sold in bulk into the deli section. Their most recent product entry is an extension of the bulk salads -- "Salad Singles" brand -- which plans to go national with packaged individual portions of non-lettuce salads. Currently, the brand has 30% market coverage in Philadelphia, Los Angeles, New York, Chicago, Baltimore, and Washington, DC.

A strength for this company is an existing distribution network which reaches 90% of the deli sections in the US.

BLUE RIDGE FARMS Blue Ridge Farms, Brooklyn, NY, is a $55 million company in the bulk, prepared, non-lettuce salad business. It sells 102 varieties of salads into supermarket delicatessans.

CONTINENTAL SALAD PROCESSORS Continental Salad Processors, Los Angeles, CA is one of about seven "cutters" (companies serving the H/R/I market with pre-cut iceberg lettuce salad mixes) in Los Angeles. Pre-cut lettuce represents about 60% of their volume, pre-cut cabbage comprises about 20%, and the remainder is in such items as onions, celery, broccoli, carrots and zucchini. The company was founded in January 1986, and is headed by Dennis Edwards, formerly marketing manager at Ready Pac Produce, and Maurice Portnoy, formerly general production manager of the international division of DuPont. They sell primarily to jobbers and distributors, who in turn supply restaurants and hotels.

PRE-PAK Pre-Pak, Sacramento, CA, has been in the packaged vegetable business for 10 years, and have recently expanded operations to include regular fresh produce merchandising and delivery. Their primary markets for packaged pre-cut iceberg lettuce are the H/R/I markets. Their marketing area is California, north of Fresno.

CUT-N-READY Cut-N-Ready, East Bay, CA, was, at one time, a producer of specialty pre-cut iceberg-based mixes for mostly-institutional markets, and was owned by DelMonte. It was bought back by the founders and is rumored to be in bankruptcy.

CROSSET & CO. Crosset & Co., Cincinnati, OH, is reputed to be the biggest producer of salad in 4-5 states. They produce both 8 oz. and institutional sizes.

GRAND UNION Grand Union is reportedly importing 1000 packs of Salad Ready product from France weekly. This program just began, and the results are yet to be documented.

Strengths Against Competition of Lyons & Coyne, Inc.

Lyons & Coyne, Inc. will have the following advantages against competition:

- ❑ flexibility to make a quick start
- ❑ attention to continuous quality control
- ❑ a fresh start: no assumption by existing customers that the product is iceberg-based.

Competitors' Likely Market Share

Lyons & Coyne, Inc. will enjoy a time advantage against the competition of approximately 9 months in terms of ability to backwards engineer the process and know-how. However, we believe that this lead-time will protect the company from substantial competition for up to three years. We anticipate having a 60% market share after three years.

MARKETING STRATEGY

Product Characteristics and Product Mix

The initial products offered by Lyons & Coyne, Inc. will be:

Content
- ❑ A mixture of lettuces
- ❑ One single type of leaf lettuce

Package Size
- ❑ 8 oz. consumer pack
- ❑ 4 oz. consumer pack
- ❑ Institutional packs in sizes from 16 oz. to 5 lb.

All products will share the following characteristics:

- ❑ High eye appeal
- ❑ Pieces sized to consumer preference
- ❑ Long shelf-life (5-20 days)
- ❑ Branded
- ❑ Transparent polypropelene bag as packaging material
- ❑ Competitively priced with bulk, but with a value added price premium for convenience

PRICE

FOB prices will be set with three objectives in mind:
1 The price will be right in order to penetrate the market
2 The price should always cover the costs of production
3 The price should allow for profitability

Product cost will not vary greatly with size of package, since the form-fill-seal machinery has maximum speed regardless of size. Thus, price will decrease with volume of production. We estimate that the experience curve effect will allow a decrease of cost of 20% when sales volume doubles.

Allowing for 15% profit before taxes, the FOB price will be:

	12,000/day	24,000/day
8 oz packet	$0.93	$0.83
4 oz packet	$0.83	$0.66

FOB price will be adjusted every week in order to take into account daily variations in the price of the raw material (raw materials account for 20% of product cost).

Lyons & Coyne, Inc. pricing policy will be flexible enough to maintain market position once competition arrives. This will be done by providing for better quality and extra features without necessitating dramatic price reductions which may jeopardize "positioning" as a high quality product.

MARKET SELECTION AND ROLL-OUT FOR SALAD READY PRODUCTS

Geographic Market Selection

The market entry strategy is to enter regional markets progressively. San Francisco is seen as the first entry market due to its closeness to produce suppliers in the year-round Salinas growing area. San Francisco also has the demographic/up-scale profile of a Salad Ready-accepting market.

Other Markets -- Export

Lyons & Coyne, Inc. intends to explore the possibility of export to Asian markets, particularly Japan. The current unfavorable export climate caused by the strong US dollar may impede rapid development of Pacific Rim markets, but several California produce brokerages have begun to offer lettuce to Pacific Rim customers.

Other Products

Lyons & Coyne, Inc. anticipates that it will add other products to its offerings.

We also believe that we may gain a revenue source by offering to serve as a sampling medium for salad dressing companies that wish to encourage trial of new products by salad companies.

Promotional Programs and Costs

Lyons & Coyne, Inc. intends to begin with an initial promotional budget of 5% of sales. This is in line with advertising-to-sales ratios reported in the preserved fruits category by Advertising Age magazine.

Brand-building activities will include:

- ❑In-store demonstrations
- ❑Public relations activities
- ❑Point-of-purchase materials (especially important since many shop pers buy produce items on impulse)
- ❑Cooperative advertising with grocers

OPERATIONS AND MANAGEMENT

Location

The first facility will be established close to the San Francisco Bay Area market (either South Bay or East Bay). The proximity of the Salinas-Watsonville supply region will be a cost-reducing factor. A specific sity will be chosed by focusing on the following issues: wage rates, labor unions, access to transportation, taxes, and county inspections.

Facilities

The business requires a 1.5 acre industrial site with a covered space of 10,000 sq.ft.:

- ❑4,000 sq.ft. for production itself (cold room)
- ❑4,000 sq.ft. storage for raw material and final product (cold room)
- ❑2,000 sq.ft. office

Open and remaining land comprises:

- ❑30,000 sq.ft. receiving-shipping area
- ❑10,000 sq.ft. for future production-area extension

There are two ways of securing the facility:

❑Lease an existing unused facility (vegetable processing plan, dairy, etc.); improve it; bring in equipment

❑Rent production space from a packer and bring in only specific equipment

Both options will be explored in the development stage.

For the present financial forecast, we have assumed that we will be leasing an existing unused facility. Cost estimates are:

Site improvement	$100,000
Facility leasing	$9,500/mo

MANUFACTURING PROCESS

Production Line

One production line consists of the following items:

- 1 preparation table with conveyors (operated by 16 people): raw leaf lettuce heads are trimmed and cored by hand
- 1 water chiller: to maintain wash water at low temperature
- 1 automatic cutter: selected raw material is cut to required size
- 2 automatic washers: one to wash cut leaves in agitated water; one to wash and rinse cut leaves
- 5 spin dryers (operated by two people): cut leaves are dried
- 1 dumper: cut leaves return to original shape
- 1 electronic scale: cut leaves are weighed in lots
- 2 automated fill-form & seal machines: cut leaves are packaged in air-filled sealed bags
- 1 automated carton packing machine: bags are put in cartons
- 8 transfer conveyors: product is transferred from each one of above units to the next

Total acquisition cost for the equipment is $420,000 (FOB). It is anticipated that all equipment will be leased. Cost estimates involved are the following:

❑Equipment leasing cost	$16,000/mo
❑Utilities	$3,640/mo
❑Maintenance	$1,500/mo

Labor

A shift that operates an eight-hour schedule at full capacity will comprise 18 people working on the production line and two people loading and unloading supplies and final product cartons. A shift is supervised by 1.5 technicians. Cost estimates are based on conservative figures for Monterey County, where labor is heavily unionized ($7.25/hour and 30% benefits).

❑Unskilled labor	$35,200/month	(20 people and benefits)
❑Supervision	$3,250/month	(1.5 person and benefits)

Raw Materials

Raw materials used in the manufacturing process comprise:

❑ Leaf lettuce in bulk, for which cost variations have both high frequency and high range. For financial projections, an average cost of $.408/lb FOB has been assumed. Bulk lettuce will be purchased daily from wholesalers and from grower-shippers. Transportation costs by truck are estimated at $6,600/mo. Storage in cold chambers should last on the average of one day. Seasonality may lead exceptionally to a five-day storage time.

❑ Polypropylene film, for which the cost of printed film has been estimated at $.047 per 1/2 lb. pack. A 10- to 20-day inventory is to be maintained.

❑ Cartons, at an estimated cost of $.032 per 1 lb pack. A 10-day inventory is to be maintained.

Cost of Sales Breakdown

Financial productions for this business plan are based on one Salad Ready product defined as:

Net weight: 1/2 lb

Content:

romaine	30%
escarole	35%
endive	30%
radicchio	5%

Cost per pack	*1 shift*	*2 shifts*
Materials		
Raw FOB	.204	.204
Transportation	.025	.025
Film	.025	.025
Printing	.022	.022
Cartons	.031	.031
Labor		
Unskilled	.134	.134
Skilled	.012	.012
Overhead		
Building	.200	.200
Add. Land	.015	.008
Equipment	.061	.030
Utilities	.014	.007
Maintenance	.006	.003
Cost of Sales	.569	.511

SALES AND MANAGEMENT

Sales

Sales will be managed through one or more brokers. The brokers will be responsible for getting daily orders from store buyers, and for arranging pickup and distribution.

Sales expenses, including broker commissions, promotion, and administration, but excluding the Sales Manager's salary, are estimated at the rate of 15% of sales.

Management

The management team consists of four key positions:

- **General Manager** Responsible for achieving projected growth. This person is the overall supervisor of all operations and is in charge of R&D, marketing, finance, and personnel.

- **Production Manager** Directs plant operations and maintenance; manages production and quality control. The production manager proposes and implements all necessary equipment and labor changes to meet the volumes, costs, and standards planned.

- **Sales Manager** Negotiates brokers' contracts, follows up on orders; organizes customer service. The tasks of the Sales Manager include promotion and demonstration implementation.

- **Purchasing Manager** Negotiates on a day-to-day, and possibly contractual, basis with grower-shippers and wholesalers. The purchasing manager is responsible for ordering the quality and quantity of raw material necessary to meet orders and standards.

The team will be assisted in the start-up stage and in the early production stage, by the CEO of the company licensing to Lyons & Coyne, Inc. the know-how as a trade secret. As part of the licensing agreement, this executive will train the General Manager and the Production Manger and will advise management as principal consultant.

Selling and Administrative Costs

For purposes of projecting financial data, the following estimates have been selected:

Salaries = $11,500 and 30% benefits

General Manager	$5,000/mo
Prod. Manager	$3,500/mo
Sales Manager	$3,000/mo (1/2 time)
Purch. Manager	$3,000/mo (1/2 time)
Office Expenses	$700/mo
Sales Expenses	15% of sales

Cost per pack	*1 shift*	*2 shifts*
Sales Expenses	.094	.094
Promotion	.047	.047
Salaries	.057	.028
Office Expenses	.002	.002
Total Sales & Admin	.200	.171

Inception Team

Founders of Lyons & Coyne, Inc. are:

Michael Lyons, mechanical engineer and financial manager; Palo Alto, CA
Mary Coyne, medical nutritionist and marketing trainee; Palo Alto, CA

The founders have added to their venture:

Barbara Keck, management and marketing consultant, President of Keck & Co., Inc., Business Consultants; Atherton, CA
Jim Cloyd, future production manager, previously production manager with Bill Cloyd's Shredded Lettuce Plant; Salinas, CA
Sylvain Darnay, as principal consultant; CEO of Salagastronomie, the leading French Company for Salad Ready-type products; Paris, France

Design and Development Plans

Before the product is ready to be manufactured and placed on the market, several steps are required. Listed below, they are scheduled over a three-month period.

Package Design Phase No. 1

Preliminary to consumer research:
Following are the stages of this task: investigate packages currently used; identify graphic elements supporting marketing concepts; design three options for each marketing concept; check with consumer focus groups; select and refine design. The direct cost of package design is $3,000

Consumer Research

As of today, a survey of secondary buyers (store buyers) has been conducted. End-consumer reactions to the product have to be checked formally: who will buy? at what price? in what packaging? where in the store? how will they use the product? etc. Quantitative and qualitative methods will be used.

Qualitative method: Consumer focus groups (1 in Bay area; 1 in Los Angeles; 1 in New York). Direct cost is $6,600.

Quantitative method: Mall intercepts survey (6 malls in Bay area); 50 people interviewed. Direct cost is $12,000.

The two methods require actual sample product to be presented and tested by people interviewed. Two hundred bags will have to be imported. Direct cost of sample import is $1,000.

Brand-building efforts are envisioned as a result of this research. Size of the market will be derived from this research as well.

Trade Secret Transfer Agreement Preparation

Preliminary agreement between the French company that currently exploits the product process and Lyons & Coyne, Inc. has to be developed into a documented form and program that can be transferred later. Thorough description and documentation of the process has to be done, training program must be defined, and consultancy must be determined and valued. Direct cost is $4,000.

Plant Engineering Design and Installation and Operational Costs Study

Once a location has been selected, it will be necessary to evaluate how to improve the costs of supplementary equipment installation required by the manufacturing process. Operational cost will be refined as well.

Preliminary design for contractor bids will be drawn from this study as well as investment figures for start up. Direct cost for the plant engineering study is $12,000.

Incorporation

To secure proper financing rounds and stockholder structure, Lyons & Coyne, Inc. will have to be incorporated. State fees and legal fees will cover structure optimization research and administrative registration. The direct cost of incorporation is $2,000.

FINANCIAL PLAN

Extensive sensitivity analysis will have to be performed, with feedback from consumer research, an engineering study, transfer agreement preparation, and brand-building (advertising effort) design, with the variables being price, cost, sales volume, and preliminary investment.

Pro forma income statements, cash flow analysis, and a balance sheet will be produced. Also, the structure of the next financial round will be proposed. The direct cost of financial plan is $7,000.

OTHER TASKS AND OVERALL COORDINATION

Principals of Lyons & Coyne, Inc. will perform the following tasks, and they will provide coordination, supervision, and management of the development stage.

Trade secret agreement	$8,000
Supply plan	$4,000
Equipment plan	$4,000
Plant site selection	$4,000
Institutional mkt analysis	$6,000
Distribution plan	$8,000
Coordination, management	$27,000
Subtotal	$61,000
Total Capital Expenditure for Development Stage	$108,600

CRITICAL RISKS: COMPANY RESPONSE

The major risks of this business venture are listed below, along with an ouline of how the management of Lyons & Coyne, Inc. is planning to react if the risks materialize.

Competitor Starts Marketing its Product Before Lyons & Coyne, Inc.

We will buy the competitor's product and test it for quality, freshness, and shelf life. We will then make results available to store buyers and consumer groups. Meanwhile, we will prepare to enter this market with better standards than the competitor, making any necessary modification of our production line quality control measures.

We may also enter markets where competition already exists with products signficantly differentiated from the competitive product. This may require us to replace packaging materials or graphics, or modify our mix of lettuces.

A delicate balance must be maintained between pushing for market share (since this may bring in qualified competitors who then set standards not compatible with our own, but with products at a loss-leader price), and being "second-in" (in order to benefit from the experience and mistakes of competitors).

Price Cutting by Competitors

The price of our product will be sustained or even increased. Value will be added with more expensive and exotic types of raw materials and complimentary items (salad dressing samples, aromatic herb packs, etc.).

Poor Quality Marketed by Competitors

Advertising, promotion, and demonstration techniques will be used to ensure that consumers differentiate our company's product from others.

Difficulties Encountered in the Supply of Raw Materials

If domestic supplies of common types of lettuce cannot be met economically, because of bad weather, strikes, etc., raw materials will be purchased through import wholesalers and brokers. The price will be revised accordingly and accepted because of efficient previous market penetration.

Larger-Than-Expected Innovation and Development Costs to Stay Competitive

The development plan will be re-evaluated, and, if appropriate, the partnership will be opened to another financing round.

Software Developer

BUSINESS PLAN

DATA TECHNOLOGIES CORPORATION

1117 Huron St.
East Traverse, OH 31790

July 17, 1992

As one of the many new software developers in the United States, Data Technologies Corporation is trying to find and fill a niche immediately. DataTech has mapped out a strategy for creating a new product they hope will accomplish that goal. This plan is intended to persuade prospective investors and lenders that their financial support is deserved.

- REASONS FOR ADDITIONAL FUNDING
- BUSINESS OBJECTIVES
- ORGANIZATIONAL STRUCTURE
- PRODUCTS AND SERVICES
- EXECUTIVE SUMMARY OF PROJECT X
- WHAT IS THE PROJECT?
- IS THERE A MARKET FOR X?
- WHAT IS THE FUNDING REQUIREMENT?
- HOW WILL FUNDING BE OBTAINED?
- WHAT WILL PROJECT X DO FOR DATATECH?

SOFTWARE DEVELOPER BUSINESS PLAN

REASONS FOR ADDITIONAL FUNDING

Data Technologies Corporation develops computer software and supplies related technical support to the business community. In order to market and expand its current product line, DataTech is seeking a capital infusion of $200,000.

DataTech's orientation at the moment is toward marketing previously developed products. While interest has been high in DataTech's products locally, many of them are professionally specialized and aimed at a national market. To exploit these possibilities, trade shows and publications must be utilized at considerable expense to DataTech. Therefore, its management anticipates employing two-thirds of any funds received in marketing.

The second reason for requesting financial assistance is to adapt software specifically designed for one type of hardware to others. During the past several months, DataTech has been hired to custom design software for several companies for which it maintains the rights. Three of DataTech's key software programs could thus be re-oriented to run on a variety of computer systems. Insodoing, their accessibility as well as affordability will be considerably enhanced, particularly for small businesses owning name-brand micro-computer hardware. The cost of this form of product development is estimated to be $75,000.

While DataTech is a new company, the management feels that $200,000 is realistic not only in terms of need but also in view of managing debt obligations. Since its incorporation, DataTech has had reasonable sales of its products as it released them to the marketplace. Product orders for the fourth quarter of 1986 are improving significantly. In the same quarter, the company will meet ninety percent of its operating expenses with income generated from its consulting activities.

DataTech's greatest attributes are a well-considered business plan, a strong desire to fully participate in advanced computer technology, and an experienced, enthusiastic staff. The management and employees are very encouraged by the amount of interest their products and services have generated in the respective business communities. The entire management team is confident that DataTech will be able not only to meet any debt obligations, but expand through its own resources within the next six months.

BUSINESS OBJECTIVES

DataTech's primary goal is to provide quality software products and related computer services to the business community. To achieve this goal, it offers the following services:

- Development of specialized application software for specific vertical markets or specific functions in a horizontal market.

- Software support for general business management, such as accounting, financial analysis, office administration, and decision support systems.

- Technical assistance to businesses as they apply advanced computer techniques to their operations.

- Development and support of custom-software on a contractual basis.

DataTech's major interest is in developing and marketing specialized application software. To this end, it has created two such products with strong market appeal. Utilizing these software packages as a foundation, DataTech intends to position itself as an industry leader in application software. The two products are as follows:

The Limousine Management System

As large sectors of the American society have become more affluent and leisure-oriented, the limousine industry has grown tremendously throughout the country. DataTech has developed a comprehensive software to help such businesses become more efficient. In researching the industry, no similar product has been discovered. DataTech believes that it can become the leading software vendor nationally in this market.

Human Resource Planning System (HRPS)

Although there are many personnel software systems in use throughout the United States, few address the planning aspects of human resource management. DataTech recently developed a human resource software package for Burroughs Corporation that can assist the company in such areas as locating qualified employees to fill specialized positions, monitor the individual employee's work history and goals, and provide demographic data on the company's workforce in general. Burroughs and DataTech are now discussing the terms for adapting this for Sperry, Burrough's recent acquisition.

One of DataTech's major product development goals is to make this software compatible with a variety of hardware systems. Several major companies and health care providers have expressed interest in a "generic" version of the product when it becomes available. Most corporations with large hierarchies, very specialized personnel, or many employees are potential customers. The system is also ideal for university/college placement offices. It could be utilized to quickly connect students with employers based on education, special skills, pay requirements, etc. In addition, it could provide the educational institution with up-to-date information on student employment rates for academic planning purposes.

The solutions that this software tries to provide for human resource managers lend themselves very well to the techniques of a brand of artificial intelligence called expert system. Therefore, DataTech's major research and development effort is to transform the software into an expert system. The funding requirement for this effort is about one million dollars. DataTech will attempt to secure most of the funding from venture capital sources. This effort has already begun and will be pursued aggressively through next year.

ORGANIZATIONAL STRUCTURE

DataTech was formed began operations on January 2, 1986. It started with three employees. By the fifth month, DataTech employed two part-time employees who contributed about 60 hours of work per week. Today, it has five full-time and two part-time employees. DataTech is in current need of a full-time marketing representative.

The five full-time employees are utilized in the following manner:

Marketing, client relations and consulting .... 2 persons

Product development and support .... 3 persons

The part-time employees are utilized in the following manner:

Clerical duties and accounting .... 1 person

Documentation for new products .... 1 person

Although DataTech is today a small company, it has developed a generic organization structure to set the foundation for a well organized team. As new employees are added over the next few years, the structure will become more apparent. This generic structure will be reviewed during the annual planning process. The current structure is as follows:

- President and CEO
  - Vice President of Engineering
  - Vice President of Marketing
  - Controller
  - Executive Committee (President, VP - Engineering, VP - Marketing, Controller)
    - Strategic Planning
    - Financial Planning
    - Human Resource Planning
    - Product Management
    - Legal Affairs
    - Large Scale Contractual Jobs

Other committees will be formed as the need arises.

Personnel

Eventually, as personnel are added, DataTech will employ the following structure:

Vice President of Engineering (Executive)

Advanced Research
Product Development
Phase II Customer Support (Response to problems beyond Marketing ability)

Positions:

1. Research Scientist (Job level 23)
2. Senior Research Engineer (17,19)
3. Research Engineer (13,15)
4. Senior Software Engineer (11,13)
5. Software Engineer (7,9)
6. Assistant Software Engineer (5)
7. Co-Op (no level)

Managers will be appointed as the need arises.

Vice President of Marketing (Executive)

Advertising
Customer Support
Market Planning
Public Relations
Sales
Systems Consulting

Positions:

1. Project Manager (20,22)
2. Account Manager (18,20)
3. Systems Consultant (16,18)
4. Assistant Account Manager (16)
5. Senior Marketing Representative (14)
6. Senior Customer Support Rep (14)
7. Marketing Rep (10)
8. Customer Support Rep (10)
9. Assistant Marketing Rep (6)

Managers will be appointed as the need arises.

Personnel *...continued*

Controller (25)

Accounting
Budgeting
Corporate Policies
Financial Analysis
Personnel Administration
Office and General Administration

Positions:
Assistant Controller (20)
Accountant (12,14)
Administrative Assistant (5,7)
Secretary (1,3)

PRODUCTS AND SERVICES

DataTech sells business application systems and technical support to the business community. Systems presently available for sale as follows:

Lease Management System

DATALEASE is a software product designed for auto and equipment leasing companies. The software was developed exclusively by DataTech. It runs on MS-DOS systems (any computer compatible with the IBM-PC). It was completed in July, 1986. There is currently one company using the system, and five others have expressed interest in the product. DataTech plans to market it in Michigan and surrounding states.

Limousine Management System (Including Full Accounting)

DATALIMO is a software product designed for luxury limousine companies. The software was developed exclusively by DataTech. The software was completed in August, 1986. Currently, one company is using the system, and three others have expressed interest. DataTech plans to market it nationwide. Our research indicates that there is currently no such software being marketed in the U.S.

Job Cost System (Including Full Accounting)

The Job Cost System is a software product designed for the construction industry. Software was originally acquired from Information Analysis and Control, Inc. in Portland, Oregon. DataTech enhanced the product extensively. Our revisions were completed in August, 1986. One company is using the system, and four others have expressed interest in the product. DataTech plans to market it in Michigan and the midwest.

Commercial Lines Rating Software

The Commercial Lines Rating Software is a software product designed for insurance agencies. The software was developed by Capitol Computers Plus, Inc. DataTech and Capitol Plus entered into an agreement in August, 1986, allowing DataTech exclusive rights to sell and support the software in the United States. Capitol Plus will continue to develop other modules, including full accounting, commercial auto rating, client tracking, as well as personal, auto and homeowners lines, all to be fully integrated. When DataTech acquired the product, there were already five agencies using it. Three more were recently added. It runs on Unix operating systems (IBM-PC and clones). DataTech plans to market it in Michigan, the midwest and eastern seaboard area.

OTHER PRODUCTS AND SERVICES

DataTech provides contractual services to develop and support business application systems. One such contract is between DataTech and Burroughs Corporation. In July, DataTech completed the development of the Burroughs Human Resource Planning System, called HRPS. Currently there are seven sites within Burroughs, including a facility in Great Britain, that are using the system. By the summer of 1987, the system will be in use worldwide in most of Burroughs' facilities. DataTech and Burroughs are finalizing an agreement for DataTech to provide support directly to the end-users of HRPS.

DataTech owns the rights to the software. Currently, the software is being generalized to help medium- to large-sized companies in a variety of industries to utilize their personnel more efficiently. Two hospitals in San Francisco have already heard about the software and are interested in employing DataTech to customize it to their needs. DataTech is now trying to obtain contracts from these hospitals.

DataTech also serves as a dealer for several computer hardware and software companies, including the following:

- Burroughs Corporation (small business systems - hardware and software)
- Alpha Micro Corporation (full line of products)
- Parameter Driven Software (full line of software products)
- Sperry Computers (small business systems)
- MasterSoft (Sales Analysis Software)

DataTech provides consulting services to small- and medium- sized companies unfamiliar with or unsure about the application of computer technology to their business operations. DataTech staff will help firms review their needs and suggest DataTech technological companies that can offer compatible products.

OTHER PRODUCTS AND SERVICES

DataTech is currently researching and developing a prototype artificial intelligence software (EXPERT system) presently called X. X is an advanced progression of the employee resource planning system that was developed for Burroughs Corporation.

DataTech provides a computerized payroll service for companies that do not want to perform this function in-house.

HUMAN RESOURCE PLANNING SOFTWARE

The Human Resource Planning Software (HRPS) is designed to assist a corporation in locating qualified employees to fill specialized positions, monitor the individual employee's work history and goals, and provide demographic data on the company's workforce in general. HRPS is unique in its planning aspects for human resource management. It can be of use to human resource personnel in five broad areas.

Employee Development

The system stores, in abbreviated form, a development plan agreed upon by the manager and employee as a result of a career-related discussion. This record can be easily called up and reviewed at any time.

The development plan includes measurable action to be taken to correct weaknesses and reinforce strengths, and the dates by which these actions should be completed. The plan can be monitored throughout the year to assess employees' improved effectiveness on the job.

Career Management

HRPS provides space for the employee to express his or her career interests, for the manager to suggest the best next job(s) for the employee, and a rough date of position availability. These are stored in both text and coded form to allow for easy comparison of attributes between large numbers of personnel. When there is a job opening in another part of the company for which the employee is interested and qualified, the employee can be easily identified as a potential candidate. HRPS can help the manager prevent employee stagnation by allowing him or her to quickly locate a position that best serves the interest of the individual and the company.

For example, a standardized HRPS report could list such data as the names and titles of all employees who have had job changes in a given period, whether they have been inter- or intra-departmental, and whether they have been vertical or lateral moves.

As the years progress, one can determine at a glance whether career plans have been carried out by comparing previous years' job plans to the current year for a particular employee.

Succession Planning & Organizational Planning

HRPS can provide early identification and grooming of possible replacement candidates, which reduces the transition period associated with filling the positions of key managers and executives who leave or are reassigned.

HRPS can also help the human resource manager identify potential conflicts between the aggregate impact of individual career plans and overall corporate objectives. For example, while the individual career plans collectively call for 30 job moves in the next 12 months, the manager knows that there have traditionally been 16-18 job openings in that unit for any one year. Aware of his/her employees' expectations, the manager can more effectively deal with possible morale or attrition problems due to the shortage of promotions.

Broad organizational planning is also possible. One can determine whether a unit has the right mix of experience, training, and interests to meet the business needs of next year and beyond.

Candidate Selection for Specific Positions

HRPS has powerful search capabilities designed to allow a manager to find employees who meet virtually any criteria he/she determines. For example, the manager can ask for the names of employees who have the following characteristics:

> ... between level 9 and 11, presently performing either financial planning or analysis, have an interest in product pricing, whose managers suggest are ready for product pricing as a lateral broadening experience, and already live in the same geographical area where the opening exists.

> ... between 15 and 17, have a law degree, have been with the company for at least three years, have an interest in contract law, and are willing to relocate.

Once a candidate list is generated, a detailed print-out on each person can be produced. HRPS has fifteen standard reports providing a different subset of information on each candidate.

Management Reporting

The report function can be used for more than just candidate searches. It can provide general demographic information for a wide variety of management needs. For example, it can answer these questions and others:

- List of all employees who are in Field Support but work outside of Headquarters. Sort them according to geographic location.

- Of all supervisors above level 12 in Marketing, how many are minorities? How many are women?

- Among senior managers throughout the company, what are the three most often mentioned development needs?

- By level, show how many people have second level managerial responsibility. How many have first level managerial responsibility? Print their names and titles. Arrange them by Group.

Management Reporting
...continued

This type of broad statistical data can be utilized in public relations material, hiring, interviews, and a host of other applications in addition to human resource planning.

HRPS is a flexible, easy-to-use tool for personnel planners. It provides current and specialized information for management as well as a simple method for employees to assess and plan their careers. Most importantly, however, HRPS allows both groups the opportunity to maximize efficiency and satisfaction.

EXECUTIVE SUMMARY OF PROJECT X

Introduction

The following material is a summary of DataTech's plans for a new expert system. As the current literature in computer technology suggests, an expert system is the newest and most exciting manifestation of the artificial intelligence phenomenon in computers. Basically, the system is structured to mimic the thought patterns and decisions of a human expert in a particular field. Because they depend on the user answering a set of questions, such systems tend to be very user friendly. For management, the greater accessibility of rare, specialized knowledge could represent a tremendous boom to productivity. The market for these systems is thus growing tremendously.

In this summary, we will explain how DataTech can participate in this boom.

What is the Project?

DataTech's most promising and important task for now is to develop an expert system software called X. X is intended to serve as a human resource planning expert, providing advice to organizations with large human resource bases. X will be designed to run on microcomputer systems with the capabilities to share information within a network of mainframe and microcomputer systems. The specific brand of the microcomputer has not yet been selected. This decision will be made during the project planning phase.

How might X benefit a client organization? X's purpose is to provide the following services:

- maintenance of extensive employee profiles
- application of consistent career movement policies
- easy explanation of trends due to certain policies or occurrences
- instant identification of employees affected by particular circumstances
- keeping human resource managers alert to actions or practices that have caused problems in the past
- simulation of situations that could have profound implications for the long-term career plans of employees
- expansion of the knowledge base. X will be ale to be updated on a continual basis, thus creating an expert that is abreast of the organization's ever-changing environment.

The following are two examples of questions that X will be able to answer:

Example 1

User's question:
What has been the general career path for employees who were hired over the past five years with M.S. degrees in computer science?

Response from X:
About half have stayed in Engineering taking on supervisory positions;the other half have been scattered in various positions with no specific pattern.

Alternate X:
I don't know; the question is too general for my response knowledge base. Since you seem to be interested in career paths, I will ask you questions to try and make your question specific.

X will then ask the user questions to which he may respond using answers such as YES, NO, PROBABLY, UNLIKELY, or HIGHLY UNLIKELY. In essence, X will engage in a dialogue with the user just as a human expert would. By the end of the dialogue, X will have acquired sufficient information to be able to answer the user's original question.

Example 2

User's question:
How can I help an employee who has low productivity?

Response from X:
here are many ways depending on the specific circumstances; therefore, let us try to narrow the problem to specific performance situations. Please respond to the following questions:

<Dialogue begins>

X: I presume that there is a performance problem; would you agree?
User: Yes.
X: How long ago did you notice a performance problem?
User: About 6 months.
X: How was his/her performance before then?
User: Somewhat fair.
X: Was that satisfactory, in your judgement?
User: Not really.

X will continue to prompt the user, until the expert has acquired sufficient information to narrow the performance problem to a specific situation. It can then safely draw conclusions based on that definition.

In X, general or vague questions will normally trigger a dialogue. X will have a vocabulary of general words and phrases that will be used to initiate these exchanges. Each dialogue will have a synopsis to inform the user about the specific problem that X attempts to solve in that dialogue. There will be many help features available to guide the user from a seemingly vague situation to a specific one. For example, he/she will be able to review X's vocabulary of words, phrases, dialogues, or acceptable answers. One of the best features of X will be it's ability to help the user solve a problem without overwhelming him/her in a technical manner.

IS THERE A MARKET FOR X?

Nearly every organization that has to concern itself with the careers of a large number of people is a potential user. Expert system technology is very new, and while its successful applications are well publicized, there are very few commercial ones. Most of these commercial systems involve financial ones. We currently know of no applications in human resource planning. Furthermore, it is safe to say that career management is one of the challenges intrinsic to nearly any organization with a substantial population base. The issue of fairness in an organization's procedures is a crucial aspect of the American work place. X can help an organization apply policies consistently and will quickly alert it to potential problems.

Most existing expert systems concentrate on offering advice that is essentially that of a human expert. X will do more. X will be able to monitor the career movement of people and track the effects of policies and practices on their careers. One of its most powerful features will be its ability to answer questions reasonably in hypothetical scenarios. The typical organizational user will be able to use X for sophisticated "WHAT IF" situations against its human resource base. A tool of this power would, we believe, make human resource planners more efficient.

DataTech has already developed a microcomputer-based software system capable of monitoring the career movement of people. This software, called HRPS (Human Resource Planning System), is the starting point for X. All companies using HRPS and wanting to upgrade its system, would be potential users of X. By the time X is fully developed, HRPS will be employed by major companies, such as Burroughs, which will serve as first-wave users. This will help draw the second and third-wave users and allay any serious apprehension they may have about a new product of X's sophistication. During the next two years, the market will be ripe for expert systems such as X. In addition, our intention to run X on popular microcomputers will make it even more accessible, both literally and psychologically, to organizations and their leaders.

WHAT IS THE FUNDING REQUIREMENT?

It will cost from $600,000 to $900,000 to develop and market X. $300,000 to $450,000 will be earmarked for engineering and development. $200,000 to $350,000 is intended for marketing purposes. The remaining $100,000 is to be set aside in a contingency fund. When DataTech is able to secure $900,000, the first phase of X will be completed in eighteen months. The conceptual model has already been designed. The only features that would be missing from this phase would be those that pertain to the user's ability to access information in a sophisticated network environment. Those features would be part of the second phase. Given this funding level, both phases can be completed in two years.

If the required $900,000 cannot be readily obtained, delays will be inevitable. A funds pool of $600,000 would stretch the development period to a total of three years. Given the volatility of X's intended market and the economy as a whole, such a delay could significantly change X's profitability, albeit to an unknown degree.

How Will Funding Be Obtained?

As a small, very new company, DataTech has few available funding sources. There are essentially three financing alternatives that DataTech could utilize to fund the project. In the next few paragraphs, the benefits and problems associated with each concept are outlined.

Funding Alternative I:

DataTech could apply for a long term loan. The current shareholders would have to guarantee the loan. However, the internal shareholders, those who makeup the management of DataTech, do not have, individually or collectively, adequate financial strength to secure such a large sum. Only the outside shareholders could be considered for this amount of loan. In this case, these shareholders must be convinced that DataTech can insure the project's profitability. If the company did very well financially in its first year of operation, these shareholders might be persuaded to back the plan for X.

Funding Alternative II:

DataTech could seek venture capital. There are a number of venture capital sources that are interested in expert systems technology. The chances are good that DataTech could raise the needed capital for Project X. However, considering the revenue of the company in its first year of operation, its financial worth is far less than the capital needed for Project X. This means that a significant percentage of its ownership would have to be compromised to attract appropriate backers. Also, it is likely that the venture capitalists would want a strong voice in the management of the company. In all likelihood, DataTech would lose some of its independence. The advantage of this alternative over the first one is that the current shareholders would not have to underwrite a huge loan.

By approaching venture capitalists, the conceptual design of X would be divulged. There is always the risk of exposing a secret plan when one seeks venture capital. Capitalists usually insist that they be provided with a detailed plan of action. The risk here is that there are many software companies that could develop X if exposed to its development plans. Therefore, DataTech would have to be very selective if this alternative were pursued.

FUNDING...*continued*

Funding Alternative III:

Using its special contacts, DataTech could solicit sponsorship from Burroughs Corporation for the development of X. If Burroughs were to back the project, it would want to get involved to the extent of understanding the engineering of X. That would put DataTech at a disadvantage in terms of it having exclusive technical knowledge of X. On the surface, it would seem that DataTech could protect its ideas by copyrighting the design of X. However, it would not, in practice, be easy to protect the system.

Burroughs-Sperry, the second largest computer manufacturer in the world, could easily redesign X by simply having cursory access to the concepts of X. Even if it were easy to copyright the design of X, it would not be adequate to protect the concepts of X from a company such as Burroughs. Therefore, approaching Burroughs could be a giveaway if it used its vast internal sources to develop an X-like system.

The success of this alternative weighs heavily on personal lobbying within Burroughs. Since Burroughs is the largest user of HRPS, it will likely view X as the logical, advanced progression from HRPS. Its competent personnel will quickly grasp the concepts of X and see its market value. Therefore, the probability of success for this alternative is high. The risk remains, however, that DataTech's ideas could become Burroughs'.

WHAT WILL X DO FOR DATATECH?

X could transform DataTech into a very successful advanced technology company. Many software houses are scrambling to grasp the new technological frontier of the expert system. Over the past few decades, computers have quickly permeated the American work place. Expert systems are the next phase of the computer revolution. They will raise the sophistication of computers to unbelievable heights. Some of these computers are available today. However, commercially they are not available at affordable rates to every company that wants one. Over the past few years, the technology has advanced dramatically. Within the next five years, most businesses are going to be shopping for expert systems with expertise in their lines of business. Today, the opportunity to become a powerhouse of commercial expert systems is excellent.

DataTech management has no doubt about its ability to develop an expert system. This statement should not suggest, however, that DataTech is in position to monopolize commercial expert systems development. In fact there are many, many software companies with the potential to develop expert systems. The crux of the matter is that searching for a practical application with strong market appeal is difficult. The fact that it has conceptualized a real application sets DataTech apart from other such firms. X is a very sound application that is saleable. It has a broad utility in business. It emanates from a product already developed. That product also runs on microcomputer systems as opposed to mainframe computers, which makes it broadly accessible. Therefore, X is not a pipe dream. It could be feasible within two years.

X could mean many good things for DataTech. Specifically, there are three that are salient. Foremost is, of course, financial success. Second is the national recognition, and third is the many byproducts and derivatives that could emerge from X.

Financial Success from X

The bottom line for pursuing X is that it be a financially profitable venture. The financial success of X will depend largely on the marketplace readiness for systems as sophisticated as X and the extent of competition. At this point in time, both conditions are very favorable to DataTech. It is not possible to associate precise dollar figures with X at this point. By conservative estimates, however, DataTech could realize revenues on the order of tens of million dollars.

If this figure sounds unrealistic, one has only to go back in recent history and observe the software companies that were at the forefront of commercializing the new technology. Some specific examples are Ashton-Tate, MicroSoft Corp., and Lotus Development Corp.

Ashton-Tate was started in 1980 with $7500 in capital to compete against the major software program houses in the country. The company offered discounts, fast delivery, strong customer support, and a toll-free number. Growth was marginal until the founder, George Tate, purchased what he perceived to be a revolutionary software package from NASA engineer who had developed it in his spare time. As a result, the engineer became a multi-millionaire and Ashton-Tate sold over 200,000 copies of the product called dBASE II within two years of its introduction. By 1985, annual sales reached $121 million and the number of employees grew to 400. Only one year before, the company sold stock to the public and raised $15 million. Tate himself sold 220,000 shares at that time, collecting $3.1 million -- and he still owned 34 percent of the company, worth about $100 million.

MicroSoft Corporation was organized in 1975 because its founders saw a great opportunity in adapting the computer language BASIC for use in microcomputers. As the personal computer industry exploded, MicroSoft emerged from the pack as a pacesetter in the development of standardized software that makes hardware more accessible to users. The signal event for the company was its selection by IBM to develop the operating system for its new personal computer due in August 1981. The resulting product, MS-DOS (MicroSoft-Disk Operating System), has since been established as the dominant operating system in the microcomputer industry. Sales for 1984 hit $100 million and the number of employees grew to 600 with offices in Europe and Asia.

Mitch Kapor, founder of Lotus Development Corp., correctly presumed that the 16-bit processor PC introduced by IBM in 1981 was the wave of the future and that software geared to the 16-bit processor would provide the company an incalculable lead over potential competition. The project required significant funding and he was able to raise $4.7 million from a group of investors. Most of this capital was used in a major advertising blitz for this single product. The product, Lotus 1-2-3, was introduced in 1982 and within six months sold 60,000 copies. Eighteen months after Lotus was founded, Kapor received $5.4 million in a public stock offering and the venture capitalists saw their $4.7 million investment mushroom to $226 million.

National Recognition from X

X could easily bring national recognition to DataTech. Considering the intense national interest in expert systems technology and the fact that its so new, any appreciable success in the field, particularly commercially, is bound to get national attention. For DataTech, national attention would mean three things: increased business activity, easy access to more investment capital, and substantial contractual work from major, reputable firms. This would be a unique opportunity.

X has been presented to have a database of employee profiles and a knowledge base of a human resource expert. It has the potential to be adapted to a multitude of uses, however. If, for example, X had police records and a criminal expert was substituted for the human resources expert, X could be used to help law enforcement agencies fight crime. Using the same kind of substitution, an X-like system could be built as a product specialist with an extensive knowledge base on a company's various products.

Once X is developed, it will be easy to generate byproducts or derivatives of it. The technical structures will be well in place. This will make DataTech prolific in the development of advanced software systems for business.

BALANCE SHEET

January-August 1986

Revenue	$87,662
Cost of Goods	($35,278)
Gross Profits	$52,384
Operating Costs	
Selling Expenses	($13,324)
Gen & Admin	($106,586)
Total Operating Costs	($119,910)
Net Profit	($67,526)

PROFIT/LOSS STATEMENT

ASSETS

Current Assets		
Cash	$9,378	
Accounts Receivable	$12,779	
Total Current Assets		$22,168
Fixed Assets		
Furniture & Fixtures		
Deprec-Furn & Fix		
Computer Equipment		
Deprec-Comp Equip		
Office Equipment		
Deprec-Office Equipment	$00000	
Total Assets		$22,168

LIABILITIES

Current Liabilities		
Current Payable	$19,629	
Payroll Taxes	$2,144	
Fed Tax Payable		
State Tax Payable	$271	
Local Tax Payable		
Other Current Liabilities	$2,000	
Long Term Liabilities	$15,650	
Total Liabilities		$39,694

Toiletry Company

BUSINESS PLAN

VERDE

227 Parklane Ave.
Mission River, ID 57731

June 15, 1992

Verde is the manufacturer of a full line of men's-only toiletries. Because of its up and down history of financial success and failure, the new management has designed this plan to attract investors.

COMPANY HISTORY

1984 Verde incorporated

1985 Bullock's and Macy's openings; *GQ* article, *Cosmetic World* cover

1986 *Soap, Cosmetic & Chemical Specialties* cover; *New York Times* article; *Playboy* feature; *Esquire* catalog; ABC radio hour; NACD packaging award; joint venture with Wilkinson Sword; America's Cup exclusive supplier; Saks, Foley's, Goldwater's, Kaufmann's, Bloomingdale's launches; private placement

1987 PBS feature; *Drug & Cosmetic Industry* reference; showcased in 98 department stores; preparation for IPO

1988 IPO; fragrance introduced; Revenues reach $3 million

1989 Campeau bankruptcy; Verde goes into receivership; corporation dissolved

1990 Marcus VanDermeer buys out of receivership

1993 After two and a half years of decline, VanDermeer decides to sell

POSITIONING

Verde sells a line of high performance skin and hair care products for men. The complete line contains twelve products for a man's basic daily skin and hair maintenance:

- Aloe Cream Shave
- Aloe After Shave
- Daily Face Scrub
- Moisture Formula
- Daily Body Wash
- Aloe Body Lotion
- Revitalizing Shampoo
- Revitalizing Conditioner
- Nutrient Complex For Hair
- Aloe Hair Gel
- Natural Deodorant
- Sunscreen (SPF6 Self Tan and SPF20 Block)

The line currently suffers from a weak identity. The original positioning of the product was "green" - Verde translates to "green" in Spanish; the advertising featured "Natural Grooming Products For Men." Current management believes the "green" identity does not carry the strength, sustainability, or differentiation for today's market. In addition, key elements of the line were inconsistent with this positioning: brightly colored packaging; bold, high-tech graphics; department store distribution.

Repositioning of the Verde line is the critical first step. Verde is a simple, efficient daily maintenance regimen of complementary precision products. The Verde system is built for the modern man. Its basic simplicity appeals to a large, underserved market. Focusing on the performance aspect of the product satisfies a strong and newly recognized theme in men's grooming aids.

The Verde "performance" message is reinforced with brightly colored packaging, recyclable materials, clean graphics and logical coding. The new management team believes that a strong performance message stressing practicality and sensibility can be a powerful motivator for men in the '90s. The positioning statement is key, and speaks to our clientele:

Verde!
Dominate the Field

TARGET MARKET

The Verde management team believes that this underserved segment of men represents 30-40% of all men. The Verde man is:

- Bold in action
- Willing to accept a challenge
- Self-assured
- Willing to take a calculated risk
- Master of his trade/profession
- A survivor who emerges from battle stronger
- A man with a few close friends; not "every guy's friend"

Mail order health and beauty aids (HBA) for men is a $23 million segment within the $2.25 billion men's market. A targeted distribution and positioning strategy will focus on generating trial customers and leading to continuity customers and developing a loyal base of 66,000 customers within three years. Distribution will be focused on mail order during years 1 and 2. Year 3 plans include the possibility of expanding to specialty retail distribution channels. These channels include: sporting goods stores, health & fitness clubs, and country clubs.

MARKETING STRATEGY

Seven key marketing tactics will be employed to build the customer base and increase volumes:

♦ Starter kits will be packaged with different product combinations at a variety of price points. New customers will be invited to try a starter kit, introducing products at a deep discount and featuring the Verde no-risk return guarantee.
♦ Routine usage will be promoted with a continuity reordering option.
♦ An aggressive customer referral program will reward existing customers and encourage product trial.
♦ Standard retail tactics will keep the product line fresh in customers' minds:
- •Purchase with purchase
- •Gift with purchase
- •Sampling

♦ A toll-free 800 number will enhance customer service/product support

Consistent with Verde's "performance" message, the product purchase/distribution will be streamlined and accelerated through:

♦ Toll-free customer support hotline.
♦ Overnight delivery.
♦ On-line (touchtone or modem) ordering.
♦ Continuity option.

THE COMPETITION

The men's grooming aids market is segmented by distribution channel and positioning theme. Expensive designer lines (Ralph Lauren, Aramis, Clinique, Origins) are generally available through department stores; mid-range products (Body Shop, H20, Eddie Bauer) are sold through specialty retail and mail-order; low-end products (Gillette, Canoe, Bodycology) are sold at drugstores and supermarkets. There are six main positioning themes:

- •Clinical (Clinique)
- •"Green" (Origins, Body Shop, H20 Plus)
- •Performance (unserved)
- •Exotic (Ralph Lauren Safari, Eddie Bauer Adventurer)
- •Nautical/sport (Canoe, Ralph Lauren Polo Sport)
- •Tech (Gillette Cool Wave)
- •Some lines use combined themes--clinitech (Aramis Lab Series), or technosport (Gillette Right Guard Power products).

VERDE VS. THE COMPETITION

- ❑Verde specializes, selling only skin and hair care products; unlike designer labels that brand clothes, fragrances and home furnishings.
- ❑Verde products are designed specifically for men, unlike other product lines that are simply an extension or repackaging of a women's line.
- ❑Verde offers a complete line of men's daily maintenance products, unlike competitors whose lines are incomplete or too expensive for daily use.
- ❑ Verde is uniquely positioned to capture men who demand performance in every aspect of their lives.

MANAGEMENT

Verde will require the following skill sets from its management:

- ♦Knowledge of health and beauty aids industry.
- ♦Knowledge of the mail order business.
- ♦Strategic marketing and product positioning.
- ♦Financial management and planning.
- ♦Negotiation and coordination of independent vendors/sales reps.
- ♦Experience in telephone-based customer service.
- ♦Data management skills.
- ♦Magazine advertising/direct response.
- ♦Public relations/editorial placement experience.

FINANCIAL REQUIREMENTS

Verde requires a capital infusion of $200,000, which will be used:

- •To bring inventory up to necessary levels.
- •To purchase targeted mailing lists and advertising.
- •For general working capital.

Assumptions

Given this investment and the assumptions described below, Verde projects:

- •Trials = 4% of purchased names
- •Trial customers fall into one of four categories, with the characteristics listed:

Customer	Conversion %	Order Cycle	Annual Fall off %	Value* 1 Yr	Value* 2 Yr
Continuity	25%	3 mon	15%	$76	$80
Frequent	20%	4 mon	18%	$69	$68
Infrequent	10%	6 mon	40%	$47	$35

**Note: Annual customer value does not include initial trial package dollars.*

- ♦ 33% of customer base will make 1-2 referrals during a calendar year.
- ♦ 33% of these referrals will become part of the customer base.
- ♦ Purchased names cost $0.10 per name.
- ♦ Referred names cost $15 per name for a free trial kit and customer bonus.
- ♦ Fulfillment averages $2.50 per order.
- ♦ Shipping averages $6 per order; the customer and the company split this cost evenly.
- ♦ There are no office rent charges the first year.

Results

	Year 1	Year 2	Year 3
Total Names Purchased	800,000	1,200,000	1,200,000
Customer Base	18,314	40,063	65,642
Continuity Customers	8,083	18,234	30,436
Sales	$1,792,000	$3,818,000	$5,893,000
COGS	594,000	1,249,000	1,907,000
Gross Margin	1,198,000	2,569,000	3,986,000
Fulfillment	147,000	307,000	465,000
Rent & Utilities	0	30,000	30,000
Marketing	348,000	537,000	697,000
Miscellaneous	48,000	48,000	48,000
Net Before Taxes & Salary Distributions	$655,000	$1,647,000	$2,746,000

Toy Company

BUSINESS PLAN

TOYS FOR A NEW GENERATION INC.

557 Univeristy South
Copper Harbor, DE 57842

January 19, 1991

With two lines of "Do-it-Yourself" educational cards for young people already on the market, Toys for a New Generation expects to increase its market and product ranges significantly. The following plan details the new card ideas and outlines the manner in which they will be introduced.

TOY COMPANY BUSINESS PLAN

MISSION STATEMENT

To develop, manufacture, and market high quality products forchildren that are enjoyable for the child, have educational benefits for the child, and are a good value for the purchaser.

EXECUTIVE SUMMARY

Purpose of Plan

Toys for a New Generation Inc. is currently financed by personal funds of the founder and a line of credit from First Bank of Boston. However, our rapid growth has exhausted funds from these sources. Since 15 products are currently developed and being sold, we feel confident enough in our products and concepts to look for outside sources. This plan has been written to summarize our history and to state our goals and plans to achieve them.

The Company

People buying items for children want value for their dollars. They want products that are both enjoyable to children and worthwhile. Toys for a New Generation is committed to supplying products that fulfill these requirements.

We currently have 15 products that are being sold nationwide. Thesehave been introduced in phases.

Phase I Box O' Cards, is a line of kits that include everything children need to make their own greeting cards - pictures to color, envelopes, colored pencils, a pencil sharpener, and stickers in a plastic travel case: We currently have seven kits in this line.

Phase II products, Card Facts, are a set of collector cards rather than greeting cards. The front of each card has a picture to color while the back has six questions about that subject. The answers are in small print, upside-down. Once the child has colored the picture and mastered their facts, they then affix their "I Know My Facts" blue ribbon sticker. We have eight sets of cards, including a custom product. Many more sets of cards are planned on various subjects. There are also many opportunities to customize sets for tourist attractions and market them as the "ideal souvenir."

Market Analysis

The products need to be designed to appeal to children between the ages of four and ten. However, the actual purchasing will be done by adults, so they must be presented in a manner that conveys value to the adult. A network of manufacturer's representatives is being established, and home office sales efforts concentrate on identified niche markets. Current plans target the continental United States, but international opportunities are being evaluated as they are received. Currently, we have been approached about a possible licensing arrangement for Europe, and inquiries have been received from distributors in Canada, Mexico, and Australia.

Organization

Toys for a New Generation Inc. was created in February, 1987 by a sole proprietor. In May, 1988, the business was incorporated in the State of Delaware. The daily operation is managed by a supervisor with an educational background in marketing, including a Bachelor of Business Administration degree from Boston University and graduate work on the MBA program at the University of Connecticut. Her work experience includes 18 years of commercial and industrial marketing and one and a half years as a Project Manager.

Additional office and sales support personnel are used on a part-time basis as needed. All other functions are contracted out to other firms. Most of the printing and some assembly of the kits are done by a workshop for mentally retarded citizens.

Financial Data

Three years of history and two years of projections are available upon request for reference, as well as proposed programs for 1991 and their impact on future financial performance.

Additional information may also be requested.

PROCEDURES

Company Description

Nature of the Business

As a parent of three young children, personal experiences have helped me to identify various product opportunities. The products help strengthen children's skills and also represent a good value to the purchaser. The products are being grouped together into related families and are being introduced in phases. The phases already in production are:

Phase I, Box O' Cards, has everything children need to make their own greeting cards: cards to color, envelopes, colored pencils, a pencil sharpener, and stickers for decorating.

Phase II is a series of collector's cards, known as Card Facts, that children color and use to learn facts about the subject in order to earn a blue ribbon sticker. These kits also come with colored pencils and a pencil sharpener.

Several additional phases for future product lines have also been identified and are described later in this plan.

While the products are designed for children, it is recognized that adults will do the purchasing in most cases. Most adults are potential customers, not just parents of young children. Between 70 and 80% of the adult population have children on their gift lists. This is the group that will be the purchasers. We must target our marketing efforts at the buyers and wholesale distributors that will make our products available to these purchasers.

Distinctive Competencies

Toys for a New Generation products are distinct in that they present items that children enjoy in a manner that encourages skill development, while giving the purchaser a quality product.

An additional unique factor about our products is that many are printed and assembled by a sheltered workshop where mentally retarded citizens learn skills to help them find jobs in local industry. The purchaser usually feels that they are helping a worthy cause while they get a good product. Use of a sheltered workshop also conveys a sense of cost containment.

Using this facility does help keep the costs down, but it also gives us greater flexibility and quick turnaround on new products. This will be even more important as we get into more customized products.

Product Description, Background and Parameters

Products currently in production and being distributed nationwide:

Phase I: Box O' Cards

Description

Each kit, packed in a plastic travel case, contains everything children need to make their own greeting card: six cards with outline drawings to color, six mailable envelopes, six coordinated stickers for decorating, six colored pencils, and a pencil sharpener. The seven kits currently in our line are:

- Clown Birthday
- Clown Thank You
- Clown Get Well
- Balloon New Brother
- Balloon New Sister
- Merry Christmas
- Happy Hanukkah

Background

Like most young children, my son and two daughters enjoy making things and they enjoy giving their creations to friends and family. At birthdays and holidays they spent a great deal of time creating that "special card." The only one who dreaded these artistic sessions was me. I would always hear "Mom, where are the scissors?" "Mom, what should I draw?" "Mom, I'm done." "Do you have an envelope?" One day the thought came to me that it would be nice to have everything in one place for my children to make their own cards. Maybe some kind of a kit... Thus, Phase I was born.

Parameters

Each kit is to meet the following parameters:

Give the child a head start by including a drawing for them to color. The different skill levels of the children should be recognized by having pictures with varying degrees of detail. There should also be plenty of open spaces for children to add their own words and decorations.

Include colored pencils in the kit. Children really enjoy them more than crayons and the finished products are much nicer. Colored pencils are also not as subject to breakage in shipping and are not as sensitive to temperatures in storage. Including a pencil sharpener completes the kit while giving added value.

Stickers are very popular with children to decorate the card as well as the envelope. Including the stickers adds color to the product to make it more attractive and eye-catching to the purchaser. This added value also gives our product a competitive edge.

There must be an envelope for each card. The envelopes are to be mailable and of high quality paper so children can color and decorate them as well.

The end-user target price should be 85 to 95 cents a card to make it an attractive value to the purchaser.

All of these parameters have been met with the current line of kits.

Phase II : Card Facts

Description

A pack consists of six collector cards with pictures to color on the front. On the back of the cards are six questions about that subject. The answers are provided at the bottom, in small print, upside down. Once the child has mastered all the facts and has completed coloring the picture with the colored pencils provided in the package, they can affix their blue ribbon sticker that says "I Know My Facts." The eight packs currently available are:

- ♦ Dinosaurs
- ♦ History of Aviation
- ♦ Birds in Your Yard
- ♦ Our Solar System
- ♦ Zoo Friends
- ♦ Spacecraft of the U.S.
- ♦ Woodland Animals
- ♦ Ellis Island

Background

As a family with three small children, we are always going on outings where souvenirs are offered for sale. I am amazed at the prices charged for items that I find are usually of poor quality and little value. The question always comes to my mind, "Why don't they offer something that the children will enjoy and at the same time get some benefit from it?"

During the normal search for customers for the line of card making kits, I contacted Sea World and offered to do a customized kit for them using their characters. The buyer was interested and asked for a prototype to be put together. While working on it I ran into several problems:

- ❑Should the cards be Birthday, Thank You, Get Well, or a non- specific note card?

- ❑When talking to my children about the possibility of a Sea World kit they all were excited about coloring Shamu, but they did NOT want to send him to anyone. They wanted to keep the card for themselves. This defeated the purpose of a greeting card of any kind.

- ❑To do a custom sticker (and in the future for all customized kits) would raise the per unit cost because of low volume runs for the custom stickers.

- ❑Then one night on the way home from seeing a movie with my children, I was asking them questions about the story and characters. When one of them got an answer correct, my daughter gave them a pretend sticker. The concept fell in place.

Parameters

Each kit will have six different cards in it and each card will have six questions on it. The questions will teach the child some basic facts about the subject, but in a fun way. To present them as a "school lesson" would discourage children from wanting to complete it and from wanting to do other sets.

A standardized Blue Ribbon sticker will be used for all sets of cards. The sticker will be printed on clear material so that no matter where the child places the sticker on the picture, the picture will show through and the ribbon will simulate a prize such as given at a fair.

The sets are packaged in a manner similar to the card making kits so customers will know they come from the same company. This will help to increase brand awareness and hopefully create in purchasers of one line a desire to try other products.

The cards will be printed on heavy stock so they will be durable. The cards will have rounded corners to give them a finished look and to keep them from fraying while children complete and collect them.

Children will be encouraged to collect all the different packs. A collector's album as an accessory is being considered as a future product.

Flexibility must be maintained so that we can provide quick turn around and low minimum order quantities to encourage customized kits.

The current line of Card Facts meets all these parameters.

There is a large potential for customized Card Facts. We have just completed our first one, which was done for the company that has the concession contract at Ellis Island. Product was shipped in time for the re-opening. Sales so far have pleased the buyer, who is considering customized sets for some of their other tourist locations. Every major tourist attraction is a potential candidate. While we cannot sell the Ellis Island cards to anyone else, we can show it as an example of our customizing capabilities. In fact, we have recently done a press release on this product and are contacting major tourist attractions to show them what we can do.

Other programs currently in varying stages of development.

Phase III: Young Artist Cards

Description

This will be an expansion of the collector card line. These packs will feature a particular famous artist. Five cards will be outline drawings of the artist's most famous paintings, while the sixth card will be a portrait of the artist. The higher skill levels needed to master these cards should increase the target age range to 12 or 14 years of age.

Background

Visits to art exhibits are always fun for children, but they can be overwhelming. There is really no way they can comprehend all that they see and understand the significance of it. Some type of souvenir that would let them become involved in the artist and his subjects would be fun for them and help to reinforce what they saw at the museum. If a child can learn six facts about an artist, and then become familiar with five of their works, any teacher or parent would feel the experience was worthwhile.

Parameters

The general concept will follow the format of the existing collector card sets to allow for use of standard items.

If this channel proves to be successful, a general set on art will be created for the younger children so that there will be something in this series for all age ranges.

Our standard collector card sets are currently doing well with science and natural history museums. We have had preliminary conversations with some representatives and some art museums, all of whom are excited about these proposed products. We have had offers from some curators and educational staff members to help in the product's development.

Phase IV: Licensed Characters--Description

The rights to use certain characters on our products is being pursued. If obtained, some will be used in our existing product families. Others will open up new product opportunities for new items. Due to the early stages of negotiating and the confidentiality of some of the potential products, identification of the characters is being withheld from this plan.

Phase V and Phase VI: Other Products--Description

Two other lines of totally different products have been identified and prototypes have been assembled. Since there are possible patent and copyrights involved, no further information can be provided at this point.

Market Analysis

General Market Analysis

Phase I products fall into the greeting card product market, which is a $3.6 billion a year business in the US. However, many of the sales outlets carrying our card-making kits serve the toy market, which is another $12.5 billion market a year in the US. Toys for a New Generation sales projections represent only a fraction of 1% penetration. Such a low level of penetration means that even if the total markets maintain or even decline, it is such a large market that we could meet the forecasted sales and possibly even gain market share. We are after a very small piece of a very large market.

The end-users of our products are children ages four to 12 years. Phase III products may increase this target age range to 13 and 14 years. However, it would take resources far beyond our current abilities to develop product awareness in children to the point that they request our products be bought for them.

Our products will be purchased by adults who buy products for children. They will make the final purchase, but in most cases this purchase will not be made directly from us. We will be making sales to retail stores and wholesale distributors. This is where we must concentrate our efforts. Our products must be presented to them in a manner that will convey our dedication to providing quality products, in attractive displays, at a price that allows stores to attain their customary mark-up. We must also be committed to supply a flow of new products. New sells -- and we want the stores to sell.

We want stores to sell - but what stores? The general gift and toy market is so vast that our limited resources would not be able to make much impact. Instead, we are identifying niche markets where we can make an impact. The markets identified and current plans are as follows:

Hospital Gift Shops ($1 billion per year)

We have advertised in, and had several free write-ups in, Get Well Soon Magazine, a management guide for hospital gift shop owners. Results have been good. We exhibited at a hospital gift shop show in New York in June, 1989, and wrote orders for 33% of the hospitals attending.

We have recently participated in a card deck mailed out to the 7000+ recipients of Get Well Soon Magazine. Response was very good, with a fair number of inquiries converting to orders.

Souvenir Market

- ❑Zoos (112 nationwide)
- ❑Museums (8411 nationwide)
- ❑ Amusement parks (8549 nationwide)

Zoo and museum gift shops have responded well to our standard products, plus they are all likely candidates for a customized Card Facts featuring their own displays.

The same card sent in the hospital mailing has been sent to the 10,000+ recipients of the U.S. Museums Magazine. Responses were even better than with the hospital mailing.

An ad for Card Facts has run in Souvenir Nationwide, Amusement Park Gifts Magazine, and Souvenir. A large quantity of inquiries were received but a disappointing number of these converted to orders. The reason for low conversion needs to be addressed before more ads are run.

Premium Market

We had an inquiry from a large manufacturing company that contacted us to develop a new product for them to use in a promotion. A prototype was developed. There is also interest by this company for a customized Card Facts for another program. So far, we do not have a commitment for either program, but the quantities requested for each program are more than double our entire 1991 forecast. This is an indication of the size of the premium marked that is out there.

Completion of either of these will be used as a basis for a campaign to let other companies know what we can do for them with a specialized product.

School Supply Wholesalers (315 nationwide)

While exhibiting at various gift shows, there has been interest expressed for use of our Card Facts in schools. Teachers could use the cards as part of their study plan. However, they do not need to have the pencils and expensive packaging. To serve this market we need to bulk pack the cards and stickers only.

Fund Raiser Program

Elementary and pre-schools are always looking for unique fund raiser programs; everyone is tired of selling magazines, candy bars, and cookbooks. The intensive one-to-one exposure to lots of people who have young children offered by this market could lead to a great response for our products. The organizations could earn over 50% of sales while giving our products tremendous exposure. Gathering information on this channel has begun.

"One-on-One" Campaign

Since Card Facts were first started, articles from newspapers and trade journals have been saved covering potential customers for our products. These articles often give the buyer's name and detail their goals and objectives. The information in the article is then used to write a "one-on-one" letter to that buyer stating how our products help fill their needs. A sample of a product and a catalog is also sent. For under $10, we get a direct "sales pitch" to the person who can take action. So far, we have been successful with this campaign twice. These two accounts have already given us orders for many thousands of dollars.

Military Exchanges

Since our products are ideal for children away from family and friends and who have idle time, we feel there is a place for them in the military exchanges around the world. All major buying operations for all the branches of the armed services have been sent catalogs and a sample. We also included a letter of certification that is a woman owned enterprise. Since Federal agencies are required to take affirmative action in support of businesses owned by women, this may give us an edge on getting product placed in the military exchanges. The initial results have been disappointing. More attention must be given to this potentially large channel. We are also looking for a representative sales organization that specializes in this channel.

Mail Order Catalogs

There are literally hundreds of mail order catalogs in existence. Of these, about 50 have children's items in them and can be considered potential outlets for our products. Each of these potentials is being contacted as time permits. So far, we have made sales to, and are in, three catalogs.

Free Publicity

Trade journals as well as consumer publications are always looking for new items to tell their readers about. So far we have had many free write-ups, and continuous efforts are made to get as much free publicity as possible.

Trade Shows

The proposed trade show schedule includes the American International Toy Fair and the International Stationery Show. Both take place in New York City. While these are the shows selected as the most appropriate to achieve our goals, no commitments have been made, pending availability of resources.

Competitive Analysis: Greeting Cards

Several similar products are currently on the market:

Creative Art Co.

Christmas card kit sold through Abbey Press mail order catalog. Each kit contains 12 cards (two each of five different designs and two blank cards), 12 envelopes, six small tubes of paint, and one paint brush. The cost is $9.95 (.829

cents per card), including shipping and handling.

The card designs are very poor, and while the package stated 12 cards, the kit received only had 10 in it.

Create-A-Card

Purchased at Imagination Toys in St. Louis, MO. Each kit contains eight cards, eight envelopes, and five markers, and are available in either Party Invitations (four different versions), Christmas cards, or assorted all occasion cards that include two blank cards. The cost is $5.00 (.625 cents per card).

The card designs are very simple. The kits are packaged in a very large sectioned plastic bag so that the whole package is about 16" by 12".

Cards for Kids

Distributed in gift shops, mass merchandise stores, and some mail order catalogs. The cards comes with child-like pictures already drawn and colored on them. Inside are blank spaces for children to fill in, such as: "Dear ________, Thank you for my ______. Love, __________." There is no room for the child to add any personal message or picture.

The Birthday and Get Well cards come eight to a pack and include envelopes. These wholesale for $2.25 a pack. Thank You notes, Invitations, Birth Announcements, and Moving Announcements are fold-over type cards that seal with a Cards for Kids sticker. These wholesale for $2.00 a pack. The end-user cost has been seen at prices ranging form $3.99 a pack to over $5.00 a pack via mail order.

We do not feel that these are truly competitive to our products because they do not allow the child any opportunity for creativity of their own; nor do they come with markers or decorative stickers. However, buyers who are familiar with this line do compare us to it. This is usually negative for us since we have not found any stores that have done well with this line.

Hallmark Make-Your-Own-Greeting Cards

Hallmark has recently introduced a line of "do-it-yourself" cards. The entire line takes up the end of an aisle display. A kit is available that includes four cards with printed messages but no pictures, four envelopes, and a piece of red foil to cut apart and use for decorating. The card stock is very good and the cards are a little larger than ours. The cost is $4.50 ($1.125 per card).

Individual cards are also available in a variety of styles. The individual card looks like a standard tri-fold four color card. When it is opened, the other side has an outline drawing to color. Some are designed for the person receiving the card to color; others are designed for the sender to color. In addition each card comes with a coordinated color envelope.

The quality of the individual cards is very good, and they are the same size as the cards in the kits.

The display also has Crayola crayons and markers that can be purchased to go along with the cards. The crayons are $.10 each and the markers are $.50 each.

Color Cards, for Kids

Literature has been received on this line, but we have not seen the actual product. Nor do we know how the makers are distributing their products.

Each kit contains 6 different card designs, 6 envelopes, and 4 crayons. The kits are available in Thank You, Every day, Christmas, Valentines, and Easter. The cost is $5.00 ($.833 per card).

The drawings are rather detailed to complete with crayons, and the packaging is very simple.

In general, having these competitive products on the market should not hinder our sales but, in effect, should help promote the concept of creating individualized cards. Our quality is equalled only by the Hallmark products where we have a large cost advantage. To have a comparable quantity of cards and markers from Hallmark the purchaser would spend between $8.75 and $9.50 and they still would not have any stickers. Our kits, including stickers, are retailing between $4.95 and $7.99.

After reviewing all the competitive greeting card products currently found on the market, we feel confident that we have the best value available.

Competitive Analysis: Card Facts

We have found nothing on the market that combines all the elements in our Card Facts. The closest has been several card quiz games on dinosaurs that ranged in price from $3.50 to $8.95. Our Card Facts are retailing between $3.95 and $5.99.

Product Life Cycle

Box O' Cards

The general kits should be consumed within six months of the child receiving it. The holiday series will be used within one to seven days of the child being given the kit to start preparing for that holiday event.

Card Facts

The kits should be completed within a week of the child receiving it. Once they are completed, the child will keep them as collectable items among their possessions for a minimum of six months to a year or more.

Both product families are designed to appeal to a child at the age of four. The skill level of the products vary so that as the child matures and gains better fine motor skills, there are products that still appeal to them. Currently products appeal to children up to 10 or l2 years old. The Young Artist Series (Phase III) should extend this to l4 years or older.

As a child grows out of our targeted age bracket, other children will just be growing into it. Hopefully, some of those new candidates for products will be in families with older children who are already familiar with our products. The adult would then just continue to buy products that they have already purchased and been satisfied with over the years.

The designs on the cards and stickers and the subjects for the general Card Facts have been chosen to have a long range and universal appeal. While additional designs may be added, there is no reason not to foresee the current kits still in our line 5 years from now.

Copyrights and Patents

Name searches have bean conducted on Box O' Cards, Card Facts, and Toys for a New Generation. The Trademark symbol is used on our products with all these terms.

There is nothing unique about any of our current products that merits a patent. However, all our artwork and printed material has the copyright symbol. The Card Facts line is in the process of being federally registered.

Research and Development

Market Research: Box O' Cards

Research for Box O' Cards was conducted by a team from Cleveland State University. They conducted focus groups and did personal interviews. The major points of their findings are:

- Mothers encourage their children to make their own cards but do not like to help their children step-by-step in the process.
- Children do not like writing thank you notes. A picture to color was much more interesting for the child.
- Reaction when shown the products was enthusiastic.
- Some thought the packaging should be more colorful, but did like the clear plastic bag so they could see what was inside. (A package re-design program was completed in early 1990 that resolved this issue.)
- Cards were thought to be of good quality and designs were not faddish and will hold the child's attention.

- There was some concern that the upper end of the retail price range was too high and that a price of over $4.00 would keep them from buying it.

- Several members of the focus group said they would choose a card made at a workshop for mentally retarded citizens over a card from Hallmark because it was helping a worthy cause.

- Interviews with teachers were very positive. They liked the varying degrees of difficulty and the open spaces for children to add their own words or pictures.

- Interviews with medical professionals were unanimous in that they thought the products were of excellent quality and of therapeutic value to patients.

Market Research: Card Facts

Research for Card Facts was done in house by showing prototypes to prospective buyers, customers, distributors, and representatives. General comments received were:

- The package is very colorful and professional.

- The possible subjects for additional Card Facts were endless. Most people immediately had one or two ideas for a new line of Card Facts.

- Reps and distributors were very interested in the potential for customized Card Facts.

- Not one comment was received that a $1.98 wholesale cost, with a suggested retail of $3.95, was too high. Any comments on price were that it was a great price and should sell well.

New Product Development: Box O' Cards

The only new Box O' Cards in active development is the specialized product for the promotion previously mentioned. Depending on the outcome of the licensing negotiations, there is the possibility of two or four new Box O' Cards with the licensed characters on them.

We are also in the very early stages of negotiation with a firm to put their copyrighted art on a line of greeting cards for them to sell through their zoo and tourist attraction channels.

Another current customer recently talked to us about doing these two kits in Spanish. If they decide to go with the items, we will also be able to sell them through our normal channels of distribution as well.

Other Box O' Cards kits that are under consideration but for which no resources have been committed are:

- Ethnic Birthday: Hispanic and African-American
- Ethnic Thank You : Hispanic and African-American

New Product Development: Card Facts

Many new Card Facts are being considered and are in various stages of development:

Sea Animals and Aquarium Life - We have received requests from several aquariums and sea animal parks. The University of South Florida has already contributed to research on the questions. The next step is to commit for artwork development.

Musical Instruments

A prototype has been completed in response to a request from the American Symphony League. We still need to follow with the league's members for commitments before going ahead with final development.

American Indians

Our western reps have accounts that are interested in this one. In addition, the Smithsonian Institute is constructing a new American Indian Museum due to open soon, so American Indians will be a "hot" subject in the next few years.

Pond Pals and Interesting Insects

These both fit in well with the park, zoo, and museum channels, as well as the educational distributor channel.

Farm Animals

This would be a super-easy Card Facts and could be the first in a Card Facts Series to interest the younger children. It would be of interest to the zoo channel since many have children's petting zoos. The educational distributor channel could also approach the pre-school customers.

Ballet and Gymnastics

These would add products attractive to girls. The gymnastics one would be in position to benefit from the next Olympic Games.

Jewish Holidays

A request was made for this by a distributor of Jewish products who is selling a lot of Hanukkah Box O' Cards sets. Research on questions is complete. Commitment has not been made on the artwork.

Biblical Stories

To be introduced as the "partner" to the Jewish Holidays Card Facts. This would also open up religious book store and school channels.

Young Artists Series

A program of the first four types has been put together but no commitment to artwork has been made, pending availability of funding.

Operations

Sales Force

We are developing a network of manufacturers reps and wholesale distributors across the country to supplement our home office activity. Most reps carry both of our lines and call on gift shops, card shops, drug stores, toy shops, zoos, museums, and hospital gift shops. Some rep organizations have showrooms at the major gift marts. We have found that it is not a prerequisite to do well with our products. Just being displayed in various showrooms does not generate many orders. We need rep organizations that are out on the road calling on the stores, telling them about our products.

We started out with most of our representatives in the gift industry. Since adding the Card Facts to our offerings, we have picked up many representatives in the toy channel. While the majority of their orders are for Card Facts, they do write some Box O' Cards orders. Since the toy and gift channels are so separate, we have some areas where two different reps cover the same territory.

We are always evaluating the rep organization, looking for additional coverage and replacing the unproductive reps.

To assure we maintain a good flow of communication with this increasing family of reps, a newsletter has been established and is sent out as needed.

Home Office

Concentrates efforts on certain functions:

Trade Shows

General gift shows as well as specialized shows have been done. All shows have been successful in that direct orders were written, new reps were located, and contacts were made with media reps that lead to free write-ups. We have worked with reps who exhibit at shows and have arranged to have our lines exhibited at some regional shows. Results were marginal.

Answering Inquiries

Advertisements that have run and free write-ups have generated many inquiries. All are promptly answered with a flyer, and in some cases, a sample. The leads are then passed on to the appropriate representative for follow-up.

Direct Mail Campaigns

While our original, unsuccessful attempt at direct mail was aimed at the end-user, we feel there is an opportunity to do some direct mail at the wholesale level. Many of our channels are niche markets that can be covered well by direct mail. Programs have been developed for a hospital direct-mail campaign and an art museum campaign for introduction of the Young Artist Series. However, none of these have been committed to at this time.

One-on-one Campaign

We generate individual letters to various potential customers that we read about in papers and magazines. This has been very successful and will be continued in the future.

Production Planning

All our cards were originally printed at Automated Industries, a sheltered workshop in Chesterland, Ohio. Turn around on printing can be three to four days in a rush situation. Normal lead time is two to three weeks. Due to the quick turn around, we can allow inventory of cards to get low before re-ordering.

Recently, however, our volume is exceeding the ability of AI to keep us in full supply. The printing of Card Facts has been contracted to a commercial printer. This requires a larger run which, in turn, increase the cash outlay. Turn-around time is still two weeks. We have also gone to an outside printer for several versions of Box O' Cards where we needed additional volume.

The components that are supplied by other firms have longer lead times and larger minimum order quantities. New suppliers are always being investigated to assure we are getting the best possible quality, price, terms, and service. Cost trade-offs are reviewed before an order is placed to evaluate the advantages of larger run sizes versus the larger cash outlay and cost to carry in inventory. Since so many of our items are printed materials, the cost per unitcan vary greatly depending on the size of the run. Our pricing structure was established using existing costs, so future cost reductions due to longer runs will greatly enhance our profit level.

Many of our kits are assembled at Automated Industries. They can currently assemble our needs with their existing staff. As our volume grows, they are prepared to add additional people. There is a backlog of people waiting for positions there, so they will be able to handle our volume for the near future. When volume exceeds their capability there are three possible actions:

- Workshop Industries, another employer of mentally ill residents, has already quoted on assembly and are competitive.

- Automated packaging would increase the per worker output at Automated Industries. There are several levels of automation that could be introduced as needed. The equipment would be purchased and donated or leased to AI, where it would be located and maintained. Their staff would operate it.

- Bring production in-house. An on-going volume is necessary to assure continual flow of production.

Lead time

Currently we ship orders within 48 hours of receipt. The response by reps and buyers that "Everything is in stock, ready to ship" has been excellent. They usually mark on their orders to ship complete, backorders will not be accepted. Current staffing levels can handle this volume with room for a lot of growth before additional personnel are needed. When order rates are particularly heavy, three temporary staff people are identified and trained to fill orders.

Packaging

Our original plans were to open a mail-order business. Packaging is not significant with that type of business because the product is purchased before it is shipped. Once we decided to concentrate on the wholesale channels, packaging became much more important. When Card Facts were first introduced, we used a nationally known design firm to create our package. Feedback from reps and buyers was very positive. We then converted the Box O' Cards line over to similar packaging. However, within six months it became apparent that our re-order rate was below an acceptable level. By interviewing buyers, reps, outside consultants and even other toy manufacturers, we learned that our package was too compact. While reps and buyers liked it and we continually received positive letters from people who had purchased our products, they were getting lost on the store shelves.

In early 1990 a new package was developed and introduced in New York. This appears to have solved the problems and the re-order rate is much better. There is still about $10,000 of old type packaging in stock that is being sold to unique channels where the packaging is not an issue.

Legal Structure

Toys for a New Generation was started in February, 1987, as a sole proprietorship. Then, on May 11, 1988, it was incorporated in the state of Ohio. Officer positions include President, Vice President, and Secretary/Treasurer.

Management and Staffing

The founder of the company and author of this business plan has an educational background in marketing, with a Bachelor of Business Administration degree from Boston University, and graduate work in the MBA program at the University of Delaware. I have over 18 years of work experience in various product planning and program management positions. I then spent 1 1/2 years doing extensive work in advertising, public relations, trade show planning, and product sourcing.

I currently handle all product development, advertising, public relations, establishment of distribution channels, and home office sales contacts.

During the first three and one-half years I have not drawn a salary. During 1990, in lieu of a salary, monthly payouts on the "Loan Payable" have been taken. The amount targeted for 1991 will be $1000 a month, but will be adjusted as the available funds of the company dictate.

One employee is currently working 20 to 24 hours a week in customer service, handling all the order activities. She has extensive background in service and is available for increased hours as the volume builds.

Another employee is active in the daily operation. He handles inventory, shipping, and responding to inquires received. He contributes about 10 to 15 hours a week to the operation while still maintaining outside employment. There are no plans at this time for him to join the operation on a full-time basis.

Our final regular employee is available on an as-needed basis. He averages five to ten hours a week filling in wherever he is needed.

Other part time personnel to help fill orders are trained and available on an as-needed basis.

There are other services that are contracted out, such as graphic designing, computer programming and updating, and accounting. We have identified a pool of workers we are tapping into that is very efficient for us...mothers. There are many mothers available who want to work, but do not want to commit to a full-time position due to a desire to spend more time with their children. They have talents and skills that are going unused. We are using them whenever possible. This allows us a great deal of flexibility. Even when our volume reaches the point of needing more permanent staffing, part-time and job sharing will be programs that we will use heavily.

Future Additions The next staff addition needs to be someone to concentrate efforts on sales, both through direct action and by overseeing the representative network. We will look for someone with strong sales abilities and pay a base salary plus a commission program. Time of addition will depend on sales volume building to handle the additional expense for a three month time frame while this person gets up to speed. After the initial three month time, their salary should be covered by the incremental sales that they generate.

Funding: Current

Personal funds of the owner, a line of credit at the First Bank of Boston, and extended terms by many of our suppliers have brought our business to this point. We can continue to operate with no changes in the financial structure. However, we cannot implement any new programs at this time, nor can we commit to any of the trade shows for the coming year. To accomplish quicker growth by adding new products and gaining the exposure from the trade shows, we are looking for outside investors.

In addition to funds for the 1991 growth programs, we are interested in additional investment dollars to replace some of our existing debt. Our current interest payments could then be used for additional marketing efforts.

Financial Data

Historical data for the last year and a projection for 1990 year-end has been prepared, as well as our forecasts for the next four years. The forecasts have been done showing results with current resources. There is also a presentation of programs that we would like to do over the next year. Most of these programs are quick to implement once funds are available.

$100,000 WISH LIST

If we had access to $100,000 in equity funding, we would do the following:

- ❑Implement our programs for the upcoming year
- ❑Purchase a van
- ❑Reduce outstanding debt by $62,050

Implementation of Upcoming Year's Programs

Development plans for the upcoming year consist of five areas. Each area will be detailed below. Furthermore, a chart is available upon request for each of the five areas, as well as in summary form for the entire year's plan.

Direct Mail Campaign

Both our Box O' Cards and Card Facts products have a real niche market in hospital gift shops, especially hospitals with maternity units. Many hospitals use a service from First Pic Inc. which takes pictures of the newborns in the hospital. Then the new mothers order a picture package by mail. In the catalog describing the different picture packages available, they also offer other "new baby" related merchandise. For the last two years, our Box O' Cards kits have been included in their catalog. As a result, First Pic has continuously ordered Box O' Card kits totaling several thousand units.

There are, however, many hospitals that do not use this service. Instead, they handle taking the pictures and selling them to the new mothers. In those cases, the gift shop is a prime target to carry our Box O' Cards.

While we are developing an extensive network of sales representatives across the country, many of them do not call on hospitals. The best way then to access this market is by a direct mail campaign. This program addresses this potential market by developing a direct mail piece for this market, purchasing a mail list of all hospitals in the U.S. with maternity wards, and doing a bulk mailing to them. This should result in a new customer base with continued reorders that are not seasonal and may extend to the gift shops carrying our other products as well.

Toy Fair Exhibit

Toys for a New Generation Inc. has exhibited at various gift shows, the Dallas Toy Show, and twice at the International Stationery Show, but never at Toy Fair, the biggest toy show in the country.

At the International Stationery Show this last May, the new deluxe product lines were shown. While we received orders from many different types of accounts, we consistently received orders from those customers that were in the toy business. It became evident that we must be at the next Toy Fair.

While the show is not until February, 1991, commitments to exhibit must be made by late 1990. The show traditionally sells out of exhibit space.

Stationery Show Exhibit

Toys for a New Generation Inc. has been able to sub-lease a small section of a booth for the last couple of Stationery Shows. That opportunity should be available to us for the next show as well, but we must commit to taking the space before the end of this year.

By sub-leasing the booth space, we can save a great deal of money while still getting exposure at the show. The display itself can be a modification of the display used earlier in the year at Toy Fair.

Exhibiting at both the Stationery Show and Toy Fair is not duplication. While some toy and children's stores attend both, Toy Fair is attended by stores in the toy channel while the Stationery Show is the gift and card market channel. They are very separate markets. Our Card Facts line predominates in the toy market, while our Box O' Cards line is featured at the Stationery Show.

Card Facts: Young Artist Cards Four New Products

Toys for a New Generation Inc. does very well in the museum channel. Currently, we have nothing for the art museum channel. To fill this product void, we plan to do a Young Artist Cards of Card Facts. Each kit would have five of the major works of that particular artist and the sixth card would be a portrait of the artist, with questions on that artist.

To introduce this series we will do the following artists: Michelangelo, Leonardo da Vinci, Raphael, and Donatello.

The theme of the introduction would be "Don't let this generation grow up thinking Michelangelo, Leonardo, Raphael, and Donatello are deformed creatures living in the sewers." A rough direct mail piece has already been developed showing a bunch of turtle figures with Michelangelo in the middle. The headline is "Will the real Michelangelo please stand up?"

By using these four particular artists, we can draw on the momentum of the turtle characters and get a lot of press coverage in the trade journals. Not only will this help with sales of the Young Artists Series, but should pull through to our other products as well.

The Young Artist Cards, while designed for the art museum niche market, has appeal for the general educational toy market as well. It would be a good series to introduce at Toy Fair in February. Preliminary research has been started, so if artwork can be started by mid-December, product should be available by Toy Fair. The "turtle" theme could then be the basis for the booth display and should attract a lot of attention.

Card Facts: Aquarium and Sea Life Two New Products

One of our target markets is the tourist attraction channel. We are trying to position Card Facts as the ideal souvenir. A large segment of the tourist business is in aquariums and sea life parks. We currently have no products to serve this market.

This market is a concise, niche market that can be approached by a direct mail campaign to get right at the primary target market. In addition, there is a strong secondary market through general toy and gift channels.

Preliminary research has been started. If artwork is started by mid-December, product should be available for Toy Fair in February.

Purchase of a Van

The personal van of the founder is currently being used. It has approximately 90,000 miles and is not dependable for long trips. A van is necessary for picking up materials, transporting them to Automated Industries, and bringing finished goods back for shipment.

Reliable transportation would also allow us to participate in regional trade shows which can be done economically by driving. Due to outstanding debts incurred to establish the business, personal purchase of a new van is not an option.

Reduction of Current Line of Credit

While most investors do not like to hear of using investment money to reduce existing debt, we need to do so. The amount of interest currently being paid is significantly hindering our growth; currently over 14% of our expenditures are interest. Converting some outstanding debt to equity would help us reduce our interest payment so that more of our income can be re-invested in growth programs.

FINANCIAL DATA

A comprehensive review of financial data is available upon request through various charts and graphs. The following is a general breakdown of what is available:

- ❑ Sales summary for the past five years
- ❑ Balance sheet of both assets and liabilities and equity
- ❑ Company income statement
- ❑ Breakeven analysis for the current year, including a chart
- ❑ Projected operating statements chart for the next 3 years
- ❑ Cash flow forecast for the next 3 years
- ❑ Income statement and balance sheet from the original Box O' Cards product

Virtual Reality

BUSINESS PLAN

BUILDING AIDS INC.

123 Main St.
Simpson Grove, CA 37911

July 10, 1993

Building Aids Inc. is a new company formed to take advantage of virtual reality technology in its application to new home design and construction. The company will develop and provide virtual reality tours and "blue prints" of homes in order to assist both architects and prospective purchasers. The following plan outlines the company's structure, present and future goals, and need for capital.

VIRTUAL REALITY BUSINESS PLAN

EXECUTIVE SUMMARY

The formation of Building Aids Inc. as aspecialized service company is the result of exploration of the high technological advancements of computer graphic design integrated with eighteen years of personal commitment to quality work for, in, and around various areas of the building industry. The initial goal is to provide home owners and builders, architects, designers, and related manufacturers and suppliers with the innovative concept of three-dimensional graphic designs integrated with virtual reality (V.R.) definition. The designs will be made available as real-time animations on computer discs and video cassette tapes. To date, no one has approached the home plan publications market with sales revenues in excess of three billion ($3,000,000,000) dollars with such a unique and affordable concept. With the assistance of the Hawaii Small Business Development Center, Building Aids Inc. will have the unique opportunity to participate in an Incubator Program, which will provide office space at little or no cost, at their EDIC Center located at 45 Maple Ln.

A major obstacle that exists for architects and builders as well as for the consumer is the difficulty to conceptualize the finished product. It is very difficult, if not impossible, to transfer a two-dimensional perspective into a three-dimensional one. In October of 1991 I began researching alternative solutions to this problem. By integrating computer software programs, I have created an application for three dimensional virtual reality (V.R.) animated movies.

Forecasters project that this technology will take years to become affordable to the public. Virtual Reality technologists and multimedia producers state, "within ten years the virtual reality market will be affordable to consumers with home electronic toys, games, and entertainment systems. It will be used in public attractions like rides, movies and exhibits. It will be an extension of the 'human computer' used in training, physical therapy, medical research, and practices of non-invasive surgery, by schools and universities."

The more advanced technology already exists and has been pursued primarily by government agencies (e.g. NASA) and corporations with the investment capital that can afford the high cost of the main frame data banks. Transferring data to video tape eliminates large capital outlays and minimizes resources, resulting in a high quality multimedia product with built-in flexibility for rapid change.

Inexpensive demonstration tapes will allow consumers to explore the three-dimensional realm of virtual reality by viewing custom home designs by "walking" from room to room. Plans would be available for purchase from the Building Aids library. These tapes will also demonstrate the capabilities of scanning a design or 2-D building plan with a computer and transforming them into a 3-D environment. It will allow one to walk around the outside and through the inside of their home before it is actually built.

The company's initial year will largely be an organizational one due to the high growth rates the company will undergo. It is essential that suitable systems and procedures be implemented at the onset to achieve the financial goals that have been established. To experience a successful start-up and ongoing development, funding in the amount of two hundred thousand dollars ($200,000) is necessary. This will allow for the purchase of equipment; initial operating costs, including but not limited to the consultation and contracting of an attorney, accountants, marketing, and sales; management team salaries; and debt service for the first year of operation.

The management team of Building Aids Inc. consists of highly specialized individuals with training in both the building and computer-aided design technologies. The General Manager will establish the company and its facilities, implement market and sales, and conduct research and design development. The Technical Operations Manager will assist in research, design/developments and production control. The Senior Engineer will make purchase recommendations and maintain and upgrade the equipment, as well as assist in the design and production of home plans. The Administrative Assistant will set up database programs for accounting, sales, and distribution of products, as well as maintain customer relations.

The company will have a limited number of competitors in its target market. Some of these competitors are larger than Building Aids Inc. and have access to more financial resources than the company, but these companies have not developed the interactive process to approach the market with the technical and marketing strategies of our company.

Marketing Strategy

Building Aids Inc. is a company providing the following services:

❑ Custom plans and designs to worldwide market of:

- ♦ Do-It-Yourself consumers
- ♦ Residential home owners and builders
- ♦ Commercial developers
- ♦ Industrial suppliers

❑ The marketing of these services will consist primarily of Computerized directories (e.g. Procurement Automated Source System (PASS))

❑ Direct mail

- ♦ National Trade Associations of the U.S. and Canada
- ♦ Professional Associations of the U.S. and Canada

- ❑Telemarketing
- ❑Newspapers and Periodicals
    - ♦The Babson Entrepreneurial Review
    - ♦Small Business Reporter
    - ♦Wall Street Journal, New York Times
- ❑Consumer Publications (e.g. Better Homes & Garden)
    - ♦Home Magazine
    - ♦Personal Computing Mac User, Byte
    - ♦AI, Architectural Digest, Victorian Homes
    - ♦Mac World, PC Magazine, PC Computing
    - ♦Home Office, Amiga World
- ❑Trade magazines
    - ♦Builder
    - ♦Fine Home Building
    - ♦Architectural Record
- ❑Newsletters
- ❑Reprints to targeted audiences
- ❑Trade Shows
- ❑Visual Presentations
- ❑Videos
- ❑Computer Bulletin Boards
    - ♦America Online, Inc.
    - ♦GEnie
    - ♦HouseNet & Prodigy Services, Co.
- ❑Exhibit creativity and innovative solutions (not only within design and problem solving areas, but for use with others approach to marketing and client communications)

Management Team

Building Aids Inc. will be established as a Limited Liability Corporation.

- ❑Principal Managers/Staff and their titles:
    - ♦General Manager, Phil Orlando
    - ♦Administrative Assistant, Carrie Green
    - ♦Technical Operations Manager, Susan Selden
    - ♦Senior Engineer, Linda Cardinale

❑Objectives of the Management Team:

Building Aids Inc.'s initial year will consist of organizing and developing. Since the company will be providing office facilities, this eliminates one major activity in the company's development. After obtaining the start-up capital, efforts in the first year will be concentrated in the following key areas:

- ♦Legal organization
- ♦Purchasing and installing equipment
- ♦Development of information management and design libraries
- ♦Marketing and sales

Initial sales of the company will consist of demonstration tapes and custom designed homes. These sales will generate cash flow and establish Building Aids in the marketplace.

Financial Considerations

The projected Income Statement has been compiled from the 1991-92 editions of the following: *Industry Norms and Key Business Ratios*, published by Dun and Bradstreet; *Thomas Register*, *Value Line*, and *International Economic Indicators*, and *The State of Small Businesses: A Report of The President.* The sales forecast for the first year is a worse case scenario.

Operating expenses are based on the industry standards with minimum salaries for the management team, independent contractors, marketing and sales, expenses, and repayment of debt service beginning on the seventh month of operation as cash flow is being established. Positive cash flow appears in month ten with year end expenses exceeding total sales.

Second year sales will show a major increase with target market being extended to 80% of potential market. Operating expenses may fluctuate depending on needs and demands. Salary increases, along with other options, will be in proportion to productivity,performance and achievement of individual goals.

Third year sales are still forecasted at conservative percentage increases based on actual economic indicators for the industry. Production and sales will increase as additional employees are added to the technical and design staff.

Anticipated profits for the first three years of operations are as follows:

Year 1	<$23,308.00>
Year 2	$140,505.00
Year 3	$150,125.00

Funds to be distributed:

Equipment Purchase	$82,000.00
Operating Costs	$26,500.00
Consultation/Contracting	$40,000.00
Salaries	$60,900.00
Total	$209,400.00

PRODUCT AND SERVICES - FIRST YEAR

Computerized three-dimensional enhancements of home plans with a virtual reality walk-through beginning from the exterior of the home through the front door and into each room of the house. Virtual Reality presentations can be purchased as floppy discs or as a VCR video tape.

Additional Services:

- Energy calculations for specific geographical areas
- Cost analysis for geographical area regarding R-values of insulation, window and door comparisons, heating/air conditioning units and gas appliances by cost and efficiency.
- Interior design - scanned photo images of actual furniture, cabinetry, lighting fixtures etc.
- Material lists.
- Design alterations - change room dimension, etc.
- Landscaping presentations.

Product Costs (Suggested Retail Price):

❑Demonstration Tape - $20.00 - examples of walkthroughs, three dimensional designs, marketing uses and sales presentations.

❑Video/Floppy Discs - Starting at $250.00.

- Energy Calculation - $85.00.
- Complete Comparative Cost Analysis - $100.00
- Design Alterations - $1.50/sq. ft.
- Landscapes - $.75/sq. ft.
- Scanned Images and Consultation - $50.00/hr.

FUTURE PRODUCTS AND SERVICES

❑ With five employees in the second year and inclusion of additional target market:

- ♦ Design and Concept Development
- ♦ Layouts and Computer Three Dimensional Graphics
- ♦ Illustrations
- ♦ Virtual Reality Presentation Material:
  Slides, Videos, Imaging, Posters, Large Scale Displays and Exhibits, Photo Imaging and Elevation, and Sectional Perspectives Renderings

❑ With seven employees in the third year, including expansion into commercial and industrial markets. Also offering franchises of information management libraries and technical support.

❑ Proprietary Features-- will apply for:

- ♦ Patents
- ♦ Copyrights
- ♦ Trademark

THE MARKET

$3 Billion Annual Growth

❑ Individuals

- ♦ Home Owners
- ♦ New Home Buyers
- ♦ Retirees
- ♦ Do It Yourselfers - Adding on or remodeling

❑ Professionals

- ♦ Builders
- ♦ Developers
- ♦ Architects
- ♦ Designers
- ♦ Resources: American Institute of Building Design (AIBD)
  Sacramento, CA 95815

❑ Commercial/Industrial Companies

- ♦ Building Supply
- ♦ Home Improvement Centers
- ♦ Industrial Suppliers
- ♦ Manufacturers (doors, windows, heating, etc.)

THE COMPETITION

No direct competition exists at the present time.

❑ Existing Companies

- Commercial Design\Graphic Corporations - $5M+
- CADCAM, Inc - $5M+, Dayton, Ohio.
- Circuit CAD Corp. - $1M+
- CACI, Inc. - $50M+, Chesapeake, Virginia.

❑ CAD Designers

- Turbo Scan International - $9M+, Coral Gables, Florida.
- Willow Peripherals - (NR) $1M+, Bronx, New York.

❑ Residential Home Plan Books

- Home Magazines - $20.00/plan book, $330 minimum, Newport Beach, California.
- Better Homes and Gardens - $425 minimum, Des Moines, Iowa.
- Builder (NAHB) - $350 minimum, Washington, D.C.
- Custom Builder - $385 minimum, Yarmouth, Maine.
- Princeton Plans Press - $330+, Princeton, New Jersey.
- W.D. Farmers Homes - Planbooks - $69.00, Atlanta, Georgia.

Estimate sales and revenues with comparative products and services. No availability of three-dimensional virtual reality technology.

❑ Architects and Designers - charge on percentage basis of building costs. Average cost to build a 1400 sq. ft. house in 1991 = $117,000.00. Architect fee @ 10% - $11,700.00.

❑ Design Services (e.g. RCM Corporation, Columbia, Maryland).
Three phase design services

Preliminary	$2,000.00
Design Phase	$2,000.00
Complete	$2.000.00
Total services	$6,000.00

MARKETING OBJECTIVES AND STRATEGIES

After extensively researching the Commercial and Private marketing opportunities, I have concluded that the most effective and efficient approach to initiate the marketing of products and services is by market segmentation and the use of direct as well as indirect methods of advertising.

The direct method will be aggressive. It will entail new product releases in key industrial/commercial as well as consumer publications, computer billboard announcements, together with sending out demonstration tapes to the architectural, design, construction, home improvement, and development industries. In addition, trade show attendance and participation will allow product introduction and overall industry awareness to take place. This extensive exposure with appropriate follow-up will generate an at-large industry demand. The indirect strategy will consist of identifying sales representative agencies, wholesalers, distributors, and retailers in key locations to nationally and internationally represent Building Aids Inc. Specially modified and custom demonstration videos will be prepared so that the indirect agencies are equipped to target market and be successful in their efforts. Creative and innovative agency training programs as well as compensation packages will be used to motivate the indirect sales force.

Production and Distribution Corporate offices will be located at 123 Main. The first six months will be spent organizing an information management library for immediate and direct access to designs and energy calculations. This will allow Building Aids to generate some "bread and butter" cash flow as it further invests efforts to get the direct and indirect marketing strategies underway. As part of reaching and informing the consumer, a composite demonstration video highlighting capabilities will be produced. Credit toward the customers' order will be made in the event that a custom design order is placed. The equipment required for development and production of virtual reality animations consists of three separate main computers with monitors, scanners, printers, plotters, GVP Impact Controllers, Processor Cards, Video Cameras, VHS & VCR recorders and controllers, modems, copiers, video monitors and relative software programs.

COMPANY STRUCTURE

Building Aids Inc. will be established as a Limited Liability Company incorporated under the laws of the state of Hawaii. The General Manager will be Phil Orlando. The two key management members will be Susan Selden and Linda Cardinale.

A quasi Board of Directors will be set up as an alternative to a formal Board of Advisors and Consultants.

Virtual Reality

BUSINESS PLAN

CineMedia Studios, Inc.

37404 Bedlington Park Pl.
Bedlington, WA 56390

June 23, 1992

CineMedia Studios is an aggressive developer of unique virtual reality entertainment products. Catering to the intelligent user seeking a game with intellect, it is seeking additional capital to fund more projects in its already well-received line. Following is an outline of a progressive company plan that can provide insight into product development and marketing.

VIRTUAL REALITY BUSINESS PLAN

EXECUTIVE SUMMARY

In 1990, CineMedia Studios was formed to fill the void in the marketplace for intelligent, sophisticated, interactive entertainment. The studio has grown to create world-class, interactive multimedia software products designed to take advantage of the rapidly expanding market. CineMedia Studios follows an artistic vision of interactive storytelling and entertainment, defining new boundaries of personal involvement with computer-based cinema. It continually explores the territory of this new media, charting ways to bring together user interaction, video, text, graphics, animation, music and sound.

CineMedia Studios now intends to capitalize on the immediate opportunities for growth in this explosive market by building our business to the next tier, expanding our operations to encompass publishing as well as production, and significantly increasing the number of innovative titles we produce each year.

Background

For the last several years, this industry has been geared towards children, and sales of computer games and equipment have risen steadily. Unfortunately, parents have found it much more difficult to find computer software that will challenge as well as entertain. This trend will continue as the Nintendo generation grows up; one need only take a look at all of the computers being used in classrooms around the country to see the potential adult market.

CineMedia Studios believes adults are hungry for intelligent, interactive entertainment that takes advantage of the computer but jettisons the adolescent trappings of computer and video games. The advent of the large installed base of CD-ROM drives coupled with the increased sophistication of computer technology has now made the delivery of this kind of content possible. According to a new study done by Simba Information, Inc., the market for consumer-based CD-ROM titles is expected to double this year, generating over $300 million. With the increased penetration of CD-ROM drives leaving consumers searching for more diverse content, audiences are clearly ready for the titles that CineMedia creates.

In the past, CineMedia Studios has developed distribution arrangements in order to produce our interactive software. We now seek capital to develop our own titles, and to establish a publishing arm. This will solidify the future of our development, and is designed to capitalize on the enormous opportunity in this industry - one that, like the golden age of Hollywood, may never come again.

Our company developed The Lunacy of Ronald, which sold out of its initial run by the end of 1993. We have operated at a break-even position ever since because every dollar we make is immediately put back into the development of the company and additional software products. Revenue projected for fiscal year

1995 is expected to be $2,000,000. Annual growth is projected to be at least 50-60% per year through 1996. We are now ready to expand our operation to achieve maximum growth in the next five years.

Concept

CineMedia Studios' target market includes educated adults ages 18 to 45 who have the latest in computer technology available in their homes and a disposable income. This combines the current market of "early adopters" with females 21-40 and college-educated families with growing children.

Our strategy for dominating the competition is through the continued development of products, each as entertaining and technologically advanced as the last. Future products, will be strategically designed to chart a course for the market, and then follow up with products that will capture the interest of our audience again and again, building brand awareness and encouraging repeat customers.

Our work on CD-ROM has already broken new ground and will continue to lead the industry in interactive cinema. Our competition is just now entering the market and must develop the expertise and experience we already bring to our titles. The ability to develop award-winning interactive films from the ground up is unique to CineMedia. Our customers expect intelligent, engrossing entertainment and leading-edge technology when they reach for our products. Since our products take a completely different approach of the traditional computer game, we've found a niche others have not been able to capture.

We have just completed the development of Astral Gate: No One Sleeps Here, a full-length, interactive movie. The press we've received for this product has been voluminous, and our proprietary method of presentation, AbsoluteCinema (patent pending), is setting the standard for interactive movie entertainment.

All products from CineMedia Studios are protected by trademark, copyright laws, and patents.

We are currently developing two titles, Astral Gate II and Gateways, an interactive movie theater environment that contains ten interactive films: six new films and four others that have already garnered multiple awards, including two Best of Shows at QuickTime™ Festivals.

In addition to our existing products, we have written treatments for another dozen software products that will build on the technology available and the demands of the market. We also have a project list of seventy other titles.

Other services include teaching and speaking engagements by our CEO and founder, James St. Clair. We are also beginning to involve other members of our organization in these capacities, including our resident composer, our computer programming team, and our award-winning digital architect.

CineMedia has been watching the movement of the interactive industry, and we have now decided to move into a strong growth phase, both to keep up with the sheer number of CD-ROM titles being distributed every year, and to capitalize on the current market opportunities for a company such as ours. This approach is generating a tremendous amount of interest throughout our industry. For example, CineMedia's recent signing with the Agency for the Performing Arts in Hollywood resulted in coverage on the front page of the Business Section in the Los Angeles Times Sunday edition.

Responses from customers and the press indicate that our software titles are enjoying an excellent reputation, and a shelf life that is far above average. Inquiries from prospective customers suggest a considerable demand. Relationships with leading retailers, manufacturers and other distributors substantiate the expectation of CineMedia Studios for rapid growth and accomplishment in our industry.

Objectives

Our current objective is to people the company into a prominent market position. We feel that within two years CineMedia Studios will be in a suitable position for even greater expansion or an initial public offering. To accomplish this goal we have developed a comprehensive plan to intensify and accelerate our marketing and sales activities, product engineering and development, and customer service.

We also intend to take on a strategic partner, either a distributor or a publisher, who can guide us into the future while providing us with some of the necessary services that CineMedia inherently avoids. We will implement a publishing division designed to bring unique, marketable titles to an expanding audience. Our partner will help get these properties into retail channels in a time when shelf space is becoming scarce, and will also help us achieve our goal of marketing our titles through innovative sales channels.

To implement our two-year plan, we require an initial investment of $2 million, followed by a second tier funding of $6-10 million for the following purposes:

❑ Develop ten new innovative, interactive software titles for the mainstream market.

❑ Solidify relationships with strong strategic partners/distributors, exploring innovative new sales channels.

❑ Hire and develop a small, focused publishing team that will bring in new products and collaborate with the marketing department to sell them through known or unique channels.

❑ Develop a campaign to promote our current products and services, in order to maximize sales, educating and exciting our customers as we go.

❑ Augment company staff to support and sustain prolonged growth under the new marketing plan.

❑ Increase Research & Development to create additional technologies as well as to further fine-tune our competitive advantages through our existing proprietary software tools.

Management

Our Management team consists of seven men and women:

James St. Clair, MFA, is our founder, CEO, and Artistic Director. His background consists of over ten years' experience as an award-winning actor, director and author combined with eight years' computer experience. He is now on the faculty of San Diego State University's Multimedia Studios Program and a coveted lecturer all over the world.

Evelyn Hallstrom, President, has seven years' experience in sales and marketing and single-handedly propelled CineMedia from a two-person operation to the leading-edge growth company it is today.

Katherine Mailor, Executive Vice-President, serves as an integral part of the day-to-day management of the company, acting as both Director of Human Resources and Production Coordinator.

Jack Lockheart, Vice-President and Chief Marketing Officer, has fourteen years of sales and marketing experience in various arenas, including the Live Aid Concert where he raised over $20 million, the 1984 Los Angeles Olympics, and most recently, major motion pictures.

Diane Armstrong, Vice President and Chief Financial Officer, has seven years of financial, corporate development, management and systems consulting experience; in her last position, she worked with American General Life Insurance Company.

Thomas Calloway, Vice-President of Technology, has twelve years' experience in systems engineering and design, including nine years with NASA and other aerospace development companies.

Michael Peters, Vice President of Audio Production, is a musician with twenty years' experience in the music industry. He composed, arranged, performed, recorded, produced and engineered the complete soundtracks for both of our interactive films.

In addition, our Advisory Council offers outside management advice and consultation. This nine member council provides tremendous support for management decisions and creativity. A list of council members is available on request.

Marketing

Overall, our company can be characterized as a high profile producer of world-class interactive multimedia entertainment.

The fundamental thrust of our marketing strategy in the short term involves reaching the audience searching for intelligent adult entertainment, through traditional software retail stores as well as untapped channels.

In the near future, we plan to lead the industry in the production of interactive movies for television and theater, and computer platforms. We anticipate a campaign aimed at filmgoers, and intend to reach this market segment by placing a variety of advertisements in industry publications and mailing a full-color catalog to retail outlets every three months.

A partial list of current customers incudes:

- Warner Music Enterprises, Inc. (client)
- Arthur Anderson Consulting, Inc. (client)
- Media Vision, Inc. (distributor)
- Micro Warehouse, Inc. (catalog distributor)
- Tiger Software (retailer)
- Educorp, Inc. (retailer)

Also, we are targeting Europe as a strong future market: a deal is being negotiated for distribution and localization of The Lunacy of Ronald throughout Japan and Australia, and 35,000 copies of Astral Gate I: No One Sleeps Here have already been shipped overseas, resulting in very favorable press.

Finance

Based on conservative estimates, CineMedia Studios' asset baseapproximates $3,000,000, including cash, receivables, equipment and the value of copyrights and patents pending. In just two years we will have grossed $28,000,000 in sales and our investors will be able to collect a return on investment within five years.

Vision

CineMedia Studios' long-term strategy is keyed to the future of interactive media. We are currently pursuing all possible trademarks, copyrights, and patents, in order to increase the value of our intellectual property and our technology. We are already negotiating to license the appropriate material to other companies who seek to duplicate our methods of interactive filmmaking and its related elements.

CineMedia is very aware of the changing face of the industry, and is constantly preparing for the future. For example, raw film assets are archived at the highest possible levels for repurposing in a future iteration of the medium. Possibilities might include a port to another platform, interactive television, and forms of new media that have yet to be invented. Our proprietary perspective-switching technique is ideally suited for feature-like films, delivered via interactive television, and AbsoluteCinema is equally appropriate for virtual reality-based programs.

CineMedia Studios is a content producer first and foremost, and until a standard is established, will continue to work on whatever platform is exciting and commercially viable.

Conclusion

CineMedia Studios enjoys an established track record as a unique supplier of interactive entertainment to our audience. By carving the niche in the marketplace for interactive cinema, we intend to continue our advances in the multimedia marketplace with many more exciting entertainment products, geared toward a sophisticated, educated customer.

PRESENT SITUATION

Market Environment

This fledgling industry is only now beginning to be taken seriously by investors and market forecasters. Fortunately, we had already begun our groundwork over three years ago when interactive multimedia is just beginning to develop and digital video was not yet a reality for the desktop. CineMedia Studios is poised on the cutting edge of a rapidly changing growth environment, better positioned than other companies who are just now facing the challenges of this industry.

Products and Services

We currently have two titles on the market: the critically acclaimed interactive novel, The Lunacy of Ronald and Astral Gate I: No One Sleeps Here, the first interactive movie to take advantage of the technology of AbsoluteCinema. (patent pending).

We have just completed work on a Macintosh version of Astral Gate, and by September will have finished. Astral Gate II for the MPC. We are developing an interactive CD-ROM version of Warner Music Enterprises' "**rock**video monthly," which will begin shipping in January, and will start work this fall on The Lunacy of Ronald Book II, which has just received a development contract. We also have twelve products in various stages of development, including four interactive movies. Written treatments for these products are available on request.

Product Life Cycle

Because our work is leading edge, our products have shown themselves to have a long life cycle. For example, The Lunacy of Ronald earned awards a full year after it was introduced and its sales reflected this.

Pricing and Profitability

Current prices are decreasing, but profits are rising far more rapidly. As price points continue to drop, market awareness and profitability will grow.

Customers

Current customers are using our products for their own entertainment; our titles have also been used by many professors as teaching tools. Our customers are requesting more of the same -- intelligent titles with universal themes.

Distribution

Currently we make available Astral Gate I: No One Sleeps Here through a distributor that does not have right of first refusal on any new products we develop. We distribute The Lunacy of Ronald through various catalog retailers around the world and are about to ink a distribution relationship for this title (a letter of agreement has already been signed).

Management

Our management team is largely in place. We have proven we have the right talent to develop world-class interactive cinema, and our business, simultaneously. However, as the studio expands, we certainly intend to bring on more strong, dedicated talent, including a COO.

Financial Resources

Current cash available is $55,765

Our Current Ratio is:

Assets/Liabilities=1.8:1

Our Quick Ratio is:

(Cash & Equivalents + Accounts Receivable
+ Notes Receivable)/ Total Current Liabilities = 10:1

OBJECTIVES

The primary objectives of our organization are to:

- Continue to create world-class interactive cinema, literature and entertainment.
- Grow the company in two significant steps that will allow CineMedia to go public within two years, ensuring that investors receive a substantial return on investment within five years.
- Expand our technological and employee base as the market expands, exploring new arenas in the interactive multimedia frontier.
- Create a commercial niche as creators of leading-edge titles.
- Produce unique, highly-marketable products resulting in a library of titles that will drive this industry forward.
- Establish a marketing and communications model that exploits untapped new and existing revenue channels for multimedia titles.

Business Goals

The business goals of CineMedia Studios, in order of their importance are as follows:

❑**Quality Products.** CineMedia is in the business of producing the highest quality products. This is our number one priority and our greatest strength.

❑**Profits/Customer Satisfaction.** We must remain profitable to sustain the company in this rapidly changing industry; with our software products, we are fulfilling a customer demand that others in this field have not been able to meet.

❑**Growth.** We realize the vital importance of growth at this phase in the marketing cycle in interactive multimedia products. We would like to take CineMedia Studios public within two years - our interim plan includes employee and market share growth to accomplish our goal of producing at least ten titles each year.

❑**Management.** Up to now, our company is been self-managed, but we recognize the need for a special type of developer management structure as growth takes hold. When small developers are purchased by large distributors, we have often witnessed the unfortunate drop in product quality; the management paradigm is entirely different, and developers cannot operate within the confines of a traditional corporate management structure. We, therefore, intend to add additional strong management personnel to allow us to remain self-managed within a more non-traditional structure.

❑**People.** The people who work for CineMedia Studios are the best in their fields, and we not only utilize their specific industry skills, we incorporate their special talents into our company's vision.

Rationale

Based on our previous work and the talented management of this company, we are poised to create inroads in the technology of this medium, where others are just now learning the basics. Our work is innovative and marketable because we have the industry experience, technological innovation, and creative content, combined with marketing and management savvy to stay on the leading edge in a rapidly changing business.

The New Market

The market for interactive cinema will be comprised of the "early adopters" of new media, and traditional moviegoers who are open to new forms of entertainment. These will include both men and women, both game-players and computer neophytes. Just as the home market is expanding to become the fastest-growing segment of computer users (Multimedia News, June, 1994), so is the market for interactive cinema growing to accommodate users who now have something intelligent, innovative, and engaging to purchase.

Interactive cinema is certainly not designed to replace linearfilm. With the advent of Hollywood, movies did not replace the traditional theatre, which remains a worldwide form of entertainment after seventy years of filmmaking. However, movies became a distinct, profitable venture, and found overwhelming acceptance despite the early years of nay-sayers and the now apocryphal stories of people running screaming from the theater because they thought the locomotive would run them down. When people have something to watch, they will begin to embrace interactive film as an alternative, and even an enhancement, to traditional movies; the positive international attention CineMedia has received for its work only endorses this theory.

Position for Growth

- ❑Understand customers, competition and industry
- ❑Develop product/channel/customer congruency, & new revenue channels
- ❑Achieve short-term goals while strategically planning for long-term
- ❑Monitor and manage product life cycles
- ❑Monitor growth by fields of interest
- ❑Balance people/management/business goals
- ❑Transition from single-point to distributed management
- ❑Hire the best people
- ❑Grow to 50 employees
- ❑Continue to develop our vision

Within the next year, we will ally ourselves with a major motion picture studio or a major name director, in order to further facilitate the acceptance of interactive films as true entertainment. Also, we will take on the first portion of growth capital as CineMedia charts its course for the future.

We expect to develop a market niche dominated by CineMedia Studios, Inc. We will sign at least one strategic partnership with a distributor this year, in addition to finding distributors for specific products. We will work with various companies as we search for a distributor who understands and believes in our family of products and the company vision.

FINANCIAL PROJECTIONS

Projecting Returns in a Growth Industry

According to a study completed in June 1994 by Frost & Sullivan, an international high-technology research firm, the U.S. market for multimedia hardware and software will more than quadruple from $4.9 billion in 1993 to over $22 billion by the end of the decade.

"End-users are increasingly aware of the impact multimedia can have on a range of applications prominently including training and education, business presentations and home entertainment," Frost & Sullivan note. "And multimedia's ability to bring together sound, animation, motion video and still images together with text on a PC or workstation will eventually make it the dominant form of computing."

In this type of growth industry, financial projections can be difficult to make. The urge is to be optimistic, and in the short history of multimedia, not unfounded. A long-term track record has not yet been established, although all signs suggest massive growth.

With the success of the video game markets and sales in the billions of dollars, the potential profits into the year 2000 are very lucrative indeed. All of this movement in the industry by hardware developers is excellent for CineMedia Studios. The demand for content to fill the vacuum established by better hardware is already a familiar cry; the need for more entertaining and unique software to run on these machines will soon be overwhelming.

Use of Funding Proceed

CineMedia Studios has developed a line of interactive multimedia software products that is entertaining, leading-edge, and unique, pioneering its own niche in the industry. In order to service the identified target markets and the potential markets with these exceptional products, significant capital infusion is required.

Specifically, the required $2 million will be allocated appropriately to:

Marketing Advertising	$100,000
Equipment	$200,000
Research & Development	$200,000
Operational Expenses	$500,000
Title Development	$1,000,000
Total	$2,000,000

Financial Reports

The following pages contain historical financial information, current figures (as 4/30/94), and projections. These reports are included:

- CineMedia Studios Balance Sheet 1992, 1993
- CineMedia Studios Balance Sheet as of 4/30/94
- CineMedia Studios Income Statement 1992, 1993
- CineMedia Studios Income Statement (month of 4/94)

Balance Sheet

ASSETS		
	1992	1993
Current Assets		
Cash	3,960	16,317
Accounts Receivable	0	708,428
Fixed Assets		
Furniture & Fixtures	1,934	7,519
Computer Equipment	23,67420	1,176
Computer Software	0	30,741
Music Equipment	0	19,872
Other Equipment	0	17,833
Accumulated Depreciation	-4,406	-4,406
Total Assets	$25,161	997,479
LIABILITIES & EQUITY		
Accounts Payable	0	4,255
Loans Payable	0	35,000
Equipment Lease Payable	0	224,673
Total Liabilities	0	331,220
STOCKHOLDERS EQUITY		
Retained Earnings	14,718	-84,540
Current Earnings	10,443	750,799
Total Equity	25,1616	66,259
TOTAL LIABILITIES & EQUITY	25,1619	97,479

Balance sheet

As of 4/30/94

ASSETS	
Bank and Cash Accounts	
Checking Account I	0.00
Checking Account II	55,764.69
Total Bank and Cash Accounts	55,764.69
Other Assets	
Accounts Receivable	201,628.80
Accumulated Depreciation	(4,406.33)
Computer Hardware	289,194.94
Computer Software	71,039.29
Filming Equipment	53,746.48
Furniture & Fixtures	15,280.34
Sound Equipment	22,341.48
Total Other Assets	648,825.00
Total Assets	704,589.69
LIABILITIES	
Credit Cards	5,032.79
Other Liabilities	
Accounts Payable	20,549.92
Equipment Lease Payable	350,490.13
Loans Payable 1	4,999.00
Payroll Taxes Payable	0.00
Total Other Liabilities	386,039.05
Total Liabilities	391,071.84
NET WORTH	313,517.85

Income and Expense Statement (1992-1993)

	1992	1993
INCOME		
The Lunacy of Ronald	35,000	86,927
IMAGINaction magazine	2,526	-570
Astral Gate I: Macintosh	0	157,104
Astral Gate I: MPC	0	572,308
RADS	5,000	0
Gateways: Macintosh	0	125,150
Astral Gate II: MPC	0	358,071
Gateways: MPC	0	190,263
Teaching Income	0	3,720
Miscellaneous Income	27,567	24,211
Total Income	70,093	1,517,184
COST OF GOODS SOLD		
Cost of Sales	14,494	17,502
GROSS PROFIT	55,599	1,499,682
EXPENSES		
Salaries	0	133,987
Contract Labor Costs	0	214,374
Consulting Fees	0	27,428
Payroll Taxes	0	76,835
Advertising	0	15,474
Art Expenses	90	2,221
Bank Service Charges	81	321
Conference Fees	1,042	5,974
Cost of Credit	0	385
Dues & Subscriptions	102	2,069
Entertainment	2,363	2,598
Filming Expense	52 2	9,714
Gifts	0	372
Insurance	0	3,634
Interest Expense	0	481
Licenses	50	970
Travel Lodging	200	4,505
Travel Meals	828	4,490
Travel-Airline Expense	1,520	19,574
Moving Expense	0	13,131
Miscellaneous Expense	21,079	140,835
Music Expense	160	35
Office Expense	7,537	7,595
Patents/Copyrights	0	11,745
Postage/Freight	1,797	8,190
Rent-Office	1,130	6,655
Rent-Equipment	4,258	25,205
Rent-Vehicles	0	2,453

Income and Expense Statement (1992-1993)...*continued*

Rent-Other	1,786	643
Repairs & Maintenance	0	24
Telephone	1,082	6,466
Total Expenses	$45,157	748,883
NET OPERATING INCOME	10,443	750,799

Income Statement 4/1/94-4/30/94

INCOME	
The Lunacy of Ronald	
Catalog	10,620.79
Individual order	242.63
Retailer	599.60
Total The Lunacy of Ronald	11,463.02
Other Income	
Teaching	1,340.00
Total Other Income	1,340.00
Gateways	
Gateways MPC Milestones	4,341.45
Total Gateways	4,341.45
Astral Gate II	
AGII MPC Milestones	178,594.86
Total Astral Gate II	178,594.86
Rock Video Monthly	
Development	3,000.00
Total Rock Video Monthly	3,000.00
Stock Sale	
Common Non-Voting 3	31,194.00
Total Stock Sale	31,194.00
Income-Unassigned	0.00
TOTAL INCOME	229,933.33

Income Statement 4/1/94-4/30/94

EXPENSES		
Advertising		
Contest Fees	500.00	
Press Kit Supplies	106.89	
Public Relations	846.30	
Reprints	175.00	
Total Advertising		1,628.19
Art Expenses		
Creative	223.61	
Print Materials	356.78	
Supplies	8.20	
Tools	57.32	
Total Art Expenses		645.91
Bank Charges		
Service Fee	16.00	
Total Bank Charges		16.00
Entertainment		
Meals	35.85	
Total Entertainment		35.85
Filming Expense		
Actor Airfare	424.00	
Actor Expenses Other	511.50	
Actor Insurance	3,733.90	
Meals	238.04	
Miscellaneous	5.50	
Stage Rental	10,956.12	
Tapes/Film/CDs	266.54	
Total Filming Expense		16,135.60
Insurance		
Equipment	165.00	
Group Health	447.87	
Life	2,215.00	
Worker's Comp	2,771.97	
Total Insurance		5,599.84
Licenses		
State	35.00	
Total Licenses		35.00
Miscellaneous		
Fines/Charges/Fees	559.83	
Total Miscellaneous		559.83

INCOME STATEMENT
4/1/94-4/30/94...*continued*

Office Expenses		
Books/Magazines	140.53	
Food/Meals	182.00	
Moving Costs	(11,000.00)	
On-Line Services	587.65	
Postage/Freight	4,464.10	
Repairs	457.15	
Supplies	1,012.27	
Total Office Expenses		(4,156.30)
Payroll		
Contractors	25,616.00	
Employees	60,645.97	
Total Payroll		86,361.97
Rental Expense		
Computer Equipment	370.88	
Total Rental Expense		370.88
Tax		
Payroll Tax	25,616.69	
State Sales Tax	1,567.78	
Total Tax		27,184.47
Travel		
Airfare	2,219.00	
Booth Expenses	750.00	
Conference Fee	63.45	
Ground Transportation	48.36	
Hotel Movies	59.53	
Lodging	607.47	
Meals	235.20	
Miscellaneous	35.28	
Phone Calls	73.09	
Total Travel		4,091.38
Utilities		
Telephone	687.20	
Total Utilities		687.20
TOTAL EXPENSES		139,195.82
INCOME LESS EXPENSES		90,737.51

MANAGEMENT

"Generally, management of many is the same as management of few. It is a matter of organization."

--Sun Tzu, *The Art of War*

How We Started

CineMedia Studios was founded in 1990 by James St. Clair. He was joined by Evelyn Hallstrom, Michael Peters, Thomas Calloway and Sarah St. Clair, who formed a general partnership in 1992 after realizing the work they were doing in interactive multimedia was unique and marketable.

On October 1, 1993, the partnership incorporated into a C corporation. This was the most appropriate move for the company given its growth potential and current exposure.

Founding Partners

Of the twenty-three people who make up the company staff, there are four founders who hold the following positions:

James St. Clair, Artistic Director and CEO
Evelyn Hallstrom, President
Thomas Calloway, Vice President of Technology
Michael Peters, Vice President of Audio Production, Composer

Of the five founders, each has been provided with a percentage of the original stock issue. Sarah St. Clair serves on our advisory council, but is not involved in the day-to-day operations of the company.

Management Team Overview

Three other members of our staff, while not among the original founders, are an invaluable part of our management team.

Katherine Mailor, Executive Vice President
Diane Armstrong, Vice President of Finance, CFO
Jack Lockheart, Vice President of Marketing, CMO

The founders and key managers of CineMedia Studios have combined experience exceeding forty years in the artistic, computer and business industries.

The strength of the CineMedia management team stems from synergistic expertise in artistic, management and technical areas. This has produced outstanding results over the past two years.

The leadership and alignment characteristics of CineMedia Studios' management team have resulted in broad and flexible goal setting, to meet the ever-changing demands of the fast-paced marketplace requiring our products. This is evident when the team responds to situations that necessitate new and innovative solutions.

Responsibilities

James St. Clair, *CEO and Artistic Director*
Conceiving, writing, directing and producing all interactive films completed by CineMedia. Managing artistic side of organization.

Evelyn Hallstrom, *President*
Strategic and organizational planning and management, organizing, actuating and controlling business side of organization. Point person for new business ventures and company growth.

Katherine Mailor, *Executive Vice President*
Managing all human resource functions for company, coordinating all aspects of production, acting as liaison between Artistic Director and production teams, President and employees. In charge of special projects as requested by Artistic Director and/or President.

Thomas Calloway, *Vice President of Technology*
Managing all product technology development, including quality control, product design, new product development improvement, and improvements on existing products.

Diane Armstrong, *Vice President of Finance, Chief Financial Officer*
Managing working capital including receivables, inventory, cash and marketable securities. Performing financial forecasting, including capital budgeting, cash budget, pro forma financial statements, and external financing requirements.

Jack Lockheart, *Vice President of Communications, Chief Marketing Officer*
Managing market planning, advertising, public relations, sales promotions, and merchandising. Identifying new markets (including foreign markets), corporate scope and market research.

Michael Peters, *Vice President of Audio Production*
Composing, arranging, performing, recording, producing and engineering all soundtracks and music for CineMedia Studios' interactive films. Managing all sound production and editing for films, as well as other employees in sound department.

Outside Support

Our Advisory Council, including highly qualified business and industry experts, assists our management team in making appropriate decisions in order to take the most effective actions.

Board of Directors

Our Board of Directors is made up of the original founding partners and our Chief Financial Officer.

People/Talent We Require

CineMedia Studios' development team recognizes that additional staff is required to properly support marketing, sales, systems administration, and support functions.

Currently, CineMedia is composed of twenty-three people; a total of up to fifty will be required to meet the demands of the projected market over the next five years. Our company expects to expand in the following direction:

Management	4 new hires, including a COO
Computer Programmers	4 new hires
SoftImage experts	2 new hires
Marketing/PR	5 new hires
Administration	5 new hires
Filming/Sound	4 new hires
Financial	3 new hires

Government Regulations

CineMedia Studios is operating in the multimedia/film industry, and we are under regulation of the State Licensing Bureau, Incorporation law, the IRS, and the Screen Actors Guild.

Currently, all appropriate legal requirements have been met, and all appropriate licenses, patents, and copyrights have been applied for and are in the process of being granted. When we prepare our initial public offering, licenses with the SEC will be processed.

PRODUCT/SERVICE DESCRIPTION

Proprietary information pertaining to product proposals is available to investors upon signature of a Non-disclosure Agreement.

Our principle product, interactive multimedia software, currently includes The Lunacy of Ronald, Astral Gate I: No One Sleeps Here (MPC & Macintosh), and IMAGINaction: the Art of Storytelling.

Under production at this time is the sequel to Astral Gate, called Astral Gate II: Incubus. Also in production is an interactive cineplex theater called Gateways that will feature ten films, four of which have already garnered multiple awards including Best of Show, Best Narrative Film, and Best Other Film at the First Annual QuickTime Film Festival; Best of Show and Best Interactive at the Second Annual QuickTime Movie Festival; Best Narrative at the second QuickTime Film Festival, and an Award of Merit at the 1993 InVision Multimedia Awards.

All of our current and future titles offer intelligent, stimulating entertainment for a mainstream audience prepared for something besides the traditional computer game.

Interactive movies work in many ways, but all allow the user to affect the movement and experience of the story/movie. Your choices ultimately determine the outcome of the story, or in AbsoluteCinema, the reactions of the characters you encounter. This individual control is a capability unique to VirtualCinema and is greatly enjoyed by our customers.

Current Products/Services

The Lunacy of Ronald Based on the story of a knight in the service of Charlemagne, this interactive novel is told through several different points of view through which the reader can move at will. Each character tells their own, often contradictory, version of the story. Ronald uses 256-color paintings, animation, QuickTime video, original music, professional "radio theatre" narration, hypertextual links and a complete soundtrack to transport you to the world of Charlemagne's France.

The Lunacy of Ronald is the winner of numerous awards including Top 50 CD-ROMs (#12) MacUser Magazine; Best Interactive, QuickTime Movie Festival, 1992; Best Interactive, QuickTime Film Festival, 1993; and Best of Show at the Dot.Pixel.Image National Graphic Design Contest, 1993.

Astral Gate 1: No One Sleeps Here In this interactive science fiction storyworld, the viewer assumes the perspective of Drew Griffin, a young medical student stationed on an alien planet. Earth's armed forces are there, at least officially, to protect a vital mission: to mine material needed to counteract terrible ecological damage, wrought by centuries of mankind's destructive use of technology. As Griffin, the viewer interacts with complex characters in situations that demand a search for truth far more sophisticated than virtual reality (VR) battle suits and seemingly dangerous aliens might suggest.

Astral Gate was named a Business Week Best Product of the Year the month it was released, and has gone on to win a silver medal for Best Interactive Movie at the 1994 InVision Multimedia Awards, and a MultiMedia World Reader's Choice Award for Best Interactive Movie.

IMAGINaction: the Art of Storytelling The first product developed by CineMedia Studios, features interactive fiction, art, political satire and music in a magazine format. Winner of numerous awards, including Editor's Choice for A+/InCider Magazine and the MacUser Top 100. This product is on hiatus until resources can be devoted to its production needs, but will return as a formidable contender in the newly emerging interactive magazine format, where it was the first pioneer.

Work For Hire CineMedia now accepts work for hire on a project-by-project basis, as a way of expanding our horizons and bringing in additional funds. Our current project is "**rock**video monthly" for Warner Music Enterprises, a monthly

CD-ROM that will ship in up to five different formats. CineMedia has planned the interactive interface design from the ground up, and will also perform the work each month on the CD-ROMs, which will be shipped to an installed base of CD-ROM owners for a nominal fee. CineMedia has already been approached by two other companies to perform similar tasks for them.

Pay Back

For most customers, our products pay for themselves immediately in terms of hours of sophisticated, exciting entertainment not previously available. Our software is robust, requiring minimum maintenance, and customers are beginning to see a brand name identity they can count on in CineMedia's titles, and are starting to anticipate a certain quality of product from us -- an expectation we encourage.

Key Benefits of All Products/ Services

The major benefit for customers of our AbsoluteCinema products is entirely entertainment-based: complete immersion into the storyworlds we create, while allowing the user freedom to experience the story in their own personal way. Our titles offertrue interaction with filmic experiences that are world-class, entertaining and exciting.

Product/Service Life Cycle

Our products have been on the shelves for a relatively short period of time, but judging by the continued press coverage for Ronald, and its recent new distribution deal, the life cycle for our software is three to five years. This is mostly due to the fact that nothing else like it exists currently. Over the next few years, many other developers will attempt to produce products to compete with ours, so this shelf life may decrease.

In the meantime, we are developing at least four titles or ports by the end of the year, and we will continue to produce many new products each year to keep ahead of the competition. By bringing on a significant amount of capital by the end of the year, we anticipate being able to grow the company to achieve this level of commitment to the industry.

Planned Products

CineMedia Studios plans to continually develop new products and enhance existing products. New products currently being developed include Gateways and Astral Gate II: Incubus, plus ports of Astral Gate I and Gateways to other viable platforms. The Lunacy of Ronald has just been ported to the MPC platform, and the new, hybrid MPC/Mac version of the product will include QuickTime 2.0 for the Macintosh, complete with full-screen video and MIDI sound.

Concepts for our next generation of interactive products include a ghostly western, Western InSpecter; a swashbuckler, Barbary Coast; a "Three Musketeers" film, Sword & Saber; a hard-hitting modern action film called Mission; and a rock music flight simulator game called RockFlight. A complete listing of our more than seventy project ideas is available on request.

INTERACTIVE MOVIE MARKETING

Advertising & Promotion

CineMedia Studios' titles are vastly different from the traditional CD-ROM games. This presents a marketing challenge, approached by highlighting the unique product features, for example, interactive movies and AbsoluteCinema. To illustrate, CineMedia's campaign for Astral Gate I & II, which will be presented as true interactive movies, is outlined below. This includes all publicity and marketing efforts.

Distributors often encourage collaboration with us, because they recognize that the emerging market niche of interactive movies requires unique marketing techniques. As detailed below, we will guide our distributors in defining an aspect of their publishing division as "interactive movies."

General Positioning Ideas For Astral Gate (Mac) and Astral Gate II

- ❑ Highlight interactive movie features and AbsoluteCinema
- ❑ Overcome consumer expectations of Astral Gate being game through initiating a movie image campaign
- ❑ Create hype over AbsoluteCinema as a hook for publicity and consumer attention
- ❑ Add marketing and publicity milestones to title production to properly and completely develop our CD-ROM titles

Promotion

- ❑ Conduct interactive movie "screening" promotions in conjunction with national retailers

Design & Advertising

- ❑ Design all product packaging and advertising to reflect movies, not games
- ❑ Offer distinctive product packaging

Publicity

- ❑ Launch publicity campaigns for each title as if they were movie
- ❑ Produce electronic press kits for national distribution, just as if this were a feature film

Bundling

- ❑ Bundle CineMedia titles with the distributor hardware (if possible), then spotlight the benefits of true interactive movies playing well on new home entertainment multimedia systems

At CineMedia, we are already moving forward with many interactive movie marketing strategies. We have created an electronic press kit (EPK) and seen immediate success, with segments airing on national and local broadcast media. Publicity events focused on "the movie" and AbsoluteCinema angles have earned us great attention. Also, we have conceptual designs for packaging, and overall promotional program ideas that will affect the thrust of "interactive movies" in the industry.

We know distributors and other publishers recognize the success of emphasizing the movie marketing angle from traditional linear films. CineMedia offers strong design, advertising development and communications services for all products and seeks financial support program ideas that will affect the thrust of "interactive movies" in the industry.

We know distributors and other publishers recognize the success of emphasizing the movie marketing angle from traditional linear films. CineMedia offers strong design, advertising development and communications services for all products and seeks financial support for these efforts as a part of the complete development of CD-ROM titles.

A complete plan of marketing and communication milestones is under development for inclusion as a part of our future product development. This will be presented to the distributors and publishers of all CineMedia products. This plan will add additional revenue and advantageously position CineMedia and its products in the marketplace.

Selling Tactics

The following is an outline of an interactive movie screening promotion to be sponsored by the distributors and publishers of CineMedia Studios products.

Objective

Identify and introduce qualified multimedia users (including prospective system buyers) to the distributor's interactive movies and other CD-ROM titles. Also, offer them incentives for purchasing all the distributor titles (especially CineMedia interactive movie titles), as well as other products, through co-sponsoring retailers. Additionally, establish thedistributor as specialists in publishing interactive movies. The number one selling point for both movies and CD-ROM titles is word-of-mouth. Nothing accomplishes word-of-mouth better than preview screenings and product sampling.

Program

On a first come, first served basis, our targeted audience is invited to a facility for the distributor's Interactive Movie Premier Screenings. The evening consists of door prizes, limited refreshments, one-night only product sales discounts, sales coupons, and a 90-minute preview of one or more of the distributor's interactive movie titles. This may include an opening of 60-second spots (like coming attractions) of other titles, or new hardware product announcements from the distributor.

Overview

- ❑ Multimedia screening nights sponsored by the distributor & national retail chains
- ❑ One or two interactive movie titles by the distributor are partially screened
- ❑ Initial test held in top ten or limited nationwide markets at retailer sites, nearby movie theater, or college campus
- ❑ Screening of new (and current) interactive movie titles published by the distributor
- ❑ Complete direct-mail, promotion, publicity & advertising campaign in each market

Promotion & Publicity

- ❑ Press release distributed nationwide with saturation at local screening markets
- ❑ Electronic press kits for feature title(s) distributed to screening market media
- ❑ Press representatives on-site at each event stocked with review copies and publicity materials
- ❑ Distributor & co-sponsor announcements will be made before the film begins
- ❑ Developers attend and demonstrate as appropriate
- ❑ Distributor uses passes and event as an incentive to area distributors and local sellers

Promotional Materials

For each screening:

- ❑ All materials include the distributor and retailer logos
- ❑ Screening passes (mailed, or picked up at participating retailer)
- ❑ Survey cards with limited market research question for the distributor & retailer
- ❑ Movie programs with the distributor advertisements listing several titles
- ❑ Ad posters posted around participating retailer and screening facility
- ❑ Movie posters distributed

Advertising

- ❑ Cooperative local print and radio advertising campaign
- ❑ Direct mail including:
    - Databases from registered owners of the distributor & multimedia buyer's club
    - Purchased lists
    - Print advertising response cards
    - 800 number responses
    - Retailer's consumer databases
    - Online announcement inquiries
    - User Group memberships
    - Databases of developers whose titles are previewed
- ❑ Event site & point of purchase signage

Coupons & Giveaways

❑Distributor gifts, door prizes, interactive movie title merchandise, and coupons will be distributed at each event
❑ Distributor CD-ROM sampler given to guests as they return a completed survey card

Distributor & Coming Attractions

❑A medley of movie trailer-style CD-ROM previews by the distributor are run before the main features

Next Step

Develop a proposal for the most appropriate retail chain (e.g., COMP USA) for co-sponsorship participation. This entire program may be sponsored exclusively by a single publisher (e.g. Viacom Interactive, Electronic Arts) as a vehicle to solidity distributor and retailer relationships in addition to publicity and consumer awareness. After approval in concept, the screening markets would be identified, followed by the selection of a third party promotional agency for implementation.

"Image" Advertising & Limited Sales

Select Print Advertising Campaign 1/3 page size column ads highlighting all current and announcing upcoming releases. Specifying the distributor's 800 number to buy product, CineMedia number for general info; also identifying new project deals, major trade shows and speaking engagements, awards, and company vision. A few possibilities:

- Multimedia World
- New media
- Wired
- Compute
- Specialty publications

On-line Services Places listing with opportunity to communicate,buy or call us for CineMedia titles and list company vision in every possible area, then keep track and respond promptly!

- America Online
- Compuserve
- AppleLink
- Genie
- User Groups

Special targeted advertising efforts and discounted product offers would be made to reach user groups.

Direct Mail Continue to build major database for quick response for moving announcement, new product releases, company vision, CineMedia product owner communique, etc.

Mailings will include

- Reader response cards from print ads and publicity "bingo cards"
- The Lunacy of Ronald registration cards
- Rented mailing lists

Direct Sales

- Catalog sales of The Lunacy of Ronald on a limited basis.
- Response card sales from direct mail
- Sales at trade shows to offset expenses

Trade Shows & Speaking Engagements Several select shows a year. Since James often presents or conducts seminars, shows can easily be chosen to coincide with speaking engagements for maximum exposure.

CineMedia Newsletter One major full-color piece produced bi-annually with an occasional two-color smaller version distributed (four times annually). Distributed to our entire collective database of media, industry, customers and prospects.

Advance Product Demos, Teasers and Broadcast Video For each title we will produce teaser footage and demos to be included into our internal milestone schedule. The distributor will provide demos if they have an installed base of kiosks to be utilized.

Demo & Video Plans

- Video version montage e.g., movie fast-cutting teaser trailer
- Actual title demo 2-3 months in advance to create retailer pull-through

New Business Development

- Music business
- New major projects based on our project proposals
- Greeting cards
- Monitor interactive advertising pursuits
- Entertainment Agencies

Communications

Milestones

Our CineMedia Studios titles must be presented as interactive movies to consumers, the industry and especially to our publisher. We have repeatedly discovered that we are the best source to introduce titles properly. Therefore, the production/milestone schedule will include communications and marketing elements. This involves incorporating both simple and involved steps into our production schedule. We will schedule steps and projects that will generate abundant resources for advance publicity, market anticipation and ultimately sales.

Press Releases

We will create a schedule for press releases corresponding to product news, shipping releases and all major media events.

Publicity

A wide variety of publicity materials is available and constantly updated. This includes screen shots, publicity skills and candid shots, sell sheets (one-sheets), a standard press kit, and an electronic press kit. The most effective way to maximize the current buzz surrounding multimedia is through personal accessibility and making an abundance of publicity materials available. CineMedia also holds regular media days on the set while shooting our interactive films. These are an integral part of CineMedia's successful publicity campaign.

E.P.K. - Electronic Press Kit

Created in standard feature film publicity format, highlighting AbsoluteCinema, the purpose is to stimulate broadcast media and print coverage.

Items for inclusion into title development milestone schedule:

- Product photography
- Media events surrounding production phases
- Main title/logo design
- Step by Step "making of" screen captures and PICT files
- Newsworthy software usage, Beta testing (e.g., Adobe, QuickTime, etc.)
- Advance screen shots for 35mm slides
- Demo creation (kiosks, promotional videos)
- Electronic Press Kit development (for each title)
- Copy prepared from storyline for all materials
- Trade show, conference title preview preparation
- Packaging/carton design
- Jewel case insert
- Registration card
- Print advertisement full page layouts
- Suggested Standee, poster, and POP design

Customers

CD-ROM buyers are expanding to include computer users of all ages, and even those most familiar with games are reaching out to widen their spectrum. Consumers brought to computer entertainment through Nintendo have grown up, and are starved for something more. This consumer demand added to the exploding installed as of CD-ROM drives leaves an open niche for interactive movies.

Currently, the new media market is broken into four distinct segments; business, home user, education, and professional. The new media home user markets primarily consist of productivity, entertainment, education, and home business applications.

At the end of 1992, multimedia market share was dominated by the professional market, followed by business, education, and home computer use. By 1996, the home computer user market will be the largest segment.

CineMedia's customers are familiar with movies, demand more intelligent content than the market currently holds, and expect innovative technological artistry. Our studio satisfies these needs.

Competition

Some developers claim they create interactive movies as a selling point. But often the claim of "movie" is where the resemblance to interactive films ends. They produce games with little or no story content. In fact, their addition of video elements, live actors, and a movie declaration typically detracts from what their products really are: games. Though other developers are beginning to come on the scene who are following our lead, CineMedia is the definitive leader in the creation of interactive movies, as exemplified by our recent awards. This is the niche we have created and defined, as we educate consumers about a new type of entertainment. Now it is our intention to own and dominate this niche, evinced by CineMedia's recent signing to a major Hollywood agency, The Agency for Performing Arts. These extensive efforts will lead us to the peak of CD-ROM sales and into interactive TV and beyond.

TECHNOLOGY DEVELOPMENT & ACQUISITION

Responsibilities of the Technology Division

The charter of the Technology Division of CineMedia Studios is:

- To provide the computer-based framework of our interactive titles.
- To provide and maintain the computer environment necessary to build our titles and run our business.
- To provide and implement the strategic plans for positioning our company at the technological forefront of the interactive film niche.

The type of entertainment products that CineMedia Studios creates relies on powerful technology. For the purposes of explanation, these are divided into three primary areas that correspond to the division's charter:

Area 1

Develop and maintain the software portion of our products.

Develop the software systems that drive our titles This includes building/using proprietary software engines, using third-party title authoring tools and building/using hybrids (generally third-party tools with sections of proprietary software linked in). A large part of this area involves working with the artistic director to define realms of feasibility for envisioned artistic goals.

Testing our products Alpha testing is the responsibility of the Technology division. Beta testing can be handled by the title's distributor (e.g., the Astral

Gate series), or can be done on a formal basis with a number of industry contacts who have the necessary skills to beta test.

Maintenance and customer technical support In-house maintenance of title support software is performed in order to build a better foundation for new titles. Any patch-maintenance of title software required to solve current user problems falls under the domain of customer technical support. For our current set of titles, Media Vision has responsibility for full customer support of the Astral Gate series, and Gateways. CineMedia has responsibility for The Lunacy of Ronald, which averages approximately three technical support questions per month, each one resolved without additional software support.

Area 2

Management of software, hardware and data:

Software tools Used to build our titles, including assetauthoring tools, project administration tools, and miscellaneous proprietary tools: the technology division recommends appropriate toolsets and makes purchases after reaching consensus with planners. In some instances, proprietary tools may be developed for in-house use if they cannot be found elsewhere.

Hardware systems Used to build our titles, including computer workstations, networks, video and sound equipment: the technology division recommends appropriate platforms and makes purchases after reaching consensus with planners.

Configuration and maintenance of hardware, software and data Includes data backup, archiving and cataloging, as well as software upgrade and license management. These tasks make up the jobs of system, network and data administration, and are performed in-house.

Maintaining vendor relations Acquire media used by our daily operations, including floppy disks, write-once CD-ROMs anddata cartridge tapes. Other video and audio media used by the company are the responsibility of the various departments that use them.

Area 3

Research and development of enabling and supporting technology.

The early stage of this industry forces developers to explore many of their own methods, to build the technology that enables these methods and supports the final project.

Planning the proper use of our development resources (striking the proper balance between "make versus buy"). It is important for a company of our size that the investments we make in technology development give us what we cannot buy from a third party, and not waste valuable time developing technology that is readily available to us elsewhere.

Maintaining knowledge regarding the state of current software and hardware architectures and development systems. This informs decisions on how to shape our development environment, as well as the plans described above.

In all of these areas, the technology that we develop is designed for internal use only. However, we are open to consider licensing technology to interested parties who may initiate such negotiations. We have already been approached regarding our AbsoluteCinema technology. This is very worthwhile for us, as the act of licensing a technology to at least one other agent has the effect of increasing the value of that technology, and thus the value of our company.

In addition, we use other technologies in order to bring our products to market.

Area 4

CD-ROM disc mass production; printing, cutting and assembly of product boxes; assembly of product with jewel case, product box and shrink wrap. The tasks performed in this area are not performed by the technology division -- they are contracted out-of-house, and the distributor of our titles is typically in charge of negotiating and maintaining these contracts.

Develop Versus Acquire

In the first two primary technology areas, we decided whether to develop the system or tool using in-house expertise, or to acquire the system or tool from a third party. The technology division supports these decisions by analyzing costs of development versus acquisition, as well as benefits from owning versus licensing. We do not develop hardware; the decision is purchase versus lease; presently, much of our equipment is leased from an independent vendor.

Research and Development

The technology division supports decisions on hardware acquisition by providing technical and pricing information, but is not soley responsible for all equipment purchase recommendations. Such decisions are made jointly with the company's core team members who do strategic planning.

One of the technology division's primary responsibilities is in the area of long-term strategic planning of technology needs. Responsibilities include:

- ❑Evaluating proposals for new titles to determine technical feasibility and resources required.
- ❑Evaluating new technologies for appropriateness for current and new title work.
- ❑Maintaining a library of software either developed or acquired by us to support title development.

New Titles Under Production

The following titles are currently in production. A document of base technology and enhancements to be developed to support these titles follows.

New Titles Under Production
...continued

- •Astral Gate II, Incubus for MPC
- •Gateways for Macintosh
- •Gateways for MPC
- •Astral Gate: No One Sleeps Here for Macintosh (just completed)

New Titles Under Evaluation

The technology division is responsible for developing a document of baseline technology required for the following titles, and making recommendations for development versus acquisition when necessary. To illustrate, several examples are listed below:

Barbary Coast	Candidate to use AbsoluteCinema engine
Mission	Candidate to use AbsoluteCinema engine
Sword & Saber	Candidate to use AbsoluteCinema engine
Western InSpecter	Candidate to use AbsoluteCinema engine
RockFlight	Requires significant technology development or licensing

Technology Base and Enhancements for Astral Gate II for MPC

Astral Gate II will use the same multimedia delivery engine as Astral Gate I. Some of the aspects of the story script require new capabilities to be created for this engine. Following is a list of the three primary features to be added -- Ubernarrative, Dreamscape and evolving diary.

Ubernarrative

This term was coined to represent what is typically referred to as a drama's subtext. Here it is an active portion of the narrative that provides an arc over the whole piece, and joins all elements together. The unique aspect of the ubernarrative is that its essence changes in reaction to the viewer's choices, thus providing a subtext that echoes the viewer even as it draws them into the central character's experience -- the central character, controlled by the user, is thus tailored to them.

This idea was conceived for Astral Gate I, but was cut from that project due to short development time. Since then, the concept has evolved, from the main character's voice-over thoughts into several new dimensions: colors, textures and music will all be tailored to reflect the user's choices. In addition, certain character interactions will be chosen, based on the current "Uberstate."

The mechanism driving the ubernarrative will be an external database/query system. This maintains a representation of the main character's emotional state, which is driven by the user's choices. Three extremes of emotion are chosen: angry, balanced, and secretive. Balanced is the "content" state, which exists between angry and secretive.

This technology will prove useful for many of our upcoming titles. The process of developing it is helping to bring AbsoluteCinema to its full potential.

Primary support required by Ubernarrative: weighted average object functionality, and corresponding database of weights and thresholds.

Dreamscape

A new level of user interactivity will be introduced with the ability to move about a landscape of dreams. The viewer will find themselves moving forward through floating images that come to life when approached; if the user continues to explore the moving image, it will enlarge to become a full screen movie, which will play one of the main characters' dreams.

The technology used for the 3D battle sequence in Astral Gate I is being modified to accommodate this dream exploration mechanism. Primary modifications are:

- ❑All current 3D and graphic objects (pyramids, friends, bugs, etc.) will be removed, and there will be no horizon, since the player is meant to be flying through the air.

- ❑Dreams will appear as panels of various size and aspect ratio, above and below the viewer's perspective. This requires texture mapping a movie onto a flat plane in perspective, and has already been developed.

- ❑The viewer will be constantly in motion; the mouse will control turning left/ right and flying higher or lower, but there is no need to use arrow keys to initiate forward movement.

The video architecture used for the dreamscape technology will be Microsoft Video for Windows 1.1, which includes a very impressive full-screen full-motion mode that is suitable for the dream compositions.

Primary support required by dreamscape: texture mapping movies onto flat planes is perspective. This is nearly complete.

Evolving Diary

As the story proceeds, the main character's journal will grow to include text that recalls this encounters; the emotions underlying the text will be taken from the Ubernarrative database, and will match the user's style of interacting with the story. In addition, charcoal-like sketches of places and people will be included. These too will vary in nature according to the engine's perception of the viewer's mood: from heavy black rough strokes indicating a reading of anger to finer shadings for a more balanced interpretation. Finally, a sketch of the user's painted "imago" will appear if they choose to create one for themselves.

Primary support required by the evolving diary: truetype font functionality; Ubernarrative functionality to select appropriate passages based on viewer's choices.

Technology Base and Enhancements Required for Astral Gate I for Macintosh

There were no significant changes made to Astral Gate I during its port to the Macintosh platform. We made two moderate changes to the video game segment in order to enhance playability. First, we modified the behavior of enemies so that there are fewer of them and they are more difficult to kill, with more interesting behavior for avoiding the player. Second, we reduced the load time of the game from 30 to 2 seconds. Neither of these enhancements added to the time required for porting the entire title. In fact, due to the dedication of the team involved in the work, the product was available for shipping one month ahead of its internal schedule.

Technology Base and Enhancements Required for Gateways for Macintosh

By far, the bulk of Gateways for Macintosh will be realized using existing authoring tools: Macromedia Director 4.0 in conjunction with a simple shell written using HyperCard 2.2 or possibly SuperCard 1.6. There is one feature that will require additional software development support -- "The Actor Variations" will provide a simple movie editing environment. SuperCard is easily capable of programming such a tool, as is HyperCard with the addition of some third party XCMDs.

Technology Base and Enhancements Required for Gateways for MPC

The primary authoring environment for Gateways for MPC will be the multimedia engine developed and enhanced for Astral Gate II. The movie editing functionality will require further tool development, to provide multiple windows and an editing capability.

Development Environment

Currently, the technology division has the following computer platforms at its disposal for software development and testing:

- (3) IBM PC-compatible 486/DX2/66 with CD-ROM and external monitoring for code debugging.
- (4) IBM PC-compatible 486/DX2/66 with CD-ROM.
- (1) IBM PC-compatible 386/SX/33 for low-end platform testing.
- (1) Macintosh Centris 650 with CD-ROM and external monitor for debugging.
- (2) Macintosh Centris 650 with CD-ROM.
- (1) Macintosh Quadra 800 with CD-ROM and large external disks for fileservice.

The software platform used for development on the PC side is Microsoft Visual C++ with CodeView for symbolic debugging and Microsoft Assembler. The code analyzers Bounds Checker and PcLint are used to assure quality. The Defect Control System is used to collect, track and manage errors.

The software platform used for development on the Macintosh side is Apple's Macintosh Programmer's Workshop (MPW) Development System with

Development Environment
...continued

MacApp, MPW C++, MPW Assembler, SADE debugger, SourceServer code control system, and other tools.

All of these computers are networked together using Apple's system 7 filesharing capability for Macintosh, and Farallon's PhoneNet PC for IBM-compatibles. PhoneNet PC makes a PC platform look and work like a Macintosh to the network, the only difference being that PCs are not implicitly visible to other computers and require the use of an additional program (Timbuktu) to implement direct communication between users. The network architecture is Ethernet, cabled as 10 base-T. We use 10 base-T hub architecture now, and as our network traffic grows, we may consider buying a router in order to split off some workstations that typically require high volume network transfers into a separate zone.

Fileservice in general is handled by a set of distributed fileservers throughout our organization. The primary fileserver is a Quadra 800 with 6 gigabytes of external storage, to be used by anyone in the organization. Certain divisions within the company have reserved directories for their use. Daily backups are performed. Since the data are so voluminous, the backup plan alternates days; one part of the cycle covers the internal disk drives of all Macintosh programmer's workstations.

Other fileservers are:

- Primary graphics station; 1 gigabyte external; backups performed daily, including 500 megabytes on the secondary graphics station.
- Sound station; 2 gigabytes external; backups performed remotely from the movie conversion station on a weekly basis.
- Primary movie editing stations (2); each with more than 3 gigabytes external;backups performed as necessary.
- Secondary movie editing station; 4 gigabytes external; backups performed remotely from the main fileserver on a weekly basis.
- Movie conversion station; 2 gigabytes external; backups performed daily, including three other administrative stations on alternate days.

The E-mail system in place is QuickMail, used by both PCs and Macintoshes.

Media required to support development operations are:

- 3.5" floppy disks, 1.4 MB capacity (DSHD). Volume is approximately 50 per month.
- 5.25" floppy disks, 1.2 MB capacity. Volume is approximately 1 per month.
- 4mm data cartridge tapes, 90 meter length, 1.3 gigabyte capacity. Volume is approximately 20 per month. 120 meter length tapes are preferred, but are not yet manufactured for data quality tapes. These should be available in second-quarter 94.
- 5" write-once CD-ROM discs, 74 minute length,680 megabyte capac ity. Volume is approximately 25 per month.

Due to the nature of computer hardware and software, there are three types of maintenance that must be performed on a regular basis:

❑Maintenance of software configuration of machines, including system software and applications. This also includes preventative maintenance of directory structures, which can become corrupted during system crashes.

❑Maintenance of computer hardware, including internal components and peripherals. There are some in-house software applications that can solve some of the problems; other difficulties require repairs, and replacement of the part with a working substitute, if available.

❑Maintenance of network hardware and configuration, including regular analysis of packet traffic speed and line transmission quality. This also includes maintenance of any individual or network modem hardware and software.

There is one area of simple hardware repair that is performed in-house when necessary: cable assembly offers an opportunity to cut back on a low level of cash flow, plus the time required to order specialty cables and have them delivered or picked up.

Software Quality

The robustness of the software we create and its ease of use (especially for PC installation software) is very important to the success of the title. Typically, two primary methods assure the quality of software: detailed design and extensive testing. However, due to the aggressive nature of our schedules, we are not afforded the luxury of long design or testing periods.

We rely quite heavily on the technical expertise of our software engineers to build code designs, structures and modules that are of high quality and performance. We evaluate progress on a very frequent basis, and strive to address concerns about performance, quality of presentation and compatibility with other platforms.

There are three forms of testing that we perform: unit testing, integration (alpha) testing, and beta testing. Our software engineers perform the unit and integration testing as they proceed, and also do a portion of the beta testing. Beta testing is performed chiefly by people who did not develop the software; other in-house personnel fulfill a portion of this role.

People

The positions that make up the technology division are:

- Director of Technology
- Senior Software Design Engineer
- Software Design Engineer (SDE)
- Systems Administrator

At present, there is one director (who also performs most of the systems administration duties), a co-manager, one senior SDE, and two SDEs. All have the bulk of their experience programming on the PC, and the junior SDEs are now programming on the Macintosh platform, using their experience on the PC to port the Astral Gate engine from there.

We are currently using other in-house personnel to asist with systems administration and will hire a full-time systems administrator as soon as a large development opportunity arises.

Conclusion

Like the company itself, the technology division is young, growing and learning. We have a good work environment that promotes satisfaction among the engineers who work here, and they do consistently good, often inspired, work.

In summary, the goals of this division are to produce high quality software to support title development, to equip and maintain the computer/working environment of the entire company, and to blaze trails into new areas of technology, helping us to deliver titles of unequaled satisfaction for the consumer.

CONCLUSIONS AND SUMMARY

CineMedia Studios is a promising, thriving company, ready to infuse growth capital into this business. In order to take advantage of our current market position and to continue to produce world-class, award-winning multimedia entertainment, we must obtain project funding.

Profits expected from this infusion of capital, already outlined in this plan, will allow our company to realize our vision; that is to:

Develop and pursue an artistic vision of interactive entertainment that defines new boundaries of personal involvement with computer-based media. CineMedia Studios will continue to explore the territory of this burgeoning growth market, charting ways to bringing together text, graphics, animation, sound, music, video and reader interaction to the complete satisfaction of ourselves and our customers.

Glossary

Glossary of Small Business Terms

ACE
See Active Corps of Executives

Accounts payable
See Trade credit

Active Corps of Executives (ACE)
(See also Service Corps of Retired Executives)
A group of volunteers for a management assistance program of the U.S. Small Business Administration; volunteers provide one-on-one counseling and teach workshops and seminars for small firms.

Adaptation
The process whereby an invention is modified to meet the needs of users.

Adaptive engineering
The process whereby an invention is modified to meet the manufacturing and commercial requirements of a targeted market.

Adverse selection
The tendency for higher-risk individuals to purchase health care and more comprehensive plans, resulting in increased costs.

Agency costs
Costs incurred to insure that the lender or investor maintains control over assets while allowing the borrower or entrepreneur to use them. Monitoring and information costs are the two major types of agency costs.

Antitrust immunity
(See also Collective ratemaking)
Exemption from prosecution under antitrust laws. In the transportation industry, firms with antitrust immunity are permitted—under certain conditions—to set schedules and sometimes prices for the public benefit.

Applied research
Scientific study targeted for use in a product or process.

Asians
A minority category used by the U.S. Bureau of the Census to represent a diverse group that includes Aleuts, Eskimos, American Indians, Asian Indians, Chinese, Japanese, Koreans, Vietnamese, Filipinos, Hawaiians, and other Pacific Islanders.

Assets
Anything of value owned by a company.

Average cost
Total production costs divided by the quantity produced.

Balance Sheet
A financial statement listing the total assets and liabilities of a company at a given time.

Bankruptcy
The condition in which a business cannot meet its debt obligations and petitions a federal district court either for reorganization of its debts or for liquidation of its assets.

Basic research
Theoretical scientific exploration not targeted to application.

Basket clause
A provision specifying the amount of public pension funds that may be placed in investments not included on a state's legal list (see separate citation).

BDC
See Business development corporation

BIDCO
See Business and industrial development company

Birth
See Business birth

Blue chip security
A low-risk, low-yield security representing an interest in a very stable company.

Blue sky laws
A general term that denotes various states' laws regulating securities.

Bond
(See also General obligation bond; Taxable bonds; Treasury bonds)
A written instrument executed by a bidder or contractor (the principal) and a second party (the surety or sureties) to assure fulfillment of the principal's obligations to a third party (the obligee or government) identified in the bond. If the principal's obligations are not met, the bond assures payment to the extent stipulated of any loss sustained by the obligee.

Bonding requirements
Terms contained in a bond (see separate citation).

Brand name
The part of a brand, trademark, or service mark that can be spoken. It can be a word, letter, or group of words or letters.

Bridge financing
A short-term loan made in expectation of intermediate-term or long-term financing. Can be used when a company plans to go public in the near future.

Broker
One who matches resources available for innovation with those who need them.

Business and industrial development company (BIDCO)
A private, for-profit financing corporation chartered by the state to provide both equity and long-term debt capital to small business owners (see separate citations for equity and debt capital).

Business birth
The formation of a new establishment or enterprise. The appearance of a new establishment or enterprise in the Small Business Data Base (see separate citation).

Business contractions
The number of establishments that have decreased in employment during a specified time.

Business death
The voluntary or involuntary closure of a firm or establishment. The disappearance of an establishment or enterprise from the Small Business Data Base (see separate citation).

Business development corporation (BDC)
A business financing agency, usually composed of the financial institutions in an area or state, organized to assist infinancing businesses unable to obtain assistance through normal channels; the risk is spread among various members of the business development corporation, and interest rates may vary somewhat from those charged by member institutions. A venture capital firm in which shares of ownership are publicly held and to which the Investment Act of 1940 applies.

Business dissolution
For enumeration purposes, the absence of a business that was present in the prior time period from any current record.

Business entry
See Business birth

Business exit
See Business death

Business expansions
The number of establishments that added employees during a specified time.

Business failure
Closure of a business causing a loss to at least one creditor.

Business format franchising
(See also Franchising)
The purchase of the name, trademark, and an ongoing business plan of the parent corporation or franchisor by the franchisee.

Business license
A legal authorization in document form issued by municipal and state governments and required for business operations.

Business name
(See also Business license; Trademark)
Enterprises must register their business names with local governments usually on a "doing business as" (DBA) form. (This name is sometimes referred to as a "fictional name.") The procedure is part of the business licensing process and prevents any other business from using that same name for a similar business in the same locality.

Business norms
See Financial ratios

Business permit
See Business license

Business plan
A document that spells out a company's expected course of actionfor a specified period, usually including a detailed listing and analysis of risks and uncertainties. For the small business, it should examine the proposed products, the market, the industry, the management policies, the marketing policies, production needs, and financial needs. Frequently, it is used as a prospectus for potential investors and lenders.

Business proposal
See Business plan.

Business service firm
An establishment primarily engaged in rendering services to other business organizations on a fee or contract basis.

Business start
For enumeration purposes, a business with a name or similar designation that did not exist in the prior time period.

Cafeteria plan
See Flexible benefit plan

Capacity
Level of a firm's, industry's, or nation's output corresponding to full practical utilization of available resources.

Capital
Assets less liabilities, representing the ownership interest in a business. A stock of accumulated goods, especially at a specified time and in contrast to income received during a specified time period. Accumulated goods devoted to production. Accumulated possessions calculated to bring income.

Capital intensity
(See also Debt capital; Equity midrisk venture capital; Informal capital; Internal capital; Owner's capital; Second-hand capital; Seed capital; Venture capital)
The relative importance of capital in the production process, usually expressed as the ratio of capital to labor but also sometimes as the ratio of capital to output.

Caribbean Basin Initiative
An interdisciplinary program to support commerce among the businesses in the nations of the Caribbean Basin and the United States. Agencies involved include the Agency for International Development, the U.S. Small Business Administration, the International Trade Administration of the U.S. Department of Commerce, and private sector groups.

Catastrophic care
Medical and other services for acute and long-term illnesses that cost more than insurance coverage limits or that cost the amount most families may be expected to pay with their own resources.

CDC
See Certified development corporation

Certified development corporation (CDC)
A local area or statewide corporation or authority (for profit or nonprofit) that packages U.S. Small Business Administration (SBA), bank, state, and/or private money into financial assistance for existing business capital improvements. The SBA holds the second lien on its maximum share of 40 percent involvement. Each state has at least one certified development corporation. This program is called the SBA 503 Program.

Certified lenders
Banks that participate in the SBA guaranteed loan program (see separate citation). Such banks must have a good track record with the U.S. Small Business Administration (SBA) and must agree to certain conditions set forth by the agency. In return, the SBA agrees to process any guaranteed loan application within three business days.

Champion
An advocate for the development of an innovation.

Closely held corporation
A corporation in which the shares are held by a few persons, usually officers, employees, or others close to the management; these shares are rarely offered to the public.

Code of Federal Regulations
Codification of general and permanent rules of the federal government published in the Federal Register.

Code sharing
See Computer code sharing

Coinsurance
(See also Cost sharing)
Upon meeting the deductible payment, health insurance participants may be required to make additional health care cost-sharing payments. Coinsurance is a payment of a fixed percentage of the cost of each service; copayment is usually a fixed amount to be paid with each service.

Collateral
Securities, evidence of deposit, or other property pledged by a borrower to secure repayment of a loan.

Collective ratemaking
(See also Antitrust immunity)
The establishment of uniform charges for services by a group of businesses in the same industry.

Commercial insurance plan
See Underwriting

Commercialization
The final stage of the innovation process, including production and distribution.

Common stock
The most frequently used instrument for purchasing ownership in private or public companies. Common stock generally carries the right to vote on certain corporate actions and may pay dividends, although it rarely does in venture investments. In liquidation, common stockholders are the last to share in the proceeds from the sale of a corporation's assets; bondholders and preferred shareholders have priority. Common stock is often used in first-round start-up financing.

Community development corporation
A corporation established to develop economic programs for a community and, in most cases, to provide financial support for such development.

Computer code sharing
An arrangement whereby flights of a regional airline are identified by the two-letter code of a major carrier in the computer reservation system to help direct passengers to new regional carriers.

Consortium
A coalition of organizations such as banks and corporations for ventures requiring large capital resources.

Consumer price index
A measure of the fluctuation in prices between two points in time.

Continuation coverage
Health coverage offered for a specified period of time to employees who leave their jobs and to their widows, divorced spouses, or dependents.

Contractions
See Business contractions

Convertible preferred stock
A class of stock that pays a reasonable dividend and is convertible into common stock (see separate citation). Generally the convertible feature may only be exercised after being held for a stated period of time. This arrangement is usually considered second-round financing when a company needs equity to maintain its cash flow.

Convertible securities
A feature of certain bonds, debentures, or preferred stocks that allows them to be exchanged by the owner for another class of securities at a future date and in accordance with any other terms of the issue.

Copayment
See Coinsurance

Copyright
A legal form of protection available to creators and authors to safeguard their works from unlawful use or claim of ownership by others. Copyrights may be acquired for works of art, sculpture, music, and published or unpublished manuscripts. All copyrights should be registered at the Copyright Office of the Library of Congress.

Corporate financial ratios
(See also Industry financial ratios)
A relationship between key figures found in a company's financial statement. The relationship is in the form of a numeric value, and is used to evaluate risk and company performance. Also known as Financial averages, Operating ratios, and Business ratios.

Corporation
A legal entity, chartered by a state or the federal government, recognized as a separate entity having its own rights, privi-

leges, and liabilities distinct from those of its members.

Cost containment

Actions taken by employers and insurers to curtail rising healthcare costs; for example, increasing employee cost sharing (see separate citation), requiring second opinions, or preadmission screening.

Cost sharing

The requirement that health care consumers contribute to their own medical care costs through deductibles and coinsurance (see separate citations). Cost sharing does not include the amounts paid in premiums. It is used to control utilization of services; for example, requiring a fixed amount to be paid with each health care service.

Cottage industry

(See also Home-based business)
Businesses based in the home in which the family units are the labor force and family-owned equipment is used to process the goods.

Credit Rating

A letter or number calculated by an organization(such as Dun & Bradstreet) to represent the ability and disposition of a business to meet its financial obligations.

Cyclical peak

The upper turning point in a business cycle.

Cyclical trough

The lower turning point in a business cycle.

DBA

See Business name

Death

See Business death

Debenture

A certificate given as acknowledgment of a debt (see separate citation) secured by the general credit of the issuing corporation. A bond, usually without security, issued by a corporation and sometimes convertible to common stock.

Debt

(See also Long-term debt; Mid-term debt; Securitized debt; Short-term debt)
Something owed by one person to another. Financing in which a company receives capital that must be repaid; no ownership is transferred.

Debt capital

Business financing that normally requires periodic interest payments and repayment of the principal within a specified time.

Debt financing

See Debt capital

Debt securities

Loans such as bonds and notes that provide a specified rate of return for a specified period of time.

Deductible

A set amount that an individual must pay before any benefits are received.

Demand shock absorbers

A term used to describe the role that some small firms play by expanding their output levels to accommodate a transient surge in demand.

Demonstration

Showing that a product or process has been modified sufficiently to meet the needs of users.

Deregulation

The lifting of government restrictions; for example, the lifting of government restrictions on the entry of new businesses, the expansion of services, and the setting of prices in particular industries.

Disaster loans

Various types of physical and economic assistance available to individuals and businesses through the U.S. Small Business Administration (SBA). This is the only SBA loan program available for residential purposes.

Diseconomies of scale

The condition in which the costs of production increase faster than the volume of production.

Dissolution

See Business dissolution

Distribution

Delivering a product or process to the user.

Doing business as (DBA)
See Business name

Economic efficiency
The use of productive resources to the fullest practical extent in the provision of the set of goods and services that is most preferred by purchasers in the economy.

Economically disadvantaged
See Socially and economically disadvantaged

Economies of scale
See Scale economies

8(a) Program
A program authorized by the Small Business Act that directs federal contracts to small businesses owned and operated by socially and economically disadvantaged individuals.

Employee leasing
A contract by which employers arrange to have their workers hired by a leasing company and then leased back to them for a management fee. The leasing company typically assumes the administrative burden of payroll and provides a benefit package to the workers.

Employee tenure
The length of time an employee works for a particular employer.

Employer identification number
The business equivalent of a social security number. Assigned by the U.S. Internal Revenue Service.

Enterprise
An aggregation of all establishments owned by a parent company. An enterprise may consist of a single, independent establishment or include subsidiaries and other branches under the same ownership and control.

Entrepreneur
A person who takes the risk of organizing and operating a new business venture.

Entry
See Business entry

Equity
(See also Common Stock; Equity midrisk venture capital) The ownership interest. Financing in which partial or total ownership of a company is surrendered in exchange for capital. An investor's financial return comes from dividend payments and from growth in the net worth of the business.

Equity capital
See Equity; Equity midrisk venture capital

Equity financing
See Equity; Equity midrisk venture capital

Equity midrisk venture capital
An unsecured investment in a company. Usually a purchase of ownership interest in a company that occurs in the later stages of a company's development.

Equity partnership
A limited partnership arrangement for providing start-up and seed capital to businesses.

Equity securities
See Equity

Equity-type
Debt financing subordinated to conventional debt.

Establishment
A single-location business unit that may be independent (a single-establishment enterprise) or owned by a parent enterprise.

Establishment and Enterprise Microdata File
See U.S. Establishment and Enterprise Microdata File

Establishment birth
See Business birth

Establishment Longitudinal Microdata File
See U.S. Establishment Longitudinal Microdata File

Evaluation
Determining the potential success of translating an invention into a product or process.

Experience rating
See Underwriting

Exit
See Business exit

Export license
A general or specific license granted by the U.S. Department ofCommerce required of anyone wishing to export goods. Some restricted articles need approval from the U.S. Departments of State, Defense, or Energy.

Failure
See Business failure

Fair share agreement
(See also Franchising)
An agreement reached between a franchisor and a minority business organization to extend business ownership to minorities by either reducing the amount of capital required or by setting aside certain marketing areas for minority business owners.

Feasibility study
A study to determine the likelihood that a proposed product or development will fulfill the objectives of a particular investor.

Fictional name
See Business name

Fiduciary
An individual or group that hold assets in trust for a beneficiary.

Financial analysis
The techniques used to determine money needs in a business. Techniques include ratio analysis, calculation of return on investment, guides for measuring profitability, and break-even analysis to determine ultimate success.

Financial intermediary
A financial institution that acts as the intermediary between borrowers and lenders. Banks, savings and loan associations, finance companies, and venture capital companies are major financial intermediaries in the United States.

Financial ratios
See Corporate financial ratios; Industry financial ratios

Financing
See First-stage financing; Second-stage financing; Third-stage financing

First-stage financing
(See also Second-stage financing; Third-stage financing)
Financing provided to companies that have expended their initial capital, and require funds to start full-scale manufacturing and sales. Also known as First-round financing.

503 Program
See Certified development corporation

Flexible benefit plan
A plan that offers a choice among cash and/or qualified benefits such as group term life insurance, accident and health insurance, group legal services, dependent care assistance, and vacations.

FOB
See Free on board

Format franchising
See Business format franchising; Franchising

Franchising
A form of licensing by which the owner—the franchisor—distributes or markets a product, method, or service through affiliated dealers called franchisees. The product, method, or service being marketed is identified by a brand name, and the franchisor maintains control over the marketing methods employed. The franchisee is often given exclusive access to a defined geographic area.

Free on board (FOB)
A pricing term indicating that the quoted price includes the cost of loading goods into transport vessels at a specified place.

Frictional unemployment
See Unemployment

Full-time workers
Generally, those who work a regular schedule of more than 35 hours per week.

Garment registration number
A number that must appear on every garment sold in the United States to indicate the manufacturer of the garment, which may not be the same as the label under which the garment is sold. The U.S. Federal Trade Commission assigns garment registration numbers.

Gatekeeper
A key contact point for entry into a network.

GDP
See Gross domestic product

General obligation bond
A municipal bond secured by the taxing power of the municipality. The Tax Reform Act of 1986 limits the purposes for which such bonds may be issued and establishes volume limits on the extent of their issuance.

GNP
See Gross national product

Goods sector
All businesses producing tangible goods, including agriculture, mining, construction, and manufacturing businesses.

GPO
See Gross product originating

Gross domestic product (GDP)
The part of the nation's gross national product (see separate citation) generated by private business using resources from within the country.

Gross national product (GNP)
The most comprehensive single measure of aggregate economic output. Represents the market value of the total output of goods and services produced by a nation's economy.

Gross product originating (GPO)
A measure of business output estimated from the income or production side using employee compensation, profit income, net interest, capital consumption, and indirect business taxes.

HAL
See Handicapped assistance loan program

Handicapped assistance loan program (HAL)
Low-interest direct loan program through the U.S. Small Business Administration (SBA) for handicapped persons. The SBA requires that these persons demonstrate that their disability is such that it is impossible for them to secure employment, thus making it necessary to go into their own business to make a living.

Health maintenance organization (HMO)
An organization of physicians and other health care professionals who provide a wide range of services to subscribers and their dependents on a prepaid basis

Health provider
An individual or institution that gives medical care. Under Medicare, an institutional provider is a hospital, skillednursing facility, home health agency, or provider of certain physical therapy services.

Hispanic
A person of Cuban, Mexican, Puerto Rican, Latin American (Central or South American), European Spanish, or other Spanish-speaking origin or ancestry.

HMO
See Health maintenance organization

Home-based business
(See also Cottage industry)
A business with an operating address that is also a residential address (usually the residential address of the proprietor).

Hub-and-spoke system
A system in which flights of an airline from many different cities (the spokes) converge at a single airport (the hub). After allowing passengers sufficient time to make connections, planes then depart for different cities.

Idea
An original concept for a new product or process.

Income
Money or its equivalent, earned or accrued, resulting from the sale of goods and services.

Income statement
A financial statement that lists the profits and losses of a company at a given time.

Incorporation
The filing of a certificate of incorporation with a state's secretary of state, thereby limiting the business owner's liability.

Incubator
A facility designed to encourage entrepreneurship and minimize obstacles to new business formation and growth, particu-

larly for high-technology firms, by housing a number of fledgling enterprises that share an array of services, such as meeting areas, secretarial services, accounting, research library, on-site financial and management counseling, and word processing facilities.

Independent contractor
An individual considered self-employed (see separate citation) and responsible for paying Social Security taxes and income taxes on earnings.

Indirect health coverage
Health insurance obtained through another individual's health care plan; for example, a spouse's employer-sponsored plan.

Industrial development authority
The financial arm of a state or other political subdivision established for the purpose of financing economic development in an area, usually through loans to nonprofit organizations, which in turn provide facilities for manufacturing and other industrial operations.

Industry financial ratios
(See also Corporate financial ratios)
Corporate financial ratios averaged for a specified industry. These are used for comparison purposes and reveal industry trends and identify differences between the performance of a specific company and the performance of its industry. Also known as Industrial averages, Industry ratios, Financial averages, and Business or Industrial norms.

Inflation
Increases in volume of currency and credit, generally resulting in a sharp and continuing rise in price levels.

Informal capital
Financing from informal, unorganized sources; includes informal debt capital such as trade credit or loans from friends and relatives and informal equity capital from informal investors.

Initial public offering (IPO)
A corporation's first offering of stock to the public.

Innovation
The introduction of a new idea into the marketplace in the form of a new product or service or an improvement in organization or process.

Internal capital
Debt or equity financing obtained from the owner or through retained business earnings.

Intrapreneurship
The state of employing entrepreneurial principles to nonentrepreneurial situations.

Invention
The tangible form of a technological idea, which could include a laboratory prototype, drawings, formulas, etc.

IPO
See Initial public offering

Job tenure
A period of time during which an individual is continuously employed in the same job.

Joint marketing agreements
Agreements between regional and major airlines, often involving the coordination of flight schedules, fares, and baggage transfer. These agreements help regional carriers operate at lower cost.

Joint venture
Venture in which two or more people combine efforts in a particular business enterprise, usually a single transaction or a limited activity, and agree to share the profits and losses jointly or in proportion to their contributions.

Labor force
Civilians considered eligible for employment who are also willing and able to work.

Labor force participation rate
The civilian labor force as a percentage of the civilian population.

Labor intensity
(See also Capital intensity)
The relative importance of labor in the production process, usually measured as the capital-labor ratio; i.e., the ratio of units of capital (typically, dollars of tangible assets) to the number of employees. The higher the capital-labor ratio exhibited by a firm or industry, the lower the capital intensity of that firm or industry is said to be.

Labor surplus area
An area in which there exists a high unemployment rate. In

procurement (see separate citation), extra points are given to firms in counties that are designated a labor surplus area; this information is requested on procurement bid sheets.

Laboratory prototype
See Prototype

Large business-dominated industry
Industry in which a minimum of 60 percent of employment or sales is in firms with more than 500 workers.

LBO
See Leveraged buy-out

Legal list
A list of securities selected by a state in which certain institutions and fiduciaries (such as pension funds, insurance companies, and banks) may invest. Securities not on the list are not eligible for investment. Legal lists typically restrict investments to high quality securities meeting certain specifications. Generally, investment is limited to U.S. securities and investment-grade blue chip securities (see separate citation).

Leveraged buy-out (LBO)
The purchase of a business or a division of a corporation through a highly leveraged financing package.

License
(See also Business license)
A legal agreement granting to another the right to use a technological innovation.

Limited partnerships
See Venture capital limited partnerships

Liquidity
The ability to convert a security into cash promptly.
Loans.

Loans
See Disaster loans; SBA direct loans; SBA guaranteed loans; SBA special lending institution categories

Local development corporation
An organization, usually made up of local citizens of a community, designed to improve the economy of the area by inducing business and industry to locate and expand there. A local development corporation establishes a capability to finance local growth.

Long-haul rates
Rates charged by a transporter in which the distance travelled is more than 800 miles.

Long-term debt
An obligation that matures in a period that exceeds five years.

Low-grade bond
A corporate bond that is rated below investment grade by the major rating agencies (Standard and Poor's, Moody's).

Macro-efficiency
(See also Economic efficiency)
Efficiency as it pertains to the operation of markets and market systems.

Management and technical assistance
A term used by many programs to mean business (as opposed to technological) assistance.

Management Assistance Programs
See SBA Management Assistance Programs

Mandated benefits
Specific treatments, providers, or individuals required by law to be included in commercial health plans.

Market evaluation
The use of market information to determine the sales potential of a specific product or process.

Market failure
The situation in which the workings of a competitive market do not produce the best results from the point of view of the entire society.

Market information
Data of any type that can be used for market evaluation, which could include demographic data, technology forecasting, regulatory changes, etc.

Market research
A systematic collection, analysis, and reporting of data about the market and its preferences, opinions, trends, and plans; used for corporate decision-making.

Master Establishment List (MEL)
A list of firms in the United States developed by the U.S. Small Business Administration; firms can be selected by industry, region, state, standard metropolitan statistical area (see separate citation), county, and zip code.

Maturity
(See also Term)
The date upon which the principal or stated value of a bond or other indebtedness becomes due and payable.

Medicaid (Title XIX)
A federally aided, state-operated and administered program that provides medical benefits for certain low-income persons in need of health and medical care who are eligible for one of the governments's welfare cash payment programs, including the aged, the blind, the disabled, and members of families with dependent children where one parent is absent, incapacitated, or unemployed.

Medicare (Title XVIII)
A nationwide health insurance program for disabled and aged persons. Health insurance is available to insured persons without regard to income. Monies from payroll taxes cover hospital insurance and monies from general revenues and beneficiary premiums pay for supplementary medical insurance.

MEL
See Master Establishment List

Metropolitan statistical area (MSA)
A means used by the government to define large population centers that may transverse different governmental jurisdictions. For example, the Washington, D.C., MSA includes the District of Columbia and contiguous parts of Maryland and Virginia because all of these geopolitical areas comprise one population and economic operating unit.

Mezzanine financing
See Third-stage financing

MESBIC
See Minority enterprise small business investment corporation

MET
See Multiple employer trust

Micro-efficiency
(See also Economic efficiency)
Efficiency as it pertains to the operation of individual firms.

Microdata
Information on the characteristics of an individual business firm.

Mid-term debt
An obligation that matures within one to five years.

Midrisk venture capital
See Equity midrisk venture capital

Minimum premium plan
A combination approach to funding an insurance plan aimed primarily at premium tax savings. The employer self-funds a fixed percentage of estimated monthly claims and the insurance company insures the excess.

Minority Business Development Agency
Contracts with private firms throughout the nation to sponsor Minority Business Development Centers to provide minority firms with advice and technical assistance on a fee basis.

Minority enterprise small business investment corporation (MESBIC)
A federally funded private venture capital firm licensed by the U.S. Small Business Administration to provide capital to minority-owned businesses (see separate citation).

Minority-owned business
Businesses owned by those who are socially or economically disadvantaged (see separate citation).

Mom and Pop business
A small store or enterprise having limited capital, principally employing family members.

Moonlighter
A wage-and-salary worker with a side business.

MSA
See Metropolitan statistical area

Multi-employer plan
A health plan to which more than one employer is required to contribute and that may be maintained through a collective bargaining agreement and required to meet standards prescribed by the U.S. Department of Labor.

Multiple employer trust (MET)
A self-funded benefit plan generally geared toward small employers sharing a common interest.

National income
Aggregate earnings of labor and property arising from the production of goods and services in a nation's economy.

Net assets
See Net worth

Net income
The amount remaining from earnings and profits after all expenses and costs have been met or deducted. Also known as Net earnings.

Net worth
(See also Capital)
The difference between a company's total assets and its total liabilities.

Network
A chain of interconnected individuals or organizations sharing information and/or services.

Nonbank bank
A bank that either accepts deposits or makes loans, but not both. Used to create many new branch banks.

Noncompetitive awards
A method of contracting whereby the federal government negotiates with only one contractor to supply a product or service.

Nonprofit
An organization that has no shareholders, does not distribute profits, and is without federal and state tax liabilities.

Norms
See Financial ratios

Optimal firm size
The business size at which the production cost per unit of output (average cost) is, in the long run, at its minimum.

Owner's capital
Debt or equity funds provided by the owner(s) of a business; sources of owner's capital are personal savings, sales of assets, or loans from financial institutions.

P & L
See Profit and loss statement

Part-time workers
Normally, those who work less than 35 hours per week. The Tax Reform Act indicated that part-time workers who work less than 17.5 hours per week may be excluded from health plans for purposes of complying with federal nondiscrimination rules.

Part-year workers
Employees who work less than 50 weeks per year.

Partnership
Two or more parties who enter into a legal relationship to conduct business for profit. Defined by the U.S. Internal Revenue Code as joint ventures, syndicates, groups, pools, and other associations of two or more persons organized for profit that are not specifically classified in the IRS code as corporations or proprietorships.

Patent
A grant made by the government to an inventor, assuring the sole right to make, use, and sell an invention for a period of 17 years.

PC
See Professional corporation

Peak
See Cyclical peak

Pension
A series of payments made monthly, semiannually, annually, or at other specified intervals during the lifetime of the pensioner. The term is sometimes used to denote the portion of the retirement allowance financed by the employer's contributions.

Pension fund
A fund established to provide for the payment of pension benefits; the collective contributions made by all of the parties to the pension plan.

Permit
See Business license

Plan
See Business plan

Pooling
An arrangement for employers to achieve efficiencies and lower health costs by joining together to purchase group health insurance or self-insurance.

PPO
See Preferred provider organization

Preferred lenders program
See SBA special lending institution categories

Preferred provider organization (PPO)
A contractual arrangement with a health care services organization that agrees to discount rates in return for faster payment and/or a patient base.

Premiums
The amount of money paid to an insurer for health insurance under a policy. The premium is generally paid periodically (e.g., monthly), and often is split between the employer and the employee. Unlike deductibles and coinsurance or copayments (see separate citations), premiums are paid for coverage whether or not benefits are actually used.

Prime-age workers
Employees 25 to 54 years of age.

Prime contract
A contract awarded directly by the U.S. Federal Government.

Private company
See Closely held corporation

Private placement
A method of raising capital by offering for sale an investment or business to a small group of investors (generally avoiding registration with the Securities and Exchange Commission or state securities registration agencies). Also known as Private financing or Private offering.

Procurement
(See also 8(a) Program; Small business set asides)
A contract from an agency of the federal government for goods orservices from a small business.

Product development
The stage of the innovation process where research is translated into a product or process through evaluation, adaptation, and demonstration.

Product franchising
An arrangement for a franchisee to use the name and to produce the product line of the franchisor or parent corporation.

Production
The manufacture of a product.

Production prototype
See Prototype

Professional corporation (PC)
Organized by members of a profession such as medicine, dentistry, or law for the purpose of conducting their professional activities as a corporation. Liability of a member or shareholder is limited in the same manner as in a business corporation.

Profit and loss statement (P & L)
The summary of the incomes (total revenues) and costs of a company's operation during a specific period of time. Also known as income and expense statement.

Proposal
See Business plan

Proprietorship
The most common legal form of business ownership; about 85 percent of all small businesses are proprietorships. The liability of the owner is unlimited in this form of ownership.

Prospective payment system
A cost-containment measure included in the Social Security Amendments of 1983 whereby Medicare payments to hospitals are based on established prices, rather than on cost reimbursement.

Prototype
A model that demonstrates the validity of the concept of an invention (laboratory prototype); a model that meets the needs of the manufacturing process and the user (production prototype).

Prudent investor rule or standard
A legal doctrine that requires fiduciaries to make investments using the prudence, diligence, and intelligence that would be used by a prudent person in making similar investments. Because fiduciaries make investments on behalf of third-party beneficiaries, the standard results in very conservative in-

vestments. Until recently, most state regulations required the fiduciary to apply this standard to each investment. Newer, more progressive regulations permit fiduciaries to apply this standard to the portfolio taken as a whole, thereby allowing a fiduciary to balance a portfolio with higher-yield, higher-risk investments. In states with more progressive regulations, practically every type of security is eligible for inclusion in the portfolio of investments made by a fiduciary, provided that the portfolio investments, in their totality, are those of a prudent person.

Public equity markets
Organized markets for trading in equity shares such as common stocks, preferred stocks, and warrants. Includes markets for both regularly traded and nonregularly traded securities.

Public offering
General solicitation for participation in an investment opportunity. Interstate public offerings are supervised by the U.S. Securities and Exchange Commission.

Rate of return
(See also Yield)
The yield obtained on a security or other investment based on its purchase price or its current market price. The total rate of return is current income plus or minus capital appreciation or depreciation.

Realignment
See Resource realignment

Recession
Contraction of economic activity occurring between the peak and trough (see separate citations) of a business cycle.

Regulated market
A market in which the government controls the forces of supply and demand, such as who may enter and what price may be charged.

Regulation D
A vehicle by which small businesses make small offerings andprivate placements of securities with limited disclosure requirements. It was designed to ease the burdens imposed on small businesses utilizing this method of capital formation.

Regulatory Flexibility Act
An act requiring federal agencies to evaluate the impact of their regulations on small businesses before the regulations are issued and to consider less burdensome alternatives.

Research
The initial stage of the innovation process, which includes idea generation and invention.

Research and development financing
A tax-advantaged partnership set up to finance product development for start-ups as well as more mature companies.

Resource mobility
The ease with which labor and capital move from firm to firm or from industry to industry.

Resource realignment
The adjustment of productive resources to interindustry changes in demand.

Resources
The sources of support or help in the innovation process, including sources of financing, technical evaluation, market evaluation, management and business assistance, etc.

Retained business earnings
Business profits that are retained by the business rather than being distributed to the shareholders as dividends.

Risk capital
See Venture capital

S corporations
See Sub chapter S corporations

SBA
See Small Business Administration

SBA direct loans
Loans made directly by the U.S. Small Business Administration (SBA); monies come from funds appropriated specifically for this purpose. In general, SBA direct loans carry interest rates slightly lower than those in the private financial markets and are available only to applicants unable to secure private financing or an SBA guaranteed loan.

SBA 503 Program
See Certified development corporation

SBA guaranteed loans
Loans made by lending institutions in which the U.S. Small

Business Administration (SBA) will pay a prior agreed-upon percentage of the outstanding principal in the event the borrower of the loan defaults. The terms of the loan and the interest rate are negotiated between the borrower and the lending institution, within set parameters.

SBA loans
See Disaster loans; SBA direct loans; SBA guaranteed loans; SBA special lending institution categories

SBA Management Assistance Programs
(See also Active Corps of Executives; Service Corps of Retired Executives; Small business institutes program)
Classes, workshops, counseling, and publications offered by the U.S. Small Business Administration (SBA).

SBA special lending institution categories
U.S. Small Business Administration (SBA) loan program in which the SBA promises certified banks a 72-hour turnaround period in giving its approval for a loan, and in which preferred lenders in a pilot program are allowed to write SBA loans without seeking prior SBA approval.

SBDB
See Small Business Data Base

SBDC
See Small business development centers

SBI
See Small business institutes program

SBIC
See Small business investment corporation

SBIR Program
See Small Business Innovation Development Act of 1982

Scale economies
The decline of the production cost per unit of output (average cost) as the volume of output increases.

Scale efficiency
The reduction in unit cost available to a firm when producing at a higher output volume.

SCORE
See Service Corps of Retired Executives

Second-stage financing
(See also First-stage financing; Third-stage financing)
The working capital for the initial expansion of a company that is producing and shipping and has growing accounts receivable and inventories. Also known as Second-round financing.

Secondary market
A market established for the purchase and sale of outstanding securities following their initial distribution.

Secondary worker
Any worker in a family other than the person who is the primary source of income for the family.

Secondhand capital
Previously used and subsequently resold capital equipment (e.g., buildings and machinery).

Securitized debt
A marketing technique that converts long-term loans to marketable securities.

Seed capital
Venture financing provided in the early stages of the innovation process, usually during product development.

Self-employed person
One who works for a profit or fees in his or her own business, profession, or trade, or who operates a farm.

Self-funding
A health benefit plan in which a firm uses its own funds to pay claims, rather than transferring the financial risks of paying claims to an outside insurer in exchange for premium payments.

Service Corps of Retired Executives (SCORE)
(See also Active Corps of Executives)
Volunteers for the SBA Management Assistance Program who provideone-on-one counseling and teach workshops and seminars for small firms.

Service firm
See Business service firm

Service sector
Broadly defined, all U.S. industries that produce intangibles, including the five major industry divisions of transportation, communications, and utilities; wholesale trade; retail trade;

finance, insurance, and real estate; and services.

Set asides
See Small business set asides

Short-haul service
A type of transportation service in which the transporter supplies service between cities where the maximum distance is no more than 200 miles.

Short-term debt
An obligation that matures in one year.

SIC codes
See Standard Industrial Classification codes

Single-establishment enterprise
See Establishment

Small business
An enterprise that is independently owned and operated, is not dominant in its field, and employs fewer than 500 people. For SBA purposes, the U.S. Small Business Administration (SBA) considers various other factors (such as gross annual sales) in determining size of a business.

Small Business Administration (SBA)
An independent agency of the federal government which provides assistance in loans, management, and advocating interests before other federal agencies.

Small Business Data Base
(See also U.S. Establishment and Enterprise Microdata File; U.S. Establishment Longitudinal Microdata File)
A collection of microdata (see separate citation) files on individual firms developed and maintained by the U.S. Small Business Administration.

Small business development centers (SBDC)
Centers that provide support services to small businesses, such as individual counseling, SBA advice, seminars and conferences, and other learning center activities. Most services are free of charge, or available at minimal cost.

Small business development corporation
See Certified development corporation

Small business-dominated industry
Industry in which a minimum of 60 percent of employment or sales is in firms with fewer than 500 employees.

Small Business Innovation Development Act of 1982
Federal statute requiring federal agencies with large extramural research and development budgets to allocate a certain percentage of these funds to small research and development firms. The program, called the Small Business Innovation Research (SBIR) Program, is designed to stimulate technological innovation and make greater use of small businesses in meeting national innovation needs.

Small business institutes (SBI) program
Cooperative arrangements made by U.S. Small Business Administration district offices and local colleges and universities to provide small business firms with graduate students to counsel them without charge.

Small business investment corporation (SBIC)
A privately owned company licensed and funded through the U.S. Small Business Administration and private sector sources to provide equity or debt capital to small businesses.

Small business set asides
Procurement (see separate citation) opportunities required by law to be on all contracts under $10,000 or a certain percentage of an agency's total procurement expenditure.

Smaller firms
For U.S. Department of Commerce purposes, those firms not included in the Fortune 1000.

SMSA
See Metropolitan statistical area

Socially and economically disadvantaged
Individuals who have been subjected to racial or ethnic prejudice or cultural bias because of their identity as a member of a group, without regard to their qualities as individuals, and whose abilities to compete are impaired because of diminished opportunities to obtain capital and credit.

Sole proprietorship
An unincorporated, one-owner business, farm, or professional practice.

Special lending institution categories
See SBA special lending institution categories

Standard Industrial Classification (SIC) codes
Four-digit codes established by the U.S. Federal Government to categorize businesses by type of economic activity; the first two digits correspond to major groups such as construction and manufacturing, while the last two digits correspond to subgroups such as home construction or highway construction.

Standard metropolitan statistical area (SMSA)
See Metropolitan statistical area

Start
See Business start

Start-up financing
Financing provided to companies either completing product development and initial marketing or already in business for one year or less, but that have not sold their product commercially.

Stock
(See also Common stock; Convertible preferred stock)
A certificate of equity ownership in a business.

Stop-loss coverage
Insurance for a self-insured plan that reimburses the company for any losses it might incur in its health claims beyond a specified amount.

Structural unemployment
See Unemployment

Sub chapter S corporations
Corporations that are considered noncorporate for tax purposes but legally remain corporations.

Subcontract
A contract between a prime contractor and a subcontractor, or between subcontractors, to furnish supplies or services for performance of a prime contract or a subcontract.

Surety bonds
Bonds providing reimbursement to an individual, company, or the government if a firm fails to complete a contract. The U.S. Small Business Administration guarantees surety bonds in a program much like the SBA guaranteed loan program (see separate citation).

Swing loan
See Bridge financing

Target market
The clients or customers sought for a business' product or service.

Tax number
(See also Employer identification number)
A number assigned to a business by a state revenue department that enables the business to buy goods wholesale without paying sales tax.

Taxable bonds
An interest-bearing certificate of public or private indebtedness. Bonds are issued by public agencies to finance economic development.

Technical assistance
See Management and technical assistance

Technical evaluation
The assessment of technological feasibility.

Technology
The method in which a firm combines and utilizes labor and capital resources to produce goods or services; the application of science for commercial or industrial purposes.

Technology transfer
The movement of information about a technology or intellectual property from one party to another for use.

Tenure
See Employee tenure

Term
(See also Maturity)
The length of time for which a loan is made.

Terms of a note
The conditions or limits of a note; includes the interest rate per annum, the due date, and transferability and convertibility features, if any.

Third-party administrator
An outside company responsible for handling claims and performing administrative tasks associated with health insurance plan maintenance.

Third-stage financing
(See also First-stage financing; Second-stage financing)
Financing provided for the major expansion of a company whose sales volume is increasing and that is breaking even or profitable. These funds are used for further plant expansion, marketing, working capital, or development of an improved product. Also known as Third-round or Mezzanine financing.

Time deposit
A bank deposit that cannot be withdrawn before a specified future time.

Trade credit
Credit extended by suppliers of raw materials or finished products. In an accounting statement, trade credit is referred to as "accounts payable."

Trade name
The name under which a company conducts business, or by which its business, goods, or services are identified. It may or may not be registered as a trademark.

Trademark
A graphic symbol, device, or slogan that identifies a business. A business has property rights to its trademark from the inception of its use; however, it is still prudent to register all trademarks with the Trademark Office of the U.S. Department of Commerce.

Translation
See Product development

Treasury bills
Investment tender issued by the Federal Reserve Bank in amounts of $10,000 that mature in 91 to 182 days.

Treasury bonds
Long-term notes with maturity dates of not less than seven and not more than twenty-five years.

Treasury notes
Short-term notes maturing in less than seven years.

Trough
See Cyclical trough

UL
See Underwriters Laboratories

Underwriters Laboratories (UL)
One of several private firms that tests products and processes to determine their safety. Although various firms can provide this kind of testing service, many local and insurance codes specify UL certification.

Underwriting
A process by which an insurer determines whether or not and on what basis it will accept an application for insurance. In an experience-rated plan, premiums are based on a firm's or group's past claims; factors other than prior claims are used for community-rated or manually rated plans.

Unfunded accrued liability
The excess of total liabilities, both present and prospective, over present and prospective assets.

Unemployment
The joblessness of individuals who are willing to work, who are legally and physically able to work, and who are seeking work. Unemployment may represent the temporary joblessness of a worker between jobs (frictional unemployment) or the joblessness of a worker whose skills are not suitable for jobs available in the labor market (structural unemployment).

Uniform product code (UPC)
A computer-readable label comprised of ten digits and stripes that encodes what a product is and how much it costs. The first five digits are assigned by the Uniform Produce Code Council, and the last five digits, by the individual manufacturer.

Unit cost
See Average cost

UPC symbol
See Uniform product code

U.S. Establishment and Enterprise Microdata (USEEM) File
A cross-sectional database containing information on employment, sales, and location for individual enterprises and establishments with employees that have a Dun & Bradstreet credit rating.

U.S. Establishment Longitudinal Microdata (USELM) File
A database containing longitudinally linked sample microdata on establishments drawn from the U.S. Establishment and

Enterprise Microdata file (see separate citation).

U.S. Small Business Administration 503 Program
See Certified development corporation

USEEM
See U.S. Establishment and Enterprise Microdata File

USELM
See U.S. Establishment Longitudinal Microdata File

VCN
See Venture capital network

Venture capital
(See also Equity; Equity midrisk venture capital)
Money used to support new or unusual business ventures that exhibit above-average growth rates, significant potential for market expansion, and are in need of additional financing to sustain growth or further research and development; equity or equity-type financing traditionally provided at the commercialization stage, increasingly available prior to commercialization.

Venture capital company
A company organized to provide seed capital to a business in its formation stage, or in its first or second stage of expansion. Funding is obtained through public or private pension funds, commercial banks and bank holding companies, small business investment corporations licensed by the U.S. Small Business Administration, private venture capital firms, insurance companies, investment management companies, bank trust departments, industrial companies seeking to diversify their investment, and investment bankers acting as intermediaries for other investors or directly investing on their own behalf.

Venture capital limited partnerships
Designed for business development, these partnerships are an institutional mechanism for providing capital for young, technology-oriented businesses. The investors' money is pooled and invested in money market assets until venture investments have been selected. The general partners are experienced investment managers who select and invest the equity and debt securities of firms with high growth potential and the ability to go public in the near future.

Venture capital network (VCN)
A computer database that matches investors with entrepreneurs.

Withholding
Federal, state, social security, and unemployment taxes withheld by the employer from employees' wages; employers are liable for these taxes and the corporate umbrella and bankruptcy will not exonerate an employer from paying back payroll withholding. Employers should escrow these funds in a separate account and disperse them quarterly to withholding authorities.

Working capital
Refers to a firm's short-term investment of current assets, including cash, short-term securities, accounts receivable, and inventories.

Yield
(See also Rate of return)
The rate of income returned on an investment, expressed as a percentage. Income yield is obtained by dividing the current dollar income by the current market price of the security. Net yield or yield to maturity is the current income yield minus any premium above par or plus any discount from par in purchase price, with the adjustment spread over the period from the date of purchase to the date of maturity.

Small Business Development Centers

Small Business Development Centers

A listing of Small Business Development Centers (SBDCs) throughout the United States, Puerto Rico, and the U.S. Virgin Islands organized alphabetically by state or country name, then region within state where applicable.

ALABAMA

John Sandefur, State Director
Alabama SBDC Consortium
University of Alabama at Birmingham
Medical Towers Building
1717 11th Ave. South, Suite 419
Birmingham, AL 35294-4410
(205)934-7260 Fax:(205)934-7645

Kim Kuerten
Auburn University SBDC
108 COB Bldg.
Auburn, AL 36849-5243
(205)844-4220

Vernon Nabors
University of Alabama at Birmingham SBDC
1601 11th Avenue S.
Birmingham, AL 35294
(205)934-6760

Dr. William S. Stewart
Univeristy of North Alabama SBDC
Box 5017 Keller Hall
Florence, AL 35632-0001
(205)760-4629

Jeff Thompson
Northeast Alabama Regional SBDC
Alabama A&M and the University of Alabama in Huntsville
225 Church St. N.W.
Huntsville, AL 35804-0343
(205)535-2061

Pat W. Shaddix
Jacksonville State University SBDC
113 B Merrill Hall
Jacksonville, AL 36265
(205)782-5271

Yolanda Devine
Livingston University SBDC
Station 35
Livingston, AL 35470
(205)652-9661 ext.439

Cheryl Coleman
University of South Alabama SBDC
BMSB 101
Mobile, AL 36688
(205)460-6004

Jacqueline Gholston
Alabama State University SBDC
915 South Jackson Street
Montgomery, AL 36195
(205)269-1102

Janet W. Bradshaw
Troy State University SBDC
Bibb Graves, Room 102
Troy, AL 36082-0001
(205)670-3771

Nisa Miranda
University of Alabama SBDC
Box 870396
400 N. Martha Parham West
Tuscaloosa, AL 35487-0396
(205)348-7621

Paavo Hanninen
University of Alabama
International Trade Center
Box 870397
400 S. Martha Parham West
Tuscaloosa, AL 35487-0397
(205)348-7011

ALASKA

Jan Fredericks, State Director
University of Alaska Anchorage SBDC
430 West Seventh Ave., Suite 110
Anchorage, AK 99501
(907) 274-7232 Fax: (907) 274-9524

Tom Brodersen, Director
University of Alaska Anchorage SBDC
Rural Outreach
430 West Seventh Ave, Suite 110
Anchorage, AK 99501
(907) 274-7232 Fax: (907) 274-9524

Theresa Proenza, Interim Director
Small Business Development Center
510 Second Avenue, Suite 115
Fairbanks, AK 99701
(907) 456-1701 Fax: (907) 456-8817

Blake Kazama, Director
University of Alaska Southeast SBDC
124 West Fifth Street
Juneau, AK 99801
(907) 463-3789 Fax: (907) 463-5670

Marian Romano, Director
University of Alaska, Mat-Su SBDC
1801 Parks Highway, Suite C-18
Wasilla, AK 99654
(907) 373-7232 Fax: (907) 373-2560

ARIZONA

Mike York, Acting State Director
Arizona SBDC Network
2411 West 14th Street, Suite 132
Tempe, AZ 85281
(602) 731-8720 Fax: (602) 731-8729

Dr. Bill Phillips
Central Arizona College
141 N. Main St.
Coolidge, AZ 85228
(602)723-4037 Fax:(602)426-4234

MaryAnn Stanton
Conconina Co. Community College
3000 N. 4th St., Suite 25
Flagstaff, AZ 86004
(602)459-9778 Fax: (602)526-8693

Joel Eittreim
Small Business Development Center
Northland Pioneer College
P.O. Box 610
Holbrook, AZ 86025
(602) 537-2976 Fax: (602) 524-2227

Bonnie Mocek
Small Business Development Center
Mohave Community College
1971 Jagerson Avenue
Kingman, AZ 86401
(602)757-0894

Kathy Evans
Small Business Development Center
Gateway Community College
108 N. 40th St.
Phoenix, AZ 85008
(602)392-5220

Marti McCorkindale
Small Business Development Center
Rio Salado Community College
301 W. Roosevelt, Suite B
Phoenix, AZ 85003
(602)238-9603 Fax:(602)776-2193

Richard Senopole
Small Business Development Center
Yavapai College
1100 E. Sheldon St.
Prescott, AZ 86301
(602) 776-2373 Fax: (602) 776-2193

Frank Granberg
Small Business Development Center
Eastern Arizona College
1111 Thatcher Blvd.
Safford, AZ 85546
(602) 428-7603 Fax: (602) 428-8462

Debbie Elver
Small Business Development Center
Cochise College
901 N. Colombo, Room 411
Sierra Vista, AZ 85635
(602) 459-9778 Fax: (602) 459-9764

Small Business Development Center
Pima Community College
655 North Alvernon, #110
Tuscon, AZ 85711
(602) 884-6306 Fax: (602) 884-6306

Richard Meyer
Small Business Development Center
Arizona Western College
281 W. 24th St. #128 Century Plaza
Yuma, AZ 85364
(602) 341-1650 Fax: (602) 341-0234

ARKANSAS

Paul McGinnis, State Director
Small Business Development Center
University of Arkansas at Little Rock
100 S. Main St., Suite 401
Little Rock, AR 72201
(501) 324-9043 Fax: (501) 324-9049

Bill Akin, Director
Small Business Development Center
Henderson State University
P.O. Box 7624
Arkadelphia, AR 71923
(501) 246-5511

Dr. Don Cook, Director
Small Business Development Center
University of Arkansas at Fayetteville
College of Business, BA 117
Fayetteville, AR 72701
(501) 575-5148

Twig Branch, Business Specialist
Regional Office - UALR
1109 S. 16th Street
P.O. Box 2067
Fort Smith, AR 72901
(501) 785-1376

Bob Penquite, Business Specialist
Regional Office - UALR
1313 Highway 62-65-412 North
P.O. Box 190
Harrison, AR 72601
(501) 741-8009

Richard Evans, Business Specialist
Regional Office - UALR
835 Central Avenue, Box 402D
Hot Springs, AR 71901
(501) 624-5448

Stephen Bryant, Business Specialist
Regional Office - UALR
1801 Stadium Boulevard
P.O. Box 1403
Jonesboro, AR 72403
(501) 932-3957

John Harrison, Business Specialist
State Office - UALR
100 S. Main, Suite 401
Little Rock, AR 72201
(501) 324-9043

Lairie Kincaid, Business Specialist
Regional Office - UALR
600 Bessie, P.O. Box 767
Magnolia, AR 71753
(501)234-4030

Mike Brewer, Business Specialist
Regional Office - UALR
The Enterprise Center III
400 Main, Suite 117
Pine Bluff, AR 71601
(501)536-0654

Gerald Jones, Director
Small Business Development Center
Arkansas State University
Drawer 2650
St. University, AR 72467
(501)972-3517

Ronny Brothers, Business Specialist
Regional Office - UALR
301 S. Grand, Suite 101
Stuttgart, AR 72160
(501)673-8707

CALIFORNIA

Barbara Hayes, State Director
Department of Commerece
801 K St., Suite 1700
Sacramento, CA 95814
(916)324-5068 Fax: (916)322-5084

Elza Minor, Director
Central Coast SBDC
6500 Soquel Drive
Aptos, CA 95003
(408)479-6136 Fax: (408)479-5743

Mary Wollesen, Director
Sierra College SBDC
560 Wall Street, Suite J
Auburn, CA 95603
(916)885-5488 Fax: (916)823-4704

Jeffrey Johnson, Director
Weill Institute SBDC
2101 K Street Mall
Bakersfield, CA 93301
(805)395-4148 Fax: (805)395-4134

Kay Zimmerlee, Director
Butte College Tri-County SBDC
260 Cohasset Avenue
Chico, CA 95926
(916)895-9017 Fax: (916)895-9099

Mary Wylie, Director
Southwestern College Small Business Development and Intl. Trade Center
900 Otay Lakes Road, Bldg. 1600
Chula Vista, CA 91910
(619)482-6393 Fax: (619)482-6402

Fran Clark, Director
North Coast SBDC
882 H Street
Cresent City, CA 95531
(707)464-2168 Fax: (707)465-6008

Duff Heuttner, Business Counselor
North Coast Satellite Center
408 7th Street, Suite "E"
Eureka, CA 95501
(707)445-9720

Dennis Winans, Director
Central Valley SBDC
2208 Tuolumne Street
Fresno, CA 93721
(209)278-4946 Fax: (209)278-6964

Peter Graff, Director
Gavilan College SBDC
5055 Santa Teresa Boulevard
Gilroy, CA 95020
(408)847-0373 Fax: (408)847-0393

Tiffany Haugen, Interim Director
Accelerate Technology Assistance Small Business Development Center
Graduate School of Management
University of California Irvine
Irvine, CA 92717-4125
(209) 278-4946 Fax: (714) 856-8469

Jeff Lucas, Interim Advisor
Lake County Satellite
341 North Main Street
Lakeport, CA 95453
(707) 263-6180 Fax: (707) 263-0920

Maria Morris, Director
Greater San Diego Chamber of Commerce SBDC
4275 Executive Square, Suite 920
La Jolla, CA 92037
(619) 453-9388 Fax: (619) 450-1997

Gladys Moreau, Director
Export Small Business Development Center of Southern California
110 E. 9th, Suite A761
Los Angeles, CA 90079
(213) 892-1111 Fax: (213) 892-8232

Joan Sullivan, Director
Merced Satellite Center
1632 "N" Street
Merced, CA 95340
(209) 385-7312 Fax: (209) 383-4959

Kelly Bearden, Director
Valley Sierra SBDC
1012 Eleventh Street, Suite 300
Modesto, CA 95354
(209) 521-6177 Fax: (209) 521-9373

Michael Kauffman, Director
Napa Valley College SBDC
1556 First Street, Suite 103
Napa, CA 94559
(707) 253-3210 Fax: (707) 253-3068

Selma Taylor, Director
East Bay SBDC
Oakland, CA 94612
(510) 893-4114 Fax: (510) 893-5532

Jana Goldsworthy, Director
Export Satellite Center
300 Esplanade Drive, Suite 1010
Oxnard, CA 93030
(805) 981-4633

Toni Valdez, Director
East Los Angeles County SBDC
363 S. Park Avenue, Suite 100
Pomona, CA 91766
(714) 629-2247 Fax: (714) 629-8310

Teri Corrazini, Director
Inland Empire SBDC
1860 Chicago Avenue, Bldg. I
Suite 1
Riverside, CA 92507
(714) 781-2345 Fax: (714) 781-2353

Deborah Travis, Director
Greater Sacramento SBDC
1787 Tribute Road, Suite A
Sacramento, CA 95815
(916) 920-7949 Fax: (916) 920-7940

Daniel Aloot, Director
Silicon Valley/San Mateo County SBDC
111 N. Market Street, #150
San Jose, CA 95113
(408) 298-7694 Fax: (408) 971-0680

Phyllis Schneider, Director
San Mateo County Satellite Center
1730 S. Amphlett Blvd., Suite 208
San Mateo, CA 94402
(415) 358-0271 Fax: (415) 358-9450

Gregory Kishel, Director
Orange County SBDC
901 East Santa Ana Blvd., Suite 108
Santa Ana, CA 92701
(714) 647-1172 Fax: (714) 835-9008

Stuart Sudduth, Interim Director
Redwood Empire SBDC
2300 County Center Drive, Suite B177
Santa Rosa, CA 95403
(707) 527-4435

Gillian Murphy, Director
San Joaquin Delta College SBDC
814 N. Hunter
Stockton, CA 95202
(209) 474-5089 Fax: (209) 474-5605

Edward Schlenker, Director
Solano County SBDC
320 Campus Lane
Suisan, CA 94585
(707) 864-3382 Fax: (707) 864-3386

Bart Hoffman, Interim Director
Southwest Los Angeles County SBDC
21221 Western Avenue, Suite 110
Torrance, CA 90501
(310) 782-3861 Fax: (310) 782-8607

Roy Muto, Director
Northern Los Angeles SBDC
14540 Victory Boulevard, Suite #206
Van Nuys, CA 91411
(818) 373-7092 Fax: (818) 373-7740

COLORADO

Rick Garcia, State Director
Small Business Development Center
Office of Business Development
1625 Broadway, Suite 1710
Denver, CO 80202
(303) 892-3809 Fax: (303) 892-3848

Patricia Skroch
Small Business Development Center
Adams State College
Alamosa, CO 81102
(719) 589-7372 Fax: (719) 589-7522

Kathy Scott
Small Business Development Center
Community College of Aurora
16000 E. Centretech Pkwy., #A201
Aurora, CO 80011-9036
(303) 360-4745 Fax: (303) 360-4761

Lewis Hagler
Small Business Development Center
Front Range Community College
2440 Pearl Street
Boulder, CO 80302
(303) 442-1475 Fax: (303) 938-8837

Elwin Boody
Small Business Development Center
Pueblo Community College
402 Valley Road
Canon City, CO 81212
(719) 275-5335 Fax: (719) 275-4400

Harry Martinez
Small Business Development Center
Pikes Peak Community College
CO Springs Chamber of Commerce
P.O. Drawer B
Colorado Springs, CO 80901-3002
(719) 635-1551 Fax: (719) 635-1571

Ken Farmer
Small Business Development Center
Colorado Northwestern Comm. College
50 Spruce Dr.
Craig, CO 81625
(303) 824-7078 Fax: (303) 824-3527

Larry Fay
Small Business Development Center
Delta Montrose Vocational School
1765 US Highway 50
Delta, CO 81416
(303) 874-8772 Fax: (303) 874-8796

Carolyn Love
Small Business Development Center
Community College of Denver
Greater Denver Chamber of Commerce
1445 Market St.
Denver, CO 80202
(303) 620-8076 Fax: (303) 534-3200

Bard Heroy
Small Business Development Center
Fort Lewis College
484 Turner Dr., Bldg. B
Durango, CO 81301
(303) 247-9634 Fax: (303) 247-9513

Barbara Brown
Small Business Development Center
Front Range Community College
P.O. Box 270490
Fort Collins, CO 80527
(303) 226-0881 Fax: (303) 825-6819

Randy Johnson
Small Business Development Center
Morgan Community College
300 Main St.
Fort Morgan, CO 80701
(303) 867-4424 Fax: (303) 867-3352

Tom Bolger
Small Business Development Center
Mesa State College
304 W. Main St.
Grand Junction, CO 81505-1606
(303) 248-7314 Fax: (303) 241-0771

David Sanchez
Small Business Development Center
Aims Community College
Greeley/Weld Chamber of Commerce
1407 8th Ave.
Greeley, CO 80631
(303) 352-3661 Fax: (303) 352-3572

Jeff Seifried
Small Business Development Center
Red Rocks Community College
13300 W. 6th Ave.
Lakewood, CO 80401-5398
(303) 987-0710 Fax: (303) 969-8039

Elwood Gillis
Small Business Development Center
Lamar Community College
2400 S. Main
Lamar, CO 81052
(719) 336-8141 Fax: (719) 336-2448

Selma Kristel
Small Business Development Center
Arapahoe Community College
South Metro Chamber of Commerce
7901 SouthPark Plaza, Suite 110
Littleton, CO 80120
(303) 795-5855 Fax: (303) 795-7520

Gil Sanchez
Small Business Development Center
Pueblo Community College
900 W. Orman Ave.
Pueblo, CO 81004
(719) 549-3224 Fax: (719) 546-2413

Roni Carr
Small Business Development Center Morgan Community College
P.O. Box 28
Stratton, CO 80836
(719) 348-5596 Fax: (719) 348-5887

Paul Cordova
Small Business Development Center
Trinidad State Junior College
600 Prospect St., Davis Bldg.
Trinidad, CO 81082
(719) 846-5645 Fax: (719) 846-5667

Jim Kraft
Small Business Development Center
Colorado Mountain College
1310 Westhaven Dr.
Vail, CO 81657
(303) 476-4040 Fax: (303) 479-9212
(800)621-1647

Michael Lenzini
Small Business Development Center
Front Range Community College
3645 W. 112th Ave.
Westminster, CO 80030
(303) 460-1032 Fax: (303) 466-1623

CONNECTICUT

John O'Connor, State Director
Small Business Development Center
University of Connecticut
Box U-41, Rm 422
368 Fairfield Rd.
Storrs, CT 06269-2041
(203) 486-4135 Fax: (203) 486-1576

Bernard Friedlander
Small Business Development Center
University of Bridgeport
141 Linden Avenue
Bridgeport, CT 06601
(203)576-4538

Juan Scott
Small Business Development Center
Bridgeport Regional Business Council
10 Middle St., P.O. Box 999
Bridgeport, CT 06601
(203)335-3800

William Anthony, Asst. Dir.
University of Bridgeport
141 Linden Avenue
Bridgeport, CT 06601
(203)576-4538

Roger Doty
Small Business Development Center
Quinebaug Valley Comm. College
742 Upper Maple Street, P.O. Box 59
Danielson, CT 06239-1440
(203) 774-1130309

William Lockwood
Small Business Development Center
University of Connecticut
1084 Shennecossett Rd.
Administration Bldg. Rm 313
Groton, CT 06340-6097
(203)449-1188

Charles Kalal
Small Business Development Center
Middlesex County Cham. of Comm.
393 Main St.
Middletown, CT 06457
(203)344-2158

Neal Wehr
Small Business Development Center
Greater New Haven Cham. of Comm.
195 Church Street
New Haven, CT 06506
(203) 773-0782

George Ahl
Small Business Development Center
SW Area Comm. & Industry Assc. (SACIA)
One Landmark Square
Stamford, CT 06901
(203)359-3220

Maurice Dougherty, Assoc. Director
Small Business Development Center
University of Connecticut
Box U-41, Rm 422
368 Fairfield Rd.
Storrs, CT 06269-2041
(203) 486-4135 Fax: (203) 486-1576

Small Business Development Center
Greater Waterbury Cham. of Comm.
83 Bank Street
Waterbury, CT 06702
(203)757-0701

Richard Rogers
Small Business Development Center
University of Connecticut
1800 Asylum Avenue
West Hartford, CT 06117
(203)241-4986

Bob Suchy
University of Connecticut
1800 Asylum Avenue
West Hartford, CT 06117
(203)241-4986

Roger Doty
Small Business Development Center
Eastern CT State University
83 Windham Street
Willimantic, CT 06226-2295
(203)456-5349

DELAWARE

Clinton Tymes, State Director
Small Business Development Center
University of Delaware
Purnell Hall, Suite 005
Newark, DE 19716-2711
(302) 831-2747 Fax: (302) 831-1423

DISTRICT OF COLUMBIA

Nancy Flake, State Director
Metropolitan Washington D.C. Small Business Development Center Network
Howard University
Small Business Development Center
2600 Sixth Street, Room #128
Washington, DC 20059
(202) 806-1550 Fax: (202) 806-1777

Susan Jones
Small Business Development Center
George Washington University
Small Business Clinic
720 20th St., N.W.
Washington, DC 20052
(202) 994-7463 Fax: (202) 994-4946

Charlie Partridge, Director
Small Business Development Center
National Business League of Southern Maryland, Inc.
9200 Basil Court, Suite 210
Landover, MD 20785
(301) 772-3683 Fax: (301) 772-0730

FLORIDA

Jerry Cartwright, State Director
Florida SBDC Network
University of West Florida
11000 University Parkway
Pensacola, FL 32514
(904) 474-3016 Fax: (904) 474-2030

Mark Hosang, Director
Small Business Development Center
Florida Atlantic University
P.O. Box 3091
Boca Raton, FL 33431
(407) 367-2273 Fax: (407) 367-2272

Linda Krepel, Associate Director
Office of International Trade
Florida Atlantic University
P.O. Box 3091
Boca Raton, FL 33431
(407) 367-2271 Fax: (407) 367-2272

Glen Morgan, Regional Manager
Small Business Development Center
Seminole Community College
4590 South Highway 17-92
Casselberry, FL 32707
(407)834-4404

Anita Moore
Small Business Development Center
Brevard Community College
1519 Clearlake Road
Cocoa, FL 32922
(407) 951-1060 ext. 2045

William Healy, Regional Manager
Small Business Development Center
46 S.W. 1st Avenue
Dania, FL 33304
(305) 987-0100

John Duizen, Regional Manager
Small Business Development Center
Stetson University
School of Business Administration
P.O. Box 8417
DeLand, FL 32720
(904) 822-7326 Fax: (904) 822-8832

John Hudson, Regional Manager
Small Business Development Center
Florida Atlantic University
Commercial Campus
1515 West Commercial Blvd., Room 11
Fort Lauderdale, FL 33309
(305) 771-6520 Fax: (305) 776-6645

Small Business Development Center
Edison Community College
8099 College Parkway, SW
Fort Myers, FL 33906-6210
(813) 489-9200

Don Bell, Regional Manager
Small Business Development Center
Indian River Community College
3209 Virginia Avenue, Room 114
Ft. Pierce, FL 34981-5599
(407) 468-4756

Walter Craft, Manager
Small Business Development Center
University of West Florida
1170 Freedom Way
Fort Walton Beach, FL 32547
(904) 863-6543 Fax: (904) 863-6564

William Stensgaard, Regional Manager
Small Business Development Center
University of North Florida
214 W. University Ave., P.O. Box 2518
Gainesville, FL 32601
(904) 377-5621

Pam Riddle, Director
Florida Product Innovation Center
2622 N.W. 43rd Street, Suite B-3
Gainesville, FL 32606
(904) 334-1680 Fax: (904) 334-1682

Lowell Salter, Director
Small Business Development Center
University of North Florida
College of Business
Building 11, Room 2163
4567 St. John's Bluff Road, South
Jacksonville, FL 32216
(904) 646-2476 Fax: (904) 646-2594

SBDC Training Center
Skipper Palms Shopping Center
14612 Livingston Avenue
Lutz, FL 33549
(813) 974-4371

Royland Jarrett, Regional Manager
Small Business Development Center
Florida International University
North Miami Campus
NE 151 & Biscayne Blvd.
Academic Bldg. #1, Room 350
Miami, FL 33181
(305) 940-5790

Marvin Nesbit, Director
Small Business Development Center
Florida International College
Trailer MO1, Tamiami Campus
Miami, FL 33199
(305) 348-2272 Fax: (305) 348-2965

Frederick Bonneau
Small Business Development Center
Miami Dade Community College
NW 27th Avenue
Miami, FL 33150
(305) 237-1900

Small Business Development Center
110 E. Silver Springs Blvd.
P.O. Box 1210
Ocala, FL 32670
(904) 629-8051

Small Business Development Center
Valencia Community College
P.O. Box 3028
Orlando, FL 32802
(407) 299-5000 ext. 1624

Al Polfer, Director
Small Business Development Center
University of Central Florida
BA Suite 309, P.O. Box 161530
Orlando, FL 32816-1530
(407) 823-5554 Fax: (407) 823-3073

Donald Clause, Director
Small Business Development Center
University of West Florida, Building 8
11000 University Parkway
Pensacola, FL 32514
(904) 474-2908 Fax: (904) 474-2126

Pete Singletary, Dir. of Procurement
Small Business Development Center
University of West Florida, Building 8
11000 University Parkway
Pensacola, FL 32514
(904) 474-2919 Fax: (904) 474-2126

Small Business Development Center
St. Petersburg Community College
3200 34th Street, South
St. Petersburg, FL 33711
(813) 341-4414

Patricia McGowan, Director
Small Business Development Center
Florida A & M University
1715-B South Gadsden Street
Tallahassee, FL 32301
(904) 599-3407 Fax: (904) 561-2395

Scott Faris, Director
Small Business Development Center
University of South Florida
College of Business Administration
4202 E. Fowler Avenue, BSN 3403
Tampa, FL 33620
(813) 974-4274

Bobbie McGee, Regional Manager
Small Business Development Center
Florida Atlantic University
Prospect Place, Suite 123
3111 South Dixie Highway
West Palm Beach, FL 33405
(407) 837-5311

GEORGIA

Henry Logan, State Director
Small Business Development Center
University of Georgia
Chicopee Complex
1180 East Broad St.
Athens, GA 30602-5412
(706) 542-5760 Fax: (706) 542-6776

Sue Ford, District Director
Southwest Georgia District SBDC
Business & Technology Center
230 S. Jackson St., Suite 333
Albany, GA 31701
(912) 430-4303 Fax: (912) 430-3933

Gary Selden, Assoc. State Director
University of Georgia
Chicopee Complex
1180 East Broad St.
Athens, GA 30602-5412
(706) 542-5760 Fax: (706) 542-6776

Harold Roberts, District Director
Northeast Georgia District SBDC
University of Georgia
Chicopee Complex
1180 E. Broad St.
Athens, GA 30602-5412
(706) 542-7436 Fax: (706) 542-6825

Lee Quarterman
Georgia State University SBDC
University Plaza, Box 874
Atlanta, GA 30303-3083
(404) 651-3550 Fax: (404) 651-1035

Morris Brown College SBDC
643 Martin Luther King, Jr., Dr., NW
Atlanta, GA 30314
(404) 220-0224 Fax: (404) 688-5985

Augusta SBDC
1061 Katherine St.
Augusta, GA 30910
(706) 737-1790 Fax: (706) 731-7937

Brunswick SBDC
1107 Fountain Lake Dr.
Brunswick, GA 31520
(912) 264-7343 Fax: (912) 262-3095

Columbus SBDC
928 45th St., North Bldg., Room 523
Columbus, GA 31995
(404) 649-7433 Fax: (404) 649-1928

DeKalb SBDC
DeKalb Chamber of Commerce
750 Commerce Dr.
Decatur, GA 30030
(404) 378-8000 Fax: (404) 378-3397

James C. Smith
Gainesville SBDC
455 Jesse Jewel Parkway, Suite 302
Gainesville, GA 30501-4203
(706) 531-5681 Fax: (706) 531-5684

Gwinnett SBDC
Gwinnet Technical Institute
1250 Atkinson Rd.
Lawrenceville, GA 30246
(404) 963-4902 Fax: (404) 962-7985

David Mills, District Director
Central Georgia District SBDC
P.O. Box 13212
Macon, GA 31208-3212
(912) 751-6592 Fax: (912) 751-6661

Carlotta Roberts
Kennesaw State College SBDC
P.O. Box 444
Marietta, GA 30061
(404) 423-6450 Fax: (404) 423-6564

Clayton State College SBDC
P.O. Box 285
Morrow, GA 30260
(404) 961-3440 Fax: (404) 961-3428

Betty Nolen
Floyd College SBDC
P.O. Box 1864
Rome, GA 30163
(404) 295-6326 Fax: (404) 295-6732

Harry O'Brien, District Director
Southeast Georgia District SBDC
450 Mall Blvd., Suite H
Savannah, GA 31416-1418
(912) 356-2755 Fax: (912) 353-3033

Statesboro SBDC
Landrum Center, Box 8156
Statesboro, GA 30460
(912) 681-5194 Fax: (912) 681-0648

Valdosta SBDC
Baytree Office Park, Suite 9
Baytree Rd.
Valdosta, GA 31601
(912) 245-3738 Fax: (912) 245-3741

Warner Robins SBDC
151 Osigian Blvd.
Warner Robins, GA 31088
(912) 953-9356 Fax: (912) 953-9376

HAWAII

Janet M. Nye, State Director
Hawaii SBDC Network
University of Hawaii at Hilo
523 W. Lanikaula St.
Hilo, HI 96720-4091
(808) 933-3515 Fax: (808) 933-3683

Frank Hatstat, Center Director
Small Business Development Center
University of Hawaii at Hilo
523 W. Lanikaula St.
Hilo, HI 96720-4091
(808) 933-3515

Jim O'Donnell, Center Director
Small Business Development Center
Kauai Community College
8-1901 Kaumualii Highway
Lihue, HI 96766
(808) 245-8287

David Fisher, Center Director
Small Business Development Center
Maui Community College
Maui Research & Technology Center
590 Lipoa Parkway
Kihei, HI 96753
(808) 242-7646

IDAHO

Ronald R. Hall, State Director
Small Business Development Center
Boise State University
1910 University Drive
Boise, ID 83725
(208) 385-1640 Fax: (208) 385-3877

Ted Rudder
Small Business Development Center
Boise State University
1910 University Drive
Boise, ID 83725
(208) 385-3875

Jim Hunter, Director
Small Business Development Center
Panhandle Area Council
11100 Airport Drive
Hayden, ID 83835
(208) 772-0587

Mary E. Capps, Regional Director
Small Business Development Center
Idaho State University
2300 N. Yellowstone
Idaho Falls, ID 83401
(208) 523-1087

Helen Le Boeuf, Director
Small Business Development Center
Lewis Clark State College
8th Avenue & 6th Street
Lewiston, ID 83501
(208) 799-2465

Paul Cox
Small Business Development Center
Idaho State University
1651 Alvin Ricken Drive
Pocatello, ID 83201
(208) 232-4921

John Thielbahr
Small Business Development Center
Box 724
Sandpoint, ID 83864
(208) 263-4073

Cindy Brown
Small Business Development Center
P.O. Box 1238
Twin Falls, ID 83303-1238
(208) 733-9554

ILLINOIS

Jeff Mitchell, Statewide Admin.
Small Business Development Center
Dept. of Commerce & Comm. Affairs
620 East Adams St., 6th Floor
Springfield, IL 62701
(217) 524-5856 Fax: (217) 785-6328

Mike O'Kelley, Director
Small Business Development Center
Waubonsee Community College
Aurora Campus, 5 East Galena Blvd.
Aurora, IL 60506
(708) 892-3334

Dennis Cody, Director
Small Business Development Center
Southern Illinois University - Carbondale
Carbondale, IL 62901-6702
(618) 536-2424 Fax: (618) 453-5040

David Taylor, Director
Small Business Development Center
John A. Logan College
RR2
Carterville, IL 62918
(618) 985-6506 Fax: (618) 985-2248

Richard McCullum, Director
Small Business Development Center
Kaskaskia College
Shattuc Road
Centralia, IL 62801
(618) 532-2049 Fax: (618) 532-4983

Paul Ladniak, Director
Small Business Development Center
Back of the Yards Neighborhood Council
751 West 47th Street
Chicago, IL 60609
(312) 523-4419 Fax: (312) 254-3525

Patsy Mullins, Director
Small Business Development Center
Daley College
7500 South Pulaski Road, Bldg. 200
Chicago, IL 60652
(312) 735-3000 315 Fax: (312) 838-4876

Maria Munoz, Director
Eighteenth Street Devel. Corporation
1839 South Carpenter
Chicago, IL 60608
(312) 733-2287 Fax: (312) 733-7315

Dan Immergluck, Director
Small Business Development Center
Greater North Pulaski Devel. Corp.
4054 West North Avenue
Chicago, IL 60639
(312) 384-2262 Fax: (312) 384-3850

Andrew Goldsmith, Director
Small Business Development Center
Industrial Council of NW Chicago
2023 West Carroll
Chicago, IL 60612
(312) 421-3941

Lisa Christian, Director
Small Business Development Center
Latin American Chamber of Commerce
2539 North Kedzie, Suite 11
Chicago, IL 60647
(312) 252-5211 Fax: (312) 252-7065

Carson Gallagher, Director
Loop SBDC
DCCA State of Illinois Center
100 West Randolph, Suite 3-400
Chicago, IL 60601
(312) 814-6111 Fax: (312) 814-1749

Jerry Chambers, Director
Small Business Development Center
Olive-Harvey Community College
Heritage Pullman Bank
1000 East 111th St., 7th Floor
Chicago, IL 60628
(312) 291-6296 Fax: (312) 660-4847

Helen Brown, Director
Small Business Development Center
Women's Business Dev. Center
8 South Michigan, Suite 400
Chicago, IL 60603
(312) 853-3477 Fax: (312) 853-0145

Don Glaze, Director
Small Business Development Center
McHenry County College
8900 U.S. Highway 14
Crystal Lake, IL 60012-2761
(815) 455-6098 Fax: (815) 455-3999

Dianna Kirk, Director
Small Business Development Center
Danville Area Community College
28 West North Street
Danville, IL 61832
(217) 442-7232 Fax: (217) 442-6228

Maureen Ruski, Director
Small Business Development Center
Richland Community College
One College Park
Decatur, IL 62521
(217) 875-7200 Fax: (217) 875-6965

Larry Rouse, Director
Small Business Development Center
Northern Illinois University
Department of Management
305 East Locust
Dekalb, IL 60115
(815) 753-1403 Fax: (815) 753-6366

Tom Gospodarczyk, Director
Small Business Development Center
Sauk Valley Community College
173 Illinois Route #2
Dixon, IL 61021-9110
(815) 288-5605 Fax: (815) 288-5958

Donna Scalf, Director
Small Business Development Center
Black Hawk College
301 42nd Avenue
East Moline, IL 61244
(309) 752-9759 Fax: (309) 755-9847

Karen Pinkston, Director
Small Business Development Center
DCCA, State Office Building
10 Collinsville
East St. Louis, IL 62201
(618) 583-2272 Fax: (618) 588-2274

Chuck Behn, Director
Small Business Development Center
Southern Illinois University-Edwardsville
Campus Box 1107
Edwardsville, IL 62026
(618) 692-2929 Fax: (618) 692-2647

Craig Fowler, Director
Small Business Development Center
Elgin Community College
1700 Spartan Drive
Elgin, IL 60123
(708) 697-1000 Fax: (708) 888-7995

Tom Parkinson, Director
Small Business Development Center
Evanston Business and Technology Center
1840 Oak Avenue
Evanston, IL 60201
(708) 866-1841 Fax: (708) 866-1841

Chuck Mufich, Director
Small Business Development Center
Highland Community College
206 South Galena
Freeport, IL 61032
(815) 232-1366 Fax: (815) 235-1366

David Gay
Small Business Development Center
College of DuPage
22nd and Lambert Road
Glen Ellyn, IL 60137
(708) 858-2800 Fax: (708) 790-1197

Arthur Cobb, Jr., Director
Small Business Development Center
College of Lake County
19351 West Washington Street
Grayslake, IL 60030
(708) 223-3633 Fax: (708) 223-9371

Becky Williams, Director
Small Business Development Center
Southeastern Illinois College
325 East Poplar, Suite A
Harrisburg, IL 62946-1528
(618) 252-8528 Fax: (618) 252-0210

Lisa Payne, Director
Small Business Development Center
Rend Lake College
Route #1
Ina, IL 62846
(618) 437-5321 Fax: (618) 437-5321 385

Denise Mikulski, Director
Small Business Development Center
Joliet Junior College
Renaissance Center, Room 319
214 North Ottawa Street
Joliet, IL 60431
(815) 727-6544 1313 Fax: (815) 722-1895

JoAnn Seggebruch, Director
Small Business Development Center
Kankakee Community College
4 Dearborn Square
Kankakee, IL 60901
(815) 933-0376 Fax: (815) 933-0380

Dan Voorhis, Director
Small Business Development Center
Western Illinois University
216 Seal Hall
Macomb, IL 61455
(309) 298-1128 Fax: (309) 298-2520

Daniel Sulsberger, Director
Small Business Development Center
Lake Land College
South Route #45
Mattoon, IL 61938-9366
(217) 235-3131 Fax: (217) 258-6459

Carol Cook, Director
Small Business Development Center
Maple City Business andTechnology Center
620 South Main St.
Monmouth, IL 61462
(309) 734-4664 Fax: (309) 734-8579

Maureen Ruski, Director
Small Business Development Center
Heartland Community College
1226 Towanda Plaza
Normal, IL 61761
(217) 875-7200 Fax: (217) 875-6965

Boyd Palmer, Director
Small Business Development Center
Illinois Valley Community College
Bldg. 11, Route 1
Oglesby, IL 61348
(815) 223-1740 Fax: (815) 224-3033

John Spitz, Director
Small Business Development Center
Illinois Eastern Communtiy College
233 East Chestnut
Olney, IL 62450
(618) 395-3011 Fax: (618) 392-2773

Tom Parkinson, Director
Small Business Development Center
William Rainey-Harper College
1200 West Algonquin Road
Palatine, IL 60067
(708) 397-3000 Fax: (708) 866-1841

Hillary Gereg, Director
Small Business Development Center
Moraine Valley College
10900 South 88th Avenue
Palos Hills, IL 60465
(708) 974-5468 Fax: (708) 974-0078

Roger Luman, Director
Small Business Development Center
Bradley University
141 North Jobst Hall, 1st Floor
Peoria, IL 61625
(309) 677-2992 Fax: (309) 677-3386

Susan Gorman, Director
Small Business Development Center
Illinois Central College
124 S.W. Adams Street, Suite 300
Peoria, IL 61602
(309) 676-7500 Fax: (309) 676-7534

Edward Van Leer
Procurement Assistance Center
301 Oak Street
Quincy, IL 62301
(217) 228-5511

Meredith Jaszczek, Director
Small Business Development Center
Triton College
2000 Fifth Avenue
River Grove, IL 60171
(708) 456-0300 Fax: (708) 456-0049

Beverley Kingsley, Director
Small Business Development Center
Rock Valley College
1220 Rock Street
Rockford, IL 61102
(815) 968-4087 Fax: (815) 968-4157

Tom Halfman, Director
Small Business Development Center
South Suburban College
15800 South State Street
South Holland, IL 60473
(708) 569-2000 Fax: (708) 596-1125

Freida Schreck, Director
Small Business Development Center
Lincoln Land Community College
200 West Washington
Springfield, IL 62701
(217) 524-3060 Fax: (217) 782-1106

Donald Denny, Director
Small Business Development Center
Shawnee Community College
Shawnee College Road
Ullin, IL 62992
(618) 634-9618 Fax: (618) 634-9028

Christine Cochrane, Director
Small Business Development Center
Governors State University
University Park, IL 60466
(708) 534-4929 Fax: (708) 534-8457

INDIANA

Indiana SBDC
One North Capitol, Suite 420
Indianapolis, IN 46204
(317) 264-6871 Fax: (317) 264-3102

David Miller
Bloomington Area SBDC
116 West 6th Street
Bloomington, IN 47404
(812) 339-8937 Fax: (812) 336-0651

Tim Tichenoe
Columbus SBDC
4920 North Warren Drive
Columbus, IN 47203
(812) 372-6480 Fax: (812) 372-0228

Jeff Lake
Southwestern Indiana SBDC
100 N.W. Second Street, Suite 200
Evansville, IN 47708
(812) 425-7232 Fax: (812) 421-5883

Cheri Maslyk
Fort Wayne SBDC
1830 Wayne Trace
Fort Wayne, IN 46803
(219) 426-0040 Fax: (219) 424-0024

Patricia Stroud
Southern Indiana SBDC
1613 E. Eighth Street
Jeffersonville, IN 47130
(812) 288-6451 Fax: (812) 284-8314

Stephen G. Thrash
Central Indiana SBDC
1317 West Michigan
Indianapolis, IN 46202
(317) 274-8200 Fax: (317) 274-3997

Todd Moser
Kokomo/Howard County SBDC
106 North Washington
Kokomo, IN 46903
(317) 457-5301 Fax: (317) 452-4564

Susan Davis
Greater Lafayette Area SBDC
122 N. Third
Lafayette, IN 47901
(317) 742-2394 Fax: (317) 742-6276

Rose Marie Roberts
Southeastern Indiana SBDC
301 East Main Street
Madison, IN 47250
(812) 265-3127 Fax: (812) 265-2923

Jeanenne Holcomb
Northwest Indiana SBDC
8002 Utah Street
Merrillville, IN 46410
(219) 942-3496 Fax: (219) 942-5806

Nancy Stoll
East Central Indiana SBDC
401 South High Street
Muncie, IN 47308
(317) 284-8144 Fax: (317) 741-5489

Patricia Stirn
Richmond-Wayne County SBDC
33 South 7 St.
Richmond, IN 47374
(317) 962-2887 Fax: (317) 966-0882

Carolyn Anderson
South Bend SBDC
300 North Michigan
South Bend, IN 46601
(219) 282-4350 Fax: (219) 282-4344

Williams Minnis
Terre Haute Area SBDC
Indiana State University
School of Business, Room 510
Terre Haute, IN 47809
(812) 237-7676 Fax: (812) 237-7675

IOWA

Ronald Manning, State Director
Iowa SBDC
State Administrative Office
Iowa State University
137 Lynn Avenue
Ames, IA 50010
(515) 292-6351 Fax: (515) 292-0020
(800) 373-7232

Steve Carter, Director
Iowa State University SBDC
137 Lynn Avenue
Ames, IA 50010
(515) 292-6351 Fax: (515) 292-0020

Sherry Shafer, Branch Manager
Iowa State University SBDC
111 Lynn Avenue, Suite 1
Ames, IA 50010
(515) 292-6355 Fax: (515) 292-0020
(800) 373-7232

Lori Harmening-Webb, Branch Manager
Audubon SBDC
Circle West Incubator
P.O. Box 204
Audubon, IA 50025
(712) 563-2623 Fax: (712) 563-2301

Lyle Bowlin, Director
University of Northern Iowa SBDC
University of Northern Iowa
Suite 5, Business Bldg.
Cedar Falls, IA 50614-0120
(319) 273-2696 Fax: (319) 273-6830

Ronald Helms, Director
Iowa Western SBDC
Iowa Western Community College
2700 College Road, Box 4C
Council Bluffs, IA 51502
(712) 325-3260 Fax: (712) 325-0189

Paul Havick, Director
Southwestern SBDC
Southwestern Community College
1501 West Townline
Creston, IA 50801
(515) 782-4161 Fax: (515) 782-3312

Jon Ryan, Director
Eastern Iowa SBDC
Eastern Iowa Comm. College District
304 West Second Street
Davenport, IA 52801
(319) 322-4499 Fax: (319) 322-3956

Benjamin Swartz, Director
Drake University SBDC
Drake University
Drake Business Center
Des Moines, IA 50311-4505
(515) 271-2655 Fax: (515) 275-4540

Charles Tonn, Director
Northeast Iowa SBDC
Dubuque Area Chamber of Commerce
770 Town Clock Plaza
Dubuque, IA 52001
(319) 588-3350 Fax:(319) 557-1591

Paul Heath, Director
University of Iowa SBDC
University of Iowa, Oakdale Campus
106 Technology Innovation Center
Iowa City, IA 52242
(319) 335-4057 Fax: (319) 335-4489
(800)253-7232

Carol Thompson, Director
Kirkwood SBDC
Kirkwood Community College
2901 10th Avenue
Marion, IA 52302
(319) 377-8256 Fax: (319) 377-5667

Richard Petersen, Director
North Iowa Area SBDC
North Iowa Area Community College
500 College Drive
Mason City, IA 50401
(515) 421-4342 Fax: (515) 423-0931

Bryan Ziegler, Director
Indian Hills SBDC
Indian Hills Community College
525 Grandview Avenue
Ottumwa, IA 52501
(515) 683-5127 Fax: (515)683-5263

Dennis Bogenrief, Director
Western Iowa Tech SBDC
Western Iowa Tech. Community College
5001 E. Gordon Drive
Box 265
Sioux City, IA 51102-0265
(712) 274-6302 Fax: (712) 274-6342
(800)352-4649

Clark Marshall, Director
Iowa Lakes SBDC
Iowa Lakes Community College
Gateway North Shopping Center
Highway 71 North
Spencer, IA 51301
(712) 262-4213 Fax: (712) 262-4047

Deb Dalziel, Director
Southeastern SBDC
Southeastern Community College
Drawer F
West Burlington, IA 52655
(319) 752-2731 103 Fax: (319) 752-4957
(800) 828-7322

KANSAS

Tom Hull, State Director
Kansas Small Business Devel. Centers
Wichita State University
1845 Fairmount
Wichita, KS 67260-0148
(316) 689-3193 Fax: (316) 689-3647

Joan Warren, Director
Small Business Development Center
Cowley County Community College
125 S. 2nd
Arkansas City, KS 67005
(316) 442-0430

Terry Courter, Director
Small Business Development Center
Butler County Community College
420 Walnut
Augusta, KS 67010
(316) 775-1124

Robert Selby, Director
Small Business Development Center
Colby Community College
1255 South Range
Colby, KS 67701
(913) 462-3984

Harold Marconnette, Director
Small Business Development Center
Dodge City Community College
2501 N. 14th Ave.
Dodge City, KS 67801
(316) 225-1321

Lisa Brumbaugh, Regional Director
Small Business Development Center
Emporia State University
207 Cremer Hall
Emporia, KS 66801
(316) 343-5308

Regional Director TBD
Small Business Development Center
Garden City Community College
801 Campus Drive
Garden City, KS 67846
(316) 276-7611

Marvin Bahr, Director
Small Business Development Center
Barton County Comm. College
115 Admin. Bldg.
Great Bend, KS 67530
(316) 792-2701

Clark Jacobs, Director
Small Business Development Center
Hutchinson Community College
9th and Walnut, #225
Hutchinson, KS 67501
(316) 665-4950

Clare Gustin, Regional Director
Small Business Development Center
Fort Hays State University
1301 Pine Street
Hays, KS 67601
(913) 628-5340

Dan Pacheco, Director
Small Business Development Center
Kansas City Kansas Comm. College
7250 State Ave.
Kansas City, KS 66112
(913) 334-1100

Mike O'Donnell, Director
Small Business Development Center
University of Kansas
734 Vermont, Suite 104
Lawrence, KS 66044
(913) 843-8844

Bob Carder, Director
Small Business Development Center
Seward County Community College
1801 N. Kansas
Liberal, KS 67901
(316)624-1951

Fred Rice, Regional Director
Small Business Development Center
Kansas State University
2323 Anderson Ave., Suite 100
Manhattan, KS 66502-2912
(913)532-5529

Lori Kravets, Director
Small Business Development Center
Ottawa University
College Ave., Box 70
Ottawa, KS 66067
(913)242-5200

Glenda Sapp, Regional Director
Small Business Development Center
Johnson County Comm. College
CEC Bldg., Room 305I
Overland Park, KS 66210-1299
(913)469-3878

Kathryn Richard, Regional Director
Small Business Development Center
Pittsburg State University
Shirk Hall
Pittsburg, KS 66762
(316)231-8267

Pat Gordon, Director
Small Business Development Center
Pratt Community College
Highway 61
Pratt, KS 67124
(316)672-5641

John Gosney, Regional Director
Small Business Development Center
Kansas College of Technology
2409 Scanlan Ave.
Salina, KS 67401
(913)825-0275

Wayne Glass, Regional Director
Small Business Development Center
Washburn University of Topeka
School of Business
101 Henderson Learning Center
Topeka, KS 66621
(913)295-6305

Chip Paul, Regional Director
Small Business Development Center
Wichita State University
Brennan Hall, 2nd Floor
Campus Box 148
Wichita, KS 67208
(316)689-3193

KENTUCKY

Janet Holloway, State Director
Kentucky Small Business Dev. Center
Center for Business Development
College of Business & Economics Bldg.
University of Kentucky
225 Business & Economics Building
Lexington, KY 40506-0034
(606)257-7668 Fax: (606)258-1907

David Barber, Director
Ashland SBDC
Boyd-Greenup County Cham. of Comm.
P.O. Box 830, 207 15th Street
Ashland, KY 41105-0830
(606)329-8011

Richard S. Horn, Director
Bowling Green SBDC
Western Kentucky University
245 Grise Hall
Bowling Green, KY 42101
(502)745-2901

Cortez Davis, Director
Southeast SBDC
Southeast Community College
Room 113, Chrisman Hall
Cumberland, KY 40823
(606)589-4514

Denver Woodring, Director
Elizabethtown SBDC
University of Kentucky
238 West Dixie Avenue
Elizabethtown, KY 42701
(502)765-6737

Sutton Landry, Director
Northern Kentucky SBDC
Northern Kentucky University
BEP Center 463
Highland Heights, KY 41099-0506
(606)572-6524

Michael Cartner, Director
Hopkinsville SBDC
300 Hammond Drive
Hopkinsville, KY 42240
(502)886-8666

William Morley, Director
Lexington Area SBDC
University of Kentucky
227 Business and Economics Building
Lexington, KY 40506-0034
(606)257-7666

Thomas G. Daley, Director
Bellarmine College SBDC
Bellarmine College, School of Business
2001 Newburg Road
Louisville, KY 40205-0671
(502)452-8282

Lou Dickie, Director
Univ of Louisville SBDC (Technology)
University of Louisville, Center for Entrepreneurship and Technology
Room 122 Burhans Hall, Shelby Campus
Louisville, KY 40292
(502)588-7854

Wilson Grier, District Director
Morehead SBDC
Morehead State University
207 Downing Hall
Morehead, KY 40351
(606)783-2895

Rosemary Miller, Director
Murray State University
College of Business and Public Affairs
Murray, KY 42071
(502)762-2856

Mickey Johnson, Director
Owensboro SBDC
3860 U.S. Highway 60 West
Owensboro, KY 42301
(502)926-8085

Michael Morley, Director
Pikeville SBDC
222 Hatcher Court
Pikeville, KY 41501
(606)432-5848

Donald R. Snyder, Director
South Central SBDC
East Kentucky University
107 W Mt. Vernon St
Somerset, KY 42501
(606)678-5520

LOUISIANA

Dr. John Baker, State Director
Louisiana SBDC
Northeast Louisiana University
College of Business Administration
700 University Ave.
Monroe, LA 71209-6435
(318)342-5506 Fax: (318)342-5510

Mr. Greg Spann, Director
Capital SBDC
Southern University
9613 Interline Ave.
Baton Rouge, LA 70809
(504)922-0998

Mr. Daniel Monistere, Director
SBDC
Southeastern LA University
College of Business Administration
SLU Station, Box 522
Hammond, LA 70402
(504)549-3831

Mr. Dan Lavergne, Interim Director
Acadiana SBDC
College of Business Administration Box 43732
Lafayette, LA 70504
(318)262-5344

Mr. Paul Arnold, Director
SBDC
McNeese State University
College of Business Administration
Lake Charles, LA 70609
(318)475-5529

Mr. Chad J. Acosta, Operations Mgr.
SBDC
Northeast LA University
Adm. 2-57
Monroe, LA 71209
(318)342-5506

Dr. Paul Dunn, Director
SBDC
Northeast Louisiana University
College of Business Administration
Monroe, LA 71209
(318)342-1224

Dr. Lesa Lawrence, Assoc. State Dir.
SBDC
Northeast Louisiana University
Monroe, LA 71209
(318)342-5506

Dr. Jerry Wall, Consultant
Special Project Director
LA Electronic Assist. Program
College of Business Administration
Northeast Louisiana University
Monroe, LA 71209
(318)342-1215

Ms. Mary Lynn Wilkerson, Director
SBDC
Northwestern State University
College of Business Administration
Natchitoches, LA 71497
(318)357-5611

Mr. Ruperto Chavarri, Coordinator
International Trade Center
University of New Orleans
College Business Administration
Lakefront Campus
New Orleans, LA 70148
(504)286-6978

Dr. Ivan Miestchovich, Director
SBDC
University of New Orleans
College of Business Administration
Lakefront Campus
New Orleans, LA 70148
(504)286-6978

Dr. Ronald H. Schroeder, Director
SBDC
Loyola University
Box 134
New Orleans, LA 70118
(504)865-3474

Mr. Jon Johnson, Director
SBDC
Southern University
College of Business Administration
New Orleans, LA 70126
(504)286-5308

Mr. Art Gilbert, Director
SBDC
Louisiana Tech University
Box 10318, Tech Station
Ruston, LA 71272-0046
(318)257-3537

Ms. Charlotta Nordyke, Director
SBDC
LSU-Shreveport
College of Business Administation
1 University Place
Shreveport, LA 71115
(318)797-5144

Director
SBDC
Nicholls State University
P.O. Box 2015
Thibodaux, LA 70310
(504)448-4242

MAINE

Charles Davis, State Director
Small Business Development Center
University of Southern Maine
96 Falmouth St.
Portland, ME 04103
(207) 780-4420 Fax: (207) 780-4810

John Jaworski
Small Business Development Center
Androscoggin Valley Council of Govt.
125 Manley Rd.
Auburn, ME 04210
(207)783-9186

Michael Aube
Small Business Development Center
Eastern Maine Development Corp.
1 Cumberland Place, Suite 300
P.O. Box 2579
Bangor, ME 04401-8520
(207)942-6389

Robert P. Clark
Small Business Development Center
N. Maine Reg. Plann. Commission
P.O. Box 779
2 Main Street
Caribou, ME 04736
(207)498-8736

Dr. William Little
Small Business Development Center
University of Maine at Machias
Math and Science Bldg.
Machias, ME 04654
(207)255-3313

Madge Baker
Small Business Development Center
Southern Maine Regional Plann. Comm.
Box Q, 255 Main Street
Sanford, ME 04073
(207)324-0316

W. Elery Keene
Small Business Development Center
N. Kennebec Regional Planning Comm.
7 Benton Ave.
Winslow, ME 04901
(207)873-0711

Ron Phillips
Small Business Development Center
Coastal Enterprises Incorporated
Middle Street, Box 268
Wiscasset, ME 04578
(207)882-7552

MARYLAND

Woodrow McCutchen, State Director
Maryland SBDC Network
State Administrative Office
Dept. of Econ. & Employment Devel.
217 East Redwood St., 10th Floor
Baltimore, MD 21202
(410) 333-6995 Fax: (410) 333-4460

Dr. John P. Faris
Central Region SBDC
1414 Key Highway
Baltimore, MD 21230
(301)234-0505

Ms. Janice Carmichael
Montgomery College
7815 Woodmount Avenue
Bethesda, MD 20814
(301)656-7482

Mr. Robert Douglas
Western Region SBDC
Three Commerce Drive
Cumberland, MD 21502
(8004)57-7233

Ms. Charlie M. Partridge
Suburban Washington Region SBDC
9200 Basil Court, Room 403
Landover, MD 20785
(301)925-5032

Dr. Richard Palmer
Eastern Shore Region SBDC
1101 Camden Avenue
Salisbury, MD 21801
(800)999-SBDC

Ms. Yolanda Flemming
Southern Region SBDC
235 Smallwood Village Center
Waldorf, MD 20602-1852
(800)762-SBDC

MASSACHUSETTS

John Ciccarelli, State Director
MSBDC Network, State Office
University of Massachusetts
School of Management, Rm 205
Amherst, MA 01003
(413)545-6301 Fax: (413)545-1273

Joseph France
Minority Business Assistance Center
P.O. Box 3437
Boston, MA 02101
(617)457-4444

John McKiernan, Reg. Director
Metro Boston MA Regional Office SBDC
Boston College
Rahner House
96 College Road
Chestnut Hill, MA 02167
(617)552-4091

Don Rielly
Capital Formation Service
Boston College
Rahner House
96 College Road
Chestnut Hill, MA 02167
(617)552-4091

Clyde Mitchell, Reg. Director
Southeastern MA Regional Office SBDC
University of Massachusetts/Dartmouth
P.O. Box 2785
200 Pocasset Street
Fall River, MA 02722
(508)673-9783

Dianne Fuller Doherty, Reg. Director
Western MA Regional Office SBDC
University of Massachusetts/Amherst
101 State St., Suite 424
Springfield, MA 01103
(413)737-6712

Laurence Marsh
Central MA Regional Office SBDC
Clark University
Graduate School of Management
950 Main Street
Worcester, MA 01610
(617)793-7615

Frederick Young
North Shore Regional Office SBDC
Salem State College
197 Essex Street
Salem, MA 01970
(508)741-6343

MICHIGAN

Dr. Norman J. Schlafmann, State Dir.
Michigan SBDC
2727 Second Ave.
Detroit, MI 48201
(313)577-4848 Fax: (313)577-4222

Kenneth Rizzio, Executive Director
Michigan SBDC
Ottawa County Econ. Dev. Office, Inc
6676 Lake Michigan Drive
Allendale, MI 49401
(616)892-4120 Fax: (616)895-6670

Carl Osentoski, Director
Michigan SBDC
Huron County Econ. Development Corp.
Huron County Building, Room 303
Bad Axe, MI 48413
(517)269-6431 Fax: (517)269-7221

Mark Clevey, SBDC Director
MERRA Speciality Business Devel. Center
2200 Commonwealth, Suite 230
Ann Arbor, MI 48105
(313)930-0034 Fax: (313)663-6622

Mark O'Connel, Director
Kellogg Community College SBDC
450 North Avenue
Battle Creek, MI 49017-3397
(616)965-3023 Fax: (616)965-4133
(800)955-4KCC

James Converse, Director
Lake Michigan SBDC
Corporation and Comm. Development
2755 E. Napier
Benton Harbor, MI 49022-1899
(616)927-3571 Fax: (616)927-4491

Lora Swenson, Director
Ferris State University SBDC
Alumni 226
901 S. State Street
Big Rapids, MI 49307
(616)592-3553 Fax: (616)592-3539

Ronald Andrews, Director
Wexford-Missaukee BDC
117 W. Cass Street, Suite 1
Cadillac, MI 49601-0026
(616)775-9776 Fax: (616)775-1440

James McLoskey, Director
Michigan SBDC
Tuscola County Econ. Devel. Corp.
1184 Cleaver Road, Suite 800
Caro, MI 48723
(517)673-2849 Fax: (517)673-2517

Raymond Genick, Director
Wayne State University SBDC
School of Business Administration
2727 Second Avenue
Detroit, MI 48201
(313)577-4850 Fax: (313)577-8933

Dorothy Benedict, Director
Comerica SBDC
8300 Van Dyke
Detroit, MI 48213
(313)571-1040

Mark Carley, Director
NILAC-Marygrove College SBDC
8425 W. McNichols
Detroit, MI 48221
(313)345-2159 Fax: (313)864-6670

Myron Miller, Director
International Business Devel. Center
Michigan State University
6 Kellogg Center
East Lansing, MI 48824-1022
(517) 353-4336 Fax: (517) 336-1009
(800) 852-5727

David Gillis, Director
1st Step, Inc. Business Devel. Center
2415 14th Avenue, S.
Escanaba, MI 49829
(906) 786-9234 Fax: (906) 786-4442

Genesee Economic Area Revitalization, Inc. SBDC
412 S. Saginaw Street
Flint, MI 48502
(313) 238-7803 Fax: (313) 238-7866

Michelle Sayers, Director
Grand Rapids Community College SBDC
Grand Rapids Community College
Applied Technology Center
151 Fountain N. E.
Grand Rapids, MI 49503
(616) 771-3600 Fax: (616) 771-3605

Charles Persenaire, Exe. Director
Michigan SBDC
Oceana Econ. Development Corporation
P.O. Box 168
Hart, MI 49420-0168
(616) 873-7141 Fax: (616) 873-3710

James Hainault, Program Manager
Michigan Technological University SBDC
Bureau of Industrial Development
1400 Townsend Drive
Houghton, MI 49931
(906) 487-2470 Fax: (906) 487-2858

Richard Tieder, Bureau Director
MTU Forest Products Industry
Assistance Center
Bureau of Industrial Development
1700 College Avenue
Houghton, MI 49931
(906) 487-2470 Fax: (906) 487-2858

Dennis Whitney, Director
Livingston County BDC
404 E. Grand River
Howell, MI 48843
(517) 546-4020 Fax: (517) 546-4115

Kenneth Warren, SBDC Director
Kalamazoo College SBDC
Stryker Center for Mgmt. Studies
1327 Academy Street
Kalamazoo, MI 49007
(616) 383-8602 Fax: (616) 383-5663

Deleski Smith, Director
Lansing Community College SBDC
Post Office Box 40010
Lansing, MI 48901
(517) 483-1921 Fax: (517) 483-9616

Deleski Smith, Director
Handicapper Business Speciality Center
Lansing Comm. College, HBSC-63
P.O. Box 40010
Lansing, MI 48910
(517) 483-9948 Fax: (517) 483-9740

Patricia Crawford-Lucas, Director
Michigan SBDC
Lapeer Development Corporation
449 McCormick Drive
Lapeer, MI 48446
(313) 667-0080 Fax: (313) 667-3541

Marvin Pichla, Director
Thumb Area Community Growth
Alliance SBDC
3270 Wilson Street
Marlette, MI 48453
(517) 635-3561 Fax: (517) 635-2230

Peter Cambier, SBDC Director
Northern Economic Initiative Corporation SBDC
1009 West Ridge Street
Marquette, MI 49855
(906) 228-5571 Fax: (906) 228-5572

Donald Morandini, Director
Michigan SBDC
Macomb County Busines Assistance Network
115 South Groesbeck Hwy.
Mt. Clemens, MI 48043
(313) 469-5118 Fax: (313) 469-6787

Charles Fitzpatrick, Director
Central Michigan University SBC
256 Applied Business Studies Complex
Mt. Pleasant, MI 48859
(517) 774-3270 Fax: (517) 774-2372

Michael Wright, Director
Muskegon Econ. Growth Alliance BDC
349 W. Webster Avenue, Suite 104
P.O. Box 1087
Muskegon, MI 49443-1087
(616) 722-3751 Fax: (616) 728-7251

Laurie Garvey, Director
Michigan SBDC
Sanilac County Economic Growth
175 East Aitken Road
Peck, MI 48466
(313) 648-4311 Fax: (616) 648-4617

Robert F. Stevens, Director
St. Clair County Community BDC
323 Erie Street
P.O. Box 5015
Port Huron, MI 48061-5015
(313) 984-3881 Fax: (313) 984-2852

JoAnn Crary, Director
Saginaw Future Inc. SBDC
301 E. Genesee, 4th Floor
Saginaw, MI 48607
(517) 754-8222 Fax: (517) 754-1715

Mark Bergstrom, Director
Michigan SBDC
West Shore Community College
Business and Industrial Devel. Institute
3000 North Stiles Road
Scottville, MI 49454-0277
(616) 845-6211 Fax: (616) 845-0207

Phil Lund, Montcalm Tomorrow Dir.
Michigan SBDC
Montcalm Community College
2800 College Drive SW
Sidney, MI 48885
(517) 328-2111 Fax: (517) 328-2950

Lillian Adams-Yanssens, Exec. Dir.
Michigan SBDC
Sterling Heights Area Chamber of Commerce
12900 Paul, Suite 110
Sterling Heights, MI 48313
(313) 731-5400

Janet Masi, Vice Pres., Econ. Devel.
Michigan SBDC Warren, Center Line
Sterling Heights Chamber of Commerce
30500 Van Dyke, #118
Sterling Heights, MI 48313
(313) 751-3939 Fax: (313) 751-3995

Charles Blankenship, President
Traverse City SBDC
Traverse Bay Economic Devel. Corp.
202 E. Grandview Parkway
P.O. Box 387
Traverse City, MI 49685-0387
(616) 946-1596 Fax: (616) 946-2565

Richard Beldin, Chief Admin. Officer
Greater Northwest Regional CDC
2200 Dendrinos Drive
Traverse City, MI 49685-0506
(616) 929-5000

Cheryl Throop, Director
Michigan SBDC
Northwest Michigan College
Center for Business & Industry
1701 E. Front Street
Traverse City, MI 49685-0387
(616) 922-1105

Matthew Meadors, Manager
Traverse City Area Chamber of Commerce BDC
202 E. Grandview Parkway
P.O. Box 387
Traverse City, MI 49685-0387
(616) 947-5075

Dorothy Heyart, Executive Director
Walsh-O.C.C. Business Enterprise
Development Center
340 E. Big Beaver, Suite 100
Troy, MI 48083
(313) 689-4094 Fax: (313) 689-4398

Jo Ann Peterson, Director
Michigan SBDC
Saginaw Valley State University
Business and Industrial Dev. Institute
2250 Pierce Road
University Center, MI 48710
(517) 790-4000 Fax: (517) 790-1314

MINNESOTA

Randall Olson, State Director
Minnesota SBDC
500 Metro Square
121 7th Place East
St. Paul, MN 55101-2146
(612) 297-5770 Fax: (612) 296-1290

Arthur R. Gullette
Small Business Development Center
Bemidji State University
1500 Birchmont Drive, N.E.
Bemidji, MN 56601
(218) 755-2750

Heather Huseby
Small Business Development Center
Normandale Community College
9700 France Ave., South
Bloomington, MN 55431
(612) 832-6395

Gordy Winzenburg
Small Business Development Center
Brainerd Technical Institute
300 Quince St.
Brainerd, MN 56401
(218) 828-5302

Robert Heller
Small Business Development Center
University of Minnesota - Duluth
10 University Dr., 150 SBE
Duluth, MN 55811
(218) 726-8761

James Wolf
Small Business Development Center
Faribault City Hall
208 N.W. First
Faribault, MN 55021
(507) 334-2222

Joe Wood
Small Business Development Center
19 N.E. Third St.
Grand Rapids, MN 55744
(218) 327-2241

Carol Moore
Small Business Development Center
Hibbing Community College
1515 East 25th St.
Hibbing, MN 55746
(218) 262-6700

Duane F. Ommen
Small Business Development Center
Rainy River Community College
Highway 11 & 71
International Falls, MN 56649
(218) 285-2255

Gary Hannem
Small Business Development Center
Mankato State University
Box 145
Mankato, MN 56001
(507) 389-1648

Jack Hawk
Small Business Development Center
Southwest State University
ST #105
Marshall, MN 56258
(507) 537-7386

Jim S. Hayes
Small Business Development Center
Minnesota Project Outreach Corp.
The Mill Place, Suite 400
111 Third Avenue South
Minneapolis, MN 55401-2254
(612)672-3490

Leonard Sliwoski
Small Business Development Center
Moorhead State University
Box 303 - MSU
Moorhead, MN 56563-0001
(218)236-2289

John Sparling
Small Business Development Center
Pine Tech. Inst., 1000 Fourth Street
Pine City, MN 55063
(612)629-7340

Danelle Wolf
Small Business Development Center
Hennepin Technical College
1820 North Xenium Lane
Plymouth, MN 55441
(612)559-3535

Ken Henricksen
Small Business Development Center
Red Wing Technical Institute
Highway 58 at Pioneer Rd.
Red Wing, MN 55066
(612)388-4079

Tony Sinkiewicz
Small Business Development Center
Rochester Community College
Highway 14 East
851 30th Ave., S.E.
Rochester, MN 55904-499
(507)285-7536

Tom Trutna
Small Business Development Center
Dakota County Technical Institute
1300 145th Street, East
Rosemount, MN 55068
(612)423-8262

Tim Allen
Small Business Development Center
St. Cloud State University
Business Resource Center
St. Cloud, MN 56304
(612)255-4842

William Connelly
Small Business Development Center
University of St. Thomas
23 Empire Drive
St. Paul, MN 55103
(612)223-8663

Jan Hoff
Small Business Development Center
Thief River Falls Tech. Institute
Highway One East
Thief River Falls, MN 56701
(218)681-5424

Robert Wagner
Small Business Development Center
Mesabi Community College
905 West Chestnut
Virginia, MN 55792
(218)749-7729

Paul Kinn
Small Business Development Center
Wadena Technical Institute
222 Second Street, SE
Wadena, MN 56482
(218)631-2674

Robert Rodine
Small Business Development Center
Northeast Metro Technical Institute
3554 White Bear Avenue
White Bear Lake, MN 55110
(612)779-5764

Tracy Thompson
Small Business Development Center
Winona State University
Winona, MN 55987
(507)457-5088

MISSISSIPPI

Raleigh Byars, Executive Director
Small Business Development Center
Old Chemistry Bldg., Suite 216
University, MS 38677
(601) 232-5001 Fax: (601) 232-5650

John Brandon
Small Business Development Center
Delta State University
P.O. Box 3235 DSU
Cleveland, MS 38733
(601) 846-4236 Fax: (601) 846-4443

Martha Heffner
Small Business Development Center
Mississippi Delta Community College
1656 East Union Street
Greenville, MS 38702
(601) 378-8183

Lucy Betcher
Small Business Development Center
Pearl River Community College
Route 9, Box 1325
Hattiesburg, MS 39401
(601) 544-0030 Fax: (601) 544-0032

Van Evans
Small Business Development Center
MS Dept. of Economic & Comm. Devel.
P.O. Box 849
Jackson, MS 39205
(601) 359-3179 Fax: (601) 359-2832

Marvel Turner
Small Business Development Center
Jackson State University
Suite A1, Jackson Enterprise Center
931 Highway 80 West
Jackson, MS 39204
(601) 968-2795 Fax: (601) 968-2358

Rebecca Montgomery, Director
Small Business Development Center
University of Southern Mississippi
USM Gulf Park Campus
Long Beach, MS 39560
(601) 865-4578 Fax: (601) 865-4544

J.W. (Bill) Lang, Director
Small Business Development Center
Meridian Community College
5500 Highway 19 North
Meridian, MS 39307
(601) 482-7445 Fax: (601) 482-5803

Estel Wilson, Director
Small Business Development Center
Mississippi State University
P.O. Box 5288
McCool Hall, Room 229
Mississippi State, MS 39762
(601) 325-8684 Fax: (601) 325-8686

Robert D. Russ
Small Business Development Center
Copiah-Lincoln Community College
Natchez Campus
Natchez, MS 39120
(601) 445-5254 Fax: (601) 446-9967

Marguerite Wall
SBDC/International Trade Center
Hinds Community College
P.O. Box 1170
Raymond, MS 39154
(601) 857-3537 Fax: (601) 857-3535

Bobby Wilson
Small Business Development Center
Itawamba Community College
653 Eason Boulevard
Tupelo, MS 38801
(601) 842-5621

Jeffrey Van Terry
Small Business Development Center
University of Mississippi
Suite 216, Old Chemistry Bldg.
University, MS 38677
(601) 234-2120 Fax: (601) 232-5650

MISSOURI

Max E. Summers, State Director
Missouri SBDC (State Office)
University of Missouri
300 University Place
Columbia, MO 65211
(314) 882-0344 Fax: (314) 884-4297

Frank "Buz" Sutherland, Director
Small Business Development Center
Southeast Missouri State University
222 North Pacific
Cape Girardeau, MO 63701
(314) 290-5965 Fax: (314) 651-5005

Frank Siebert, Director
Small Business Development Center
University of Missouri - Columbia
1800 University Place
Columbia, MO 65211
(314) 882-7096 Fax: (314) 882-6156

Charles Luther, Director
Small Business Development Center
Mineral Area College
P.O. Box 1000
Flat River, MO 63601
(314)431-4593 Fax:(314)431-6807

Dr. Tom Buchanan, Director
Small Business Development Center
Business and Industrial Specialists
University Extension
2507 Industrial Drive
Jefferson City, MO 65101
(314)634-2824

Sharon Gulick, Director
Small Business Development Center
DED - Missouri Product Finder
301 West High, Room 770
P.O. Box 118
Jefferson City, MO 65102
(314) 751-4892 Fax: (314) 751-8394

Jim Krudwig, Director
Small Business Development Center
Missouri Southern State College
3950 Newman Rd, #107, Matthews Hall
Joplin, MO 64801-1595
(417) 625-9313 Fax: (816) 926-4588

Judith Burngen, Director
Small Business Development Center
Rockhurst College
1100 Rockhurst Road
Kansas City, MO 64110-2599
(816) 926-4572 Fax: (816) 926-4588

Glen Giboney, Director
Small Business Development Center
Northeast Missouri State University
207 East Patterson
Kirksville, MO 63501
(816) 785-4307 Fax: (816) 785-4181

James H. MacKinnon, Director
Small Business Development Center
Northwest Missouri State University
127 South Buchanan
Maryville, MO 64468
(816) 562-1701 Fax: (816) 562-1900

John Bonifield, Director
Small Business Development Center
Three Rivers Community College
Business Incubator Bldg.
3019 Fair Street
Poplar Bluff, MO 63901
(314) 686-3499 Fax: (314) 686-5467

Bob Laney, Director
Small Business Development Center
University of Missouri - Rolla
223 Engineering Management Building
Rolla, MO 65401-0249
(314) 341-4561 Fax: (314) 341-2071

Don Myers, Director
Center for Tech. Trans. & Econ. Devel.
Univ. of Missouri - Rolla
Rm 104, Bldg. 1, Nagogami Terrace
Rolla, MO 65401-0249
(314) 341-4559 Fax: (314) 341-4992

James H. MacKinnon, Director
Small Business Development Center
Missouri Western State College
4525 Downs Drive
Student Union 108
St. Joseph, MO 64507
(816) 271-4364

Virginia Campbell, Director
Small Business Development Center
Saint Louis University
3642 Lindell Boulevard
St. Louis, MO 63108
(314) 534-7232 Fax: (314) 836-6337

Jane Peterson, Director
Small Business Development Center
Center for Business Research
S.W. Missouri State University
Box 88, 901 South National
Springfield, MO 65804-0089
(417) 836-5685 Fax: (417) 836-6337

Wes Savage, Coordinator
Small Business Development Center
Central Missouri State University
Grinstead #75
Warrensburg, MO 64093-5037
(816) 543-4402 Fax: (816) 747-1653

Bernie Sarbaugh, Coordinator
Center for Technology
Central Missouri State University
Grinstead #75
Warrensburg, MO 64093-5037
(816) 543-4402 Fax: (816) 747-1653

MONTANA

Dave Elenbaas, Interim Director
Helena SBDC
Montana Department of Commerce
1424 Ninth Avenue
Helena, MT 59620
(406) 444-4780 Fax: (406) 444-2808

Al Jones
Billings SBDC
Billings Area Business Incubator
115 N. Broadway, 2nd Floor
Billings, MT 59101
(406) 256-6875 Fax: (406) 255-7175

Darrell Berger
Bozeman SBDC
321 East Main, Suite 413
Bozeman, MT 59715
(406) 587-3113 Fax: (406) 587-9565

Ralph Kloser
Butte SBDC
REDI
305 West Mercury, Suite 211
Butte, MT 59701
(406) 782-7333 Fax: (406) 782-9675

Tony Preite
Havre SBDC
Bear Paw Development Corporation
P.O. Box 1549
Havre, MT 59501
(406) 265-9226 Fax: (406) 265-3777

Dan Manning
Kalispell SBDC
Flathead Valley Community College
777 Grandview Drive
Kalispell, MT 59901
(406) 756-8333 Fax: (406) 756-3815

Bill Chumrau
Missoula SBDC
Missoula Business Incubator
127 N. Higgins, 3rd Floor
Missoula, MT 59802
(406) 728-9234 Fax: (406) 721-4584

Randal D. Hanson
Sidney SBDC
123 West Main
Sidney, MT 59270
(406) 482-5024 Fax: (406) 482-5306

NEBRASKA

Robert Bernier, State Director
University of Nebraska at Omaha
60th & Dodge Sts.
CBA Room 407
Omaha, NE 68182
(402) 554-2521 Fax: (402) 554-3747

Cliff Hanson, Center Director
NBDC - Chadron
Chadron State College
Administration Bldg.
Chadron, NE 69337
(308) 432-6282

Kay Payne, Center Director
NBDC - Kearney
University of Nebraska at Kearney
Welch Hall, 19th & College Dr.
Kearney, NE 68849
(308) 234-8344

Larry Cox, Center Director
NBDC - Lincoln
University of Nebraska - Lincoln
Cornhusker Bank Bldg.
11th & Cornhusker Hwy., Suite 302
Lincoln, NE 68521
(402) 472-3358

Dean Kurth, Center Director
NBDC - North Platte
Mid Plains Community College
416 N. Jeffers, Room 26
North Platte, NE 69101
(308) 534-5115

Jacki Staudt-Netzel, Center Director
NBDC - Omaha
University of Nebraska at Omaha
Peter Kiewit Conference Center
1313 Farnam-on-the-Mall, Suite 132
Omaha, NE 68182-0248
(402) 595-2381

Herb Patten, Center Director
NBDC - OBTC
Omaha Business & Technology Center
2505 North 24 St., Suite 101
Omaha, NE 68110
(402) 595-3511

Dottie Holliday, Center Director
NBDC - Peru
Peru State College
T.J. Majors Hall, Room 248
Peru, NE 68421
(402) 872-2274

Ingrid Battershell, Center Director
NBDC - Scottsbluff
Nebraska Public Power Building
1721 Broadway, Room 408
Scottsbluff, NE 69361
(308) 635-7513

Terry Henderson, Center Director
NBDC - Wayne
Wayne State College
Connell Hall
Wayne, NE 68787
(402) 375-7575

NEVADA

Sam Males, State Director
Small Business Development Center
University of Nevada, Reno
College of Business Administration-032
Room 411
Reno, NV 89557-0100
(702) 784-1717 Fax: (702) 784-4337

John Pryor, Director
Small Business Development Center
Northern Nevada Community College
901 Elm Street
Elko, NV 89801
(702) 738-8493

Sharolyn Craft, Director
Small Business Development Center
University of Nevada at Las Vegas
College of Business & Economics
4505 Maryland Parkway
Las Vegas, NV 89154
(702) 739-0852

Larry Osborne, Executive Director
Small Business Development Center
Carson City Chamber of Commerce
1900 South Carson Street, #100
Carson City, NV 89702
(702) 882-1565

Sharlet Berentsen, Director
Small Business Development Center
Tri-County Development Authority
50 West Fourth Street
Winnemucca, NV 89445
(702) 623-5777

Evan Childers, Business Dev. Specialist
Small Business Development Center
19 West Brooks Avenue
North Las Vegas, NV 89030
(702) 399-6300

Elwood Miller, Director
Small Business Development Center
University of Nevada, Reno
Cooperative Extension Service
College of Agriculture
Reno, NV 89557-0016
(702) 784-1679

NEW HAMPSHIRE

Helen Goodman, State Director
SBDC
University of New Hampshire
108 McConnell Hall
Durham, NH 03824
(603) 862-2200 Fax: (603) 862-4468

Kit McCormick, Regional Manager
SBDC, Kingham Farm
University of New Hampshire
Durham, NH 03824
(603) 743-3995 Fax: (603) 743-3997

Michelle Sweet, Special Proj. Dir.
SBDC
University of New Hampshire
108 McConnell Hall
Durham, NH 03824
(603) 862-2200 Fax: (603) 862-4468

Dick Gorges, Regional Manager
SBDC
Keene State College
Blake House
Keene, NH 03431
(603) 358-2602 Fax: (603) 756-4878

Liz Matott, Regional Manager
SBDC
P.O. Box 786
Littleton, NH 03561
(603) 444-1053

Bob Ebberson, Regional Manager
SBDC
1001 Elm Street
Manchester, NH 03101
(603) 624-2000 Fax: (603) 623-3972

Kate Durnin
SBDC
c/o Nashua Chamber of Commerce
One Tara Blvd., Suite 211
Nashua, NH 03062
(603) 891-2471 Fax: (603) 891-2474

Janice Kitchen, Regional Manager
SBDC
Plymouth State College
Hyde Hall
Plymouth, NH 03264
(603) 535-2523 Fax: (603) 535-2526

NEW JERSEY

Brenda Hopper, State Director
Small Business Development Center
Rutgers University
180 University Ave.
3rd Floor- Ackerson Hall
Newark, NJ 07102
(201)648-5950 Fax:(201)648-1110

John DeYoung
Small Business Development Center
Greater Atlantic City Chamber of Commerce
1301 Atlantic Ave.
Atlantic City, NJ 08401
(609)345-5600

Patricia Peacock, Ed.D.
Small Business Development Center
Rutgers Univ. Schools of Business
P.O. Box 93800C
Camden, NJ 08101-3800
(609)225-6221 Fax:(609)225-6231

Bill Nunnally
Small Business Development Center
Brookdale Community College
Newman Springs Road
Lincroft, NJ 07738
(201)842-1900

Gordon Haym
Small Business Development Center
Rutgers University at Newark
3rd Floor - Ackerson Hall
180 University Ave.
Newark, NJ 07102
(201)648-5950

Herbert Spiegel
Small Business Development Center
Mercer County Community College
1200 Old Trenton Road
Trenton, NJ 08690
(609)586-4800

Mira Kostak
Small Business Development Center
Kean College
Morris Ave. and Conant
Union, NJ 07083
(201)527-2413

Dianne L. Latona
Small Business Development Center
Warren County Community College
Route 57 West, Rd #1 Box 55A
Washington, NJ 07882
(201)689-7613

NEW MEXICO

Randy Grissom, State Director
NMSBDC Lead Center
Santa Fe Community College
P.O. Box 4187
Santa Fe, NM 87502-4187
(505)438-1362 Fax:(505)438-1237

Dwight Harp
Small Business Development Center
New Mexico State University at Alamogordo
1000 Madison
Alamogordo, NM 88310
(505)434-5272

Roslyn Block
Small Business Development Center
Albuquerque Tech.-Vocational Inst.
525 Buena Vista SE
Albuquerque, NM 87106
(505)224-4246

Larry Coalson
Small Business Development Center
New Mexico State University at Carlsbad
P.O. Box 1090
Carlsbad, NM 88220
(505)887-6562

Roy Miller
Small Business Development Center
Clovis Community College
417 Schepps Blvd.
Clovis, NM 88101-8345
(505)769-4136

Darien Cabral
Small Business Development Center
Northern New Mexico Comm. College
1002 N. Onate Street
Espanola, NM 87532
(505)753-7141, ext. 248

Brad Ryan
Small Business Development Center
San Juan College
203 W. Main Street, Suite 201
Farmington, NM 87401
(505)326-4321

Barbara Stanley
Small Business Development Center
University of New Mexico-Gallup
P.O. Box 1395
Gallup, NM 87305
(505)722-2220

Clemente Sanchez
Small Business Development Center
New Mexico State University at Grants
709 E. Roosevelt Ave.
Grants, NM 87020
(505)287-8221

Don Leach
Small Business Development Center
New Mexico Junior College
5317 Lovington Highway
Hobbs, NM 88240
(505)392-4510

Michael Elrod
Small Business Development Center
NM State University - Dona Ana Branch
Box 30001, Dept. 3DA
Las Cruces, NM 88003-0001
(505)527-7601

Small Business Development Center
Luna Vocational-Technical Institute
P.O. Drawer K
Las Vegas, NM 87701
(505)454-2595

Jim Greenwood
Small Business Development Center
University of New Mexico at Los Alamos
P.O. Box 715
Los Alamos, NM 87544
(505)662-0001

Andrew Thompson
Small Business Development Center
University of New Mexico at Valencia
280 La Entrada
Los Lunas, NM 87031
(505)865-9596, ext. 317

Eugene Simmons
Small Business Development Center
Eastern New Mexico University at Roswell
P.O. Box 6000
Roswell, NM 88201-6000
(505)624-7133

Emily Miller
Small Business Development Center
Santa Fe Community College
P.O. Box 4187
Santa Fe, NM 87502-4187
(505)438-1343

Linda Kay Jones
Small Business Development Center
Western New Mexico University
P.O. Box 2672
Silver City, NM 88062
(505)538-6320

Richard Spooner
Small Business Development Center
Tucumcari Area Vocational School
P.O. Box 1143
Tucumcari, NM 88401
(505)461-4413

NEW YORK

James L. King, State Director
Small Business Development Center
State University of New York
SUNY Central Plaza S-523
Albany, NY 12246
(518)443-5398 Fax: (518)465-4992

Peter George
Small Business Development Center
SUNY at Albany
Draper Hall, 107
135 Western Ave.
Albany, NY 12222
(518)442-5577

Joanne Bauman
Small Business Development Center
SUNY at Binghamton
P.O. Box 6000, Vestal Parkway East
Binghamton, NY 13902-6000
(607)777-4024

Thomas Canavan
Small Business Development Center
Long Island University
Humanities Building, 7th Floor
One University Plaza
Brooklyn, NY 11201
(718)852-1197

Susan McCartney
Small Business Development Center
State University College at Buffalo
BA 117, 1300 Elmwood Ave.
Buffalo, NY 14222
(716)878-4030

Judy Smith
Small Business Development Center
24-28 Denison Parkway West
Corning, NY 14830
(607)962-9461

Joseph Schwartz
Small Business Development Center
State University College of Technology at Farmingdale
Laffin Admin. Bldg., Room 007
Farmingdale, NY 11735
(516)420-2765

James A. Heyliger
Small Business Development Center
York College, Science Bldg, Rm 107
The City University of New York
Jamaica, NY 11451
(718)262-2880

Irene Dobies
Small Business Development Center
Jamestown Community College
P.O. Box 20
Jamestown, NY 14702-0020
(716)665-5220

Dr. William J. Lawrence
Small Business Development Center
Pace University, Pace Plaza
New York, NY 10038
(212)346-1899

Small Business Development Center
Clinton Community College
Alpert Bldg., Rt. 9
Plattsburgh, NY 12901
(518)564-7232

Dr. Frederick Greene
Small Business Development Center
Manhattan College, Farrell Hall
Riverdale, NY 10471
(212)884-1880

Colette Dorais
Small Business Development Center
Monroe Community College
1000 East Henrietta Road
Rochester, NY 14623
(716)292-2000 ext. 3030

Wilfred Bordeau
Small Business Development Center
Niagara County Community College
3111 Saunders Settlement Road
Sanborn, NY 14132
(716)693-1910

Judith McEvoy
Small Business Development Center
State University at Stony Brook
Harriman Hall, Rm 109
Stony Brook, NY 11794
(516)632-9070

Jean Morris
Small Business Development Center
Ulster County Community College
Stone Ridge, NY 12484
(914)687-5272

Thomas J. Morley
Small Business Development Center
Rockland Community College
145 College Road
Suffern, NY 10901
(914)356-0370

Robert Varney
Small Business Development Center
Greater Syracuse Incubator Center
1201 East Fayette Street
Syracuse, NY 13210
(315)475-0083

Thomas Reynolds
Small Business Development Center
SUNY Institute of Tech. Utica/Rome
P.O. Box 3050
Utica, NY 13504-3050
(315)792-7546

John F. Tanner
Small Business Development Center
Jefferson Community College
Watertown, NY 13601
(315)782-9262

NORTH CAROLINA

Scott Daugherty, Executive Director
NC SBDC Headquarters Office
University of N. Carolina at Chapel Hill
4509 Creedmoor Road, Suite 201
Raleigh, NC 27612
(919)571-4154 Fax: (919)571-4161
(800)2580-UNC

Judy Ball, Consultant
Northwestern Regional Center
Appalachian State University
Walker College of Business
Boone, NC 28608
(704)262-2095

Chris Moore, Director
Southern Piedmont Regional Center
University of North Carolina at Charlotte
The Ben Craig Center
8701 Mallard Creek Road
Charlotte, NC 28262
(704)548-1090

R. Daniel Parks, Director
Central Carolina Regional Center
University of N. Carolina at Chapel Hill
608 Airport Road, Suite B
Chapel Hill, NC 27514
(919)962-0389

Tom McClure, Director
Western Regional Center
Western Carolina University
Center for Improving Mountain Living
Cullowhee, NC 28723
(704)227-7494

Michael Twiddy, Assistant Director
Northeastern Regional Center
Elizabeth City State University
Weeksville Road, P.O. Box 874
K.E. White Graduate Center
Elizabeth City, NC 27909
(919)335-3247

Dr. Sid Gautam, Director
Cape Fear Area Center
Fayetteville State University
P.O. Box 1334
Fayetteville, NC 28302
(919)486-1727

Walter Fitts, Director
Eastern Regional Center
East Carolina University
Corner 1st and Reade Streets
Greenville, NC 27858-4353
(919)757-6157

Cynthia Clemons, Associate Director
Northern Piedmont Regional Center-Eastern Office
The University of N. Carolina at Grensboro
P.O. Box D-22
Greensboro, NC 27411
(919)334-7005

Marc King, Director
Capital Regional Center
North Carolina State University
4509 Creedmoor Rd, Suite 201
Raleigh, NC 27612
(919)571-4154

Ted Jans, Director
Northern Piedmont Regional Center
Winston-Salem State University
P.O. Box 13025
Winston-Salem, NC 27110
(919)750-2030

Bill Dowe, Director
Northern Piedmont Regional Center
P.O. Box 13025
Winston-Salem, NC 27110
(919)750-2030

NORTH DAKOTA

Walter (Wally) Kearns, State Dir.
State Center/Grand Forks
118 Gamble Hall, UND
Box 7308
Grand Forks, ND 58202-7308
(701) 777-3700 Fax: (701) 777-5099

Jan Peterson, Regional Director
Bismark Regional Center
Small Business Development Center
400 E. Broadway, Suite 421
Bismark, ND 58501
(701) 223-8583 Fax: (701) 222-3843

Bryan Vendsel, Regional Director
Dickinson Regional Center
Small Business Development Center
314 3rd Ave., West, Drawer L
Dickinson, ND 58602
(701) 227-2096 Fax: (701) 225-5116

Gordon Snyder, Regional Director
Grand Forks Regional Center
Small Business Development Center
The Hemmp Center
1407 24th Avenue S., Suite 201
Grand Forks, ND 58201
(701) 772-8502 Fax: (701) 775-2772

Jon Grinager, Regional Director
Fargo Regional Center
Small Business Development Center
417 Main Avenue
Fargo, ND 58103
(701) 237-0986 Fax: (701) 235-6706

George Youngerman, Regional Center
Minot Regional Center
Small Business Development Center
1020 20th Ave. SW
P.O. Box 940
Minot, ND 58702
(701) 852-8861 Fax: (701) 838-2488

OHIO

Holly Schick, State Director
Small Business Development Center
77 South High St.
P.O. Box 1001
Columbus, OH 43226
(614) 466-2711 Fax: (614) 466-0829

Barbara Lange
Womens Entrepreneurial SBDC
58 W. Center St.
Akron, OH 43309
(216)535-9346

Charles Way
Small Business Development Center
Akron Regional Development Board
8th Floor, One Cascade Plaza
Akron, OH 44308
(216)379-3170

Don Wright
Small Business Development Center
Northwest Technical College
Box 245-A, Route 1
Archbold, OH 43502
(419)267-3331

Bernie Tuttle
Small Business Development Center
Ohio Hi-Point JVC
2280 State Route 540
Bellefontaine, OH 43311
(513)559-3010

Richard Knight
Small Business Development Center
Stark Development Board
800 Savannah Ave., N.E.
Canton, OH 44704
(216)453-5900

Maryann Huey
Small Business Development Center
City of Cambridge
1131 Steubenville Ave.
Cambridge, OH 43725
(614)439-2822

Dr. Tom Knapke
Small Business Development Center
Wright State Branch Campus
7600 State Route 703
Celina, OH 45822
(419)586-2365

William A. Fioretti
Small Business Development Center
University of Cincinnati
IAMS Research Park
1111 Edison Dr. Mail Loc. #189
Cincinnati, OH 45216
(513)948-2082

Russ Molinar
Small Business Development Center
Council of Smaller Enterprises
690 Huntington Bldg.
Cleveland, OH 44115
(216)621-3300

Burton Schildhouse
Small Business Development Center
37 North High Street
Columbus, OH 43216
(614)221-1321

Doug Peters
Small Business Development Center
Chamber Plaza: 5th and Main St.
Dayton, OH 45402
(513)226-8213

Joe Wilson
Small Business Development Center
Terra Technical College
1220 Cedar Street
Freemont, OH 43420
(419)334-3886

Charles Wright
Small Business Development Center
Southern State Community College
100 Hobart Drive
Hillsboro, OH 45133
(513)393-3431

Larry Kramer
Small Business Development Center
36 West Walnut Street
Jefferson, OH 44047
(216)576-9126

W. C. Dyer
Small Business Development Center
Lima Technical College
545 West Market St., Suite 305
Lima, OH 45801
(419)229-5320

Frank DeTillio
Small Business Development Center
Greater Lorain Chamber of Commerce
204 Fifth Street
Lorain, OH 44052
(216)244-2292

Fred Moritz
Small Business Development Center, Mid-Ohio
P.O. Box 1208
Mansfield, OH 44901
(419)525-1614

Dr. Michael Broida
Small Business Development Center
Miami University
DSC Department
311 Upham Hall
Oxford, OH 45056
(513)529-4841

Jon Heffner
Small Business Development Center
Upper Valley Joint Vocational School
8811 Career Drive
Piqua, OH 45358
(513)778-8419

Stephen Weir
Small Business Development Center
Department of Dev. of CIC
100 E. Main Street
St. Clairsville, OH 43950
(614)695-9678

James Ackley
Small Business Development Center
Sandusky City Schools
407 Decatur Street
Sandusky, OH 44870
(419)626-6940

Lou Ann Walden
Small Business Development Center
Lawrence County Chamber of Commerce
US Route 52 and Solida Road
P.O. Box 488
Southpoint, OH 45680
(614)894-3838

Terry Sterling
Small Business Development Center
Department of Dev. of CIC
Ohio Valley Towers
Steubenville, OH 43952
(614)282-6226

Joseph D. Kelly
Small Business Development Center
218 North Huron Street
Toledo, OH 43604
(419)243-8191

Patricia Veisz
Small Business Development Center
Youngstown State University
Cushwa Center for Industrial Devel.
Youngstown, OH 44555
(216)742-3495

Cheri Ater
Small Business Development Center
Zanesville Area Chamber of Commerce
217 North Fifth Street
Zanesville, OH 43701
(614)452-4868

OKLAHOMA

Grady Pennington, State Director
Small Business Development Center
Southeastern Oklahoma State University
P.O. Box 2584, Station A
Durant, OK 74701
(405) 924-0277 Fax: (405) 924-7071

Tom Beebe
Small Business Development Center
East Central University
1036 East 10th
Ada, OK 74820
(405) 436-3190

David Pecha
Small Business Development Center
Northwesten State University
Alva, OK 73717
(405) 327-5883

Herb Manning
Small Business Development Center
Southeastern State University
517 University Blvd.
Durant, OK 74701
(405) 924-0277

Sue Urbach
Small Business Development Center
Central State University
100 North University Blvd.
Edmond, OK 73034
(405) 359-1968

Enid Satellite Center
Small Business Development Center
Phillips University,
100 South University Ave.
Enid, OK 73701
(405) 242-7989

Robert Allen
Small Business Development Center
Langston University Center
P.O. Box 667
Langston, OK 73050
(405) 466-3924

Lawton Satellite Center
Small Business Development Center
601 SW D, Suite 209
Lawton, OK 73501
(405) 248-4946

Carl Echols
International Trade Office
Rose State College, 6420 S.E. 15th
Midwest City, OK 73110
(405) 736-0328

Judy Robbins
Procurement Specialty Center
Rose State College
6420 Southeast 15th
Midwest City, OK 73110
(405) 733-7348

Muskogee Satellite Center
Small Business Development Center
400 West Broadway
Muskogee, OK 74401
(918) 683-5762

Mary Crumrine
Small Business Development Center
Oklahoma Department of Commerce
6601 Broadway Extension
Oklahoma City, OK 73116
(800) 999-6652

Poteau Satellite Center
Small Business Development Center
Carl Albert Junior College
1507 South McKenna
Poteau, OK 74953
(918) 647-4019

Dr. Constance VanScoy
Small Business Development Center
N.E. Oklahoma State University
Tahlequah, OK 74464
(918)458-0802

Tulsa Satellite Center
Small Business Development Center
100 Petroleum Club Bldg.
601 S. Boulder
Tulsa, OK 74119
(918)587-8324

Chuck Felz
Small Business Development Center
S.W. Oklahoma State University
100 Campus Drive
Weatherford, OK 73096
(405)774-1040

OREGON

Edward Cutler, Ph.D., State Director
Small Business Development Center
Lane Community College
99 W. 10th Ave., Suite 216
Eugene, OR 97401
(503) 726-2250 Fax: (503) 345-6006

John Pascone, Director
Small Business Development Center
Linn-Benton Community College
6500 S.W. Pacific Boulevard
Albany, OR 97321
(503) 967-6112 Fax: (503) 967-6550

Small Business Development Center
Southern Oregon State College
Regional Services Institute
Ashland, OR 97520
(503) 482-5838 Fax: (503) 482-1115

Bob Newhart, Director
Small Business Development Center
Central Oregon Community College
2600 N.W. College Way
Bend, OR 97701
(503) 385-5524 Fax: (503) 385-5497
(800)422-3041 ext. 524

Jon Richards, Director
Small Business Development Center
Southwestern Oregon Comm. College
340 Central
Coos Bay, OR 97420
(503) 267-2300 Fax: (503) 269-0323

Bob Cole, Director
Small Business Development Center
Columbia Gorge Community College
212 Washington
The Dalles, OR 97058
(503) 296-1173 Fax: (503) 296-2107

Jane Scheidecker, Director
Small Business Development Center
Lane Community College
1059 Willamette Street
Eugene, OR 97401
(503) 726-2255 Fax: (503) 686-0096

Lee Merritt, Director
Small Business Development Center
Rogue Comm. College
290 N.E. "C" St.
Grants Pass, OR 97526
(503)471-3515

Don King, Director
Small Business Development Center
Mount Hood Community College
323 NE Roberts Street
Gresham, OR 97030
(503) 667-7658 Fax: (503) 666-1140

Jamie Albert, Director
Small Business Development Center
Oregon Institute of Technology
3201 Campus Drive South 314
Klamath Falls, OR 97601
(503) 885-1760 Fax: (503) 885-1115

Joni Gibbens, Counselor
Eastern Oregon State College
Regional Services Institute
Lagrande, OR 97850
1-800-452-8639 Fax: (503) 962-3668

Mike Lainoff, Director
Small Business Development Center
Oregon Coast Community College
P.O. Box 419
4157 NW Highway 101, Suite 123
Lincoln City, OR 97367
(503) 994-4166 Fax: (503) 996-4958

Liz Shelby, Director
Small Business Development Center
S. Oregon State College/Medford
Regional Service Institute
229 N. Barlett
Medford, OR 97501
(503) 772-3478 Fax: (503) 776-2224

Jan Stennick, Director
Small Business Development Center
Clackamas Community College
7616 SE Harmony Road
Milwaukee, OR 97222
(503) 656-4447 Fax: (503) 652-0389

Kathy Simko, Director
Small Business Development Center
Treasure Valley Community College
88 SW Third Avc
Ontario, OR 97914
(503) 889-2617 Fax: (503) 889-8331

Garth Davis, Director
Small Business Development Center
Blue Mountain Community College
37 SE Dorion
Pendleton, OR 97801
(503) 276-6233

Robert Keyser, Interim Director
Small Business Development Center
Portland Community College
123 NW Second Ave., Suite 321
Portland, OR 97209
(503) 273-2828 Fax: (503) 294-0725

John Otis, Director
Small Business Development Center
International Trade Program
121 SW Salmon Street, Suite 210
Portland, OR 97204
(503) 274-7482 Fax: (503) 228-6350

Terry Swagerty, Director
Small Business Development Center
Umpqua Community College
744 SE Rose
Roseburg, OR 97470
(503) 672-2535 Fax: (503) 672-3679

Bobbie Clyde, Director
Small Business Development Center
Chemeketa Community College
365 Ferry St. SE
Salem, OR 97301
(503) 399-5181 Fax: (503) 581-6017

Robin Buzzard, Director
Small Business Development Center
Clatstop Community College
1240 South Holladay
Seaside, OR 97138
(503) 738-3347 Fax: (503) 738-3347

Mike Harris, Director
Small Business Development Center
Tillamook Bay Community College
401 B Main Street
Tillamook, OR 97141
(503) 842-2551 Fax: (503) 842-2555

PENNSYLVANIA

Gregory L. Higgins, State Director
Small Business Development Center
University of PA, The Wharton School
444 Vance Hall, 3733 Spruce Street
Philadelphia, PA 19104-6374
(215) 898-1219 Fax: (215) 573-2135

Dr. John Bonge
Small Business Development Center
Lehigh University, Rauch Business Center #37
Bethlehem, PA 18015
(215)758-3980

Dr. Woodrow Yeaney
Small Business Development Center
Clarion University of Pennsylvania
Dana Still Building
Clarion, PA 16214
(814)226-2060

Mr. Ernie Post
Small Business Development Center
Gannon Univ, Carlisle Bldg, 3rd Flr.
Erie, PA 16541
(814)871-7714

Jack Fabean
Small Business Development Center
St. Vincent College
Alfred Hall, Fourth Floor
Latrobe, PA 15650
(412)537-4572

Dr. Charles Coder
Small Business Development Center
Bucknell University
Dana Engineering Bldg., 1st Floor
Lewisburg, PA 17837
(717)524-1249

John A. Palko
Small Business Development Center
St. Francis College, Business Resource Ctr.
Loretto, PA 15940
(814)472-3200

Dr. Keith Yackee
Small Business Development Center
PA State University, The Capital College
Crags Building - Route 230
Middletown, PA 17057
(717)948-6069

Linda Karl
Small Business Development Center
LaSalle University
20th and Olney Ave.
Philadelphia, PA 19141
(215)951-1416

Geraldine Perkins
Small Business Development Center
Temple University
Room 6 - Speakman Hall-006-00
Philadelphia, PA 19122
(215)787-7282

David B. Thornburgh
Small Business Development Center
University of Pennsylvania
The Wharton School, 409 Vance Hall
Philadelphia, PA 19104
(215)898-4861

Clarence F. Curry
Small Business Development Center
University of Pittsburgh
Room 343 Mervis Hall
Pittsburgh, PA 15260
(412)648-1544

Dr. Mary T. McKinney
Small Business Development Center
Duquesne University, Rockwell Hall
Rm 10 Concourse, 600 Forbes Ave.
Pittsburgh, PA 15282
(412)434-6233

Elaine M. Tweedy
Small Business Development Center
University of Scranton
St. Thomas Hall, Room 588
Scranton, PA 18503
(717)941-7588

Edmund Sieminski
Small Business Development Center
Wilkes University, 192 South Franklin Street
Wilkes-Barre, PA 18766
(717)824-4651

PUERTO RICO

Jose M. Romaguera, State Director
Small Business Development Center
University of Puerto Rico
P.O. Box 5253 College Station
Mayaguez, PR 00681
(809) 834-3590 Fax: (809) 834-3790

Nydia Figueroa
Small Business Development Center
Interamerican University
Casa Llompart
P.O. Box 1293
Hato Rey, PR 00917
(809) 765-2335

Joy C. Camacho
Small Business Development Center
University of Puerto Rico at Humacao
Box 10226, CUH Station
Humacao, PR 00661
(809) 850-2500

Marian Diaz
Small Business Development Center
University of Puerto Rico at Mayaguez
P.O. Box 5253 College Station
Mayaguez, PR 00709
(809) 834-3590

Elma Santiago
Small Business Development Center
University of Puerto Rico at Ponce
P.O. Box 7186
Ponce, PR 00732
(809) 841-2641

Oscar Cordero
Small Business Development Center
University of Puerto Rico at Rio Piedras
P.O. Box 21417, UPR Station
Rio Piedras, PR 00931
(809) 763-5933

RHODE ISLAND

Douglas Jobling, State Director
State Administrative Office
Bryant College RISBDC
1150 Douglas Pike
Smithfield, RI 02917
(401) 232-6111 Fax: (401) 232-6416

Thomas F. Policastro, Manager
RISBDC
University of Rhode Island
24 Woodward Hall
Kingston, RI 02881
(401) 792-2451 Fax: (401) 792-4017

Cheryl Faria, Case Manager
Aquidneck Island RISBDC
28 Jacome Way
Middletown, RI 02840
(401) 849-6900 Fax: (401) 849-0815

Erwin Robinson, Program Manager
Bryant College RISBDC
Downtown Providence Office
7 Jackson Walkway
Providence, RI 02903
(401) 831-1330 Fax: (401) 454-2819

Judith Shea, Manager
RISBDC
Community College of RI
Providence Campus
One Hilton Street
Providence, RI 02905
(401) 455-6042 Fax: (401) 455-6047

Sue Barker, Assistant Director
Bryant College RISBDC
1150 Douglas Pike
Smithfield, RI 02917
(401) 232-6115

SOUTH CAROLINA

John Lenti, State Director
The Frank L. Roddey Small Business Development Center
College of Business Administration
University of South Carolina
Columbia, SC 29201-9980
(803) 777-4907 Fax: (803) 777-4403

Martin Goodman, Area Manager
USC Beaufort SBDC
800 Carteret Street
Beaufort, SC 29902
(803) 521-4143 Fax: (803) 521-4198

Tom Koontz, Area Manager
Charleston SBDC
Trident Technical College
P.O. Box 20339
Charleston, SC 29413-0339
(803) 727-2020 Fax: (803) 727-2013

Rebecca Hobart, Regional Director
Clemson Regional SBDC
425 Sirrine Hall
Clemson University
Clemson, SC 29634-1392
(803) 656-3227 Fax: (803) 656-4869

Bill Tumblin, Energy Consultant
Clemson Regional SBDC
425 Sirrine Hall
Clemson University
Clemson, SC 29634-1392
(803) 656-3227 Fax: (803) 656-4869

Russ Madray, Area Manager
Clemson Regional SBDC
425 Sirrine Hall
Clemson University
Clemson, SC 29634-1392
(803) 656-3227 Fax: (803) 656-4869

Dean Kress, Area Manager
USC Regional SBDC
University of South Carolina
College of Business Administration
Columbia, SC 29201-9980
(803) 777-5118 Fax: (803) 777-4403

Jim Brazell, Regional Director
USC Regional SBDC
University of South Carolina
College of Business Administration
Columbia, SC 29201-9980
(803) 777-5118 Fax: (803) 777-4403

Patrick King, Area Manager
Coastal Carolina SBDC
School of Business Administration
Coastal Carolina
Conway, SC 29526
(803) 349-2169 Fax: (803) 349-2990

Harriette Edwards, Area Manager
Greenville SBDC
Greenville Technical College
Box 5616, Station B - GHEC
Greenville, SC 29606
(803) 271-4259 Fax: (803) 250-8514

David Raines, Area Manager
Florence Darlington Tech, SBDC
P.O. Box 100548
Florence, SC 29501-0548
(803) 661-8324 or (803) 661-8041

George Long, Area Manager
Upper Savannah Council of Government
SBDC Exchange Building
222 Phoenix Street, Suite 200
P.O. Box 1366
Greenwood, SC 29648
(803) 227-6110 Fax: (803) 229-1869

Jim DeMartin, Consultant
USC Hilton Head SBDC
Suite 300, Kiawah Building
10 Office Park Road
Hilton Head, SC 29928
(308) 785-3995 F ax: (803) 777-0333

Jackie Moore, Area Manager
Aiken/North Augusta SBDC
Triangle Plaza
215-B Edgefield Road
North Augusta, SC 29841
(803) 442-3670 Fax: (803) 641-3445

John Gadson, Regional Director
SC State Regional SBDC
School of Business Administration
South Carolina State University
Orangeburg, SC 29117
(803) 536-8445 Fax: (803) 536-8066

Francis Heape, Area Manager
School of Business Administration
SC State University
Orangeburg, SC 29117
(803) 536-8445 Fax: (803) 536-8066

Nate Barber, Regional Director
Winthrop Regional SBDC
Winthrop University
119 Thurmond Building
Rock Hill, SC 29733
(803) 323-2283 Fax: (803) 323-4281

Dianne Hockett, Area Manager
Winthrop Regional SBDC
Winthrop University
119 Thurmond Bldg.
Rock Hill, SC 29733
(803) 323-2283 Fax: (803) 323-4281

Robert Grooms, Area Manager
Spartanburg Chamber of Commerce/SBDC
P.O. Box 1636
Spartanburg, SC 29304
(803) 594-5080 Fax: (803) 594-5055

SOUTH DAKOTA

Donald Greenfield, State Director
Small Business Development Center
University of South Dakota
414 East Clark
Vermillion, SD 57069
(605) 677-5279 Fax: (605) 677-5272

Ron Kolbeck, Area Director
Small Business Development Center
226 Citizens Bldg.
Aberdeen, SD 57401
(605) 225-2252

Wade Druin, Area Director
Small Business Development Center
105 South Euclid, Suite C
Pierre, SD 57501
(605) 773-5941

Ron Adinolfi, Marketing Consultant
Small Business Development Center
444 Mount Rushmore Road, #208
P.O. Box 7715
Rapid City, SD 57709
(605) 394-5311

Bob Domalewski, Area Director
Small Business Development Center
444 Mount Rushmore Road, #208
Rapid City, SD 57709
(605) 394-5311

Nancy Straw, Area Director
Small Business Development Center
200 North Phillips, L103
Sioux Falls, SD 57102
(605) 330-6008

Jeffrey Heisinger, Business Consultant
Small Business Development Center
University of South Dakota
414 East Clark
Vermillion, SD 57069
(605) 677-5279

TENNESSEE

Kenneth J. Burns, State Director
Small Business Development Center
Memphis State University
Bldg. 1, South Campus
Memphis, TN 38152
(901) 678-2500 Fax: (901) 678-4072

Rick Layne
Small Business Development Center
Southeast Tennessee Dev. District
100 Cherokee Boulevard, Suite 201
Chattanooga, TN 37405
(615)752-4308

John Volker
Small Business Development Center
Austin Peay St. Univ, College of Business
Clarksville, TN 37044
(615)648-7674

Don Green
Small Business Development Center
Cleveland State Community College
Adkisson Drive, P.O. Box 3570
Cleveland, TN 37320
(615)478-6247

Harold Holloway
Small Business Development Center
Tennessee Technological University
College of Business Administration
P.O. Box 5023
Cookeville, TN 38505
(615)372-3648

Bob Wylie
Small Business Development Center
Dyersburg State Community College
Office of Extension Services
P.O. Box 648
Dyersburg, TN 38024
(901)286-3267

Debbie Bishop
Small Business Development Center
Jackson State Community College
2046 North Parkway Street
Jackson, TN 38305
(901)424-5389

Robert Justice
Small Business Development Center
East Tennessee State University
College of Business
Johnson City, TN 37614
(615)929-5630

Joe Andrews
Small Business Development Center
Pellissippi State Tech. Comm.
P.O. Box 22990, 3435 Division St.
Knoxville, TN 37933
(615)694-6661

Dr. Carl Savage
Small Business Development Center
University of Tennessee at Martin
Pepsi Building, 402 Elm St.
Martin, TN 38238
(901)587-7236

Earnest Lacey
Small Business Development Center
Memphis St. University, 320 S. Dudley St.
Memphis, TN 38104
(901)527-1041

Mr. Jack Tucker
Small Business Development Center
Walters State Community College
500 S. Davy Crockett Parkway
Morristown, TN 37813
(615)587-9722

Dr. Jack Forrest
Small Business Development Center
Middle Tennessee State University
School of Business, 1417 East Main St.
Murfreesboro, TN 37132
(615)898-2745

Billy Lowe
Small Business Development Center
Tennessee State University
School of Business
330 10th Ave. North
Nashville, TN 37203
(615)251-1178

TEXAS--DALLAS

Beth Huddleston, Interim Director
North Texas-Dallas SBDC
1 J. Priest Institute for Economic Development
1402 Corinth St.
Dallas, TX 75215
(214) 565-5833 Fax: (214) 565-5813

Judy Loden, Director
Small Business Development Center
Trinity Valley Community College
500 South Prairieville
Athens, TX 75751
(903)675-6230

Small Business Development Center
Sam Rayburn Library
Bonham, TX 75148
(214)583-7025

Gary M. Burns, Director
Small Business Development Center
120 North 12th St.
Corsicana, TX 75110
(903)874-0658

Joe Berry
Small Business Development Center for Government Contracting
1402 Corinth
Dallas, TX 75215
(214) 565-5842 Fax: (214) 565-5857

Elizabeth Huddleston, Director
International SBDC
2050 Stemmons Fwy, Suite #150
World Trade Ctr, P.O. Box 58299
Dallas, TX 75258
(214)653-1777 Fax: (214) 748-5774

Neil Small, Dir. of Counseling
Small Business Development Center
Dallas County Comm. College
1402 Corinth
Dallas, TX 75215
(214) 565-5836 Fax: (214) 565-5857

Jerry Linn, Director
Small Business Development Center
Grayson County College
6101 Grayson Dr.
Denison, TX 75020
(903) 463-8654 Fax: (214) 463-5284

Carolyn Birkhead, Coordinator
Small Business Development Center
P.O. Box P
Denton, TX 76201
(817) 382-7151 Fax: (817) 382-0040

Herb Kamm, Director
Small Business Development Center
1001 N. Beckley, Suite 606D
DeSoto, TX 75115
(214)228-3783

Jim Emery, Director
Small Business Development Center
Tarrant County Junior College
1500 Houston Suite 163
Ft. Worth, TX 76102
(817)877-9254

Cathy Keeler, Director
Small Business Development Center
1525 West California
Gainesville, TX 76240
(817) 665-4785 Fax: (817) 668-6049

Small Business Development Center
SOS Building
P.O. Box 619
Hillsboro, TX 76645
(817) 582-2555, ext. 382

Chris Mullins, Director
Small Business Development Center
Kilgore College, 300 South High
Longview, TX 75601
(903) 763-2642

Robert Wall, Director
Small Business Development Center
N.E. Texas Comm. Coll, P.O. Box 1307
Mt. Pleasant, TX 75455
(903) 572-1911 Fax: (903) 572-6712

Pat Bell, Director
Small Business Development Center
Paris Jr College, 2400 Clarksville St.
Paris, TX 75460
(903) 784-1802

Steve Hardy, Director
Small Business Development Center
Collin County Community College
Piano Market Square
1717 E. Spring Creek Pkwy, #109
Piano, TX 75074
(214) 881-0506

Glen Galiga, Director
Small Business Development Center
Tyler Jr. College
1530 South S.W. Loop 323, Suite 100
Tyler, TX 75701
(903) 510-2975 Fax: (903) 510-2978

Lu Billings, Director
Small Business Development Center
McLennan Community College
4601 North 19th Street
Waco, TX 76708
(817) 750-3600 Fax: (817) 756-0776

TEXAS--HOUSTON

Dr. Elizabeth Gatewood
Regional Director
Small Business Development Center
University of Houston
601 Jefferson, Suite 2330
Houston, TX 77002
(713) 752-8444 Fax: (713) 752-8484

Gina Mattel
Small Business Development Center
Alvin Community College
3110 Mustang Rd.
Alvin, TX 77511-4898
(713) 388-4686

Kenneth Voytek, Director
Small Business Development Center
Lee College, Rundell Hall
511 S. Whiting St.
Baytown, TX 77520-4796
(713) 425-6309 Fax: (713) 425-6307

Roy Huckaby, Director
Small Business Development Center
John Gray Institute/Lamar University
855 Florida Ave.
Beaumont, TX 77705
(409) 880-2367 Fax: (409) 880-2201
(800) 722-3443

Phillis Nelson, Director
Small Business Development Center
Blinn College
902 College Ave.
Brenham, TX 77833
(409) 830-4137 Fax: (409) 830-4116

Frank Murphy, Director
Small Business Development Center
Bryan/College Station Chamber of Commerce
401 S. Washington
Bryan, TX 77803
(409) 823-3034 Fax: (409) 822-4818

Joe Harper, Director
Small Business Development Center
Galveston College
4015 Avenue Q
Galveston, TX 77550
(409) 740-7380 Fax: (409) 740-7381

Susan Macy, Director
Small Business Development Center
Houston Lead Center SBDC
601 Jefferson, Suite 2330
Houston, TX 77002
(713) 752-8400 Fax: (713) 752-8484

J.R. Maxfield, Director
Small Business Development Center
Texas Product Development Center
601 Jefferson, Suite 2330
Houston, TX 77002
(713)752-8400

Jack Ruoff, Director
Small Business Development Center
Texas Info. Procurement Service
601 Jefferson, Suite 2330
Houston, TX 77002
(713) 752-8477 Fax: (713) 752-8484

Luis Saldarriaga, Director
International Trade Center
601 Jefferson, Suite 2330
Houston, TX 77002
(713)752-8404

Joe Harper, Director
Small Business Development Center
Sam Houston State University
College of Business Administration
P.O. Box 2056
Huntsville, TX 77341
(409) 294-3737 Fax: (409) 294-3612

Ray Laughter, Director
Small Business Development Center
N. Harris County College, Admin. Bldg. Rm 104
20000 Kingwood Dr.
Kingwood, TX 77339
(713) 359-1677 Fax: (713) 359-1612

Linda Fields, Director
Small Business Development Center
Brazosport College
500 College Dr.
Lake Jackson, TX 77566
(409) 265-7208 Fax: (409) 265-2944

Chuck Stemple, Director
Small Business Development Center
Angelina College
P.O. Box 1768
Lufkin, TX 75902-1768
(409) 639-1887 Fax: (409) 634-8726

John Fishero, Director
Small Business Development Center
Houston Community College System
13600 Murphy Road
Stafford, TX 77477
(713) 499-4870 Fax: (713) 499-8194

Ed Socha
Small Business Development Center
College of the Mainland
8419 Emmett F. Lowry Expressway
Texas City, TX 77591
(713) 499-4870 Fax: (713) 499-8194

Lynn Polson, Director
Small Business Development Center
Wharton County Jr. College
Admin. Bldg. Room 102
911 Boling Hwy.
Wharton, TX 77488-0080
(409) 532-4560 Fax:(409)532-2201

TEXAS--LUBBOCK

Craig Bean, Region Director
Northwest Texas SBDC
Center for Innovation
2579 South Loop 289, Suite 114
Lubbock, TX 79423
(806) 745-3973 Fax: (806) 745-6207

Stuart Hall
Caruth SBDC
Abilene Christian University
ACU Station, Box 8307
Abilene, TX 79699
(915) 674-2776 Fax: (915) 674-2507

Don Taylor
Panhandle SBDC
1800 S. Washington, Suite 110
Amarillo, Texas 79102
(806) 372-5151 Fax: (806) 372-3939

David Montgomery
Texas Tech University
Small Business Development Center
Center for Innovation
2579 South Loop 289, Suite 210
Lubbock, Texas 79423
(806) 745-1637 Fax: (806) 745-6207

Corbett Gaulden
Small Business Development Center
4901 E. University
Odessa, TX 79762
(915) 563-0400 Fax: (915) 561-5534

Rusty Freed
Small Business Development Center
Tarleton State University
College of Business Administration Box T-158
Stephenville, TX 76402
(817) 968-9330 Fax: (817) 968-9329

Tim Thomas
Small Business Development Center
Midwestern State University
3400 Taft Blvd.
Wichita Falls, TX 76308
(817) 696-6738 Fax: (817) 696-8303

TEXAS--SAN ANTONIO

Robert M. McKinley, Reg. Director
UTSA South Texas Border SBDC
UTSA Downtown Center
801 S. Bowie Street
San Antonio, TX 78205
(210) 224-0791 Fax: (512) 222-9834

Joe Morin, Director
Austin SBDC
2211 South IH 35, Suite 103
Austin, TX 78741
(512) 326-2256 Fax: (512) 447-9825

R. J. Sandoval, Director
Corpus Christi Chamber of Comm. SBDC
1201 North Shoreline
Corpus Christi, TX 78403
(512) 882-6161 Fax: (512) 888-5627

Ms. Carminia Oris, Director
University of Texas-Pan American SBDC
1201 West University
Edinburg, TX 78539-2999
(512) 381-3361 Fax: (512) 381-2322

Roque Sequra, Director
El Paso Community College SBDC
103 Montana Ave., Suite 202
El Paso, TX 79902-3929
(915) 534-3410 Fax: (915) 534-3420

Ms. Cathy Myers, Director
Kingsville Chamber of Commerce SBDC
635 E. King
Kingsville, TX 78363
(512) 595-5088 Fax: (512) 592-0866

Ms. Andriana Lopez, SBDC Manager
Laredo Development Foundation SBDC
616 Leal Street
Laredo, TX 78041
(512) 722-0563 Fax: (512) 722-6247

Harlan Bruha, Director
Angelo State University SBDC
2601 West Avenue N
Campus Box 10910
San Angelo, TX 76909
(915) 942-2098 Fax: (915) 942-2038

Morrison Woods, Director
UTSA SBDC
801 S. Bowie Street
San Antonio, TX 78205
(210) 224-0791 Fax: (512) 222-9834

Ms. Sara Jackson, Director
UTSA International SBDC
801 S. Bowie Street
San Antonio, TX 78205
(210) 227-2997 Fax: (512) 222-9834

Raul Zamora, Director
Middle Rio Grande Development Council SBDC
209 North Getty St.
Uvalde, TX 78801
(512) 278-2527 Fax: (512) 278-2929

Jack Whitmire, Director
University of Houston-Victoria SBDC
700 Main Center, Suite 102
Victoria, TX 77901
(512) 575-8944 Fax: (512) 575-8852

UTAH

David A. Nimkin, Executive Director
Utah SBDC
University of Utah
102 West 500 South #315
Salt Lake City, UT 84101
(801) 581-7905 Fax: (801) 581-7814

Ed Harris, Director
Utah SBDC
Southern Utah University
351 West Center
Cedar City, UT 84720
(801) 586-5400 Fax: (801) 586-5493

Lynn Schiffman, Director
Utah SBDC
Snow College
345 West 1st North
Ephraim, UT 84627
(801) 283-4021 Fax: (801) 283-6913

Franklin C. Prante, Director
Utah SBDC
Utah State University
East Campus Building
Logan, UT 84322-8330
(801) 750-2277 Fax: (801) 750-3317

Bruce Davis, Director
Utah SBDC
Weber State University
College of Business & Economics
Ogden, UT 84408-3806
(801) 626-7232 Fax: (801) 626-7423

Nate McBride, Director
Utah SBDC
College of Eastern Utah
451 East 400 North
Price, UT 84501
(801) 637-1995 Fax: (801) 637-4102

Kathy Buckner, Director
Utah SBDC
Brigham Young University
School of Management
790 Tanner Building
Provo, UT 84602
(801) 378-4022 Fax: (801) 378-4501

Scott Bigler, Director
Uintah Basin Applied Technology Center
Utah SBDC
1100 East Lagoon
P.O. Box 124-5
Roosevelt, UT 84066
(801) 722-4523 Fax: (801) 722-5804

Eric Pederson, Director
Utah SBDC
Dixie College
225 South 700 East
St. George, UT 84770
(801) 673-4811455 Fax: (801) 673-8552

VERMONT

Donald L. Kelpinski, State Director
Vermont SBDC
Vermont Technical College
P.O. Box 422
Randolph, VT 05060
(802) 728-9101 Fax: (802) 728-3026

William A. Farr, SBDC Specialist
Northwestern Vermont SBDC
Greater Burlington Industrial Corp.
P.O. Box 786
Burlington, VT 05402-0786
(802) 862-5726 Fax: (802) 860-1899

James B. Stewart, SBDC Specialist
Southwestern Vermont SBDC
Rutland Industrial Dev. Corp.
P.O. Box 39
Rutland, VT 05701-0039
(802) 773-9147 Fax: (802) 773-5709

Joseph P. Wynne, SBDC Specialist
Northeastern Vermont SBDC
Northeastern Vermont Dev. Corp.
P.O. Box 640
St. Johnsbury, VT 05819-0640
(802) 748-5181 Fax: (802) 748-1223

Norbert B. Johnston, SBDC Specialist
Southeastern Vermont SBDC
Springfield Regional Dev. Corp.
P.O. Box 58
Springfield, VT 05156-0058
(802) 885-2071 Fax: (802) 885-3027

VIRGINIA

Dr. Robert Smith, State Director
Virginia SBDC
1021 East Cary Street, 11th Floor
Richmond, VA 23219
(804) 371-8253 Fax: (804) 371-8185

Paul Hall, Director
Arlington SBDC
GMU Arlington Campus
3401 N. Fairfax Drive
Arlington, VA 22201
(703) 993-8128 Fax: (703) 993-8130

Helen Duncan, Director
Southwest SBDC
Mt. Empire Community College
Drawer 700, Route 23 South
Big Stone Gap, VA 24219
(703) 523-6529 Fax: (703) 523-4130

Michael Hensley, Director
Western VA SBDC Consortium
VPI & SU
Economic Development Assistance Center
404 Clay Street
Blacksburg, VA 24061-0539
(703) 231-5278 Fax: (703) 953-2307

Dave Shanks, Director
New River Valley SBDC
Bldg. D, Plaza 1
200 Country Club Drive
Blacksburg, VA 24061-0548
(703) 231-4004 Fax: (703) 552-0047

Charles Kulp, Director
Central Virginia SBDC
918 Emmet Street North, Suite 200
Charlottesville, VA 22903-4878
(804) 295-8198 Fax: (804) 979-3749

Gerald L. Hughes, Director
Longwood SBDC
Longwood College, 515 Main Street
Farmville, VA 23901
(804) 395-2086 Fax: (804) 395-2359

Michael Kehoe, Director
Northern Virginia SBDC
4260 Chainbridge Road, Suite B-1
Fairfax, VA 22030
(703) 993-2131 Fax: (703) 993-2126

Joseph Amato, Director
Rappahannock Region SBDC
1301 College Ave.
Seacobeck Hall
Fredricksburg, VA 22401
(703) 899-4076 Fax: (703)899-4373

Karen Wigginton, Director
James Madison University SBDC
JMU College of Business
Zane Showker Hall, Rm. 523
Harrisonburg, VA 22807
(703) 568-3227 Fax: (703) 568-3299

Barry Lyons, Director
Lynchburg Regional SBDC
147 Mill Ridge Road
Lynchburg, VA 24502
(804) 582-6100 Fax: (804) 582-6106

Linda Decker, Director
Dr. William E.S. Flory SBDC
10311 Sudley Manor Drive
Manassas, VA 22110
(703) 335-2500 Fax: (703) 335-1700

William J. Holloran, Jr., Director
SBDC of Hampton Roads, Inc.
P.O. Box 327, 420 Bank Street
Norfolk, VA 23501
(804) 622-6414 Fax: (804) 622-5563

R. Victor Brungart, Director
Southwest SBDC
SW VA Community College
P.O. Box SVCC
Richlands, VA 24641
(703) 964-7345 Fax: (703) 964-9307

Cynthia Arrington, Assoc. State Dir.
Virginia SBDC
1021 East Cary Street, 11th Floor
Richmond, VA 23219
(804) 371-8253 Fax: (804) 371-8185

Taylor Cousins, Director
Capital Area SBDC
403 East Grace Street
Richmond, VA 23219
(804) 648-7838 Fax: (804) 648-7849

John Jennings, Director
Western VA SBDC Consortium
The Blue Ridge SBDC
310 First St., S.W. Mezzanine
Roanoke, VA 24011
(703) 983-0717 Fax: (703) 983-0723

Carroll Thackston, Business Analyst
Longwood SBDC South Boston Branch
P.O. Box 1116
515 Broad Street
South Boston, VA 24592
(804) 575-0044 Fax: (804) 572-4087

Joseph Messine, Director
Loudoun County SBDC
One Steeplechase at Dulles
21736 Atlantic Blvd., Suite 100
Sterling, VA 22170
(703) 430-7222 Fax: (703) 430-9562

Jeffrey Sneddon, Director
Warsaw SBDC
P.O. Box 490
106 West Richmond Rd.
Warsaw, VA 22572
(804) 333-0286 Fax: (804) 333-0187

Rob Edwards, Director
Western VA SBDC Consortium
Wytheville SBDC
Wytheville Community College
1000 E. Main Street
Wytheville, VA 24382
(703) 228-5541 314 Fax: (703) 228-2542

VIRGIN ISLANDS

Chester Williams, Acting State Dir.
Small Business Development Center
University of the Virgin Islands
Grand Hotel Building, Annex B
P.O. Box 1087
St. Thomas, VI 00804
(809) 776-3206 Fax: (809) 775-3756

Chester Williams
Small Business Development Center
University of the Virgin Islands
United Plaza Shopping Center
Suite 1, Sion Farm
St. Croix, VI 00820
(809) 778-8270

WASHINGTON

Lyle M. Anderson, State Director
Small Business Development Center
Washington State University
245 Todd Hall
Pullman, WA 99164-4727
(509) 335-1576 Fax: (509) 335-0949

Bill Huenefeld
Small Business Development Center
Bellevue Community College
13555 Bel-Red Road #208
Bellevue, WA 98005
(206) 643-2888

Lynn Trzynka
Small Business Development Center
Western Washington University
415 Park Hall
Bellingham, WA 98225-9073
(206) 676-3899

Don Hays
Small Business Development Center
Centralia Community College
600 West Locust Street
Centralia, WA 98531
(206) 736-9391

Jack Wicks
Small Business Development Center
Edmonds Community College
917 134th St. S.W.
Everett, WA 98204
(206) 745-0430

Glynn Lamberson
Small Business Development Center
Columbia Basin College
TRIDEC, 901 North Colorado
Kennewick, WA 99336
(509) 735-6222

Ed Baroch
Small Business Development Center
Big Bend Community College
7662 Chanute Street
Moses Lake, WA 98837
(509) 762-6289

Peter Stroosma
Small Business Development Center
Skagit Valley College
2405 College Way
Mt. Vernon, WA 98273
(206) 428-1282

Douglas Hammel
Small Business Development Center
Washington State University
721 Columbia St. S.W.
Olympia, WA 98501
(206) 753-5616

Earl True
Business Development Specialists
DTED Business Assistance Center
919 Lakeridge Way, Suite A
Olympia, WA 98502
(206) 586-4854

Ron Nielsen
Small Business Development Center
Wenatchee Valley College
P.O. Box 1042
Omak, WA 98841
(509)826-5107

Ann Tamura
Small Business Development Center
North Seattle Community College
International Trade Institute
9600 College Way North
Seattle, WA 98103
(206)527-3733

Bill Jacobs
Small Business Development Center
2001 6th Ave, Suite 2608
Seattle, WA 98121
(206)464-5450

Ruth Ann Halford
Small Business Development Center
Duwamish Ind. Educational Center
6770 East Marginal Way South
Seattle, WA 98108
(206)764-5375

John King
Small Business Development Center
WSU-Spokane, West 601 1st Street
Spokane, WA 99204
(509)456-2781

Neil Delisanti
Small Business Development Center
950 Pacific Ave., Suite 300
P.O. Box 1933
Tacoma, WA 98401
(206)272-7232

Dennis Hanslits
Small Business Development Center
Columbia River EDC
100 East Columbia Way
Vancouver, WA 98660-3156
(206)693-2555

Nick Gerde
Small Business Development Center
Grand Central Building
25 North Wenatchee Ave.
Wenatchee, WA 98801
(509)662-8016

Janice Durnil
Small Business Development Center
Yakima Valley College
P.O. Box 1647
Yakima, WA 98907
(509)575-2284

WEST VIRGINIA

Eloise Jack, State Director
Small Business Development Center
Governor's Office of Comm. & Ind.
1115 Virginia Street
East Capitol Complex
Charleston, WV 25301
(304) 558-2960 Fax: (304) 558-0127

Greg Helbig
Small Business Development Center
Concord College
Center for Economic Action
Box D-125
Athens, WV 24712
(304)384-5103

Keith Zinn
Small Business Development Center
Bluefield State College
Bluefield, WV 24701
(304)327-4107

Wanda Chenoweth
Small Business Development Center
Governor's Office of Community and Industrial Develoment
1115 Virginia St., East
Charleston, WV 25301
(304)348-2960

Dale Bradley
Small Business Development Center
Fairmont State College
Fairmont, WV 26554
(304)367-4125

Elaine Hayslett
Small Business Development Center
Marshall University
1050 Fourth Ave.
Huntington, WV 25701
(304)696-6789

Sharon Butner
Small Business Development Center
Potomac State College
Keyser, WV 26726
(304)788-3011

James Epling
Small Business Development Center
West Virginia Inst. of Technology
Room 102, Engineering Bldg.
Montgomery, WV 25136
(304)442-5501

Stan Kloc
Small Business Development Center
West Virginia University
P.O. Box 6025
Morgantown, WV 26506
(304)293-5839

Barry Lyons
Small Business Development Center
West VA University at Parkersburg
Route 5, Box 167-A
Parkersburg, WV 26101
(304)424-8277

Fred Baer
Small Business Development Center
Shepherd College
White Hall - Room 101
Shepherdstown, WV 25443
(800)344-5231

Small Business Development Center
West Virginia Northern Comm. College
College Square
Wheeling, WV 26003
(304)233-5900

WISCONSIN

William H. Pinkovitz, State Dir.
Small Business Development Center
University of Wisconsin
432 North Lake Street, Room 423
Madison, WI 53706
(608)263-7794 Fax: (608)262-3878

Fred Waedt
Small Business Development Center
University of Wisconsin- Eau Claire
Schneider Hall #113
Eau Claire, WI 54701
(715)836-5811

Jim Holly
Small Business Development Center
University of Wisconsin at Green Bay
Wood Hall, Suite 460
Green Bay, WI 54311
(414)465-2089

Patricia Duetsch
Small Business Development Center
University of Wisconsin at Parkside
234 Tallent Hall
Kenosha, WI 53141
(414)553-2620

Dr. A. William Pollman
Small Business Development Center
University of Wisconsin at La Crosse
323 N. Hall
La Crosse, WI 54601
(608)785-8782

Joan Gillman
Small Business Development Center
University of Wisconsin at Madison
905 University Ave.
Madison, WI 53706
(608)263-2221

Patrick Milne
Small Business Development Center
University of Wisconsin at Milwaukee
929 North Sixth Street
Milwaukee, WI 53203
(414)227-3226

John Mozingo
Small Business Development Center
University of Wisconsin at Oshkosh
Clow Faculty Building - Rm 157
Oshkosh, WI 54901
(414)424-1453

Mark Stover
Small Business Development Center
University of Wisconsin, Lower Level
Stevens Point, WI 54481
(715)346-2004

Tuula Harris
Small Business Development Center
University of Wisconsin at Superior
29 Sundquist Hall
Superior, WI 54880
(715)394-8352

Carla Lenk
Small Business Development Center
University of Wisconsin at Whitewater
2000 Carlson Bldg.
Whitewater, WI 53190
(414)472-3217

WYOMING

Jim Glover, State Director
WSBDC/State Network Office
951 North Poplar
Casper, WY 82601
(307)235-4825 Fax: (307)473-7243
(800)281-4825 (in state)

Barbara Stuckert
WSBDC/Casper College
350 W. A St., Suite 200
Casper, WY 82601
(307)235-4827 Fax: (307)472-7243

Jim Lamprecht
WSBDC/Laramie County Comm. College
1400 E. College Drive
Cheyenne, WY 82007
(307)778-1222

Jay Nielson
WSBDC/Eastern Wyoming College
203 N. 6th St.
Douglas, WY 82633
(307)358-4090 Fax: (307)358-5629

Judith Semple
WSBDC/Northern Wyoming Comm. College District-Gillete
720 W. 8th St.
Gillette, WY 82716
(307)686-0297 Fax: (307)686-0339

Bruce Armentrout
WSBDC/Central Wyoming College
360 Main St.
Lander, WY 82520
(307)332-3394
(800)735-8394

Gail Mattheus
WSBDC/University of Wyoming
P.O. Box 3275
Laramie, WY 82071
(307)766-2363 Fax: (307)766-4028

Lloyd Snyder
WSBDC/Northwest College
146 S. Bent St.
Powell, WY 82435
(307) 754-3746 Fax: (307) 754-9368

Ron Johnson
WSBDC/Western Wyoming Comm. College
P.O. Box 428
Rock Springs, WY 82902
(307) 382-1830 Fax: (307) 382-7665

WSBDC/NWCCD-Sheridan (Satellite)
(307) 674-6446 ext. 180 Fax: (307) 672-6157

WSBDC/Uinta/Lincoln Counties (Satellite)
(800)824-0335 ext. 211 Fax: (307) 789-9572

Bibliography

Bibliography

Adams, Robert L. *Ten Second Business Forms.* Holbrook, MA: Bob Adams, Inc., 1990.

Alexander, T.M., Sr. *Beyond the Timberline: The Trials & Triumphs of a Black Entrepreneur.* Edgewood, MD: M.E. Duncan Company, Inc., 1992.

Andreasen, Alan R. *Cheap but Good Market Research.* Homewood, IL: Business One Irwin, 1991.

Bailey, C.J. *Thoughts to Be Added to...: How One Successful Entrepreneur Thinks.* Morehead, KY: Entrepreneur Projects, 1987.

Baird, Michael L. *Engineering Your Start-Up: A Guide for the High-Tech Entrepreneur.* Belmont, CA: Professional Publications, Inc., 1992.

Ballas, George C. *The Making of an Entrepreneur: Keys to Your Success.* Englewood Cliffs, NJ: Prentice Hall, 1980.

Bandele, Gabriel. *Do for Self: One Hundred of the Best Businesses for Africans in the 21st Century.* Washington, DC: Bandele Publications, 1992.

Banfe, Charles. *Entrepreneur: From Zero to Hero.* New York, NY: Van Nostrand Reinhold, 1991.

Bangs, David H., Jr. *Cash Flow Control Guide: Methods to Understand & Control Small Business's Number One Problem.* Dover, NH: Upstart Publishing Company, Inc., 1989.

-----. *Managing by the Numbers: Financial Essentials for the Growing Business.* Dover, NH: Upstart Publishing Company, Inc., 1992.

-----. *The Market Planning Guide: Gaining & Maintaining the Competitive Edge.* Dover, NH: Upstart Publishing Company, Inc., 1989.

-----. *The Personnel Planning Guide: Successful Management of Your Most Important Asset.* Dover, NH: Upstart Publishing Company, Inc., 1989.

-----. *The Start Up Guide: A One-Year Plan for Entrepreneurs.* Dover, NH: Upstart Publishing Company, Inc., 1989.

Barkemeyer, Erica. *Eighty-Plus Great Ideas for Making Money at Home: A Guide for the First-Time Entrepreneur.* New York, NY: Walker & Co., 1992.

-----. *Eighty-Plus Great Ideas for Making Money: A Guide for the First-Time Entrepreneur.* New York, NY: Ivy Books, 1993.

Barreto, Humberto. *The Entrepreneur in Micro-Economic Theory: Disappearance & Explanation.* New York, NY: Routledge, Chapman & Hall, Inc., 1990.

Barrow, Colin. *The Economist Pocket Entrepreneur.* Cambridge, MA: Blackwell Publishers, 1987.

Basye, Jennifer. *How to Become a Successful Weekend Entrepreneur: Secrets of Making an Extra 100 Dollars or More Each Week Using Your Spare Time.* Roseville, CA: Prima Publishing, 1993.

Batchelor, Andrew J., Jr. *Business Planning for the Entrepreneur.* Sausalito, CA: Tangent Publishing, 1990.

Beale, Dorr D. *Dorr Entrepreneur.* New York, NY: Carlton Press, Inc., 1992.

Bell, J. Perry. *Doing Business with Integrity: One Man's Story.* De Forest, WI: Bell Press.

Bell, Judy K. *Disaster Survival Planning: A Practical Guide for Businesses: Everything You Need to Know to Develop, Implement, & Test Your Own Recovery Plans.* Port Hueneme, CA: Disaster Survival Planning, Inc., 1991.

Benson, Benjamin. *Your Family Business.* Homewood, IL: Business One Irwin, 1991.

Berle, Gustav. *The Green Entrepreneur: Business Opportunities That Can Save the Earth & Make You Money.* Blue Ridge Summit, PA: TAB Books, 1991.

Brenner, Gary. *Complete Handbook for the Entrepreneur.* Englewood Cliffs, CA: Prentice Hall, 1989.

Brogdon, Anthony. *Being an Entrepreneur in Alabama.* Detroit, MI: Multi Business Concepts, 1991.

-----. *Being an Entrepreneur in California.* Detroit, MI: Multi Business Concepts, 1991.

-----. *Being an Entrepreneur in Colorado.* Detroit, MI: Multi Business Concepts, 1991.

-----. *Being an Entrepreneur in Florida.* Detroit, MI: Multi Business Concepts, 1991.

-----. *Being an Entrepreneur in Georgia.* Detroit, MI: Multi Business Concepts, 1989.

-----. *Being an Entrepreneur in Illinois.* Detroit, MI: Multi Business Concepts, 1991.

-----. *Being an Entrepreneur in Louisiana.* Detroit, MI: Multi Business Concepts, 1991.

-----. *Being an Entrepreneur in Maryland.* Detroit, MI: Multi Business Concepts, 1991.

-----. *Being an Entrepreneur in Michigan.* Detroit, MI: Multi Business Concepts, 1991.

-----. *Being an Entrepreneur in Minnesota.* Detroit, MI: Multi Business Concepts, 1991.

-----. *Being an Entrepreneur in New Jersey.* Detroit, MI: Multi Business Concepts, 1991.

-----. *Being an Entrepreneur in New York.* Detroit, MI: Multi Business Concepts, 1991.

-----. *Being an Entrepreneur in Ohio.* Detroit, MI: Multi Business Concepts, 1991.

-----. *Being an Entrepreneur in Pennsylvania.* Detroit, MI: Multi Business Concepts, 1991.

-----. *Being an Entrepreneur in Texas.* Detroit, MI: Multi Business Concepts, 1991.

-----. *Being an Entrepreneur in Washington, DC.* Detroit, MI: Multi Business Concepts, 1991.

-----. *Twenty-Three Principles to Being a Successful Entrepreneur: The Block Buster.* Detroit, MI: Multi Business Concepts, 1989.

Brown, John O. *The Small Business Guide to the Malcolm Baldrige National Quality Award: Proven Strategies for Building Quality into Your Organization.* Homewood, IL: Business One Irwin, 1995.

Building Wealth. Dover, NH: Upstart Publishing Company, Inc., 1992.

Bursten, Steven C. *The Bootstrap Entrepreneur.* Nashville, TN: Thomas Nelson Inc., 1993.

Business of Your Own Staff. *So You're Thinking about Starting a Business: A Comprehensive Business Start up Manual.* Nashville, TN: Business of Your Own, 1988.

-----. *Starting a Business to Sell Your Artwork.* Nashville, TN: Business of Your Own, 1988.

-----. *Starting a Business to Sell Your Craft Items.* Nashville, TN: Business of Your Own, 1988.

-----. *Starting a Clothing Boutique.* Nashville, TN: Business of Your Own, 1988.

-----. *Starting a Day Care Center.* Nashville, TN: Business of Your Own, 1988.

------. *Starting a Franchise.* Nashville, TN: Business of Your Own, 1988.

-----. *Starting a Gift Shop.* Nashville, TN: Business of Your Own, 1988.

-----. *Starting a Home Based Business.* Nashville, TN: Business of Your Own, 1988.

-----. *Starting a Mail Order Business.* Nashville, TN: Business of Your Own, 1988.

-----. *Starting a Secretarial Service.* Nashville, TN: Business of Your Own, 1988.

-----. *Starting an Antique Shop.* Nashville, TN: Business of Your Own, 1988.

Business Planning Guide. Dover, NH: Upstart Publishing Company, Inc., 1992.

Buskirk, Richard H. *Program for Writing Winning Business Plans.* Denver, CO: Creative Management Unlimited, Inc.

Casson, Mark. *The Entrepreneur: An Economic Theory.* Brookfield, VT: Ashgate Publishing Co., 1992.

Chandler, Marsha K. *Homegrown Computer Profits: A Comprehensive Guide for the Home Business* Entrepreneur. Cincinnati, OH: Betterway Books, 1989.

Cohen, William A. *The Entrepreneur & Small Business Marketing Problem Solver.* New York, NY: John Wiley & Sons, Inc., 1991.

-----. *The Entrepreneur & Small Business Problem Solver.* New York, NY: John Wiley & Sons, 1990.

Common Sense Editors. Creating Customers. Dover, NH: Upstart Publishing Company, Inc., 1992.

The Computer Entrepreneur: How to Get a Second Income Using Your Personal Computer. New York, NY: Gordon Press, Publishers, 1987.

Three Keys to Obtaining Venture Capital. Coopers & Lybrand.

Cook, James R. The *Start-Up Entrepreneur: How You Can Succeed in Building Your Own Company into a Major Enterprise Starting From Scratch.* New York, NY: HarperCollins Publishers, Inc., 1987.

Covello, Joseph A. *The Complete Book of Business Plans: Simple Steps to Writing a Powerful Business Plan.* Naperville, IL: Sourcebooks, Inc., 1992.

Crowner, Robert P. *Developing a Strategic Business Plan with Cases: An Entrepreneur's Advantage.* Homewood, IL: Richard D. Irwin, Inc., 1990.

Cullinane, John J. *Entrepreneur's Survival Guide: One Hundred One Tips for Managing in Good Times & Bad.* Homewood, IL: Business One Irwin, 1992.

Cushman, Robert F., ed. *Business Opportunities in the United States: The Complete Reference Guide to Practices & Procedures.* Homewood, IL: Business One Irwin, 1992.

Dailey, Gene. *Secrets of a Successful Entrepreneur: How to Start & Succeed at Running Your Own Business.* Pleasanton, CA: K & A Publications, 1993.

Daughtery, David E. *From Technical Professional to Entrepreneur: A Guide to Alternative Careers.* New York, NY: John Wiley & Sons, 1986.

Davidson, Jeffrey P. *Marketing for the Home-Based Business.* Holbrook, MA: Bob Adams, Inc., 1990.

Dawson, George M. *Borrowing for Your Business: Winning the Battle for the Banker's Yes.* Dover, NH: Upstart Publishing Company, Inc., 1991.

Dears, Donn D. *The Entrepreneur as CEO: Building a Business.* Plano, TX: WDD Corporation Publishing Divison, 1991.

-----. *The New Entrepreneur: How to Get Started in Business.* Plano, TX: WDD Corporation Publishing Division, 1992.

Dible, Donald M. *Up Your Own Organization: A Handbook for Today's Entrepreneur.* New York, NY: Simon & Schuster Trade.

Doyle, Patricia A. *Sit & Grow Rich: Petsitting & Housesitting for Profit.* Dover, NH: Upstart Publishing Company, Inc., 1993.

Dwyer, Don. Target Success: *How You Can Become a Successful Entrepreneur -- Regardless of Your Background.* Holbrook, MA: Bob Adams, Inc., 1993.

Eckert, Lee A. *Small Business: An Entrepreneur's Plan.* Fort Worth, TX: Dryden Press, 1993.

Entrepreneur Magazine Staff. *Complete Guide to Owning a Home Based Business*. New York, NY: Bantam Books, Inc., 1990.

-----. *One Hundred & Eleven Businesses You Can Start for Under $10,000.* New York, NY: Bantam Books, Inc., 1991.

-----. *One Hundred & Sixty-Eight More Businesses Anyone Can Start & Make a Lot of Money*. New York, NY: Bantam Books, Inc., 1991.

-----. *One Hundred Eighty-Four Businesses Anyone Can Start.* New York, NY: Bantam Books, Inc., 1990.

Fallek, Max. *How to Write Your Own Business Plans*. Minneapolis, MN: American Institute of Small Business, 1989.

Fasiska, Edward J. *The Fingerprint of the Entrepreneur: Your Entrepreneurial Profile*. Hadley, MA: Laserlight Publishing, 1987.

Ferrell, O.C. *Business: A Changing World*. Homewood, IL: Richard D. Irwin, Inc., 1992.

Foegen, George J. *Business Plan Guidebook with Financial Spreadsheets*. Fort Worth, TX: Dryden Press, 1990.

Freeley, James. *Are You an Entrepreneur? The Characteristics & Skills Needed to Start Your Own Business*. Elka Park, NY: Business Resource Network, Inc., 1989.

Freiberg, Bill D. *Racing Failure: What it Takes to Become an Entrepreneur... & Make it!* Cedar Falls, IA: Freiberg Publishing Company, 1989.

From Tech Professional to Entrepreneur. Los Angeles, CA: T/C Publications.

Gelder, Alice A. *World Business Desk Reference: How to Do Business with 192 Countries by Phone, Fax, & Mail.* Homewood, IL: Business One Irwin, 1994.

Gilbert, Dale L. *Complete Guide to Starting a Used Bookstore*. Dover, NH: Upstart Publishing Company, Inc., 1991.

Gottschalk, Jack. *Promoting Your Professional Services.* Homewood, IL: Business One Irwin, 1991.

Growth Company Starter Kit: "How to" for: Business Plans, Financing, Operations. Coopers & Lybrand.

Harfer, M. *The Private Marketing Entrepreneur & Rural Development: Case Studies and Commentary*. Lanham, MD: UNIPUB, 1982.

Harper, Stephen C. *The McGraw-Hill Guide to Starting Your Own Business: A Step-by-Step Blueprint for the First-Time Entrepreneur.* New York, NY: McGraw-Hill, Inc., 1991.

Hebert, Robert F. *The Entrepreneur: Mainstream Views & Radical Critiques*. Westport, CT: Greenwood Publishing Group, Inc., 1988.

Helm, Kathy K. *Becoming an Entrepreneur in Your Own Setting*. Chicago, IL: American Dietetic Association, 1990.

Henze, Geraldine. *Winning Career Moves: A Guide to Improving Your Work Life*. Homewood, IL: Business One Irwin, 1992.

Hisrich, Robert D. *Entrepreneurship*. Homewood, IL: Richard D. Irwin, Inc., 1989.

-----. *On Your Own*. Homewood, IL: Business One Irwin, 1991.

-----. *The Woman Entrepreneur: Starting, Financing, & Managing a Successful Business*. New York, NY: Free Press, 1990.

Hodgetts, Richard. *Effective Small Business Management.* Fort Worth, TX: Dryden Press, 1992.

Holtz, Herman. *Complete Work-at-Home Companion: Everything You Need to Know to Prosper as a Home-Based Entrepreneur or Employee.* Roseville, CA: Prima Publishing, 1993.

Jackson, Gordon E. *Labor & Employment Law Desk Book.* Englewood Cliffs, CA: Prentice Hall, 1986.

Jacobs, Joseph J. *Anatomy of an Entrepreneur: Family, Culture, & Ethics*. San Francisco, CA: ICS Press, 1991.

Kao, John. *The Entrepreneur*. Englewood Cliffs, CA: Prentice Hall, 1990.

Kiam, Victor. *Going for it: How to Succeed as an Entrepreneur.* New York, NY: Morrow, 1986.

Klein, Fred. *Handbook on Building a Profitable Business: An Expert's Step-by-Step Presentation on How to Make Money in Business.* Seattle, WA: Entrepreneurial Workshops Publications, 1990.

Knight, Brian, & the Associates of Country Business Inc. Staff. *Buy the Right Business -- At the Right Price.* Dover, NH: Upstart Publishing Company, Inc.

Kozmetsky, Ronya. *Women in Business: Succeeding as a Manager, Professional, or Entrepreneur.* Houston, TX: Gulf Publishing Company, 1989.

Kraft, Elmer. *Beats Wages.* Bend, OR: Maverick Publications, 1982.

Kraft, Ronald D. *Strategic Planning for the Entrepreneur.* La Mesa, CA: Center Publications, 1991.

Kuehl, Charles. *Small Business: Planning & Management.* Fort Worth, TX: Dryden Press, 1990.

Kuratko, Donald F. *Entrepreneurship: A Contemporary Approach.* Fort Worth, TX: Dryen Press, 1989.

Levine, Jeffrey P. *Doing Business in Chicago.* Homewood, IL: Business One Irwin, 1990.

Levine, Sumner N., ed. *The Business One Irwin Business & Investment Almanac, 1992.* Homewood, IL: Business One Irwin, 1991.

Levitt, Mortimer. *How to Start Your Own Business Without Losing Your Shirt: Secrets of the Artful Entrepreneur.* New York, NY: MacMillan Publishing Company, Inc., 1988.

Lisoskie, Pete. *Networking Your Way to Profits: How to Create a Customer Network That Keeps Them Coming Back.* Newbury Park, CA: Business Toolbox, 1992.

Lownes, Millicent G. *Entrepreneurially Yours: A Compilation of Articles about Starting and Managing a Small Business.* Nashville, TN: Business of Your Own, 1990.

-----. *The Purple Rose Within: A Woman's Basic Guide for Developing a Business Plan.* Business of Your Own, 1989.
Ludden, LaVerne. *Mind Your Own Business: Getting Started as an Entrepreneur.* Indianapolis, IN: JIST Works, Inc., 1993.

Lynn, Richard. *Entrepreneur.* Woodstock, NY: Beekman Publishers, Inc., 1973.

Malburg, Christopher R. *Business Plans to Manage Day to Day Operations: Real-Life Results for Small Business Owners & Operators.* New York, NY: John Wiley & Sons, Inc., 1993.

Matthews, John. *The Beginning Entrepreneur.* Lincolnwood, IL: NTC Publishing Group, 1993.

Mazzo, William L. *A Business Plan & Evaluation: Simple As One-Two-Three -- Three Easy Steps for a Do-It-Yourself Business Plan -- Just Fill in the Blanks.* St. Augustine, FL: Business Plan Publishing, 1987.

McGarty, Terrence B. *Business Plans That Win Venture Capital.* New York, NY: John Wiley & Sons, Inc., 1989.

McKenzie, R.A. *Successful Business Plans for Architects.* New York, NY: McGraw-Hill, Inc., 1992.

Megginson, William L. *Small Business Management: An Entrepreneur's Guide to Success.* Homewood, IL: Richard D. Irwin, Inc., 1993.

Miller, Jack V. *Fat Hogs & Dead Dogs: How to Use Ideas, Inventions & Patents to Win the War for Your Markets & Profits.* Pasadena, CA: Design Technology Corporation, 1990.

Mitchell, Lee. *A Moving Stairway: From Home-Making to Business-Making in Eight Dynamic Steps.* Dunbridge, OH: Selective Marketing Corporation, 1991.

Mooney, Sean. *Insuring Your Business: What You Need to Know to Get the Best Insurance Coverage for Your Business.* New York, NY: Insurance Information Institute, 1993.

Moskowitz, Robert K. *The Small Business Computer Book: A Guide in Plain English.* Dover, NH: Upstart Publishing Company, Inc., 1993.

National Center for Research in Vocational Educational Staff. *Determining Your Potential as an Entrepreneur Module, PACE: A Program for Acquiring Competence in Entrepreneurship.* Columbus, OH: Center on Education & Training Employment, 1983.

National Nurses in Business Association. *How I Became a Nurse Entrepreneur: Tales from Fifty Nurses in Business.* Petaluma, CA: National Nurses in Business Association, 1991.

National Plan Service, Inc. Staff, Ed. *America's Best Project Plans.* Elmhurst, IL: National Plan Service, Inc., 1990.

Nitschke, Martha. *How to Start Your Own One Hundred Thousand Dollar Nursing Agency: With As Little As One Week's Salary.* Wilmington, NC: Entrepress, 1991.

O'Donnell, Michael. *Writing Business Plans That Get Results: A Step-by-Step Guide.* Chicago, IL: Contemporary Books, Inc., 1991.

Parkin, Bond L. *The Florida Entrepreneur.* Sarasota, FL: Pineapple Press, Inc., 1993.

Pence. *Financial Management for the Entrepreneur.* Acton, MA: Copley Publishing Group, 1991.

Perkins, Ron. *How to Find Your Treasure in a Gift Basket.* Costa Mesa, CA: Home Income Publishing, 1991.

Pinson, Linda. *The Home-Based Entrepreneur: The Complete Guide to Working at Home.* Dover, NH: Upstart Publishing Company, Inc., 1993.

-----. *Keeping the Books: Basic Recordkeeping & Accounting for the Small Business.* Dover, NH: Upstart Publishing Company, Inc., 1993.

-----. *The Woman Entrepreneur.* Tustin, CA: Out of Your Mind & Into the Marketplace, 1992.

Pratt, Shannon. *Valuing Small Businesses & Professional Practices.* Homewood, IL: Business One Irwin, 1993.

Ratliff, Susan. *How to Be a Weekend Entrepreneur: Making Money at Craft Fairs, Trade Shows & Swap Meets.* Phoenix, AZ: Marketing Methods Press, 1991.

Restaurant Planning Guide. Dover, NH: Upstart Publishing Company, Inc., 1992.

Rich, Stanley R. *Business Plans That Win: Lessons from the MIT Enterprise Forum.* New York, NY: HarperCollins Publishers, Inc., 1987.

Rifkin, Glenn. *The Ultimate Entrepreneur: The Story of Ken Olsen & Digital Equipment Corporation.* Roseville, CA: Prima Publishing, 1990.

Rosen, Al. *Business Rescue: How to Fix a Company That's Losing Money.* Brea, CA: Business University Press, 1989.

Ryan, J.D. *Small Business: An Entrepreneur's Plan.* Fort Worth, TX: Dryden Press, 1990.

Schell, Jim. *The Brass Tacks Entrepreneur.* New York, NY: Henry Holt & Company, 1993.

Schutt, David and Yong Lim, Eds. *Pratt's Guide to Venture Capital Sources.* New York, NY: Venture Economics Inc., 1992.

Sitterly, Connie. *The Female Entrepreneur.* Menlo Park, CA: Crisp Publications, Inc., 1993.

Skloot, Edward, Ed. *The Nonprofit Entrepreneur: Creating Ventures to Earn Income.* New York, NY: The Foundation Center, 1988.

Smith, Allan. *List n' Forms for Businesses.* Palm Beach Gardens, FL: Success Publishing, 1989.

Smith, Jerald R. *Entrepreneur: A Simulation.* Boston, MA: Houghton Mifflin Co., 1987.

Smith, Ruth Q., ed. *Starting a Public Relations Firm.* Business of Your Own, 1988.

Sotkin, Joan. *Starting Your Own Business: An Easy-to-Follow Guide for the New Entrepreneur.* Laguna Hills, CA: Build Your Business, Inc., 1993.

Sperry, Paul S. *Complete Guide to Selling Your Business.* Dover, NH: Upstart Publishing Company, Inc., 1992.

Stapleton, Richard J. *The Entrepreneur: Concepts & Cases on Creativity in Business.* Lanham, MD: University Press of America, 1985.

Stevens, Chris. *The Entrepreneur's Guide to Developing a Basic Business Plan.* Northbrook, IL: S.K. Brown Publishing, 1991.

Stevens, Mark. *The Ten-Minute Entrepreneur.* New York, NY: Warner Books, Inc., 1985.

Stevenson, Howard H. *New Business Ventures & the Entrepreneur.* Homewood, IL: Richard D. Irwin, Inc., 1994.

Taylor, Ted. M. *Secrets to a Successful Greenhouse Business.* Melbourne, FL: Green Earth Publishing Company, 1991.

Timmons, Jeffrey A. *The Entrepreneurial Mind.* New Boston, NH: BrickHouse Publishing Company, 1989.

Tolman, Ruth. *Lesson Plans for a Woman's Guide to Business & Social Success.* Bronx, NY: Milady Publishing Company, 1983.

Torrence, Ronald. *The Entrepreneur Survival Handbook.* Englewood Cliffs, CA: Prentice Hall, 1985.

Update Publicare Research Staff. *Small Business or Entrepreneur Related Newsletters & Periodicals: An Updating Reference.* Denver, CO: Prosperity & Profits Unlimited, Distribution Services, 1983.

Warner, Alice S. *Mind Your Own Business: A Guide for the Information Entrepreneur.* New York, NY: Neal-Schuman Publishers, Inc., 1987.

Warshaw, Stanley. *How to Become a Financially Successful Paperhanging Entrepreneur.* Rutland, VT: U.S. School of Professional Paperhanging, Inc., 1981.

Weidlein, Marianne S. *Visions & Business: Support & Tools for the Entrepreneur.* Lafayette, CA: Business Plan Plus, 1987.

Wolf, Jack S. *Export Profits: A Guide for Small Business.* Dover, NH: Upstart Publishing Company, Inc., 1992.

Woman Entrepreneur. Dover, NH: Upstart Publishing Company, Inc., 1993.

Wylie, Peter. *Can This Partnership Be Saved? Improving (or Salvaging) Your Key Business Relationships.* Dover, NH: Upstart Publishing Company, Inc., 1993.

Zagury, Carolyn S. *Nurse Entrepreneur: Building the Bridge of Opportunity.* Long Branch, NJ: Vista Publishing, Inc., 1993.

Ziegler, Mel. *The Republic of Tea: Letters to a Young Entrepreneur.* New York, NY: Doubleday, 1992.

Zoghlin, Gil. *From Executive to Entrepreneur: Making the Transition.* New York, NY: AMACOM, 1991.

Zuckerman, Laurie B. *On Your Own: A Woman's Guide to Building a Business.* Dover, NH: Upstart Publishing Company, Inc., 1990.